COMPLETE HOME GUIDE TO MEDICATION

Other books by Dr Warwick Carter

FOR LAY PEOPLE

*More Than 500 Questions You've Always
    Been Afraid to Ask Your Doctor*
*Macquarie Home Guide to Health and
    Medicine*
*Complete Home Guide to Medical
    Illnesses*
Australian Home Guide to Medications
1001 Medical Questions and Answers
The Complete Family Medical Guide
Encyclopedia of Medical Symptoms
Dr. Wickham – The Book
Medical Matters

FOR DOCTORS

Pathinterp
Pathognosis
Sympinterp
Signinterp
Therognosis
Syndromecum
Doctor's Companion

Dr Warwick Carter
MB BS, FRACGP

D1393182

For Vern

Cover Design: Sam Grimmer

Published in 2004 by Hinkler Books Pty Ltd
17–23 Redwood Drive
Dingley VIC 3172 Australia
www.hinklerbooks.com

ISBN 1 7412 1282 0
Printed and bound in Australia

CONTENTS

INTRODUCTION
Preface

All medications on the market have been extensively tested for effectiveness and lack of serious side effects. Nevertheless, every medication has potential problems, inter-actions, adverse reactions and correct methods of use. For these reasons it is important for everyone who takes any medication that they know as much as possible about its uses and actions.

This book is designed to educate users of medication in simple language about the medications they are taking. If you have any concerns, discuss them further with your doctor or pharmacist.

Every entry has a standard format and entries are extensively cross referenced. Every prescription medication available in the country (with the exception of general anaesthetics and some injections used in operating theatres and for exotic cancer treatments) is explained, as well as many non-prescription pharmacy only medicines.

The terminology of medications can be confusing. Every medication has at least three names—a chemical name which is normally only used by scientists, a generic (common) name which is specific to that medication and a trade name (or several trade names) which is given to the medication by the various manufacturers.

For example:

Chemical name: Acetyl salicylic acid

Generic name: Aspirin

Trade names: Angettes, Caprin, Disprin etc.

Every medication also belongs to a class of similar medications (some belong to two or more classes). Aspirin belongs to the Analgesic, Salicylate and Nonsteroidal Anti-inflammatory (NSAID) classes. Common drug classes are listed with the drug generic names in the main part of the book.

The main entries are either under the medication's generic name or its drug class. It will depend on the complexity of the listing if all medications in one drug class can be listed together (e.g. all Proton Pump Inhibitors are listed together) or separately (e.g. the various forms of Penicillin are listed separately). These entries are listed in alphabetical order in the body of the book and are cross-referenced between generic drug name and drug class so that looking up either will lead you to the required entry.

If you wish to find a medication by its trade name, consult the index where you will be directed to the appropriate entry.

If you wish to find different medications that treat the same condition (e.g. epilepsy), look up one medication that treats the condition, see which drug class it is in (e.g. Anticonvulsant) and under that drug class you will find listed other medications that will treat that condition.

Some illegal drugs (cocaine, marijuana and heroin) and commonly used herbs are also covered in this book.

New medications are introduced onto the market at the rate of about a dozen every month, while others are removed because they have been superseded, are found to have unacceptable complications or they are not profitable. Other medications have additional uses or side-effects determined, are found to interact with other medications, or may become more readily available without prescription. This second edition of the *Complete Home Guide to Medication* therefore contains thousands of alterations and additions that reflect these changes. More than 90% of the entries have been modified for this edition.

Understanding the medications patients are using by referring to this book will help them cope with their condition and enable them to understand why their doctor has chosen a particular course of action.

Dr. Warwick Carter MB BS, FRACGP, FAMA

February 2004

Format

Generic Name or

DRUG GROUP
(Alternative Name)

TRADE NAMES, or

TRADE and GENERIC NAMES:

Trade Names of medication listed above, or **Trade Name** followed by generic names within a drug group. The specific ingredient that is being discussed in this entry is <u>underlined</u> when there is any possibility of confusion.

DRUG CLASS:

Class of drug to which medication belongs. Only common drug classes are mentioned, as not all medications can be put into a drug class that has any meaning outside university laboratories.

USES:

The conditions that can be treated by the medication.

DOSAGE:

 The way in which the medication should be taken. Normal adult dose shown.

FORMS:

The ways in which the medication is presented e.g. capsules, mixture, injection (colour and storage precautions in brackets).

Aerosol spray

Atomiser spray, Inhaler

Capsule
Rotacap

Cream, Gel,
Lotion,
Ointment, Paste

Drops

Elixer, Liquid,
Gargle, Infusion,
Mixture, Solution,
Suspension

Lozenge,
Pessary, Supository

Nasal spray

Paint,
Tincture

Powder

Ampoule,
Intravenous injection,
Syringe, Injection,

Flimtabs,
Tablets

Syrup
1 Teaspoon = 5mL
1 Desertspoon = 10mL
1 Tablespoon = 15mL

PRECAUTIONS:

The precautions that a doctor or pharmacist should warn a patient about if taking this medication, including its use in pregnancy (with pregnancy risk categorisation in brackets after the word 'pregnancy'—see below), breast feeding and children.

Do not take if:

- suffering from certain conditions
- under other circumstances

SIDE EFFECTS:

The vast majority of medications have been very extensively tested and are very safe as well as being effective, although a minority of patients may experience some side effects with some medications.

Common: Unwanted problems that many patients may experience.

Unusual: Less common problems that fewer than 3% of patients may experience.

Severe but rare (stop medication, consult doctor): Rare and serious complications.

INTERACTIONS:

Other drugs:
- Drug name that may interact with medication. This interaction may affect the medication unfavourably, increase or decrease its action or side effects or increase or decrease its excretion from the body. Many interactions have only a minimal effect on most patients. Some interactions may improve the effects of the drug. Discuss any possible interaction with your doctor or pharmacist.

Herbs:
- herbs that cause reaction.

Other substances:
- reactions with substances such as alcohol, caffeine, foods, exercise etc.

PRESCRIPTION:

Whether a prescription is required for the medication.

PERMITTED IN SPORT:

Can the medication be taken legally while competing in high standards of sport.

OVERDOSE:

The effects of an overdose and the first aid treatment of an overdose. See section on 'Overdose' and 'Poisoning' in Introduction for further information.

OTHER INFORMATION:

Other relevant and interesting information about the medication, including problems with addiction and long term use.

See also Other Related Medication.

DRUG GROUP NAME

DISCUSSION:

An explanation of drug group action and discussion on its effects.

See Generic Name(s).

Generic Name

See DRUG GROUP NAME.

Pregnancy Risk Categorisation

The following system is used in this book. The risk category is shown in the
PRECAUTIONS section of most entries in brackets after the word 'pregnancy'.
The definitions of the categories are:

A	No proven direct or indirect harmful effects to the foetus.
B1	Studies in animals have shown no evidence of increased foetal damage.
B2	Studies in animals are inadequate, but available data shows no evidence of increased foetal damage.
B3	Studies in animals have shown evidence of increased foetal damage, but the significance of this in humans is uncertain.
C	May cause harmful effects to the foetus but not malformations. These effects may be reversible.
D	Cause an increased incidence of foetal malformations, other irreversible damage and/or adverse pharmacological effects on the foetus.
X	High risk of permanent damage to the foetus. Should not be used if pregnancy is even a possibility.

Safe Storage of Medication

Accidental overdoses of medications, even common ones like paracetamol (e.g. Calpol)
can kill children. Many tablets and capsules are brightly coloured and naturally attractive
to little people who want to find out what they are like.

A safe storage area for all medications is absolutely essential. A high, locked
cupboard with a child proof latch is best.

Home Medicine Chest

**A comprehensive home medical chest
should contain the following items:**

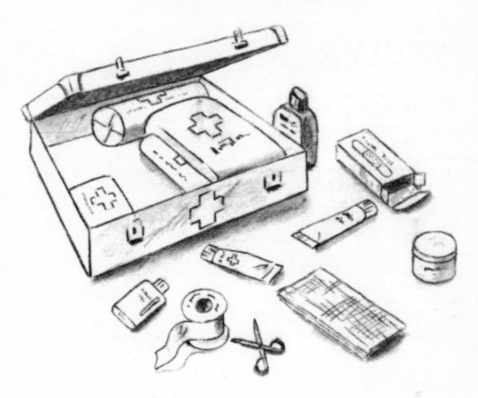

Paracetamol Tablets
Paracetamol Liquid
Charcoal Tablets or Solution
(for overdose)
Lotion for bites and stings
Anti-itch Cream
Antiseptic Cream
Antiseptic Liquid
Pseudoephedrine Tablets and/or Liquid
(for nasal congestion)
Oxymetazoline Nose Drops
Menthol Inhalant

Cough Syrup
Antiseptic Ear Drops
Antiseptic Eye Drops
Sunscreen Lotion or Cream
Splinter Forceps
Scissors
Triangular Bandage (sling)
Adhesive Dressing (various sizes)
Elastic Bandages (wide)
Cotton Gauze (NOT cotton wool)
Adhesive Tape

EMERGENCIES

Allergy reaction

An allergy is excess sensitivity to a substance that produces a reaction in the body.

Allergies may occur on exposure to almost any type of chemical. As well as medications, animal hair, dust, milk, eggs, pollen, fish, fruit, insect bites, moulds and parasites are just a few of the thousands of possible allergic substances.

An allergen is a substance (such as a medication) that causes an allergic reaction. When the body first encounters an allergen, the defence mechanisms of the body are triggered, but there is usually no detectable effect. On the second and subsequent occasions of exposure to the allergen, the defence mechanism over-reacts, causing effects that may be merely a nuisance, or severe and life threatening (see Anaphylactic Reaction below), in different areas of the body.

In an allergic reaction, a substance called histamine is released. It causes rapid swelling of the tissue, which in the nose or lungs then secretes copious amounts of watery phlegm and becomes intensely itchy.

The body gradually breaks down the histamine itself and the reaction disappears, but this process can be speeded up by the use of antihistamine drugs that are taken by mouth or injection to destroy the histamine that is causing the allergy reaction.

In an emergency, anyone exposed to a medication or substance to which they have an allergic reaction should be given antihistamines by mouth and then taken to a doctor. Antihistamines are available without prescription from chemists.

Tests may be performed to determine whether or not you are allergic to a particular medication, but because there are so many possibilities, the patient must have some idea of which medication is causing the problem before the tests are commenced. The tests may take the form of skin pricks with a number of suspected substances, or blood tests that can detect the body's reaction to an allergen.

If someone is found to be highly allergic to a specific substance, they can be desensitised so that they do not react as strongly, or sometimes do not react at all. This process is often long and involved and unfortunately does not always work, but many people have had life threatening and disabling allergies cured or reduced by this procedure.

Allergies are usually annoying rather than serious, but in a small number of people, they may become a life threatening anaphylactic reaction (see below). Those who know they may have a life threatening allergy should always carry adrenaline with them, to be self-injected if they have an attack.

Anaphylactic reaction

An anaphylactic reaction is an immediate, severe, life-threatening allergic reaction. Death may occur within minutes if medical help is not immediately available.

The patient becomes rapidly sweaty, develops widespread pins and needles, swelling develops in one or more parts of the body (possibly including the tongue and throat), starts wheezing, becomes blue around the lips, may become incontinent of urine, loses consciousness, convulses and stops breathing.

Swelling of the tongue and throat alone may be enough to cause death if air is unable to pass into the lungs. The terrified victim suffocates.

First aid can give only limited assistance. The patient must be placed on their back with the neck extended to give the best possible airway, and mouth to mouth resuscitation, and external cardiac massage may be necessary.

Medical treatment must be sought urgently, as an injection of drugs such as adrenaline, aminophylline, hydrocortisone or an antihistamine will reverse the allergic reaction rapidly and save the patient's life.

Patients who are aware that they may have an anaphylactic reaction usually carry an injectable form of adrenaline with them at all times to be used in an emergency.

Insect stings (e.g. bees, hornets, wasps and ants) and injected drugs are the most likely substances to produce acute anaphylaxis. It is rare for inhaled, touched or eaten substances to cause this reaction.

Choking

If a piece of food or other foreign body is caught in the windpipe, the person may die from asphyxiation in a few minutes. It is essential to dislodge the blockage as rapidly as possible.

If a child is choking, turn them upside down and while holding them by the feet, bang firmly on the back.

In an older child or adult, with the patient sitting or standing, place your arms around them from behind and cross your wrists over the breast bone. Firmly compress the chest by pressure on the breast bone to force the air out of the lungs and hopefully the foreign body out of the windpipe.

Alternatively, lie the patient in the coma position on their side on the floor, give several sharp blows between the shoulder blades and then if necessary, give several firm quick pushes on the side of the chest wall below the arm pit.

If unsuccessful, lie the patient on a table or bed, with the body above the waist hanging over the edge and bang on the back several times before repeating the chest compression. These manoeuvres are successful in the vast majority of cases.

If you fail to dislodge the food blocking the windpipe and the patient is turning blue, mouth to mouth resuscitation should be started, in an attempt to force some air past the blockage and into the lungs.

Diarrhoea

Diarrhoea has causes that vary from the serious (cancer, ulcerative colitis), to the annoying (food poisoning, drug reactions), but the most common type of diarrhoea is that caused by a viral infection of the gut.

A virus may infect your bowel to cause diarrhoea, in the same way that another may cause a cold by infecting your nose and throat. The virus particles enter the gut on food or droplets of breath, they are swallowed and immediately start multiplying into incredibly large numbers. Billions upon trillions of them will eventually be present.

Once in the stomach in these vast numbers, viruses irritate the tissue around them. This in turn causes the lining of the gut to secrete large amounts of fluid and it also interferes with the normal absorption of food from the intestine, so anything eaten passes straight through.

The third effect is an irritation of the gut, causing it to go into repeated spasms. This causes severe, colic-like pain and anything that is inside the gut is pushed out through the nearest appropriate orifice (mouth or anus) by these strong contractions.

The upper part of the gut is normally attacked first, causing six to twelve hours of vomiting. This settles as the virus moves down the intestine, and the lower gut becomes inflamed, causing diarrhoea that may last from one to three days.

Because the infection is caused by a virus, antibiotics have no effect on the disease—they may in fact, make the diarrhoea worse.

It is not desirable in most circumstances to use drugs to stop the diarrhoea either, as all this does is hold the virus in the body and allow it to reproduce further. The body is cleaning the infection from the gastrointestinal system with the diarrhoea and within reason, it is best to allow this process to proceed.

The treatment of viral gastroenteritis is therefore primarily rest and diet. Fluids and food should be taken in small amounts frequently, not large amounts occasionally.

For the first 24 hours, only clear fluids should be taken by mouth. Commercial preparations that contain salts and sugars are ideal, but clear soups, cordial and very dilute cordials with a pinch of salt added may also be used as a short term substitute. Freezing the liquid and allowing the child to lick the resultant block is an excellent way to get fluids into a vomiting child.

Plain water should not be drunk, as the body requires the salts and sugars for the absorption of fluids from the gut.

On the second and subsequent days, food should be gradually introduced. Cereals, bread, rice and dry biscuits are the first foods to be tried and if they cause no problems, boiled vegetables, fruit and white meat can be added.

It is important to avoid all dairy products, eggs, fatty and fried foods until you are completely better.

Only if the vomiting lasts more than twelve hours, or the diarrhoea is excessively severe or prolonged, is further medical attention and medication required.

Extra care must be observed with young children, as severe diarrhoea may cause dehydration in less than a day.

Overdose

Excessive doses of medication can be taken by accident (e.g. children finding a bottle of pills, confused elderly people) or deliberately (e.g. suicide attempt). The appropriate first aid by the person discovering the overdose may be lifesaving.

Some medications are far more dangerous than others when taken in excess. These relative dangers are discussed in the 'Overdose' section in the section on each medication in the main part of this book.

For virtually all medication overdosages, the first aid treatment is to administer charcoal to neutralise the medication. Activated charcoal solutions are readily available from chemists without a prescription and should be included in any home medicine chest.

If activated charcoal is not available and there will be some delay in obtaining medical attention it is preferable to induce vomiting rather than allow the medication to be absorbed. Vomiting should NOT be induced if the patient is unconscious or otherwise liable to inhale any vomitus.

Activated charcoal should be given at any time after the overdose being taken. Induction of vomiting is most beneficial within 30 minutes of the overdose being taken, but even up to two hours later it may be beneficial. Many medications cause vomiting as part of their overdose effects, but by this time, the drug has already been absorbed and the vomiting is unlikely to reduce the effects of the drug significantly.

Vomiting can be induced by giving Ipecacuanha syrup and water, by giving soapy water to drink, by applying pressure to the upper belly or by putting a finger down the back of the persons throat (be careful not to be bitten, particularly if patient likely to convulse). The patient should be lying on their side with the neck extended, or sitting up and leaning over to avoid inhaling vomitus.

Carers should seek medical advice as soon as possible and sometimes urgent medical attention must be obtained.

Advice is available from your own general practitioner or local hospital.

See also 'Poisoning'.

Poisoning

Innumerable substances in our environment can poison the human body.
A brief summary of common poisons and their treatment follows,
but if in doubt, contact your general practitioner or local hospital.

CHEMICAL/DRUG	EFFECT OF POISON	FIRST AID TREATMENT
Alkalis (household bleaches)	Burning, vomiting, shock, difficult breathing.	Dilute with milk, allow vomiting, give vinegar.
Aspirin (Aspro, Disprin etc.)	Rapid breathing, brain disturbance, coma, kidney failure.	Give activated charcoal or induce vomiting.
Barbiturates	Drowsiness, confusion, coma, breathing difficulty.	Give activated charcoal or induce vomiting, black coffee, assist breathing.
Codeine (in pain killers, cough mixtures, antidiarrhoeals)	Constipation, reduced breathing, stupor, coma, heart attack.	Give activated charcoal or induce, assist breathing.
Digoxin (Lanoxin)	Vomiting, irregular pulse, heart failure.	Dilute with milk or water then give activated charcoal or induce vomiting.
Insecticides	Vomiting, diarrhoea, difficult breathing, convulsions.	Dilute with large amount of milk, give activated charcoal or induce vomiting, assist breathing.
Lysol and creosote	Burning of throat, vomiting, shock, breathing difficulty.	Dilute with large amount of milk. Do NOT induce vomiting.
Mushrooms	Varies depending on type.	Dilute with water, give activated charcoal or induce vomiting, assist breathing.
Narcotics (Morphine, heroin)	Headache, nausea, excitement, weak pulse, shock, coma.	Give activated charcoal or induce vomiting if narcotic swallowed, assist breathing.
Paracetamol (Panadol, Dymadon, Panamax etc.)	Vomiting, low blood pressure, liver damage, death [>50 tabs].	Give activated charcoal or induce vomiting.
Petroleum products (petrol, kerosene, etc.)	Liver damage, lung damage.	Do NOT induce vomiting, dilute with milk.
Tranquillisers (Phenothiazines)	Drowsiness, low blood pressure, rapid pulse, convulsions, coma.	Give activated charcoal or induce vomiting.
Tricyclic antidepressants (Sinequan, Tofranil, Prothiaden, Tryptanol etc.).	Coma, muscle spasm, convulsions, death.	Give activated charcoal or induce vomiting, assist breathing.

Vomiting

The stomach and sometimes the upper part of the small gut, will go into spasm and discharge their contents via the gullet and mouth for a very wide variety of reasons. Some causes of vomiting are common and innocuous, but others may indicate serious disease.

By far the most common reason to vomit is a toxin irritating the gut. This is food poisoning and a contaminated prawn, sausage or other foodstuff is usually responsible. The vomiting occurs two to eight hours after eating the food and is usually sudden, violent and short-lived. It is unusual for the problem to persist for more than a few hours and is only occasionally accompanied by diarrhoea.

Gastroenteritis is the other very common cause of vomiting. In this, a virus enters the stomach, causing it to become inflamed. In this state it secretes excess amounts of digestive juices and can go into spasm very easily, particularly if any further food is eaten. Initially the upper part of the gut is affected and as the virus moves down through the alimentary canal, the large bowel is involved. When the gut goes into spasm, its contents are expelled causing vomiting and/or diarrhoea and may be associated with painful abdominal cramps.

The virus can easily spread from one person to another and so one member of the family after another may become infected. Spread is avoided by hand washing, especially after toilet and before eating. Fortunately, the disease is self limiting and a strict diet for a few days is all that is normally required for treatment.

Nausea (the feeling that you want to be sick) and vomiting often accompany migraine type headaches. Some patients find that their migraine actually eases after vomiting.

Overindulgence in food and alcohol is another common cause of this distressing condition. Although today, sympathy for a self-induced condition is not often forthcoming, 2000 years ago, the Romans sometimes left a feast to vomit so that they could consume even greater amounts of the delicacies being offered.

Other people who may induce vomiting in themselves are those suffering from bulimia and anorexia nervosa. They have a compulsive desire to be thin and may appear to eat normally, but later regurgitate their food. They steadily loose weight and may become extremely ill as a result.

Vomiting after a head injury is a sign that there may be some brain damage. One or two vomits are not unusual, but if it becomes prolonged, urgent medical attention should be sought.

Sinusitis and colds may be associated with nausea and vomiting because of the large amounts of infected phlegm that are swallowed. Medications are available to dry up the phlegm and control the sinus infection.

Many rarer diseases from meningitis and stomach cancer to liver disease and pregnancy may be associated with vomiting. If you suffer from this condition and it does not settle rapidly, have the cause diagnosed and treated by your family doctor.

MEDICATIONS

Abacavir

TRADE NAME:

Ziagen.
Trizivir (with lamivudine and zidovudine).

DRUG CLASS:

Antiviral.

USES:

Treatment of AIDS and HIV infection.

DOSAGE:

 One tablet or 15mLs solution twice a day.

FORMS:

Tablet (300mg), solution.

PRECAUTIONS:

Intolerance to fructose in solution.

SIDE EFFECTS:

Common: liver damage, diarrhoea, tiredness, sensitivity reactions, fever, loss of appetite.
Severe but rare (stop medication, consult doctor): allergy reaction (cease immediately and never use again).

INTERACTIONS:

Other drugs:
• retinoids.

PRESCRIPTION:

Yes.

PERMITTED IN SPORT:

Yes.

OVERDOSE:

Effects not known.

OTHER INFORMATION:

Released in 1999 as one of numerous medications that may be beneficial in slowing the progress of AIDS.
See also Efavirenz, Indinavir, Lamivudine, Nelfinavir, Nevirapine, Ritonavir, Saquinavir, Stavudine, Tenofovir, Zalcitabine, Zidovudine.

Abciximab

TRADE NAME:

Reopro.

DRUG CLASS:

Anticoagulant.

USES:

Prevents blood clots during heart and artery surgery.

DOSAGE:

 Given by injection via a drip only.

FORMS:

Injection vial.

PRECAUTIONS:

Used only under strict supervision in hospital. May cause abnormal and excessive bleeding.

SIDE EFFECTS:

Common: unwanted bleeding.
Unusual: development of antibodies to the medication.

INTERACTIONS:

None serious.

PRESCRIPTION:
Yes.

PERMITTED IN SPORT:
Yes.

OVERDOSE:
May cause excessive bleeding.

OTHER INFORMATION:
Drug introduced in 1996 for prevention of complications of surgery on heart and arteries.
See also Heparin, Ticlopidine.

Acamprosate

TRADE NAME:
Campral EC.

USES:
Reduces desire for alcohol in alcoholics.

DOSAGE:
 One or two tablets three times a day.

FORMS:
Tablets of 333mg.

PRECAUTIONS:
Reduce dose in elderly and small body weight patients.
Use with caution in pregnancy (B2) and breast feeding.
Not to be used until completely withdrawn from alcohol.
Do not take if:
 • suffering from severe kidney disease, severe liver disease.

SIDE EFFECTS:
Common: diarrhoea.
Unusual: itch, red skin, reduced libido.

INTERACTIONS:
Other drugs:
• psychotropic drugs.

PRESCRIPTION:
Yes.

PERMITTED IN SPORT:
Yes.

OVERDOSE:
Serious effects unlikely.

OTHER INFORMATION:
Introduced in 1999.
See also Disulfiram, Naltrexone.

Acarbose

TRADE NAME:
Glucobay.

DRUG CLASS:
Hypoglycaemic.

USES:
Maturity onset diabetes type 2.

DOSAGE:
 50 to 200mg two to three times a day.

FORMS:
Tablets of 50mg and 100mg.

PRECAUTIONS:
Use with caution in pregnancy (B3) breast feeding and children. Regular blood tests to check sugar levels and liver function.

SIDE EFFECTS:
Common: low blood sugar, nausea, diarrhoea.
Unusual: liver abnormalities.

INTERACTIONS:
Other drugs:
• other hypoglycaemics (medications that lower blood sugar levels), neomycin, cholestyramine.
Herbs:
• alfalfa, celery, eucalyptus, fenugreek, garlic, ginger.

PRESCRIPTION:

Yes.

PERMITTED IN SPORT:

Yes.

OVERDOSE:

May cause coma due to excessively low blood sugar levels. Give activated activated charcoal or induce vomiting if medication taken recently. Seek medical assistance.

OTHER INFORMATION:

Introduced in 1998 as an additional form of treatment for difficult to control maturity onset diabetes.

See also Glibenclamide, Gliclazide, Glimepride, Glipizide, Gliquidone, INSULINS, Metformin, Repaglinide, Rosiglitazone, Tolbutamide.

Acebutolol

TRADE NAME:

Sectral.
Secadrex (with hydrochlorothiazide).

USES:

High blood pressure.

DOSAGE:

 200 to 800mg a day.

FORMS:

Tablets of 400mg, capsules of 100mg and 200mg.

PRECAUTIONS:

Should be used in pregnancy (C) only if medically essential. Eye drops unlikely to cause problems in pregnancy.
Safe to use in breast feeding.
May be used with caution in children.
Use with care if suffering from alcoholism, liver or kidney failure or about to have surgery.

Do not take if:

- suffering from diabetes, asthma, or allergic conditions.
- suffering from heart failure, shock, slow heart rate, or enlarged right heart.
- undertaking prolonged fast.

SIDE EFFECTS:

Common: low blood pressure, slow heart rate, cold hands and feet, asthma.
Unusual: loss of appetite, nausea, diarrhoea, impotence, tiredness, sleeplessness, nightmares, rash, loss of libido, hair loss, noises in ears.
Severe but rare (stop medication, consult doctor): severe asthma.

INTERACTIONS:

Other drugs:
- calcium channel blockers, disopyramide, clonidine, adrenaline, other medications for irregular heart beat, lignocaine, ergotamine, indomethacin, chlorpromazine.

Herbs:
- goldenseal, guarana, hawthorn, Korean ginseng, liquorice.

PRESCRIPTION:

Yes.

PERMITTED IN SPORT:

No.

OVERDOSE:

Slow heart rate, low blood pressure, asthma and heart failure may result. Administer activated charcoal or induce vomiting if tablets taken recently. Use Salbutamol or other asthma sprays for difficulty in breathing. Seek medical assistance.

OTHER INFORMATION:

Except for asthmatics, very safe and effective.

See also BETA-BLOCKERS.

Aceclofenac

TRADE NAME:

Preservex.

DRUG CLASS:

NSAID (Nonsteroidal anti-inflammatories drug).

USES:

All forms of arthritis, inflammatory disorders, gout, back pain, ankylosing spondylitis.

DOSAGE:

 One tablet twice a day.

FORMS:

Tablets of 100mg.

PRECAUTIONS:

Should not be used in pregnancy (C) unless medically essential. Breast feeding should be ceased if necessary to use NSAID. Not for use in children under two. Gel safe in pregnancy.
Use tablets and capsules with caution in psychiatricaly disturbed patients, epilepsy, severe infection, heart failure and kidney disease.
Lower doses required in elderly, who may suffer more side effects.

Do not take if:

- suffering from peptic ulcer at present or in recent past.
- due for surgery (including dental surgery).
- suffering from bleeding disorder or anaemia.

SIDE EFFECTS:

Common: stomach discomfort, diarrhoea, constipation, heartburn, nausea, headache, dizziness.
Unusual: blurred vision, stomach ulcer, ringing noise in ears, retention of fluid, swelling of tissue, drowsiness, itch, rash, shortness of breath.

Severe but rare (stop medication, consult doctor): vomiting blood, passing blood in faeces, other unusual bleeding, asthma induced by medication.

INTERACTIONS:

Other drugs:
- must never be used with anticoagulants (e.g. warfarin)
- probenecid, diuretics, lithium, methotrexate, beta-blockers, ACE inhibitors, digoxin, cyclosporin, diabetes medication (hypoglycaemics), steroids.

Herbs:
- feverfew.

PERMITTED IN SPORT:

Yes.

OVERDOSE:

Causes nausea, vomiting, severe headache, dizziness, confusion and convulsions. Administer activated charcoal or induce vomiting if taken recently. Seek medical assistance.

OTHER INFORMATION:

Significant side effects (particularly on the stomach) in about 5% of patients. Limit its use.

See also Acemetacin, Dexketoprofen, Diclofenac, Diflunisal, Etodolac, Felbinac, Fenbufen, Fenoprofen, Flurbiprofen, Ibuprofen, Indomethacin, Ketoprofen, Mefenamic acid, Meloxicam, Nabumetone, Naproxen, NSAID, Piroxicam, Salicylic acid, Sulindac, Tenoxicam, Tiaprofenic Acid, Tolfenamic acid.

ACE INHIBITORS
(Angiotensin Converting Enzyme Inhibitors)

TRADE and GENERIC NAMES:

Accupro (Quinapril).
Accuretic (Quinapril with hydrochlorothiazide).
Acepril, Capoten (Captopril).

Capozide (Captopril with hydrochlorothiazide).
Carace, Zestril (Lisinopril).
Carace Plus, Zestoretic (Lisinopril with hydrochlorothiazide).
Coversyl (Perindopril).
Gopten, Odrik (Trandolapril).
Innovace (Enalapril).
Innozide (Enalapril with hydrochlorothiazide).
Perdix (Moexipril).
Staril (Fosinopril).
Tanatril (Imidapril).
Tarka (Trandolapril with verapamil).
Triapin, Triapin Mite (Ramipril with felodipine).
Tritace (Ramipril).
Vascace (Ciliazapril).

DRUG CLASS:

Antihypertensive.

USES:

High blood pressure, heart failure, improves survival after heart attack.

DOSAGE:

 Different forms are longer acting than others. Follow doctor's instructions.
Dosage varies from one capsule or tablet a day, to two capsules or tablets three times a day.
Do not vary dosage without medical advice.

FORMS:

Tablets, capsules, injection and mixture.

PRECAUTIONS:

Should not be used in pregnancy (D). Should be used only if specifically medically indicated and with caution in children and while breast feeding.
Do not take if:
 • suffering from severe kidney disease, reduced blood supply to brain or taking immunosuppressive drugs.

SIDE EFFECTS:

Common: dry cough, swelling of ankles and other tissue, rash.
Unusual: stomach upsets, abnormal taste.
Severe but rare (stop medication, consult doctor): abnormal bleeding.

INTERACTIONS:

Other drugs:
• interacts with Diuretics, and some arthritis drugs, but often carefully used with these drugs
• reacts with Lithium, potassium increasing drugs, Tetracycline, Vasodilators.

PRESCRIPTION:

Yes.

PERMITTED IN SPORT:

Yes.

OVERDOSE:

May cause low blood pressure. First aid involves giving activated charcoal or induction of vomiting and seeking medical attention.

OTHER INFORMATION:

Relatively new group of drugs that are rapidly becoming the first choice in the treatment of high blood pressure and heart failure. First released early 1980s, but many new forms coming onto the market in the mid 1990s. Angiotensin is a hormone that naturally increases blood pressure. ACE Inhibitors reduce the amount of angiotensin produced in the body to reduce blood pressure.

See also Angiotensin II Receptor Antagonists.

Acemetacin

TRADE NAME:

Emflex.

DRUG CLASS:

NSAID (Nonsteroidal anti-inflammatories drug).

USES:

Osteoarthritis, rheumatoid arthritis, inflammatory disorders, back pain.

DOSAGE:

 One tablet two or three times a day.

FORMS:

Capsule of 60mg.

PRECAUTIONS:

Should not be used in pregnancy (C) unless medically essential. Breast feeding should be ceased if necessary to use NSAID. Not for use in children under two. Gel safe in pregnancy.

Use tablets and capsules with caution in psychiatricaly disturbed patients, epilepsy, severe infection, heart failure and kidney disease.

Lower doses required in elderly, who may suffer more side effects.

Do not take if:

- suffering from peptic ulcer at present or in recent past.
- due for surgery (including dental surgery).
- suffering from bleeding disorder or anaemia.

SIDE EFFECTS:

Common: stomach discomfort, diarrhoea, constipation, heartburn, nausea, headache, dizziness.

Unusual: blurred vision, stomach ulcer, ringing noise in ears, retention of fluid, swelling of tissue, drowsiness, itch, rash, shortness of breath.

Severe but rare (stop medication, consult doctor): vomiting blood, passing blood in faeces, other unusual bleeding, asthma induced by medication.

INTERACTIONS:

Other drugs:
- must never be used with anticoagulants (e.g. warfarin)
- probenecid, diuretics, lithium, methotrexate, beta-blockers, ACE inhibitors, digoxin, cyclosporin, diabetes medication (hypoglycaemics), steroids.

Herbs:
- feverfew.

PERMITTED IN SPORT:

Yes.

OVERDOSE:

Causes nausea, vomiting, severe headache, dizziness, confusion and convulsions. Administer activated charcoal or induce vomiting if taken recently. Seek medical assistance.

OTHER INFORMATION:

Significant side effects (particularly on the stomach) in about 5% of patients. Limit its use.

See also Aceclofenac, Dexketoprofen, Diclofenac, Diflunisal, Etodolac, Felbinac, Fenbufen, Fenoprofen, Flurbiprofen, Ibuprofen, Indomethacin, Ketoprofen, Mefenamic acid, Meloxicam, Nabumetone, Naproxen, NSAID, Piroxicam, Salicylic acid, Sulindac, Tenoxicam, Tiaprofenic Acid, Tolfenamic acid.

Acetazolamide

TRADE NAME:

Diamox.

USES:

Glaucoma, retention of fluid, swelling, petit mal and some other forms of epilepsy.

DOSAGE:

 Complex. Depends on condition being treated, its severity and weight of patient. Must be individually determined for each patient by doctor.

FORMS:

Tablets (white) of 250mg.

PRECAUTIONS:

Not to be used in pregnancy (B3). Use with caution in breast feeding and children.
Care must be used in long term use. Regular blood tests to check blood chemistry advisable.
Use with caution in emphysema.
Do not exceed recommended dose.

Do not take if:

- suffering from disorders of blood chemistry, liver disease, kidney disease, adrenal gland disease.

SIDE EFFECTS:

Common: pins and needles, frequent passing of urine, loss of appetite.
Unusual: biochemical imbalances in blood.

INTERACTIONS:

Other drugs:
- aspirin, hypoglycaemics, anticoagulants, phenytoin, digoxin.

Herbs:
- willow bark.

PRESCRIPTION:

Yes.

PERMITTED IN SPORT:

No.

OVERDOSE:

Significant abnormalities in blood chemistry may occur. Give activated charcoal or induce vomiting if medication taken recently. Seek medical assistance.

OTHER INFORMATION:

In glaucoma, usually taken in combination with eye drops.

See also Apraclonidine, Betaxolol, Bimatoprost, Brimonidine, Brinzolamide, Carbachol, Dipivefrine, Dorzolamide, Latanoprost, Levobunolol, Phenylephrine, Pilocarpine, Timolol, Travoprost.

Acetic acid

TRADE NAME:

Aci-Jel, EarCalm.
Otomize (with dexamethasone, neomycin).

USES:

Ear drops: EarCalm removes water from ears to prevent swimmers ear.
Otomize treats swimmers ear.
Gel: Restores vaginal acidity.

DOSAGE:

Ear drops: 4 to 6 drops in each ear after swimming.
Gel: 1 applicator full of gel twice a day.

FORMS:

Ear drops, vaginal gel.

PRECAUTIONS:

Ear drops: safe in pregnancy.
Gel: not for use in pregnancy.

Do not use ear drops if:

- suffering from ear infection, ear discharge, blocked ear canals, perforated ear drum.
- grommets inserted.

SIDE EFFECTS:

Ear drops: Ear canal irritation.
Gel: Minimal.

INTERACTIONS:

None.

PRESCRIPTION:

Aci-Jel, EarCalm: No.
Otomize: Yes.

PERMITTED IN SPORT:

Yes.

OVERDOSE:

Not likely to be harmful if swallowed.

Acetaminophen

See Paracetamol.

Acetylcholine chloride

TRADE NAME:

Miochol-E.

DRUG CLASS:

Miotic.

USES:

Rapid contraction of the pupil in the eye during eye surgery for cataracts.

DOSAGE:

 As determined by doctor.

FORMS:

Eye drops.

PRECAUTIONS:

Use with caution in pregnancy (B2). Drops must be prepared immediately before use.

SIDE EFFECTS:

Reduced vision in dull light.

INTERACTIONS:

None significant.

PRESCRIPTION:

Yes.

PERMITTED IN SPORT:

Yes.

OVERDOSE:

Unlikely to have adverse effects if swallowed.

OTHER INFORMATION:

Used only by ophthalmologists (eye doctors) in their rooms or hospital.
See also Carbachol.

Acetylcysteine

TRADE NAME:

Parvolex.
Ilube (with hypromellose).

USES:

Injection: paracetamol overdose.
Eye drops: dry eyes with excess mucus.

DOSAGE:

 Eye drops: one or two drops, three or four times a day.
Injection: as determined by doctor.

FORMS:

Eye drops, injection.

PRECAUTIONS:

Use with caution in pregnancy (B2), worsening asthma.
Do not take if:

 • suffering from severe liver or kidney disease.
• wearing soft contact lenses.

SIDE EFFECTS:

Eye drops: minimal.
Injection: asthma.

INTERACTIONS:

None significant.

PRESCRIPTION:

Yes.

PERMITTED IN SPORT:

Yes.

OTHER:

Should be used within ten hours of paracetamol overdose. Minimal benefit after 15 hours.

Acetylsalicylic Acid

See Aspirin.

Aciclovir

TRADE NAME:

Zovirax.

DRUG CLASS:

Antiviral.

USES:

Treatment of genital herpes, shingles, cold sores, chickenpox and herpes eye infections.

DOSAGE:

 Tablets: 200mg to 800mg every four to eight hours.
Cream: apply five times a day starting as soon as possible after onset of symptoms.
Eye ointment: insert five times a day for 14 days.

FORMS:

Tablets of 200mg, 400mg and 800mg: suspension, injection, eye ointment, skin cream.

PRECAUTIONS:

Use in pregnancy (B3) and breast feeding only when medically essential. May be used in children.
Lower doses necessary in elderly.
Use tablets with caution in serious kidney disease, dehydration, brain disorders.

SIDE EFFECTS:

Common: minimal.
Unusual: tablets—Nausea, vomiting, headache.

INTERACTIONS:

Other drugs:
• probenecid, diuretics (fluid tablets), interferon, methotrexate.

PRESCRIPTION:

Yes.

PERMITTED IN SPORT:

Yes.

OVERDOSE:

Exacerbation of side effects likely.

OTHER INFORMATION:

Very safe and effective medication that has a very high success rate in treating Herpes infections. Chickenpox and shingles are caused by Herpes zoster and cold sores and genital herpes by Herpes simplex. It is vital that any patient who suspects they have shingles must see their doctor immediately as Aciclovir only works if started within 72 hours of onset of rash. Chickenpox and cold sores are normally only treated under special circumstances as the medication is quite expensive. Eye infections with Herpes may cause blindness if not treated rapidly and effectively. Cream effective against cold sores only if started as soon as symptoms appear.

ACIDS

See Eicosapentaenoic acid, Lactic acid, Salicylic acid.

Acipimox

TRADE NAME:

Olbetam.

DRUG CLASS:

Hypolipidaemic.

USES:

Some types of high blood cholesterol and triglycerides.

DOSAGE:

 Maximum of 1200mg a day divided into two or three doses.

FORMS:

Capsule.

PRECAUTIONS:

Do not use in pregnancy (B2) and breast feeding.
Regular blood tests to check liver and kidney function and blood fat levels recommended.
Use with caution with low blood pressure and poor liver or kidney function.

Do not take if:

- suffering from peptic ulcer, stomach upsets, recent heart attack, severe kidney disease, diabetes, gout, heart disease, gall bladder disease, glaucoma, tendency to bleed easily.

SIDE EFFECTS:

Common: rashes, red skin, stomach upsets, nervousness, headache, tiredness.
Unusual: dry skin, skin pigmentation.
Severe but rare (stop medication, consult doctor): yellow skin.

INTERACTIONS:

Other drugs:
- drugs used to treat high blood pressure
- steroids, hallucinogens, reserpine, chlordiazepoxide.

PRESCRIPTION:

Yes.

PERMITTED IN SPORT:

Yes.

OVERDOSE:

Causes flushing, itch, vomiting, diarrhoea, heartburn, belly cramps, fainting. Induce vomiting if tablets taken recently. Seek medical assistance.

OTHER INFORMATION:

Derived from nicotinic acid.
See also Nicotinic Acid.

Acitretin

TRADE NAME:

Neotigason.

DRUG CLASS:

Keratolytic.

USES:

Severe psoriasis.

DOSAGE:

 Determined individually for each patient. 25 to 50mg a day.

FORMS:

Capsules of 10mg and 25mg.

PRECAUTIONS:

Absolutely forbidden in pregnancy (X). Use with caution in children and adolescents. Use with great caution in liver and kidney disease.

SIDE EFFECTS:

Common: dry skin, itchy skin, rashes, fragile skin.
Unusual: kidney and liver abnormalities, eye irritation, increased blood fat and cholesterol levels, bone and brain growths.
Severe but rare (stop medication, consult doctor): rare and serious complications.

INTERACTIONS:

Other drugs:
- mini-contraceptive pill, tetracycline antibiotics, phenytoin.
Other substances:
- vitamin A, alcohol.

PRESCRIPTION:

Yes. Hospitals only.

PERMITTED IN SPORT:

Yes.

OVERDOSE:

May cause headache, vomiting, flushing, mouth soreness and dryness, abdominal pain, flushing and incoordination. Seek medical assistance.

OTHER INFORMATION:

First introduced in 1997 to replace etretinate. A very potent and potentially dangerous drug, but if used correctly can dramatically and often permanently cure severe chronic psoriasis. Use in pregnancy will always cause severe damage to foetus. Vitamin A derivative.

Acriflavine

TRADE NAME:

Acriflavine.

DRUG CLASS:

Antiseptic.

USES:

Minor skin abrasions.

DOSAGE:

 Apply once or twice.

FORMS:

Solution.

PRECAUTIONS:

Do not mix with detergents or other chemicals.
Safe in pregnancy.

SIDE EFFECTS:

Minor skin irritation.

INTERACTIONS:

None significant on the skin.

PRESCRIPTION:

No.

PERMITTED IN SPORT:

Yes.

OVERDOSE:

May cause vomiting and diarrhoea if swallowed.

OTHER INFORMATION:

Old fashioned skin antiseptic.

Acrivastine

See ANTIHISTAMINES, NON-SEDATING.

Actinomycin D
(Dactinomycin)

TRADE NAME:

Cosmegen Lyovac

DRUG CLASS:

Cytotoxic.

USES:

Cancer of the kidney (Wilms tumour), brain, testes, uterus and bone.

DOSAGE:

 By drip into vein as determined for each patient by doctor.

FORMS:

Injection.

PRECAUTIONS:

Not to be used in pregnancy (D), breast feeding or infants.
Use with caution in children.
Use with caution if having radiotherapy.
Do not allow solution to touch skin— extremely corrosive. Ensure there is no leakage from drip into tissues outside vein.
Regular blood tests essential to check function of liver, kidney, bone marrow and blood cells.

Do not take if:

 • suffering from chickenpox or shingles.

SIDE EFFECTS:

Common: skin rashes, nausea, vomiting, tiredness, muscle pain, fever, anal pain, belly pain, loss of appetite.
Unusual: liver damage, anaemia.

INTERACTIONS:

None significant.

PRESCRIPTION:

Yes.

PERMITTED IN SPORT:

Yes.

OVERDOSE:

Very serious. Only given under strict medical supervision.

Activated Charcoal

See Charcoal.

Adapalene

TRADE NAME:

Differin.

USES:

Severe acne.

DOSAGE:

 Apply thinly once a day at bedtime to clean dry skin.

FORMS:

Gel, cream.

PRECAUTIONS:

Do not use if pregnant (D). Use with caution in children and breast feeding. Avoid eyes, lips, mouth, nostrils. Do not apply to broken skin, moist skin, moist tissues, eczema, dermatitis. Avoid sun exposure.

SIDE EFFECTS:

Common: red skin, dry skin.
Unusual: itch, burning, scaly skin.

INTERACTIONS:

Other drugs:
• retinoids, astringents, drying agents.
Other substances:
• abrasive cleansers.

PRESCRIPTION:

Yes.

PERMITTED IN SPORT:

Yes.

OVERDOSE:

Wash affected area thoroughly.

Adefovir

TRADE NAME:

Hepsera.

DRUG CLASS:

Antiviral.

USES:

Treatment of chronic hepatitis B.

DOSAGE:

 One tablet a day.

FORMS:

Tablets of 10mg.

PRECAUTIONS:

Not for use in pregnancy, breast feeding and children.
Patients must be closely monitored with blood tests regularly for at least six months after ceasing treatment.
Use with caution if suffering from kidney disease, obese or suffering from hepatitis C or hepatitis D.
Use with increased caution in elderly.

SIDE EFFECTS:

Common: nausea, diarrhoea, tiredness.
Unusual: belly pain, headache, kidney damage.
Severe but rare (stop medication, consult doctor): kidney failure.

INTERACTIONS:

Other drugs:
• reacts with numerous medications excreted through the kidneys.

PRESCRIPTION:

Yes.

PERMITTED IN SPORT:

Yes.

OVERDOSE:

Very serious. Seek urgent medical attention.

OTHER INFORMATION:

Introduced in 2002 for the treatment of serious liver disease due to hepatitis B.

Adenosine

TRADE NAME:

Adenocor.

DRUG CLASS:

Antiarrhythmic.

USES:

Control of some types of irregular heart beat starting in the upper chambers of the heart (the atria).
Dilates arteries of heart to allow adequate x-ray pictures to be taken.

DOSAGE:

 Given rapidly by injection into a vein.

FORMS:

Injection.

PRECAUTIONS:

Use with caution in pregnancy (B2), children and breast feeding.
Must only be used if type of irregular heart rhythm has been definitely established.

SIDE EFFECTS:

Common: flushed face, headache.
Unusual: shortness of breath, pressure in chest, light headedness, nausea, very slow heart rate.

INTERACTIONS:

Other drugs:
• carbamazepine, xanthines, dipyridamole.

PRESCRIPTION:

Yes. Used in hospital only.

PERMITTED IN SPORT:

Yes.

OVERDOSE:

Serious. Always given under close medical supervision.

Adrenaline

TRADE NAMES:

Anapen, Epipen.
Often combined with various local anaesthetics (e.g. lignocaine).

DRUG CLASS:

Vasoconstrictor, mydriatic.

USES:

Constriction of blood vessels to prolong effect of medication (e.g. local anaesthetics).
Control of very severe allergy reactions and asthma.
Dilates the size of the pupil in eye surgery and examination.
Treatment of certain type of glaucoma (chronic simple glaucoma).
Emergency treatment of some forms of heart disease.

DOSAGE:

 Eye drops: one drop in affected eye once or twice a day.
Injection: self inject for severe allergic reaction.

FORMS:

Injection, injection pen, eye drops.

PRECAUTIONS:

May be used in pregnancy, breast feeding and children.

Very safe to use as anal suppository or cream.

Eye drops should not be used for prolonged periods.

Injections only used by doctors in emergency situations. Never inject into ear, fingers, toes or penis. Never inject into artery or vein.

Use with caution if suffering from overactive thyroid gland, heart disease, high blood pressure, psychiatric conditions or diabetes.

SIDE EFFECTS:

Common: eye drops: eye pain, headache, brow ache, red eye.

Injection: rapid heart rate, reduced circulation at site of injection, difficulty in breathing, dizziness, weakness, tremor, headache, irritability, anxiety, fear.

INTERACTIONS:

Other drugs:
• injection may interact with tricyclic antidepressants, thyroxine and some antihistamines.

Other substances:
• do not use alcohol or caffeine, or undertake vigourous exercise.

PRESCRIPTION:

Yes.

PERMITTED IN SPORT:

Eye drops: yes.
Injection: no.

OVERDOSE:

Eye drops: flush eye with water.
Injection: very serious. May result in stroke, heart attack and death. Extremely urgent medical attention required to administer counter acting drugs.

OTHER INFORMATION:

Widely used to prolong effect of local anaesthetics and reduce bleeding at operation site. Effective in extreme cases of severe allergy to reduce effects of swelling.

See also Isoprenaline.

AIDS (HIV) TREATMENTS

See Abacavir, Delavirdine, Didanosine, Efavirenz, Indinavir, Lamivudine, Nelfinavir, Nevirapine, Ritonavir, Saquinavir, Stavudine, Tenofovir, Valganciclovir, Zalcitabine, Zidovudine.

Alclometasone

TRADE NAME:

Modrasone.

DRUG CLASS:

Corticosteroid.

USES:

Eczema, dermatitis.

DOSAGE:

 Apply thinly two or three times a day.

FORMS:

Cream, ointment.

PRECAUTIONS:

Should be used with caution in pregnancy and breast feeding. Safe for use in children.

Avoid eyes.

Use for shortest period of time possible.

Do not use if:

 • suffering from any form of skin infection, skin ulcers, acne or cracked lips.

SIDE EFFECTS:

Minimal.

INTERACTIONS:

None significant.

PRESCRIPTION:

Yes.

PERMITTED IN SPORT:

Yes.

OTHER INFORMATION:

Extremely effective and useful medication, particularly on the face, on delicate skin and in children. Lowest dose and shortest possible course should be used. Not addictive. Introduced late 1980s.

ALCOHOLS

See Ethanol, Isopropyl alcohol.

Alendronate

TRADE NAME:

Fosamax.

DRUG CLASS:

Bisphosphonate.

USES:

Osteoporosis, Paget's disease.

DOSAGE:

 Up to 10mg a day. Take one or two tablets a day 30 minutes before eating or drinking after waking in morning. Remain erect until after eating.
70mg tablets: take one tablet a week 30 minutes before first food or drink of day with full glass of water. Do not lie down for 30 minutes and until after first food.

FORMS:

Tablets of 5mg and 70mg.

PRECAUTIONS:

Use with great caution in pregnancy (B3), breast feeding and children.
Use with caution with recent peptic ulcer and kidney damage.

Calcium and vitamin D levels must be monitored.
Do not take any other medications within two hours.

Do not take if:

 • suffering from peptic ulcer.

SIDE EFFECTS:

Common: nausea, vomiting, indigestion.
Unusual: ulceration of oesophagus and stomach, mouth ulcers, peptic ulcers, muscle pain, headaches.
Severe but rare (stop medication, consult doctor): vomiting blood, black motions.

INTERACTIONS:

Other drugs:
• calcium supplements, antacids, biphosphonates, aspirin
• may affect almost any medication taken by mouth.

PRESCRIPTION:

Yes.

PERMITTED IN SPORT:

Yes.

OVERDOSE:

Very low blood levels of calcium may occur. This may interfere with the function of nerves and other tissues. Other symptoms may include indigestion and vomiting. Induce vomiting if medication taken recently or drink large amounts of milk.

OTHER INFORMATION:

Potent and effective medication for osteoporosis introduced in 1996. Once a week dose (70mg) introduced in 2001 has dramatically increased ease of use.
See also Residronate.

Alfacalcidol

TRADE NAME:

One-Alpha.

USES:

Severe body calcium chemistry diseases involving the parathyroid glands and/or kidneys (e.g. renal osteodystrophy), rickets, osteomalacia.

DOSAGE:

 As determined by doctor.

FORMS:

Capsules, mixture.

PRECAUTIONS:

Not for use in pregnancy and breast feeding.
Blood tests required regularly to monitor calcium levels.

Do not take if:

 • suffering from kidney failure.

INTERACTIONS:

Other drugs:
• barbiturates, anticonvulsants, danazol, digoxin, antacids, thiazide diuretics, sucralfate, colestipol, cholestyramine.

Other substances:
• mineral oils.

PRESCRIPTION:

Yes.

PERMITTED IN SPORT:

Yes.

OVERDOSE:

Serious. Seek urgent medical attention.

Alfentanil

TRADE NAME:

Rapifen.

DRUG CLASS:

Narcotic.

USES:

Pain relief while under anaesthesia.

DOSAGE:

 Calculated by anaesthetist for each individual patient.

FORMS:

Injection.

PRECAUTIONS:

Must not be used in pregnancy (C) or children under 12 years.
Use with caution in head injuries, obesity and elderly.

Do not take if:

 • suffering from liver failure, underactive thyroid gland.

SIDE EFFECTS:

Unusual: reduced ability to breathe, muscle rigidity, slow heart rate, low blood pressure, throat spasm.

INTERACTIONS:

Other drugs:
• some anaesthetics, erythromycin, cimetidine, MAOI, medications that depress brain function.

PRESCRIPTION:

Yes. Controlled drug.

PERMITTED IN SPORT:

No.

See also Buprenorphine, Codeine, Dextromoramide, Dextropropoxyphene, Fentanyl, Heroin, Hydromorphone, Methadone, Morphine, Oxycodone, Pentazocine, Pethidine.

Alfuzosin

TRADE NAME:

Xantral.

USES:

Enlarged prostate gland.

DOSAGE:

 One tablet three times a day after meals.

FORMS:

Tablet.

PRECAUTIONS:

Not for use in pregnancy, breast feeding and children.
Use with caution in heart, kidney and liver disease.
Blood pressure should be checked regularly.

Do not take if:

- suffering from prostate cancer, low blood pressure or significant liver disease.
- angina or chest pain occurs.
- having a general anaesthetic.

SIDE EFFECTS:

Common: dizziness, giddiness, headache, nausea, diarrhoea.
Unusual: low blood pressure, fainting, tiredness, rapid heart rate, palpitations, rash, itch, flushes, swelling of feet and hands.
Severe but rare (stop medication, consult doctor): angina. (chest pain).

INTERACTIONS:

Other drugs:
- medications that lower blood pressure, other medications that reduce prostate gland size.

PRESCRIPTION:

Yes.

PERMITTED IN SPORT:

Yes.

OVERDOSE:

Serious. May cause diarrhoea, vomiting, difficulty in breathing, weakness, low blood pressure, slow heart rate and heart attack. Seek urgent medical attention.

Alginic acid

See ANTACIDS.

ALKYLATERS

See CANCER TREATING DRUGS.

Allantoin

TRADE NAMES:

Available only in combination with other medications.
Actinac (with chloramphenicol, hydrocortisone, sulphur and other ingredients).
Alphosyl HC (with tar, hydrocortisone).
Alphosyl (with tar).

USES:

Repairs damaged skin, minor burns, grazes, acne, psoriasis.

DOSAGE:

 Apply several times a day.

FORMS:

Powder, cream, ointment, lotion.

PRECAUTIONS:

Safe to use in pregnancy, breast feeding and children.
Avoid eye contact.

SIDE EFFECTS:

Minimal.

INTERACTIONS:

None significant.

PRESCRIPTION:

Alphosyl: No.
Others: Yes.

PERMITTED IN SPORT:

Yes.

ALLERGEN EXTRACTS

TRADE NAMES:

Allergens against a wide range of plants, foods, animals, moulds, insects etc, are available.

DRUG CLASS:

Antiallergen.

USES:

Reduction of allergy reaction to specific substances.

DOSAGE:

 Complex. Series of injections over many months in very slowly increasing concentrations and doses as determined by doctor.

FORMS:

Injection.

PRECAUTIONS:

Patient must wait in surgery for 30 minutes after injection given in case of serious allergy reaction.
Injection must be given subcutaneously (just under the skin) and not into muscle or a vein.
Should not be used in pregnancy, but unlikely to be serious consequences if administered inadvertently.

Do not take if:

 • allergy reaction at time of planned injection.

SIDE EFFECTS:

Common: local redness of skin at site of injection.
Unusual: widespread redness and itching of skin around site of injection.
Severe but rare: generalised severe anaphylactic (allergy) reaction that may be life threatening unless treated promptly.

INTERACTIONS:

None.

PRESCRIPTION:

Yes.

PERMITTED IN SPORT:

Yes.

OVERDOSE:

Very severe, life threatening anaphylactic (allergy) reaction may occur. Adrenaline should be injected subcutaneously every few minutes to counteract anaphylaxis. Doctor may need to give oxygen and cardiopulmonary resuscitation.

Allopurinol

TRADE NAME:

Zyloric.

DRUG CLASS:

Uricosuric.

USES:

Prevention of gout and its complications.

DOSAGE:

 One or two tablets once a day.

FORMS:

Tablets of 100mg and 300mg.

PRECAUTIONS:

Use with caution in pregnancy (B2) and breast feeding. Not for use in children. Use with caution in kidney and liver disease, and haemochromatosis.

Do not take if:

 • suffering from acute gout.

SIDE EFFECTS:

Common: minimal.
Unusual: fever, arthritis, nausea.
Severe but rare (stop medication, consult doctor): rash.

INTERACTIONS:

Other drugs:
• azathioprine, mercaptopurine, sulfinpyrazone, probenecid, aspirin.
Other substances:
• alcohol may aggravate gout.

PRESCRIPTION:

Yes.

PERMITTED IN SPORT:

Yes.

OVERDOSE:

May cause vomiting, diarrhoea and dizziness.

OTHER INFORMATION:

Widely used, very safe and effective medication for the prevention of gout. Does not cause dependence or addiction.
See also Probenecid.

Almotriptan

TRADE NAME:

Almogran.

DRUG CLASS:

Antimigraine.

USES:

Treatment of acute migraine.

DOSAGE:

 One tablet at onset of headache. Repeat once only if necessary after two hours.

FORMS:

Tablet (white) of 12.5mg.

PRECAUTIONS:

Should not be used in pregnancy (B3) unless medically essential. Should be used with caution in breast feeding. Not for use in children under 12 years. Should be used with caution in epilepsy, asthma, liver and kidney disease, heart disease and in elderly.

Not to be used for prevention of migraine, only treatment of acute attacks.

Do not take if:

 • suffering from angina, poor circulation to heart or limbs, recent heart attack, severe high blood pressure, recent stroke, irregular heart beat, significant liver disease.
• Ergotamine used in previous 24 hours.

SIDE EFFECTS:

Common: chest pain, pain at injection site, tingling sensation, heat, heaviness, flushing, tightness, dizziness, weakness.
Unusual: fatigue, drowsiness, nausea, vomiting.
Severe but rare (stop medication, consult doctor): significant chest pain (angina), fitting.

INTERACTIONS:

Other drugs:
• ergotamine, MAOI.
Herbs:
• St John's wort.
Other substances:
• does not interact with alcohol.

PRESCRIPTION:

Yes.

PERMITTED IN SPORT:

Yes.

OVERDOSE:

Exacerbation of side effects only.

OTHER INFORMATION:

Other relevant and interesting information about the medication, including problems with addiction and long term use.
See also Ergotamine, Naratriptan, Sumatriptan, Zolmitriptan.

ALPHA BLOCKERS

DISCUSSION:

Alpha receptor blockers are drugs that block the reception of certain nerve

signals to the arteries and if these signals are not received, the artery relaxes, allowing more blood to flow through at a lower pressure, thus easing high blood pressure. These drugs have undergone considerable refinement over the years, and most of the earlier ones that had significant side effects are no longer used.
See Doxazosin, Indoramin, Labetalol, Prazosin, Tamsulosin, Thymoxamine.

Alpha tocopherols

See Tocopherols.

Alprostadil
(Prostaglandin E1)

TRADE NAMES:

Caverject, Muse, Prostin VR, Viridal.

USES:

Prostin VR: To keep arteries open in newborn babies with heart defects.
Others: Inability to obtain an erection in the male penis.

DOSAGE:

 Caverject, Virida: Inject into shaft of penis as directed by doctor. Muse: Insert pellet with applicator into urethral opening at end of penis. Prostin: As determined by doctor.

FORMS:

Injection, pellet.

PRECAUTIONS:

Do not use for erection if:

- suffering from blood borne diseases.
- partner pregnant.
- suffering from curvature or deformity of penis.
- penile implant inserted.

SIDE EFFECTS:

Common: pain during injection and erection, bruising.

Unusual: prolonged erection, scarring and curvature of penis.

INTERACTIONS:

Other drugs:
- warfarin, heparin.
Other substances:
- reactions with substances such as alcohol, caffeine, foods, exercise etc.

PRESCRIPTION:

Yes.

PERMITTED IN SPORT:

Yes.

OVERDOSE:

Prolonged painful erection, diarrhoea, depression, rapid breathing. Medical attention essential for any penile erection lasting longer than four hours.

OTHER INFORMATION:

Injection introduced in 1996 as a safe and effective form of treatment for impotence. Muse introduced in 1998 as an alternative to injected form.
See also Sildenafil, Tadalafil.

Alteplase

See FIBRINOLYTICS.

Aluminium chloride

TRADE NAMES:

Anhydrol Forte, Driclor.

USES:

Excessive sweating from arm pits, hands and feet.

DOSAGE:

 Apply nightly initially, reducing to once or twice a week depending on response.

FORMS:

Solution.

PRECAUTIONS:

Safe to use in pregnancy, breast feeding and children over six years.
Avoid contact with eyes.
Do not use on broken or damaged skin.
Do not shave arm pit within 24 hours of use.
Do not bathe immediately before use.

SIDE EFFECTS:

None significant.

INTERACTIONS:

None.

PRESCRIPTION:

No.

PERMITTED IN SPORT:

Yes.

OVERDOSE:

Seek medical attention if swallowed.

OTHER INFORMATION:

One of the more useful treatments for the distressing condition of hyperhidrosis (excess sweating).

Aluminium oxide

TRADE NAME:

Brasivol.

DRUG CLASS:

Keratolytic.

USES:

Acne.

DOSAGE:

 Apply once a day to dry skin. Rub into affected area then rinse skin. Start with strength 1, progress to strength 2 after several weeks if necessary.

FORMS:

Suspension in two strengths.

PRECAUTIONS:

Safe in pregnancy. Not for use in children.
Avoid eye contact.
Do not use for rosacea and superficial veins.

SIDE EFFECTS:

Common: skin irritation.

INTERACTIONS:

None significant.

PRESCRIPTION:

No.

PERMITTED IN SPORT:

Yes.

See also KERATOLYTICS.

Aluminium salts

See ANTACIDS.

Alverine Citrate

TRADE NAMES:

Spasmonal.
Spasmonal Fibre (with sterculia).

DRUG CLASS:

Antispasmodic.

USES:

Irritable bowel syndrome, bowel spasms.

DOSAGE:

 Capsules: one or two, two or three times a day.
Fibre: one or two heaped teaspoons once or twice a day.

FORMS:

Capsules, granules.

PRECAUTIONS:

Ensure adequate fluid intake with fibre. Use with caution in pregnancy. Safe in breast feeding.

Do not take if:

- suffering from obstructed bowel or bowel cancer.

SIDE EFFECTS:

Common: mild feeling of belly distension.

INTERACTIONS:

Other drugs:
- may interfere with the absorption of many medications.

PRESCRIPTION:

No.

PERMITTED IN SPORT:

Yes.

OVERDOSE:

Take additional water. Belly discomfort and passing excess wind only effects.

See also Dicyclomine, Mebeverine.

Amantadine

TRADE NAMES:

Lysovir, Symmetrel.

DRUG CLASS:

Antiparkinsonian.

USES:

Parkinson's disease, prevention of influenza type A.

DOSAGE:

Parkinson's disease: increase slowly over several weeks under doctor's instructions.
Influenza A prevention: one capsule twice a day.

FORMS:

Capsule of 100mg.

PRECAUTIONS:

Use in pregnancy (B3) only if medically essential. Use in breast feeding with considerable caution. Not for use in children under nine years.
Use with caution in glaucoma, enlarged prostate gland, confused or psychiatricaly disturbed patients, heart failure, low blood pressure, liver and kidney disease. Do not stop suddenly, but reduce dose slowly.
Lower dose required in elderly.

SIDE EFFECTS:

Common: indigestion, excitement, dizziness, poor concentration, dry mouth, blurred vision, constipation, anxiety, confusion, swelling of ankles and feet.
Unusual: tremor, headache, slurred speech, incoordination, sleeplessness, palpitations, difficulty in passing urine.
Severe but rare (stop medication, consult doctor): unable to pass urine, convulsions, irrational behaviour.

INTERACTIONS:

Other drugs:
- other antiparkinsonians, L-Dopa.
Other substances:
- reacts adversely with alcohol and caffeine.

PRESCRIPTION:

Yes.

PERMITTED IN SPORT:

Yes.

OVERDOSE:

May cause confusion, hallucinations, delirium, rapid heart rate, rapid breathing, vomiting, dry mouth and retention of urine. Deaths have not been reported. Induce vomiting if medication taken recently. Seek medical attention.

OTHER INFORMATION:

Widely used for decades to help Parkinsonism, but has the additional benefit of protecting against one form (the less common form) of influenza, which may be useful during an epidemic.

See also Apomorphine, Benzhexol, Benztropine, Biperiden, Bromocriptine, Entacapone, LEVODOPA COMPOUNDS,

Orphenadrine, Pergolide, Pramipexole, Procyclidine, Ropinirole, Selegiline.

Amethocaine
See ANAESTHETICS, LOCAL.

Amfebutamone
See Bupropion.

Amifostine

TRADE NAME:

Ethyol.

USES:

Decreases damage to white blood cells and kidneys in patients having chemotherapy for cancer.

DOSAGE:

 Complex. As determined for each patient by doctor.

FORMS:

Injection.

PRECAUTIONS:

Use with caution in pregnancy (B3), elderly and children.
Blood pressure and blood calcium levels must be checked regularly.
Use with caution in kidney, liver, heart and brain disease.

SIDE EFFECTS:

Common: low blood pressure, nausea, vomiting, flushing, chills, dizziness, tiredness.
Unusual: hiccups, sneezing.

INTERACTIONS:

Other drugs:
• drugs that lower blood pressure and blood calcium levels.

PRESCRIPTION:
Yes.

PERMITTED IN SPORT:
Yes.

Amikacin

TRADE NAME:

Amikin.

DRUG CLASS:

Aminoglycoside antibiotic.

USES:

Short term treatment of serious infections.

DOSAGE:

 As determined by doctor.

FORMS:

Injection.

PRECAUTIONS:

Must not be used in pregnancy (D). Use with caution in elderly, children and during breast feeding.
Not designed for long term use as it may accumulate in body.
Adequate fluid intake essential.

Do not take if:

 • suffering from severe kidney disease.

SIDE EFFECTS:

Unusual: adverse effects on ears, kidneys and brain.

INTERACTIONS:

Other drugs:
• other antibiotics, fluid removing medications (diuretics), anaesthetics and muscle relaxants.

PRESCRIPTION:

Yes.

PERMITTED IN SPORT:

Yes.

OVERDOSE:

Causes ringing in ears, dizziness, deafness which may be permanent, rash, fever, headache, pins and needles sensation and kidney failure. Seek urgent medical attention so that blood dialysis can be performed.

See Gatifloxacin, Gentamicin, Neomycin, Tobramycin.

Amiloride

TRADE NAMES:

Only available in Britain in combination with diuretics (fluid removers).
Amil-Co, Moducren, Moduret, Moduretic (with hydrochlorothiazide).
Burinex A (with bumetanide).
Fru-Co, Frumil, Lasoride (with frusemide).
Kalten (with atenolol and hydrochlorothiazide).
Navispare (with cyclopenthiazide).

DRUG CLASS:

Potassium sparing diuretic (removes fluid from body through kidneys without excess loss of potassium).

USES:

High blood pressure, conserving potassium within body, excess fluid in body.

DOSAGE:

 One to four tablets in morning.

FORMS:

Tablets.

PRECAUTIONS:

Should only be used in pregnancy (C) and breast feeding if medically essential. Should not be used in children.

Should be used with caution in diabetes or liver disease.

Do not take if:

 • suffering from kidney disease.

SIDE EFFECTS:

Common: minimal.
Unusual: nausea, loss of appetite, belly discomfort, rash, excess wind.

INTERACTIONS:

Other drugs:
• lithium.
• do not use with potassium supplements or triamterene.
Herbs:
• celery, dandelion, uva ursi.

PRESCRIPTION:

Yes.

PERMITTED IN SPORT:

No.

OVERDOSE:

Dehydration may occur. Induce vomiting if tablets taken recently. Give extra fluids.

See also See also Amiloride, Bumetanide, Ethacrynic Acid, Frusemide, Indapamide, Spironolactone, THIAZIDE DIURETICS, Triamterene.

Aminobenzoic Acid
(Potassium p-Aminobenzoate)

TRADE NAME:

Potaba.

USES:

Peyronie disease (deformed erect penis), scleroderma.

DOSAGE:

 Six tablets or capsules, four times a day.

FORMS:

Tablets and capsules of 500mg, powder in sachet.

PRECAUTIONS:

Not to be used in pregnancy, breast feeding or children.

Do not take if:

 • suffering from kidney disease.

SIDE EFFECTS:

Common: loss of appetite, nausea.

INTERACTIONS:

Other drugs:
• sulphonamide antibiotics.

PRESCRIPTION:

No.

PERMITTED IN SPORT:

Yes.

OVERDOSE:

Seek medical advice. Vomiting likely.

with caution in children.
Regular checking of blood pressure essential.
Regular blood tests to check thyroid gland and blood chemistry essential.

Do not take if:

 • suffering from porphyria.

SIDE EFFECTS:

Common: tiredness, incoordination, dizziness, rash, nausea.
Unusual: confusion, vomiting, fever.

INTERACTIONS:

Other drugs:
• dexamethasone, anticoagulants, hypoglycaemics (used for diabetes).

PRESCRIPTION:

Yes.

OVERDOSE:

May cause incoordination, sedation, difficulty in breathing and coma. Death unlikely. Induce vomiting if medication taken recently. Seek urgent medical assistance.

Aminoglutethamide

TRADE NAME:

Orimeten.

USES:

Breast cancer, Cushing's syndrome.

DOSAGE:

 Must be individualised for each patient by doctor depending on disease.

FORMS:

Tablets (white) of 250mg.

PRECAUTIONS:

Must not be used in pregnancy (D) unless the mother's life is at risk. Breast feeding must be ceased before use. May be used

AMINOGLYCOSIDES

DISCUSSION:

Aminoglycosides are a group of less commonly used antibiotics that can destroy certain types of bacteria causing infections in the urinary tract, skin and bloodstream.

See Amikacin, Gentamicin, Neomycin, Tobramycin.

Aminophylline

TRADE NAME:

Phyllocontin.

DRUG CLASS:

Bronchodilator.

USES:

Asthma, emphysema, chronic bronchitis.

DOSAGE:

 One or two tablets twelve hourly.

FORMS:

Tablets of 100mg (orange), 225mg (cream), and 350mg (yellow).

PRECAUTIONS:

Safe to use in pregnancy (A), breast feeding and children.
Use with caution in infants.
Use with caution in heart disease, stomach ulcers, heartburn, kidney disease and liver disease.
Lower doses necessary in elderly and lighter patients.
Higher doses may be necessary in smokers.
Blood tests to monitor drug levels may be necessary.

SIDE EFFECTS:

Common: nausea, vomiting, belly discomfort, rapid heart rate, tremor, palpitations.
Unusual: irregular heart rate, convulsions, angina.

INTERACTIONS:

Other drugs:
• cimetidine, erythromycin.
Other substances:
• reacts with alcohol, caffeine and nicotine.

PRESCRIPTION:

No.

PERMITTED IN SPORT:

Yes.

OVERDOSE:

Serious. May cause vomiting, headache, irritability, rapid heart rate, confusion, fever, delirium and convulsions. Seek urgent medical assistance.

OTHER INFORMATION:

An early treatment for asthma that is still very useful. Dose must be finely adjusted to give adequate clinical response while avoiding side effects.
See also Theophylline.

Aminosalicylic Acid

See Mesalazine.

Amiodarone

TRADE NAME:

Cordarone X.

DRUG CLASS:

Antiarrhythmic.

USES:

Severe rapid irregular heart beat.

DOSAGE:

 One tablet, one to three times a day.

FORMS:

Tablet of 100mg and 200mg, injection.

PRECAUTIONS:

Should not be used in pregnancy (C) unless medically essential. Not to be used in breast feeding or children.
Regular cardiograph (ECG) and blood test monitoring may be required.
Should be used with caution in heart failure and liver disease.
Do not take if:

 • suffering from slow heart rate, thyroid disease or iodine sensitivity.

SIDE EFFECTS:

Common: serious heart irregularities,

slow heart rate, sensitivity to sunburn increased, nausea.

Unusual: grey skin pigmentation, rashes, vomiting, loss of appetite, metallic taste, constipation, tremor, sleeplessness, headache, dizziness, anxiety, shortness of breath.

Severe but rare (stop medication, consult doctor): angina, weight loss, restlessness.

INTERACTIONS:

Other drugs:
• beta-blockers, calcium channel blockers, digoxin, anticoagulants (e.g. warfarin).
• other drugs for treatment of irregular heartbeat.

Herbs:
• echinacea.

Other substances:
• alcohol use should be restricted.
• smoking should be ceased.
• caffeine intake should be restricted.

PRESCRIPTION:

Yes.

PERMITTED IN SPORT:

Yes.

OVERDOSE:

Exaggerated side effects only response. If tablets taken recently, give activated charcoal or induce vomiting. Seek medical advice.

OTHER INFORMATION:

Medication reserved for the most serious forms of heart arrhythmia.

See also Disopyramide, Flecainide, Mexiletine, Procainamide, Propafenone, Quinidine, Sotalol, Verapamil.

Amisulpride

TRADE NAME:

Solian.

DRUG CLASS:

Antipsychotic.

USES:

Some types of schizophrenia.

DOSAGE:

 400mg to 1200mg a day in divided doses.

FORMS:

Tablets of 50mg, 100mg, 200mg and 400mg (white).

PRECAUTIONS:

Use in pregnancy (B3) and breast feeding only if essential. Not for use in children. Use with caution in kidney disease, epilepsy, Parkinson's disease, slow heart rate, low potassium levels in blood, abnormal heart rhythm.

Do not take if:
• suffering from prolactin dependent tumours, phaeochromocytoma.

SIDE EFFECTS:

Common: inability to sleep, cessation of menstrual periods.

Unusual: abnormal heart rhythm, incoordination, production of breast milk.

Severe but rare (stop medication, consult doctor): high fever (neuroleptic malignant syndrome).

INTERACTIONS:

Other drugs:
• quinidine, disopyramide, amiodarone, sotalol, cisapride, erythromycin, pentamidine, levodopa, lithium, calcium channel blockers, beta-blockers, clonidine, digoxin, diuretics, amphotericin, steroids and some antidepressants and blood pressure medications.

Herbs:
• evening primrose (linoleic acid).

Other substances:
• alcohol.

PRESCRIPTION:

Yes.

PERMITTED IN SPORT:

Yes.

OVERDOSE:

Serious. If tablets taken recently, give activated charcoal or induce vomiting. Seek urgent medical advice.

See also Droperidol, Flupenthixol, Haloperidol, Lithium Carbonate, Olanzapine, PHENOTHIAZINES, Pimozide, Quetiapine, Risperidone, Thiothixene, Zuclopenthixol.

Amitriptyline

See TRICYCLICS.

Amlodipine

TRADE NAME:

Istin.

DRUG CLASS:

Calcium channel blocker (calcium antagonist).

USES:

High blood pressure, angina.

DOSAGE:

 2.5 to 10mg a day.

FORMS:

Tablets (white) of 5mg and 10mg.

PRECAUTIONS:

Should only be used in pregnancy (C) and breast feeding if medically essential. Not designed for use in children.

Do not take if:

 • suffering from severe heart failure, low blood pressure, atrial flutter or fibrillation.

SIDE EFFECTS:

Common: constipation, tiredness, headache, dizziness, indigestion, swelling of feet and ankles.
Unusual: flushing, palpitations, slow heart rate, scalp irritation, depression, flushes, nightmares, excess wind.
Severe but rare (stop medication, consult doctor): fainting.

INTERACTIONS:

Other drugs:
• beta-blockers (e.g. propranolol), cyclosporin, digoxin, cimetidine, diazepam, amiodarone, quinidine, rifampicin, phenytoin, cisapride, theophylline, terbutaline, salbutamol, diltiazem
• additive effect with other medications for high blood pressure.
Herbs:
• goldenseal, guarana, hawthorn, Korean ginseng, liquorice.
Other substances:
• smoking may aggravate conditions that these medications are treating.
• grapefruit juice.

PRESCRIPTION:

Yes.

PERMITTED IN SPORT:

Yes.

OVERDOSE:

May continue to be absorbed for up to 48 hours after overdose. Administer activated charcoal or induce vomiting. Purging should be encouraged to eliminate drug from gut. Overdose may cause low blood pressure, irregular heart rhythm, difficulty in breathing, heart attack and death. Obtain urgent medical attention.

OTHER INFORMATION:

Commonly used as a first line medication in high blood pressure and to prevent angina.

See also Diltiazem, Felodipine, Nifedipine, Nimodipine, Verapamil.

Ammonium chloride

TRADE NAMES:

Found in numerous over the counter cough mixtures and bladder infection treatments.

DRUG CLASS:

Urinary acidifier, cough suppressant.

USES:

Maintains acid urine, increases urine production, eases coughs.

DOSAGE:

 Take every four hours.

FORMS:

Tablets, mixture.

PRECAUTIONS:

Safe for use in pregnancy (A), breast feeding and children.
Blood tests to check level of potassium recommended if used long term.

Do not take if:

 • suffering from kidney or liver disease.

SIDE EFFECTS:

Common: nausea.
Unusual: vomiting, belly pains, low blood potassium.

INTERACTIONS:

None significant.

PRESCRIPTION:

No.

PERMITTED IN SPORT:

Yes.

OVERDOSE:

Exacerbation of side effects likely.

Amorolfine

TRADE NAME:

Loceryl.

DRUG CLASS:

Antifungal.

USES:

Fungal infections of the nails.

DOSAGE:

 Apply lacquer to affected nails once or twice a week.
Apply cream to skin once a day in evening.

FORMS:

Nail lacquer, cream.

PRECAUTIONS:

Should not be used in pregnancy (B3).
Use with caution in children.
Do not apply to skin.

SIDE EFFECTS:

Common: temporary burning sensation, itching.
Unusual: redness, nail discolouration, scaling of nail.

INTERACTIONS:

None.

PRESCRIPTION:

Yes.

PERMITTED IN SPORT:

Yes.

OVERDOSE:

Serious effects if swallowed. Seek urgent medical attention.

OTHER INFORMATION:

Introduced in 1996 as a very effective way of treating severe fungal infections of nails that caused disfigurement.

Amoxapine

See TRICYCLIC ANTIDEPRESSANTS.

Amoxycillin

TRADE NAMES:

Amoxil.
Augmentin (with clavulanic acid).
Heliclear (with lansoprazole and clarithromycin).

DRUG CLASS:

Penicillin antibiotic.

USES:

Treatment of infections caused by susceptible bacteria.
Heliclear used to destroy *Helicobacter pylori*, a bacteria that may be responsible for peptic ulcers.

DOSAGE:

 Most forms: one or two capsules every eight hours before food.
Heliclear: complex dosage schedule of multiple capsules taken three times a day.
Course (usually five to seven days) should be completed.

FORMS:

Capsules, mixture (store in door of refrigerator), injection.

PRECAUTIONS:

Safe in pregnancy (A), children and breast feeding.
Use with caution in kidney failure and leukaemia.
Do not take if:
 • allergic to penicillin.
• suffering from glandular fever.

SIDE EFFECTS:

Common: mild diarrhoea, nausea, vomiting.
Unusual: genital itch or rash, headache, dizziness, hot flushes, tiredness.
Severe but rare (stop medication, consult doctor): itchy rash, hives, severe diarrhoea, jaundice, muscle pains, throat tightness.

INTERACTIONS:

Other drugs:
• allopurinol.
Other substances:
• alcohol should be avoided
• may cause false positive results for glucose in urine.

PRESCRIPTION:

Yes.

PERMITTED IN SPORT:

Yes.

OVERDOSE:

Not life threatening unless allergic to penicillin. Vomiting and diarrhoea likely.

OTHER INFORMATION:

One of the most commonly used antibiotics. Does not cause dependence or addiction.
See also Ampicillin, Benzathine penicillin, Benzyl penicillin, Dicloxacillin, Flucloxacillin, Phenoxymethyl penicillin, Piperacillin, Procaine penicillin, Ticarcillin.

AMPHETAMINES

See Dexamphetamine.

Amphotericin

TRADE NAMES:

Abelcet, Ambisome, Amphocil, Fungilin, Fungizone.

DRUG CLASS:

Antifungal.

USES:

Injection: severe internal fungal infections.
Other forms: fungal infections of gut and mouth.

DOSAGE:

 Suspension: 1mL four times a day with meals.
Lozenges and tablets: one four times a day.

FORMS:

Lozenges, suspension, tablets, injection.

PRECAUTIONS:

Must be used with caution in pregnancy (B2). May be used in breast feeding and children.
Use medication without a break for full course or until infection resolves.

SIDE EFFECTS:

Suspension, tablets and lozenges: nil.
Injection: causes significant and varied effects in most patients.

INTERACTIONS:

Other drugs:
• flucytosine.

PRESCRIPTION:

Yes.

PERMITTED IN SPORT:

Yes.

OVERDOSE:

Unlikely to be serious.

OTHER INFORMATION:

Amphotericin is very well tolerated and effective when taken by mouth as it is not absorbed from the gut, but when given by injection for severe life threatening fungal infections it can cause significant side effects which must be balanced against the severity of the infection.
See also Fluconazole, Griseofulvin, Itraconazole, Ketoconazole, Terbinafine.

Ampicillin

TRADE NAMES:

Penbritin.
Magnapen (with flucloxacillin).

DRUG CLASS:

Penicillin antibiotic.

USES:

Treatment of infections caused by susceptible bacteria.

DOSAGE:

 One or two capsules every eight hours before food. Course (usually seven days) should be completed.

FORMS:

Capsule, injection.

PRECAUTIONS:

Safe in pregnancy (A), children and breast feeding.
Use with caution in leukaemia.
Do not take if:
 • allergic to penicillin.
• suffering from glandular fever.

SIDE EFFECTS:

Common: mild diarrhoea, nausea, vomiting.
Unusual: headache, dizziness, black tongue, tiredness.
Severe but rare (stop medication, consult doctor): itchy rash, hives, severe diarrhoea, yellow skin (jaundice), throat tightness.

INTERACTIONS:

Other drugs:
• allopurinol.
Other substances:
• alcohol should be avoided
• may cause false positive results for glucose in urine.

PRESCRIPTION:

Yes.

PERMITTED IN SPORT:

Yes.

OVERDOSE:

Vomiting and diarrhoea only likely effects.

OTHER INFORMATION:

Widely used in the 1970s, but has been superseded in most cases by amoxycillin. Does not cause dependence or addiction.

See also Amoxycillin, Benzathine penicillin, Benzyl penicillin, Dicloxacillin, Flucloxacillin, Phenoxymethyl penicillin, Piperacillin, Procaine penicillin, Ticarcillin.

Amprenavir

TRADE NAME:

Agenerase.

DRUG CLASS:

Antiviral.

USES:

HIV infection, AIDS.

DOSAGE:

 1200mg twice a day. Lower dosage if combined with other antiviral medication.

FORMS:

Capsules of 50mg and 150mg, solution.

PRECAUTIONS:

Not for use in pregnancy, breast feeding and children under four years.

Do not take if:

 • suffering from kidney or liver disease.

SIDE EFFECTS:

Common: nausea, diarrhoea.
Unusual: vomiting, pins and needles sensation around mouth, rash.

Severe but rare (stop medication, consult doctor): rash involving inside of mouth.

INTERACTIONS:

Other drugs:
• terfenadine, oral contraceptives, lignocaine, tricyclic antidepressants, quinidine, warfarin, methadone, antacids, amiodarone, phenobarbitone, phenytoin, triazolam, pimozide, cisapride, diazepam, midazolam, flurazepam, rifampicin.

Herbs:
• St John's wort.

PRESCRIPTION:

Yes.

PERMITTED IN SPORT:

Yes.

OVERDOSE:

Very serious. Induce vomiting or give activated charcoal if swallowed recently. Seek urgent medical attention.

OTHER INFORMATION:

Released in 2002 for the treatment of severe cases of AIDS.

See also Abacavir, Delavirdine, Didanosine, Efavirenz, Lamivudine, Nelfinavir, Nevirapine, Ritonavir, Saquinavir, Stavudine, Tenofovir, Zidovudine.

Amsacrine

TRADE NAME:

Amsidine.

DRUG CLASS:

Antineoplastic.

USES:

Leukaemia not responding to other treatment.

DOSAGE:

 As determined by doctor.

FORMS:

Intravenous infusion.

PRECAUTIONS:

Must not be used in pregnancy (D) or breast feeding.
Must be given by a drip into a centrally located vein.
Regular blood tests to monitor blood cells necessary.
Use with caution in heart disease.
Adequate fluids must be given through drip or by mouth.

Do not take if:

- suffering from bone marrow depression or significant infection.

SIDE EFFECTS:

Common: multiple including diarrhoea, vomiting, mouth ulcers, hair loss and heart rhythm irregularities.
Unusual: liver and kidney damage, rash.
Severe but rare (stop medication, consult doctor): brain function disturbances.

INTERACTIONS:

None significant.

PRESCRIPTION:

Yes.

PERMITTED IN SPORT:

Yes.

OVERDOSE:

Very serious. Seek urgent medical attention.

OTHER INFORMATION:

Introduced in 1998 for very serious forms of leukaemia.
See also CANCER TREATING DRUGS, VINCA ALKALOIDS.

Amylmetacresol

TRADE NAMES:

Found in some over the counter throat lozenges.

DRUG CLASS:

Antiseptic.

USES:

Minor mouth and throat infections.

DOSAGE:

 One lozenge dissolved in mouth every two or three hours.

FORMS:

Lozenges.

PRECAUTIONS:

Safe in pregnancy and children.

Do not take if:

- suffering from diabetes.

SIDE EFFECTS:

None.

INTERACTIONS:

None.

PRESCRIPTION:

No.

PERMITTED IN SPORT:

Yes.

OVERDOSE:

Diarrhoea only likely result.

Amylobarbitone

See BARBITURATES.

ANABOLIC STEROIDS

DISCUSSION:

Anabolic steroids are drugs that repair and build up body tissue. They are used illegally by athletes and body builders to increase muscle mass and are available as tablets and injections. There are many serious side effects and problems associated with their long-term use, including liver disease and damage, the development of male characteristics and cessation of periods in women, stunting of growth and early onset of puberty in children, swelling of tissue, water retention, infertility, personality disorders and voice changes.

See also Methenolone, Nandrolone, Stanozolol.

ANAESTHETICS, LOCAL

TRADE and GENERIC NAMES:

AAA Spray (<u>Benzocaine</u>).
Ametop (<u>Amethocaine</u>).
Betnovate Rectal (<u>Lignocaine</u>, betamethasone, phenylephrine).
Bradosol Plus (<u>Lignocaine</u>, domiphen bromide).
Calgel (<u>Lignocaine</u>, cetylpyridinium chloride).
Citanest (<u>Prilocaine</u>).
Depo-Medrone with Lidocaine (<u>Lignocaine</u> with methylprednisolone).
Dequaspray (<u>Lignocaine</u>).
EMLA (<u>Lignocaine</u>, <u>prilocaine</u>).
Hemocane (<u>Lignocaine</u>, zinc oxide, bismuth oxide, benzoic acid, cinnamic acid).
Instillagel (<u>Lignocaine</u>, chlorhexidine and other ingredients).
Intralgin (<u>Benzocaine</u>, salicylamide).
Marcain (<u>Bupivacaine</u>).
Merocaine (<u>Benzocaine</u>, cetylpyridinium).
Minims Lignocaine and Fluorescein (<u>Lignocaine</u>, fluorescein dye).
Minims Local Anaesthetic (<u>Amethocaine</u>, OR <u>lignocaine</u>, OR <u>oxybuprocaine</u> OR <u>proxymetacaine</u>).
Minims Proxymetacaine and Fluorescein (<u>Proxymetacaine</u>, fluorescein dye).
Naropin (<u>Ropivacaine</u>).
Perinal (<u>Lignocaine</u>, hydrocortisone).
Proctosedyl (<u>Cinchocaine</u>, hydrocortisone).
Scheriproct (<u>Cinchocaine</u>, prednisolone).
Ultraproct (<u>Cinchocaine</u>, corticosteroids and other ingredients).
Uniroid HC (<u>Cinchocaine</u>, hydrocortisone)
Xylocaine (<u>Lignocaine</u> with or without adrenaline).
Xyloproct (<u>Lignocaine</u>, aluminium acetate, zinc oxide, hydrocortisone).
NB: generic medications with the suffix '-caine' and <u>underlined</u> are local anaesthetics.

USES:

Relief of superficial pain of skin, mouth, lips, vagina, penis, anus and other areas.
Lignocaine injection may relieve migraine and irregular heart beat.

DOSAGE:

 Skin preparations: apply three to four times a day.
Mouth and lip preparations: apply or use every two to four hours.
Anal and vaginal preparations: apply or use three or four times a day
Eye drops and injections used by doctors only.

FORMS:

Cream, eye drop, gel, injection, lozenge, ointment, paint, paste, patch, spray, suppository.

PRECAUTIONS:

Safe in pregnancy (A), breast feeding and children.
Use skin preparations with care on thin

skin, genitals, broken skin, eczema or infected skin.

Elderly may need lower doses.

Special precautions apply to eye preparations and injections. Eye must be protected after use.

Drops should not be used for prolonged period.

Area injected must be protected from inadvertent injury.

Advise doctor before injection if:
• suffering from heart disease, over active thyroid gland.

SIDE EFFECTS:

Common: injections: nervousness, dizziness, blurred vision, tremor, drowsiness, ringing in ears, numbness, nausea, vomiting, low blood pressure, slow heart rate.

Eye preparations: eye irritation, stinging. Other preparations: adverse reactions rare.

Unusual: injections: Convulsions, allergy.

Severe but rare: injection: Unconsciousness, cessation of breathing.

INTERACTIONS:

Other drugs:
• creams: Other local anaesthetics, sulfonamides.
• injection: Drugs acting on heart, cimetidine, anticonvulsants.

PRESCRIPTION:

Most creams, ointments, gels, lozenges etc: no.
Eye drops, patches, anal preparations, injections: yes.

PERMITTED IN SPORT:

Yes.

OVERDOSE:

No serious effects except from injection. Effects of injection overdose are very serious and include irregular heart beat, cessation of breathing, heart attack and death.

OTHER INFORMATION:

All local anaesthetics are derived from

cocaine, but are not addictive. Widely used in many forms for relief of pain and discomfort, and generally very safe. Poorly absorbed through skin, but well absorbed through mucous membranes of mouth, anus, vagina etc.

See also Cocaine.

ANALGESICS

DISCUSSION:

Drugs that reduce the sensation of pain are called analgesics. There are three main types—narcotics, salicylates (see also NSAIDs) and paracetamol. Many analgesic preparations are combinations of two or more different medications.

See Aspirin, Benorylate, Buprenorphine, Capsaicin, Codeine, Dextromoramide, Dextropropoxyphene, Dihydrocodeine, Fentanyl, Heroin, Meptazinol, Methadone, Morphine, Nefopam, NSAID, Oxycodone, Paracetamol, Pentazocine, Pethidine, SALICYLATES, Tramadol.

Anastrozole

TRADE NAME:

Arimidex.

DRUG CLASS:

Antineoplastic.

USES:

Treatment of advanced breast cancer.

DOSAGE:

 One tablet a day.

FORMS:

Tablet of 1mg.

PRECAUTIONS:

Must not be used in pregnancy (C), breast feeding or children.

Caution with use before the menopause, liver and kidney disease.

SIDE EFFECTS:

Common: hot flushes, dry vagina, nausea, thinning of hair.
Unusual: vaginal bleeding, tiredness, headache, rash, vomiting, diarrhoea, increase in blood cholesterol.
Severe but rare (stop medication, consult doctor): liver or kidney failure.

INTERACTIONS:

Other drugs:
• oestrogen.

PRESCRIPTION:

Yes.

PERMITTED IN SPORT:

Yes.

OVERDOSE:

Very serious. Seek urgent medical attention. Induce vomiting or administer activated charcoal.

OTHER INFORMATION:

Introduced in 1996. Acts to destroy oestrogen producing cells in the body.

ANGINA MEDICATIONS

DISCUSSION:

These medications are used to treat angina (chest pain caused by a poor blood supply to the heart).
See Glyceryl trinitrate, Isosorbide nitrate, Nicorandil, Perhexiline.

ANGIOTENSIN CONVERTING ENZYME INHIBITORS

See ACE Inhibitors.

ANGIOTENSIN II RECEPTOR ANTAGONISTS

TRADE and GENERIC NAMES:

Amias (Candesartan).
Aprovel (Irbesartan).
CoAprovel (Irbesartan, hydrochlorothiazide).
Cozaar (Losartan).
Cozaar-Comp (Losartan, hydrochlorothiazide).
Diovan (Valsartan).
Micardis (Telmisartan).
Micardis Plus (Telmisartan, hydrochlorothiazide).
Teveten (Eprosartan).

DRUG CLASS:

Antihypertensives.

USES:

High blood pressure (hypertension), congestive heart failure.

DOSAGE:

 Usually one tablet a day, but may be increased to two a day.

FORMS:

Tablets.

PRECAUTIONS:

Not to be used in pregnancy (D) or breast feeding. No trials on use in children have been performed.
Use with caution in heart failure, primary hyperaldosteronism, dehydration, heart valve disease and kidney transplant.
Do not take if:
 • severe kidney, liver or bile duct disease.

SIDE EFFECTS:

Common: minimal.
Unusual: diarrhoea, back and muscle pain.
Severe but rare (stop medication, consult doctor): liver damage.

INTERACTIONS:

Other drugs:
- potassium supplements.

Herbs:
- goldenseal.

PRESCRIPTION:

Yes.

PERMITTED IN SPORT:

Yes.

OVERDOSE:

Low blood pressure most likely effect. Take activated charcoal to reduce absorption. Seek medical attention.

OTHER INFORMATION:

Very similar in action to ACE Inhibitors (see separate entry) but with fewer side effects. Some forms combined with a thiazide diuretic (fluid tablet— hydrochlorothiazide) to increase effectiveness. Only released on to market between 1998 and 2000.

See also ACE Inhibitors.

ANORECTICS

DISCUSSION:

Anorectic drugs are used to reduce appetite. These drugs do NOT reduce weight but act as an aid to controlling appetite while the patient complies with a strictly controlled diet. They are available in tablet and capsule form only. Anorectics should not be used for long periods, as dependence can occur. Some are stimulants, which may cause insomnia if used in the evening and are used illegally by long-distance drivers and other who wish to remain awake for long periods of time. Many drugs in this class have been removed from the market in recent years because of abuse, interactions and side effects.

See Methylcellulose, Orlistat, Silbutramine.

ANTACIDS

TRADE and GENERIC NAMES:

Algicon, Maalox, Mucogel (Aluminium hydroxide, magnesium salts).
Alu-Cap (Aluminium hydroxide).
Asilone (Aluminium hydroxide, magnesium salts, dimethicone).
Gastrocote (Alginic acid, aluminium hydroxide, sodium bicarbonate).
Gaviscon Advance (Alginates, potassium bicarbonate).
Gaviscon Infant (Alginates).
Gaviscon Liquid (Alginic acid, calcium carbonate, bicarbonates).
Gaviscon Tablets (Alginic acid, aluminium hydroxide, magnesium salts, bicarbonates).
Kolanticon (Aluminium hydroxide, dimethicone, dicyclomine)
Mucaine (Aluminium salts, magnesium salts, oxethazine).
Peptac (Sodium bicarbonate, calcium carbonate, alginates)
Pyrogastrone (Alginic acid, carbenoxolone, aluminium hydroxide, magnesium salts, bicarbonates)
Topal (Aluminium hydroxide, magnesium salts, alginic acid).

USES:

Heartburn, acid reflux, peptic ulcer, gastritis, hiatus hernia, reduce stomach acid, diarrhoea.

DOSAGE:

 Multiple presentations. Follow instructions on packaging, or from doctor or pharmacist. Take immediately before meals or one hour after meals.

FORMS:

Mixture, tablets, capsules, granules, powder, chewable tablets.

PRECAUTIONS:

Safe in pregnancy (A), children and breast feeding.

Care required in patients with kidney disease, bleeding from stomach, irregular bowels.

Should not be taken for prolonged period without medical advice.

Do not take if:

- suffering from severe belly pain
- you have recently had kidney or bladder stones.

SIDE EFFECTS:

Common: mild.
Unusual: constipation, loss of appetite.
Severe but rare (stop medication, consult doctor): severe abdominal pain, muscle weakness, bone pain.

INTERACTIONS:

Other drugs:
- tetracycline antibiotics, beta-blockers, digoxin.

Herbs:
- ginger, garlic, parsley, senega, ginkgo biloba, alfalfa, capsicum, eucalyptus.

Other substances:
- food and alcohol reduce antacid effect.

PRESCRIPTION:

No.

PERMITTED IN SPORT:

Yes.

OVERDOSE:

Very unlikely to be life threatening but may cause weakness, dizziness, tiredness and confusion.

OTHER INFORMATION:

Widely used preparations for minor stomach upsets, antacids are drugs that neutralise acid in the stomach. A very large number of these medications are available without prescription as both mixtures and tablets. Sometimes they cause problems with the absorption of other medications if taken at the same time. They often contain multiple ingredients.

See also Cimetidine, Cisapride, Famotidine, Misoprostol, Nizatadine, PROTON PUMP INHIBITORS, Ranitidine, Simethicone, Sucralfate.

Antazoline

TRADE NAME:

Otrivine-Anthistin (with xylometazoline).

DRUG CLASS:

Vasoconstrictor.

USES:

Allergic conjunctivitis, inflamed eyes.

DOSAGE:

 One or two drops in eye three or four times a day.

FORMS:

Eye drops.

PRECAUTIONS:

May be used in pregnancy and breast feeding. Use with caution in children. Not to be used for more than two weeks without medical review.

Do not take if:

- suffering from glaucoma.

SIDE EFFECTS:

Common: stinging on inserting drops.

INTERACTIONS:

None significant.

PRESCRIPTION:

No.

PERMITTED IN SPORT:

Yes.

OTHER INFORMATION:

Widely used and effective treatment for tired, itchy, watery, red eyes. If symptoms do not settle rapidly, seek medical advice.

See also VASOCONSTRICTORS.

ANTHELMINTICS

DISCUSSION:

Helminths are different types of worms that infect the gut. The drugs that destroy these unwanted internal worms are called anthelmintics. There are many different types of helminths, including threadworms, hookworms, roundworms, and a number of rarer worms. Most common anthelmintics can be purchased without prescription in mixture, tablet and granule formulations. It is important to treat all family members and to carefully wash clothing and bedding at the time of treatment. A number of prescription drugs are available for the treatment of resistant cases or rarer types of infection.

See Mebendazole, Piperazine.

ANTIALLERGEN

DISCUSSION:

Medications that reduce allergy reactions.
See Allergen extracts.

ANTIANDROGEN

DISCUSSION:

Medications that act against the male hormone, testosterone.
See Cyproterone, Flutamide.

ANTIANGINALS

DISCUSSION:

Medications that relieve or prevent angina (heart pain).
See BETA BLOCKERS, CALCIUM CHANNEL BLOCKERS, Glyceryl trinitrate, Isosorbide, Nicorandil.

ANTIARRHYTHMICS

DISCUSSION:

Antiarrhythmics are the drugs that keep the heart beating regularly. If the heart rhythm is uneven, beats are being missed or extra beats are causing palpitations, doctors will prescribe an antiarrhythmic. There is a wide range of medications in this class that work in different ways depending on the type of heart rhythm irregularity.

See Adenosine, Amiodarone, Bretyllium, Disopyramide, Flecainide, Lignocaine, Mexiletine, Procainamide, Propafenone, Quinidine, Sotalol, Verapamil.

ANTIBIOTICS

DISCUSSION:

Every sixth prescription written by doctors is for an antibiotic. They are thus the most widely prescribed group of drugs, but most patients understand very little about them. Although there were chemical compounds used against infection before the Second World War, the isolation of penicillin from a mould grown in a laboratory represented the first real exploitation of a purified natural substance that could kill bacteria. The very first supplies of penicillin came from the mould grown, due to wartime exigencies, in large numbers of bedpans. Most antibiotics today are produced as the result of chemical reactions (i.e. synthesised) as opposed to harvesting the drug from primitive life forms grown in bulk in areas that resembled mushroom farms.

Antibiotics are only effective against bacteria and not against viral infections. Most of the infections seen by a general practitioner are caused by viruses and there is no need for antibiotics in these cases.

Antibiotics are used by doctors in several situations:

- If the infection appears to be bacterial, the appropriate antibiotic will be selected to cure it. Samples or swabs may be taken so that the infecting bacteria and the correct antibiotic to kill it can be identified in a laboratory.
- if the problem is not clear-cut or if there is some doubt as to the cause of a problem, an antibiotic may be prescribed to cover one of the possibilities. This may be the case with a severely sore throat.
- If a person has reduced immunity, is elderly, frail, liable to recurrent infections or due for an operation, an antibiotic may be used to prevent a bacterial infection. Women with recurrent bladder infections are one example.

Major problems can occur with the overuse of antibiotics. Cost is the first one and as the government pays part of the cost of everyone's antibiotics, this is a problem affecting you. Side effects are another problem, including stopping the oral contraceptive pill from working. The most important problem is the development of resistance which can enable bacteria to change in a way which makes them able to resist the actions of an antibiotic that was previously very effective. The need for new antibiotic agents is therefore always with us. Their development is a long and costly process involving huge investments by the drug companies. A good antibiotic deserves a long and effective life and the needs of the public will be best served by the prescribing of antibiotics only when they are really needed, thus reducing the rate at which resistant strains develop.

See **Amoxycillin, Ampicillin, Azithromycin, Aztreonam, Bacitracin, Benzyl penicillin, CEPHALOSPORINS, Chloramphenicol, Chlortetracycline, Cilastatin and Imipenem, Ciprofloxacin, Clarithromycin, Clavulanic acid, Clindamycin, Demeclocycline, Doxycycline,** **Erythromycin, Flucloxacillin, Framycetin, Fusafungine, Gentamicin, Gramicidin, Levofloxacin, Meropenem, Metronidazole, Minocycline, Mupirocin, Nalidixic acid, Neomycin, Netimicin, Nitrofurantoin, Norfloxacin, Ofloxacin, Oxytetracycline, Penicillin G, Piperacillin, Pivmecillinam, Polymyxin B, Potassium clavulanate, Potassium hydroxyquinolone, Silver sulfadiazine, Sodium fusidate, Sulphamethoxazole, Sulphasalazine, SULPHONAMIDES, Tazobactam, Telcoplanin, Telithromycin, Tetracycline, Ticarcillin, Tinidazole, Tobramycin, Trimethoprim, Vancomycin.**

ANTICANCER DRUGS

See **CANCER TREATING DRUGS.**

ANTICHOLINERGICS

DISCUSSION:

A group of drugs that act as drying agents, relieve spasm of gut and other hollow organs (e.g. bladder) and dilate the pupil of the eye.

See **Atropine, Dicyclomine, Homatropine methylbromide, Hyoscine, Ipratropium, MYDRIATICS, Oxitropium, Oxybutynin, Propiverine, Tiotropium, Tolterodine, Trospium.**

ANTICHOLINESTERASES

DISCUSSION:

A group of drugs used to treat difficulty in passing urine and the rare condition myasthenia gravis.

See **Distigmine, Donepezil, Neostigmine, Pyridostigmine, Rivastigmine.**

ANTICOAGULANTS

DISCUSSION:

Anticoagulants are drugs that stop blood from clotting at the normal speed. They are used in patients who have had strokes due to blood clots, clots in leg veins and clots in heart and lung arteries. Aspirin is also a mild anticoagulant and can be used in small doses to prevent strokes. All anticoagulants should be stopped before any surgical procedure.

Patients on the stronger anticoagulants listed below, must be monitored carefully by their doctors and have blood tests regularly to ensure that the clotting factors in their blood are kept at the desirable level. Patients using anticoagulants will bruise and bleed more easily than normal and care must be taken when using some antiarthritic medications, as they may cause bleeding into the gut while the patient is on anticoagulants. There are many precautions necessary with these drugs that make compliance with a doctor's instructions vital.

See Abciximab, Aspirin, Clopidrogel, Dalteparin, Dipyridamole, Enoxaparin, Heparin, Nicoumalone, Phenindione, Ticlopidine, Warfarin.

ANTICONVULSANTS

DISCUSSION:

This large group of drugs is used to control and prevent fits and convulsions caused by epilepsy and other diseases. Barbiturates (see separate entry) and benzodiazepines (see separate entry) are also used for this purpose. Patients must sometimes take quite large quantities of anticonvulsants or combinations of several drugs to control their problem and blood levels are usually checked to arrive at the correct dosage. Side effects from anticonvulsants vary widely from one person to another and between drugs.

They are usually worst when treatment is first started and wear off as time passes. All these drugs have a tendency to interact with other drugs and the doctor must be made aware of all medications being taken and any other diseases (e.g. diabetes) that may be present.

See BARBITURATES, BENZODIAZEPINES, Carbamazepine, Clonazepam, Ethosuximide, Gabapentin, Lamotrigine, Levetiracetam, Oxcarbazepine, Phenytoin, Piracetam, Primidone, Sodium valproate, Topiramate, Valproic acid, Vigabatrin.

ANTIDEPRESSANTS

DISCUSSION:

Antidepressants are used to control depression. This is as much a disease as diabetes or high blood pressure but is often thought to be a mental disorder that patients can 'pull themselves out of'. Nothing could be further than the truth. Depression is caused by a biochemical imbalance in the brain and requires appropriate medication to correct it before a tragedy occurs. There are many sub-classes of antidepressants including MAOI, RIMA, SNRI, SSRI, tetracyclics and tricyclics.

See Citalopram, Escitalopram, Fluoxetine, Fluvoxamine, MAOI, Maprotiline, Mirtazapine, Moclobemide, Nefazodone, Paroxetine, Reboxetine, Sertraline, Trazodone, TRICYCLIC ANTIDEPRESSANTS, Venlafaxine.

ANTIDIARRHOEALS

DISCUSSION:

Antidiarrhoeals are one of the most popular drug groups with patients. When you just have to go and go and go—and you want to stop—antidiarrhoeals are just the thing to help. There are some types of diarrhoea that they are not suitable for, including those associated with jaundice (yellow skin), bacterial gut infections, and diarrhoea during pregnancy. Diarrhoea has a vast number of causes and the exact treatment chosen will depend on that cause. Many types of diarrhoea require no medication but a correct diet.

See Atropine, Codeine, Diphenoxylate, Kaolin, Loperamide, Pectin.

Antidiuretic hormone

See Vasopressin.

ANTIDIURETICS

DISCUSSION:

The antidiuretics are used to reduce the amount of urine produced by the kidneys in bed wetting, diabetes insipidus and in some other even rarer conditions. They are unusual in that some forms are given routinely as a nasal spray or injection.

See Desmopressin acetate, Vasopressin.

ANTIDOTES

DISCUSSION:

Medications that counteract poisons or a drug overdose.

See Charcoal, Methionine, Naloxone.

ANTIEMETICS

DISCUSSION:

Antiemetics are medicines that stop vomiting. They are often difficult to give in tablet or mixture form, so many of them are also available as an injection or suppository (for insertion into the back passage). There are many different drugs in this category, from the mild over-the-counter travel sickness pills, to the more effective and potent prescription drugs such as prochlorperazine, domperidone

and metoclopramide. These are also available as injections.

See ANTIHISTAMINES—SEDATING, Cyclizine, Domperidone, Granisetron, Hyoscine, Metoclopramide, Ondansetron, PHENOTHIAZINES, Prochlorperazine.

ANTIFUNGALS

DISCUSSION:

Antifungals treat fungal infections. Fungi are members of the plant kingdom and are one of the types of microscopic life that can infect human beings in many diverse ways. The most common site of infection is the skin, where they cause an infection that is commonly known as tinea. Fungi are also responsible for many gut infections, particularly in the mouth and around the anus. It is a rare infant that escapes without an attack of oral thrush. Around the anus, the fungus can cause an extremely itchy rash, but in women it may spread forward from the anus to the vagina to cause the white discharge and intense itch of vaginal thrush or candidiasis. The most serious diseases develop when fungal infections occur deep inside the body in organs such as the lungs, brain and sinuses. These diseases are very difficult to treat and it may take many months with potent antifungal drugs to bring them under control. Fortunately, this type of condition is relatively rare.

See Amorolfine, Amphotericin, Atovaquone, Fluconazole, Flucytosine, Griseofulvin, IMIDAZOLES, Iodine, Itraconazole, Ketoconazole, Methyl undecanoate, Nystatin, Potassium hydroxyquinolone, Selenium sulfide, Sulconazole, Terbinafine, Tolnaftate, Undecenoic acid, Voriconazole.

ANTIHISTAMINES, NON-SEDATING

TRADE and GENERIC NAMES:

Neoclarityn (Desloratadine).
Telfast (Fexofenadine).

USES:

Allergy reactions, hay fever, urticaria (hives).

DOSAGE:

 Once a day.

FORMS:

Capsules, tablets and mixture.

PRECAUTIONS:

Should be used with caution in pregnancy (B1). Fexofenadine (B2). Should not be used in breast feeding.

Do not take if:

 • suffering from severe liver disease.

SIDE EFFECTS:

Common: None.
Unusual: increase in appetite, fainting, dry mouth, gastric upset, blurred vision, muscle pains, tremor, sweating, rash.

INTERACTIONS:

Other drugs:
• fexofenadine may react with ketoconazole (antifungal) and erythromycin (antibiotic) to cause heart problems.

PRESCRIPTION:

Yes.

PERMITTED IN SPORT:

Yes.

OVERDOSE:

Mild effects only. Possible heart beat irregularities. First aid involves induction of vomiting and then observing in hospital for a day.

OTHER INFORMATION:

Antihistamines are divided into two broad groups—those that cause sedation and those that do not. In an allergy reaction, a substance called histamine is released from special cells (mast cells) to cause swelling, itching and increase in secretions. Antihistamines counteract this reaction. The non-sedating antihistamines will not have any effect on excessive secretions from causes other than allergy (e.g. they have no effect on runny noses caused by the common cold).

See also ANTIHISTAMINES, SEDATING.

ANTIHISTAMINES, SEDATING

TRADE and GENERIC NAMES:

Atarax, Ucerax (<u>Hydroxyzine embonate</u>).
Avomine, Phenergan (<u>Promethazine</u>).
Dimotane (<u>Brompheniramine</u>).
Dimotane Plus (<u>Brompheniramine</u>, phenylephrine).
Galpseud Plus (<u>Chlorpheniramine</u>, pseudoephedrine).
Haymine (<u>Chlorpheniramine</u>, ephedrine).
Mizollen (<u>Mizolastine</u>).
Pamergan P100 (<u>Promethazine</u>, pethidine).
Periactin (<u>Cyproheptadine</u>).
Piriton (<u>Chlorpheniramine</u>),
Sudafed Plus (<u>Triprolidine</u>, pseudoephedrine).
Tavegil (<u>Clemastine</u>).
Vallergan (<u>Trimeprazine</u>).
Xepin (<u>Doxepin hydrochloride</u>).
Xyzal (<u>Levocetirizine</u>).
Zirtek (<u>Cetirizine</u>).
NB: antihistamines are <u>underlined</u>. Sedating antihistamines may be found in many other over the counter cold and cough remedies that are distributed locally.

USES:

Allergies (e.g. hay fever, hives, urticaria), drug allergies, drying of secretions, itchy skin.
PLUS
Pheniramine, Promethazine: nausea, vomiting, motion sickness, Ménière's disease.
Hydroxyzine embonate: anxiety.
Cyproheptadine: prevention of migraine
Doxepin hydrochloride: itchy eczema.
Promethazine, Trimeprazine: Sedation.

DOSAGE:

 Follow directions on packaging. Some antihistamines are far longer acting than others. Dose will vary from once a day to four times a day.

FORMS:

Tablets, capsules, mixture, cream.

PRECAUTIONS:

Promethazine and trimeprazine should only be used in pregnancy (C) and breast feeding on medical advice.
All other sedating antihistamines are safe in pregnancy (A) and breast feeding.
All are safe in children over two years. Seek medical advice if using in younger children.
All should be used with caution in patients with liver disease, heart disease, glaucoma, chronic lung disease, enlarged prostate or severe peptic ulcer.

Do not take if:

 • operating machinery or undertaking tasks that require concentration and coordination.
• Drinking alcohol.

SIDE EFFECTS:

Common: drowsiness, dry mouth, constipation, restlessness in children, incoordination, blurred vision.
Unusual: upper belly discomfort, loss of appetite, nausea, diarrhoea, irritability.
Severe but rare (stop medication, consult doctor): unusual bleeding.

INTERACTIONS:

Other drugs:
• may interfere with anticoagulants, MAOI (monoamine oxidase inhibitors), sedatives and relaxants
• skin preparations have no significant interactions.
Other substances:
• do not use alcohol with sedating antihistamines.

PRESCRIPTION:

Varies depending on form and product.

PERMITTED IN SPORT:

Yes.

OVERDOSE:

May result in convulsions, hallucinations, delirium, anxiety, muscle spasms, rapid heart rate, flushing, dry skin, dry mouth and coma. First aid involved inducing vomiting and seeking urgent medical attention.

OTHER INFORMATION:

Antihistamines are widely used to dry the excessive secretions of hay fever and common colds. Taken in the correct dosage, they are very safe, but care must be taken with drowsiness.
Antihistamines are divided into two broad groups—those that cause sedation and those that do not. In an allergy reaction, a substance called histamine is released from special cells (mast cells) to cause swelling, itching and increase in secretions. Antihistamines counteract this reaction. The non-sedating antihistamines will not have any effect on excessive secretions from causes other than allergy (e.g. they have no effect on runny noses caused by the common cold). Sedating antihistamines are available in a huge range of cold and flu remedies. They are added to pain killers to relax muscles and tension.

See also Azelastine, Cinnarizine, Cyclizine, Emedastine, Ketotifen, Levocabastine, Metoclopramide, Prochlorperazine.

ANTIHYPERTENSIVES

DISCUSSION:

A very mixed bag of medications that treat high blood pressure in many different ways.

See ACE INHIBITORS, Amlodipine, ANGIOTENSIN II RECEPTOR ANTAGONISTS, Atenolol, Carvedilol, Clonidine, Diazoxide, Diltiazem, Doxazosin, Felodipine, Hydralazine, Indapamide, Indoramin, Labetalol, Lercanidipine, Methyldopa, Metoprolol, Minoxidil, Moxonidine, Nifedipine, Oxprenolol, Pindolol, Prazosin, Propranolol, Sotalol, Tamsulosin, THIAZIDE DIURETICS, Thymoxamine, Verapamil.

ANTIMALARIALS

DISCUSSION:

Antimalarials treat and prevent malaria. Malaria is becoming an increasing problem in the world, as many forms of the disease are becoming resistant to the commonly used medications. Millions of people die of malaria in tropical countries every year and the most resistant and virulent form in the world can be found in our nearest neighbour country, Papua New Guinea. It is essential for travellers to any tropical country to discuss with their doctor, at least a month before their departure, the appropriate medications necessary to prevent malaria.

Because it is spread by mosquitoes, insect repellents, protective clothing and mosquito nets also play an important part in preventing malaria.

Generally speaking, the same drugs are used for both prevention and treatment of malaria, but they are given in much higher dosages for treatment.

See Artemether, Atovaquone, Chloroquine, Doxycycline, Hydroxychloroquine, Mefloquine, Proguanil, Pyrimethamine, Quinine bisulphate.

ANTIMETABOLITES

See CANCER TREATING DRUGS.

ANTIMIGRAINE

DISCUSSION:

Medications that prevent and treat migraine.

See ANALGESICS, Almotriptan, BETA BLOCKERS, Clonidine, Eletriptan, Ergotamine, Frovatriptan, Methysergide, Naratriptan, NSAIDs, Pizotifen, Rizatripan, Sumatriptan, Zolmitriptan.

ANTINEOPLASTICS

See CANCER TREATING DRUGS.

ANTIPARASITICS

DISCUSSION:

Medications that kill skin parasites.

See Benzyl benzoate, Crotamiton, Permethrin.

ANTIPARKINSONIANS

DISCUSSION:

Medications that treat and slow the progression of Parkinson's disease.

See Amantadine, Apomorphine, Benzhexol, Benztropine, Biperiden, Bromocriptine, Entacapone, LEVODOPA COMPOUNDS, Orphenadrine, Pergolide, Pramipexole, Procyclidine, Ropinirole, Selegiline.

ANTIPSYCHOTICS

DISCUSSION:

A psychosis is a serious mental disorder,

in which the patients normally have no idea that there is anything wrong with them. There are a large number of specific mental diseases that fit into this category and different antipsychotic drugs are known to be more useful in treating some types psychoses.

Psychoses are often characterised by agitation, anxiety, tension, personality changes and emotional disturbances. Common psychotic diseases include mania, some types of depression and schizophrenia. Nearly all of the drugs that can correct these problems are available as tablets and some as mixtures and injections. The main class of antipsychotics is the phenothiazines.

See Amisulpride, Flupenthixol, Haloperidol, Lithium Carbonate, Olanzapine, PHENOTHIAZINES, Pimozide, Quetiapine, Risperidone, Sulpiride, Thiothixene, Zotepine, Zuclopenthixol.

ANTIPYRETICS

DISCUSSION:

These medications reduce fevers as well as easing pain.
See Aspirin, Ibuprofen, Paracetamol.

ANTIRHEUMATICS

DISCUSSION:

An amazingly diverse range of drugs can be placed in the category of relieving rheumatoid arthritis and other rheumatic conditions. Most of them have found their place here serendipitously, when patients being treated for other diseases found that their rheumatoid arthritis was improved. There is no cure for rheumatoid arthritis, but by the use of painkillers, physiotherapy, NSAIDs (see separate entry) and the antirheumatic drugs, control is normally possible.
See Chloroquine, CORTICOSTEROIDS,

GOLD, Hydroxychloroquine, Methotrexate, NSAIDs, Penicillamine, Sulfasalazine.

ANTISEPTICS

DISCUSSION:

Antiseptics are drugs that kill bacteria and other infecting organisms on the skin, in the mouth or other areas, without being absorbed into the body or blood. They may also be used to sterilise medical instruments and equipment. Something that is 'septic' is infected, so antiseptics act against infection.
See Acriflavine, Azelaic acid, Benzalkonium chloride, Cetrimide, Cetylpyridinium, Chlorhexidine, Chloroxylenol, Clioquinol, Crotamiton, Dequalinium chloride, Hexachlorophane, Hexetedine, Hydrogen peroxide, Iodine, Povidone-iodine, Pyrithione zinc, Sodium perborate.

ANTISEPTICS, URINARY

DISCUSSION:

Medications that can be used on a long term basis to prevent urine infections.
See Hexamine hippurate.

ANTISPASMODICS

DISCUSSION:

Antispasmodics prevent or treat painful muscular spasm of hollow tubes within the body, such as the gut. If the gut goes into spasm, severe intermittent pains can develop in the abdomen. Irritable bowel syndrome, infantile colic, gastroenteritis and gut infections are just a few of the diseases that can cause this problem. There are a large number of antispasmodic drugs for the gut that vary from mild over-the-counter tablet and mixture preparations to potent prescription tablets such as dicyclomine, mebeverine, hyoscine and propantheline. Some of these are also available as injections.

See Alverine citrate, Atropine, Dicyclomine, Flavoxate, Hyoscine, Mebeverine, Peppermint Oil.

ANTITHYROIDS

DISCUSSION:

An overactive thyroid gland can cause a multiplicity of serious problems. The excess production of thyroxine hormone by the gland must be reduced before serious damage occurs to other organs in the body. The antithyroid drugs that act against the thyroid gland are carbimazole and propylthiouracil. Because of their significant side effects, these tablets are used only in the acute situation, until a cure by means of surgery or irradiation is undertaken.

See Carbimazole.

ANTIVENOMS

TRADE NAMES:

Antivenoms against numerous snakes, spiders and ticks are available.

USES:

Treatment of bites by specific toxic animal.

DOSAGE:

 As determined by doctor depending on patient's condition and weight.

FORMS:

Injection.

PRECAUTIONS:

May be used in pregnancy, breast feeding and children if medically indicated.
All patients must be carefully monitored

and any signs of allergy reaction treated early.
Use with caution in asthma, eczema and previous history of allergy.
Use with caution if antivenom used previously.

SIDE EFFECTS:

Common: minimal.
Unusual: allergy reaction, generalised illness.

INTERACTIONS:

None significant.

PRESCRIPTION:

Yes.

PERMITTED IN SPORT:

Yes.

OVERDOSE:

May cause serious allergy reaction.

OTHER INFORMATION:

Life saving, but must be given as soon as possible after any bite.
Most venoms are large compounds and spread very slowly from the site of the bite. The spread of venom can be prevented by applying a firm bandage (not too tight to cut off circulation) while arranging urgent medical care. Keep any dressing or material contaminated by the venom as it can be used to identify the type of animal responsible.

ANTIVIRALS

DISCUSSION:

Medications that can be used to treat a limited number of viral infections (mainly HIV/AIDS and Herpes infections such as shingles and genital herpes).

See also Abacavir, Aciclovir, Amantadine, Amprenavir, Didanosine, Efavirenz, Ganciclovir, Idoxuridine, Indinavir, Lamivudine, Nevirapine, Penciclovir, Ritonavir, Saquinavir, Stavudine, Tribavirin, Valaciclovir, Valganciclovir, Zanamivir, Zidovudine.

ANXIOLYTICS

DISCUSSION:

Medications that relieve both anxiety and muscle spasm.

See Clobazam, Diazepam, Lorazepam.

Apomorphine hydrochloride

TRADE NAMES:

APO-Go, Uprima.

DRUG CLASS:

Antiparkinsonian.

USES:

Severe Parkinson's disease, impotence.

DOSAGE:

 For parkinson's disease, as determined by doctor for each individual patient.
For impotence, one tablet dissolved under the tongue 20 minutes prior to sexual activity, no more than once every eight hours.

FORMS:

Injection (injector pen), tablets of 2mg and 3mg.

PRECAUTIONS:

Use injection with caution in pregnancy (B3) and during breast feeding.
Tablets not for use in women or children.
Use both forms with caution in elderly.
Use with caution with penile deformity, liver or kidney disease, or uncontrolled high blood pressure.

Do not take if:

 • suffering from dementia and some psychiatric disorders, low blood pressure, angina and other unstable heart diseases, poor blood circulation to brain or poor brain function
• sensitive to morphine or levodopa.

SIDE EFFECTS:

Common: nausea, diarrhoea, drowsiness, headache, dizziness.
Unusual: vomiting, watery nose discharge, sore throat, cough, flushing, abnormal taste, sweating, nodule at injection site, allergy reaction.

INTERACTIONS:

Other drugs:
• some drugs affecting brain function, some antihypertensives, glyceryl trinitrate.
• other medications used for impotence.
Other substances:
• alcohol.

PRESCRIPTION:

Yes.

PERMITTED IN SPORT:

Yes.

Apraclonidine

TRADE NAME:

Iopidine.

USES:

Certain forms of severe glaucoma.

DOSAGE:

 One drop to affected eye three times a day. Apply pressure to tear duct at inside corner of eye following application.

FORMS:

Eye drops.

PRECAUTIONS:

Use with caution in pregnancy (B3), children and breast feeding.
Do not use for more than 60 days.
Use with caution in high blood pressure, severe heart disease, depression, liver disease, kidney disease.

SIDE EFFECTS:

Common: eye irritation.
Unusual: excessive response.

INTERACTIONS:

Other drugs:
• MAOI, sympathomimetics, tricyclic antidepressants, beta-blockers, digoxin, clonidine, antihypertensives, brain depressants.

PRESCRIPTION:

Yes.

PERMITTED IN SPORT:

Yes.

See also Acetazolamide, Betaxolol, Bimatoprost, Brimonidine, Brinzolamide, Carbachol, Dipivefrine, Dorzolamide, Latanoprost, Levobunolol, Phenylephrine, Pilocarpine, Timolol, Travoprost.

Aprotinin

TRADE NAME:

Trasylol.

DRUG CLASS:

Fibrinolytic.

USES:

Prevention of excessive blood loss during heart surgery and after serious injury.

DOSAGE:

 As determined by doctor for individual patient. Test dose must be given initially.

FORMS:

Injection.

PRECAUTIONS:

Relatively safe in pregnancy (B1) and children.
May cause severe allergy reaction if used a second time.

SIDE EFFECTS:

Common: excessive sensitivity.

INTERACTIONS:

Other drugs:
• thrombolytics.

PRESCRIPTION:

Yes.

PERMITTED IN SPORT:

Yes.

OVERDOSE:

Very serious. Always given under strict medical supervision.

Arachis Oil

TRADE NAMES:

Fletcher's Oil.
Cerumol Ear Drops (with chlorbutol, paradichlorobenzene).
Polytar (with coal tar and other ingredients).
Used as an ingredient in numerous other non-prescription preparations.

USES:

Softens ear wax, faeces and dry skin.

DOSAGE:

 Ear drops: two drops daily for three days.
Liquid: use as shampoo once or twice a week.
Enema: use 100 to 130 mLs once only.

FORMS:

Ear drops, liquid, enema.

PRECAUTIONS:

Safe in pregnancy and breast feeding. No significant precautions.

SIDE EFFECTS:

None significant.

INTERACTIONS:

None significant.

PRESCRIPTION:

No.

PERMITTED IN SPORT:

Yes.

OVERDOSE:

Diarrhoea only likely effect if swallowed.

Artemether and Lumefantrine

TRADE NAME:

Riamet.

DRUG CLASS:

Antimalarial.

USES:

Treatment of malaria.

DOSAGE:

 Four tablets at once then at intervals of eight, 24, 36, 48 and 60 hours.

FORMS:

Tablets (yellow).

PRECAUTIONS:

Use with caution in pregnancy (B3)and children under 12 years.
Not for use if breast feeding.
Use with caution if suffering from irregular heart rhythm, heart disease, electrolyte (blood chemistry) disturbances, anorexia nervosa, liver and kidney disease.

SIDE EFFECTS:

Common: headache, loss of appetite, muscle pains.
Unusual: fever, tiredness.
Severe but rare (stop medication, consult doctor): irregular heart rhythm.

INTERACTIONS:

Other drugs:
• severe interaction with erythromycin, ketoconazole, metoprolol, itraconazole, cimetidine, flecainide, imipramine, amitriptyline, clomipramine.
• other antimalarials.

PRESCRIPTION:

Yes.

PERMITTED IN SPORT:

Yes.

OVERDOSE:

Very serious. Heart rhythm abnormalities may cause sudden death. Induce vomiting or give activated charcoal if taken recently. Seek urgent medical attention.

OTHER INFORMATION:

Released in 2003. These medications are only available in this combination.
See also Atovaquone, Chloroquine, Doxycycline, Hydroxychloroquine, Mefloquine, Proguanil, Pyrimethamine, Quinine bisulphate.

Ascorbic acid
(Sodium ascorbate, Vitamin C)

TRADE NAMES:

A large number of preparations include ascorbic acid (vitamin C) alone or in combination with other medications.

DRUG CLASS:

Vitamin.

USES:

Scurvy, vitamin deficiency, convalescence.

DOSAGE:

 Recommended daily allowance: Males 40mg, Females 30mg.

FORMS:

Tablets, capsules, mixture, drops, injection.

PRECAUTIONS:

Safe in pregnancy, breast feeding and children.
Do not take in high doses or for prolonged periods of time.
Use with caution in kidney disease.

SIDE EFFECTS:

Common: minimal.
Unusual: kidney stones if taken in excessive doses.

INTERACTIONS:

None significant.

PRESCRIPTION:

No.

PERMITTED IN SPORT:

Yes.

OVERDOSE:

May cause kidney damage if taken in high doses long term.

OTHER INFORMATION:

Ascorbic acid is a water soluble vitamin found in citrus fruit, tomatoes and greens. Its level in food is reduced by mincing, grating and contact with copper utensils. It is essential for the formation and maintenance of bone, cartilage and teeth. Remember, vitamins are merely chemicals that are essential for the functioning of the body and if taken to excess, act as a drug. There is unfortunately, no evidence that it helps the common cold.

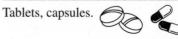

Aspirin
(Acetylsalicylic Acid)

TRADE NAMES:

Angettes, Caprin, Nu-seals.
Asasantin Retard (with dipyridamole).
Imazin XL (with isosorbide mononitrate).

DRUG CLASS:

Analgesic (pain killer), NSAID (anti-inflammatory), anticoagulant (stops blood clotting), antipyretic (reduces fever).

USES:

Relief of pain, reduction of fever, reduction of inflammation, prevention of blood clots and strokes.

DOSAGE:

 Prevention of blood clots and strokes: 75mg to 150mg once a day.
Other uses: 600mg (usually two tablets) every four hours.
Maximum 4500mg a day.

FORMS:

Tablets, capsules.

PRECAUTIONS:

Aspirin should not be used in pregnancy (C) unless medically essential. Should be used with caution in breast feeding and children. Not for use in infants, or children under 15 years with a fever.
Do not take if:
- suffering from bleeding disorders, peptic ulcer, fluid retention
- surgery planned in next few days, or recent surgery performed.

SIDE EFFECTS:

Common: gut irritation, heartburn, nausea.
Unusual: vomiting, blood in faeces, rash, aggravation of asthma, hay fever, ringing in ears.
Severe but rare (stop medication, consult doctor): unusual bleeding, asthma.

INTERACTIONS:

Other drugs:
- anticoagulants, NSAIDs, phenytoin, allopurinol, sodium valproate, sulfonamides, methotrexate, spironolactone.
Herbs:
- garlic, tamarind.
Other substances:
- reacts adversely with alcohol.

PRESCRIPTION:

No.

PERMITTED IN SPORT:

Yes.

OVERDOSE:

Adult lethal dose is over 25000mg (about 85 tablets). Symptoms include dizziness, ear noises, deafness, sweating, nausea, vomiting, headache, confusion, fever, rapid breathing, restlessness and coma. If tablets swallowed recently, induce vomiting. Seek medical assistance.

OTHER INFORMATION:

First synthesised in 1899, Aspirin is now one of the oldest and most widely used medications in the world.

See also NSAIDs.

Atenolol

TRADE NAMES:

Tenormin.
Beta-Adalat, Tenif (with nifedipine).
Kalten (with amiloride and hydrochlorothiazide).
Tenben (with bendrofluazide).
Tenoret 50, Tenoretic (with chlorthalidone).

DRUG CLASS:

Beta-blocker.

USES:

High blood pressure, angina, rapid heart rate, irregular heart beat, paroxysmal atrial tachycardia, heart attack.

DOSAGE:

 One to three tablets a day.

FORMS:

Tablets, injection.

PRECAUTIONS:

Should be used in pregnancy (C) only if medically essential.
Safe to use in breast feeding.
May be used with caution in children.
Use with care if suffering from alcoholism, liver or kidney failure or about to have surgery.

Do not take if:

- suffering from diabetes, asthma, or allergic conditions
- suffering from heart failure, shock, slow heart rate, or enlarged right heart
- if undertaking prolonged fast.

SIDE EFFECTS:

Common: low blood pressure, slow heart rate, cold hands and feet, asthma.
Unusual: loss of appetite, nausea, diarrhoea, impotence, tiredness, sleeplessness, nightmares, rash, loss of libido, hair loss, noises in ears.
Severe but rare (stop medication, consult doctor): severe asthma.

INTERACTIONS:

Other drugs:

- calcium channel blockers, disopyramide, clonidine, adrenaline, other medications for irregular heart beat, lignocaine, ergotamine, indomethacin, chlorpromazine.

Herbs:

- goldenseal, guarana, hawthorn, Korean ginseng, liquorice.

PRESCRIPTION:

Yes.

PERMITTED IN SPORT:

No.

OVERDOSE:

Slow heart rate, low blood pressure, asthma and heart failure may result. Administer activated charcoal or induce vomiting if tablets taken recently. Use Salbutamol or other asthma sprays for difficulty in breathing. Seek medical assistance.

OTHER INFORMATION:

Except for asthmatics, very safe and effective. First developed in 1960s.

See also Carvedilol, Esmolol, Labetalol, Metoprolol, Oxprenolol, Pindolol, Propranolol, Sotalol.

Atorvastatin

TRADE NAME:

Lipitor.

DRUG CLASS:

Hypolipidaemic.

USES:

Lowers blood cholesterol level.

DOSAGE:

 10mg to 40mg once a day.

FORMS:

Tablets (white) of 10mg, 20mg, 40mg and 80mg.

PRECAUTIONS:

Not to be used in pregnancy, breast feeding or children.
Use with caution in liver and kidney disease.
Regular blood tests to check cholesterol level and liver function advisable.

Do not take if:
- suffering from active liver disease
- previous adverse effects (e.g. muscle pain or weakness) experienced from other medication used to lower cholesterol.

SIDE EFFECTS:

Common: altered bowel habits (diarrhoea or constipation), indigestion, heartburn, nausea, headache.
Unusual: belly pain, sleeplessness, rash, itch.

Severe but rare (stop medication, consult doctor): swelling of face or lips, muscle pain, muscle damage, tingling in hands and feet.

INTERACTIONS:

Other drugs:
- digoxin, erythromycin, rifampicin, phenytoin, oral contraceptives, immunosuppressives, antifungals, other medications used to lower cholesterol levels.

Other substances:
- alcohol.

Herbs:
- alfalfa, fenugreek, garlic, ginger.

PRESCRIPTION:

Yes.

PERMITTED IN SPORT:

Yes.

OVERDOSE:

Liver and muscle damage possible. Induce vomiting or give activated activated charcoal if taken recently. Seek medical assistance.

OTHER INFORMATION:

Introduced in 1998 as an improved version of similar drugs. Much more effective in lowering cholesterol levels in blood and has fewer side effects than other hypolipidaemics. Designed for long term use as it controls high cholesterol but does not cure the problem. Stopping the medication without advice from a doctor may lead to a rapid increase in cholesterol to the pre-treatment level. High cholesterol levels increase the risk of heart attack and stroke.

See also Cholestyramine, Colestipol, Fluvastatin, Gemfibrizol, Nicotinic acid, Pravastatin, Simvastatin.

Atobisan

TRADE NAME:

Tractocile.

USES:

Delays onset of labour of childbirth when immediate delivery of the infant is not desired due to prematurity.

DOSAGE:

 As determined by the doctor.

FORMS:

Injection.

PRECAUTIONS:

Not for use in pregnancy before 24 weeks or over 33 weeks. Not for use in breast feeding, children or males.
Use with caution in premature rupture of the membranes.
Use with caution in kidney and liver disease.
Use with caution on second and subsequent occasions.
Careful monitoring of both mother and infant essential during use.

Do not take if:

- infant is showing signs of distress, retarded growth
- suffering from eclampsia, bleeding from the vagina, infection of the uterus or placental abnormality.

SIDE EFFECTS:

Common: nausea, headache, dizziness.
Unusual: vomiting, hot flushes, rapid heart rate, excess blood sugar level, low blood pressure, reaction at injection site.
Severe but rare (stop medication, consult doctor): distress of foetus, bleeding from mother.

INTERACTIONS:

Other drugs:
- not known.

PRESCRIPTION:

Yes.

OTHER INFORMATION:

Introduced in 2000 to prevent premature labour.
See also Ritodrine.

Atovaquone

TRADE NAMES:

Wellvone.
Malarone (with proguanil).

DRUG CLASS:

Antifungal and antimalarial.

USES:

Wellvone: treatment of specific fungal infections caused by *Pneumocystis carinii* in AIDS patients.
Malarone: treatment of malaria.

DOSAGE:

 Wellvone: 5mLs twice a day.
Malarone: once a day with food.

FORMS:

Wellvone: suspension.
Malarone: tablets, pink.

PRECAUTIONS:

Use with caution in pregnancy (B2), breast feeding and children.
Use with caution in patients with lung and intestinal diseases.
Malarone: use with caution if malaria affects brain and other complicated cases.

SIDE EFFECTS:

Common: loss of appetite, diarrhoea, nausea, rash, headache, belly pain.
Unusual: vomiting, fever, sleeplessness, dizziness, muscle pains.

INTERACTIONS:

Other drugs:
* metoclopramide, rifampicin, paracetamol, benzodiazepines, aciclovir, morphine, pethidine, codeine, cephalosporins, antidiarrhoeals, laxatives, many other drugs.

PRESCRIPTION:

Yes.

PERMITTED IN SPORT:

Yes.

OVERDOSE:

Severe intestinal effects. Seek urgent medical treatment. Vomiting will probably occur spontaneously.

OTHER INFORMATION:

Wellvone introduced in 1997 for treatment of severe complication of AIDS infection. Malarone introduced in 1999.

See also Artemether and Lumefantrine, Chloroquine, Doxycycline, Hydroxychloroquine, Mefloquine, Primaquine, Proguanil, Pyrimethamine, Quinine bisulphate, Sulfadoxine.

Atropine

TRADE NAMES:

Atropine Injection, Minims Atropine Isopto Atropine (with hypromellose). **Lomotil** (with diphenoxylate hydrochloride).

DRUG CLASS:

Mydriatic, Anticholinergic.

USES:

Tablets: diarrhoea, intestinal cramps, drying of secretions.
Eye drops: enlargement of pupil.
Injection: drying of secretions and saliva.

DOSAGE:

 Depends on usage. Follow directions on pack or doctor's advice.

Lomotil: one or two tablets four times a day as required for diarrhoea.

FORMS:

Tablets, eye drops, injection.

PRECAUTIONS:

Safe in pregnancy and children.
Injection and tablets should be used with caution in elderly or debilitated patients.

Do not take if:

* as eye drops if suffering from glaucoma
* in other forms if suffering from rapid heart rate, heart failure, lung failure or over active thyroid gland.

SIDE EFFECTS:

Common: dry mouth, dilated pupils, dry eyes, difficulty in passing urine, rapid heart rate.
Unusual: flushing, palpitations, constipation, dry skin, rash, drowsiness, vomiting, mood changes.

INTERACTIONS:

Other drugs:
* additive effect with antihistamines, phenothiazines, and tricyclic antidepressants.

PRESCRIPTION:

Yes.

PERMITTED IN SPORT:

Yes.

OVERDOSE:

Eye drops: no problem.
Other forms: may be very serious, depending upon dose and form. Seek urgent medical advice.

OTHER INFORMATION:

Widely used for over a century to dry secretions before an operation, to dilate the pupil to aid examination of the eye, and to ease intestinal cramps and diarrhoea. Occurs naturally in certain herbal extracts.

Auranofin
(Gold)

TRADE NAME:
Ridaura.

DRUG CLASS:
Antirheumatic.

USES:
Rheumatoid arthritis.

DOSAGE:

One tablet two or three times a day with food.

FORMS:
Tablets of 3mg (pale yellow).

PRECAUTIONS:
Should be used with caution in pregnancy (B3), breast feeding and children.
Use with caution in liver and kidney disease, inflammatory bowel disease.
Lower doses required in elderly.
Regular blood and urine tests required to assess kidney and liver function, blood cells and effectiveness of treatment.

Do not take if:

• suffering from severe diabetes, severe kidney or liver disease, severe high blood pressure, heart failure, severe dermatitis, bone marrow damage, systemic lupus erythematosus, Sjögren syndrome, eczema, blood diseases or colitis.

SIDE EFFECTS:
Common: dermatitis, itch, mouth ulcers, flushing, fainting.
Unusual: sweating, dizziness, weakness, feeling unwell, nausea, diarrhoea, light sensitive skin, eye damage.
Severe but rare (stop medication, consult doctor): severe rash, unusual bleeding or bruising.

INTERACTIONS:
Other drugs:
• phenylbutazone, hydroxychloroquine, immunosuppressives, warfarin, dextropropoxyphene, clonidine, penicillamine, antimalarials, cytotoxics, phenylbutazone, oxphenbutazone, levamisole, high dose steroids.

PRESCRIPTION:
Yes.

PERMITTED IN SPORT:
Yes.

OTHER INFORMATION:
An unusual but remarkably effective treatment that has been used for over thirty years. Careful monitoring of blood tests and skin reactions essential. Gold is not addictive when swallowed or injected, only when collected!
See also Sodium aurothiomalate.

Aurothiomalate
See Sodium aurothiomalate.

Azapropazone

TRADE NAME:
Rheumox.

DRUG CLASS:
NSAID (Nonsteroidal anti-inflammatory drug).

USES:
Gout, ankylosing spondylitis and rheumatoid arthritis when other treatments have failed.

DOSAGE:

One tablet or capsule two to four times a day with food.

FORMS:
Tablets of 600mg, capsules of 300mg.

PRECAUTIONS:
Should not be used in pregnancy (C) unless medically essential. Breast feeding should be ceased. Not for use in children. Use with caution in psychiatricaly disturbed patients, epilepsy, severe infection, heart failure and kidney disease.

Lower doses required in elderly, who may suffer more side effects.

Do not take if:

- suffering from peptic ulcer at present or in recent past
- due for surgery (including dental surgery)
- suffering from bleeding disorder or anaemia
- suffering from proctitis (suppository only).

SIDE EFFECTS:
Common: stomach discomfort, diarrhoea, constipation, heartburn, nausea, headache, dizziness, sun sensitivity.
Unusual: blurred vision, stomach ulcer, ringing noise in ears, retention of fluid, swelling of tissue, drowsiness, itch, rash, shortness of breath.
Severe but rare (stop medication, consult doctor): vomit blood, pass blood in faeces, other unusual bleeding, asthma induced by medication.

INTERACTIONS:
Other drugs:
- must never be used with anticoagulants (e.g. warfarin)
- probenecid, digoxin, cimetidine, phenytoin, hypoglycaemics (used for diabetes), diuretics, lithium, methotrexate, beta-blockers, ACE inhibitors.

Herbs:
- feverfew.

PRESCRIPTION:
Yes.

PERMITTED IN SPORT:
Yes.

OVERDOSE:
Causes nausea, vomiting, severe headache, dizziness, confusion and convulsions. Administer activated charcoal or induce vomiting if taken recently. Seek medical assistance.

See also Aceclofenac, Acemetacin, Aspirin, Dexketoprofen, Diclofenac, Diflunisal, Etodolac, Felbinac, Fenbufen, Fenoprofen, Flurbiprofen, Ibuprofen, Indomethacin, Ketoprofen, Ketorolac trometanol, Mefenamic acid, Meloxicam, Nabumetone, Naproxen, Phenylbutazone, Piroxicam, Salicylic acid, Sulindac, Tenoxicam, Tiaprofenic Acid, Tolfenamic acid.

Azathioprine

TRADE NAME:
Imuran.

DRUG CLASS:
Immunomodifier.

USES:
Prevents rejection of transplanted organ, autoimmune diseases.

DOSAGE:
Complex. Must be determined individually for each patient by doctor.

FORMS:
Tablets of 25mg (orange) and 50mg (yellow), injection.

PRECAUTIONS:
Not to be used in pregnancy (D) unless mother's life at risk. Breast feeding must be ceased before use. May be used with caution in children.

Regular blood tests to monitor response essential.

Use with caution in liver and kidney disease.

Do not take if:

- undertaking dental procedures without consulting doctor.
- having live virus vaccine (e.g. Sabin for polio).

SIDE EFFECTS:

Very complex. Wide range of side effects may occur and must be discussed with doctor before use of medication. Report any unusual effects to doctor.

INTERACTIONS:

Other drugs:
- allopurinol, oxypurinol, thiopurinol, cancer treating medications, captopril, many others.

Other substances:
- reacts with alcohol.

PRESCRIPTION:

Yes.

PERMITTED IN SPORT:

Yes.

OVERDOSE:

May cause damage to immune system which leads to multiple infections, ulceration of mouth and throat, bruising and bleeding. Seek medical assistance.

OTHER INFORMATION:

Potent medication that must be finely balanced to prevent rejection of donated organ but allow protection of body against infection.

Azelaic acid
See KERATOLYTICS.

Azelastine

TRADE NAMES:

Opilast, Rhinolast.

DRUG CLASS:

Antihistamine.

USES:

Hay fever, allergic conjunctivitis.

DOSAGE:

Nose spray: one spray into each nostril twice a day.
Eye drops: one drop in each eye twice a day. Increase to four times a day if necessary. Do not use for more than six weeks.

FORMS:

Nasal spray, eye drops.

PRECAUTIONS:

May be used with caution in pregnancy (B3), breast feeding and and children under five years. Eye drops not recommended under four years.
Use with caution in elderly.

SIDE EFFECTS:

Common: bitter taste in mouth (bend head forward when spraying to reduce this effect).
Unusual: nose irritation.

INTERACTIONS:

Other drugs:
- sedatives.

Other substances:
- alcohol is theoretically (but probably not practically) a problem.

PRESCRIPTION:

No.

PERMITTED IN SPORT:

Yes.

OVERDOSE:

May cause convulsions, hallucinations, delirium, anxiety, muscle spasms, rapid heart rate, flushing, dry skin, dry mouth and coma if contents of bottle drunk. First aid involved inducing vomiting and seeking urgent medical attention.

OTHER INFORMATION:

Introduced in 2000 as a way of controlling hay fever with minimal side effects as occurs with other antihistamines that are usually swallowed. **See also ANTIHISTAMINES, SEDATING.**

Azithromycin

TRADE NAME:

Zithromax.

DRUG CLASS:

Macrolide antibiotic.

USES:

Infections caused by susceptible bacteria (e.g. bronchitis, sinusitis, throat infection).

DOSAGE:

 Once a day, away from meals.

FORMS:

Capsules (white) of 250mg, tablets (white) of 500mg.

PRECAUTIONS:

Use in pregnancy (B3) only if medically necessary. Use with caution in breast feeding and children.
Lower doses necessary in elderly and debilitated.
Use with caution in liver and kidney disease.

SIDE EFFECTS:

Common: nausea, diarrhoea, belly pains.
Unusual: vomiting, palpitations, dizziness, vaginal thrush, rash, headache.

INTERACTIONS:

Other drugs:
• theophylline, antacids, cyclosporin, digoxin, zidovudine, warfarin.

PRESCRIPTION:

Yes.

PERMITTED IN SPORT:

Yes.

OVERDOSE:

Exacerbation of side effects likely. Induce vomiting if medication taken recently. Seek medical assistance.

OTHER INFORMATION:

Introduced 1995 to treat difficult infections.
See Zidovudine.

AZT

See Zidovudine.

Aztreonam

TRADE NAME:

Azactam.

DRUG CLASS:

Antibiotic.

USES:

Severe bacterial infections.

DOSAGE:

 As determined by doctor for each individual patient.

FORMS:

Injection.

PRECAUTIONS:

Relatively safe in pregnancy (B1), breast feeding and children.
Use caution in use with severe kidney and liver disease.
Use caution in use with premature infants and elderly.
Must be used with caution in gynaecological infections.

SIDE EFFECTS:

Common: minimal.
Unusual: development of resistant infections.
Severe but rare (stop medication, consult doctor): bowel inflammation (pseudomembranous colitis).

INTERACTIONS:

Other drugs:
• frusemide.

PRESCRIPTION:

Yes.

PERMITTED IN SPORT:

Yes.

OVERDOSE:

Always given by infusion or injection under strict medical supervision.

OTHER INFORMATION:

Only used after other antibiotics have been proved to be ineffective.

B

Bacitracin

TRADE NAMES:

Available only in combination with other medications.
Cicatrin (with neomycin).
Polyfax (with polymyxin B).

DRUG CLASS:

Antibiotic.

USES:

Skin infections.

DOSAGE:

 Apply three or four times a day.

FORMS:

Cream, ointment, powder.

PRECAUTIONS:

Used on the skin, safe in pregnancy, breast feeding and children.
Do not use on large areas that are weeping or lacking in good quality skin. Not designed for long term use.

SIDE EFFECTS:

Common: skin irritation.

INTERACTIONS:

None significant.

PRESCRIPTION:

Yes.

PERMITTED IN SPORT:

Yes.

Baclofen

TRADE NAME:

Lioresal.

DRUG CLASS:

Muscle relaxant.

USES:

Muscle spasm in multiple sclerosis, muscle spasm in spinal injury, muscle spasm in cerebral palsy, bladder spasm.

DOSAGE:

 5mg to 25mg three times a day.

FORMS:

Tablets of 10mg (white).
Liquid.
Injection for use in spinal cord.

PRECAUTIONS:

Use in pregnancy (B3) only if medically essential. Use with caution in breast feeding and children.
Use with caution in psychiatric disorders, peptic ulcer, heart disease, stroke, lung disease, liver or kidney disease, diabetes, difficulty in passing urine.
Lower doses required in elderly.
Do not stop suddenly, but reduce dosage slowly.

Do not take if:

 • suffering from epilepsy or brain injury.

SIDE EFFECTS:

Common: dose related. Sedation, drowsiness, nausea
Unusual: dry mouth, vomiting, confusion, dizziness, headache, sleeplessness, mood changes.
Severe but rare (stop medication, consult doctor): convulsions.

INTERACTIONS:

Other drugs:
- tricyclics, sedatives, medications for lowering blood pressure, L-dopa, diazepam.

Other substances:
- reacts with alcohol to increase sedation.

PRESCRIPTION:

Yes.

PERMITTED IN SPORT:

Yes.

OVERDOSE:

Drowsiness, difficulty in breathing, confusion, hallucinations, slow heart rate, coma and rarely death may occur. Administer or induce vomiting if medication taken recently and patient alert. Seek urgent medical attention.

OTHER INFORMATION:

Used successfully in a number of difficult conditions that cause distressing muscle spasms.

Balsalazide

TRADE NAME:

Colazide.

DRUG CLASS:

Salicylate.

USES:

Treatment and prevention of ulcerative colitis.

DOSAGE:

 Treatment: Three capsules three times a day with food.
Prevention: Two capsules twice a day with food.

FORMS:

Capsule of 750mg (beige).

PRECAUTIONS:

Not to be used in pregnancy (D), breast feeding or children.
Use with caution in asthma, bleeding disorders, peptic ulcer or stomach inflammation, mild kidney or liver disease.
Regular blood and urine tests necessary during treatment.

Do not take if:

- suffering from significant liver or kidney disease
- allergic to salicylates (e.g. aspirin).

SIDE EFFECTS:

Common: headache, nausea, diarrhoea.
Unusual: belly pain, gall stone formation.
Severe but rare (stop medication, consult doctor): abnormal bleeding, bruising, sore throat, excessive tiredness.

INTERACTIONS:

Other drugs:
- digoxin, methotrexate.

PRESCRIPTION:

Yes.

PERMITTED IN SPORT:

Yes.

OVERDOSE:

Symptoms include dizziness, ear noises, deafness, sweating, nausea, vomiting, headache, confusion, fever, rapid breathing, restlessness and coma. If tablets swallowed recently, induce vomiting. Seek medical assistance.

Bambuterol

TRADE NAME:

Bambec.

DRUG CLASS:

Beta agonist.

USES:
Asthma, spasm of airways.

DOSAGE:
 One tablet a day at night.

FORMS:
Tablets of 10mg and 20mg (white).

PRECAUTIONS:
Use with caution in pregnancy and breast feeding. Not for use in children.
Use with caution in kidney disease, poor heart function, diabetes and hyperthyroidism (overactive thyroid gland).
Regular blood tests to check blood potassium levels may be necessary.

Do not take if:

 • suffering from liver disease or heart enlargement.

SIDE EFFECTS:
Common: tremor, headache, muscle cramps.
Unusual: low blood potassium, palpitations, allergic rash.

INTERACTIONS:
Other drugs:
• beta-blockers, suxamethonium.

PRESCRIPTION:
Yes.

PERMITTED IN SPORT:
Yes, but only under specific conditions set out by each sport. Must be declared by athlete to sport administrators.

OVERDOSE:
Exacerbation of side effects likely. May be dangerous in patients with heart disease or high blood pressure.

OTHER INFORMATION:
Introduced in 2002.
See also Salbutamol, Salmeterol.

BARBITURATES

TRADE and GENERIC NAMES:
Amytal, Sodium Amytal (Amylobarbitone).
Phenobarb (Phenobarbitone).
Not generally available.
Seconal (Quinalbarbitone).
Soneryl (Butobarbitone).
Tuinal (Amylobarbitone and quinalbarbitone).

DRUG CLASS:
Sedative/hypnotic, anticonvulsant.

USES:
Sedation, insomnia (sleeplessness), epilepsy.

DOSAGE:
 One or two tablets one to three times a day.

FORMS:
Tablets, injection.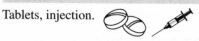

PRECAUTIONS:
Should not be taken in pregnancy (D), particularly early pregnancy, unless medically essential (e.g. for uncontrolled epilepsy). May be used in breast feeding and children.
Lower doses required in elderly.
Should not be stopped suddenly if used for long period constantly, but dose should be reduced gradually. Use intermittently if possible.

Do not take if:

 • suffering from poor lung function, porphyria, severe liver or kidney disease, uncontrolled pain
• likely to develop a drug dependency
• history of alcohol or drug abuse.

• operating machinery, driving a vehicle or undertaking tasks that require concentration and alertness.

SIDE EFFECTS:

Common: drowsiness, incoordination, slow breathing, hangover sensation, slow heart rate, low blood pressure, nausea, diarrhoea, dependence on drug.
Unusual: memory defects, dizziness, paradoxical excitement, nightmares, hallucinations, constipation, vomiting, headache.
Severe but rare (stop medication, consult doctor): loss of consciousness.

INTERACTIONS:

Other drugs:
• griseofulvin, folic acid, pethidine, morphine, phenytoin, rifampicin, oral contraceptives, chlorpromazine, tricyclic antidepressants, warfarin, antihistamines, MAOI.
Herbs:
• valerian, kava kava, goldenseal, valerian, St John's wort.
Other substances:
• reacts with alcohol to cause sedation.

PRESCRIPTION:

Yes.

PERMITTED IN SPORT:

Yes.

OVERDOSE:

Very serious. Low blood pressure, coma, cessation of breathing and death may occur. Induce vomiting if tablets taken recently. Seek urgent medical assistance.

OTHER INFORMATION:

Used for many decades to sedate, calm and ease sleeplessness. Dependency problem limits its use today mainly to the control of some forms of epilepsy.
See also BENZODIAZEPINES, Carbamazepine, Clonazepam, Ethosuximide, Gabapentin, Lamotrigine, Levetiracetam, Oxcarbazepine, Phenytoin, Primidone, Sodium valproate, Sulthiame, Tiagabine, Topiramate, Vigabatrin.

BCG vaccine
(Tuberculosis vaccine)

TRADE NAME:
BCG Vaccine.

DRUG CLASS:
Vaccine.

USES:
Prevention of tuberculosis (TB).

DOSAGE:
 Single vaccination (skin scratch, not injection).

FORMS:
Ampoule.

PRECAUTIONS:
Vaccination during pregnancy (B2) is not recommended, but unintentional or necessary vaccination is unlikely to have any adverse effects. May be used safely in breast feeding, children and infants. Prevent vaccination fluid from being inhaled.
Use with caution near any skin disorder.

Do not take if:
 • suffering from significant illness or reduced immunity.

SIDE EFFECTS:
Common: skin irritation at site of vaccination.

INTERACTIONS:
Other drugs:
• other vaccines.

PRESCRIPTION:
Yes.

PERMITTED IN SPORT:
Yes.

OTHER INFORMATION:
Routine use is restricted to immigrants. Widely used in poorer countries.

Becaplermin

TRADE NAME:

Regranex.

USES:

Healing diabetic skin ulcers.

DOSAGE:

 Remove surface debris from ulcer. Apply a thin layer of gel across whole ulcer area once a day and cover with a moist saline dressing. Treatment may be necessary for several months.

FORMS:

Gel.

PRECAUTIONS:

Not for use in pregnancy, breast feeding and children.
Ensure adequate blood supply to area before use.

Do not take if:

 • suffering from skin cancer at or near ulcer site
• underlying skin or bone infection or malignancy.

SIDE EFFECTS:

Common: infection, redness of skin, pain.
Unusual: blistering skin reaction.
Severe but rare (stop medication, consult doctor): swelling of tissue.

INTERACTIONS:

Other drugs:
• other creams, ointments and gels on same area.

PRESCRIPTION:

Yes.

PERMITTED IN SPORT:

Yes.

OVERDOSE:

Redness, blistering and swelling of skin only likely effect if excess applied. Seek medical attention if swallowed.

OTHER INFORMATION:

Introduced in 1999 for treatment of difficult diabetic skin ulcers.

Beclomethasone dipropionate

TRADE NAMES:

Aerobec, Asmabec, Beclazone, Becloforte, Becodisks, Beconase, Becotide, Filair, Nasobec, Propaderm, Pulvinal, Qvar, Rino Clenil.

DRUG CLASS:

Corticosteroid.

USES:

Prevention of asthma, prevention of hay fever, severe dermatitis, psoriasis.

DOSAGE:

 Asthma: one or two inhalations, two to four times a day.
Nasal spray: one spray in each nostril twice a day.
Cream (Propaderm): use sparingly once or twice a day.

FORMS:

Inhaler, rotacaps, nebuliser solution, nasal spray, cream.

PRECAUTIONS:

Use with caution in pregnancy (B3), breast feeding and children.
Use with caution in lung, nose or throat infection and tuberculosis.
Lung function should be checked regularly to ensure adequate dose is received.

Do not take if:

 • cream if suffering from fungal skin infection.

INTERACTIONS:

Other drugs:
- phenothiazines, MAOI, antihistamines, antidepressants, disopyramide, amantadine.

PRESCRIPTION:

Yes.

PERMITTED IN SPORT:

Yes.

OVERDOSE:

Serious. Seek urgent medical attention. Induce vomiting or give activated charcoal if swallowed recently.

See also Amantadine, Apomorphine, Benztropine, Biperiden, Bromocriptine, Entacapone, LEVODOPA COMPOUNDS, Orphenadrine, Pergolide, Pramipexole, Procyclidine, Ropinirole, Selegiline.

Benzocaine

See ANAESTHETIC, LOCAL.

BENZODIAZEPINES

DISCUSSION:

Benzodiazepines all sedate and may cause dependency and they also relieve anxiety, but the degree of sedation and dependency varies dramatically from one drug to another and one patient to another. Dependency should not be a problem unless the drugs are used inappropriately. Some of these drugs (e.g. diazepam) can also be used to relax muscle spasm and control convulsions. They should be stopped slowly, with a gradual reduction in dosage if they have been used for a long time. They will increase the effects of alcohol and care should be taken with driving and using machinery while taking them.

See Buspirone, Clobazam, Clonazepam, Diazepam, Flunitrazepam, Lorazepam, Midazolam, Nitrazepam, Temazepam.

Benzoic acid

See KERATOLYTICS.

Benzoyl peroxide

See KERATOLYTICS.

Benzthiazide

See THIAZIDE DIURETICS.

Benztropine

TRADE NAME:

Cogentin.

DRUG CLASS:

Antiparkinsonian.

USES:

Parkinsonism.

DOSAGE:

 Individualised dose depending on response. Must be closely monitored by doctor.

FORMS:

Tablet of 2mg (white), injection.

PRECAUTIONS:

Use with caution in pregnancy (B2) and breast feeding. Not for use in children under three years.
Use with caution with enlarged prostate gland, rapid heart rate, psychiatric conditions, glaucoma.

SIDE EFFECTS:

Common: rapid heart rate, constipation, dry mouth, nausea, confusion, blurred vision.
Unusual: vomiting, hallucinations, difficulty passing urine, rash.

INTERACTIONS:

Other drugs:
- phenothiazines, tricyclic antidepressants, haloperidol.

PRESCRIPTION:

Yes.

PERMITTED IN SPORT:

Yes.

OVERDOSE:

Confusion, nervousness, psychiatric disturbances, dizziness, weakness, rapid heart rate, incoordination, palpitations and vomiting may occur. Administer activated charcoal or induce vomiting if medication taken recently. Seek medical assistance.

Benzydamine hydrochloride

TRADE NAMES:

Difflam, Difflam Oral.

DRUG CLASS:

Topical anti-inflammatory.

USES:

Reduces inflammation and pain.

DOSAGE:

 Cream: massage into affected area three to six times a day.
Oral: use every 90 minutes as required.

FORMS:

Cream, gargle, mouth spray.

PRECAUTIONS:

Safe in pregnancy, breast feeding and children.
Avoid eyes with all preparations.
Cream should not be used in mouth, nose, anus and vagina.
Use with caution in severe liver disease.

SIDE EFFECTS:

Common: minimal.
Unusual: skin reaction.

INTERACTIONS:

None significant.

PRESCRIPTION:

No.

PERMITTED IN SPORT:

Yes.

OVERDOSE:

Unlikely to be a problem.

OTHER INFORMATION:

Does not cause addiction or dependence.
See also Heparinoid, LINIMENTS.

Benzyl benzoate

TRADE NAMES:

Ascabiol.
Anugesic HC (with hydrocortisone, paramoxine, zinc oxide, bismuth oxide and other ingredients).
Anusol HC (with hydrocortisone, zinc oxide, bismuth oxide and other ingredients).

DRUG CLASS:

Antiparasitic.

USES:

Scabies, head and body lice. Used in combination with other ingredients for piles and anal itch.

DOSAGE:

 Lotion: apply to small area of skin for ten minutes before using to test for sensitivity. Apply to whole body from neck down after a hot bath. Remove by washing after one day. Repeat after five days. More applications may be necessary for lice.
Suppositories and anal cream: insert into and apply around anus twice a day.

FORMS:

Lotion, cream, suppository.

PRECAUTIONS:

Use with caution in pregnancy (B2). Safe for use in breast feeding. Dilute for use in children.
Avoid use on face, head and around vagina, head of penis and anus.

SIDE EFFECTS:

Common: skin irritation.
Unusual: skin burning.

INTERACTIONS:

None significant.

PRESCRIPTION:

No.

PERMITTED IN SPORT:

Yes.

OVERDOSE:

If swallowed, administer activated charcoal or induce vomiting if medication taken recently. May cause convulsions. Seek urgent medical advice.

OTHER INFORMATION:

Commonly used and effective treatment for parasites. All members of family must be treated at same time. Change and wash all bed linen and clothing in hot water with each treatment.

Benzyl penicillin

See Penicillin G.

BETA-2 AGONISTS
(β2 AGONISTS)

DISCUSSION:

The bronchi are the tubes in the lung that contain air. Bronchodilators open these tubes to their maximum extent to allow more air to enter and leave the lungs.

The most common bronchodilators are the beta-2 agonists. They are available as pressure pack sprays, nebuliser additives,various inhalers mixtures, tablets and injections. They act very rapidly if inhaled or injected but more slowly and with more side effects, if taken as a mixture or tablet. Some forms have a very long action and can act effectively as both a preventer and a treatment.

See Bambuterol, Eformoterol, Fenoterol, Salbutamol, Salmeterol, Terbutaline.

BETA-BLOCKERS
(β ADRENERGIC BLOCKING AGENTS)

DISCUSSION:

High blood pressure, migraine, irregular heartbeat, stage fright, prevention of heart attack, exam nerves, angina, overactive thyroid gland, tremors and glaucoma—all these diseases can be controlled, or treated, by the amazingly versatile group of drugs called beta-blockers. Some beta-blockers are very specific for particular diseases (e.g. timolol is used only in eye drop form for glaucoma; atenolol acts mainly on the heart), but others (e.g. propranolol) can act in virtually all areas. Beta receptors are present on certain nerves in the body and blocking the action of these nerves with beta-blockers produces the desired effects. Because they can control a fine tremor and anxiety over performance, these drugs are banned in the Olympic and Commonwealth games, as they would give athletes such as archers and shooters an unfair advantage. Beta-blockers are generally very safe medications but cannot be used in asthmatics and must be used with care in diabetics.

See Atenolol, Betaxolol, Bisoprolol, Carteolol, Carvedilol, Celiprolol, Esmolol, Labetalol, Levobunolol, Metipranolol,

Metoprolol, Nadolol, Oxprenolol, Pindolol, Propranolol, Sotalol, Timolol.

Betacarotene
(Vitamin A)

TRADE NAMES:

A form of vitamin A (retinol is another form) found in numerous vitamin and mineral preparations, as well as soothing and healing creams and lotions.

DRUG CLASS:

Vitamin.

USES:

Vitamin A deficiency, malnutrition, poor diet, soothing agent in creams for minor burns.

DOSAGE:

 Recommended daily allowance: 2500 International Units a day.

FORMS:

Capsules, tablets, mixture, lotion, cream.

PRECAUTIONS:

Must not be used in pregnancy (D) as high doses may cause birth defects. May be used in breast feeding and with caution in children. Skin preparations safe in pregnancy.
Do not exceed recommended dose.
Use with caution in Vitamin K deficiency.

SIDE EFFECTS:

Common: minimal.
Severe but rare (stop medication, consult doctor): yellow skin, particularly of palms and soles.

INTERACTIONS:

None significant.

PRESCRIPTION:

No.

PERMITTED IN SPORT:

Yes.

OVERDOSE:

Chronic overdosage will lead to carotenaemia in which excess Betacarotene is deposited in skin (causes it to turn yellow) and may cause damage to organs.

OTHER INFORMATION:

Fat soluble vitamin. Dangerous in pregnancy and overdose. Remember, vitamins are merely chemicals that are essential for the functioning of the body and if taken to excess, act as a drug.

See also Cod liver oil, Retinols.

Betahistine

TRADE NAME:

Serc.

DRUG CLASS:

Vasodilator.

USES:

Ménière's syndrome, dizziness, nausea, vomiting, noises in ears (tinnitus), some forms of poor hearing.

DOSAGE:

 Two tablets three or four times a day.

FORMS:

Tablet of 8 and 16mg (white).

PRECAUTIONS:

Should not be used in pregnancy, breast feeding or children.
Do not take if:
 • suffering from phaeochromocytoma, asthma, peptic ulcer.

SIDE EFFECTS:

Common: minimal.
Unusual: rash, diarrhoea, dizziness, headache, nausea, sleeplessness.

INTERACTIONS:

None significant.

PRESCRIPTION:

Yes.

PERMITTED IN SPORT:

Yes.

OVERDOSE:

No serious effects.
See also Diazoxide, Guanethidine, Nicotinic Acid.

Betaine

TRADE NAME:

Kloref (with potassium salts).

DRUG CLASS:

Detoxifying agent.

USES:

Treatment of the rare metabolic condition homocystinuria. In combination with potassium used to treat potassium deficiency.

DOSAGE:

 One or two tablets three times a day dissolved in water.

FORMS:

Effervescent tablet.

PRECAUTIONS:

Not to be used in pregnancy (C) or breast feeding.

SIDE EFFECTS:

Common: nausea, diarrhoea.

INTERACTIONS:

Other drugs:
• affects the absorption of all other medications taken at the same time.

PRESCRIPTION:

No.

PERMITTED IN SPORT:

Yes.

OVERDOSE:

Significant diarrhoea only likely effect.

Betamethasone

TRADE NAMES:

Betacap, Betnelan, Betnesol, Betnovate, Bettamousse, Diprosone.
Betnesol N, Betnovate N (with neomycin).
Betnovate C (with clioquinol).
Diprosalic (with salicylic acid).
Duvobet (with calcipotriol).
Fucibet (with fusidic acid).
Lotriderm (with clotrimazole).

DRUG CLASS:

Corticosteroid.

USES:

Skin preparations: severe inflammation of skin (eczema, dermatitis, psoriasis etc.). Tablets, injections: above uses plus severe asthma, rheumatoid and other forms of severe arthritis, autoimmune diseases (e.g. Sjögren Syndrome), severe allergy reactions, and other severe and chronic inflammatory diseases.

DOSAGE:

 Tablets: one to ten tablets a day as directed by doctor.
Creams, ointments: apply two or three times a day.
Lotions, mousse: apply once or twice a day.

FORMS:

Tablets, cream, ointment, gel, lotion, hair mousse, injection.

PRECAUTIONS:

Should be used in pregnancy (C), breast feeding and children only on specific medical advice.
Skin preparations safe in pregnancy, breast feeding and children over three years.
Use tablets and injections with caution if under stress and in patients with under active thyroid gland, liver disease, diverticulitis, high blood pressure, myasthenia gravis or kidney disease.
Avoid eyes with all forms.
Use for shortest period of time possible.

Do not use if:

- suffering from any form of infection, peptic ulcer, or osteoporosis
- having a vaccination.

SIDE EFFECTS:

Common: skin preparations: minimal.
Tablets and injections: may cause bloating, weight gain, rashes and intestinal disturbances.
Unusual: skin preparations: thinning of skin, premature ageing, itching, scarring of skin.
Tablets and injections: biochemical disturbances of blood, muscle weakness, bone weakness, impaired wound healing, skin thinning, tendon weakness, peptic ulcers, gullet ulcers, bruising, increased sweating, loss of fat under skin, premature ageing, excess facial hair growth in women, pigmentation of skin and nails, acne, convulsions, headaches, dizziness, growth suppression in children, aggravation of diabetes, worsening of infections, cataracts, aggravation of glaucoma, blood clots in veins and sleeplessness.
Most significant side effects occur only with prolonged use of tablets or injections.

Medication should not be ceased abruptly, but dosage should be slowly reduced.
Severe but rare (stop medication, consult doctor): any significant side effect should be reported to a doctor immediately.

INTERACTIONS:

Other drugs:
- tablets and injections may be affected by oral contraceptives, barbiturates, phenytoin, and rifampicin.

PRESCRIPTION:

Yes.

PERMITTED IN SPORT:

Tablets, injections: no.
Skin preparations: yes.

OVERDOSE:

Medical treatment is required. Serious effects and death rare.

OTHER INFORMATION:

Extremely effective and useful medication if used correctly. Tablets must be used with extreme care under strict medical supervision. Lowest dose and shortest possible course should be used. Not addictive.

See also Desoxymethasone, Diflucortolone, Halcinonide, Hydrocortisone, Methylprednisolone, Mometasone, Triamcinolone.

Betaxolol

TRADE NAMES:

Betoptic, Kerlone.

DRUG CLASS:

Beta-blocker.

USES:

Glaucoma, high blood pressure.

DOSAGE:

 Drops: one drop twice a day.
Tablets: one tablet a day.

FORMS:

Eye drops, tablet of 20mg (white).

PRECAUTIONS:

Should be used with caution in pregnancy (C), but eye drops unlikely to cause problems.
Safe to use in breast feeding.
May be used with considerable caution in children.
Use with care if suffering from alcoholism, liver or kidney failure or about to have surgery.
Use with caution with enlarged right heart, diabetes or allergic conditions.

Do not take if:

- suffering from heart failure, slow heart rate, asthma.

SIDE EFFECTS:

Common: low blood pressure, slow heart rate, burning eyes, stinging, asthma.
Severe but rare (stop medication, consult doctor): severe asthma.

INTERACTIONS:

Other drugs:

- calcium channel blockers, disopyramide, clonidine, adrenaline, other medications for irregular heart beat, lignocaine, ergotamine, indomethacin, chlorpromazine, beta-blocker tablets.

PRESCRIPTION:

Yes.

PERMITTED IN SPORT:

Eye drops: yes.
Tablets: not permitted in some sports.

OVERDOSE:

Unlikely to be serious effects if eye drops swallowed.

See also Bimatoprost, Latanoprost, Levobunolol, Timolol, Travoprost.

Bethanechol

TRADE NAME:

Myotonine.

USES:

Inability to pass urine, reflux of stomach contents in children.

DOSAGE:

 10 to 25mg, three or four times a day.

FORMS:

Tablets of 10 and 25mg.

PRECAUTIONS:

Use with caution in pregnancy (B2).
Use with caution if taking blood pressure medication.

Do not take if:

 • suffering from bowel obstruction, over active thyroid gland, asthma, peptic ulcer, epilepsy, slow heart rate, low blood pressure, heart failure or urinary tract infection.

SIDE EFFECTS:

Common: discomfort in the belly, excess production of saliva, flushing of skin, sweating.
Unusual: tiredness, headache, diarrhoea, nausea, belching.
Severe but rare (stop medication, consult doctor): severe belly pain, asthma attack.

INTERACTIONS:

None significant.

PRESCRIPTION:

Yes.

PERMITTED IN SPORT:

Yes.

OVERDOSE:

Atropine is a specific antidote. Seek medical assistance.

Bezafibrate

TRADE NAMES:

Bezalip, Zimbacol.

DRUG CLASS:

Hypolipidaemic.

USES:

Some types of excess lipids (fats such as cholesterol and triglyceride) in blood.

DOSAGE:

 One to three tablets a day with or after food.

FORMS:

Tablets of 200 and 400mg.

PRECAUTIONS:

Not to be used in pregnancy, breast feeding and children.
Use with caution with any kidney disease.
Do not take if:

 • suffering from severe liver or kidney disease (e.g. nephrotic syndrome).

SIDE EFFECTS:

Common: diarrhoea, nausea, rash.
Unusual: vomiting, muscle damage.
Severe but rare (stop medication, consult doctor): impotence, hair loss.

INTERACTIONS:

Other drugs:
• warfarin, anticoagulants, MAOI, other hypolipidaemics, hypoglycaemics (used in diabetes).

PRESCRIPTION:

Yes.

PERMITTED IN SPORT:

Yes.

See also HYPOLIPIDAEMICS.

Bicalutamide

TRADE NAME:

Casodex.

DRUG CLASS:

Antineoplastic.

USES:

Severe cancer of the prostate gland.

DOSAGE:

 One tablet a day.

FORMS:

Tablets (white) of 50 and 150mg.

PRECAUTIONS:

Not to be used in women or children.
Use with caution in liver disease.

SIDE EFFECTS:

Common: hot flushes, itchy skin, breast enlargement and tenderness, nausea, diarrhoea, tiredness.
Unusual: liver damage, vomiting, depression, hair loss, poor libido, blood in urine.

INTERACTIONS:

Other drugs:
• warfarin, astemizole, cisapride, midazolam, calcium channel blockers, cyclosporin, antivirals, carbamazepine, quinidine, cimetidine, ketoconazole.

PRESCRIPTION:

Yes.

PERMITTED IN SPORT:

Yes.

OVERDOSE:

Serious, seek urgent medical attention.

OTHER INFORMATION:

Introduced in 1997 to treat cases of prostate cancer that are not responding to other treatment.

Bicarbonates

See ANTACIDS.

Bimatoprost

TRADE NAME:

Lumigan.

DRUG CLASS:

Beta-blocker.

USES:

Glaucoma.

DOSAGE:

 One drop in affected eye once a day. Apply pressure to inner corner of eye (tear duct) immediately after use. Wait five minutes before using in other eye if necessary.

FORMS:

Eye drops.

PRECAUTIONS:

Use with caution in pregnancy (B3), Not for use in children.
Use with caution in severe lung, liver and kidney disease.
Do not use with contact lenses.

Do not take if:

 • breast feeding
• under other circumstances.

SIDE EFFECTS:

Common: eyelid darkening, increased eyelash growth, pigment formation in iris (coloured part of eye).
Unusual: red eye, itchy eye, tiredness, headache.
Severe but rare (stop medication, consult doctor): slow heart rate, asthma attack.

INTERACTIONS:

None.

PRESCRIPTION:

Yes.

PERMITTED IN SPORT:

Yes.

OVERDOSE:

Unlikely to be serious effects if eye drops swallowed.

OTHER INFORMATION:

Introduced in 2002 as an advance in the treatment of glaucoma.

See also Betaxolol, Brimonidine, Brinzolamide, Pilocarpine, Timolol.

Biotin
(Vitamin H)

TRADE NAMES:

A large number of preparations include biotin (vitamin H) alone or in combination with other vitamins and minerals.

DRUG CLASS:

Vitamin.

USES:

No specific medical use.

DOSAGE:

 Recommended daily allowance: 100 to 200 µg per day.

FORMS:

Tablets, capsules, mixture.

PRECAUTIONS:

Safe in pregnancy, breast feeding and children.
Do not take in high doses or for prolonged periods of time.

SIDE EFFECTS:

Minimal.

INTERACTIONS:

None significant.

PRESCRIPTION:

No.

PERMITTED IN SPORT:

Yes.

OVERDOSE:

Unlikely to have serious adverse effects.

OTHER INFORMATION:

Remember, vitamins are merely chemicals that are essential for the functioning of the body and if taken to excess, act as a drug.

Biperiden

TRADE NAME:

Akineton.

DRUG CLASS:

Antiparkinsonian.

USES:

Parkinson's disease, night time leg cramps, some movement disorders.

DOSAGE:

 Night time leg cramps: one or two tablets at night.
Other conditions: half to two tablets three or four times a day.

FORMS:

Tablets of 2mg (white).

PRECAUTIONS:

Use with caution in pregnancy (B2) and breast feeding.
Use with caution in prostate gland disease, rapid heart rate.
Do not take if:
 • suffering from glaucoma, megacolon, intestinal obstruction.

SIDE EFFECTS:

Common: dry mouth, drowsiness, blurred vision, dizziness.
Unusual: rapid heart rate, confusion, constipation, rash, uncoordinated movements, difficulty in passing urine, insomnia.
Severe but rare (stop medication, consult doctor): severe constipation, glaucoma.

INTERACTIONS:

Other drugs:
• other antiparkinsonian drugs, quinidine, tricyclic antidepressants, tetracyclic antidepressants, metoclopramide.
Other substances:
• reacts with alcohol to cause sedation.

PRESCRIPTION:

Yes.

PERMITTED IN SPORT:

Yes.

OVERDOSE:

May be serious. Induce vomiting if taken recently. Seek urgent medical attention.

Biphasic Insulin

See INSULINS.

Bisacodyl

TRADE NAME:

Dulcolax.

DRUG CLASS:

Laxative.

USES:

Constipation, preparing bowel for surgery or x-rays.

DOSAGE:

 Tablets: two to four tablets at night.
Suppository: one or two at night.

FORMS:

Tablets of 15mg (yellow), suppository.

PRECAUTIONS:

Safe in pregnancy (A), breast feeding and children.
Designed for short term use only.

Do not take if:

- suffering from belly pains or bowel obstruction.

SIDE EFFECTS:

Common: minimal.
Unusual: diarrhoea, belly discomfort.
Severe but rare (stop medication, consult doctor): severe belly pain.

INTERACTIONS:

Other drugs:
- do not take antacids within 30 minutes of bisacodyl.

PRESCRIPTION:

No.

PERMITTED IN SPORT:

Yes.

OVERDOSE:

Diarrhoea and belly pain only effects likely.

OTHER INFORMATION:

Widely used and very safe.

See also Docusate sodium, Fibre, Glycerol, Frangula, Lactulose, Paraffin, Psyllium, Senna, Sodium phosphate, Sodium picosulfate, Sorbitol, Sterculia.

Bismuth

See Tripotassium dicitratobismuthate.

Bisoprolol

TRADE NAMES:

Cardicor, Emcor, Monocor.

DRUG CLASS:

Beta-blocker.

USES:

Stable chronic heart failure, high blood pressure.

DOSAGE:

Slowly increase from 1.25mg a day to necessary dose. Maximum 10mg a day.
Usually prescribed with an ACE inhibitor.

FORMS:

Tablets of 1.25mg, 2.5mg, 3.75mg, 5mg, 7.5mg, 10mg.

PRECAUTIONS:

Not to be used in pregnancy (C), breast feeding and children.
Use with caution in diabetes, liver and kidney disease, congenital heart disease, cardiomyopathy, recent heart attack, Prinzmetal angina, asthma, thyrotoxicosis, psoriasis.
Use with care in the elderly.

Do not take if:

- suffering from acute heart failure, low blood pressure, sick heart sinus syndrome, slow heart rate, severe asthma, emphysema, poor circulation, Raynaud syndrome, phaeochromocytoma.

SIDE EFFECTS:

Common: cold numb feeling in hands and feet, tiredness, dizziness, headache, diarrhoea.

INTERACTIONS:

Other drugs:
- calcium antagonists, clonidine, monoamine oxidase inhibitors, insulin, drugs used to control heart rhythm,

hypoglycaemics, digoxin, ergotamine, tricyclic antidepressants, barbiturates, phenothiazines, other beta-blockers, rifampicin, mefloquine.

PRESCRIPTION:

Yes.

PERMITTED IN SPORT:

Yes.

OVERDOSE:

Likely to be serious. Slow heart rate, low blood pressure, asthma and heart failure may result. Administer activated charcoal or induce vomiting if tablets taken recently. Use Salbutamol or other asthma sprays for difficulty in breathing. Seek medical assistance.

OTHER INFORMATION:

Introduced in 2001 for the management of patients whose heart failure or hypertension could not be controlled by other medications.

BISPHOSPHONATES

DISCUSSION:

Medications that prevent the loss of bone density in osteoporosis.

See Alendronate, Disodium clodronate, Etidronate, Pamidronate, Risedronate, Sodium clodronate, Tiludronic acid.

Bosentan

TRADE NAME:

Tracleer.

USES:

High blood pressure in lungs.

DOSAGE:

 62.5mg to 125mg twice a day.

FORMS:

Tablets of 62.5mg and 125mg (orange/white).

PRECAUTIONS:

Must never be used in pregnancy (X) as serious damage to the baby will occur. Use with care in breast feeding and children.
Adequate contraception essential in non-menopausal women.
Use with caution if suffering from low blood pressure and anaemia.
Regular blood tests to check blood cells and liver function recommended.

Do not take if:

 • suffering from liver disease.

SIDE EFFECTS:

Common: headache, flushing.
Unusual: leg swelling.
Severe but rare (stop medication, consult doctor): liver damage (jaundice), blood cell damage.

INTERACTIONS:

Other drugs:
• severe interaction with cyclosporin A, glibenclamide.
• ketoconazole, warfarin, digoxin, simvastatin.

PRESCRIPTION:

Yes.

PERMITTED IN SPORT:

Yes.

OVERDOSE:

Severe liver damage possible. Induce vomiting or give activated charcoal if taken recently. Seek urgent medical attention.

OTHER INFORMATION:

Introduced in 2003 as the first effective treatment for the very complex condition of isolated high blood pressure in the lungs which may be due to scleroderma.

Botulinum toxin

TRADE NAMES:

Botox, Dysport, Neurobloc.

USES:

Spasms of eyelids, facial nerve disorders, facial muscle spasms, foot spasticity and deformity in children with cerebral palsy, spasm of cervix.

DOSAGE:

 Complex. As determined by doctor for each individual patient.

FORMS:

Injection.

PRECAUTIONS:

Use with caution in pregnancy (B3), breast feeding and children.
Use with caution in myasthenia gravis, Eaton-Lambert syndrome, amyotrophic lateral sclerosis, other nerve-muscle diseases.
Avoid areas of local inflammation when injecting.

SIDE EFFECTS:

General: nerve damage, muscle weakness and pain, rash, irregular heart rhythm.
Eyelid injections: eye irritation, drooping eyelid, dry eye surface and ulceration.
Facial spasm: blurred vision, facial muscle weakness.
Severe but rare (stop medication, consult doctor): heart attack.

INTERACTIONS:

Other drugs:
• aminoglycosides, drugs acting on nerves and muscles.

PRESCRIPTION:

Yes.

PERMITTED IN SPORT:

Yes.

OVERDOSE:

Potentially fatal.

OTHER INFORMATION:

Derived from the bacteria that causes botulism, one of the most severe forms of food poisoning.

Brimonidine tartrate

TRADE NAME:

Alphargan.

USES:

Glaucoma.

DOSAGE:

 One drop in affected eye twice a day.

FORMS:

Eye drops (keep refrigerated).

PRECAUTIONS:

Use with caution in pregnancy (B1), breast feeding and children.
Use with caution in severe heart disease, poor liver and kidney function, poor blood supply to heart or brain, low blood pressure.
May aggravate Raynaud phenomenon.
Eye drops are absorbed into the bloodstream and may cause effects in other parts of the body.

Do not take if:

 • using soft contact lenses.

SIDE EFFECTS:

Common: dry mouth, red eyes, irritated eyes, eye stinging, eye itching, headache, tiredness.
Unusual: eye irritation, eye ulceration, light sensitivity of eye, swelling of eyelid, inflamed eye, intestinal upset.

INTERACTIONS:

Other drugs:
- must not be used with MAOI (see separate entry).

PRESCRIPTION:

Yes.

PERMITTED IN SPORT:

Yes.

OVERDOSE:

Unlikely to be serious if swallowed. Wash out eye thoroughly with water if excess drops used.

OTHER INFORMATION:

Introduced in 1998 for forms of glaucoma that cannot be controlled by other medications.

See also Betaxolol, Bimatroprost, Brinzolamide, Levobunolol, Pilocarpine.

Brinzolamide

TRADE NAME:

Azopt.

USES:

Additional treatment in difficult cases of glaucoma.

DOSAGE:

 One drop in affected eye two or three times a day.

FORMS:

Eye drops.

PRECAUTIONS:

Use with caution in pregnancy. Not for use in breast feeding and children.
Use with caution in some types of glaucoma, dry eyes and with contact lenses (wait 15 minutes after using drops before inserting lenses).
Use with caution in diabetes.
Progress and eye pressure must be monitored closely.

Do not take if:

- suffering from significant liver or kidney disease
- allergic to sulpha.

SIDE EFFECTS:

Common: blurred vision, eye discomfort, red eye.
Unusual: eye pain, dry eye, eye discharge, headache, taste disturbance.

INTERACTIONS:

Other drugs:
- some other drops and tablets used for glaucoma.

PRESCRIPTION:

Yes.

PERMITTED IN SPORT:

Yes.

OVERDOSE:

Eye damage possible. Wash out eye thoroughly with water if excess drops used.

OTHER INFORMATION:

Introduced in 1999 for otherwise uncontrolled glaucoma.

See also Betaxolol, Bimatroprost, Brimonidine, Levobunolol, Pilocarpine.

Bromocriptine

TRADE NAME:

Parlodel.

DRUG CLASS:

Antiparkinsonian.

USES:

Parkinson's disease, acromegaly, abnormal production of breast milk, stopping production of breast milk when breast feeding ceased.

DOSAGE:

 Depends on purpose. Usually start low, and increase slowly until desired result obtained. Taken three or four times a day.

FORMS:

Tablets, capsules.

PRECAUTIONS:

Safe in pregnancy (A). Not to be used during breast feeding or in children.

Use with caution in psychiatric conditions, high or low blood pressure, heart disease, diabetes, peptic ulcer, eye disease and liver disease.

Use with caution in women who wish to fall pregnant, as bromocriptine may reduce fertility.

Do not take if:

- suffering from high blood pressure in or immediately after pregnancy, after pregnancy if breast feeding desired, toxaemia of pregnancy, significant heart disease.

SIDE EFFECTS:

Common: nausea very common. Dizziness, headache, nasal congestion, vomiting, tiredness, reduced blood pressure (fainting).

Unusual: hallucinations, confusion, behavioural disturbances, unwanted muscle movements, psychiatric disturbances, peptic ulcer.

Severe but rare (stop medication, consult doctor): vomiting blood, severe psychiatric disturbances.

INTERACTIONS:

Other drugs:
- medications that lower blood pressure, erythromycin.

Other substances:
- reacts adversely with alcohol.

PRESCRIPTION:

Yes.

PERMITTED IN SPORT:

Yes.

OVERDOSE:

May cause vomiting, tiredness, low blood pressure and hallucinations. Not likely to be life threatening. Administer activated charcoal or induce vomiting if taken recently. Seek medical assistance.

OTHER INFORMATION:

A very useful drug with an extraordinary range of activities. Tumours of the pituitary gland in the brain cause both acromegaly (excess bone growth) and abnormal breast milk production (in both sexes).

Brompheniramine

See ANTIHISTAMINES, SEDATING.

BRONCHODILATORS

DISCUSSION:

Wide range of inhaled and oral medications that open the airways (bronchi) in the lungs to treat conditions such as asthma, chronic bronchitis and emphysema.

See BETA-2 AGONISTS, Eformoterol, Ephedrine, Fenoterol, Ipratropium bromide, Orciprenaline, Salbutamol, Salmeterol, Terbutaline, THEOPHYLLINES.

Buclizine

TRADE NAME:

Only available in combination with other ingredients.

Migraleve Pink (with paracetamol, codeine).

USES:

Relieves nausea of migraine and causes sedation.

DOSAGE:

Two pink tablets at onset of migraine attack.

FORMS:

Tablets (pink). Yellow Migraleve tablets do not contain Buclizine.

PRECAUTIONS:

Use with caution in pregnancy, breast feeding and children.

SIDE EFFECTS:

Common: sedation.

INTERACTIONS:

Other drugs:
• other sedatives and pain relievers.

PRESCRIPTION:

Yes.

PERMITTED IN SPORT:

Yes.

OVERDOSE:

May be very serious due to paracetamol in contents of tablets (see separate entry). Buclizine alone unlikely to have serious effects.

Budesonide

TRADE NAMES:

Budenofalk, Entocort, Pulmicort, Rhinocort Aqua.
Symbicort (with eformoterol).

DRUG CLASS:

Corticosteroid.

USES:

Prevention of asthma, prevention of hay fever and chronic nasal drip, Crohn's disease.

DOSAGE:

 Asthma spray (Pulmicort, Symbicort): one or two inhalations, once a day.
Nasal sprays (Rhinocort): one spray, once a day in each nostril.
Capsules (Budenofalk, Entocort): one three times a day.
Enema (Entocort): one at night.

FORMS:

Inhaler, nasal spray, nebuliser solution, capsule, enema.

PRECAUTIONS:

Use with caution in pregnancy (B3), breast feeding and children.
Sprays and inhalers: Use with caution in lung or throat infection and tuberculosis. Lung function should be checked regularly to ensure adequate dose is received.
Capsules and enema: Use with caution in high blood pressure, diabetes, osteoporosis, peptic ulcer, glaucoma, cataracts and liver disease.
Do not use capsules or enema if:
• suffering from bacterial, fungal or viral infections.

SIDE EFFECTS:

Common: fungal (thrush) infections of mouth, sore throat and mouth, dry mouth. *Unusual:* hoarseness, unusual bleeding and bruising, slowed growth, stomach upsets, muscle weakness, high blood pressure.

INTERACTIONS:

Inhalers and sprays:
• none significant.
Capsules and enema:
• cholestyramine, ketoconazole, digoxin, diuretics, live vaccines, some high blood pressure medications.
Herbs:
• liquorice.

PRESCRIPTION:

Yes.

PERMITTED IN SPORT:

Yes.

OVERDOSE:

Unlikely to have any serious effects.

OTHER INFORMATION:

The introduction of the turbuhaler for the inhalation of Budesonide was a major advance in asthma prevention as it is far easier to use than pressurised sprays. Budesonide is extremely effective in preventing hay fever and other forms of constantly dripping nose. Inhalers and sprays designed for long term use, but capsules and enemas should not be used for more than a couple of months. Does not cause dependence or addiction.

See also Beclomethasone, Fluticasone, Mometasone.

Bumetanide

TRADE NAMES:

Burinex.
Burinex A (with amiloride).
Burinex K (with potassium).

DRUG CLASS:

Diuretic.

USES:

Excess fluid in body.

DOSAGE:

 One or more tablets in morning to maximum of 10mg.

FORMS:

Tablets, injection.

PRECAUTIONS:

Should not be used in pregnancy (C) unless medically essential. Should not be used in breast feeding or children.
Use with caution in elderly, diabetes, gout and heart failure.
May require regular blood tests to check on level of salts (electrolytes) in blood.

Do not take if:

 • suffering from severe kidney or liver disease.

SIDE EFFECTS:

Common: muscle cramps, dizziness, headache, nausea.
Unusual: deafness, rash, itch, weakness, arthritis, belly pains, vomiting.
Severe but rare (stop medication, consult doctor): fainting.

INTERACTIONS:

Other drugs:
• digoxin, lithium, probenecid, anticoagulants, indomethacin
• medications that lower blood pressure.
Herbs:
• celery, dandelion, uva ursi.

PRESCRIPTION:

Yes.

PERMITTED IN SPORT:

No.

OVERDOSE:

May lead to severe dehydration and blood clots. Symptoms include weakness, dizziness, confusion, cramps and vomiting. Induce vomiting if tablets taken recently. Give extra fluids. Seek medical assistance.

OTHER INFORMATION:

Introduced in 1980s. Similar to Frusemide, but faster and shorter acting.

See also Amiloride, Frusemide, Indapamide, Spironolactone, THIAZIDE DIURETICS.

Bupivacaine

See ANAESTHETICS, LOCAL.

Buprenorphine

TRADE NAMES:

Subutex, Temgesic, Transtec.

DRUG CLASS:

Narcotic, analgesic.

USES:

Moderate to severe pain not responding to non-narcotic pain relievers.

DOSAGE:

 One or two tablets under tongue every six to eight hours as required.
One or two patches applied every 72 hours to non-hairy area of skin. Always remove old patch before applying new.

FORMS:

Tablets for use under tongue, patch, injection.

PRECAUTIONS:

Should not be used in pregnancy (C) unless medically essential. Not for use in breast feeding or children.
Use with caution in head injury, liver disease and severe lung disease.

Do not take if:

• operating machinery or driving a vehicle.

SIDE EFFECTS:

Common: drowsiness, nausea.
Unusual: headache, vomiting, dry mouth, constipation, dizziness, difficulty in passing urine.
Severe but rare (stop medication, consult doctor): difficulty in breathing.

INTERACTIONS:

Other drugs:
• MAOI, benzodiazepines, sedatives, other narcotics, some antifungals, erythromycin, calcium channel antagonists.
Other substances:
• alcohol should be avoided.

PRESCRIPTION:

Yes (very restricted).

PERMITTED IN SPORT:

No.

OVERDOSE:

Symptoms may include drowsiness, confusion, difficulty in breathing and coma. Induce vomiting if medication taken recently and patient alert. Seek urgent medical attention.

OTHER INFORMATION:

May cause addiction or dependence if used inappropriately. Introduced in the late 1980s for use in more intractable pain conditions and now sometimes used to treat drug addiction.

See also Alfentanil, Codeine, Dextromoramide, Dextropropoxyphene, Fentanyl, Heroin, Hydromorphone, Methadone, Morphine, Oxycodone, Pentazocine, Pethidine.

Bupropion
(Amfebutamone)

TRADE NAME:

Zyban.

USES:

Aids cessation of smoking and counteracts nicotine addiction.

DOSAGE:

 One tablet a day for three days, increasing if necessary to one tablet twice a day.

FORMS:

Tablet of 150mg (white).

PRECAUTIONS:

Not to be used in pregnancy, breast feeding and children.
Use with caution in any liver or kidney disease, head injury, brain tumour, alcoholism and diabetes.
Blood pressure should be checked regularly.

Do not take if:

- suffering from epilepsy or other condition causing seizures, bipolar disorder, eating disorder, severe liver disease (e.g. cirrhosis).

SIDE EFFECTS:

Common: sleeplessness, headache, fever, dry mouth, nausea, flushing, rapid heart rate.
Unusual: diarrhoea or constipation, brain irritation, skin reaction, taste disorders, poor concentration, loss of appetite.
Severe but rare (stop medication, consult doctor): convulsion, high blood pressure.

INTERACTIONS:

Other drugs:
- MAOI, antipsychotics, antidepressants, theophylline, steroid tablets, benzodiazepines, medications used to treat epilepsy and convulsions, levodopa, beta-blockers.

Other substances:
- alcohol, stimulants.

PRESCRIPTION:

Yes.

PERMITTED IN SPORT:

No.

OVERDOSE:

May be serious. Drowsiness, hallucinations, seizures, coma and rarely death may occur. Seek urgent medical attention. Administer activated charcoal or induce vomiting if tablets taken recently and patient alert.

OTHER INFORMATION:

Introduced in 2000 as an additional aid in the fight against smoking.
See also Nicotine.

Buserelin

TRADE NAMES:

Suprecur, Suprefact.

USES:

Endometriosis, prostate cancer, control of ovulation during in vitro fertilisation for infertility.

DOSAGE:

Nasal sprays as determined by doctor for each patient, depending on condition.

FORMS:

Nasal spray.

PRECAUTIONS:

Must not be used in pregnancy, breast feeding or children.
Barrier contraception must be used.
Use with caution if patient at risk of osteoporosis.

Do not take if:

- suffering from undiagnosed vaginal bleeding
- testes have been surgically removed.

SIDE EFFECTS:

Common: hot flushes, nasal irritation, loss of libido, dry vagina, emotional upsets, headache, breast tenderness.
Unusual: change in breast size, ovarian cysts.

INTERACTIONS:

Other drugs:
- contraceptive pill, nasal decongestants, sex hormones.

PRESCRIPTION:

Yes.

PERMITTED IN SPORT:

Yes.

OVERDOSE:

Seek medical attention. Exacerbation of side effects likely.

Buspirone

TRADE NAME:

Buspar.

DRUG CLASS:

Anxiolytic.

USES:

Relief of anxiety.

DOSAGE:

 5mg to 20mg (one to three tablets), three times a day.

FORMS:

Tablets of 5mg and 10mg (white).

PRECAUTIONS:

Should only be used in pregnancy if medically essential. Breast feeding should be ceased before Buspirone taken. Not for use in children.
Should be used with caution in epilepsy, liver and kidney disease.
Lower doses required in elderly.

Do not take if:

- suffering from severe liver disease
- operating machinery, driving a vehicle, or undertaking tasks that require concentration, alertness and coordination.

SIDE EFFECTS:

Common: dizziness, sleeplessness, drowsiness, light headedness, nausea, headache, nasal congestion.
Unusual: excitement, chest pain, nightmares, rapid heart rate, palpitations, blurred vision, muscle pains, pins and needles sensation, tremor.

INTERACTIONS:

Other drugs:
- benzodiazepines and other anxiolytics.
- MAOI.

Other substances:
- no reaction with alcohol
- food increases absorption of buspirone.

PRESCRIPTION:

Yes.

PERMITTED IN SPORT:

No.

OVERDOSE:

May cause vomiting, drowsiness and stomach pains. Not believed to be serious. Administer activated charcoal or induce vomiting if tablets taken recently and patient alert. Seek medical attention.

OTHER INFORMATION:

Introduced in early 1990s as an non-addictive alternative to Benzodiazepines. Does not cause dependence. Very safe, but not as rapid in its effect as other Anxiolytics.
See also Clobazam, Diazepam, Lorazepam, Oxazepam.

Busulphan

TRADE NAME:

Myleran.

DRUG CLASS:

Alkylater.

USES:

Leukaemia, polycythaemia rubra vera, myelofibrosis, thrombocythaemia.

DOSAGE:

 Must be individualised by doctor for each patient depending on disease, severity, age and weight of patient.

FORMS:

Tablets of 2mg (white).

PRECAUTIONS:

Must not be used in pregnancy (D) unless mother's life is at risk as damage to the

foetus may occur. Breast feeding must be ceased before use. May be used in children if medically essential.
Regular blood tests to monitor blood cells and liver function essential.
Adequate contraception must be used by women while medication taken.
Must be used with caution in all patients.

SIDE EFFECTS:

Common: damage to bone marrow, skin pigmentation.
Unusual: nausea, vomiting, diarrhoea, lung damage (cough), eye damage, hair loss, rash, itch.

INTERACTIONS:

Other drugs:
• phenytoin, itraconazole, thioguanine.

PRESCRIPTION:

Yes.

PERMITTED IN SPORT:

Yes.

OVERDOSE:

Very serious. Permanent damage to bone marrow with subsequent death likely. Administer activated charcoal or induce vomiting if medication taken recently. Seek urgent medical assistance.

OTHER INFORMATION:

Although busulphan has serious side effects, it may be life saving in patients with some types of malignancy or blood disorders.
See also VINCA ALKALOIDS.

Butobarbitone
See BARBITURATES.

Butoxyethyl nicotinate

TRADE NAME:

Only available in Britain in combination with other ingredients.
Actinac (with chloramphenicol, hydrocortisone, allantoin, sulphur compounds).

USES:

Acne. When used alone acts as a liniment.

DOSAGE:

 Apply twice a day for four days, then once a day.

FORMS:

Powder and solvent to make lotion.

PRECAUTIONS:

Safe in pregnancy and breast feeding. Do not use on infants.
Avoid eyes, mouth, nose, ears, anus and vagina.
Do not use on broken, diseased, infected or inflamed skin.

SIDE EFFECTS:

Common: skin irritation and redness.

INTERACTIONS:

None significant.

PRESCRIPTION:

Yes.

PERMITTED IN SPORT:

Yes.

Cabergoline

TRADE NAMES:

Cabaser, Dostinex.

USES:

Parkinson's disease, stopping breast milk production, excess production of the hormone prolactin.

DOSAGE:

 Stopping breast feeding: two 0.5mg. tablets taken once.
Excess prolactin production: 0.5 to 2mg, once a week.
Parkinson's disease: 1 to 6mg a day in divided doses. Increase dose very slowly.

FORMS:

Tablets.

PRECAUTIONS:

Not to be used in pregnancy (C), breast feeding and children.
Use with caution in heart disease, kidney disease, liver disease, peptic ulcer disease. May aggravate some psychiatric conditions.
High blood pressure after childbirth may be made worse.

SIDE EFFECTS:

Common: low blood pressure, fainting, dizziness, headache, tiredness.
Unusual: fatigue, depression, stomach upsets, breast pain, hot flushes.
Severe but rare (stop medication, consult doctor): pleural effusion (collection of fluid around lungs, chest pain and shortness of breath).

INTERACTIONS:

Other drugs:
• ergot alkaloids, methylergotamine, dopamine agonists, drugs that inhibit liver function, metoclopramide.

PRESCRIPTION:

Yes.

PERMITTED IN SPORT:

Yes (restricted to specific purposes).

Cadexomer Iodine

TRADE NAMES:

Iodoflex, Iodosorb.

USES:

Chronic skin ulcers.

DOSAGE:

 Apply paste, powder or ointment every one to three days.

FORMS:

Ointment, powder, paste.

PRECAUTIONS:

Use with caution in in pregnancy (C) and breast feeding.
Not for use in children under 12 years.
Use with caution on large ulcers.
Do not use for more than three months.
Do not take if:
 • suffering from kidney failure, Hashimoto thyroiditis, goitre
• sensitive to iodine.

SIDE EFFECTS:

Common: skin irritation.
Unusual: swelling of tissue.
Severe but rare (stop medication, consult doctor): thyroid gland abnormalities (e.g. goitre).

INTERACTIONS:

Other drugs:
• lithium, mercury based antiseptics (e.g. Mercurochrome).

PRESCRIPTION:

No.

PERMITTED IN SPORT:

Yes.

OTHER INFORMATION:

Introduced in 2001 as a new form of treatment for persistent skin and leg ulcers.

Caffeine

TRADE NAMES:

Found in multiple non-prescription minor stimulants, foods and beverages.
Cafergot (with ergotamine).
Migril (with ergotamine, cyclizine).

DRUG CLASS:

Stimulant.

USES:

Fatigue, additive to assist motion sickness and migraines.

DOSAGE:

 One tablet every three hours or as directed by doctor.
One suppository up to three times a day.

FORMS:

Tablets, suppository.

PRECAUTIONS:

Safe in pregnancy and breast feeding. Use with caution in children.

Do not take if:

 • suffering from peptic ulcer, heartburn.

SIDE EFFECTS:

Common: anxiety, nervousness, sleeplessness, passing increased amount of urine.

INTERACTIONS:

Other substances:
• reacts with coffee, tea and cola drinks containing caffeine.

PRESCRIPTION:

Cafergot, Migril: yes.
Other forms: no.

PERMITTED IN SPORT:

No.

OVERDOSE:

Anxiety, restlessness, irritability and sleeplessness are likely.

OTHER INFORMATION:

Used for centuries in tea and coffee as a mild stimulant. Also found in cola drinks and chocolate.
100mL of brewed coffee contains 60 to 130mg of caffeine.
100mL of instant coffee contains 40 to 100mg caffeine.
100mL of tea contains 40 to 60mg caffeine.
100mL of cola drink contains 10mg of caffeine.
100g of chocolate contains 20 to 30mg of caffeine.

Calamine

TRADE NAMES:

Found in numerous soothing non-prescription preparations.
Calamine lotion.
Vasogen (with dimethicone, zinc oxide).

USES:

Minor skin irritations, insect bites, sunburn, leg ulcers.

DOSAGE:

 Apply several times a day as required.

FORMS:

Cream, lotion.

PRECAUTIONS:

Safe to use in pregnancy, breast feeding and children.
Avoid eyes, mouth and nostrils.

Do not take if:

 • suffering from blistered, raw or oozing skin.

SIDE EFFECTS:

Minimal.

INTERACTIONS:

None.

PRESCRIPTION:

No.

PERMITTED IN SPORT:

Yes.

OTHER INFORMATION:

Widely used, effective old fashioned treatment for everything from bites to chickenpox.

Calciferol

See Calcitriol, Cholecalciferol and Ergocalciferol (Vitamin D).

Calcipotriol

TRADE NAMES:

Dovonex.
Dovobet (with betamethasone).

USES:

Psoriasis.

DOSAGE:

 Apply twice a day. Reduce frequency if possible.

FORMS:

Ointment, cream, scalp lotion.

PRECAUTIONS:

Use with caution in pregnancy (B1), breast feeding and children.
Avoid contact with eyes.
Use with caution on face, scalp and in skin flexures.
Use with care long term.
Avoid sun exposure during use.

Do not take if:

 • suffering from disorders of calcium metabolism
• suffering from severe or pustular psoriasis.

SIDE EFFECTS:

Common: skin irritation, sun sensitivity.
Unusual: skin pigmentation, excess calcium levels in blood with excess use.

INTERACTIONS:

Other drugs:
• calcium, vitamin D supplements.

PRESCRIPTION:

Yes.

PERMITTED IN SPORT:

Yes.

OVERDOSE:

Skin damage possible if overused.

Calcitonin

See Salcatonin.

Calcitriol

TRADE NAMES:

Calcijex, Rocaltrol, Silkis.

DRUG CLASS:

A form of vitamin D.

USES:

Osteoporosis prevention and treatment, rickets, hypoparathyroidism, some types of hypocalcaemia.
Used externally for psoriasis.

DOSAGE:

One or two tablets twice a day.
Apply ointment twice a day.

FORMS:

Capsules of 0.25µg, injection, ointment.

PRECAUTIONS:

Use with caution in pregnancy (B3),
breast feeding and children. Use with
caution in infants.
Use with caution in kidney disease.
Regular blood tests necessary if using
tablets.
Ensure adequate fluid intake.
Avoid face with ointment.

Do not take if:

- suffering from hypercalcaemia,
  vitamin D sensitivity.

SIDE EFFECTS:

Common: drowsiness, nausea, weakness,
constipation or diarrhoea, itchy skin.
Unusual: calcium deposits in tissue,
dehydration, kidney damage.

INTERACTIONS:

Other drugs:
- cholestyramine, thiazide diuretics,
  digoxin, magnesium, corticosteroids.

PRESCRIPTION:

Yes.

PERMITTED IN SPORT:

Yes.

OVERDOSE:

Serious. Symptoms include loss of
appetite, tiredness, vomiting, diarrhoea,
sweating, excess urine production,
extreme thirst and headache. This may
progress to high blood pressure and
kidney failure. Administer activated
charcoal or induce vomiting if taken
recently. Seek medical assistance.
**See also Cholecalciferol, Ergocalciferol
(Vitamin D).**

Calcium

TRADE NAMES:

Calcium in various forms is found in
numerous nutritional supplements,
dressings and antacids, some of which are
listed below.
Adcal-D3, Calceos (Calcium carbonate,
vitamin D).
Cacit, Calcichew (Calcium carbonate).
Calcium-Sandoz (Calcium lactobionate,
calcium glubionate).
Gaviscon, Peptac (Calcium carbonate
with antacids).
Sandocal (Calcium lactate gluconate,
calcium carbonate).
Titralac (Calcium carbonate, glycine).

DRUG CLASS:

Mineral.

USES:

Antacid, improves circulation, poor
nutrition, osteomalacia, osteoporosis,
excess phosphate in body, lack of calcium
in body.

DOSAGE:

Recommended daily intake
800mg per day.

FORMS:

Tablets, capsules, mixtures, injections.

PRECAUTIONS:

Safe in pregnancy, breast feeding and
children.
Use with caution in kidney stones, kidney
disease and diabetes.

Do not take if:

- suffering from severe kidney
  disease, high blood calcium.

SIDE EFFECTS:

Common: constipation, hot flushes,
sweating.
Unusual: low blood pressure.

Severe but rare (stop medication, consult doctor): kidney stones (severe loin pain).

INTERACTIONS:

Other drugs:
- iron, digoxin, tetracycline, fluoride, calcium channel blockers, vitamin D.

PRESCRIPTION:

No.

PERMITTED IN SPORT:

Yes.

OVERDOSE:

Exacerbation of side effects likely.

OTHER INFORMATION:

Essential mineral found mainly in dairy products (e.g. cheese, milk, yoghurt), bony fish (e.g. sardines, salmon) and to a lesser extent in peas, beans, broccoli, almonds and whole grain cereals.
See also ANTACIDS; Calcium acetate; Calcium alginate.

Calcium acetate

TRADE NAME:

Phosex.

USES:

Control of excessively high phosphate levels in blood from kidney failure.

DOSAGE:

 One to four tablets three times a day with meals.

FORMS:

Tablets (yellow) of 1000mg.

PRECAUTIONS:

Not to be used in pregnancy or children unless medically essential. Breast feeding should be ceased before use.
Regular blood tests to monitor kidney function, calcium and phosphate levels essential.

Do not take if:

 • suffering from high blood calcium.

SIDE EFFECTS:

Common: nausea, vomiting, constipation, loss of appetite.

INTERACTIONS:

Other drugs:
- calcium supplements, tetracycline, digoxin, ciprofloxacin, enoxacin, norfloxacin, verapamil.

PRESCRIPTION:

Yes.

PERMITTED IN SPORT:

Yes.

OVERDOSE:

Serious. May cause extremely high levels of calcium in blood with consequent confusion, delirium and coma. Induce vomiting if tablets taken recently and patient alert. Seek urgent medical assistance.

Calcium alginate

TRADE NAMES:

Kaltogel, Kaltostat, Sorbalgon, Sorbsan.

USES:

Discharging, purulent, contaminated wounds and ulcers.

DOSAGE:

 Dressing applied directly to wound. Changed every 12 to 72 hours depending on nature of wound.

FORMS:

Dressing.

PRECAUTIONS:

Inert agent. Safe to use on all patients. Not for use on dry wounds or if

significant infection present.
Infected wounds may need antibiotics to reduce infection.

SIDE EFFECTS:

None.

INTERACTIONS:

None.

PRESCRIPTION:

No.

PERMITTED IN SPORT:

Yes.

OTHER INFORMATION:

Derived from seaweed. Soaks up exudate from weeping wounds to keep them dry and aid healing. Forms a protective thick gel over healing tissue.

Calcium carbonate

See ANTACIDS; Calcium.

CALCIUM CHANNEL BLOCKERS
(CALCIUM ANTAGONISTS)

DISCUSSION:

Calcium is essential for the contraction of the tiny muscles around the arteries. When these muscles contract, the artery becomes smaller and narrower. Calcium channel blockers prevent the calcium from entering the muscle cells through tiny channels in the membrane surrounding the cell. These muscle cells cannot then contract easily, remain relaxed, and do not narrow the artery. The wider an artery, the less resistance is placed on the blood flowing through it, and the lower the blood pressure. Because they prevent the contraction of all arteries, they reduce the strain on the heart and some of these drugs can therefore be used to treat angina (a lack of blood to the heart muscle).

Calcium channel blockers are quite safe and are normally used in tablet form, although some can be given as injections.
See Amlodipine, Diltiazem, Felodipine, Isradipine, Lacidipine, Lercanidipine, Nicardipine, Nifedipine, Nimodipine, Nisoldipine, Verapamil.

Calcium folinate
(Calcium leucoverin, Folinic acid)

TRADE NAME:

Refolinon.

USES:

Deficiencies in the body's folic acid level caused by cancer treatment, inadequate intake or anaemia, Methotrexate overdose.

DOSAGE:

 Depends on disease, and severity of folic acid deficiency.

FORMS:

Tablets (pale yellow) of 15mg, injection.

PRECAUTIONS:

May be used safely in pregnancy (A) and children. Use with caution in breast feeding.

Do not take if:

 • suffering from pernicious anaemia.

SIDE EFFECTS:

Common: minimal.
Unusual: fever.

INTERACTIONS:

Other drugs:
• methotrexate, droperidol.

PRESCRIPTION:

Yes.

PERMITTED IN SPORT:

Yes.

OVERDOSE:

No adverse effects expected.

OTHER INFORMATION:

Folic acid is essential for formation of red blood cells, but the bacteria that produce it in the gut are destroyed by many anticancer drugs.

Calcium Heparin

TRADE NAME:

Calciparine.

DRUG CLASS:

Anticoagulant.

USES:

Prevention and treatment of blood clots.

DOSAGE:

 As determined by doctor.

FORMS:

Injection.

PRECAUTIONS:

Should only be used in pregnancy (C) if medically essential. Breast feeding should be ceased if heparin treatment necessary. May be used in children.
Lower doses required in elderly.
Regular blood tests to monitor blood clotting time essential.

Do not take if:

- suffering from bleeding disorders, threatened abortion, heart infection, peptic ulcer, severe high blood pressure, severe liver or kidney disease
- due for surgery.

SIDE EFFECTS:

Common: excessive bleeding, bruising.

Unusual: nose bleeds, vomiting blood, blood in faeces, rash, itch, asthma.

INTERACTIONS:

Other drugs:
- other anticoagulants, aspirin.

PRESCRIPTION:

Yes.

PERMITTED IN SPORT:

Yes, but not advised in any active sport.

OVERDOSE:

Extremely serious. Massive bleeding may occur. Antidote available.

OTHER INFORMATION:

Only administered by doctors by injection in hospital, or strictly controlled outpatient basis.

See also Dalteparin, Enoxaparin, Heparin.

Calcium Leucoverin

See Calcium folinate.

Calcium Salts

See ANTACIDS; Calcium.

Camphor

TRADE NAMES:

Widely used in many cough mixtures, ointments, creams, liniments, lotions and inhalations.
Balmosa (with menthol, methyl salicylate and other ingredients).

DRUG CLASS:

Expectorant, rubefacient (liniment).

USES:

Soothes muscle and joint pains, and burns.
Eases productive coughs.
Eases nasal congestion.

DOSAGE:

 Take every four to six hours.
Apply to affected areas or inhale as required.

FORMS:

Mixture, ointment, cream, liniment, lotion, inhalation, spray.

PRECAUTIONS:

Safe to use in pregnancy, breast feeding and children.
Not to be swallowed.

SIDE EFFECTS:

Minimal.

INTERACTIONS:

None significant.

PRESCRIPTION:

No.

PERMITTED IN SPORT:

Yes.

OVERDOSE:

Unlikely to cause any significant adverse effects.

See also Benzydamine, Capsaicin, Guaiphenesin, Heparinoid, Menthol.

CANCER TREATING DRUGS
(Alkylaters, Antimetabolites, Antineoplastics, Cytotoxics)

DISCUSSION:

The cytotoxics and antineoplastics form a large, diverse group of drugs that are used to destroy cancer cells within the body in a process known as chemotherapy. 'Cyto' means cell, so 'cytotoxic' means toxic (harmful) to cells, while antineoplastic means 'against cancer'. These drugs can be given by tablet or injection and different drugs are used to attack different types of cancer. Unfortunately they are not all as specific in attacking cancer cells as we would wish and normal cells may also be attacked and destroyed. The balance between giving enough of the drug to kill the cancer cells and not enough to kill too many normal cells is a very fine one.

The effectiveness of cytotoxic drugs varies dramatically from one patient to another and one disease to another. Some forms of cancer are very susceptible to cytotoxic drugs (e.g. acute leukaemias), while others are resistant. Side effects are very common, and again variable. Nausea, vomiting, diarrhoea, muscle pain, loss of hair, weight loss, fatigue and headaches are just a few of the many complications possible. Patients taking this type of medication will be closely monitored by their doctors through regular blood tests and clinic visits. Long-term treatment for many months is usually required and other medications may be added to control the side effects.

See Altretamine, Aminoglutethamide, Amsacrine, Anagrelide, Anastrozole, Bicalutamide, Bleomycin sulfate, Busulfan, Capecitabine, Carboplatin, Carmustine, Chlorambucil, Cisplatin, Cyclophosphamide, Daunorubicin, Estramustine, Etoposide, Exemestane, Fluorouracil, Flutamide, Fosfestrol, Goserelin, Hydroxyurea, Idarubicin, Imatinib, Letrozole, Leuprorelin, Medroxyprogesterone, Megestrol, Melphalan, Mercaptopurine, Methotrexate, Paclitaxel, Tamoxifen, Tegafur, Temozolomide, Toremifene, Trilostane, Uracil, VINCA ALKALOIDS.

Candesartan
See ANGIOTENSIN II RECEPTOR ANTAGONISTS.

Cannabis
See Marijuana.

Capecitabine

TRADE NAME:

Xeloda.

DRUG CLASS:

Antimetabolite.

USES:

Advanced breast and colon cancer not responding to other treatments.

DOSAGE:

 As determined by doctor for each individual patient.

FORMS:

Tablets (peach) of 150 and 500mg.

PRECAUTIONS:

Not for use in pregnancy (D) or breast feeding.
Use with caution in heart disease, liver disease, children and the elderly.

Do not take if:

 • suffering from severe kidney disease.

SIDE EFFECTS:

Common: numerous, including diarrhoea, nausea, vomiting, hand and foot discomfort, mouth ulcers and soreness, loss of appetite, rashes, tiredness.
Unusual: abdominal pain, insomnia, dizziness, taste changes, excessive skin sensitivity, pins and needles sensation, swelling of tissue.
Severe but rare (stop medication, consult doctor): damage to blood cells (regular blood tests necessary), liver damage.

INTERACTIONS:

Other drugs:
• warfarin, phenytoin.

PRESCRIPTION:

Yes.

PERMITTED IN SPORT:

Yes.

OVERDOSE:

Very serious. Seek urgent medical attention. Induce vomiting or give activated charcoal if swallowed recently.

OTHER INFORMATION:

Introduced in 2002 as a treatment of last resort for breast and colon cancer.

Capsaicin

TRADE NAMES:

Axsain, Zacin.

DRUG CLASS:

Rubefacient, analgesic.

USES:

Nerve pain in skin after shingles, diabetic nerve pain, arthritic joint pain.

DOSAGE:

 Apply to affected area three or four times a day.

FORMS:

Cream.

PRECAUTIONS:

Safe in pregnancy, breast feeding and children over two years.
Avoid eyes, mouth, nose, anus and vagina.
Avoid broken or infected skin.

Do not use if:

 • suffering from active shingles or chickenpox.

SIDE EFFECTS:

Common: minimal.
Unusual: burning, skin irritation.

INTERACTIONS:

None significant.

PRESCRIPTION:

Yes.

PERMITTED IN SPORT:

Yes.

OTHER INFORMATION:

Becoming less relevant as more effective treatments for acute shingles (e.g. Aciclovir) to prevent nerve pain have become available. Still useful for minor arthritic pain.

See also Benzydamine, Camphor, Heparinoid, Menthol.

Captopril

See ACE INHIBITORS.

Carbachol

TRADE NAME:

Isopto Carbachol (with hypromellose).

DRUG CLASS:

Miotic.

USES:

Glaucoma, eye surgery.

DOSAGE:

 Two drops three times a day.

FORMS:

Eye drops.

PRECAUTIONS:

May be used in pregnancy, breast feeding and children.
Avoid exceeding recommended dose.
Use with caution in heart failure, asthma, stomach ulcer, over active thyroid gland, Parkinson's disease, gut spasm, difficulty in passing urine.

Do not use if:

 • eye injured or grazed.

SIDE EFFECTS:

Common: blurred vision, constriction of pupil, headache.
Uncommon: heart disturbances, gut disturbances.

INTERACTIONS:

None significant.

PRESCRIPTION:

Yes.

PERMITTED IN SPORT:

Yes.

OVERDOSE:

Seek medical attention if swallowed. Antidote available.

See also Apraclonidine, Betaxolol, Bimatoprost, Brimonidine, Brinzolamide, Carbachol, Dipivefrine, Dorzolamide, Latanoprost, Levobunolol, Phenylephrine, Pilocarpine, Timolol, Travoprost.

Carbamazepine

TRADE NAMES:

Tegretol, Teril.

DRUG CLASS:

Anticonvulsant.

USES:

Epilepsy, manic states, mood stabilisation, trigeminal neuralgia (tic douloureux) other forms of neuralgia (nerve pain).

DOSAGE:

 Dosage increased slowly under medical supervision until desired effect obtained. Maximum 1200mg a day. Blood tests help check on dose required.

FORMS:

Tablets of 100, 200 and 400mg (white), controlled release tablet of 200mg (orange) and 400mg (brown), suspension, suppositories.

PRECAUTIONS:

Not to be used in pregnancy (D) unless medically essential as risk of foetal abnormality is increased by 300%. Breast feeding should be ceased before use. May be used in children over five years.
Use with caution in heart disease, glaucoma, psychiatric conditions, prostate disease, kidney and liver disease.
Use with caution in elderly.
Regular blood tests to check liver and kidney function and blood cells recommended.
Do not stop suddenly, but reduce dose slowly.

Do not take if:

- suffering from heart block, lupus erythematosus, liver failure, porphyria, bone marrow suppression
- sensitive to tricyclic anti-depressants
- drinking alcohol.

SIDE EFFECTS:

Common: some side effects are very common for the first few days then decrease. Drowsiness, incoordination, reduced alertness, dizziness, double vision, headache, nausea, skin reactions.
Unusual: vomiting, hallucinations, depression, dry mouth, fluid retention.
Severe but rare (stop medication, consult doctor): unusual bleeding or bruising.

INTERACTIONS:

Other drugs:
- other anticonvulsants, oral contraceptives, MAOI within 14 days, warfarin
Herbs:
- evening primrose (linoleic acid), Gingko biloba, St John's wort.

Other substances:
- reacts adversely with alcohol
- borage.

PRESCRIPTION:

Yes.

PERMITTED IN SPORT:

Yes.

OVERDOSE:

Serious. Symptoms very varied but may include vomiting, low blood pressure, rapid heart rate, agitation, hallucinations, blurred vision, coma and death. Administer activated charcoal or induce vomiting if medication recently taken and patient alert. Seek urgent medical assistance.

OTHER INFORMATION:

Used for many decades to control epilepsy and neuralgia. Not addictive or dependence forming. Does not cause dependence or addiction.

See also **BARBITURATES, BENZODIAZEPINES, Clonazepam, Ethosuximide, Gabapentin, Lamotrigine, Levetiracetam, Oxcarbazepine, Phenytoin, Primidone, Sodium valproate, Sulthiame, Tiagabine, Topiramate, Vigabatrin.**

Carbaryl

TRADE NAME:

Carylderm.

USES:

Head lice.

DOSAGE:

 Apply once to affected hair. Leave for 12 hours before washing out.

FORMS:

Lotion, liquid.

PRECAUTIONS:

Safe to use in pregnancy, breast feeding and children.

Use with caution under six months of age. Not for continued or repeated use. Avoid eyes and areas of broken skin or eczema.

SIDE EFFECTS:

Common: scalp irritation.

INTERACTIONS:

Other drugs:
• none significant.

PRESCRIPTION:

Yes.

PERMITTED IN SPORT:

Yes.

OVERDOSE:

If swallowed seek urgent medical attention. Administer activated charcoal or induce vomiting if medication recently taken and patient alert.

Carbenoxolone

TRADE NAMES:

Bioplex.
Pyrogastrone (with antacids).

USES:

Heals mouth ulcers.

DOSAGE:

 Use mouthwash four times a day after meals, reflux oesophagitis (heartburn).

FORMS:

Bioplex: granules to make mouthwash.
Pyrogastrone: tablets, liquid.

PRECAUTIONS:

Bioplex: safe in pregnancy, breast feeding and children. Seek medical advice if mouth ulcer not healed in two weeks. Do not swallow mouthwash.
Pyrogastrone: not for use in pregnancy, breast feeding or children. Use with caution in water and salt retention.

Do not take Pyrogastrone if:

 • suffering from heart, liver or kidney failure
• blood potassium level low
• elderly.

SIDE EFFECTS:

Bioplex: minimal.
Pyrogastrone: swelling of hands and feet, low blood potassium levels, high blood pressure.
Severe but rare (stop medication, consult doctor): heart failure.

INTERACTIONS:

None significant.
Antacids in Pyrogastrone interact with a wide range of medications.

PRESCRIPTION:

Yes.

PERMITTED IN SPORT:

Yes.

OTHER INFORMATION:

Now considered to be a rather outdated form of treatment.

Carbidopa

See LEVODOPA COMPOUNDS.

Carbimazole

TRADE NAME:

Neomercazole.

DRUG CLASS:

Antithyroid.

USES:

Over active thyroid gland.

DOSAGE:

 20 to 60mg a day in divided doses, strictly as directed by doctor.

FORMS:

Tablets (pink) of 5mg and 20mg.

PRECAUTIONS:

Not to be used in pregnancy (C) or breast feeding. Use in children only if medically essential.

SIDE EFFECTS:

Common: dose related.
Unusual: nausea, diarrhoea, headache, rash, muscle pains, joint pains, itchy skin, hair loss.
Severe but rare (stop medication, consult doctor): bone marrow damage, liver damage (detected by regular blood tests).

INTERACTIONS:

Other drugs:
• radioactive iodine.

PRESCRIPTION:

Yes.

PERMITTED IN SPORT:

Yes.

OVERDOSE:

Rash likely. Damage to bone marrow possible.

OTHER INFORMATION:

Often used to control overactive thyroid gland before surgery to remove gland or irradiation to destroy gland.

Carbocisteine

TRADE NAME:

Mucodyne.

DRUG CLASS:

Mucolytic.

USES:

Excessive thick mucus, glue ears, tracheostomy clearance in children.

DOSAGE:

 Initially 750mg three times a day, reducing to 500mg three times a day.

FORMS:

Syrup.

PRECAUTIONS:

Use with caution in pregnancy. Safe to use in children.
Use with caution if past history of peptic ulcer.

Do not take if:

 • suffering from active peptic ulcer.

SIDE EFFECTS:

Common: nausea, diarrhoea, rash.
Severe but rare (stop medication, consult doctor): peptic ulcer.

INTERACTIONS:

None significant.

PRESCRIPTION:

Yes (very restricted on NHS).

PERMITTED IN SPORT:

Yes.

OVERDOSE:

Significant stomach irritation possible.

Carbomer

See EYE LUBRICANTS.

Carboplatin

TRADE NAME:

Paraplatin.

DRUG CLASS:

Antineoplastic.

USES:

Some forms of advanced cancer of the ovary and lung.

DOSAGE:

 As determined by doctor for each patient.

FORMS:
Injection.

PRECAUTIONS:
Not to be used in pregnancy (D), breast feeding and children.
Use with caution in debilitated and elderly patients.
Regular blood tests essential.
Hearing and brain function need to be checked regularly.

Do not take if:

 • suffering from severe kidney disease.

SIDE EFFECTS:
Common: blood cell damage, kidney and liver damage, ear damage, nausea, diarrhoea, muscle pains.
Unusual: vomiting, local skin reactions.
Severe but rare (stop medication, consult doctor): liver or kidney failure.

INTERACTIONS:
Other drugs:
• other drugs used to treat cancer, aminoglycosides.

PRESCRIPTION:
Yes.

PERMITTED IN SPORT:
Yes.

OTHER INFORMATION:
Used only when no other medication will assist patient.

Carboxymethylcellulose

TRADE NAME:
Glandosane.

USES:
Artificial saliva for dry mouth.

DOSAGE:
 Use spray as required, normally three or four times a day.

FORMS:
Mouth spray.

PRECAUTIONS:
Safe to use in pregnancy and breast feeding.
Use with caution in children.

SIDE EFFECTS:
Minimal.

INTERACTIONS:
None significant.

PRESCRIPTION:
No.

PERMITTED IN SPORT:
Yes.

OVERDOSE:
Unlikely to have serious effects.

OTHER INFORMATION:
Normally used after radiotherapy to the mouth and throat or in the Sicca syndrome, but may also be useful in the elderly to moisturise the mouth.

CARDIAC GLYCOSIDE

DISCUSSION:
The cardiac glycosides are an ancient group of medications that regulate heart rate. They are derived from the foxglove flower. Only one is used in modern medicine.
See Digoxin.

Carisoprodol

TRADE NAME:
Carisoma.

DRUG CLASS:
Muscle relaxant.

USES:
Muscle spasms.

DOSAGE:

 125 to 350mg three times a day.

FORMS:

Tablets of 125 and 350mg (white).

PRECAUTIONS:

Not for use in pregnancy, breast feeding or children.
Reduce dose in elderly.
Use with caution in liver or kidney disease, alcoholism or history of drug dependence.
Avoid long term use. Do not stop suddenly but reduce dose gradually.

Do not take if:

 • suffering from acute intermittent porphyria.

SIDE EFFECTS:

Common: drowsiness, dizziness, nausea. flushes, headache, constipation.
Unusual: rash.

INTERACTIONS:

Other drugs:
• sedatives, hypnotics, anticoagulants, contraceptive pills, steroids, phenytoin, griseofulvin, tricyclic antidepressants, phenothiazines, rifampicin.
Other substances:
• alcohol.

PRESCRIPTION:

Yes.

PERMITTED IN SPORT:

Yes.

OVERDOSE:

Exacerbation of side effects likely. Induce vomiting or administer activated charcoal if swallowed recently. Seek medical attention.

OTHER INFORMATION:

May cause dependence if used inappropriately.
See also MUSCLE RELAXANTS.

Carmustine

TRADE NAME:

Bicnu.

DRUG CLASS:

Antineoplastic.

USES:

Hodgkin's disease, multiple myeloma, lymphomas, some types of brain cancer, palliation of other cancers.

DOSAGE:

 As determined by doctor for each patient.

FORMS:

Injection.

PRECAUTIONS:

Must not be used in pregnancy (D) or breast feeding. Adequate contraception essential.
Blood tests must be performed regularly to monitor liver function and blood cells.
Use with caution in lung disease.

Do not take if:

 • suffering from bleeding disorders due to low platelet count.

SIDE EFFECTS:

Common: liver and kidney damage, lung damage.
Unusual: numerous possibilities that should be discussed with your doctor.

INTERACTIONS:

None significant.

PRESCRIPTION:

Yes.

PERMITTED IN SPORT:

Yes.

OVERDOSE:

Serious organ damage likely. Only given under strict medical supervision.

Carteolol

TRADE NAMES:

Teoptic.

DRUG CLASS:

Beta-blocker.

USES:

Glaucoma.

DOSAGE:

 One drop twice a day in eye.

FORMS:

Eye drops.

PRECAUTIONS:

Should be used with caution in pregnancy (C), but eye drops unlikely to cause problems.
Safe to use in breast feeding.
May be used with caution in children.
Use with care if suffering from alcoholism, liver or kidney failure or about to have surgery.
Use with caution in heart disease, shock or enlarged right heart.

Do not take if:

 • suffering from diabetes, asthma, heart block, heart failure, slow heart rate, or allergic conditions.

SIDE EFFECTS:

Common: low blood pressure, slow heart rate, burning eyes, stinging, asthma.
Severe but rare (stop medication, consult doctor): severe asthma.

INTERACTIONS:

Other drugs:

• calcium channel blockers, disopyramide, clonidine, adrenaline, other medications for irregular heart beat, lignocaine, ergotamine, indomethacin, chlorpromazine, beta-blocker tablets.

PRESCRIPTION:

Yes.

PERMITTED IN SPORT:

Yes.

OVERDOSE:

Unlikely to be serious effects other than exacerbation of side effects if eye drops swallowed.

See also Betaxolol, Bimatroprost, Brimonidine, Brinzolamide, Levobunolol, Pilocarpine, Timolol, Travoprost.

Carvedilol

TRADE NAME:

Eucardic.

DRUG CLASS:

Beta-blocker.

USES:

Heart failure, prevention of angina, high blood pressure.

DOSAGE:

 Start with 12.5mg twice a day with food. Increase dose slowly to maximum of 25mg twice a day (may be higher for very heavy patients).

FORMS:

Tablets of 12.5 and 25mg.

PRECAUTIONS:

Should not be used in pregnancy (C) unless essential for the mother's health.
Use with considerable caution in breast feeding and children.

Use with caution in poor circulation to hands and feet, kidney disease, diabetes, overactive thyroid gland.

Do not stop medication suddenly, but reduce dose slowly.

Do not take if:

- suffering from asthma, slow heart rate, low blood pressure, heart block, poor liver function.

SIDE EFFECTS:

Common: tissue swelling, slow heart rate, low blood pressure, dizziness, diarrhoea, nausea.

Unusual: vomiting, ankle swelling, joint pain, muscle pain, blurred vision, fainting, chest pain.

Severe but rare (stop medication, consult doctor): unusual bleeding, wheezing, shortness of breath.

INTERACTIONS:

Other drugs:
- rifampicin, cimetidine, clonidine, calcium channel blockers, hypoglycaemics, insulin, quinidine, paroxetine, fluoxetine, digoxin, MAOI, reserpine, other beta-blockers.

Other substances:
- grapefruit eaten as same time as tablets taken.

PRESCRIPTION:

Yes.

PERMITTED IN SPORT:

No.

OVERDOSE:

Low blood pressure, fainting, slow heart rate, seizures, reduced breathing, collapse, heart failure and death may occur. Lie patient flat on side in coma position. Induce vomiting or administer activated charcoal if swallowed recently. Seek urgent medical attention.

OTHER INFORMATION:

Introduced in 1998, mainly to treat more difficult cases of heart failure.

See also BETA-BLOCKERS, Esmolol, Labetalol, Metoprolol, Oxprenolol, Pindolol, Propranolol, Sotalol.

Cefaclor, Cefadroxil, Cefamandole, Cefixime, Cefotaxime, Cefoxitin, Cefpiromine, Cefpodoxime, Cefprozil, Ceftazidime, Ceftriaxone, Cefuroxime.

See CEPHALOSPORINS.

Celecoxib

TRADE NAME:

Celebrex.

DRUG CLASS:

COX-2 Inhibitor.

USES:

Rheumatoid arthritis and osteoarthritis.

DOSAGE:

 100 to 400mg a day.

FORMS:

Capsules (white) of 100 and 200mg.

PRECAUTIONS:

Use with considerable caution in pregnancy (B3).

Use with caution in breast feeding and children.

Use with caution with previous peptic ulcer, high blood pressure, fluid retention, heart failure, asthma, dehydration, liver or kidney disease, sulpha allergy.

Lower doses may be necessary in the elderly and with long term use.

Do not take if:

- asthma occurs with NSAID medications or aspirin.

SIDE EFFECTS:

Common: fluid retention (swollen feet).
Unusual: gut irritation, indigestion.
Severe but rare (stop medication, consult doctor): liver and kidney damage.

INTERACTIONS:

Other drugs:
- nonsteroidal anti-inflammatory drugs (NSAID), steroids, anticoagulants (e.g. warfarin), diuretics, ACE inhibitors, lithium, antacids, fluconazole.

PRESCRIPTION:

Yes.

PERMITTED IN SPORT:

Yes.

OVERDOSE:

Lethargy, drowsiness, nausea, vomiting and indigestion may occur. Give activated charcoal. Seek medical attention.

OTHER INFORMATION:

Revolutionary new class of medications first released in 1999 to treat all forms of arthritis and inflammation with much reduced side effects.
See also Meloxicam, NSAID, Parecoxib, Rofecoxib.

Celiprolol

TRADE NAMES:

Celectol.

DRUG CLASS:

Beta-blocker.

USES:

High blood pressure.

DOSAGE:

 One tablet a day.

FORMS:

Tablets (yellow) of 200mg and 400mg.

PRECAUTIONS:

Should be used in pregnancy (C) only if medically essential.
Safe to use in breast feeding.
May be used with caution in children.
Use with care if suffering from alcoholism, liver or kidney failure or about to have surgery.

Do not take if:

- suffering from diabetes, asthma, or allergic conditions
- suffering from heart failure, shock, slow heart rate, or enlarged right heart
- if undertaking prolonged fast.

SIDE EFFECTS:

Common: low blood pressure, slow heart rate, cold hands and feet, asthma.
Unusual: loss of appetite, nausea, diarrhoea, impotence, tiredness, sleeplessness, nightmares, rash, loss of libido, hair loss, noises in ears.
Severe but rare (stop medication, consult doctor): severe asthma.

INTERACTIONS:

Other drugs:
- calcium channel blockers, disopyramide, clonidine, adrenaline, other medications for irregular heart beat, lignocaine, ergotamine, indomethacin, chlorpromazine.

Herbs:
- goldenseal, guarana, hawthorn, Korean ginseng, liquorice.

PRESCRIPTION:

Yes.

PERMITTED IN SPORT:

No.

OVERDOSE:

Slow heart rate, low blood pressure, asthma and heart failure may result. Administer activated charcoal or induce vomiting if tablets taken recently. Use Salbutamol or other asthma sprays for difficulty in breathing. Seek medical assistance.

OTHER INFORMATION:

Except for asthmatics, very safe and effective.

See also Atenolol, Carvedilol, Esmolol, Labetalol, Metoprolol, Oxprenolol, Pindolol, Propranolol, Sotalol.

Cephalexin

See CEPHALOSPORINS.

CEPHALOSPORINS

TRADE and GENERIC NAMES:

Baxan (Cefadroxil).
Cefrom (Cefpirome).
Cefzil (Cefprozil).
Ceporex, Keflex (Cephalexin).
Claforan (Cefotaxime).
Distaclor (Cefaclor).
Fortum, Kefadim (Ceftazidime).
Kefadol (Cefamandole).
Kefzol (Cephazolin).
Mefoxin (Cefoxitin).
Orelox (Cefpodoxime).
Rocephin (Ceftriaxone).
Suprax (Cefixime).
Velosef (Cephadrine).
Zinacef, Zinnat (Cefuroxime).

DRUG CLASS:

Antibiotic, broad spectrum.

USES:

Treats infections caused by susceptible bacteria.

DOSAGE:

 One or two capsules two to four times a day.

FORMS:

Capsules, tablets, suspension, injection.

PRECAUTIONS:

Safe to use in pregnancy (Cephalexin—A, other forms—B1), breast feeding and children.
Use with caution in severe kidney disease and colitis (inflammation of large bowel). Use short term if possible.

SIDE EFFECTS:

Common: diarrhoea.
Unusual: nausea, vomiting, belly pain, rash.
Severe but rare (stop medication, consult doctor): bloody diarrhoea, severe itchy rash, yellow skin (jaundice).

INTERACTIONS:

Other drugs:
• diuretics, other cephalosporins.
Other substances:
• may cause false positive test for sugar in urine.

PRESCRIPTION:

Yes.

PERMITTED IN SPORT:

Yes.

OVERDOSE:

Exacerbation of side effects only likely effect.

OTHER INFORMATION:

Cephalosporins are a group of relatively strong antibiotics. They are divided by doctors into first, second and third generation cephalosporins. In general terms, they increase in strength and the number of types of bacteria they are active against decreases as you go from first to third generation drugs.
First generation cephalosporins (cefaclor, cephalexin, cefuroxime) are commonly used by general practitioners. They are active against a very wide range of bacteria and are particularly useful in chest, urinary, skin and joint infections. Side effects are uncommon with the first generation capsules and mixtures, but more likely with the third generation cephalosporins which are given by

injection. They do not cause dependence or addiction.
See also ANTIBIOTICS.

Cephazolin, Cephradine
See CEPHALOSPORINS.

Cetalkonium chloride

TRADE NAME:

Only available in combination with other medications.
Bonjela (with choline salicylate).

DRUG CLASS:

Antiseptic.

USES:

Mouth and gum irritation, teething.

DOSAGE:

 Apply to gums every three hours.

FORMS:

Gel.

PRECAUTIONS:

Safe in pregnancy, breast feeding, children and infants over four months.

SIDE EFFECTS:

Minimal.

INTERACTIONS:

Other drugs:
• aspirin.

PRESCRIPTION:

No.

PERMITTED IN SPORT:

Yes.

OTHER INFORMATION:

Widely and safely used for infant teething.

Cetirizine
See ANTIHISTAMINES, SEDATING.

Cetomacrogol

TRADE NAMES:

Found in numerous over the counter skin moisturisers and cosmetics.

DRUG CLASS:

Moisturiser.

USES:

Dry skin, cracked skin, soap substitute.

DOSAGE:

 Apply as required.

FORMS:

Cream.

PRECAUTIONS:

Safe to use in pregnancy, breast feeding and children.

SIDE EFFECTS:

None.

INTERACTIONS:

None.

PRESCRIPTION:

No.

PERMITTED IN SPORT:

Yes.

OTHER INFORMATION:

One of the original moisturising creams that has been available for a century. Cheap and effective.

Cetrimide

TRADE NAMES:

Cetavlex.

Ceanel (with undecenoic acid).
Drapolene (with benzalkonium chloride).
Hibicet, Steripod Yellow, Tisept (with chlorhexidine).
Siopel (with dimethicone).

DRUG CLASS:

Antiseptic.

USES:

Disinfection of skin and medical equipment, acne, minor burns, grazes.

DOSAGE:

 Apply or use as required.

FORMS:

Cream, wash, lotion, liquid.

PRECAUTIONS:

Safe to use in pregnancy, breast feeding and children.
Avoid eye contact.

SIDE EFFECTS:

Minimal.

INTERACTIONS:

None significant.

PRESCRIPTION:

No.

PERMITTED IN SPORT:

Yes.

OVERDOSE:

If swallowed may cause nausea, vomiting, diarrhoea and stomach cramps.

Cetylpyridinium

TRADE NAMES:

Merocets.
Calgel (with lignocaine).
Merocaine (with benzocaine).
Also found in numerous locally produced over the counter antiseptic preparations.

DRUG CLASS:

Antiseptic.

USES:

Prevention of infection, treatment of minor infections, teething in infants.

DOSAGE:

 Use up to six times a day as directed by instructions on packaging.

FORMS:

Lozenges, gel, gargle.

PRECAUTIONS:

Safe to use in pregnancy (A), breast feeding and children.
Use with caution under three years.

SIDE EFFECTS:

None significant.

INTERACTIONS:

None significant.

PRESCRIPTION:

No.

PERMITTED IN SPORT:

Yes.

OVERDOSE:

Swallowing gargle or lozenges may cause belly discomfort, nausea and diarrhoea.

Chamomile

TRADE NAME:

Kamillosan.
Also used in herbal drinks and other soothing preparations.

USES:

Chapped skin, nappy rash, sore nipples.

DOSAGE:

 Apply two to four times a day.

FORMS:
Ointment.

PRECAUTIONS:
Safe in pregnancy, breast feeding and children.

SIDE EFFECTS:
None significant.

INTERACTIONS:
None significant.

PRESCRIPTION:
No.

PERMITTED IN SPORT:
Yes.

OVERDOSE:
Swallowing ointment has no serious effects.

Charcoal

TRADE NAMES:
Actidose-Aqua, Charcodote, Liqui-Char (activated charcoal).
Also available in numerous other brands as tablets and capsules.

USES:
Excessive amounts of burping, excessive passing of wind, gassy discomfort of stomach, may absorb some forms of poison, drug overdosage.

DOSAGE:
 Poisoning: 50 to 100g as a single dose.
Other uses: 200 to 1200mg up to four times a day.

FORMS:
Suspension, granules, capsules, tablets (store capsules away from heat and moisture).

PRECAUTIONS:
Safe in pregnancy and breast feeding. Not for use under three years of age.
Do not take from one hour before to two hours after a meal.
Do not take if:
- taking other medications as charcoal may interfere with absorption of many types of medication
- suffering from diarrhoea

SIDE EFFECTS:
Common: may alter bowel habits.

INTERACTIONS:
Other drugs:
- reduces absorption of many medications.
Other substances:
- reduces absorption of some foods.

PRESCRIPTION:
No.

PERMITTED IN SPORT:
Yes.

OVERDOSE:
Diarrhoea only likely result. No specific treatment necessary.

OTHER INFORMATION:
One of the oldest medications known to mankind and probably used since prehistoric times for stomach wind and discomfort. Very effective in reducing amount of toxic material absorbed in overdosage of medication or in poisoning. See section on First Aid at front of book.

Chickenpox vaccine
(Varicella zoster vaccine)

TRADE NAMES:
Varilrix.

DRUG CLASS:
Vaccine.

USES:

Prevention of chickenpox.

DOSAGE:

 Children from 9 months to 12 years: one injection
Over 12 years: two injections six weeks apart.

FORMS:

Injection.

PRECAUTIONS:

Not for use in pregnancy.
Use with caution in breast feeding.
Use with caution in HIV (AIDS).

Do not take if:

- sensitive to neomycin
- blood transfusion received recently
- suffering from a high fever
- under nine months of age.

SIDE EFFECTS:

Common: local soreness at injection site.
Unusual: rash. Vaccinated person may rarely pass virus onto an unvaccinated person to cause chickenpox.
Severe but rare (stop medication, consult doctor): allergic reaction.

INTERACTIONS:

Other drugs:
- other viral vaccines (e.g. measles), salicylates.

Other substances:
- interferes with TB skin tests.

PRESCRIPTION:

Yes.

PERMITTED IN SPORT:

Yes.

OTHER INFORMATION:

Introduced in 2000 as the first vaccine against chickenpox. An attenuated live virus vaccine.

See also VACCINES.

Chloral betaine

See Chloral hydrate.

Chloral hydrate

(**Chloral betaine**).

TRADE NAME:

Welldorm.

DRUG CLASS:

Sedative, hypnotic.

USES:

Insomnia (sleeplessness).

DOSAGE:

 One or two tablets at night.
15 to 45mLs at night.

FORMS:

Tablet (purple), elixir.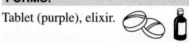

PRECAUTIONS:

Not to be used in pregnancy and breast feeding.
Use with caution in children.
Should not be used long term.

Do not take if:

- suffering from porphyria, severe liver or kidney disease, significant heart disease, gastritis (inflamed stomach).

SIDE EFFECTS:

Common: nausea, headache.
Unusual: vomiting, bloating, passing excess wind, rash.
Severe but rare (stop medication, consult doctor): allergies, bleeding disorders, blood cell damage.

INTERACTIONS:

Other drugs:
- other sedatives, anticoagulants, anticholinergics.

Other substances:
- alcohol.

PRESCRIPTION:

Yes.

PERMITTED IN SPORT:

Yes.

OVERDOSE:

Serious. Seek urgent medical attention. Liver and other organ damage possible.

OTHER INFORMATION:

Very old fashioned medication that has largely been replaced by more reliable and safer sedatives.
See also HYPNOTICS and SEDATIVES.

Chlorambucil

TRADE NAME:

Leukeran.

DRUG CLASS:

Alkyllater.

USES:

Leukaemia, breast and ovary cancer, Hodgkin's disease, lymphoma, other malignant conditions.

DOSAGE:

 Complex. Must be individualised by doctor for each patient.

FORMS:

Tablets (brown) of 2mg.

PRECAUTIONS:

Must not be used in pregnancy (D) unless the life of the mother is at risk as serious damage to the foetus is likely. Breast feeding must be ceased before use. Use in children only when medically essential. Regular blood tests to monitor blood cells and liver function essential.
Adequate contraception must be used during treatment.
Must be used with extreme caution in all patients.

SIDE EFFECTS:

Common: bone marrow damage.
Unusual: nausea, vomiting, diarrhoea, mouth ulcers, lung damage, convulsions in children.
Severe but rare (stop medication, consult doctor): yellow skin (jaundice).

INTERACTIONS:

Other drugs:
• phenylbutazone, other cancer treatments.

PRESCRIPTION:

Yes.

PERMITTED IN SPORT:

Yes.

OVERDOSE:

May cause damage to blood and bone marrow cells, convulsions, incoordination and irrational behaviour. Administer activated charcoal or induce vomiting if medication taken recently. Seek medical assistance.

OTHER INFORMATION:

Although serious side effects are possible, Chlorambucil may be life saving in some patients.
See also Amascrine, VINCA ALKALOIDS.

Chloramphenicol

TRADE NAMES:

Chloromycetin, Kemicetine, Minims Chloramphenicol.
Actinac (with hydrocortisone and other ingredients).

DRUG CLASS:

Antibiotic.

USES:

Very severe infections, eye and skin infections.

DOSAGE:

Eye drops: two drops every three hours.
Eye ointment: insert three times a day.
Cream: apply once or twice a day.

FORMS:

Cream, eye ointment, injection, eye drops.

PRECAUTIONS:

Eye drops and ointment may be used in pregnancy, breast feeding and children.
Use cream with caution in pregnancy, breast feeding and children.
Injection should not be used in any patient unless no other antibiotic can be successfully used for a severe infection.
There are further risks of using injection in pregnancy (C), breast feeding and children.
Never to be used long term.
Use with additional caution in liver and kidney disease.

SIDE EFFECTS:

Common: eye preparations—irritation.
Unusual: injection—vomiting, sore mouth, diarrhoea, headache.
Severe but rare: chloramphenicol can cause (sometimes months after the medication is taken) a severe and usually fatal blood disorder with an incidence between 1:25,000 and 1:100,000 patients using the drug. In children under three months, the 'Grey Syndrome' may occur as a result of the undeveloped liver's inability to adequately deal with the drug.

INTERACTIONS:

Other drugs:
• anticonvulsants, anticoagulants (e.g. warfarin).

PRESCRIPTION:

Yes.

PERMITTED IN SPORT:

Yes.

OVERDOSE:

Exacerbation of side effects and increased risk of serious reactions possible.

OTHER INFORMATION:

Chloramphenicol is a very effective and well tolerated antibiotic, but because if taken by mouth or injection it can rarely cause death by destroying the red blood cells, it is only used when no other antibiotic can control a severe infection. It is widely used in eye and skin preparations quite safely, as the drug is not absorbed in any significant concentration into the blood stream. The use of Chloramphenicol is usually restricted to topical creams and eye preparations. It is used by mouth or injection in certain serious life threatening situations, such as meningitis, when it worth the risk of the rare side effects.
See also ANTIBIOTICS.

Chlordiazepoxide

TRADE NAME:

Librium.

DRUG CLASS:

Anxiolytic, benzodiazepine.

USES:

Anxiety disorders, acute alcohol withdrawal, relaxation before operations, muscle spasms caused by brain injury.

DOSAGE:

Varies widely from one capsule every few days as required for mild anxiety to 300mg (30 capsules) a day in several doses for alcohol withdrawal. Most patients would not exceed one 10mg capsule three times a day. Higher dose requires strict medical supervision.

FORMS:

Capsules of 5mg and 10mg.

PRECAUTIONS:

Should not be used in pregnancy (C) unless essential. Should be used with caution in breast feeding.
Should be used with caution in patients with liver and kidney disease, chronic bronchitis, asthma, emphysema.
Should not be ceased suddenly in epileptics as this may cause a convulsion. Should only be used for short periods of time if possible.
Should not be used while driving or operating machinery.
Should be used with caution in elderly patients.

Do not take if:

- elderly and suffering from heart failure
- suffering from myasthenia gravis, glaucoma, some psychiatric conditions.

SIDE EFFECTS:

Common: drowsiness, confusion, poor coordination.
Unusual: rash, swelling, irregular periods, nausea, constipation, decreased sex drive.
Severe but rare (stop medication, consult doctor): patient becomes violent and irrational, jaundice (yellow skin) develops.

INTERACTIONS:

Other drugs:
- reacts with barbiturates, sedatives, antidepressants, phenothiazines, antihistamines and muscle relaxants to cause sedation
- reacts with cimetidine and disulfiram to cause increased effect of chlordiazepoxide
- reacts with anticonvulsants to change their effectiveness
Other substances:
- reacts with alcohol to cause sedation.

PRESCRIPTION:

Yes.

PERMITTED IN SPORT:

Yes.

OVERDOSE:

May cause drowsiness, coma and very rarely death. First aid involves inducing vomiting and seeking urgent medical attention.

OTHER INFORMATION:

May cause dependence if used long term. One of the older and more potent benzodiazepines.

Chlorhexidine

TRADE NAMES:

Corsodyl, CX Powder, Hibiscrub, Hibisol, Hibitane, Hydrex, Serotulle, Steripod Pink, Unisept, Uriflex C, Uro-Tainer.
Dermol (with paraffin, benzalkonium chloride and other ingredients).
Hibicet, Steripod Yellow, Tisept (with cetrimide).
Instillagel (with lignocaine and other ingredients).
Naseptin (with neomycin).
Nystaform (with nystatin).
Nystaform HC (with nystatin and hydrocortisone).
Also found in other locally produced antiseptics.

DRUG CLASS:

Antiseptic.

USES:

Prevention of infection, skin cleaning, minor infections of skin and mouth.

DOSAGE:

 Depends on form. Normally use several times a day.

FORMS:

Cream, solution, wash, oil, powder, tincture, gel, mouth wash, tulle (netting).

PRECAUTIONS:

Safe to use in pregnancy (A), breast feeding and children.
Avoid eye contact.
Use with caution on open wounds and in nose, mouth and ears.

SIDE EFFECTS:

Minimal.

INTERACTIONS:

Other drugs:
• none significant.
Other substances:
• detergents.

PRESCRIPTION:

No.
Prescription required for some medication combinations.

PERMITTED IN SPORT:

Yes.

OVERDOSE:

Diarrhoea, belly discomfort and vomiting only likely effects if swallowed. Seek medical advice, particularly in children.

OTHER INFORMATION:

The most widely used antiseptic cleansing agent in hospitals, general practice and operating theatres. Very safe and effective.
See also Mupirocin, Neomycin, Sodium Fusidate.

Chlormethiazole

TRADE NAME:

Heminevrin.

DRUG CLASS:

Hypnotic, sedative.

USES:

Control of alcohol withdrawal and delirium tremens, short term control of extreme agitation and confusion.

DOSAGE:

 One capsule or 5mLs three times a day, then reduce dosage slowly, ceasing within ten days. Higher doses sometimes given initially. Only prescribed in circumstances of strict medical supervision.

FORMS:

Capsules, syrup, infusion.

PRECAUTIONS:

Safe in pregnancy (A). Breast feeding should be ceased if medication necessary.
Not for use in children.
Lower doses required in elderly.
Caution needed in patients with heart disease, and severe liver disease.
Do not take if:

 • suffering from severe lung disease
• operating machinery, driving vehicles, or undertaking tasks requiring coordination, concentration and alertness.

SIDE EFFECTS:

Common: drowsiness, nasal irritation, eye irritation, facial burning.
Unusual: rash, red skin, itch, excessive phlegm in throat.

INTERACTIONS:

Other drugs:
• propranolol, cimetidine, diazoxide, sedatives.
Herbs:
• celery, camomile, goldenseal, valerian.
Other substances:
• reacts adversely with alcohol.

PRESCRIPTION:

Yes.

PERMITTED IN SPORT:

Yes.

OVERDOSE:

Low blood pressure, low body temperature, slow heart rate and coma may occur. Symptoms worse if taken with alcohol. Rarely fatal. Administer activated charcoal or induce vomiting if patient alert and tablets taken recently. Seek urgent medical attention.

OTHER INFORMATION:

Rarely used outside hospital. Very useful in very disturbed patients or alcohol withdrawal. Addictive.

See also BARBITURATES, Flunitrazepam, Midazolam, Nitrazepam, Temazepam, Triazolam, Zolpidem, Zopiclone.

Chloroquine

TRADE NAMES:

Avloclor, Nivaquine.

DRUG CLASS:

Antimalarial.

USES:

Prevention and treatment of malaria, treatment of rheumatoid arthritis, amoebic hepatitis, systemic lupus erythematosus (SLE), other collagen affecting diseases.

DOSAGE:

 Malaria prevention: two tablets on same day once a week for two weeks before and four weeks after entering malarious area.
Treatment: start with high daily dose and slowly decrease as directed by doctor.

FORMS:

Tablets.

PRECAUTIONS:

Not to be used in pregnancy (D) unless mother's life threatened by severe malaria. May be used in breast feeding and children over one year.

Use with caution in liver and kidney disease, psoriasis and porphyria.
Regular eye checks required if used daily long term.

Do not take if:

 • suffering from alcoholism
• trying to become pregnant.

SIDE EFFECTS:

Common: minimal.
Unusual: nausea, vomiting, diarrhoea, skin pigmentation, hair loss, rash.
Severe but rare (stop medication, consult doctor): deteriorating vision.

INTERACTIONS:

Other drugs:
• antacids, kaolin, cimetidine, metronidazole, ampicillin, other antimalarial drugs.
Other substances:
• reacts with alcohol.

PRESCRIPTION:

Yes.

PERMITTED IN SPORT:

Yes.

OVERDOSE:

Very serious. Depresses the function of the heart and lungs and may cause fatal liver damage. Administer activated charcoal or induce vomiting if taken recently. Seek urgent medical assistance.

OTHER INFORMATION:

Chloroquine is the traditional mainstay for the prevention of malaria, but malaria in many areas (including most of South-East Asia and New Guinea) is now resistant to chloroquine. Found serendipitously to assist in the treatment of rheumatoid and other autoimmune diseases. Very dangerous to the foetus in pregnancy and in overdose.

See also Atovaquone, Artemether and Lumefantrine, Doxycycline, Hydroxychloroquine, Mefloquine, Primaquine, Proguanil, Pyrimethamine, Quinine bisulphate, Sulfadoxine.

Chloroxylenol

TRADE NAME:

Zeasorb (with other ingredients).

DRUG CLASS:

Antiseptic.

USES:

Minor skin cuts and grazes, minor skin infections.

DOSAGE:

 Apply as required.

FORMS:

Powder.

PRECAUTIONS:

Safe in pregnancy, breast feeding and children.
Do not use for prolonged period.
Avoid eye contact.

SIDE EFFECTS:

Minimal.

INTERACTIONS:

None significant.

PRESCRIPTION:

No.

PERMITTED IN SPORT:

Yes.

Chlorpheniramine

See ANTIHISTAMINES, SEDATING.

Chlorpromazine

See PHENOTHIAZINES.

Chlortetracycline

TRADE NAMES:

Aureocort (with triamcinolone).
Deteclo (with tetracycline, demeclocycline).

DRUG CLASS:

Tetracycline, antibiotic.

USES:

Bacterial skin infections, acne.

DOSAGE:

 Ointment: apply once or twice a day.
Tablets: take one twice a day.

FORMS:

Ointment, tablet.

PRECAUTIONS:

External use during pregnancy (D) is unlikely to cause the serious adverse effects on the foetus that may occur if Tetracyclines are taken internally. May be used in breast feeding, but not on the breast. Use with caution in children. Seek further medical advice if infection does not settle rapidly.

SIDE EFFECTS:

Ointment: none significant.
Tablets: nausea, diarrhoea, rash.
Severe but rare (stop medication, consult doctor): severe headache.

INTERACTIONS:

Ointment:
• none significant.
Tablets:
• oral contraceptives, antacids, penicillins, anticoagulants
• milk, mineral supplements.

PRESCRIPTION:

Yes.

PERMITTED IN SPORT:

Yes.

OTHER INFORMATION:

Very safe and effective antibiotic for skin use. Widely used. Available for over forty years.

See also Tetracycline.

Chlorthalidone

See THIAZIDE DIURETICS.

Cholecalciferol, Calcitriol and Ergocalciferol
(Vitamin D)

TRADE NAMES:

Vitamin D consists of a number of chemicals including cholecalciferol, calcitriol and ergocalciferol. It is found in many non-prescription mineral and vitamin supplements.

Adcal-D3, Calcit D3, Calceos, Calcichew D3, Calfovit D3 (with calcium).
Calcijex, Rocaltrol (calcitriol).

DRUG CLASS:

Fat soluble essential vitamin.

USES:

Nutritional deficiency, osteomalacia, rickets, hypoparathyroidism, osteoporosis.

DOSAGE:

 Daily requirement is 5mcg. Much higher doses used to treat diseases listed above.

FORMS:

Tablets, capsules, injection.

PRECAUTIONS:

Safe for use pregnancy, breast feeding and children. Use with caution in infants. Use with caution in kidney disease.

SIDE EFFECTS:

Common: drowsiness, constipation.
Unusual: calcium deposits in tissue, dehydration.

INTERACTIONS:

Other drugs:
• cholestyramine, thiazide diuretics, digoxin, magnesium.

PRESCRIPTION:

Calcijex, Rocaltrol: yes.
Other forms: no.

PERMITTED IN SPORT:

Yes.

OVERDOSE:

Serious. Symptoms include loss of appetite, tiredness, vomiting, diarrhoea, sweating, excess urine production, extreme thirst and headache. This may progress to high blood pressure and kidney failure. Administer activated charcoal or induce vomiting if taken recently. Seek medical assistance.

OTHER INFORMATION:

Remember, vitamins are merely chemicals that are essential in minute doses for the functioning of the body and if taken to excess, act as a drug. Vitamin D can be found naturally in fatty fish (sardines, tuna, salmon, herrings etc.), margarine and egg yolk. It is also produced in the body by the action of sunlight on the skin.

CHOLESTEROL LOWERING DRUGS
(HYPOLIPIDAEMICS)

See Acipimox, Atorvastatin, Cholestyramine, Ciprofibrate, Colestipol, Fenofibrate, Fluvastatin, Gemfibrizol, Pravastatin, Simvastatin.

Cholestyramine

TRADE NAME:

Questran.

DRUG CLASS:

Hypolipidaemic.

USES:

High blood cholesterol level, relief of itch caused by liver failure, relief of diarrhoea caused by small intestine disease.

DOSAGE:

 4g to 16g of powder per day with copious fluids in divided doses through the day.

FORMS:

Powder.

PRECAUTIONS:

Should be used with caution in pregnancy (B2). Not to be used in breast feeding.
Use with caution in children.
May interfere with vitamin absorption.
Lower doses required in elderly.

Do not take if:

 • suffering from gall bladder obstruction, phenylketonuria.

SIDE EFFECTS:

Common: constipation.
Unusual: belly discomfort, excess wind, vomiting, heartburn, loss of appetite, rash, osteoporosis.
Severe but rare (stop medication, consult doctor): unusual bleeding.

INTERACTIONS:

Other drugs:
• other medications should be taken 30 minutes before cholestyramine or four to six hours after cholestyramine
• warfarin, digoxin, phenylbutazone, chlorthiazide, tetracyclines, phenobarbitone, thyroxine, oestrogen.
Herbs:
• alfalfa, fenugreek, garlic, ginger.

PRESCRIPTION:

Yes.

PERMITTED IN SPORT:

Yes.

OVERDOSE:

No significant problems. Severe constipation probable.

OTHER INFORMATION:

One of the earlier forms of treatment for excess blood cholesterol. Effective, but patient compliance often poor due to taste and method of taking.

See also Acipimox, Atorvastatin, Ciprofibrate, Colestipol, Fenofibrate, Fluvastatin, Gemfibrizol, Pravastatin, Simvastatin.

Choline salicylate

TRADE NAME:

Bonjela (with cetalkonium chloride).

DRUG CLASS:

Salicylate.

USES:

Temporary relief of gum pain.

DOSAGE:

 Apply gels every three hours.

FORMS:

Gel.

PRECAUTIONS:

Safe in pregnancy and breast feeding and children over four months.

SIDE EFFECTS:

Minimal.

INTERACTIONS:

Other drugs:
• aspirin interacts with mouth gel.

PRESCRIPTION:
No.

PERMITTED IN SPORT:
Yes.

OTHER INFORMATION:
Widely used and very safe.

Choline theophyllinate
See THEOPHYLLINES.

Chorionic gonadotrophin, human
See Gonadotrophin.

Cilastatin and Imipenem

TRADE NAME:
Primaxin (only available as combination of the two medications).

DRUG CLASS:
Antibiotic.

USES:
Serious bacterial infections of the lungs, belly, pelvis, bones, joints, heart and blood stream.

DOSAGE:
 Administered by a slow infusion through a drip into a vein, or deep injection into muscle. Dosage determined by doctor.

FORMS:
Injection.

PRECAUTIONS:
Use with caution in pregnancy (B3), breast feeding and infants.
Safe to use in children.

Use with caution in kidney disease, colitis, meningitis, brain abscess and other brain diseases.
Not for long term use.
Regular blood tests necessary during use to monitor blood and liver.

SIDE EFFECTS:
Common: rash, itch, other infections, fever, abnormal taste.
Unusual: aeizures, confusion, dizziness, tiredness, nausea, diarrhoea.
Severe but rare (stop medication, consult doctor): vein inflammation, low blood pressure, pseudomembranous colitis (bowel inflammation), abnormal blood cells, abnormal liver function.

INTERACTIONS:
Other drugs:
• other antibiotics, ganciclovir, probenecid.

PRESCRIPTION:
Yes.

PERMITTED IN SPORT:
Yes.

OTHER INFORMATION:
Introduced in 1999 for the treatment of serious infections that do not respond to other antibiotics.

Ciliazapril
See ACE INHIBITORS.

Cimetidine

TRADE NAMES:
Dyspamet, Tagamet.

DRUG CLASS:
Antiulcerant, H2 receptor antagonist.

USES:
Prevention and treatment of ulcers of the stomach, oesophagus (gullet) and duodenum (upper small intestine).

Prevention of acid reflux into the oesophagus (heartburn).
Unapproved use: treatment of widespread warts.

DOSAGE:

 Up to 1600mg a day in one, two or three doses.

FORMS:

Tablets, soluble tablets, syrup, injection.

PRECAUTIONS:

Care should be taken with use in pregnancy (B1) and breast feeding. Children under 12 may be treated at the discretion of the doctor.
Use with caution in kidney and liver disease.

Do not take if:

• suffering from severe kidney disease or phenylketonuria.

SIDE EFFECTS:

Common: headache, diarrhoea, tiredness, dizziness, drowsiness, rash.
Unusual: constipation, breast enlargement and tenderness (both sexes), confusion in elderly.
Severe but rare (stop medication, consult doctor): hepatitis (jaundice—yellow skin), pancreatitis (severe stomach pain), rapid or irregular heart beat.

INTERACTIONS:

Other drugs:
• toxicity may result with warfarin, phenytoin, lignocaine, theophylline, quinidine, procainamide, flecainide, nifedipine, antacids
• effectiveness of many medications affecting the heart, blood pressure and diabetes may be altered.
Herbs:
• alfalfa, capsicum, eucalyptus, senega.

PRESCRIPTION:

Yes.

PERMITTED IN SPORT:

Yes.

OVERDOSE:

No serious effects reported.

OTHER INFORMATION:

Introduced in 1978, cimetidine was the first of a group of drugs (H2 antagonists) that radically improved the treatment of peptic ulcers. It is very safe and available without prescription in some countries.
See also Nizatadine, Ranitidine.

Cinchocaine

See ANAESTHETICS, LOCAL.

Cinnarizine

TRADE NAME:

Stugeron.

DRUG CLASS:

Sedating antihistamine.

USES:

Poor circulation to hands and feet, Raynaud disease, dizziness, motion sickness.

DOSAGE:

 15 to 75mg, two or three times a day.

FORMS:

Tablet of 15mg. (white), capsule of 75mg (orange/cream).

PRECAUTIONS:

Use with caution in pregnancy and breast feeding.
Safe to use in children in low doses.
Not for use in infants.
Use with caution in low blood pressure and Parkinson's disease.

SIDE EFFECTS:

Common: drowsiness.
Unusual: rash.

INTERACTIONS:

Other drugs:
• sedatives and antidepressants.
Other substances:
• alcohol.

PRESCRIPTION:

No.

PERMITTED IN SPORT:

Yes.

OVERDOSE:

May result in convulsions, hallucinations, delirium, anxiety, muscle spasms, rapid heart rate, flushing, dry skin, dry mouth and coma. First aid involved inducing vomiting and seeking urgent medical attention.

See also ANTIHISTAMINES, SEDATING.

Ciprofibrate

TRADE NAME:

Modalim.

DRUG CLASS:

Hypolipidaemic.

USES:

High blood fat (e.g. cholesterol and triglyceride) levels.

DOSAGE:

 One tablet a day.

FORMS:

Tablets of 100mg (white).

PRECAUTIONS:

Use in pregnancy (B3) only if medically essential. Not for use in breast feeding and children.

Use with caution in thyroid disease. Regular blood tests to check blood fat levels, liver enzymes and blood cells are recommended.

Do not take if:

 • suffering from liver or kidney disease
• trying to get pregnant as drug may reduce fertility.

SIDE EFFECTS:

Common: headache, dizziness, rash, nausea, diarrhoea.
Unusual: muscle pain, impotence, hair loss, dizziness.
Severe but rare (stop medication, consult doctor): muscle damage.

INTERACTIONS:

Other drugs:
• warfarin, diabetes medications, oral contraceptives, other medications to lower blood fat levels (hypolipidaemics).

PRESCRIPTION:

Yes.

PERMITTED IN SPORT:

Yes.

OVERDOSE:

Exacerbation of side effects most likely. Administer activated charcoal or induce vomiting if medication taken recently.

See also HYPOLIPIDAEMICS.

Ciprofloxacin

TRADE NAMES:

Ciloxan, Ciproxin.

DRUG CLASS:

Quinolone antibiotic.

USES:

Serious bacterial infections.

DOSAGE:

Tablets: one to three tablets twice a day.
Eye drops: two drops every 15 to 60 minutes.

FORMS:

Tablets, mixture, eye drops, infusion.

PRECAUTIONS:

Use in pregnancy (B3) and breast feeding only if medically essential. Not for use in children.
Eye drops may be used with caution in pregnancy and children.
Use with caution in cystic fibrosis and kidney disease.
Designed for short term use.

SIDE EFFECTS:

Common: nausea.
Unusual: diarrhoea, vomiting, rash, restlessness, tremor, headache, dizziness, itch.

INTERACTIONS:

Other drugs:
• antacids, theophylline, probenecid, warfarin, cyclosporin, metoclopramide, glibenclamide, NSAIDs, iron, sucralfate.
Other substances:
• caffeine (coffee, stimulant drinks and tablets).

PRESCRIPTION:

Yes.

PERMITTED IN SPORT:

Yes.

OVERDOSE:

Exacerbation of side effects most likely. Administer activated charcoal or induce vomiting if medication taken recently.

OTHER INFORMATION:

Very effective and useful medication in dealing with severe bacterial infections that are not controlled by other antibiotics. Introduced in the late 1980s.
See also Norfloxacin.

Cisplatin

TRADE NAME:

Platinex.

USES:

Cancer of the ovary, testes, bladder, skin (squamous cell carcinomas) involving the head and neck.

DOSAGE:

Injections or by drip infusion as directed by doctor.

FORMS:

Injection, infusion.

PRECAUTIONS:

Not to be used in pregnancy (D) unless mother's life in danger, as damage to foetus possible. Breast feeding must be ceased before use. Use in children only if medically essential.
Regular blood tests to check blood cells and kidney function essential.
Regular hearing tests recommended.
Ensure adequate fluid intake.
Use with caution in kidney disease.
Do not take if:

• suffering from hearing disorders, kidney failure or bone marrow disease.

SIDE EFFECTS:

Common: ringing in ears, pins and needles, nausea, vomiting.
Unusual: tremor, muscle spasms, wheeze, unusual bleeding and bruising.
Severe but rare (stop medication, consult doctor): abnormal blood test results.

INTERACTIONS:

Other drugs:
• aminoglycosides, frusemide.
Other substances:
• aluminium medical instruments.

PRESCRIPTION:

Yes.

PERMITTED IN SPORT:

Yes.

OVERDOSE:

Exacerbation of side effects likely.

OTHER INFORMATION:

Despite its significant side effects, cisplatin may be life saving in some patients with cancer.

Citalopram

TRADE NAME:

Cipramil.

DRUG CLASS:

SSRI antidepressant.

USES:

Depression, panic disorders, agoraphobia.

DOSAGE:

 20mg to 60mg once a day.

FORMS:

Tablets of 10, 20 and 40mg (white), drops.

PRECAUTIONS:

Use with caution in pregnancy (B3), breast feeding and children.
Use with caution in heart disease, mania and liver disease.
Reduce dose slowly, do not stop suddenly.

Do not take if:

 • taking other SSRI antidepressants.

SIDE EFFECTS:

Common: nausea, diarrhoea, tiredness, dry mouth, impotence.
Unusual: sweating, loss of appetite, tremor, agitation, watery nose, low libido.

Severe but rare (stop medication, consult doctor): excessive bruising, bleeding or nose bleeds.

INTERACTIONS:

Other drugs:
• other SSRI and tricyclic antidepressants, MAOI, cimetidine, lithium, moclobemide, tryptophan, tramadol, sumatriptan, ketoconazole, itraconazole, macrolide antibiotics, omeprazole, metoprolol, cimetidine.
Herbs:
• St John's wort, ma huang.
Other substances:
• alcohol.

PRESCRIPTION:

Yes.

PERMITTED IN SPORT:

Yes.

OVERDOSE:

Tiredness, vomiting, rapid heart rate, tremor, sweating, poor circulation (blue tinged colour to skin), coma, convulsions and death can occur. Induce vomiting or administer activated charcoal if tablets taken recently. Seek urgent medical attention.

OTHER INFORMATION:

Introduced in 1998 as a further advance within an excellent class of drugs that are very effective in treating depression. Claimed to have a faster effect and fewer side effects than other SSRI antidepressants.

See also Fluoxetine, Fluvoxamine, Paroxetine, Sertraline, Venlafaxine.

Citric acid

See URINARY ALKALINISERS.

Clarithromycin

TRADE NAMES:

Klaricid.
Heliclear (with lansoprazole, amoxycillin).
Helimet (with lansoprazole, clarithromycin).

DRUG CLASS:

Macrolide antibiotic.

USES:

Treatment of infections caused by susceptible bacteria (e.g. Streptococcal throat infection, skin infection, bronchitis), in combination with other drugs to eradicate *Helicobacter pylori* which may cause peptic ulcers.

DOSAGE:

 250 to 500mg twice a day.

FORMS:

Tablets of 250 and 500mg, suspension, powder in sachet.

PRECAUTIONS:

Use with caution in pregnancy (B3), breast feeding and children.
Not designed for prolonged or repeated use.
Use with caution in kidney disease.
Do not take if:
• suffering from severe liver disease, jaundice (yellow skin).

SIDE EFFECTS:

Common: nausea, vomiting, diarrhoea, rash, headache.
Unusual: belly pain, loss of appetite, excess wind, dizziness, ear noises, temporary deafness.
Severe but rare (stop medication, consult doctor): yellow skin (jaundice), irregular heart beat.

INTERACTIONS:

Other drugs:
• serious interactions with cisapride and pimozide
• alprazolam, carbamazepine, cilastazol, cyclosporin, digoxin, lovastatin, methylprednisolone, midazolam, oral contraceptives, phenytoin, quinidine, sildenafil, simvastatin, theophylline, triazolam, valproate, vinblastine, warfarin, zidovudine.

PRESCRIPTION:

Yes.

PERMITTED IN SPORT:

Yes.

OVERDOSE:

Severe diarrhoea, stomach pains and deafness may occur.

OTHER INFORMATION:

Very effective and generally safe antibiotic introduced in 1998. Becoming used as a first line antibiotic in many situations.

Clavulanic acid

(Potassium clavulanate).

TRADE NAMES:

Augmentin (with amoxycillin).
Timentin (with ticarcillin).

USES:

Only available as an additive to penicillin antibiotics to decrease bacterial resistance.

DOSAGE:

 One or two capsules, two or three times a day.

FORMS:

Capsules, tablets, suspension, injection.

PRECAUTIONS:

Safe to use in pregnancy (B1), breast feeding and children.

SIDE EFFECTS:

Related to the form of Penicillin with which it is combined. Diarrhoea very common.

INTERACTIONS:

None significant.

PRESCRIPTION:

Yes.

PERMITTED IN SPORT:

Yes.

OVERDOSE:

Diarrhoea and vomiting only likely effects.

OTHER INFORMATION:

The combination of amoxycillin and potassium clavulanate is becoming very widely prescribed as very few bacteria are resistant to this potent combination.

Clemastine

See ANTIHISTAMINES, SEDATING

Clindamycin

TRADE NAMES:

Dalacin C, Dalacin Cream, Dalacin T, Zindaclin.

DRUG CLASS:

Antibiotic.

USES:

Solution: acne.
Cream: vaginal infections.
Capsules and injection: serious bacterial infections (e.g. lung, belly and skin abscesses).

DOSAGE:

 Solution: apply to acne twice a day.
Vaginal cream: once a day at night.
Capsules: one or two capsules, three or four times a day.

FORMS:

Capsules of 75 and 150mg, injection, lotion, solution, vaginal cream.

PRECAUTIONS:

Safe to use in pregnancy (A). May be used with caution in breast feeding and infants. Safe in children.
Capsules and syrup not to be used long term.
Capsules and syrup to be used with caution in kidney and liver disease.
Cream not to be used on skin or in eyes.

SIDE EFFECTS:

Common: solution—dry skin.
Capsules—nausea, rash.
Unusual: capsules—vomiting, diarrhoea, belly pains, itch.
Severe but rare (stop medication, consult doctor): severe or bloody diarrhoea, severe belly pain, yellow skin (jaundice).

INTERACTIONS:

Other drugs:
• erythromycin.
Other substances:
• capsules and syrup react with alcohol.

PRESCRIPTION:

Yes.

PERMITTED IN SPORT:

Yes.

OVERDOSE:

Exacerbation of side effects likely.

OTHER INFORMATION:

Effective medication that is reserved for more severe internal infections, but commonly used as a topical preparation to control acne.

Clioquinol

TRADE NAMES:

Only available in combination with other medications.
Betnovate C (with betamethasone).
Locacorten Vioform (with flumethasone).
Synalar C (with fluocinolone).
Vioform-Hydrocortisone (with hydrocortisone).

DRUG CLASS:

Antiseptic.

USES:

Minor bacterial and fungal infections of skin.

DOSAGE:

 Apply three or four times a day.

FORMS:

Cream, ear drops.

PRECAUTIONS:

Safe to use in pregnancy, breast feeding (avoid application to breasts) and children over two years.
Avoid eye contact.
Not designed for long term use.
May interfere with blood tests for thyroid function.

SIDE EFFECTS:

Common: staining, skin irritation.
Unusual: pimples on skin.
Severe but rare (stop medication, consult doctor): brain irritation in children.

INTERACTIONS:

Other:
• affects thyroid function tests.

PRESCRIPTION:

Yes.

PERMITTED IN SPORT:

Yes.

OTHER INFORMATION:

Dangerous brain inflammation may rarely occur if used in children under two years.

Clobazam

TRADE NAME:

Frisium.

DRUG CLASS:

Benzodiazepine (Anxiolytic).

USES:

Short term relief of anxiety and sleep disturbances.

DOSAGE:

 10 to 30mg a day.

FORMS:

Tablets of 10mg (white).

PRECAUTIONS:

Should be used with caution in pregnancy (C), but not at all if delivery of infant imminent as it may decrease desire to breathe in newborn infant. Should be used with caution in breast feeding. Not for use in children.
Lower dose required in elderly.
Should be used intermittently and not constantly as dependency may develop.
Use with caution in glaucoma, heart disease, kidney or liver disease, psychiatric conditions, schizophrenia, depression and epilepsy.

Do not take if:

 • suffering from severe lung or liver disease, confusion, myasthenia gravis, sleep apnoea
• tendency to addiction or dependence
• operating machinery, driving a vehicle or undertaking tasks that require concentration and alertness.

SIDE EFFECTS:

Common: reduced alertness, dependence, dry mouth, depression.
Unusual: incoordination, tremor, confusion, increased risk of falls in elderly, rash, low blood pressure, nausea, muscle weakness.
Severe but rare (stop medication, consult doctor): jaundice (yellow skin).

INTERACTIONS:

Other drugs:
• sedatives, other anxiolytics, disulfiram, cimetidine, anticonvulsants, narcotics, anticholinergics, lithium.
Herbs:
• guarana, kava kava, passionflower, St John's wort, valerian.
Other substances:
• reacts with alcohol to cause sedation and confusion.

PRESCRIPTION:

Yes.

PERMITTED IN SPORT:

Yes.

OVERDOSE:

Seldom life threatening. May cause drowsiness, confusion and coma. Induce vomiting if tablets taken recently. Seek medical assistance.

OTHER INFORMATION:

Very safe if used correctly. Dependency may be a problem, particularly in elderly, due to overuse.

See also Alprazolam, Bromazepam, Buspirone, Diazepam, Lorazepam, Oxazepam.

Clobetasol

TRADE NAMES:

Dermovate.
Dermovate NN (with neomycin, nystatin).

DRUG CLASS:

Corticosteroid.

USES:

Psoriasis, severe eczema and dermatitis, lichen planus, discoid lupus.

DOSAGE:

 Apply very sparingly once or twice a day.

FORMS:

Cream, ointment, scalp lotion.

PRECAUTIONS:

Use with caution in pregnancy, breast feeding and children. Not for use in infants.
Do not use around mouth, nose, nipple, vagina or anus.
Not for long term use.
Do not take if:
 • suffering from acne, scabies, broken or ulcerated skin, tuberculosis, fungal or bacterial skin infection.

SIDE EFFECTS:

Common: exacerbation of infections, skin reaction.
Unusual: skin thinning and damage, bleeding under skin, hair growth in skin.
Severe but rare (stop medication, consult doctor): swelling of tissues, weight gain.

INTERACTIONS:

None significant.

PRESCRIPTION:

Yes.

PERMITTED IN SPORT:

Yes.

OVERDOSE:

Skin damage if overused.

OTHER INFORMATION:

Very potent medication that is only used when others have failed.

Clobetasone

TRADE NAMES:

Eumovate.
Trimovate (with oxytetracycline, nystatin).

DRUG CLASS:

Corticosteroid.

USES:

Eye inflammation, eczema, dermatitis.

DOSAGE:

 Eye drops: one or two drops every three to six hours.
Skin preparations: apply three or four times a day.

FORMS:

Eye drops, cream, ointment.

PRECAUTIONS:

Do not use excessively in pregnancy, breast feeding and children. Not for use in infants.

Do not use eye drops if:

 • suffering from viral, fungal or bacterial eye infection, glaucoma, contact lenses.

Do not use if:

 • suffering from tuberculosis, broken or ulcerated skin.

SIDE EFFECTS:

Eye drops: damage to eye surface, eye irritation, worsening of eye infections, glaucoma.
Skin preparations: exacerbation of infections, skin reaction.

INTERACTIONS:

None significant.

PRESCRIPTION:

Yes.

PERMITTED IN SPORT:

Yes.

OVERDOSE:

Unlikely to be harmful.

OTHER INFORMATION:

Medium strength steroid.
See also CORTICOSTEROIDS.

Clofazime

TRADE NAME:

Lamprene.

USES:

Leprosy in combination with other drugs.

DOSAGE:

 Complex. As directed by doctor.

FORMS:

Capsules (red/brown) of 100mg.

PRECAUTIONS:

Not to be used in pregnancy (C) or breast feeding. May be used in children.
Use with caution in liver or kidney disease, history of abdominal pain or diarrhoea.
Use for more than three months should be carefully monitored.

SIDE EFFECTS:

Common: reversible discolouration of skin and hair, nausea, dry skin, diarrhoea.
Unusual: itch, light sensitive skin, acne, vomiting, belly pain, weight loss.
Severe but rare (stop medication, consult doctor): blood in faeces or urine, severe belly pain.

INTERACTIONS:

None significant.

PRESCRIPTION:

Yes.

PERMITTED IN SPORT:

Yes.

OVERDOSE:

Serious exacerbation of side effects possible. Seek medical assistance.

Clomiphene

TRADE NAME:

Clomid.

USES:

Female infertility.

DOSAGE:

 One tablet a day for five days. Repeat monthly for a maximum of six cycles.

FORMS:

Tablets (beige) of 50mg.

PRECAUTIONS:

Not to be used in pregnancy (B3), breast feeding or children.
Use with caution with ovarian cysts.
Multiple pregnancies (i.e. twins, triplets, quads etc.) possible.
Must only be used in carefully selected patients.

Do not take if:

 • suffering from liver disease, hormonal tumours, abnormal bleeding from uterus.

SIDE EFFECTS:

Common: hot flushes, belly discomfort and bloating.
Unusual: one in 200 chance of birth defect (similar to normal risk).
Severe but rare (stop medication, consult doctor): blurred vision, yellow skin (jaundice).

INTERACTIONS:

None significant.

PRESCRIPTION:

Yes.

PERMITTED IN SPORT:

Yes.

OVERDOSE:

May increase risk of foetal abnormality if taken during pregnancy. Otherwise no serious effects likely.

OTHER INFORMATION:

Stimulates ovulation in infertile women, but several eggs may be released, resulting in multiple pregnancies. Has revolutionised the lives of many infertile couples since first introduced in the 1970s.

See also Follicle Stimulating Hormone.

Clomipramine

See TRICYCLIC ANTIDEPRESSANTS.

Clonazepam

TRADE NAME:

Rivotril.

DRUG CLASSES:

Anticonvulsant, Benzodiazepine.

USES:

Epilepsy.

DOSAGE:

 Given twice a day in individually determined dosage. Follow doctors instructions carefully.

FORMS:

Tablets of 0.5 and 2mg, injection.

PRECAUTIONS:

Not to be used in pregnancy (D) unless medically essential. Use with caution in breast feeding and infants. Safe for use in children.
Use with caution in glaucoma, myasthenia gravis, low blood pressure, heart disease, kidney and liver disease,

depression and psychiatric conditions (e.g. schizophrenia).

Use with caution if operating machinery or driving a vehicle.

Do not stop taking medication suddenly, but reduce dose slowly.

Use with caution for long periods of time.

Do not take if:

• suffering from severe lung or liver disease, alcoholism.

SIDE EFFECTS:

Common: drowsiness (worse in first few days), incoordination, behaviour changes, tiredness, fatigue, muscle weakness, excess salivation, dizziness.

Unusual: low blood pressure, itch, skin pigmentation, changes in hair distribution, nausea, loss of appetite, weight changes, impotence, low libido, confusion, aggression, depression, irritability, cough.

Severe but rare (stop medication, consult doctor): unusual bruising or bleeding.

INTERACTIONS:

Other drugs:
• sedatives, stimulants, phenytoin, carbamazepine, valproate, other anticonvulsants, disulfiram, cimetidine.

Herbs:
• guarana, borage, kava kava, passionflower, St John's wort, valerian, evening primrose (linoleic acid), Gingko biloba.

Other substances:
• reacts adversely with alcohol.

PRESCRIPTION:

Yes.

PERMITTED IN SPORT:

Depends on sport. Check with governing body.

OVERDOSE:

May cause drowsiness, confusion, incoordination, slow breathing, coma and rarely death. Administer activated charcoal or induce vomiting if taken recently and patient alert. Seek urgent medical attention.

OTHER INFORMATION:

May cause dependence if used inappropriately.

See also BARBITURATES, BENZODIAZEPINES, Carbamazepine, Ethosuximide, Gabapentin, Lamotrigine, Levetiracetam, Oxcarbazepine, Phenytoin, Primidone, Sodium valproate, Sulthiame, Tiagabine, Topiramate, Vigabatrin.

Clonidine

TRADE NAMES:

Catapres, Dixarit.

DRUG CLASS:

Antihypertensive, Antimigraine.

USES:

High blood pressure, prevention of migraine and vascular headaches, treatment of menopausal flushing.

DOSAGE:

One or two tablets, three times a day to a maximum of 900mcg per day.

FORMS:

Tablets, capsules, injection.

PRECAUTIONS:

Use with significant caution in pregnancy (B3) and breast feeding.

Use with caution in children under 12 years.

Use with caution in depression, poor blood supply to brain, irregular heart beat, constipation and phaeochromocytoma.

Medication must not be stopped suddenly, but dosage must be slowly decreased over several days or weeks.

Do not take if:

• suffering from liver or kidney failure, severe heart disease, diabetes or very slow heart rate.

SIDE EFFECTS:

Common: drowsiness, dry mouth, stomach upsets.
Unusual: hair thinning, blurred vision, constipation, delusions, depression, impotence, irritability, low blood pressure on standing.

INTERACTIONS:

Other drugs:
• sedatives, hypnotics, other medications for treatment of high blood pressure, antidepressants.
Other substances:
• reacts with alcohol.

PRESCRIPTION:

Yes.

PERMITTED IN SPORT:

Yes.

OVERDOSE:

Slow heart rate, low blood pressure and coma result. First aid involves administering activated charcoal or inducing vomiting if awake and alert and seeking very urgent medical assistance.

OTHER INFORMATION:

Old fashioned, but often effective treatment for migraines. Only used for most severe forms of high blood pressure. Occasionally used to stop symptoms of narcotic withdrawal.

Clopamide

See THIAZIDE DIURETICS.

Clopidrogel

TRADE NAME:

Plavix.

DRUG CLASS:

Anticoagulant.

USES:

Prevention of blood clots (e.g. strokes, heart attack).

DOSAGE:

 One tablet a day.

FORMS:

Tablets of 75mg (pink).

PRECAUTIONS:

Not for use in pregnancy (B1). Use with caution in breast feeding and children. Use with caution in peptic ulcers, other intestinal ulcers, recent heart attack or stroke.
Cease before any elective surgery.
Do not take if:
 • suffering from liver disease or bleeding disorders.

SIDE EFFECTS:

Common: abnormal bleeding, diarrhoea, rash, agitation.
Unusual: low level of white blood cells.
Severe but rare (stop medication, consult doctor): jaundice, heavy bleeding.

INTERACTIONS:

Other drugs:
• NSAID, aspirin (but may be used with aspirin in low doses), fluvastatin, anticoagulants (e.g. warfarin, heparin), phenytoin, tamoxifen, tolbutamide.

PRESCRIPTION:

Yes.

PERMITTED IN SPORT:

Yes.

OVERDOSE:

May be very serious with excessive internal and external bleeding. Administer activated charcoal or inducing vomiting if awake and alert and seek urgent medical assistance.

OTHER INFORMATION:

Introduced 1999 as an additional treatment for patients who have recurrent episodes of abnormal blood clotting.
See also ANTICOAGULANTS.

Clotrimazole

TRADE NAMES:

Canesten.
Canesten HC (with hydrocortisone).
Lotriderm (with betamethasone).

USES:

Treatment of fungal infections of skin (tinea, athlete's foot, pityriasis versicolor) and vagina (thrush).

DOSAGE:

 Skin: apply two or three times a day.
Vagina: insert once a day at night.

FORMS:

Cream, vaginal cream, vaginal pessary, gel, lotion, solution.

PRECAUTIONS:

Safe to use in pregnancy (A), breast feeding and children.
Should not be swallowed or used in eyes.
Use with care on open wounds.

SIDE EFFECTS:

Common: none.
Unusual: skin irritation, rash.

INTERACTIONS:

None significant.

PRESCRIPTION:

No.

PERMITTED IN SPORT:

Yes.

OTHER INFORMATION:

This class of medication dramatically improved the treatment of fungal infections when introduced in the early 1970s. Very safe and effective.
See also Econazole, Fluconazole, Itraconazole, Ketoconazole, Miconazole.

Clozapine

See PHENOTHIAZINES.

Coal tar

See Tar.

Cocaine

OTHER NAMES:

Crack, coke.

DRUG CLASS:

Local anaesthetic, stimulant.

USES:

No recognised medical uses.
Used illegally as a psychoactive drug to cause euphoria (artificial happiness).

FORMS:

Used illegally in many forms including smoked, injected and sniffed.

PRECAUTIONS:

Should never be used in pregnancy (increased risk of malformation and heart disease), breast feeding or children.
Do not use if:
• suffering from psychiatric disturbances
• driving a car, operating machinery, swimming or undertaking any activity that requires concentration.

SIDE EFFECTS:

Common: damage to nostrils, fever, headache, irregular heart rate, dilation of pupils, loss of libido, infertility, impotence, breast enlargement and

tenderness in both sexes, menstrual period irregularities, psychiatric disturbances, abnormal breast milk production, may lead to desire for more frequent use or stronger drugs of addiction.
Unusual: high blood pressure, perforation of nasal septum, difficulty in breathing, convulsions, stroke, dementia, heart attack, death.

INTERACTIONS:

Other drugs:
• stimulants, MAOI (severe reaction), tricyclics, sedatives, other medications acting on the brain.
Other substances:
• reacts with alcohol, heroin and marijuana.

PRESCRIPTION:

Illegal except in hospitals.

PERMITTED IN SPORT:

No.

OVERDOSE:

Convulsions, difficulty in breathing, irregular heart rate, coma and death may occur. Seek urgent medical assistance.

OTHER INFORMATION:

The more refined version of cocaine known as 'crack' is the only form that can be smoked and is ten times more potent than cocaine base and is therefore more dangerous. Highly addictive. When smoked, sniffed or injected, cocaine works within seconds to cause euphoria (artificial happiness) and stimulates the brain to increase all sensations. After use many people feel worse than before, hence they want to repeat the artificial high. The more frequently it is used, the higher the dose necessary to achieve the same sensations and the greater the risk of serious side effects.

Codeine Phosphate

TRADE NAMES:

Galcodine.
Codafen Continus (with ibuprofen).
Kapake, Solpadol, Tylex, Zapain (with paracetamol).
Migraleve (with buclizine, paracetamol).
Also found in other locally produced cough and cold remedies and pain relievers.

DRUG CLASS:

Narcotic.

USES:

Pain, diarrhoea, coughing.

DOSAGE:

 5mg to 60mg every four to six hours.

FORMS:

Mixture as Codeine Phosphate alone. Tablets, powders and mixtures in combination with other medications.

PRECAUTIONS:

Safe in pregnancy (A). Should be used with caution in breast feeding and children.
Should be used with caution in people with an underactive thyroid gland, liver disease, an enlarged prostate gland or lung disease.
Elderly patients should take a reduced dose.
Do not take if:
 • addicted to narcotics
• operating machinery, driving a vehicle or undertaking other activity requiring concentration.

SIDE EFFECTS:

Common: constipation, nausea, drowsiness.
Unusual: dizziness, vomiting.

INTERACTIONS:

Other drugs:
- increases the effects of sedatives and hypnotics.

Herbs:
- kava kava.

Other substances:
- do not drink alcohol while taking codeine.

PRESCRIPTION:

Depends on strength and formulation.

PERMITTED IN SPORT:

Yes.

OVERDOSE:

Moderately serious. May cause initial stimulation, followed by vomiting, drowsiness, convulsions, reduced breathing, coma and very rarely death. Seek urgent medical attention.

OTHER INFORMATION:

May cause dependency or addiction if used unnecessarily for long periods. The mildest of the narcotic drugs. Very effective and except for slight risk of dependency, very safe. Widely used in many cough and cold mixtures, pain relievers and preparations for diarrhoea.

See also Alfentanil, Buprenorphine, Dextromoramide, Dextropropoxyphene, Fentanyl, Heroin, Hydromorphone, Methadone, Morphine, Oxycodone, Pentazocine, Pethidine.

Cod liver oil

TRADE NAMES:

Found in a large range of over the counter and health shop medications.

USES:

Tonic, moisturiser.

DOSAGE:

 Apply to skin as required, or take one dose a day.

FORMS:

Cream, capsule, mixture etc.

PRECAUTIONS:

Safe in breast feeding and children. Small amounts safe, but excess may cause birth defects in pregnancy (D).

SIDE EFFECTS:

Common: foul taste.
Unusual: nausea, diarrhoea.

INTERACTIONS:

None significant.

PRESCRIPTION:

No.

PERMITTED IN SPORT:

Yes.

OVERDOSE:

Vomiting and diarrhoea only likely effects.

OTHER INFORMATION:

Very old form of multivitamin (particularly A and D) and fatty acid supplementation.

See also Retinol.

Colchicine

TRADE NAME:

Colgout.

USES:

Treatment of acute gout, prevention of gout.

DOSAGE:

 Two tablets at once, then one tablet every two hours until relief obtained, diarrhoea starts or six tablets taken.

FORMS:

Tablets (white) of 500mcg.

PRECAUTIONS:

Use with caution in pregnancy (B2) and breast feeding. Not for use in children. Use with caution in heart disease, kidney disease and bowel disease. Lower doses necessary in elderly and debilitated.

SIDE EFFECTS:

Common: diarrhoea.
Unusual: reduced body temperature, reduced urge to breathe, muscle weakness, cold extremities, high blood pressure, rash.

INTERACTIONS:

Other drugs:
• sedatives.
Other substances:
• alcohol may aggravate gout.

PRESCRIPTION:

Yes.

PERMITTED IN SPORT:

Yes.

OVERDOSE:

Very serious. Symptoms may be delayed in onset and may include burning mouth, vomiting, diarrhoea, gut pain and spasms, delirium, convulsions and death. Administer activated charcoal or induce vomiting if medication taken recently. Give copious fluids. Seek urgent medical attention.

OTHER INFORMATION:

Does not cause addiction or dependence. Effective, but diarrhoea limits its usefulness.

Colestipol

TRADE NAME:

Colestid.

DRUG CLASS:

Hypolipidaemic.

USES:

Lowering high levels of cholesterol in blood.

DOSAGE:

 15g to 30g two to four times a day with water.

FORMS:

Granules (sachets of 5g).

PRECAUTIONS:

Should be used with caution in pregnancy (B2). Should not be used in breast feeding. Use only if medically essential in children.
Regular blood tests to check blood fat levels are recommended.

Do not take if:

 • suffering from underactive thyroid gland, diabetes, severe kidney or liver disease.

SIDE EFFECTS:

Common: constipation.
Unusual: vitamin deficiency.
Severe but rare (stop medication, consult doctor): chest pain, rapid heart rate.

INTERACTIONS:

Other drugs:
• numerous other drugs—check with doctor.
• do not take at same time as any other medication.
Herbs:
• alfalfa, fenugreek, garlic, ginger.

PRESCRIPTION:

Yes.

PERMITTED IN SPORT:

Yes.

OVERDOSE:

Constipation only likely problem.

See also Atorvastatin, Cholestyramine, Fluvastatin, Gemfibrizol, Nicotinic acid, Pravastatin, Simvastatin.

CONTRACEPTIVES

See Etonogestrel, Medroxyprogesterone acetate, ORAL CONTRACEPTIVES, SPERMICIDES.

Copper

TRADE NAME:

Cuplex (with salicylic and lactic acid). Also found in other non-prescription skin and cosmetic preparations and as part of intrauterine devices.

DRUG CLASS:

Mineral.

USES:

Mild antiseptic.

DOSAGE:

 Massage into skin twice a day.

FORMS:

Gel.

PRECAUTIONS:

May be used in pregnancy and breast feeding.
Not for use under two years of age.
Do not swallow mouthwash tablets.
Use with caution in kidney and liver failure.

Do not use if:

 • suffering from Wilson's disease.

SIDE EFFECTS:

Common: dry skin, skin irritation.

INTERACTIONS:

None significant.

PRESCRIPTION:

No.

PERMITTED IN SPORT:

Yes.

CORTICOSTEROIDS

See STEROIDS.

Cortisol

See Hydrocortisone.

Co-Trimoxazole

See Sulphamethoxazole, Trimethoprim.

COUGH SUPPRESSANTS

DISCUSSION:

Antitussives are the mixtures, lozenges or tablets that stop coughing. They act by directly soothing the inflamed throat, decreasing the sensitivity of the part of the brain that triggers the spasm of coughing, decreasing the amount of phlegm in the throat, anaesthetising the throat, reducing inflammation, reducing pain and by almost any combination of these methods. There are several different ingredients used in cough mixtures.

They differ from the expectorants (see separate entry), which are designed to increase coughing but make the coughing more effective so that phlegm can be cleared from the lungs and throat.

See Ammonium chloride, Codeine, EXPECTORANTS, Pholcodine.

COX-2 INHIBITORS

DISCUSSION:

Anti-inflammatory medication for the treatment of arthritis with reduced effects on the stomach compared to other nonsteroidal anti-inflammatory drugs, NSAIDs.

See Celecoxib, Meloxicam, NSAID, Parecoxib, Rofecoxib, Valdecoxib.

Cromoglycate, sodium

See Sodium cromoglycate.

Crotamiton

TRADE NAMES:

Eurax.
Eurax-HC (with hydrocortisone).

DRUG CLASS:

Antiseptic.

USES:

Itchy skin, scabies.

DOSAGE:

 Itch: apply to affected area two or three times a day.
Scabies: rub over entire body surface except scalp and face after bathing for three to five consecutive days.

FORMS:

Cream, lotion.

PRECAUTIONS:

Use with caution in first three months of pregnancy and small children. May be used safely in breast feeding (not on breasts) and older children.
Avoid eye contact.

Do not use if:

 • suffering from weeping or broken skin.

SIDE EFFECTS:

Common: slight stinging, sensitive skin.

INTERACTIONS:

None significant.

PRESCRIPTION:

No.

PERMITTED IN SPORT:

Yes.

Cyanocobalamin
(Vitamin B12)

TRADE NAMES:

Cytacon, Cytamen.
A large number of other preparations include various forms of vitamin B12 alone or in combination with other medications.

DRUG CLASS:

Vitamin.

USES:

Pernicious anaemia, pins and needles sensation of feet.

DOSAGE:

 Injection: once every three months, or as determined by doctor.
Recommended daily allowance: 2µg a day.

FORMS:

Tablets, injection.

PRECAUTIONS:

Safe in pregnancy, breast feeding and children.
Do not take in high doses or for prolonged periods of time.

Do not take if:

 • suffering from megaloblastic anaemia of pregnancy.

SIDE EFFECTS:

Common: injection site reaction.
Unusual: diarrhoea, abdominal pain, skin rash, allergy reaction.
Severe but rare (stop medication, consult doctor): vision changes (Leber's disease).

INTERACTIONS:

Other drugs:
- chloramphenicol, oral contraceptives, folic acid, colchicine, phenytoin, some antibiotics (aminoglycosides), phenobarbitone, primidone, cimetidine, ranitidine, nizatadine, famotidine.

Other substances:
- alcohol.

PRESCRIPTION:

Injection: yes.
Other forms: no.

PERMITTED IN SPORT:

Yes.

OVERDOSE:

Unlikely to cause any serious effects.

OTHER INFORMATION:

Several chemical variations of Vitamin B12 exist including cyanocobalamin and hydroxocobalamin. They are identical in their actions and use. Cyanocobalamin was the original form of vitamin B12 used medically. Vitamin B12 is a water soluble vitamin found in animal products. It is essential for the formation of red blood cells, normal growth, and normal fat and sugar metabolism. In pernicious anaemia, the body loses the ability to absorb vitamin B12 from the stomach. Remember, vitamins are merely chemicals that are essential for the functioning of the body and if taken to excess, act as a drug.

See also Hydroxocobalamin.

Cyclizine

TRADE NAMES:

Valoid.
Cyclimorph (with morphine).
Diconal (with dipipanone).
Migril (with ergotamine, caffeine).

DRUG CLASS:

Antiemetic, Antihistamine.

USES:

Vomiting caused by migraine or cancer drugs, motion sickness, dizziness.

FORMS:

Tablets, injection.

PRECAUTIONS:

Not for use in pregnancy.
Use with caution in breast feeding and children.

Do not take if:

- suffering from severe heart failure.

SIDE EFFECTS:

Common: drowsiness, dry mouth, constipation, restlessness in children, incoordination, blurred vision.
Unusual: upper belly discomfort, loss of appetite, diarrhoea, irritability.

INTERACTIONS:

Other drugs:
- may interfere with anticoagulants (e.g. warfarin), MAOI (monoamine oxidase inhibitors), sedatives and relaxants.

PRESCRIPTION:

Tablets: no.
Injection: yes.
Combined with other medications: yes.

PERMITTED IN SPORT:

Alone: yes.
Combined with narcotics: no.

OVERDOSE:

May result in convulsions, hallucinations, delirium, anxiety, muscle spasms, rapid heart rate, flushing, dry skin, dry mouth and coma. First aid involved inducing vomiting and seeking urgent medical attention.

Cyclopenthiazide

See THIAZIDE DIURETICS.

Cyclopentolate

See MYDRIATICS.

Cyclophosphamide

TRADE NAME:

Endoxana.

DRUG CLASS:

Alkylater.

USES:

Leukaemia, lymphomas, multiple myeloma, Hodgkin's disease, cancer of the ovary and retina (eye).
Prevents rejection of transplanted organs.

DOSAGE:

 Must be individualised by doctor for each patient depending on disease, severity, response, weight and age of patient.

FORMS:

Tablets, injection.

PRECAUTIONS:

Use in pregnancy (D) will cause damage or death to the foetus, and therefore cyclophosphamide must not be used unless life of mother is threatened. Breast feeding must be ceased before use. Use in children only if child's life at risk.
Regular blood tests to follow course of disease and the effect of medication on blood cells, bone marrow and liver function essential.
Adequate contraception must be used during use of cyclophosphamide.
Must be used with caution in all patients.
Ensure adequate fluid intake.

Do not take if:

 • suffering from recent surgery.

SIDE EFFECTS:

Common: nausea, vomiting, mouth ulcers, hair loss, dermatitis, nail damage, delayed wound healing, infertility.
Unusual: yellow skin (jaundice), blood in urine, fluid retention, testicle and ovary damage, skin pigmentation, diarrhoea
Severe but rare (stop medication, consult doctor): lung and kidney damage, further cancer development.

INTERACTIONS:

Other drugs:
• barbiturates, imipramine, allopurinol, phenothiazines, indomethacin, insulin, diabetic medications, digoxin, cytotoxics, warfarin.

PRESCRIPTION:

Yes.

PERMITTED IN SPORT:

Yes.

OVERDOSE:

Extremely serious. May cause severe damage to kidney, bone marrow and blood cells leading to destruction of immune system and subsequent fatal infections. Administer activated charcoal or induce vomiting if medication taken recently. Seek urgent medical assistance.

OTHER INFORMATION:

Although cyclophosphamide has multiple serious side effects, it may be life saving in patients with severe or widespread cancer or leukaemia.
See also VINCA ALKALOIDS.

Cyclosporin

TRADE NAMES:

Neoral, Sandimmun.

DRUG CLASS:

Immunomodifier.

USES:

Prevents rejection of transplanted organs (e.g. kidney, liver, heart), severe rheumatoid arthritis, severe psoriasis, nephrotic syndrome.

DOSAGE:

 Taken twice a day with milk or food.

FORMS:

Capsules, solution, infusion.

PRECAUTIONS:

Not to be used in pregnancy (C) unless mother's life at risk. Breast feeding must be ceased before use. Must be used with caution in children.
Careful monitoring of all patients by clinical examination and blood tests essential.

Do not take if:

 • suffering from high blood pressure, significant infection, immune deficiency, poor kidney function.

SIDE EFFECTS:

Common: excess hair growth, tremor, sore gums, nausea, vomiting, high blood pressure, increased risk of infection.
Unusual: fluid retention, convulsions, diarrhoea, peptic ulcer formation, acne, rash, itch, muscle cramps, headache, hearing loss, ringing in ears, confusion, tiredness, anaemia, pins and needles, flushing, sinusitis, weight loss.

INTERACTIONS:

Other drugs:
• reacts with a wide range of medications. Check all with a doctor.
Herbs:
• St John's wort, echinacea.
Other substances:
• zinc.

PRESCRIPTION:

Yes.

PERMITTED IN SPORT:

Yes.

OVERDOSE:

Serious. Administer activated charcoal or induce vomiting if medication taken recently. Seek urgent medical assistance.

OTHER INFORMATION:

Potent medication which can be of great benefit if used appropriately and carefully.

Cyproheptadine

See ANTIHISTAMINES, SEDATING.

Cyproterone Acetate

TRADE NAMES:

Androcur, Cyprostat.
Dianette (with ethinyloestradiol—see Oral Contraceptives).

DRUG CLASS:

Sex hormone.

USES:

Excessive body hair in women, loss of scalp hair in women, severe acne in women.
Reduction of sexual drive in men, premature puberty, cancer of the prostate gland.
Dianette: oral contraception.

DOSAGE:

 Androcur, Cyprostat: usually one morning and evening. Depends on use and response to medication. Follow doctors instructions.
Dianette: take one daily, including 7 days of sugar drug free pills.

FORMS:

Tablets.

PRECAUTIONS:

Not to be used in pregnancy or breast feeding. Adequate contraception must be used in sexually active women. Not to be used in girls. For use in boys only if medically indicated.
Use Androcur and Cyprone with caution if operating machinery or undertaking tasks that require concentration.
Use with caution in diabetes, liver tumours.

Do not take if:

- suffering from severe liver disease, blood clots, sickle cell anaemia, severe depression or diabetes.

SIDE EFFECTS:

Common: male infertility, reduced libido, tiredness, increased weight, nausea, headache, irregular menstrual periods (Androcur and Cyprostat only).
Unusual: breast enlargement in men, depression, breast milk production, sleeplessness, hot flushes.
Severe but rare (stop medication, consult doctor): calf or chest pain.

INTERACTIONS:

None significant.

PRESCRIPTION:

Yes.

PERMITTED IN SPORT:

Yes.

OVERDOSE:

Aggravation of side effects likely.

OTHER INFORMATION:

Does not cause addiction or dependence. Must be used strictly according to doctor's instructions.

See also Danazol, Dydrogesterone, Ethinyloestradiol, Etonogestrel, HORMONE REPLACEMENT THERAPY, Medroxyprogesterone acetate, Oestradiol, Oestriol, Oestrogen, ORAL CONTRACEPTIVES, Testosterone.

Cysteamine

TRADE NAME:

Cystagon.

DRUG CLASS:

Detoxifying agent.

USES:

Cystinosis affecting the kidneys.

DOSAGE:

 Depends on body weight. Gradually increased over six weeks to maintenance dose level.

FORMS:

Capsules of 50mg and 150mg.

PRECAUTIONS:

Use with caution in pregnancy (B2), breast feeding and children.
Use with caution if brain symptoms or rash present due to cystinosis.
Liver function and blood condition must be monitored regularly by blood tests.

Do not take if:

- hypersensitive to penicillamine.

SIDE EFFECTS:

Common: rash, drowsiness, depression, stomach ulcers, nausea.
Unusual: bleeding from bowel, vomiting blood, abnormal liver function, fever, low white blood cell count.
Severe but rare (stop medication, consult doctor): seizures, brain inflammation.

INTERACTIONS:

None significant.

PRESCRIPTION:

Yes.

PERMITTED IN SPORT:

Yes.

OTHER INFORMATION:

Introduced in 1997 for treatment of the rare condition, cystinosis.

CYTOTOXICS

See CANCER TREATING DRUGS.

D

Dactinomycin

See Actinomycin D.

Dalteparin

TRADE NAME:

Fragmin.

DRUG CLASS:

Anticoagulant.

USES:

Prevention and treatment of blood clots.

DOSAGE:

 Injection under skin into fat tissue once a day.

FORMS:

Injection.

PRECAUTIONS:

Use only if essential in pregnancy (C) as damage to foetus may occur. Use with caution in breast feeding and children. Bleeding times must be checked regularly by blood test.
Liver and kidney function must be checked regularly by blood tests if used for prolonged period.
Use with caution in osteoporosis and elderly.

Do not use if:

- suffering from bleeding disorder, active bleeding, severe coagulation disorders, heart infection, uncontrolled high blood pressure
- having eye, ear, brain or spinal cord surgery
- Using aspirin or NSAIDs (anti-inflammatory drugs used for joint pain).

SIDE EFFECTS:

Common: abnormal bruising and bleeding.
Severe but rare (stop medication, consult doctor): excessive bleeding or bruising, loss of blood from anus, vagina or mouth, coughing blood.

INTERACTIONS:

Other drugs:
- aspirin, NSAIDs, vitamin K antagonists, dipyridamole, dextran, sulfinpyrazone, probenecid, ethacrynic acid, antihistamines, digoxin, tetracycline antibiotics, ascorbic acid.

Other substances:
- vitamin C.

PRESCRIPTION:

Yes.

PERMITTED IN SPORT:

Yes.

OVERDOSE:

Very serious. May cause catastrophic excessive bleeding. Seek emergency medical treatment.

OTHER INFORMATION:

Used instead of Heparin in some patients as it is less likely to have serious side effects.

See also Heparin.

Danazol

TRADE NAME:

Danol.

DRUG CLASS:

Sex hormone.

USES:

Endometriosis, severe intractable period pain, severe abnormal menstrual bleeding,

severe breast pain, rare form of severe
tissue swelling.

DOSAGE:

 One capsule two to four times a
day for three to nine months.

FORMS:

Capsules of 100mg and 200mg.

PRECAUTIONS:

Not to be used during pregnancy (D) or
breast feeding. Adequate non-hormonal
contraception must be used by women
taking danazol. Not to be used in
children.
Regular blood tests to check liver
function recommended.
Use with caution in liver disease, high
blood pressure, heart disease, diabetes.

Do not take if:

 • suffering from undiagnosed
genital disease, severe liver
disease, pelvic infection, cancer
of sex organs, heart failure,
recent blood clot, porphyria.

SIDE EFFECTS:

Common: acne, weight gain, fluid
retention, excess body hair growth, voice
deepening, flushing, sweating, dry
vagina, menstrual period irregularities.
Unusual: oily skin, hoarseness, reduced
breast size, enlargement of clitoris,
nervousness.
*Severe but rare (stop medication, consult
doctor):* yellow skin (jaundice), blood
clot in vein, chest pain (embolism).

INTERACTIONS:

Other drugs:
• warfarin, carbamazepine, cyclosporin,
oral contraceptives, phenytoin, steroids,
diabetes medications.

PRESCRIPTION:

Yes.

PERMITTED IN SPORT:

No.

OVERDOSE:

May cause vomiting, tissue swelling and
indigestion.

OTHER INFORMATION:

Very effective medication, but significant
side effects a problem for some patients.
Used for six to nine months only. Does
not cause addiction or dependence.

**See also Cyproterone acetate,
Dydrogesterone, Ethinyloestradiol,
Etonogestrel, HORMONE REPLACEMENT
THERAPY, Medroxyprogesterone acetate,
Oestradiol, Oestriol, Oestrogen, ORAL
CONTRACEPTIVES,Testosterone.**

Dantrolene

TRADE NAME:

Dantrium.

USES:

Muscle spasm caused by cerebral palsy,
stroke, multiple sclerosis or spinal cord
injury.

DOSAGE:

 25mg once a day initially, then
slowly increase as directed by
doctor to a maximum of 100mg
four times a day.

FORMS:

Capsules of 25 and 100mg.

PRECAUTIONS:

Use with caution in pregnancy (B2),
breast feeding and children.
Use with caution in liver disease.
Regular blood tests to check on liver
function recommended.

Do not take if:

 • suffering from severe liver
disease.
• operating machinery or driving
a vehicle.

SIDE EFFECTS:

Common: drowsiness, weakness, dizziness, diarrhoea.
Unusual: constipation, bleeding from bowel, slurred speech, headache, rapid heart rate, depression, urinary frequency, skin sensitised to sunlight.
Severe but rare (stop medication, consult doctor): yellow skin (jaundice).

INTERACTIONS:

Other drugs:
• tranquillisers, verapamil, oral contraceptives.
Other substances:
• reacts adversely with alcohol.

PRESCRIPTION:

Yes.

PERMITTED IN SPORT:

Yes.

OVERDOSE:

May cause drowsiness, irregular heart rate, convulsions and coma. Induce vomiting if medication taken recently and patient alert. Seek urgent medical assistance.

OTHER INFORMATION:

Does not cause addiction or dependence.

Darbepoetin

See Epoetin.

Daunorubicin

TRADE NAMES:

Cerubidin, Daunoxome.

DRUG CLASS:

Cytotoxic.

USES:

Leukaemia, neuroblastoma, other cancers.

DOSAGE:

 As determined by doctor for each patient. Given by drip into vein.

FORMS:

Injection.

PRECAUTIONS:

Must not be used in pregnancy (D). Use with caution in breast feeding.
Second full course must not be used unless clinically essential.
Use with caution in heart, kidney and liver disease.
Regular blood tests to monitor kidney, liver and bone marrow function essential.
Ensure medication does not leak out of drip into surrounding tissues outside vein.
Do not take if:

 • suffering from suppressed bone marrow from radiotherapy or chemotherapy.

SIDE EFFECTS:

Common: nausea, vomiting, hair loss, ulceration of mouth, anus and vagina, inflammation around drip site.
Unusual: anaemia, diarrhoea, belly pain, fever, chills.
Severe but rare (stop medication, consult doctor): heart and kidney damage.

INTERACTIONS:

Other drugs:
• doxorubicin, cyclophosphamide, allopurinol, colchicine, heparin, fluorouracil, dexamethasone.

PRESCRIPTION:

Yes.

PERMITTED IN SPORT:

Yes.

OVERDOSE:

Very serious. Given under strict medical supervision.
See also VINCA ALKALOIDS.

DECONGESTANTS (SYMPATHOMIMETICS)

DISCUSSION:

Medications that clear blocked nose and sinuses in patients with a cold, flu or hay fever.

See Phenylephrine, Pseudoephedrine.

Deflazacort

TRADE NAME:

Calcort.

DRUG CLASS:

Corticosteroid.

USES:

Severe asthma, rheumatoid and other forms of severe arthritis, autoimmune diseases (e.g. Sjögren syndrome), severe allergy reactions and other severe and chronic inflammatory diseases.

DOSAGE:

 Strictly as directed by doctor.

FORMS:

Tablets.

PRECAUTIONS:

Should be used in pregnancy (C), breast feeding and children only on specific medical advice.

Use with caution if under stress and in patients with under active thyroid gland, liver disease, diverticulitis, high blood pressure, myasthenia gravis or kidney disease.

Use for shortest period of time possible. Medication should not be ceased abruptly but dosage should be slowly reduced.

Do not use if:

 • suffering from any form of infection, peptic ulcer or osteoporosis
• having a vaccination.

SIDE EFFECTS:

Most significant side effects occur only with prolonged use of tablets or rectal preparations.

Common: may cause bloating, weight gain, rashes and intestinal disturbances.

Unusual: biochemical disturbances of blood, muscle weakness, bone weakness, impaired wound healing, skin thinning, tendon weakness, peptic ulcers, gullet ulcers, bruising, increased sweating, loss of fat under skin, premature ageing, excess facial hair growth in women, pigmentation of skin and nails, acne, convulsions, headaches, dizziness, growth suppression in children, aggravation of diabetes, worsening of infections, cataracts, aggravation of glaucoma, blood clots in veins and sleeplessness.

Severe but rare (stop medication, consult doctor): any significant side effect should be reported to a doctor immediately.

INTERACTIONS:

Other drugs:
• oral contraceptives, barbiturates, phenytoin and rifampicin.

PRESCRIPTION:

Yes.

PERMITTED IN SPORT:

No.

OVERDOSE:

Medical treatment is required. Serious effects and death rare.

OTHER INFORMATION:

Extremely effective and useful medication if used correctly. Must be used with extreme care under strict medical supervision. Lowest dose and shortest possible course should be used. Not addictive.

Demeclocycline

TRADE NAMES:

Ledermycin.
Deteclo (with tetracycline hydrochloride, chlortetracycline).

DRUG CLASS:

Tetracycline antibiotic.

USES:

Infections caused by susceptible bacteria.

DOSAGE:

 One capsule four times a day.

FORMS:

Capsules, tablets.

PRECAUTIONS:

Not to be used in pregnancy (D) or children under twelve as it may cause permanent staining of teeth of foetus or child. Use with caution in breast feeding. Use with caution in kidney and liver disease.

Do not take if:

 • suffering from severe kidney disease, systemic lupus erythematosus (SLE), Staphylococcal infection.

SIDE EFFECTS:

Common: loss of appetite, nausea, sore mouth, diarrhoea, difficulty in swallowing, inflamed colon.
Unusual: vomiting, inflamed pancreas, rash, secondary fungal infection (thrush).
Severe but rare (stop medication, consult doctor): severe belly pain, severe diarrhoea, tooth discolouration.

INTERACTIONS:

Other drugs:
• anticoagulants, penicillin, antacids, iron, oral contraceptives.
Other substances:
• milk may reduce absorption from gut.

PRESCRIPTION:

Yes.

PERMITTED IN SPORT:

Yes.

OVERDOSE:

Exacerbation of side effects only likely effect.

See also Doxycycline, Methacycline, Minocycline, Tetracycline.

Dequalinium chloride

TRADE NAME:

Labosept.

DRUG CLASS:

Antiseptic.

USES:

Mouth and throat infections, mouth ulcers, denture irritation.

DOSAGE:

 One every two or three hours.

FORMS:

Lozenges.

PRECAUTIONS:

Safe in pregnancy (A), breast feeding and children.

SIDE EFFECTS:

Minimal.

INTERACTIONS:

None significant.

PRESCRIPTION:

No.

PERMITTED IN SPORT:

Yes.

Desferrioxamine

TRADE NAME:

Desferal.

DRUG CLASS:

Detoxifying agent.

USES:

Iron poisoning.

DOSAGE:

 By drip into vein as determined by doctor for each patient.

FORMS:

Injection.

PRECAUTIONS:

Use with caution in pregnancy (B3), breast feeding and children.
Not for long term use.
Not to be given rapidly.
Test eye and ear function regularly.
Use with caution in kidney disease.

Do not take if:

 • iron stores in body are normal.

SIDE EFFECTS:

Common: reaction at injection site, nausea, vomiting, diarrhoea.
Unusual: disturbances to lung, heart, blood, kidney and nerve function.
Increased risk of infection.
Severe but rare (stop medication, consult doctor): growth disturbance in children.

INTERACTIONS:

Other drugs:
• phenothiazines, prochlorperazine, methyldopa, ascorbic acid.
Other substances:
• vitamin C.

PRESCRIPTION:

Yes.

PERMITTED IN SPORT:

Yes.

OVERDOSE:

Excessively low iron levels and organ damage may occur.

Desloratadine

See ANTIHISTAMINES, NON-SEDATING.

Desmopressin acetate

TRADE NAMES:

DDAVP, Desmospray, Desmotabs, Nocutil.

DRUG CLASS:

Antidiuretic.

USES:

Diabetes insipidus, bed wetting, abnormally frequent passing of urine.

DOSAGE:

 Nasal spray: 10mcg to 40mcg a day.
Tablets: one or two at night.

FORMS:

Nasal spray, tablets, injection.

PRECAUTIONS:

Use with caution in pregnancy (B2), breast feeding and children.
Use nasal spray with caution in nasal infection and hay fever.
Use all forms with caution in heart disease and after operations.
Lower doses necessary in elderly.

Do not take if:

 • suffering from some types of von Willebrand's disease, frequent passing of urine due to habit or psychological factors, heart failure.

SIDE EFFECTS:

Common: headache, stomach pain, nausea.
Unusual: fluid retention, rapid heart rate, low blood pressure, headache, nausea, gut cramps, nasal congestion.
Severe but rare (stop medication, consult doctor): convulsions.

INTERACTIONS:

Other drugs:
• glibenclamide, clofibrate, indomethacin, tricyclic antidepressants, chlorpromazine, carbamazepine, chlorpropamide.

PRESCRIPTION:

Yes.

PERMITTED IN SPORT:

Yes.

OVERDOSE:

No serious effects expected.

OTHER INFORMATION:

One of the few effective treatments for the rare condition of diabetes insipidus which is a totally separate condition to sugar diabetes (diabetes mellitus). Very effective treatment for bed wetting.
See also Vasopressin.

Desogestrel
See ORAL CONTRACEPTIVES.

Desoxymethasone

TRADE NAMES:

Stiedex LP.
Stiedex Lotion (with salicylic acid).

DRUG CLASS:

Corticosteroid.

USES:

Inflammation of skin (eczema, dermatitis etc.).

DOSAGE:

 Apply two or three times a day.

FORMS:

Cream, lotion.

PRECAUTIONS:

Skin preparations safe in pregnancy, breast feeding and children.
Avoid eyes.
Use for shortest period of time possible.

SIDE EFFECTS:

Most significant side effects occur only with prolonged use.
Common: rarely cause adverse reactions.
Unusual: thinning of skin, scarring of skin, premature ageing of skin.

INTERACTIONS:

None significant.

PRESCRIPTION:

Yes.

PERMITTED IN SPORT:

Yes.

OVERDOSE:

Exacerbation of side effects likely.

OTHER INFORMATION:

Extremely effective and useful medication if used correctly. Lowest dose and shortest possible course should be used. Not addictive.
See also Betamethasone, Hydrocortisone, Methylprednisolone, Mometasone, Triamcinolone.

Dexamethasone

TRADE NAMES:

Decadron, Dexsol, Minims Dexamethasone.
Dexa-Rhinaspray Duo (dexamethasone isonicotinate with tramazoline).

Maxidex (with hypromellose).
Maxitrol (with hypromellose, neomycin, polymyxin B).
Otomize (with acetic acid, neomycin).
Sofradex (with framycetin, gramicidin).
Tobradex (with tobramycin).

DRUG CLASS:

Corticosteroid.

USES:

Severe inflammation of eyes, ears and nose.
Severe asthma, rheumatoid and other forms of severe arthritis, autoimmune diseases (e.g. Sjögren syndrome), severe allergy reactions, other severe and chronic inflammatory diseases.

DOSAGE:

 Eye drops: insert every two to four hours.
Ear drops: two drops three times a day.
Nose spray: one spray in each nostril two to four times a day.
Tablets: 0.5mg to 4mg a day strictly as directed by doctor.

FORMS:

Injection, tablets, eye drops, ear drops, nose spray.

PRECAUTIONS:

Should be used in pregnancy (C), breast feeding and children only on specific medical advice.
Eye, nose and ear preparations safe in pregnancy, breast feeding and children.
Use tablets with caution if under stress, and in patients with under active thyroid gland, liver disease, diverticulitis, high blood pressure, myasthenia gravis, or kidney disease.
Avoid eyes with all forms except eye drops.
Use for shortest period of time possible.

Do not use if:

 • suffering from any form of infection, peptic ulcer, or osteoporosis
• having a vaccination

SIDE EFFECTS:

Common: tablets and injection—may cause bloating, weight gain, rashes and intestinal disturbances.
Eye, ear and nose drops rarely cause adverse reactions.
Unusual: tablets and injections—biochemical disturbances of blood, muscle weakness, bone weakness, impaired wound healing, skin thinning, tendon weakness, peptic ulcers, gullet ulcers, bruising, increased sweating, loss of fat under skin, premature ageing, excess facial hair growth in women, pigmentation of skin and nails, acne, convulsions, headaches, dizziness, growth suppression in children, aggravation of diabetes, worsening of infections, cataracts, aggravation of glaucoma, blood clots in veins and sleeplessness.
Most significant side effects occur only with prolonged use of tablets.
Medication should not be ceased abruptly, but dosage should be slowly reduced.
Severe but rare (stop medication, consult doctor): any significant side effect should be reported to a doctor immediately.

INTERACTIONS:

Other drugs:
• tablets—oral contraceptives, barbiturates, phenytoin, rifampicin.
Herbs:
• echinacea.

PRESCRIPTION:

Yes.

PERMITTED IN SPORT:

Tablets and injections: no.
Eye, nose and ear drops: yes.

OVERDOSE:

Medical treatment is required. Serious effects and death rare.

OTHER INFORMATION:

Extremely effective and useful medication if used correctly. Tablets must be used with extreme care under strict medical supervision. Lowest dose and shortest possible course should be used. Not addictive.

See also CORTICOSTEROIDS, Cortisone acetate, Fludrocortisone, Flumethasone, Fluorometholone, Fluticasone, Hydrocortisone, Methylprednisolone, Prednisolone.

Dexamphetamine

TRADE NAME:

Dexedrine.

DRUG CLASS:

Stimulant, Amphetamine.

USES:

Hyperactivity disorders in children, narcolepsy.

DOSAGE:

 0.5mg to 60mg a day in several doses depending upon age, condition and response.

FORMS:

Tablets of 5mg (white).

PRECAUTIONS:

Should be used in pregnancy only if medically essential. Not for use in breast feeding. May be used in children over three years.
Use with caution in kidney disease.

Do not take if:

- suffering from heart disease, high blood pressure, overactive thyroid gland, anxiety, excitability, Tourette syndrome or twitching
- MAOI taken within two weeks
- history of drug abuse.

SIDE EFFECTS:

Common: drug dependence, dry mouth, restlessness, difficulty passing urine, sleeplessness, tremor, loss of appetite, twitching, diarrhoea, nausea, headache. *Unusual:* rapid heart rate, high blood pressure, irregular heart beat, angina.

INTERACTIONS:

Other drugs:
- urinary alkalinisers, MAOI, tricyclic antidepressants, antihistamines, medications that lower blood pressure, chlorpromazine, ethosuximide, haloperidol, lithium, pethidine, dextropropoxyphene, phenobarbitone, phenytoin.

Herbs:
- ma huang.

Other substances:
- alcohol.

PRESCRIPTION:

Yes (restricted).

PERMITTED IN SPORT:

No.

OVERDOSE:

Very serious. May cause vomiting, agitation, tremors, twitching, confusion, hallucinations, convulsions, coma and death. Administer activated charcoal or induce vomiting if tablets taken recently. Seek urgent medical attention.

OTHER INFORMATION:

May be addictive if used inappropriately. Very effective in improving the lives of some children with hyperactivity, but there are concerns that it may be used when not necessary or excessively. All forms of behaviour therapy should be tried before this is used as a last resort. Treatment rarely necessary into adult life.

Dexketoprofen

TRADE NAMES:

Keral.

DRUG CLASS:

NSAID (Nonsteroidal anti-inflammatories drug).

USES:

All forms of arthritis, inflammatory disorders, back pain, dental pain, menstrual pain.

DOSAGE:

 One tablet, every four to six hours with food.

FORMS:

Tablets (white) of 25mg.

PRECAUTIONS:

Should not be used in pregnancy (C) unless medically essential. Breast feeding should be ceased if necessary to use NSAID. Not for use in children.

Use tablets and capsules with caution in psychiatricaly disturbed patients, epilepsy, severe infection, heart failure and kidney disease.

Lower doses required in elderly, who may suffer more side effects.

Do not take if:

- suffering from peptic ulcer at present or in recent past
- due for surgery (including dental surgery)
- suffering from bleeding disorder or anaemia.

SIDE EFFECTS:

Common: stomach discomfort, diarrhoea, constipation, heartburn, nausea, headache, dizziness.

Unusual: blurred vision, stomach ulcer, ringing noise in ears, retention of fluid, swelling of tissue, drowsiness, itch, rash, shortness of breath.

Severe but rare (stop medication, consult doctor): vomiting blood, passing blood in faeces, other unusual bleeding, asthma induced by medication.

INTERACTIONS:

Other drugs:
- must never be used with anticoagulants (e.g. warfarin)
- probenecid, diuretics, lithium, methotrexate, beta-blockers, ACE inhibitors, digoxin, cyclosporin, diabetes medication (hypoglycaemics), steroids.

Herbs:
- feverfew.

PRESCRIPTION:

Yes.

PERMITTED IN SPORT:

Yes.

OVERDOSE:

Causes nausea, vomiting, severe headache, dizziness, confusion and convulsions. Administer activated charcoal or induce vomiting if taken recently. Seek medical assistance.

OTHER INFORMATION:

Significant side effects (particularly on the stomach) in about 5% of patients. Limit use.

See also Acemetacin, Azapropazone, Diclofenac, Diflunisal, Etodolac, Felbinac, Fenbufen, Fenoprofen, Flurbiprofen, Ibuprofen, Indomethacin, Ketoprofen, Meloxicam, Nabumetone, Naproxen, NSAID, Phenylbutazone, Piroxicam, Salicylic acid, Sulindac, Tenoxicam, Tiaprofenic Acid.

Dextran

See EYE LUBRICANTS.

Dextranomer

TRADE NAME:

Debrisan.

USES:

Ulcers and infected or weeping wounds.

DOSAGE:

 Apply every one to three days.

FORMS:

Micro beads, paste.

PRECAUTIONS:

Safe in pregnancy, breast feeding and children.
No other precautions.

SIDE EFFECTS:

Minimal.

INTERACTIONS:

None significant.

PRESCRIPTION:

No.

PERMITTED IN SPORT:

Yes.

OVERDOSE:

Unlikely to have serious effects if swallowed.

Dextromoramide

TRADE NAME:

Palfium.

DRUG CLASS:

Narcotic, Analgesic.

USES:

Severe pain.

DOSAGE:

 One to four tablets as required for pain before meals. Patient should lie down for 30 minutes after first dose.

FORMS:

Tablets of 5mg (white) and 10mg (peach).

PRECAUTIONS:

Should not be used in the last few weeks of pregnancy (C) as medication may cause difficulty in breathing in newborn infant. Use with caution in breast feeding and children.
Not designed for prolonged use except in patients with terminal disease.

Do not take if:

- suffering from severe lung disease, low blood pressure
- operating machinery, driving a vehicle or undertaking tasks that require concentration.

SIDE EFFECTS:

Common: lightheadedness, dizziness, drowsiness, fainting, nausea.
Unusual: vomiting, difficulty in breathing, perspiration.

INTERACTIONS:

Other drugs:
- MAOI, barbiturates, tranquillisers, anaesthetics.
Other substances:
- do not use alcohol with dextromoramide.

PRESCRIPTION:

Yes (very restricted).

PERMITTED IN SPORT:

No.

OVERDOSE:

Serious. Administer activated charcoal or induce vomiting if medication taken recently and patient alert. May cause drowsiness, difficulty in breathing, convulsions, coma and death. Especially dangerous when taken with other sedatives including alcohol. Seek urgent medical assistance. Antidote available.

OTHER INFORMATION:

May cause dependence or addiction if used inappropriately.

See also Alfentanil, Buprenorphine, Codeine, Dextropropoxyphene, Fentanyl, Heroin, Hydromorphone, Methadone, Morphine, Oxycodone, Pentazocine, Pethidine.

Dextropropoxyphene

TRADE NAMES:

Doloxene.
Distalgesic (with paracetamol).

DRUG CLASS:

Narcotic, Analgesic.

USES:

Pain relief.

DOSAGE:

 One or two capsules or tablets, three or four times a day.

FORMS:

Tablets, capsules.

PRECAUTIONS:

Should only be used in pregnancy (C) if medically essential. May cause difficulty in breathing of newborn if used during labour. Use with caution in breast feeding. Not for use in children.
Use with caution in severe lung disease. Designed for short term use.

Do not take if:

 • suffering from alcoholism
• operating machinery or driving a vehicle.

SIDE EFFECTS:

Common: sleeplessness, mood changes, rash, dizziness, sedation, nausea.

Unusual: constipation, belly pains, headache, lightheadedness, weakness, blurred vision.
Severe but rare (stop medication, consult doctor): yellow skin (jaundice).

INTERACTIONS:

Other drugs:
• sedatives, anticoagulants, orphenadrine, beta-blockers, diazepam, phenytoin, carbamazepine.
Other substances:
• do not use with alcohol.

PRESCRIPTION:

Yes.

PERMITTED IN SPORT:

No.

OVERDOSE:

Serious. Induce vomiting if medication taken recently and patient alert. Symptoms include drowsiness, convulsions, reduced breathing, low blood pressure, coma and possibly death. Seek emergency medical assistance.

OTHER INFORMATION:

Widely used for many decades to treat moderate severity pain. May cause dependence if used long term and inappropriately.

See also Alfentanil, Buprenorphine, Codeine, Dextromoramide, Fentanyl, Heroin, Hydromorphone, Methadone, Morphine, Oxycodone, Pentazocine, Pethidine.

DIABETES MEDICATIONS

See HYPOGLYCAEMICS, Insulin.

Diazepam

TRADE NAMES:

Diazemuls, Diazepam Rectubes, Stesolid, Valclair.

DRUG CLASS:

Benzodiazepine (Anxiolytic).

USES:

Short term relief of anxiety, relief of muscle spasm, withdrawal from alcohol dependence, preoperative sedation, convulsions.

DOSAGE:

 One to four tablets a day in one or more doses. Do not exceed dose directed by doctor.

FORMS:

Tablets of 2mg and 5mg, rectal infusion, injection.

PRECAUTIONS:

Should be used with caution in pregnancy (C), but not at all if delivery of infant imminent as it may decrease desire to breathe in newborn infant. Should be used with caution in breast feeding. Not for use in children.

Lower dose required in elderly.

Should be used intermittently and not constantly as dependency may develop.

Use with caution in glaucoma, heart disease, kidney or liver disease, psychiatric conditions, depression and epilepsy.

Do not take if:

- suffering from severe lung disease, confusion, myasthenia gravis, sleep apnoea or psychotic illness (e.g. schizophrenia)
- tendency to addiction or dependence
- operating machinery, driving a vehicle or undertaking tasks that require concentration and alertness.

SIDE EFFECTS:

Common: reduced alertness, dependence.
Unusual: incoordination, tremor, muscle weakness, confusion, increased risk of falls in elderly, rash, low blood pressure, nausea, muscle weakness, memory loss, nausea, diarrhoea.
Severe but rare (stop medication, consult doctor): jaundice (yellow skin).

INTERACTIONS:

Other drugs:
- sedatives, other anxiolytics, disulfiram, cimetidine, anticonvulsants (e.g. phenytoin), ketoconazole, fluvoxamine, omeprazole, cisapride, anticholinergics.

Herbs:
- guarana, kava kava, passionflower, St John's wort, valerian.

Other substances:
- reacts with alcohol to cause sedation and confusion.

PRESCRIPTION:

Yes.

PERMITTED IN SPORT:

Yes.

OVERDOSE:

Seldom life threatening. May cause drowsiness, confusion and coma. Induce vomiting if tablets taken recently. Seek medical assistance.

OTHER INFORMATION:

Widely used, and very safe if used correctly. Dependency becoming a significant problem, particularly in elderly, due to overuse. First introduced in 1960s.

See also Buspirone, Clobazam, Lorazepam.

Diazoxide

TRADE NAME:

Eudemine.

DRUG CLASS:

Vasodilator, Antihypertensive, Thiazide diuretic.

USES:

Severe high blood pressure.

DOSAGE:

 Injection into vein every four hours as necessary.

FORMS:

Injection.

PRECAUTIONS:

Use only if essential in pregnancy (C).
Use with caution in breast feeding and children.
Use with caution in kidney disease, brain damage, severe heart disease, diabetes and gout.
Patient must be monitored very carefully during use.

Do not take if:

 • suffering from arteriovenous shunt, sensitive to thiazides.

SIDE EFFECTS:

Common: high blood sugar, fluid retention, low blood pressure, headache, sensation of warmth, rapid heart rate.
Unusual: high blood salt levels, vomiting, diarrhoea.
Severe but rare (stop medication, consult doctor): heart attack, stroke, coma.

INTERACTIONS:

Other drugs:
• thiazide diuretics, anticoagulants, other medications that lower blood pressure.

PRESCRIPTION:

Yes.

PERMITTED IN SPORT:

Yes.

OVERDOSE:

Extremely serious. Only given under close medical supervision.

OTHER INFORMATION:

Only used in cases of extremely high, life threatening high blood pressure.
See also Betahistine, Guanethidine, Nicotinic Acid.

Dibromopropamidine isethionate

See Propamidine isethionate.

Diclofenac

TRADE NAMES:

Dicloflex, Diclomax, Motifene, Volsaid, Voltarol.
Arthrotec (with misoprostol).
Solaraze (with hyaluronate).

DRUG CLASS:

NSAID (Nonsteroidal anti-inflammatories drug).

USES:

All forms of arthritis, inflammatory disorders, gout, back pain, ankylosing spondylitis, bone pain, prevention of miosis (eye contraction) during eye surgery, skin keratoses.

DOSAGE:

 Tablets: one tablet, two or three times a day with food.
Gels: rub into affected area three or four times a day for up to two weeks.
Eye drops: as directed by eye doctor.
Solaraze: apply twice a day for maximum of three months.

FORMS:

Tablets, gel, eye drops.

PRECAUTIONS:

Should not be used in pregnancy (C) unless medically essential. Breast feeding should be ceased if necessary to use NSAID. Not for use in children under two. Gel safe in pregnancy.

Use tablets and capsules with caution in psychiatricaly disturbed patients, epilepsy, severe infection, heart failure and kidney disease.

Lower doses required in elderly, who may suffer more side effects.

Do not take if:

- suffering from peptic ulcer at present or in recent past
- due for surgery (including dental surgery)
- suffering from bleeding disorder or anaemia.

SIDE EFFECTS:

Common: gel—minimal.
Other forms—stomach discomfort, diarrhoea, constipation, heartburn, nausea, headache, dizziness.
Unusual: blurred vision, stomach ulcer, ringing noise in ears, retention of fluid, swelling of tissue, drowsiness, itch, rash, shortness of breath.
Severe but rare (stop medication, consult doctor): vomiting blood, passing blood in faeces, other unusual bleeding, asthma induced by medication.

INTERACTIONS:

Other drugs:
- must never be used with anticoagulants (e.g. warfarin)
- probenecid, diuretics, lithium, methotrexate, beta-blockers, ACE inhibitors, digoxin, cyclosporin, diabetes medication (hypoglycaemics), steroids.
- gel has minimal interactions.

Herbs:
- feverfew.

PRESCRIPTION:

Tablets: yes.
Gel: no.

PERMITTED IN SPORT:

Yes.

OVERDOSE:

Causes nausea, vomiting, severe headache, dizziness, confusion and convulsions. Administer activated charcoal or induce vomiting if taken recently. Seek medical assistance.

OTHER INFORMATION:

Extensively used to give excellent relief to a wide variety of inflammatory conditions. Significant side effects (particularly on the stomach) in about 5% of patients. Limit their use. Special forms with added misoprostol reduces stomach effects. Minimal side effects with gel, but less effective.

See also Aceclofenac, Acemetacin, Aspirin, Azapropazone, Dexketoprofen, Diflunisal, Etodolac, Felbinac, Fenbufen, Fenoprofen, Flurbiprofen, Ibuprofen, Indomethacin, Ketoprofen, Ketorolac trometanol,Mefenamic acid, Meloxicam, Nabumetone, Naproxen, Phenylbutazone, Piroxicam, Salicylic acid, Sulindac, Tenoxicam, Tiaprofenic Acid, Tolfenamic acid.

Dicyclomine

TRADE NAMES:

Merbentyl.
Kolanticon (with dimethicone and antacids).

DRUG CLASS:

Anticholinergic, Spasmolytic.

USES:

Spasm of the intestine, irritable bowel syndrome, colic.

DOSAGE:

 Tablets: one to four tablets, three or four times a day.
Mixture: 5 to 20mLs three or four times a day.

FORMS:

Merbentyl: tablets, mixture.
Infacol-C: mixture.

PRECAUTIONS:

Should only be used in pregnancy if medically indicated.
Should not be used while breast feeding.
Should not be used in children under six months of age.
Use with caution in glaucoma, enlarged prostate, reflux oesophagitis and hiatus hernia.

Do not take if:

- suffering from difficulty in passing urine
- suffering from ulcerative colitis, intestinal obstruction or intestinal underactivity
- suffering from myasthenia gravis.

SIDE EFFECTS:

Common: dry mouth, difficulty in passing urine, blurred vision.
Unusual: rapid heart rate, loss of taste, headache, nervousness, weakness, dizziness, constipation, sleeplessness, bloating, rashes.
Severe but rare (stop medication, consult doctor): cessation of breathing in infants.

INTERACTIONS:

None significant.

PRESCRIPTION:

Merbentyl: yes
Kolanticon: no.

PERMITTED IN SPORT:

Yes.

OVERDOSE:

Causes headache, dizziness, vomiting, hot dry skin and difficulty in swallowing.
See also Alverine, Mebeverine.

Didanosine

TRADE NAME:

Videx.

DRUG CLASS:

Antiviral.

USES:

Treatment of advanced AIDS (Acquired Immune Deficiency Syndrome).

DOSAGE:

 100 to 200mg twice a day on an empty stomach.

FORMS:

Chewable tablets (25mg, 100mg), capsules (125mg, 200mg, 250mg, 400mg), powder for solution.

PRECAUTIONS:

Should not be used in pregnancy (B2) and children unless medically essential.
Breast feeding should be ceased before use.
Use with caution in kidney and liver disease, pancreatitis.

SIDE EFFECTS:

Common: diarrhoea, nausea, vomiting.
Unusual: pins and needles, chills, fever, headache, pancreatitis, muscle pain, tiredness, convulsions, confusion, sleeplessness, rash, itch, arthritis.

INTERACTIONS:

Other drugs:
- ketoconazole, pentamidine, tetracycline, phenylalanine, allopurinol, stavudine, hydroxyurea (serious).

PRESCRIPTION:

Yes.

PERMITTED IN SPORT:

Yes.

OVERDOSE:

Liver damage likely. Seek medical assistance.

OTHER INFORMATION:

Introduced in 1993 to help slow the progress (but not cure) of HIV/AIDS.

See also Abacavir, Delavirdine, Didanosine, Efavirenz, Indinavir, Lamivudine, Nelfinavir, Nevirapine, Ritonavir, Saquinavir, Stavudine, Tenofovir, Zalcitabine, Zidovudine.

Diethylamine salicylate

TRADE NAME:

Algesal.
Numerous other ointments, creams and liniments.

DRUG CLASS:

Rubefacient.

USES:

Temporary relief of pain (e.g. muscular, arthritic, gums).

DOSAGE:

 Massage into clean dry skin two or three times a day.

FORMS:

Cream, spray.

PRECAUTIONS:

Safe in pregnancy and breast feeding.
Use with caution in children under five years.
Avoid contact with eyes, mouth, nose, anus and vagina.
Use sparingly on face, skin folds and thin skin.
May stain clothing.
Do not use if:

 • suffering from broken or infected skin.

SIDE EFFECTS:

Minimal.

INTERACTIONS:

None significant.

PRESCRIPTION:

No.

PERMITTED IN SPORT:

Yes.

OVERDOSE:

May have serious effects in the unlikely event of the liniment being swallowed.
See also Salicylic acid.

Diflucortolone

TRADE NAME:

Nerisone.

DRUG CLASS:

Corticosteroid.

USES:

Inflammation of skin (eczema, dermatitis etc.).

DOSAGE:

 Apply two or three times a day.

FORMS:

Cream, ointment.

PRECAUTIONS:

Safe on skin in pregnancy (C), breast feeding and children over three years.
Avoid eyes.
Use for shortest period of time possible.
Do not use if:

 • suffering from any form of skin infection
• having a vaccination.

SIDE EFFECTS:

Common: minimal.
Unusual: thinning of skin, premature

ageing, itching, scarring of skin. Most significant side effects occur only with prolonged use of tablets or injections.

INTERACTIONS:

None significant.

PRESCRIPTION:

Yes.

PERMITTED IN SPORT:

Yes.

See also Betamethasone, Desoxymethasone, Hydrocortisone, Methylprednisolone, Mometasone, Triamcinolone.

Diflunisal

TRADE NAME:

Dolobid.

DRUG CLASS:

NSAID (Nonsteroidal anti-inflammatories drug).

USES:

All forms of arthritis, inflammatory disorders, gout, back pain, bone pain, general pain relief.

DOSAGE:

 One tablet twice a day with food.

FORMS:

Tablets of 250mg (peach) and 500mg (orange).

PRECAUTIONS:

Should not be used in pregnancy (C) unless medically essential. Breast feeding should be ceased if necessary to use. Not for use in children.
Use with caution in Reye syndrome, epilepsy, severe infection, high blood pressure, heart failure and kidney disease.

Lower doses required in elderly, who may suffer more side effects.

Do not take if:

- suffering from peptic ulcer at present or in recent past
- due for surgery (including dental surgery)
- suffering from bleeding disorder or anaemia
- urticaria.

SIDE EFFECTS:

Common: stomach discomfort, diarrhoea, constipation, heartburn, nausea, headache, dizziness.
Unusual: blurred vision, stomach ulcer, ringing noise in ears, retention of fluid, swelling of tissue, drowsiness, itch, rash, shortness of breath.
Severe but rare (stop medication, consult doctor): vomiting blood, passing blood in faeces, other unusual bleeding, asthma induced by medication.

INTERACTIONS:

Other drugs:
- must never be used with anticoagulants (e.g. warfarin)
- Probenecid, diuretics, lithium, methotrexate, beta-blockers, ACE inhibitors.

PRESCRIPTION:

Yes.

PERMITTED IN SPORT:

Yes.

OVERDOSE:

Causes nausea, vomiting, severe headache, dizziness, confusion and convulsions. Administer activated charcoal or induce vomiting if taken recently. Seek medical assistance.

OTHER INFORMATION:

Used to give relief to a wide variety of inflammatory conditions. Significant side effects (particularly on the stomach) in about 5% of patients. Limit their use.

See also Aceclofenac, Acemetacin, Azapropazone, Dexketoprofen, Diclofenac,

Etodolac, Felbinac, Fenbufen, Fenoprofen, Flurbiprofen, Ibuprofen, Indomethacin, Ketoprofen, Meloxicam, Nabumetone, Naproxen, NSAID, Phenylbutazone, Piroxicam, Salicylic acid, Sulindac, Tenoxicam.

Digitalis

See Digoxin.

Digoxin

TRADE NAME:

Lanoxin.

DRUG CLASS:

Cardiac glycoside.

USES:

Heart failure, irregular heart beat originating in heart atrium (atrial fibrillation).

DOSAGE:

 Must be carefully individualised by regular blood tests. Usually one or two tablets once a day.

FORMS:

Tablets of 62.5, 125 and 250mg, elixir, injection.

PRECAUTIONS:

Safe in pregnancy (A), breast feeding and children.
Should be used with care in thyroid disease, malabsorption, poor kidney function and elderly.
Regular blood tests recommended to check blood level of medication.

Do not take if:

- suffering from heart block, very rapid heart rate, very slow heart rate.

SIDE EFFECTS:

Common: usually associated with overdosage. Loss of appetite, nausea.
Unusual: vomiting, weakness, breast enlargement (both sexes), depression, headache.
Severe but rare (stop medication, consult doctor): unusual bleeding, slow heart rate.

INTERACTIONS:

Other drugs:
- blood levels of digoxin increased by diuretics, lithium, steroids, carbenoxolone, amiodarone, captopril, flecainide, prazosin, quinidine, spironolactone, tetracyclines, erythromycin, propantheline and other drugs
- blood levels of digoxin decreased by antacids, kaolin, pectin, bulking agents, laxatives, cholestyramine, sulfasalazine, neomycin, rifampicin, phenytoin, metoclopramide, penicillamine and other drugs
- variable effects from calcium channel blockers.

Herbs:
- St John's wort, fenugreek, liquorice, guarana, hawthorn, ginseng, golden seal, kyushin, parsley plantain, uzara root.

PRESCRIPTION:

Yes.

PERMITTED IN SPORT:

Yes.

OVERDOSE:

May result in life threatening heart beat irregularities. Early symptom of overdosage is a slow heart rate. Administer activated charcoal or induce vomiting if tablets taken recently. Seek urgent medical assistance.

OTHER INFORMATION:

In 1785, William Withering identified the active ingredient of an English folk remedy for dropsy (heart failure) distilled from the purple foxglove as digitalis. This has been further refined into digoxin, which has been the most important medication for the treatment of heart disease for over two centuries.

Dihydrocodeine

TRADE NAMES:

DF118, DHC Continus.
Remedeine (with paracetamol).

DRUG CLASS:

Analgesic.

USES:

Severe pain.

DOSAGE:

 One or two tablets two or three times a day.

FORMS:

Tablets.

PRECAUTIONS:

Safe to use in pregnancy (A), breast feeding and children over two years.
Use with caution in severe lung disease.

SIDE EFFECTS:

Common: constipation, nausea, dizziness, headache when medication wears off.

INTERACTIONS:

Other drugs:
• sedatives, MAOI.
Other substances:
• alcohol.

PRESCRIPTION:

Yes.

PERMITTED IN SPORT:

Yes.

OVERDOSE:

Sedation and constipation only likely effects.

OTHER INFORMATION:

Safe and effective. Risk of dependence if used long term in high doses.

See also Codeine.

Dihydrotachysterol

TRADE NAME:

AT-10.

USES:

Conditions associated with low levels of calcium in the body
(e.g. hypoparathyroidism, rickets, osteomalacia, some forms of kidney and bowel failure).

DOSAGE:

 Must be determined by doctor for each patient.

FORMS:

Solution.

PRECAUTIONS:

Use with caution in pregnancy, breast feeding and children.
Use with caution in kidney stones.
Regular blood tests to check level of calcium necessary.

SIDE EFFECTS:

Common: minimal at correct dose.

INTERACTIONS:

Other drugs:
• thiazide diuretics, digoxin.

PRESCRIPTION:

Yes.

PERMITTED IN SPORT:

Yes.

OVERDOSE:

May cause effects for many weeks including weakness, fatigue, nausea, vomiting, diarrhoea, headache, and increased frequency of passing urine.
Long term overdosage may cause calcium deposits in kidneys, heart, lungs, skin and blood vessels. Give copious fluids and

seek medical attention.

OTHER INFORMATION:

Does not cause addiction or dependence. Increases absorption of calcium from intestine.

Diltiazem

TRADE NAMES:

Adizem, Angitil SR, Dilzem, Slozem, Tildiem, Viazem XL, Zemtard XL.

DRUG CLASS:

Calcium channel blocker (calcium antagonist).

USES:

High blood pressure, angina.

DOSAGE:

 120 to 240mg a day in one or more doses, depending on formulation.

FORMS:

Tablets, capsules, injection.

PRECAUTIONS:

Should only be used in pregnancy (C) and breast feeding if medically essential. Not designed for use in children.

Do not take if:

 • suffering from severe heart failure, low blood pressure, atrial flutter or fibrillation.

SIDE EFFECTS:

Common: constipation, tiredness, headache, dizziness, indigestion, swelling of feet and ankles.
Unusual: flushing, palpitations, slow heart rate, scalp irritation, depression, flushes, nightmares, excess wind.
Severe but rare (stop medication, consult doctor): fainting.

INTERACTIONS:

Other drugs:
• beta-blockers (e.g. propranolol), cyclosporin, digoxin, cimetidine, diazepam, amiodarone, quinidine, rifampicin, phenytoin, cisapride, theophylline, terbutaline, salbutamol, diltiazem.
• additive effect with other medications for high blood pressure.
Herbs:
• goldenseal, guarana, hawthorn, Korean ginseng, liquorice.
Other substances:
• smoking may aggravate conditions that these medications are treating.
• grapefruit juice.

PRESCRIPTION:

Yes.

PERMITTED IN SPORT:

Yes.

OVERDOSE:

May continue to be absorbed for up to 48 hours after overdose. Administer activated charcoal or induce vomiting. Purging should be encouraged to eliminate drug from gut. Overdose may cause low blood pressure, irregular heart rhythm, difficulty in breathing, heart attack and death. Obtain urgent medical attention.

OTHER INFORMATION:

Commonly used as a first line medication in high blood pressure and to prevent angina.

See also Amlodipine, Felodipine, Nifedipine, Nimodipine, Verapamil.

Dimethicone
(Simethicone)

TRADE NAMES:

Infacol.
Altacite Plus (with hydrotalcite).
Asilone, Maalox (with antacids).

Conotrane (with benzalkonium chloride).
Kolanticon (with dicyclomine and antacids).
Siopel (with cetrimide).
Spirilon, Vasogen (with zinc oxide).
Timodine (with nystatin and hydrocortisone).
Also found in numerous other preparations.

USES:

Skin protection, burping, indigestion, heartburn, dyspepsia, peptic ulcer.

DOSAGE:

 Skin preparations: apply freely as required.
Mixtures: use three or four times a day.

FORMS:

Cream, mixture, gel, solution, skin spray.

PRECAUTIONS:

Safe to use in pregnancy, breast feeding and children.

SIDE EFFECTS:

None.

INTERACTIONS:

Other drugs:
• tetracycline antibiotics.

PRESCRIPTION:

No.

PERMITTED IN SPORT:

Yes.

Dinoprostone

TRADE NAMES:

Propess, Prostin.

USES:

Inducing labour in late pregnancy.

DOSAGE:

 As determined by doctor for each patient.

FORMS:

Vaginal gel, tablets, pessary.

PRECAUTIONS:

Not to be used until late in pregnancy (C).
Use with caution in liver, heart and kidney disease.
Use with caution in asthma, epilepsy and glaucoma.
Contractions of uterus and health of baby must be monitored regularly.

Do not use if:

• suffering from ruptured membranes around the baby, head of baby is high, previous pregnancies delivered by Caesarean section, patient has had surgery to uterus, breech or other inappropriate presentation, abnormal vaginal bleeding, more than five previous child births.

SIDE EFFECTS:

Common: excessive contractions of uterus, altered heart rate in baby, nausea, diarrhoea, excess bleeding after delivery.
Unusual: infection after delivery.
Severe but rare: lung embolism.

INTERACTIONS:

Other drugs:
• oxytocin, alcohol.

PRESCRIPTION:

Yes.

OVERDOSE:

Excessive contractions of uterus may lead to rupture of the uterus, a condition which is potentially fatal to mother and child.

OTHER INFORMATION:

Normally used when a woman is overdue for delivery and the health of the baby is being affected by a prolonged pregnancy.

Diphenoxylate hydrochloride

TRADE NAMES:

Lomotil, Tropergen (with atropine sulfate).

DRUG CLASS:

Antidiarrhoeal.

USES:

Diarrhoea.

DOSAGE:

 Two tablets, three or four times a day as required for diarrhoea.

FORMS:

Tablets.

PRECAUTIONS:

Should not be used in the last part of pregnancy (C). Should be used with caution in breast feeding.
Should not be used in children under 12 years.

Do not take if:

- suffering from diarrhoea caused by use of antibiotics.
- suffering from jaundice, ulcerative colitis, Crohn's disease, bacterial colitis or amoebic colitis.

SIDE EFFECTS:

Common: tiredness, dizziness, confusion, rapid heart rate.
Unusual: restlessness, mood changes, headache, tissue swelling, rash, vomiting, belly discomfort.

INTERACTIONS:

Other drugs:
- interacts with barbiturates, tranquillisers and monoamine oxidase inhibitors (MAOI).

Other substances:
- should not be taken with alcohol.

PRESCRIPTION:

Yes.

PERMITTED IN SPORT:

Yes.

OVERDOSE:

Serious. May cause dry skin and mouth, restlessness, rapid heart rate, coma and reduced breathing. Seek urgent medical attention.

OTHER INFORMATION:

Possibility of addiction with prolonged use. Very effective medication.

See also Atropine, Codeine, Kaolin, Loperamide, Pectin.

Diphtheria vaccine

TRADE NAMES:

Diftavax.
ACT-HiB DTP, Infanrix-HiB (with haemophilus influenzae B, tetanus and whooping cough vaccines).
Infanrix (with tetanus and whooping cough vaccines).

DRUG CLASS:

Vaccine.

USES:

Prevention of diphtheria (life threatening throat infection).

DOSAGE:

 Three doses two months apart at two, four and six months of age; repeat at 18 months, five years and then every ten years.

FORMS:

Injection.

PRECAUTIONS:

May be used safely in pregnancy (A), breast feeding and children.

SIDE EFFECTS:

Common: local redness, soreness and lump at injection site; fever.
Unusual: tiredness, irritability.

INTERACTIONS:

None significant.

PRESCRIPTION:

Yes.

PERMITTED IN SPORT:

Yes.

OVERDOSE:

No serious effect expected if unintentional additional dose given.

OTHER INFORMATION:

Normally given in combination with other vaccines. Should be given to all infants starting at two months of age. Diphtheria is a very serious infectious disease causing severe and often fatal throat infection. It can be prevented by vaccination.

Dipipanone

TRADE NAME:

Diconal (with cyclizine).

DRUG CLASS:

Narcotic.

USES:

Moderate to severe pain.

DOSAGE:

 One tablet, two or three times a day.

FORMS:

Tablet (pink).

PRECAUTIONS:

Not for use in children.
Use with caution in pregnancy and breast feeding.
Use with caution in patients with history of narcotic dependency.

Use with caution in under active thyroid gland, low blood pressure, diabetes and enlarged prostate gland.

Do not take if:

 • suffering from severe lung disease, alcoholism, head injury, ulcerative colitis, liver or kidney disease.

SIDE EFFECTS:

Common: tolerance to drug requiring higher doses, drowsiness, dry mouth.
Unusual: blurred vision.

INTERACTIONS:

Other drugs:
• MAOI, sedatives.
Other substances:
• alcohol.

PRESCRIPTION:

Yes (restricted).

PERMITTED IN SPORT:

No.

OVERDOSE:

Moderately serious. May cause initial stimulation, followed by vomiting, drowsiness, convulsions, reduced breathing, coma and very rarely death. Seek urgent medical attention.

OTHER INFORMATION:

May cause dependency or addiction if used unnecessarily for long periods. Relatively mild narcotic drugs. Risk of dependency.

Dipivefrine

TRADE NAME:

Propine.

USES:

Some types of glaucoma.

DOSAGE:

 One drop twice a day.

FORMS:

Eye drops.

PRECAUTIONS:

May be used in pregnancy, breast feeding and children.

Do not take if:

 • suffering from narrow angle glaucoma.

SIDE EFFECTS:

Common: red eyes, eye burning and stinging.
Unusual: rapid heart rate.

INTERACTIONS:

None significant.

PRESCRIPTION:

Yes.

PERMITTED IN SPORT:

Yes.

See also Acetazolamide, Apraclonidine, Betaxolol, Bimatoprost, Brimonidine, Brinzolamide, Carbachol, Dorzolamide, Latanoprost, Levobunolol, Phenylephrine, Pilocarpine, Timolol, Travoprost.

Dipyridamole

TRADE NAMES:

**Persantin, Persantin Retard.
Asasartin Retard** (with aspirin).

DRUG CLASS:

Anticoagulant.

USES:

Prevention and treatment of blood clots and strokes, particularly in patients with previous strokes, transient ischaemic attacks (mini-strokes), kidney disease and after transplantation of heart valves.

DOSAGE:

 Persantin—one tablet four times a day one hour before meals.
Asasartin Retard, Persantin Retard—one tablet twice a day.

FORMS:

Tablet, capsule.

PRECAUTIONS:

Should be used with caution in pregnancy (B1). Not for use in breast feeding. Use with caution in children.
Use with caution in severe heart disease (e.g. unstable angina) and aortic stenosis (heart valve disease).

SIDE EFFECTS:

Common: headache.
Unusual: diarrhoea, nausea, flushing, low blood pressure, dizziness, rapid heart rate.
Severe but rare (stop medication, consult doctor): abnormal bruising or bleeding.

INTERACTIONS:

Other drugs:
• xanthinates, adenosine, blood pressure medications (but may be used with most of them).

PRESCRIPTION:

Yes.

PERMITTED IN SPORT:

Yes.

OVERDOSE:

Unlikely to be serious, but medical assistance should be sought.

OTHER INFORMATION:

Often used in combination with other Anticoagulants. Very safe and can be taken long term to prevent heart attacks and strokes.

See also Clopidrogel, Warfarin.

Disodium clodronate

TRADE NAME:

Loron.

USES:

High blood calcium blood levels, bone cancer pain.

DOSAGE:

 Two to four capsules a day in divided doses, one hour before or after food.

FORMS:

Capsules, tablets, injection.

PRECAUTIONS:

Not to be used in pregnancy, breast feeding and children.
Use with caution in kidney disease.
Blood levels of calcium and phosphate must be checked regularly during use.

Do not take if:

 • suffering severe kidney disease, mouth ulcers.

SIDE EFFECTS:

Common: nausea, diarrhoea.
Unusual: blood chemistry changes, reduced kidney function, skin reactions.
Severe but rare (stop medication, consult doctor): damage to kidney or parathyroid glands.

INTERACTIONS:

Other drugs:
• other drugs that alter calcium levels, antacids.
Other substances:
• mineral supplements.

PRESCRIPTION:

Yes.

PERMITTED IN SPORT:

Yes.

OVERDOSE:

Potentially very serious. Seek urgent medical attention.

Disodium cromoglycate

See Sodium cromoglycate.

Disodium etidronate

See Etidronate.

Disodium pamidronate

See Pamidronate.

Disopyramide

TRADE NAMES:

Rythmodan, Rythmodan Retard.

DRUG CLASS:

Antiarrhythmic.

USES:

Control of heart beat irregularities.

DOSAGE:

 Rythmodan: one or two tablets, three to four times a day.
Rythmodan Retard: one or two tablets, twice a day.

FORMS:

Capsules, tablets, injection.

PRECAUTIONS:

Should be used with caution in pregnancy (B2) and breast feeding. Not designed for use in children.
Use with caution in low blood pressure, soon after heart attack, low blood potassium, diabetes, glaucoma, prostate disease, kidney and liver failure.
Regular blood tests to check potassium levels necessary.

Do not take if:

 • suffering from heart failure.

SIDE EFFECTS:

Common: dose related effects may cause dry mouth, nausea, indigestion, belly pains, bloating, constipation, blurred

vision, difficulty in passing urine, dry eyes, dry nose.
Unusual: dizziness, angina, itch, rash, loss of appetite, bad taste, diarrhoea, frequent urination, burning on urination, impotence, tiredness, pins and needles sensation, headache.
Severe but rare (stop medication, consult doctor): unable to pass urine, yellow skin.

INTERACTIONS:

Other drugs:
• other drugs for treatment of irregular heart rhythm.
• phenothiazines, tricyclic antidepressants, phenytoin, beta-blockers, astemizole, cisapride, pentamidine, pimozide, roxithromycin, some laxatives.

PRESCRIPTION:

Yes.

PERMITTED IN SPORT:

Yes.

OVERDOSE:

Extremely serious. Administer activated charcoal or induce vomiting if conscious. Seek emergency medical assistance. Symptoms include shortness of breath, cessation of breathing, coma and death.
See also Amiodarone, Flecainide, Mexiletine, Procainamide, Quinidine, Sotalol, Verapamil.

Distigmine

TRADE NAME:

Ubretid.

DRUG CLASS:

Anticholinesterase.

USES:

Myasthenia gravis, inability to pass urine, maintenance of bowel movement after surgery, premedication before general anaesthetic.

DOSAGE:

 One to three tablets once or twice a day.

FORMS:

Tablets.

PRECAUTIONS:

Should be used in pregnancy (C) only when medically essential. Safe for use in breast feeding. Use with caution in children.
Dosage must be carefully monitored by doctor.
Use with caution in epilepsy, slow heart rate, asthma, recent heart attack, irregular heart beat, overactive thyroid gland, and peptic ulcer.

Do not take if:
 • suffering from gut obstruction.

SIDE EFFECTS:

Common: slow heart rate, headache, nausea, diarrhoea, excess salivation, cough, wheeze, bowel noises.
Unusual: confusion, slurred speech, vomiting, belly cramps, desire to pass urine, muscle cramps, contracted pupils.
Severe but rare (stop medication, consult doctor): difficulty breathing, chest pain.

INTERACTIONS:

Other drugs:
• muscle relaxants, atropine, aminoglycosides, drugs used to treat irregular heart beat, some anaesthetics.

PRESCRIPTION:

Yes.

OVERDOSE:

Serious. May cause diarrhoea, vomiting, difficulty in breathing, weakness, low blood pressure, slow heart rate and heart attack. Seek urgent medical attention.

OTHER INFORMATION:

Very useful for the few patients with the distressing muscle disease of myasthenia gravis.

Disulfiram

TRADE NAME:

Antabuse.

USES:

Alcoholism. Causes violent vomiting if alcohol taken within 24 hours.

DOSAGE:

 Half to two tablets once a day.

FORMS:

Tablets (white) of 200mg.

PRECAUTIONS:

Use in pregnancy (B2) and breast feeding only if medically essential. Not designed for use in children.

Patient and close relatives must be made completely aware of effects of medication before use.

Use with caution in diabetes, thyroid disease, epilepsy, allergic dermatitis, eczema and asthma.

Not designed for prolonged use.

Do not take if:

- suffering from significant heart disease, severe liver or kidney disease, psychiatric disturbances
- using cough mixtures or other medicines containing alcohol
- alcohol taken within previous 24 hours.

SIDE EFFECTS:

Common: numbness, tingling, pain or weakness in hands and feet.
Unusual: eye pain, blurred vision, psychiatric disturbances, impotence, headache, tiredness, bad taste.

INTERACTIONS:

Other drugs:
- metronidazole and paraldehyde must not be used
- phenytoin, isoniazid, chlordiazepoxide, diazepam, anticoagulants (e.g. warfarin).

Other substances:
- reacts severely with alcohol.

PRESCRIPTION:

Yes.

PERMITTED IN SPORT:

Yes.

OVERDOSE:

Severe adverse effects unlikely provided alcohol avoided. Induce vomiting if medication taken recently. Seek medical attention.

OTHER INFORMATION:

A very useful incentive in encouraging alcoholics to completely abstain from alcohol. Must be accompanied by appropriate counselling and support. In use for many decades. Does not cause addiction or dependence.

See also Acamprosate, Naltrexone.

Dithranol
(Anthralin)

TRADE NAMES:

Dithrocream, Micanol.
Psorin (with salicylic acid and tar).

USES:

Psoriasis, fungal skin infections.

DOSAGE:

 Apply sparingly twice a day. Wash off if redness occurs.

FORMS:

Cream, ointment.

PRECAUTIONS:

Safe in pregnancy and breast feeding. Use with caution on children.
Avoid eyes, nostrils, mouth, vagina, penis head and anus.
Use with care in skin folds and thin skin. Wash hands after use.

Do not use if:

- suffering from severe or pustular psoriasis
- suffering from broken skin.

SIDE EFFECTS:

Common: skin irritation.
Unusual: fever, skin staining.

INTERACTIONS:

None significant.

PRESCRIPTION:

No.

PERMITTED IN SPORT:

Yes.

OTHER INFORMATION:

Very effective medication for psoriasis, but must be used carefully, starting with lowest concentration cream then slowly increasing strength depending on response.

DIURETICS

DISCUSSION:

Diuretics are commonly called fluid tablets because they increase the rate at which the kidney produces urine, and therefore the frequency with which the patient has to visit the toilet to pass urine. Common diuretics all come as tablets, and some are available as injections. The most common side effect of diuretics is washing out of the body (with the increased urine production) essential elements that should remain in the body. Potassium is the element most commonly lost and as a result, many patients are given potassium (K) supplements to take while using diuretics. This side effect may also be overcome by taking the tablets only five days a week, or in some other intermittent pattern. Blood tests are often ordered to assess the levels of potassium (and other elements) in patients on diuretics.

See Amiloride, Bumetanide, Frusemide, Indapamide, Spironolactone, THIAZIDE DIURETICS, Torasemide, Triamterene.

Docosahexaenoic acid

See Fatty acids.

Docusate sodium

TRADE NAMES:

Dioctyl, Docusol, Fletchers' Enemette, Waxsol.
Normax (with danthron).

DRUG CLASS:

Laxative, softener.

USES:

Constipation, softening faeces, softening ear wax.

DOSAGE:

 Tablets: two tablets, once a day after evening meal.
Suppositories: one a day in evening.
Ear drops: ten drops nightly for two or three nights.

FORMS:

Tablets, suspension, suppository, liquid enema, ear drops.

PRECAUTIONS:

Safe in pregnancy (A), breast feeding and after medical advice in children.
Designed for short term use only, unless advised otherwise by a doctor.

Do not take if:

- suffering from belly pains or bowel obstruction.

SIDE EFFECTS:

Common: ear drops—none.
Other forms—belly discomfort.
Unusual: diarrhoea. Blood chemistry imbalances with prolonged use.
Severe but rare (stop medication, consult doctor): severe belly pains.

INTERACTIONS:

Other drugs:
- do not use within two hours of any other laxative.

PRESCRIPTION:

Normax: yes.
Others: no.

PERMITTED IN SPORT:

Yes.

OVERDOSE:

Diarrhoea and loss of vital body chemicals may occur.

OTHER INFORMATION:

Safe and frequently used medication. Use of ear drops before ear syringing makes wax removal far easier.
See also Bisacodyl, FIBRE, Glycerol, Frangula, Lactulose, Paraffin, Poloxamer, Psyllium, Senna, Sodium phosphate, Sodium picosulfate, Sorbitol, Sterculia.

DOSAGE:

One tablet or injection a day. Do not use for more than four consecutive days.

FORMS:

Tablets of 50mg (light pink) and 200mg (dark pink) injection.

PRECAUTIONS:

May be used with caution in pregnancy (B1), breast feeding and children.
Use with caution in heart and blood vessel disease.

SIDE EFFECTS:

Common: headache, dizziness, drowsiness, tiredness, sleeplessness, diarrhoea.
Unusual: altered heart rate, low blood pressure, itch, liver damage.
Severe but rare (stop medication, consult doctor): heart damage noted on ECG (electrocardiograph).

INTERACTIONS:

Other drugs:
- some drugs used for irregular heart rhythm.

PRESCRIPTION:

Yes.

PERMITTED IN SPORT:

Yes.

Dolasetron

TRADE NAME:

Anzemet.

USES:

Prevention of nausea and vomiting in patients having chemotherapy for cancer, postoperative nausea and vomiting.

Domperidone

TRADE NAMES:

Motilium.
Domperamol (with paracetamol).

DRUG CLASS:

Antiemetic.

USES:

Nausea, vomiting, delayed stomach emptying, migraine.

DOSAGE:

Motilium: one tablet, three or four times a day, 30 minutes before meals.
Domperamol: two every four hours as necessary. maximum eight a day.

FORMS:

Motilium: tablets (white) of 10mg.
Domperamol: tablet (white).

PRECAUTIONS:

Should be used with caution in pregnancy (B2) and breast feeding and children.
Use with caution in breast cancer, liver and kidney disease.

Do not take if:

• suffering from some forms of pituitary gland tumour.

SIDE EFFECTS:

Common: minimal.
Unusual: dry mouth, stomach cramps, breast enlargement, breast milk production, reduced libido, rash.
Rare: dizziness.

INTERACTIONS:

Other drugs:
• antacids, anticholinergics, imidazole antifungals, macrolide antibiotics, nefazodone.

PRESCRIPTION:

Yes.

PERMITTED IN SPORT:

Yes.

OVERDOSE:

No serious effects likely. Seek medical advice.

OTHER INFORMATION:

A remarkably safe and effective medication introduced in the mid-1980s. Marvellous for motion sickness. Does not cause dependence or addiction, but is designed for short term use.

See also Metoclopramide, Prochlorperazine.

Donepezil

TRADE NAME:

Aricept.

DRUG CLASS:

Anticholinesterase.

USES:

Mild Alzheimer's disease.

DOSAGE:

 5 to 10mg a day before bed.

FORMS:

Tablets of 5mg (white) and 10mg (yellow).

PRECAUTIONS:

Not for use in breast feeding (B3), breast feeding or children.
Use with caution in irregular heart rhythm, peptic ulcers, asthma, emphysema, seizures, difficulty in passing urine.
Only prescribed after very careful assessment of the patient's mental state and level of dementia.

SIDE EFFECTS:

Common: nausea, diarrhoea, tiredness, sleeplessness.
Unusual: muscle cramps, difficulty in passing urine, seizures, dizziness, headache, loss of appetite.
Severe but rare (stop medication, consult doctor): liver damage (jaundice), psychiatric disturbances, irregular heart rhythm, peptic ulcer.

INTERACTIONS:

Other drugs:
• some anaesthetics, beta-blockers, other anticholinergics, NSAID, ketoconazole, phenytoin, quinidine, carbamazepine,

dexamethasone, rifampicin, phenobarbitone.

PRESCRIPTION:

Yes.

PERMITTED IN SPORT:

Yes.

OVERDOSE:

Serious. May cause diarrhoea, vomiting, difficulty in breathing, weakness, low blood pressure, slow heart rate and heart attack. Seek urgent medical attention.

OTHER INFORMATION:

Introduced in 1999 as a form of treatment for the otherwise untreatable early stages of Alzheimer's disease.

See also Galantamine, Neostigmine, Pyridostigmine, Rivastigmine.

Dorzolamide hydrochloride

TRADE NAMES:

Trusopt.
Cosopt (with timolol).

USES:

Glaucoma.

DOSAGE:

 One drop two or three times a day in affected eye.

FORMS:

Eye drops.

PRECAUTIONS:

Use with caution in pregnancy (B3), breast feeding and children.
Only suitable for certain types of glaucoma (open angle glaucoma).
Use with caution in severe liver and kidney disease.
Use with caution if eye painful from ulcers on surface or other eye disease present.

Do not use if:

 • wearing contact lenses
• suffering from acute angle closure glaucoma.

SIDE EFFECTS:

Common: eye irritation, bitter taste.
Uncommon: blurred vision, eye pain, eye redness, eyelid crusting, throat irritation, wheeze.

INTERACTIONS:

Other drugs:
• oral carbonic anhydrase inhibitors (e.g. acetazolamide, dichlorphenamide, methazolamide).

PRESCRIPTION:

Yes.

PERMITTED IN SPORT:

Yes.

OVERDOSE:

May cause heart and blood pressure irregularities.

OTHER INFORMATION:

Introduced in 1996.

See also Acetazolamide, Apraclonidine, Betaxolol, Bimatoprost, Brimonidine, Brinzolamide, Carbachol, Dipivefrine, Latanoprost, Levobunolol, Phenylephrine, Pilocarpine, Timolol, Travoprost.

Dothiepin

See TRICYCLICS.

Doxazosin

TRADE NAME:

Cardura.

DRUG CLASS:

Alpha blocker.

USES:

Control of mild to moderate high blood pressure.

DOSAGE:

 Start at low dose and increase very slowly. Maximum 8mg a day in divided doses.

FORMS:

Tablets of 1, 2 and 4mg.

PRECAUTIONS:

Use with considerable caution in pregnancy (B3). Use with caution in breast feeding. Not for use in children. Use lower doses in elderly.
Use with caution in heart disease, blood vessel disease, severe liver and kidney disease.

SIDE EFFECTS:

Common: sudden drop in blood pressure to cause fainting, swelling of ankles, headache, tiredness.
Unusual: fatigue, change in heart rate.
Severe but rare (stop medication, consult doctor): low white blood cell count, severe infections.

INTERACTIONS:

None significant.

PRESCRIPTION:

Yes.

PERMITTED IN SPORT:

Yes.

OVERDOSE:

Low blood pressure, drowsiness and depressed reflexes only effects.

OTHER INFORMATION:

Introduced in 1996.
See also Prazosin.

Doxepin

See ANTIHISTAMINES, SEDATING; TRICYCLIC ANTIDEPRESSANTS.

Doxycycline

TRADE NAMES:

Periostat, Vibramycin.

DRUG CLASS:

Tetracycline antibiotic, Antimalarial.

USES:

Treatment or prevention of infections caused by susceptible bacteria.
Prevention of malaria.
Prevention of periodontal (gum) disease.

DOSAGE:

 Treatment of infection: two tablets or capsules at once, then one tablet or capsule a day.
Prevention of malaria and acne: one tablet or capsule a day.
Prevention of periodontal disease: one capsule twice a day an hour or more before food.

FORMS:

Capsules, tablets.

PRECAUTIONS:

Not to be used in pregnancy (D) or children under twelve as it may cause permanent staining of teeth of child. Use with caution in breast feeding.
Use with caution in kidney disease.
Do not take if:

 • suffering from severe kidney disease, systemic lupus erythematosus (SLE), Staphylococcal infection
• taking vitamin A or retinoids.

SIDE EFFECTS:

Common: loss of appetite, nausea, sore mouth, diarrhoea, difficulty in swallowing, inflamed colon.
Unusual: vomiting, inflamed pancreas, rash, sun sensitive skin, secondary fungal infection (thrush).
Severe but rare (stop medication, consult doctor): severe belly pain, severe diarrhoea, tooth discolouration.

INTERACTIONS:

Other drugs:
- vitamin A, retinoids, anticoagulants (e.g. warfarin), penicillin, antacids, iron, oral contraceptives, methoxyflurane, bismuth, barbiturates, anticonvulsants, acetazolamide.

Other substances:
- milk and food may reduce absorption from gut.

PRESCRIPTION:

Yes.

PERMITTED IN SPORT:

Yes.

OVERDOSE:

Exacerbation of side effects only likely effect.

OTHER INFORMATION:

Used to prevent acne and malaria. Used to treat a wide variety of bacterial infections. Does not cause dependence or addiction.

See also Demeclocycline, Methacycline, Minocycline, Tetracycline.

Drosperidone
See ORAL CONTRACEPTIVES.

Dydrogesterone

TRADE NAMES:

Duphaston.
Femoston (with oestradiol).
Femapak (with oestrogen).

DRUG CLASS:

Sex hormone.

USES:

Abnormal bleeding from uterus, failure of menstrual periods, endometriosis, painful menstrual periods.
Used with Oestrogens in postmenopausal hormone replacement.

DOSAGE:

 Duphaston: must be individualised by doctor.
Femoston: one tablet a day.
Femapak: apply new patch twice a week.

FORMS:

Tablets (white) of 10mg, patch.

PRECAUTIONS:

Not to be used in pregnancy (D), breast feeding or children.
Use with caution in high blood pressure, heart failure, fluid retention and depression.

Do not take if:

- suffering from blood clots, inflamed veins, stroke, angina, heart attack, breast or genital cancer, liver disease, jaundice, sickle cell anaemia, miscarriage, Dubin-Johnson syndrome, Rotor syndrome
- suffering undiagnosed vaginal bleeding.

SIDE EFFECTS:

Common: dizziness, breast pain.
Uncommon: headache, nausea, abnormal vaginal bleeding, weight gain, fluid retention.
Severe but rare (stop medication, consult doctor): blood clot, yellow skin (jaundice).

INTERACTIONS:

Other drugs:
- other sex hormones.

PRESCRIPTION:

Yes.

PERMITTED IN SPORT:

Yes.

OVERDOSE:

Vomiting and abnormal vaginal bleeding only likely effects.

OTHER INFORMATION:

Does not cause addiction or dependence.

See also Cyproterone acetate, Danazol, Ethinyloestradiol, Etonogestrel, HORMONE REPLACEMENT THERAPY, Medroxyprogesterone acetate, Oestradiol, Oestriol, Oestrogen, ORAL CONTRACEPTIVES, Testosterone.

Echinacea

USES:

Cold symptoms, cough, fever, mouth inflammation, minor wounds and burns.

DOSAGE:

 Up to 900mg a day, divided into several doses.

FORMS:

Capsules, liquid, tincture, cream.

PRECAUTIONS:

Do not use in pregnancy or breast feeding or children. Use with caution in children over 12 years.
Use with caution in diabetes.

Do not take if:

- suffering from AIDS, multiple sclerosis, tuberculosis, autoimmune or connective tissue diseases (e.g. SLE), allergic tendencies
- trying to fall pregnant.

SIDE EFFECTS:

Common: nausea, vomiting, rash.
Unusual: dizziness, low blood pressure.
Severe but rare (stop medication, consult doctor): breathing difficulties, swelling of face, infertility.

INTERACTIONS:

Other drugs:
- cyclosporin, steroids, some cancer treating drugs.

PRESCRIPTION:

No.

PERMITTED IN SPORT:

Yes.

OVERDOSE:

Exacerbation of side effects expected. Seek medical advice.

OTHER INFORMATION:

Not used in orthodox medicine.

Econazole

TRADE NAMES:

Ecostatin, Gyno-Pevaryl, Pevaryl. Econacort (with hydrocortisone).

USES:

Treatment of fungal infections of skin (tinea, athlete's foot, pityriasis versicolor) and vagina (thrush).

DOSAGE:

 Skin: apply two or three times a day.
Vagina: insert once a day at night.

FORMS:

Cream, vaginal cream, vaginal pessary, solution.

PRECAUTIONS:

Safe to use in pregnancy (A), breast feeding and children.
Should not be swallowed or used in eyes.
Use with care on open wounds.

SIDE EFFECTS:

Common: none.
Unusual: skin irritation, rash.

INTERACTIONS:

None significant.

PRESCRIPTION:

No.

PERMITTED IN SPORT:

Yes.

OTHER INFORMATION:

This class of medication dramatically improved the treatment of fungal infections when introduced in the early 1970s. Very safe and effective.
See also Clotrimazole, Fluconazole, Itraconazole, Ketoconazole, Miconazole.

Efavirenz

TRADE NAME:

Sustiva.

DRUG CLASS:

Antiviral.

USES:

Treatment of HIV/AIDS in combination with other medications.

DOSAGE:

 Up to 600mg once a day.

FORMS:

Capsules of 50, 100 and 200mg.

PRECAUTIONS:

Never to be used in pregnancy (D). Use with caution in breast feeding and children.
Use with caution in liver and kidney disease, psychiatric disturbances.
Use lower doses in elderly.
Monitor blood cholesterol and liver enzyme levels by regular blood tests.
Do not take if:

- suffering from severe liver disease
- using other medications to control HIV/AIDS.

SIDE EFFECTS:

Common: rash, dizziness, sleeplessness, nausea, diarrhoea, tiredness.
Unusual: poor concentration, psychotic reactions, headache.

Severe but rare (stop medication, consult doctor): liver damage.

INTERACTIONS:

Other drugs:
- astemizole, cisapride, midazolam, triazolam, ergots (all preceding give severe interaction), oral contraceptives, phenobarbitone, phenytoin, carbamazepine, warfarin, rifampicin, sertraline.

Other substances:
- grapefruit, St John's wort
- may give false positive test for cannabis use.

PRESCRIPTION:

Yes.

PERMITTED IN SPORT:

Yes.

OVERDOSE:

Serious liver and brain damage may occur. Seek urgent medical attention. Induce vomiting or give activated charcoal if alert and medication taken recently.

OTHER INFORMATION:

One of numerous antivirals that are used in combination to control HIV/AIDS.
See also Abacavir, Delavirdine, Didanosine, Indinavir, Lamivudine, Nelfinavir, Nevirapine, Ritonavir, Saquinavir, Stavudine, Tenofovir, Zalcitabine, Zidovudine.

Eformoterol

TRADE NAMES:

Foradil, Oxis.
Symbicort (with budesonide).

DRUG CLASS:

Bronchodilator.

USES:

Long term treatment of asthma.

DOSAGE:

 Powder from one or two Foradil capsules inhaled twice daily through purpose made inhaler. Use Oxis Turbuhaler and Symbicort twice a day.

FORMS:

Capsules containing powder for inhalation, inhaler.

PRECAUTIONS:

Use with caution in pregnancy (B3). Safe in breast feeding and children over five years.
Not for use in unstable or deteriorating asthma.
Do not exceed recommended dose.
Do not swallow capsules.
Use with caution in diabetes, liver, heart and thyroid disease.
Lung function should be monitored regularly by use of spirometer.

Do not take if:

• lactose sensitive.

SIDE EFFECTS:

Common: tremor, palpitations, rapid heart rate, headache, throat irritation, dizziness.
Unusual: lung irritation, nausea, taste disturbance, low blood potassium levels.
Severe but rare (stop medication, consult doctor): angina (chest pain).

INTERACTIONS:

Other drugs:
• other bronchodilators used for treatment of asthma (check with doctor)
• digoxin, beta-blockers, xanthinates, diuretics, MAOI, tricyclic antidepressants, quinidine, disopyramide, procainamide, phenothiazines, some antihistamines, oxytocin.
Other substances:
• alcohol.

PRESCRIPTION:

Yes.

PERMITTED IN SPORT:

No.

OVERDOSE:

Palpitations, tremor and exacerbation of side effects likely.

OTHER INFORMATION:

Introduced in 1996. Enables patients who would otherwise use large quantities of inhaled bronchodilators (e.g. Ventolin) to reduce their usage of these medications dramatically.
See also Salmeterol.

Eicosapentaenoic acid

TRADE NAMES:

Used as an ingredient in many skin preparations and nutritional supplements.
Maxepa, Omacor (with docosahexaenoic acid).

DRUG CLASS:

Nutritional (triglyceride) supplement, moisturiser.

USES:

Fatty acid supplement, dry skin.

DOSAGE:

 One to five capsules twice a day. Apply to skin three times a day.

FORMS:

Capsules, liquid, creams, gels.

PRECAUTIONS:

Safe in pregnancy (A), breast feeding and children.
Do not exceed recommended dose.

SIDE EFFECTS:

Common: nausea.

INTERACTIONS:

None significant.

PRESCRIPTION:

No.

PERMITTED IN SPORT:

Yes.

OVERDOSE:

Vomiting and diarrhoea only likely effects.

OTHER INFORMATION:

Derived from fish oil.

See also Fatty acids

ELECTROLYTES

TRADE and GENERIC NAMES:

Electrolytes such as sodium chloride (common salt), potassium bicarbonate, potassium chloride, sodium bicarbonate and sodium acid citrate are found in numerous preparations, sometimes in combination with antacids, laxatives and analgesics.

Algicon (Potassium bicarbonate with aluminium hydroxide, calcium carbonate, magnesium salts, and other ingredients). See Antacids entry for further details.

Aqsia, Askina, Flowfusor, Irriclens, Minims Sodium Chloride, Normasol, Optiflo S, Saline Steri-Neb, Steripod Blue, Uriflex S, Uriflex SP, Uro-Tainer (Sodium chloride).

Burinex K (Potassium chloride with bumetanide).

Dioralyte (Sodium chloride, sodium acid citrate, potassium chloride, glucose).

Diumide K, Lasikal (Potassium chloride with frusemide).

Electrolade (Sodium chloride, sodium bicarbonate, potassium chloride, glucose).

Glandosane, Luborant (Potassium chloride and sodium chloride with carboxymethylcellulose).

Iocare (Sodium chloride, potassium chloride, sodium acetate and sodium citrate with calcium chloride, magnesium chloride, sodium citrate).

Kay-Cee-L, Slow-K (Potassium chloride).

Klean-Prep, Movicol (Potassium chloride, sodium chloride and sodium bicarbonate with polyethylene glycol, and other ingredients).

Kloref (Potassium bicarbonate and potassium chloride with betaine and potassium benzoate).

Micralax (Sodium citrate with sorbic acid, sodium alkylsulphoacetate).

Microlette (Sodium citrate with glycerol, sodium lauryl sulphoacetate).

Mictral (Sodium citrate and sodium Bicarbonate with nalidixic acid).

Minims Artificial Tears (Sodium chloride with hydroxymethylcellulose).

Neo-Naclex-K (Potassium chloride with bendrofluazide).

Pyrogastrone Liquid (Potassium bicarbonate with carbenoxolone and antacids).

Rapolyte (Sodium chloride, sodium citrate, potassium chloride, dextrose).

Rehidrat (Sodium chloride, sodium bicarbonate, potassium chloride, citric acid and sugars).

Relaxit (Sodium citrate with glycerol, sodium lauryl sulphoacetate, sorbitol and other ingredients).

Sando-K (Potassium bicarbonate and potassium chloride).

Electrolytes are underlined. Electrolytes are also found in many antacids (see separate entry).

USES:

Replacement of essential electrolytes lost because of diarrhoea, vomiting, excess passing of urine, heart disease, excess nasal mucus, eye cleansing, bladder irrigation and other diseases.

DOSAGE:

 Tablets: one to four tablets a day in one or more doses.
Powder: dissolve in water and use as often as necessary to prevent dehydration.

FORMS:

Tablets, powder, mixture, nose spray, eye drops, enema, injection.

PRECAUTIONS:

Safe in pregnancy, breast feeding and children.
Be careful not to exceed necessary dose.
Blood tests to measure severity of electrolyte depletion and response to treatment may be necessary.
Use with caution in kidney and liver disease, stomach ulcers.
Dilute powders with water only, not milk, juice etc.
Use with caution in dehydration as adequate fluid replacement also necessary.

Do not take if:

- suffering from Addison's disease, severe kidney disease, severe injuries or burns.

SIDE EFFECTS:

Common: minimal.
Unusual: fluid retention.

INTERACTIONS:

Other drugs:
- triamterene, amiloride.

PRESCRIPTION:

No.

PERMITTED IN SPORT:

Yes.

OVERDOSE:

Most forms: no serious effects expected. Potassium salts: serious. May cause low blood pressure, irregular heart beat, pins and needles sensation, convulsions, paralysis, heart attack, inability to breathe and death. Administer activated charcoal or induce vomiting if medication taken recently. Seek urgent medical assistance.

OTHER INFORMATION:

Electrolytes are elements such as Potassium, Sodium, Chlorine and Magnesium that are essential for the biochemical functioning of the body. Diuretics cause increased loss of potassium and specific replacement and regular checks of blood potassium level is advisable.

Eletriptan

TRADE NAME:

Relpax.

DRUG CLASS:

5HT agonist (antimigraine).

USES:

Acute treatment of migraine.

DOSAGE:

 40mg swallowed whole at onset of migraine with water. Repeat if necessary between two and 24 hours afterwards. Maximum 80mg a day.

FORMS:

Tablets (orange) of 20mg and 40mg.

PRECAUTIONS:

Use with caution in pregnancy and breast feeding.
Not for use in elderly and children.
Use with care in mild kidney disease, at risk of heart disease or stroke.

Do not take if:

- suffering from severe liver or kidney disease, untreated high blood pressure, heart disease, angina, irregular heart rhythm, history of stroke, non-migraine headache, unusual forms of migraine.

SIDE EFFECTS:

Common: tiredness, chest pain and tightness, headache, belly pains.

Unusual: back pain, chills, throat tightness, flushing, palpitations, rapid heart rate, diarrhoea, nausea, dry mouth, muscle pain, dizziness, sweats, tingling. *Severe but rare (stop medication, consult doctor):* collapse.

INTERACTIONS:

Other drugs:
• ergotamine, methysergide.
Herbs:
• St John's wort.

PRESCRIPTION:

Yes.

PERMITTED IN SPORT:

Yes.

OVERDOSE:

Causes high blood pressure and may affect heart. Recovery within eight hours usual unless heart damaged. Seek medical attention.

OTHER INFORMATION:

Introduced in 2002 to add to range of medications available for the treatment of migraine.

See also ANALGESICS, Almotriptan, Ergotamine, Methysergide, Naratriptan, Pizotifen, Rizatripan, Sumatriptan, Zolmitriptan.

Emedastine

TRADE NAME:

Emadine.

DRUG CLASS:

Antihistamine.

USES:

Allergic conjunctivitis (eye allergy).

DOSAGE:

 One drop into affected eye(s) twice a day.

FORMS:

Eye drops.

PRECAUTIONS:

Must not be used in pregnancy (D).
Use with caution in breast feeding and kidney disease.
May be used in children over three years.
Use with caution if wearing contact lenses.
Do not use long term.
Do not take if:
• suffering from kidney or liver disease.

SIDE EFFECTS:

Common: eye irritation, blurred vision.
Unusual: eye surface swelling, headache, eye pain, runny nose.

INTERACTIONS:

None significant.

PRESCRIPTION:

Yes.

PERMITTED IN SPORT:

Yes.

OVERDOSE:

Unlikely to be serious.

OTHER INFORMATION:

Introduced in 1999.
See also Levocabastine.

Enalapril

See ACE INHIBITORS.

Enoxaparin

TRADE NAME:

Clexane.

DRUG CLASS:

Anticoagulant.

USES:

Prevention and treatment of blood clots in veins. Often used after major surgery, in unstable angina, or in bedridden patients.

DOSAGE:

 As determined by doctor for each patient.

FORMS:

Injection.

PRECAUTIONS:

Not to be used in pregnancy (C) unless essential. Use with caution in breast feeding.

Must not be injected into muscle.

Use with caution in severe kidney and liver disease, artificial heart valves, diabetic eye damage, very thin people, history of peptic ulcer and uncontrolled high blood pressure.

Not for use in association with a spinal or epidural anaesthetic.

Regular blood tests to measure effect essential.

Do not use if:

- suffering from heart infections, bleeding disorders, active peptic ulcer, stroke caused by bleeding in brain
- Taking aspirin, heparin or NSAIDs (anti-inflammatory drugs used for arthritis).

SIDE EFFECTS:

Common: abnormal bruising and bleeding, bruising at injection site.
Unusual: liver damage.
Severe but rare (stop medication, consult doctor): bleeding from anus, coughing blood.

INTERACTIONS:

Other drugs:
- warfarin, other anticoagulants, NSAIDs, aspirin, dextran, clopidrogel, steroids.

Other substances:
- celery tablets.

PRESCRIPTION:

Yes.

PERMITTED IN SPORT:

Yes.

OVERDOSE:

Very serious. Excessive bleeding may occur. Antidote available. Given under strict medical supervision.

OTHER INFORMATION:

Introduced in 1996. Has fewer side effects than Heparin.
See also Heparin.

Entacapone

TRADE NAME:

Comtess.

DRUG CLASS:

Antiparkinsonian.

USES:

Severe Parkinson's disease, unmanageable by other medications.

DOSAGE:

 One tablet, four to seven times a day.

FORMS:

Tablets of 200mg (orange).

PRECAUTIONS:

Use with caution in pregnancy (B3), breast feeding and children.

Use with caution in low blood pressure.

Avoid taking with fatty meal.

Do not cease suddenly, but reduce dose slowly.

Do not take if:

- suffering from phaeochromocytoma, liver disease.

SIDE EFFECTS:

Common: incoordination, dry mouth, nausea, diarrhoea, belly pains, discoloured urine.
Unusual: sleep disturbances, psychiatric disturbances, chest pain, confusion, shortness of breath.
Severe but rare (stop medication, consult doctor): pneumonia, anaemia.

INTERACTIONS:

Other drugs:
• MAOI, Isoprenaline, adrenaline, methyldopa, apomorphine, iron, diazepam, venlafaxine, antidepressants, ibuprofen, benserazide, levodopa, other medications used to treat Parkinson's disease.
Other substances:
• fatty foods.

PRESCRIPTION:

Yes.

PERMITTED IN SPORT:

Yes.

OVERDOSE:

Likely to be serious. Seek urgent medical attention.

OTHER INFORMATION:

Introduced in 1999 to assist the most severely affected cases of Parkinson's disease.
See also ANTIPARKINSONIANS.

Ephedrine

TRADE NAMES:

CAM.
Franol, Franol Plus (with theophylline).
Haymine (with chlorpheniramine).

DRUG CLASS:

Sympathomimetic, Bronchodilator.

USES:

Asthma, spasm of bronchi in lungs, severe allergy, bed wetting.

DOSAGE:

 One or two tablets, three or four times a day.

FORMS:

Tablets, injection.

PRECAUTIONS:

May be used in pregnancy (A), breast feeding and children.
Use with caution in heart disease, angina and prostate gland enlargement.
Do not exceed recommended dose.
Do not take if:
• suffering from narrowing of heart arteries, heart attack, glaucoma, high blood pressure, overactive thyroid gland.

SIDE EFFECTS:

Common: alertness, sleeplessness, dizziness, headache, nausea, sweating, palpitations.
Unusual: vomiting, diarrhoea, rapid heart rate, difficulty in passing urine, weakness.

INTERACTIONS:

Other drugs:
• MAOI, digoxin, theophylline, frusemide, cyclopropane, some general anaesthetics.
Other substances:
• reacts with caffeine.

PRESCRIPTION:

Yes.

PERMITTED IN SPORT:

No.

OVERDOSE:

Exacerbation of side effects leading to convulsions and possible heart attack possible. Seek urgent medical assistance.

EPILEPSY TREATMENTS
See ANTICONVULSANTS.

Epoetin
(Erythropoietin)

TRADE NAMES:

Eprex, Neorecormon.

USES:

Stimulates red blood cell production in anaemia associated with kidney failure.

DOSAGE:

 Complex. As determined by doctor for each patient. Usually one to three injections a week.

FORMS:

Injection.

PRECAUTIONS:

Use in pregnancy (B3) only if medically essential. Not for use in breast feeding or children.
Use with caution in heart disease, epilepsy, porphyria and gout.
Do not take if:

 • suffering from uncontrolled high blood pressure, severe heart disease.

SIDE EFFECTS:

Common: bone pains, muscle aches.
Unusual: high blood pressure, fits, blood clots, rash, allergy reaction.

INTERACTIONS:

Other drugs:
• cyclosporin, iron.

PRESCRIPTION:

Yes.

PERMITTED IN SPORT:

No. Occasionally used illegally in endurance sports, when it may cause blood clots and sudden death.

OTHER INFORMATION:

Has dramatically improved life expectancy and quality of life for patients on dialysis for kidney failure, but expense limits its use. Has been used illegally by athletes to improve the oxygen uptake of their body and increase endurance.

Eprosartan

See ANGIOTENSIN II RECEPTOR ANTAGONISTS.

Ergocalciferol

See Cholecalciferol, Calcitriol and Ergocalciferol (Vitamin D).

Ergometrine

TRADE NAMES:

Ergometrine.
Syntometrine (with oxytocin).

USES:

Stopping abnormal bleeding after delivery or abortion.

DOSAGE:

 One injection immediately after delivery of baby.

FORMS:

Injection.

PRECAUTIONS:

Safe to use after delivery in pregnancy (A), but should not otherwise be used in pregnancy. Safe for use in breast feeding. Not for use in children.
Use with caution in heart disease.
Do not use injection if:

 • previous caesarean section, retained placenta.

SIDE EFFECTS:

Common: rapid heart rate, retention of fluid.
Unusual: low or high blood pressure,

irregular heart rhythm, nausea, diarrhoea, dizziness, hallucinations, sweating.

INTERACTIONS:

Other drugs:
- glyceryl trinitrate, beta blockers, bromocriptine, dopamine, doxycycline, sumatriptan, erythromycin, tetracycline, general anaesthetics, methysergide, nicotine.

PRESCRIPTION:

Yes.

PERMITTED IN SPORT:

Yes.

OVERDOSE:

Unlikely to have serious effects.

OTHER INFORMATION:

Injection commonly used to increase intensity of labour and immediately after delivery to reduce bleeding.

Ergotamine

TRADE NAMES:

Migril (with caffeine, cyclizine).
Cafergot (with caffeine).

DRUG CLASS:

Antimigraine.

USES:

Migraine, vascular headaches.

DOSAGE:

 Tablets and capsules: one or two tablets or capsules immediately symptoms detected. Repeat every half hour. Maximum six a day. Suppository: one immediately symptoms detected. Maximum three a day.

FORMS:

Tablets, capsules, suppositories.

PRECAUTIONS:

Should not be used in pregnancy (C) as it may cause premature labour. Not for use in breast feeding or children.
Should not be used for prolonged period. Not designed for prevention of migraine.

Do not take if:

 • suffering from poor circulation to arms or legs, angina, high blood pressure, hardening of arteries, severe infection, severe liver or kidney disease.

SIDE EFFECTS:

Common: nausea, vomiting, diarrhoea, leg weakness, pins and needles sensation, chest pain.
Unusual: swelling of feet, itch, slow heart rate.
Severe but rare (stop medication, consult doctor): severe chest pain, irregular heart beat.

INTERACTIONS:

Other drugs:
- vasoconstrictors.

Other substances:
- alcohol, caffeine, smoking and exercise may be migraine triggers.

PRESCRIPTION:

Yes.

PERMITTED IN SPORT:

Yes.

OVERDOSE:

May be serious. Symptoms include vomiting, diarrhoea, thirst, tingling, itching, cold skin, rapid weak pulse, confusion and coma. If tablets or capsules taken recently, induce vomiting. Seek urgent medical assistance.

OTHER INFORMATION:

May become ineffective if used too frequently.
See also Dihydroergotamine, Eletriptan, Naratriptan, Sumatriptan, Zolmitriptan.

Erythromycin

TRADE NAMES:

Eryacne, Erymax, Erythroped, Stiemycin, Tiloryth.
Aknemycin Plus (with tretinoin).
Benzamycin (with benzoyl peroxide).
Isotrexin (with isotretinoin).
Zineryt (with zinc acetate and other ingredients).

DRUG CLASS:

Macrolide antibiotic.

USES:

Treatment of infections caused by susceptible bacteria, acne.

DOSAGE:

 One tablet or capsule, two to four times a day.
Gel: Apply twice a day.

FORMS:

Tablets, capsules, injection, syrup, suspension, gel.

PRECAUTIONS:

Safe to use in pregnancy (A), breast feeding and children.
Not designed for prolonged or repeated use.
Use with caution in liver disease.

Do not take if:

 • suffering from severe liver disease, jaundice (yellow skin).

SIDE EFFECTS:

Common: nausea, vomiting, diarrhoea, rash, headache.
Unusual: belly pain, loss of appetite, excess wind, dizziness, ear noises, temporary deafness.
Severe but rare (stop medication, consult doctor): yellow skin (jaundice), irregular heart beat, worsening infection, seizures, pancreatitis (severe belly pain).

INTERACTIONS:

Other drugs:
• theophylline, cisapride, pimozide, carbamazepine, warfarin, cyclosporin, triazolam, phenytoin, digoxin, oral contraceptives, dihydroergotamine, disopyramide, bromocriptine, valproate, quinidine, methylprednisolone, sildenafil, triazolam, dihydroergotamine, lovastatin, simvastatin, zopiclone.

PRESCRIPTION:

Yes.

PERMITTED IN SPORT:

Yes.

OVERDOSE:

Severe diarrhoea, stomach pains and deafness may occur.

OTHER INFORMATION:

Used for a wide range of infections in general practice. Does not cause addiction or dependence. Some forms may cause fewer side effects than others.

Erythropoietin

See Epoetin.

Escitalopram

TRADE NAME:

Cipralex.

DRUG CLASS:

Antidepressant.

USES:

Depression, panic disorders, agoraphobia.

DOSAGE:

 5mg to 20mg once a day.
Continue treatment for depression for at least six months.
Reduce dose in elderly.

FORMS:

Tablet of 10mg (white).

PRECAUTIONS:

Not for use in pregnancy, breast feeding and children.
Use with caution in liver and kidney disease, diabetes, mania, epilepsy, history of convulsions, low blood sodium levels or bleeding disorders.
Monitor carefully for suicide risk.

Do not take if:

- suffering from serotonin syndrome.

SIDE EFFECTS:

Common: nausea, sweating, tiredness.
Unusual: dizziness, insomnia, diarrhoea, poor appetite, reduced libido, impotence, fever, yawning, sinus pain.

INTERACTIONS:

Other drugs:
- MAOI, other antidepressants, anticoagulants, lithium, tryptophan, omeprazole, cimetidine.

Herbs:
- St John's wort.

PRESCRIPTION:

Yes.

PERMITTED IN SPORT:

Yes.

OTHER INFORMATION:

Introduced in 2002.

See also Citalopram, Fluoxetine, Fluvoxamine, MAOI, Mirtazapine, Moclobemide, Nefazodone, Paroxetine, Reboxetine, Sertraline, Trazodone, TRICYCLIC ANTIDEPRESSANTS, Venlafaxine.

Esmolol

TRADE NAME:

Brevibloc.

DRUG CLASS:

Beta-blocker.

USES:

Rapid or irregular heart beat, paroxysmal atrial tachycardia.

DOSAGE:

 Slow infusion. Rate determined by doctor.

FORMS:

Injection.

PRECAUTIONS:

Should be used in pregnancy (C) only if medically essential.
Safe to use in breast feeding.
May be used with caution in children.
Use with care if suffering from alcoholism, liver or kidney failure or about to have surgery.

Do not take if:

- suffering from diabetes, asthma, or allergic conditions
- suffering from heart failure, shock, slow heart rate, or enlarged right heart
- if undertaking prolonged fast.

SIDE EFFECTS:

Common: low blood pressure, slow heart rate, cold hands and feet, asthma.
Unusual: loss of appetite, nausea, diarrhoea, impotence, tiredness, sleeplessness, nightmares, rash, loss of libido, hair loss, noises in ears.
Severe but rare (stop medication, consult doctor): severe asthma.

INTERACTIONS:

Other drugs:
- calcium channel blockers, disopyramide, clonidine, adrenaline, other medications for irregular heart beat, lignocaine, ergotamine, indomethacin, chlorpromazine.

PRESCRIPTION:

Yes.

PERMITTED IN SPORT:

Yes.

OVERDOSE:

Slow heart rate, low blood pressure, asthma and heart failure may result.

See also Atenolol, Carvedilol, Labetalol, Metoprolol, Oxprenolol, Pindolol, Propranolol, Sotalol.

Esomeprazole

See PROTON PUMP INHIBITORS.

Estradiol

See Oestradiol.

Estramustine

TRADE NAME:

Estracyt.

USES:

Cancer of prostate gland.

DOSAGE:

 One to three capsules, two to three times a day depending on body weight.

FORMS:

Capsules of 140mg (off white).

PRECAUTIONS:

Must not be used in women or children. Use with caution with history of blood clots, heart disease, diabetes, bone marrow damage.

Do not take if:

 • suffering from liver disease, peptic ulcer, severe heart disease or blood clots.

SIDE EFFECTS:

Common: nausea, diarrhoea, fluid retention, breast enlargement and tenderness, reduced libido.
Unusual: blood clots, heart damage.

INTERACTIONS:

Other drugs:
• none significant.
Other substances:
• reacts with milk and milk products.

PRESCRIPTION:

Yes.

PERMITTED IN SPORT:

Yes.

OVERDOSE:

Serious exacerbation of side effects possible. Seek medical assistance.

OTHER INFORMATION:

Although significant side effects occur, this medication may prolong life.

Estropipate

TRADE NAME:

Harmogen.

DRUG CLASS:

Sex hormone.

USES:

Female hormone replacement in menopause.

DOSAGE:

 One or two tablets a day, combined with progestogen for ten to 14 days if uterus intact.

FORMS:

Tablets of 1.5mg (peach).

PRECAUTIONS:

Not to be used in pregnancy (B1), breast feeding or children. Accidental usage in these situations unlikely to be harmful.

Use with caution in epilepsy, migraine, heart failure, high blood pressure, kidney disease, diabetes, porphyria or uterine disease.

Do not take if:

 • suffering from liver disease, breast or genital cancer, blood clots.

SIDE EFFECTS:

Common: abnormal uterine bleeding, vaginal thrush, nausea, fluid retention, weight gain, breast tenderness.
Unusual: rash, blurred vision, vomiting, bloating, intestinal cramps, pigmentation of skin on face.
Severe but rare (stop medication, consult doctor): blood clots, calf or chest pain, yellow skin (jaundice).

INTERACTIONS:

Other drugs:
• other sex hormones.
Other substances:
• smoking increases risk of serious side effects.

PRESCRIPTION:

Yes.

PERMITTED IN SPORT:

Yes.

OVERDOSE:

Vomiting and abnormal vaginal bleeding only likely effects.

OTHER INFORMATION:

Does not cause addiction or dependence. Very useful in managing the effects of menopause and reduces the risk of osteoporosis and heart disease after the menopause.

See also Ethinyloestradiol, Etonogestrel, HORMONE REPLACEMENT THERAPY, Oestradiol, Oestriol, Piperazine.

Ethamsylate

TRADE NAME:

Dicynene.

DRUG CLASS:

Haemostatic (stops bleeding).

USES:

Heavy menstrual bleeding, bleeding with IUD.

DOSAGE:

 One tablet four times a day while bleeding.

FORMS:

Capsule shaped tablet of 500mg (white).

PRECAUTIONS:

Not for use in pregnancy, breast feeding and children.
Seek further medical attention if vaginal bleeding persists.

Do not take if:

 • suffering from other forms of bleeding

SIDE EFFECTS:

Common: headache, rash, nausea.

INTERACTIONS:

None significant.

PRESCRIPTION:

Yes.

PERMITTED IN SPORT:

Yes.

Ethanol

TRADE NAMES:

Ethanol is common alcohol (ethyl alcohol) and is used in a large number of medications, particularly as a solvent in mixtures, gels and lotions. Ethanol is the alcohol that is present in all alcoholic drinks (beer, wine, spirits etc.).

DRUG CLASS:
Alcohol.

USES:
In medication: dissolves other medications, acts as a preservative, mild sedative, mild cough suppressant.
In drinks: relaxes, reduces inhibitions.

DOSAGE:
 As directed or desired.

FORMS:
Mixture, liquid, gel, lotion.

PRECAUTIONS:
Use in pregnancy should be avoided. May be used in small quantities in breast feeding. Not to be given to children except when used in approved medications.

Do not take if:

- suffering from liver damage, alcoholism, depression, other psychiatric conditions, pancreatitis, any abnormal bleeding.
- operating machinery, driving a vehicle or undertaking tasks that require concentration.

SIDE EFFECTS:
Common: drowsiness, flush, rapid heart rate.
Unusual: nausea, vomiting, headache.

INTERACTIONS:
Other drugs:
- interacts with a wide range of medications. Should not be taken while using any other medication without consulting a pharmacist or doctor.

Other substances:
- reacts adversely with exercise, cocaine, marijuana and narcotics.

PRESCRIPTION:
No.

PERMITTED IN SPORT:
Yes. Impairs sport performance.

OVERDOSE:
Vomiting, poor coordination, loss of inhibitions, headache, blurred vision, loss of control of bodily functions, convulsions, coma and rarely death may occur. Seek medical assistance if massive rapid overdose consumed.

OTHER INFORMATION:
Ethanol has been produced by fermenting various fruits, vegetables and cereals for thousands of years and is mankind's most widely used drug. May cause dependence and addiction. Long term use at moderate to high dosage can cause damage to liver, brain and other organs.

Ethinyloestradiol
See MORNING AFTER PILL, ORAL CONTRACEPTIVES.

Ethosuximide

TRADE NAMES:
Emeside, Zarontin.

DRUG CLASS:
Anticonvulsant.

USES:
Petit mal epilepsy (absences).

DOSAGE:
 One to four capsules twice a day.

FORMS:
Capsule of 250mg, syrup.

PRECAUTIONS:

Not to be used in pregnancy (D) unless medically essential. Breast feeding should be ceased before use. May be used in children.

Regular blood tests to check on liver function and blood cells recommended. Do not stop medication suddenly, but reduce dosage slowly.

Use with caution if operating machinery or driving a vehicle.

SIDE EFFECTS:

Common: loss of appetite, nausea, belly cramps, drowsiness, headache.
Unusual: belly pain, weight loss, diarrhoea, hiccups, irritability, rash, abnormal liver function, incoordination, hyperactive.
Severe but rare (stop medication, consult doctor): blood cell damage (detected by blood tests).

INTERACTIONS:

Other drugs:
• other medications used to treat epilepsy.
Herbs:
• evening primrose (linoleic acid), Gingko biloba.
Other substances:
• reacts adversely with alcohol.

PRESCRIPTION:

Yes.

PERMITTED IN SPORT:

Yes.

OVERDOSE:

Administer activated charcoal or induce vomiting if medication taken recently and patient alert. Seek medical attention.

OTHER INFORMATION:

Widely and successfully used in treatment of petit mal absences. Does not cause dependence or addiction.

See also BARBITURATES, BENZODIAZEPINES, Clonazepam, Gabapentin, Lamotrigine, Levetiracetam, Oxcarbazepine, Phenytoin, Primidone, Sodium valproate, Sulthiame, Tiagabine, Topiramate, Vigabatrin.

Ethynodiol diacetate

See ORAL CONTRACEPTIVES.

Etidronate
(Disodium etidronate)

TRADE NAME:

Didronel.

DRUG CLASS:

Bisphosphonate.

USES:

Paget's disease, osteoporosis.

DOSAGE:

 Once a day at bedtime on an empty stomach. Usually combined with calcium supplement.

FORMS:

Tablets, effervescent tablet.

PRECAUTIONS:

Use in pregnancy only if medically essential. Not for use in breast feeding or children.

Use with caution in peptic ulcer, inflamed bowel, kidney stones.

Diet must contain adequate calcium and vitamin D.

Do not take if:

 • suffering from osteomalacia, bone cancer, severe kidney disease.

SIDE EFFECTS:

Common: diarrhoea, nausea.
Unusual: bone pain.
Severe but rare (stop medication, consult doctor): bleeding from bowel.

INTERACTIONS:

Other drugs:
• antacids, vitamin and mineral supplements.
Other substances:
• high calcium foods (e.g. cheese, sardines).

PRESCRIPTION:

Yes.

PERMITTED IN SPORT:

Yes.

OVERDOSE:

Unlikely to be serious unless taken long term in excessive doses.

OTHER INFORMATION:

Does not cause dependence or addiction.

Etodolac

TRADE NAME:

Lodine SR.

DRUG CLASS:

NSAID.

USES:

All forms of arthritis, rheumatoid arthritis.

DOSAGE:

 One tablet a day.

FORMS:

Tablets of 600mg (grey).

PRECAUTIONS:

Should not be used in pregnancy (C) unless medically essential. Breast feeding should be ceased if necessary to use NSAID. Not for use in children.
Use with caution in psychiatricaly disturbed patients, epilepsy, severe infection, heart failure and kidney disease.

Lower doses required in elderly, who may suffer more side effects.

Do not take if:

• suffering from peptic ulcer at present or in recent past
• due for surgery (including dental surgery)
• suffering from bleeding disorder or anaemia.

SIDE EFFECTS:

Common: stomach discomfort, diarrhoea, constipation, heartburn, nausea, headache, dizziness.
Unusual: blurred vision, stomach ulcer, ringing noise in ears, retention of fluid, swelling of tissue, drowsiness, itch, rash, shortness of breath.
Severe but rare (stop medication, consult doctor): vomit blood, pass blood in faeces, other unusual bleeding, asthma induced by medication.

INTERACTIONS:

Other drugs:
• must never be used with anticoagulants
• probenecid, diuretics, lithium, methotrexate, beta-blockers, ACE inhibitors, quinolone antibiotics, cyclosporin, digoxin, blood pressure medications, steroids, mifepristone.

PRESCRIPTION:

Yes.

PERMITTED IN SPORT:

Yes.

OVERDOSE:

Causes nausea, vomiting, severe headache, dizziness, confusion and convulsions. Administer activated charcoal or induce vomiting if taken recently. Seek medical assistance.

See also Aceclofenac, Acemetacin, Aspirin, Azapropazone, Dexketoprofen, Diclofenac, Diflunisal, Felbinac, Fenbufen, Fenoprofen, Flurbiprofen, Ibuprofen, Indomethacin, Ketoprofen, Ketorolac trometanol,Mefenamic acid, Meloxicam, Nabumetone, Naproxen, Phenylbutazone, Piroxicam, Salicylic acid, Sulindac,

Tenoxicam, Tiaprofenic Acid, Tolfenamic acid.

Etonogestrel

TRADE NAME:

Implanon.

DRUG CLASS:

Sex hormone.

USES:

Long term contraception. One implant gives three years protection.

DOSAGE:

 One implant inserted under skin at inside of upper arm every three years. Implant initially during a menstrual period.

FORMS:

Implant.

PRECAUTIONS:

Not for use in pregnancy (B3), breast feeding or children.
Implantation must be preceded by a thorough medical history and examination.

Do not take if:

- suffering from blood clots (thromboses), liver disease or tumours, breast cancer
- cause of any abnormal vaginal bleeding has not been diagnosed.

SIDE EFFECTS:

Common: breast discomfort, heavy periods, acne, headaches, belly pain, emotional upsets, weight increase, pain at implant site.
Unusual: chloasma (skin pigmentation), hair loss, dizziness, nausea, depression, increased libido.
Severe but rare (stop medication, consult doctor): blood clot in vein or artery, lumps in breast, constant vaginal bleeding, jaundice (yellow skin).

INTERACTIONS:

Other drugs:
- barbiturates, primidone, carbamazepine, oxcarbazepine, griseofulvin, rifampicin, rifabutin, other sex hormones.

PRESCRIPTION:

Yes.

PERMITTED IN SPORT:

Yes.

OTHER INFORMATION:

Introduced in 1999 as an improved long term contraceptive that requires no regular dosing schedule or planning. Must be carefully implanted in the correct position and must always be removed after three years.

See Medroxyprogesterone acetate, Oestradiol, Oestriol, Oestrogen, ORAL CONTRACEPTIVES.

Etoposide

TRADE NAMES:

Vepesid.
Etopophos (etoposide phosphate).

USES:

Leukaemia, lung cancer, Hodgkin's disease, lymphoma.

DOSAGE:

 Complex. Must be determined individually for each patient by doctor depending on diseases, severity, response and size of patient.

FORMS:

Capsules (pink) of 50mg and 100mg, drip infusion.

PRECAUTIONS:

Not to be used in pregnancy (D) unless mother's life is threatened. Breast feeding must be ceased before use. Use in children only if medically essential.

Adequate contraception must be used by women while taking Etoposide.
Regular blood tests to check blood cells, kidney and liver function essential.
Use with caution in infections.
Do not allow infusion to come in contact with skin.

Do not take if:

- suffering from severe liver or bone marrow disease.

SIDE EFFECTS:

Common: reduced blood white cells and increased risk of infection, unusual bleeding and bruising, total hair loss, nausea, vomiting, loss of appetite, sore mouth, diarrhoea.
Unusual: low blood pressure, fever, rapid heart rate, shortness of breath, pins and needles.

INTERACTIONS:

Other drugs:
- other medications used to treat cancer, cyclosporin.

PRESCRIPTION:

Yes.

PERMITTED IN SPORT:

Yes.

OVERDOSE:

Worsening of side effects likely. Seek medical attention.

OTHER INFORMATION:

Despite serious side effects, etoposide may be life saving for patients with some severe forms of cancer.

Etoricoxib

TRADE NAME:

Arcoxia.

DRUG CLASS:

Nonsteroidal anti-inflammatory (NSAID).

USES:

All forms of arthritis, rheumatoid arthritis, gout.

DOSAGE:

 One tablet a day.

FORMS:

Tablets of 60mg, 90mg and 120mg.

PRECAUTIONS:

Should not be used in pregnancy (C) unless medically essential. Breast feeding should be ceased if necessary to use NSAID. Not for use in children under 16 years.
Use with caution in psychiatricaly disturbed patients, epilepsy, severe infection, heart failure and kidney disease.
Lower doses required in elderly, who may suffer more side effects.

Do not take if:

- suffering from peptic ulcer at present or in recent past
- due for surgery (including dental surgery)
- suffering from bleeding disorder or anaemia.

SIDE EFFECTS:

Common: stomach discomfort, diarrhoea, constipation, heartburn, nausea, headache, dizziness.
Unusual: blurred vision, stomach ulcer, ringing noise in ears, retention of fluid, swelling of tissue, drowsiness, itch, rash, shortness of breath.
Severe but rare (stop medication, consult doctor): vomiting blood, passing blood in faeces, other unusual bleeding, asthma induced by medication.

INTERACTIONS:

Other drugs:
- must never be used with anticoagulants (e.g. warfarin)

- other NSAID, diuretics, lithium, methotrexate, tacrolimus, ACE inhibitors, oral contraceptives, salbutamol, digoxin, blood pressure medications, steroids, minoxidil, rifampicin.

PRESCRIPTION:

Yes.

PERMITTED IN SPORT:

Yes.

OVERDOSE:

Causes nausea, vomiting, severe headache, dizziness, confusion and convulsions. Administer activated charcoal or induce vomiting if taken recently. Seek medical assistance.

OTHER INFORMATION:

Introduced in 2002.

See also Aceclofenac, Acemetacin, Aspirin, Azapropazone, Dexketoprofen, Diclofenac, Diflunisal, Felbinac, Fenbufen, Fenoprofen, Flurbiprofen, Ibuprofen, Indomethacin, Ketoprofen, Ketorolac trometanol, Mefenamic acid, Meloxicam, Nabumetone, Naproxen, Phenylbutazone, Piroxicam, Salicylic acid, Sulindac, Tenoxicam, Tiaprofenic Acid, Tolfenamic acid.

Evening primrose oil
(Linoleic acid)

See FATTY ACIDS.

Exemestane

TRADE NAME:

Aromasin.

USES:

Advanced breast cancer.

DOSAGE:

 One tablet a day.

FORMS:

Tablet of 25mg (white).

PRECAUTIONS:

Not to be used in pregnancy (D), breast feeding or children.
Use with caution in liver and kidney disease.
Blood tests to check liver function required regularly.

Do not take if:

 • still menstruating regularly.

SIDE EFFECTS:

Common: hot flushes, nausea, fatigue, sweating, headache, dizziness, sleeplessness, muscle pain.
Unusual: rash, loss of appetite, weight loss, belly pains, depression, swelling of feet, hair loss, constipation, indigestion.
Severe but rare (stop medication, consult doctor): blood cell damage, liver damage.

INTERACTIONS:

Other drugs:
• oestrogen.

PRESCRIPTION:

Yes.

PERMITTED IN SPORT:

Yes.

OVERDOSE:

Very serious. Seek urgent medical attention.

OTHER INFORMATION:

Introduced in 1999 to treat breast cancer patients in whom no other treatment is helping.

EXPECTORANTS

DISCUSSION:

Expectorants aid the removal of phlegm and mucus from the respiratory passages of the lung and throat by coughing. They act by liquefying tenacious, sticky mucus so that it does not adhere firmly to the walls of the air passages and can be shifted up and out by the microscopic hairs that line these passages and by the forced expiration of air in coughing. They are usually combined in a mixture with other medications such as mucolytics, decongestants, antihistamines, bronchodilators or antitussives.

The traditional expectorants include senega, ammonium chloride and potassium iodide, all of which taste absolutely foul. Bromhexine is a more recently developed expectorant that has a slightly better taste. The side effects of expectorants are minimal. Many different brands are available from chemists without a prescription.

See Camphor, COUGH SUPPRESSANTS.

EYE LUBRICANTS

TRADE and GENERIC NAMES:

Geltears, Liposic, Viscotears (Carbomer).
Hypotears, LiquifilmTears, Sno Tears (Polyvinyl alcohol).
Ilube (Hypromellose with acetylcysteine).
Isopto Alkaline, Isopto Plain (Hypromellose).
Isopto Atropine (Hypromellose with atropine).
Isopto Carbachol (Hypromellose with carbachol).
Isopto Frin (Hypromellose with phenylephrine).
Lacri Lube, Lubri-Tears (Paraffin, wool fat).
Maxidex (Hypromellose with dexamethasone).

Maxitrol (Hypromellose with dexamethasone, neomycin, polymyxin).
Minims Artificial Tears (Hydroxymethylcellulose).
Oculotect (Povidone)
Tears Naturale (Hypromellose with dextran).
NB: eye lubricants are underlined.

USES:

Dry, itchy, irritated eyes.

DOSAGE:

 Use drops as required several times a day.

FORMS:

Eye drops, eye ointment, eye gel.

PRECAUTIONS:

May be used safely in pregnancy (use Carbomer 940 with caution), breast feeding and children.
Use with caution if wearing contact lenses.

SIDE EFFECTS:

Common: mild stinging, blurred vision.

INTERACTIONS:

None significant.

PRESCRIPTION:

No.

PERMITTED IN SPORT:

Yes.

OVERDOSE:

No adverse effects likely if swallowed.

OTHER INFORMATION:

Widely and commonly used for dry itchy eyes.

Famciclovir

TRADE NAME:

Famvir.

DRUG CLASS:

Antiviral.

USES:

Treatment of herpes zoster infections (genital herpes, shingles).

DOSAGE:

 Treatment: 750mg a day.
Prevention: 250mg a day.

FORMS:

Tablets (white) of 250, 500 and 750mg.

PRECAUTIONS:

Use with caution in pregnancy (B1), breast feeding and children.
Use with caution in serious kidney disease.

SIDE EFFECTS:

Common: headache.
Unusual: nausea, fatigue.

INTERACTIONS:

Other drugs:
• probenecid, diuretics (fluid tablets).

PRESCRIPTION:

Yes.

PERMITTED IN SPORT:

Yes.

OVERDOSE:

Exacerbation of side effects likely.

OTHER INFORMATION:

Introduced in 1996. Very safe and effective medication that has a very high success rate in treating Herpes infections.

Chickenpox and shingles are caused by Herpes zoster, and cold sores and genital herpes by Herpes simplex. It is vital that any patient who suspects they have shingles must see their doctor immediately as medication only works if started within 72 hours of onset of rash.
See also Aciclovir.

Famotidine

TRADE NAME:

Pepcid.

DRUG CLASS:

H2 Receptor antagonist. (Anti-ulcerant).

USES:

Treatment and prevention of ulceration and inflammation of the stomach, duodenum (upper small intestine) and oesophagus (gullet).
Zollinger-Ellison syndrome (a rare cause of severe stomach ulceration).

DOSAGE:

 20 to 40mg once a day at night.
Higher doses with Zollinger-Ellison syndrome and severe ulceration.

FORMS:

Tablets of 20mg and 40mg.

PRECAUTIONS:

Caution required in pregnancy (B1), with children and while breast feeding.
Use with caution in kidney disease.
Assess stomach with gastroscopy if not effective rapidly.
Do not take if:

 • suffering from stomach cancer, significant kidney disease.

SIDE EFFECTS:

Common: headache, dizziness, irregular bowel habits.
Unusual: dry mouth, nausea, loss of appetite, bloating, tiredness, itchy skin, arthritis.

INTERACTIONS:

Herbs:
• alfalfa, capsicum, eucalyptus, senega.

PRESCRIPTION:

Yes.

PERMITTED IN SPORT:

Yes.

OVERDOSE:

No serious adverse effects expected.

OTHER INFORMATION:

An effective and safe medication for rapidly easing the pain of peptic ulcers, and curing them. May be used safely long term.

See also Cimetidine, Nizatadine, Ranitidine.

FATTY ACIDS

TRADE and GENERIC NAMES:

Evening Primrose Oil, Gammaderm (linoleic acid).
Maxepa, Omacor (eicosapentaenoic acid, docosahexaenoic acid—triglycerides).
Fatty acids are also found in numerous other nutritional, vitamin and mineral supplements.

USES:

Fatty acid (triglyceride) deficiency.

DOSAGE:

 One or two capsules, two or three times a day with food.

FORMS:

Capsules, liquid, oil.

PRECAUTIONS:

Safe in pregnancy, breast feeding and children.
Not to be used long term.
Use with caution in hyperactive children and asthma.
Never inject liquid forms.

SIDE EFFECTS:

Common: increased bleeding time, nausea.
Unusual: vomiting.

INTERACTIONS:

Other drugs:
• anticoagulants.

PRESCRIPTION:

No.

PERMITTED IN SPORT:

Yes.

OVERDOSE:

Unlikely to have serious effects.

OTHER INFORMATION:

Does not cause addiction or dependence.

Felbinac

TRADE NAME:

Traxam.

DRUG CLASS:

Nonsteroidal anti-inflammatory drug (NSAID).

USES:

Arthritic pains, sprains, strains, bruises.

DOSAGE:

 Rub into affected area two to four times a day.

FORMS:

Gel, foam.

PRECAUTIONS:

Gel and foam may be used with caution in pregnancy, breast feeding (but not on the breasts) and children.

Do not take if:

• suffering from bleeding disorder.

SIDE EFFECTS:

Common: skin redness, dermatitis.
Unusual: itch, skin sensitivity.

INTERACTIONS:

Other drugs:
• aspirin, other NSAIDs.

PRESCRIPTION:

Yes.

PERMITTED IN SPORT:

Yes.

OTHER INFORMATION:

Only used externally for milder forms of tissue damage.

See also Aceclofenac, Acemetacin, Aspirin, Azapropazone, Dexketoprofen, Diclofenac, Diflunisal, Etodolac, Fenbufen, Fenoprofen, Flurbiprofen, Ibuprofen, Indomethacin, Ketoprofen, Mefenamic acid, Meloxicam, Nabumetone, Naproxen, Piroxicam, Sulindac, Tenoxicam, Tiaprofenic Acid, Tolfenamic acid.

Felodipine

TRADE NAMES:

Plendil.
Triapin (with ramipril).

DRUG CLASS:

Calcium channel blocker (calcium antagonist).

USES:

High blood pressure.

DOSAGE:

 2.5 to 20mg once a day.

FORMS:

Tablets of 2.5, 5 and 10mg.

PRECAUTIONS:

Should only be used in pregnancy (C) and breast feeding if medically essential. Not designed for use in children.

Do not take if:

• suffering from severe heart failure, low blood pressure, atrial flutter or fibrillation.

SIDE EFFECTS:

Common: constipation, tiredness, headache, dizziness, indigestion, swelling of feet and ankles.
Unusual: flushing, palpitations, slow heart rate, scalp irritation, depression, flushes, nightmares, excess wind.
Severe but rare (stop medication, consult doctor): fainting.

INTERACTIONS:

Other drugs:
• beta-blockers (eg, propranolol), cyclosporin, digoxin, cimetidine, barbiturates, diazepam, amiodarone, quinidine, rifampicin, phenytoin, cisapride, theophylline, terbutaline, salbutamol, diltiazem
• additive effect with other medications for high blood pressure.
Herbs:
• goldenseal, guarana, hawthorn, Korean ginseng, liquorice.
Other substances:
• smoking may aggravate conditions that these medications are treating
• grapefruit juice.

PRESCRIPTION:

Yes.

PERMITTED IN SPORT:

Yes.

OVERDOSE:

May continue to be absorbed for up to 48 hours after overdose. Administer activated charcoal or induce vomiting. Purging should be encouraged to eliminate drug from gut. Overdose may cause low blood pressure, irregular heart rhythm, difficulty in breathing, heart attack and death. Obtain urgent medical attention.

OTHER INFORMATION:

Commonly used as a first line medication in high blood pressure.

See also Amlodipine, Diltiazem, Isradipine, Lacidipine, Lercanidipine, Nicardipine, Nifedipine, Nimodipine, Verapamil.

Fenbufen

TRADE NAME:

Lederfen.

DRUG CLASS:

Propionic acid (NSAID).

USES:

Osteoarthritis, rheumatoid arthritis, ankylosing spondylitis, back pain, muscle pain.

DOSAGE:

 300mg morning and 600mg at night, or 450mg twice a day.

FORMS:

Tablets of 300mg and 450mg (light blue), capsules of 300mg (dark blue).

PRECAUTIONS:

Use with caution in pregnancy (C) and breast feeding. Not for use in late pregnancy.
May be used in children.
Use with caution in asthma, dehydration, high blood pressure, severe infection, heart failure and kidney disease.
Lower doses required in elderly, who may suffer more side effects.

Do not take if:

- suffering from peptic ulcer at present or in recent past
- sensitive to anti-inflammatories or aspirin
- due for surgery (including dental surgery)
- suffering from bleeding disorder or anaemia.

SIDE EFFECTS:

Common: stomach discomfort, diarrhoea, constipation, heartburn, nausea, headache, dizziness.
Unusual: blurred vision, stomach ulcer, ringing noise in ears, retention of fluid, swelling of tissue, drowsiness, itch, rash, shortness of breath.
Severe but rare (stop medication, consult doctor): vomiting blood, passing blood in faeces, other unusual bleeding, asthma induced by medication.

INTERACTIONS:

Other drugs:
- must never be used with anticoagulants (e.g. warfarin)
- probenecid, diuretics, lithium, methotrexate, beta-blockers, ACE inhibitors.

PRESCRIPTION:

Yes.

PERMITTED IN SPORT:

Yes.

OVERDOSE:

Causes nausea, vomiting, severe headache, dizziness, confusion and convulsions. Administer activated charcoal or induce vomiting if taken recently. Seek medical assistance.

OTHER INFORMATION:

Extensively used to give excellent relief to a wide variety of inflammatory and pain conditions. Significant side effects (particularly on the stomach) in about 5% of patients. Limit their use.

See also Aspirin, Bufexamac, Celecoxib, Diclofenac, Diflunisal, Fenoprofen, Flurbiprofen, Indomethacin, Ketoprofen, Ketorolac trometanol, Mefenamic Acid, Naproxen, Piroxicam, Rofecoxib, Salicylic acid, Sulindac, Tenoxicam, Tiaprofenic Acid.

Fenofibrate

TRADE NAMES:

Lipantil Micro, Supralip.

DRUG CLASS:

Hypolipidaemic.

USES:

Lowers blood fat (cholesterol) levels.

DOSAGE:

 67mg three times a day with food, or 160mg to 267mg once a day with food.

FORMS:

Capsules and tablets of 67mg, 160mg, 200mg and 267mg.

PRECAUTIONS:

Not to be used in pregnancy and breast feeding.
May be used in children.
Use with caution in kidney disease.

Do not take if:

 • suffering from gall stones, other gall bladder disease, severe liver or kidney disease.

SIDE EFFECTS:

Common: nausea, diarrhoea, rash.
Unusual: headache, tiredness, dizziness.
Severe but rare (stop medication, consult doctor): poor libido, muscle pain, liver damage, light sensitivity.

INTERACTIONS:

Other drugs:
• anticoagulants, phenylbutazone, diabetes medications, other medications to lower cholesterol.

PRESCRIPTION:

Yes.

PERMITTED IN SPORT:

Yes.

OVERDOSE:

No specific problems. Exacerbation of side effects likely.

OTHER INFORMATION:

Normally only used in patients who are resistant to other medications.

See also Clofibrate, HYPOLIPIDAEMICS.

Fenoprofen

TRADE NAME:

Fenopron.

DRUG CLASS:

Propionic acid (NSAID).

USES:

Osteoarthritis, rheumatoid arthritis, ankylosing spondylitis, back pain, muscle pain.

DOSAGE:

 300mg to 600mg three or four times a day.

FORMS:

Tablets of 300mg and 600mg (orange).

PRECAUTIONS:

Use with caution in pregnancy (C) and breast feeding. Not for use in late pregnancy.
Not for use in children.
Use with caution in asthma, dehydration,

high blood pressure, severe infection, heart failure and kidney disease.
Lower doses required in elderly, who may suffer more side effects.

Do not take if:

- suffering from peptic ulcer at present or in recent past
- sensitive to anti-inflammatories or aspirin
- due for surgery (including dental surgery)
- suffering from bleeding disorder or anaemia.

SIDE EFFECTS:

Common: stomach discomfort, diarrhoea, constipation, heartburn, nausea, headache, dizziness.
Unusual: blurred vision, stomach ulcer, ringing noise in ears, retention of fluid, swelling of tissue, drowsiness, itch, rash, shortness of breath.
Severe but rare (stop medication, consult doctor): vomiting blood, passing blood in faeces, other unusual bleeding, asthma induced by medication.

INTERACTIONS:

Other drugs:
- must never be used with anticoagulants (e.g. warfarin)
- probenecid, diuretics, lithium, methotrexate, beta-blockers, ACE inhibitors.

PRESCRIPTION:

Yes.

PERMITTED IN SPORT:

Yes.

OVERDOSE:

Causes nausea, vomiting, severe headache, dizziness, confusion and convulsions. Administer activated charcoal or induce vomiting if taken recently. Seek medical assistance.

OTHER INFORMATION:

Extensively used to give excellent relief to a wide variety of inflammatory and pain conditions. Significant side effects (particularly on the stomach) in about 5% of patients. Limit their use.

See also Aspirin, Bufexamac, Celecoxib, Diclofenac, Diflunisal, Fenbrufen, Flurbiprofen, Indomethacin, Ketoprofen, Ketorolac trometanol, Mefenamic Acid, Naproxen, Piroxicam, Rofecoxib, Salicylic acid, Sulindac, Tenoxicam, Tiaprofenic Acid.

Fenoterol

TRADE NAME:

Duovent (with ipratropium).
Only available in this combination in Britain.

DRUG CLASS:

Bronchodilator (Beta-2 agonist).

USES:

Asthma, chronic bronchitis.

DOSAGE:

 One or two inhalations every six to eight hours.

FORMS:

Inhaler, autohaler, nebules.

PRECAUTIONS:

Safe to use in pregnancy (A), breast feeding and children.
Not designed for long term constant use.
Use with care in high blood pressure, heart disease, overactive thyroid gland, diabetes, liver and kidney disease.
Lower doses necessary in elderly.
Seek urgent medical assistance if no response to medication.

SIDE EFFECTS:

Common: tremor, rapid heart rate, palpitations, headache.
Unusual: nausea, flush, mouth irritation.

INTERACTIONS:

Other drugs:
- sympathomimetics, beta-blockers, theophyllines, steroids, diuretics, digoxin, MAOI, tricyclic antidepressants.

PRESCRIPTION:

Yes.

PERMITTED IN SPORT:

No.

OVERDOSE:

Exacerbation of side effects likely. May be dangerous in patients with heart disease or high blood pressure.

OTHER INFORMATION:

Designed for intermittent occasional use, and not to be taken regularly. Other medication should be used to prevent asthma if repeated doses of this medication are needed. Does not cause dependence or addiction. First introduced in the 1960s, beta-agonists have revolutionised life for asthmatics, but since deregulation in the mid 1980s, they have often been used excessively and inappropriately.

See also Salbutamol, Salmeterol, Terbutaline.

Fentanyl

TRADE NAMES:

Actiq, Durogesic, Sublimaze.

DRUG CLASS:

Narcotic analgesic.

USES:

Relief of severe pain.

DOSAGE:

Patches: one patch applied every three days.
Lozenges: do not swallow or chew, allow to dissolve in mouth. Start with low dose four times a day and increase strength of lozenge as required.
Injection: intramuscular or intravenous as determined by doctor.

FORMS:

Skin patches of 25, 50, 75 and 100 µg; lozenges of 200, 400, 600, 800, 1200 and 1600 µg; injection.

PRECAUTIONS:

Not for use in pregnancy (C).
Use with caution in breast feeding and children.
Initial dose of patch should not exceed 25µg or lozenge 200µg.
Use with caution in head injuries, fevers, severe lung, kidney, liver and heart disease.
Lower doses required in elderly.

Do not take if:
- suffering from intermittent or postoperative pain.
- history of drug abuse.

SIDE EFFECTS:

Common: tolerance requiring higher doses, addiction to medication, tiredness, constipation, dry mouth, nausea, sweating.
Unusual: vomiting, confusion, abdominal pain, hallucinations, reduced breath volume, low blood pressure, itchy rash, local skin reactions at site of patch application, excessive happiness (euphoria).
Severe but rare (stop medication, consult doctor): retention of urine, irregular heart beat, chest pain (angina).

INTERACTIONS:

Other drugs:
- monoamine oxidase inhibitors (MAOI, used for severe depression), sedatives, ritonavir.

Other substances:
- alcohol, marijuana.

PRESCRIPTION:

Yes.

PERMITTED IN SPORT:

No.

OVERDOSE:

Excessive use of patches may result in worsening of side effects to the point of life threatening lung and heart complications. The effects will persist for up to 24 hours after patches removed. Antidote available. Seek urgent medical attention.

OTHER INFORMATION:

Patches introduced in 2000 and lozenges in 2002 for the treatment of persistent cancer pain with less constipation and sedation than narcotic pain killers taken by mouth or injection. Injection usually used only during a general anaesthetic.

See also Alfentanil, Buprenorphine, Codeine, Dextromoramide, Dextropropoxyphene, Heroin, Hydromorphone, Methadone, Morphine, Oxycodone, Pentazocine, Pethidine.

Fenugreek
(Trigonella)

USES:

Poor appetite, skin inflammation.

DOSAGE:

 2g three times a day.

FORMS:

Capsules, powder for tea preparation.

PRECAUTIONS:

Do not use in pregnancy or breast feeding.

SIDE EFFECTS:

Common: minimal.
Unusual: skin sensitisation.

INTERACTIONS:

Other drugs:
• hypoglycaemics (used to treat diabetes).

PRESCRIPTION:

No.

PERMITTED IN SPORT:

Yes.

OTHER INFORMATION:

Not used in orthodox medicine.

FERROUS SALTS
(Ferric ammonium citrate, Ferrous fumarate, Ferrous gluconate, Ferrous phosphate, Ferrous sulfate)

See Iron.

Feverfew
(Tanacetum parthenium)

USES:

Prevention of migraine.

DOSAGE:

 200mg to 250mg a day.

FORMS:

Capsules, tablets.

PRECAUTIONS:

Use with caution in pregnancy, breast feeding and children.
Avoid skin contact.
Rebound effects possible after cessation include headache, insomnia, muscle pains and stiffness, joint pain and tiredness.

SIDE EFFECTS:

Common: minimal.

Unusual: heartburn, belly pains, mouth irritation, anal irritation.
Severe but rare (stop medication, consult doctor): severe diarrhoea.

INTERACTIONS:

Other drugs:
• anticoagulants (e.g. warfarin).
Herbs:
• tansy, yarrow, aster, sunflower, laurel, liverwort.

PRESCRIPTION:

No.

PERMITTED IN SPORT:

Yes.

OTHER INFORMATION:

Not used in orthodox medicine.

Fexofenadine

See ANTIHISTAMINES, NON-SEDATING.

FIBRE

See Frangula, Ispaghula, Methylcellulose, Pectin, Psyllium, Sterculia.

FIBRINOLYTICS

TRADE and GENERIC NAMES:

Actilyse (Alteplase).
Streptase (Streptokinase).
Varidase (Streptokinase and streptodornase).

USES:

Lysis (destruction) of blood clots in veins and arteries, particularly in heart, lungs and brain.
Cleaning of wounds full of slough.

DOSAGE:

 As administered by doctor.

FORMS:

Injection, powder.

PRECAUTIONS:

Only used in pregnancy (C) if medically essential. Breast feeding should be ceased if medication used. Not designed for use in children, but may be necessary medically.
Do not take if:
 • recent surgery performed.

SIDE EFFECTS:

Common: minor unusual bleeding, fever.
Unusual: significant unusual bleeding, allergy reaction.

INTERACTIONS:

Other drugs:
• anticoagulants (e.g. warfarin).

PRESCRIPTION:

Yes.

PERMITTED IN SPORT:

Yes, but no vigourous activity should be undertaken for some time after use.

OVERDOSE:

Serious, but antidote available.

OTHER INFORMATION:

Injection used only in hospital for seriously ill patients. Topical forms used to clean up wound exudates.
See also Aprotinin.

Finasteride

TRADE NAME:

Proscar.

USES:

Benign enlargement of prostate gland.

DOSAGE:

 One tablet a day for six to twelve months.

FORMS:

Tablets (blue) of 5mg.

PRECAUTIONS:

Must never be used in pregnancy (X) as severe damage may be caused to foetus. Must never be used in breast feeding or children.
Must never be used in women.
Pregnant women whose male partner is using finasteride must avoid sex during pregnancy as contact with semen may cause deformities in foetus.

SIDE EFFECTS:

Common: impotence, decreased libido.
Unusual: breast enlargement in men, rash.

INTERACTIONS:

None significant.

PRESCRIPTION:

Yes.

PERMITTED IN SPORT:

Yes.

OVERDOSE:

No serious consequences expected.

OTHER INFORMATION:

Released in 1993. Extremely dangerous in pregnancy, otherwise safe and effective. May take some months for improvement in symptoms. Does not cause dependence or addiction.
See also Tamsulosin, Terazosin.

Flavoxate

TRADE NAME:

Urispas.

DRUG CLASS:

Antispasmodic.

USES:

Incontinence of urine, frequency of urination, passing urine excessively at night, pain when passing urine, pain after passing urinary catheter.

DOSAGE:

 One tablet three times a day.

FORMS:

Tablets of 200mg (white).

PRECAUTIONS:

Use with caution in pregnancy, breast feeding and children.
Exclude urinary obstruction and prostate cancer before use.
Use with caution in glaucoma.
Do not take if:
 • suffering from gut obstruction.

SIDE EFFECTS:

Common: headache, nausea, fatigue, diarrhoea.
Unusual: blurred vision, dry mouth.

INTERACTIONS:

None significant.

PRESCRIPTION:

Yes.

PERMITTED IN SPORT:

Yes.

OVERDOSE:

Exacerbation of side effects likely.

Flecainide

TRADE NAME:

Tambocor.

DRUG CLASS:

Antiarrhythmic.

USES:

Control and prevention of certain types of heart beat irregularity.

DOSAGE:

 One to three tablets twice a day.

FORMS:

Tablets of 50mg and 100mg, injection.

PRECAUTIONS:

Should be used only if essential and with caution in pregnancy (B3). Should only be used if medically essential in breast feeding and children.
Use with caution in heart failure, if pacemaker implanted, kidney or liver disease.

Do not take if:

 • suffering from recent heart attack, or certain types of heart nerve conduction defects.

SIDE EFFECTS:

Common: noises in ears, palpitations, fainting, chest pains, dizziness, rash, nausea, constipation, diarrhoea, belly pains, visual disturbances, shortness of breath.
Unusual: angina, slow heart rate, high blood pressure, swelling of tissues, vomiting, fever, sweating, impotence, discomfort on urination, arthritis, leg cramps, muscle aches, dry mouth, twitches, double vision, anxiety, confusion, tiredness.
Severe but rare (stop medication, consult doctor): jaundice, continued angina, severe shortness of breath, marked tissue swelling.

INTERACTIONS:

Other drugs:
• digoxin, disopyramide, verapamil, amiodarone.

PRESCRIPTION:

Yes (restricted to treatment of serious cardiac arrhythmias where treatment is started in hospital).

PERMITTED IN SPORT:

Yes.

OVERDOSE:

Low blood pressure and rapid heart rate likely. Administer activated charcoal or induce vomiting if tablets taken recently. Seek medical assistance.

See also Amiodarone, Disopyramide, Mexiletine, Procainamide, Quinidine bisulphate, Sotalol, Verapamil.

Flucloxacillin

TRADE NAMES:

Floxapen.
Magnapen (with ampicillin).

DRUG CLASS:

Penicillin antibiotic.

USES:

Treatment of infections caused by susceptible bacteria.

DOSAGE:

 One or two capsules every six hours 30 minutes before food. Course (usually seven days) should be completed.

FORMS:

Capsules, mixture (store in door of refrigerator), injection.

PRECAUTIONS:

May be used in pregnancy (B1), children and breast feeding if medically indicated. Use with caution in kidney failure, liver disease, premature infants and leukaemia. Not for use in eyes.

Do not take if:

 • allergic to penicillin
• suffering from glandular fever or severe liver disease.

SIDE EFFECTS:

Common: mild diarrhoea, nausea, vomiting.
Unusual: genital itch or rash.
Severe but rare (stop medication, consult doctor): itchy rash, hives, severe diarrhoea, yellow skin (jaundice), unusual bleeding or bruising.

INTERACTIONS:

Other drugs:
• probenecid, oral contraceptives.

PRESCRIPTION:

Yes.

PERMITTED IN SPORT:

Yes.

OVERDOSE:

Vomiting and diarrhoea only likely effects.

OTHER INFORMATION:

Used for more severe infections. Some bacteria can break down simpler forms of Penicillin. Cloxacillin, Dicloxacillin and Flucloxacillin are not able to be broken down this way and so can be effective when other penicillins fail. Does not cause dependence or addiction.
See also Amoxycillin, Ampicillin, Cloxacillin, Penicillin G, Piperacillin, Pivmecillinam, Ticarcillin.

Fluconazole

TRADE NAME:

Diflucan.

DRUG CLASS:

Antifungal.

USES:

Fungal infections of vagina (thrush), mouth, oesophagus, brain and other areas.

DOSAGE:

 Vaginal thrush: single tablet taken once.
More severe infections: one to four tablets a day.

FORMS:

Tablet of 50 and 200mg, suspension, infusion.

PRECAUTIONS:

Not to be used in pregnancy (B3) or children unless medically essential. Cease breast feeding before use.
Use with caution in kidney disease and dehydration.
Ensure adequate fluid intake.

SIDE EFFECTS:

Common: nausea, acne.
Unusual: headache, rash, vomiting, diarrhoea, belly discomfort.
Severe but rare (stop medication, consult doctor): liver damage, allergy.

INTERACTIONS:

Other drugs:
• never use with cisapride
• warfarin, astemizole, phenytoin, cyclosporin, diazepam, hypoglycaemics, rifampicin, theophylline, zidovudine, oral contraceptives.

PRESCRIPTION:

Yes.

PERMITTED IN SPORT:

Yes.

OVERDOSE:

Hallucinations and mental disturbance may occur. Administer activated charcoal or induce vomiting if medication taken recently. Seek medical attention.

OTHER INFORMATION:

Introduced in early 1990s. A single dose by mouth will cure most forms of thrush (Candidiasis) in the vagina, mouth or elsewhere in the body. Very useful in the treatment of fungal complications in AIDS. Very expensive.

See also Clotrimazole, Econazole, Griseofulvin, Itraconazole, Ketoconazole, Miconazole.

Flucytosine

TRADE NAME:

Ancotil.

DRUG CLASS:

Antifungal.

USES:

Generalised fungal infections.

DOSAGE:

 As determined by doctor.

FORMS:

Injection.

PRECAUTIONS:

Not to be used in pregnancy (B3) unless clinically essential. Breast feeding should be ceased before use. May be used with caution in children.
Use with caution in bone marrow disease and kidney disease.

SIDE EFFECTS:

Common: nausea.
Unusual: vomiting, rash, diarrhoea.
Severe but rare: liver and blood cell damage, irregular heart beat.

INTERACTIONS:

Other drugs:
• amphotericin B, cytarabine, corticosteroids.

PRESCRIPTION:

Yes.

PERMITTED IN SPORT:

Yes.

OVERDOSE:

May cause kidney damage. Seek medical advice.

OTHER INFORMATION:

Extremely expensive, and so reserved for the most severe fungal infections.

Fludrocortisone

TRADE NAME:

Florinef.

DRUG CLASS:

Corticosteroid.

USES:

Addison's disease, adrenogenital syndrome.

DOSAGE:

 Tablets: one to three tablets a day as directed by doctor.

FORMS:

Tablets of 0.1mg (pink).

PRECAUTIONS:

Should be used in pregnancy (C), breast feeding and children only on specific medical advice.
Use with caution if under stress, and in patients with under active thyroid gland, liver disease, diverticulitis, high blood pressure, myasthenia gravis, or kidney disease.
Medication should not be ceased abruptly, but dosage should be slowly reduced.

Do not use if:

 • suffering from any form of infection
• having a vaccination.

SIDE EFFECTS:

Common: may cause bloating, weight gain, rashes and intestinal disturbances.
Unusual: biochemical disturbances of blood, muscle weakness, bone weakness,

impaired wound healing, skin thinning, tendon weakness, peptic ulcers, gullet ulcers, bruising, increased sweating, loss of fat under skin, premature ageing, excess facial hair growth in women, pigmentation of skin and nails, acne, convulsions, headaches, dizziness, growth suppression in children, aggravation of diabetes, worsening of infections, cataracts, aggravation of glaucoma, blood clots in veins and sleeplessness.

Most significant side effects occur only with prolonged use of tablets.

Severe but rare (stop medication, consult doctor): any significant side effect should be reported to a doctor immediately.

INTERACTIONS:

Other drugs:
• oral contraceptives, barbiturates, phenytoin, rifampicin, warfarin, isoniazid, amphotericin, diabetic medications, cyclosporin, digoxin, oestrogen, ketoconazole, NSAID.

PRESCRIPTION:

Yes.

PERMITTED IN SPORT:

No.

OVERDOSE:

Medical treatment is required. Serious effects and death rare.

OTHER INFORMATION:

Extremely effective and useful medication if used correctly. Must be used with extreme care under strict medical supervision. Lowest dose possible should be used. Not addictive.

FLUID TABLETS

See DIURETICS.

Flumethasone

TRADE NAME:

Available only in combination with clioquinol.
Locacorten Vioform (with clioquinol).

DRUG CLASS:

Corticosteroid.

USES:

Eczema and inflammation of ear canal.

DOSAGE:

 Two or three drops twice a day for no more than ten days.

FORMS:

Ear drops.

PRECAUTIONS:

Ear preparations safe in pregnancy, breast feeding and children over three years.
Avoid eye contact.
Use for shortest period of time possible.

SIDE EFFECTS:

Common: minimal.
Unusual: prolonged use—thinning of skin, itching, scarring of skin.

INTERACTIONS:

None significant.

PRESCRIPTION:

Yes.

PERMITTED IN SPORT:

Yes.

Flunisolide

TRADE NAME:

Syntaris.

DRUG CLASS:

Corticosteroid.

USES:

Prevention of hay fever and chronic nasal drip.

DOSAGE:

 Initially once or two sprays in each nostril, twice a day. Reduce dose to lowest possible.

FORMS:

Nasal spray.

PRECAUTIONS:

Use with caution in pregnancy (B3), breast feeding and children.
Use with caution in lung or throat infection and tuberculosis.

SIDE EFFECTS:

Common: nasal irritation.
Unusual: fungal (thrush) infections of nose, nose bleeds.

INTERACTIONS:

None significant.

PRESCRIPTION:

Yes.

PERMITTED IN SPORT:

Yes.

OVERDOSE:

Unlikely to have any serious effects.
See also Budesonide, Beclomethasone.

Flunitrazepam

TRADE NAME:

Rohypnol.

DRUG CLASS:

Sedative/hypnotic, Benzodiazepine.

USES:

Severe insomnia (sleeplessness).

DOSAGE:

 One or two at bedtime. Quarter to one tablet in elderly.

FORMS:

Tablet of 1mg (grey green).

PRECAUTIONS:

Should be used with caution in pregnancy (C), but not at all if delivery of infant imminent as it may decrease desire to breathe in newborn infant. Should be used with caution in breast feeding. Not for use in children.
Lower dose required in elderly.
Should be used intermittently and not constantly as dependency may develop.
Stopping suddenly after prolonged constant use may cause withdrawal symptoms.
Use with caution in glaucoma, myasthenia gravis, heart disease, low blood pressure, kidney or liver disease, psychiatric conditions, schizophrenia, depression and epilepsy.

Do not take if:

- suffering from severe lung disease, confusion
- tendency to addiction or dependence
- operating machinery, driving a vehicle or undertaking tasks that require concentration, coordination or alertness within next 12 hours.

SIDE EFFECTS:

Common: confusion and falls in elderly, impaired alertness, dependency.
Unusual: dizziness, incoordination, poor memory, headache, hangover in morning, slurred speech, nightmares.

INTERACTIONS:

Other drugs:
- other medications that reduce alertness (e.g. barbiturates, antihistamines, antianxiety drugs).
- disulfiram, cimetidine, anticonvulsants, anticholinergics.

Herbs:
- guarana, kava kava, passionflower, St John's wort, valerian, celery, camomile, goldenseal.

Other substances:
• reacts with alcohol to cause excessive drowsiness.

PRESCRIPTION:

Yes (restricted).

PERMITTED IN SPORT:

Yes.

OVERDOSE:

Seldom life threatening. May cause drowsiness, confusion and coma. Induce vomiting if tablets taken recently. Seek medical assistance.

OTHER INFORMATION:

One of the most powerful sleeping tablets available. Risk of dependency is high. Should be used only intermittently and for short periods except in exceptional cases.

See also BARBITURATES, Chlormethiazole, Midazolam, Nitrazepam, Temazepam, Triazolam, Zolpidem, Zopiclone.

Fluocinolone

TRADE NAMES:

Synalar.
Synalar C (with clioquinol).
Synalar N (with neomycin).

DRUG CLASS:

Corticosteroid.

USES:

Inflammation of skin (eczema, dermatitis etc.).

DOSAGE:

 Apply two or three times a day.

FORMS:

Cream, ointment.

PRECAUTIONS:

Should be used with caution in pregnancy, breast feeding and children. Avoid eyes.
Use for shortest period of time possible.

Do not use if:

 • suffering from any form of skin infection, acne, or broken skin.

SIDE EFFECTS:

Common: minimal.
Unusual: thinning of skin, itching, burning, stinging, scarring of skin.

INTERACTIONS:

None significant.

PRESCRIPTION:

Yes.

PERMITTED IN SPORT:

Yes.

OTHER INFORMATION:

Lowest dose and shortest possible course should be used.

See also CORTICOSTEROIDS.

Fluocinonide

TRADE NAME:

Metosyn.

DRUG CLASS:

Corticosteroid.

USES:

Inflammation of skin, itchy and allergic skin conditions.

DOSAGE:

 Apply three or four times a day.

FORMS:

Cream, ointment.

PRECAUTIONS:

Should be used with caution in pregnancy, breast feeding and children.
Avoid eyes.
Use for shortest period of time possible.

Do not use if:

- suffering from any form of skin infection, acne, or broken skin.

SIDE EFFECTS:

Common: minimal.
Unusual: thinning of skin, itching, burning, stinging, scarring of skin.

INTERACTIONS:

None significant.

PRESCRIPTION:

Yes.

PERMITTED IN SPORT:

Yes.

OTHER INFORMATION:

Lowest dose and shortest possible course should be used.
See also CORTICOSTEROIDS.

Fluocortolone

TRADE NAMES:

Ultalanum.
Ultraproct (with cinchocaine).

DRUG CLASS:

Corticosteroid.

USES:

Severe inflammation of anus, piles, anal fissure.

DOSAGE:

Ointment: apply two times a day.
Suppositories: insert one into anus once a day after a bowel motion.

FORMS:

Ointment, cream, suppositories.

PRECAUTIONS:

Should be used with caution in pregnancy.
May aggravate fungal infections of skin.
Use for shortest period of time possible.

Do not use if:

- suffering from any form of skin infection, anal ulcer or broken skin.

SIDE EFFECTS:

Common: minimal.
Unusual: thinning of skin, itching, burning, stinging, scarring of skin.

INTERACTIONS:

None significant.

PRESCRIPTION:

Yes.

PERMITTED IN SPORT:

No.

OTHER INFORMATION:

Shortest possible course should be used.
Not addictive. One of the older types of steroid cream.
See also CORTICOSTEROIDS.

Fluoride
(Sodium fluoride)

TRADE NAMES:

Endekay, Fluorigard.
Fluoride is also found naturally in water, and in numerous nutritional supplements and medications, all of which are available without prescription. It is also added artificially to some water supplies.

DRUG CLASS:

Mineral.

USES:

Prevention of tooth decay, in addition to calcium and vitamin D in the treatment of osteoporosis, multiple myeloma, Paget's disease.

DOSAGE:

 One to three times a day as directed by packaging or doctor.

FORMS:

Tablets, mixture, drops.

PRECAUTIONS:

Not to be used in pregnancy and breast feeding. May be used with caution in children.
Fluoride supplements should only be used where local water supply is low in fluoride.

Do not take if:

 • suffering from severe kidney disease.

SIDE EFFECTS:

Common: none at correct dose.
Uncommon: excess dosage for a long period may cause white flecks or brown stains on teeth.

INTERACTIONS:

None significant.

PRESCRIPTION:

No.

PERMITTED IN SPORT:

Yes.

OVERDOSE:

Deliberate or accidental overdosage with a large number of tablets may cause significant poisoning. Administer activated charcoal or induce vomiting if taken recently. Symptoms of acute poisoning include vomiting, diarrhoea, convulsions, rapid weak pulse, difficulty in breathing, coma and possibly death. Seek urgent medical assistance.

OTHER INFORMATION:

Since the introduction of fluoride to water supplies, as a supplement and in tooth paste, the incidence of tooth decay in children has dropped dramatically. In areas with fluoride in the water supply additional supplements are not required.

Fluorometholone

TRADE NAME:

FML.

DRUG CLASS:

Corticosteroid.

USES:

Inflammation of eye, iritis.

DOSAGE:

 Insert one or two drops two to four times a day.

FORMS:

Eye drops.

PRECAUTIONS:

May be used with caution in pregnancy, breast feeding and children.
Use with caution in bacterial eye infections.
Not designed for prolonged use.

Do not take if:

 • suffering from any form of viral or fungal eye infection.
• suffering from tuberculosis of eye.

SIDE EFFECTS:

Common: temporary blurred vision.
Severe but rare (stop medication, consult doctor): glaucoma (halos around objects), eye pain, permanent blurred vision, weeping eye, pus in eye.

INTERACTIONS:

None significant.

PRESCRIPTION:

Yes.

PERMITTED IN SPORT:

Yes.

OTHER INFORMATION:

Must only be used strictly as directed by doctor. Infection must be excluded before use, or eye damage may result. Prolonged use may result in eye damage. Very useful in controlling severe eye inflammation.

See also CORTICOSTEROIDS.

Fluorouracil

TRADE NAME:

Efudix.

USES:

Skin cancer and sun damaged skin.

DOSAGE:

 Apply to affected skin once or twice a day with a metal applicator or using a rubber glove for four to six weeks.

FORMS:

Cream.

PRECAUTIONS:

Should not be used in pregnancy (D) as the safety of this medication in pregnancy has not been established. Should be used in breast feeding and children only if medically essential.

Cream must not be allowed to come into contact with eyes, mouth, lips, nose, anus or vagina.

Do not use on normal skin.

Avoid using cosmetics or other skin preparations on areas of skin being treated.

Avoid sun exposure to areas of skin being treated.

SIDE EFFECTS:

Common: redness, itch, burning, pigmentation.
Unusual: scarring, dermatitis, soreness, sun sensitivity.

INTERACTIONS:

None significant.

PRESCRIPTION:

Yes.

PERMITTED IN SPORT:

Yes.

OVERDOSE:

Inflammation and soreness of skin. Very serious if swallowed. Seek urgent medical assistance.

OTHER INFORMATION:

Very effective and useful in many forms of skin cancer but must be used carefully.

Fluoxetine

TRADE NAME:

Prozac.

DRUG CLASS:

SSRI antidepressant.

USES:

Depression.

DOSAGE:

 20 to 60mg, once or twice a day. Maximum 120mg a day.

FORMS:

Capsules of 20mg (green/yellow) and 60mg (yellow), liquid.

PRECAUTIONS:

Should be used in pregnancy (B2), breast feeding and children with considerable caution.

Should be used with caution in epilepsy, liver and kidney disease.

Use with caution after shock treatment.

Lower doses necessary in elderly.

Do not take if:
• MAOI antidepressants taken recently.

SIDE EFFECTS:

Common: generally minimal. Nausea, drowsiness, sweating, tremor, tiredness, dry mouth, sleeplessness, impotence, weight loss.
Unusual: headache, fever, palpitations, sweating, rash, blurred vision.
Severe but rare (stop medication, consult doctor): convulsions.

INTERACTIONS:

Other drugs:
• MAOI, lithium, diazepam, flecainide, warfarin, anticoagulants (e.g. warfarin), phenytoin, tryptophan, tramadol, sumatriptan.
Herbs:
• St John's wort, ma huang.
Other substances:
• use of alcohol is not advised.

PRESCRIPTION:

Yes.

PERMITTED IN SPORT:

Yes.

OVERDOSE:

Symptoms may include nausea, tremor, dilated pupils, dry mouth and irritability. Death or serious effects unlikely. Administer activated charcoal or induce vomiting if tablets taken recently. Seek medical attention.

OTHER INFORMATION:

One of the newer antidepressants released in the early 1990s that has dramatically improved the treatment of depression because of its safety and lack of side effects. May take up to two weeks for patient to notice any improvement in depression.
See also Citalopram, Fluvoxamine, Paroxetine, Sertraline, Venlafaxine.

Flupenthixol

TRADE NAMES:

Depixol, Fluanxol.

DRUG CLASS:

Antipsychotic.

USES:

Schizophrenia, depression and psychoses.

DOSAGE:

 One to three tablets, once or twice a day.
One injection every two to four weeks.

FORMS:

Injection, tablets.

PRECAUTIONS:

Use in pregnancy (C) only if medically essential. Use with caution in breast feeding.
Not to be used in children.
Use lower doses in elderly.
Use with caution if taking anti-vomiting drugs.
Use with caution in glaucoma, extreme heat, epilepsy, agitation states, Parkinson's disease, hardening of arteries, heart disorders, stroke, liver and kidney disease.
Do not use if:
 • suffering from brain damage, blood abnormalities, phaeochromocytoma
• sensitive to phenothiazine
• having surgery.

SIDE EFFECTS:

Common: confusion, twitches, tremors, muscle spasms, dry mouth.

INTERACTIONS:

Other drugs:
• tricyclic antidepressants, phenobarbitone, carbamazepine, hypnotics, lithium, medications that lower blood pressure, levodopa, MAOI, metoclopramide.
Herbs:
• evening primrose (linoleic acid).
Other substances:
• organophosphate insecticides
• alcohol.

PRESCRIPTION:

Yes.

PERMITTED IN SPORT:

Yes.

OVERDOSE:

Causes sedation preceded by agitation, confusion and convulsions. May proceed to collapse, failure of breathing and death. Seek urgent medical attention. Support in hospital necessary.

OTHER INFORMATION:

Used long term to prevent symptoms of schizophrenia or other psychiatric disorders.

See also Amisulpride, Haloperidol, Lithium Carbonate, Olanzapine, PHENOTHIAZINES, Pimozide, Quetiapine, Risperidone, Thiothixene, Zuclopenthixol.

Fluphenazine

See PHENOTHIAZINES.

Flurandrelone

TRADE NAME:

Haelan.

DRUG CLASS:

Corticosteroid.

USES:

Dermatitis, eczema.

DOSAGE:

 Apply two or three times a day.

FORMS:

Cream, ointment.

PRECAUTIONS:

Should be used with caution in pregnancy, breast feeding and children.

Avoid eyes.
Use for shortest period of time possible.

Do not use if:

 • suffering from any form of skin infection, acne, or broken skin.

SIDE EFFECTS:

Common: minimal.
Unusual: thinning of skin, itching, burning, stinging, scarring of skin.

INTERACTIONS:

None significant.

PRESCRIPTION:

Yes.

PERMITTED IN SPORT:

Yes.

OTHER INFORMATION:

Lowest dose and shortest possible course should be used.

See also CORTICOSTEROIDS.

Flurbiprofen

TRADE NAMES:

Froben, Ocufen, Streflam.

DRUG CLASS:

NSAID (Nonsteroidal anti-inflammatory drug).

USES:

Tablets and capsules: osteoarthritis, rheumatoid arthritis, muscle strains and pains, ankylosing spondylitis, period pain. Eye drops: prevention of miosis (eye contraction) during eye surgery. Lozenges: relied of throat pain.

DOSAGE:

 Tablets and capsules: up to 300mg a day divided into one, two or more doses after food.
Eye drops: as directed by eye doctor.
Lozenges: dissolve one in mouth every three to six hours.

FORMS:

Capsules of 200mg, tablets of 50mg and 100mg, eye drops, lozenges.

PRECAUTIONS:

Use with caution in pregnancy (C), breast feeding and children.
Care with eye drops in presence of eye infection.
Use lozenges with care in kidney, liver and heart disease.

Do not take if:

- eye drops if suffering from viral eye infection (e.g. Herpes)
- tablets, capsules and lozenges if suffering from peptic ulcer, asthma, hay fever
- sensitive to aspirin.

SIDE EFFECTS:

Common: eye drops: eye burning and stinging, delayed healing of eye wounds, increased bleeding tendency in eye.
Lozenges: abnormal taste, nausea, diarrhoea.
Tablets and capsules: stomach discomfort, diarrhoea, constipation, heartburn, nausea, headache, dizziness.
Unusual: lozenges: stomach ulcer.
Tablets and capsules: blurred vision, stomach ulcer, ringing noise in ears, retention of fluid, swelling of tissue, drowsiness, itch, rash, shortness of breath.
Severe but rare (stop medication, consult doctor): vomiting blood, passing blood in faeces, other unusual bleeding, asthma induced by medication.

INTERACTIONS:

Eye drops: none significant.
Lozenges: frusemide, other NSAIDs, warfarin, methotrexate, blood pressure medications.
Tablets and capsules.
Other drugs:
- must never be used with anticoagulants (e.g. warfarin)
- probenecid, diuretics, lithium, methotrexate, beta-blockers, ACE inhibitors, digoxin, cyclosporin, diabetes medication (hypoglycaemics), steroids.

Herbs:
- feverfew.

PRESCRIPTION:

Lozenges: no.
Eye drops: yes.
Tablets and capsules: yes.

PERMITTED IN SPORT:

Yes.

See also Aspirin, Bufexamac, Celecoxib, Diclofenac, Diflunisal, Ibuprofen, Indomethacin, Ketoprofen, Ketorolac trometanol, Mefenamic Acid, Naproxen, Piroxicam, Rofecoxib, Salicylic acid, Sulindac, Tenoxicam, Tiaprofenic Acid.

Flutamide

TRADE NAMES:

Chimax, Drogenil.

DRUG CLASS:

Antiandrogen (acts against testosterone).

USES:

Cancer of prostate gland in combination with other medication.

DOSAGE:

 One tablet three times a day.

FORMS:

Tablets (yellow) of 250mg.

PRECAUTIONS:

Not to be used by women or children.
Regular blood tests to check liver function essential.

Do not take if:

- suffering from severe liver disease.

SIDE EFFECTS:

Common: hot flushes, decreased libido, impotence, diarrhoea, nausea, vomiting, breast enlargement and tenderness.
Severe but rare (stop medication, consult doctor): yellow skin (jaundice).

INTERACTIONS:

Other drugs:
• warfarin, paracetamol, narcotics.

PRESCRIPTION:

Yes.

OVERDOSE:

Exacerbation of side effects only likely result.

OTHER INFORMATION:

Not designed to be used alone, but only in combination with other medication for prostate gland cancer.
See also Cyproterone.

Fluticasone propionate

TRADE NAMES:

Cutivate, Flixonase, Flixotide.
Seretide (with salmeterol).

DRUG CLASS:

Corticosteroid.

USES:

Prevention of asthma and hay fever, dermatitis.

DOSAGE:

 Inhaler: one to four inhalations twice a day.
Nose spray: one or two spays in each nostril once a day.
Cream: apply once a day.

FORMS:

Inhaler, disc inhaler, nose spray, cream.

PRECAUTIONS:

Inhaler:
Use with caution in pregnancy (B3), breast feeding and children over four years.
Not to be used in children under four years.
Use with caution in lung or throat infection and tuberculosis.
Lung function should be checked regularly to ensure adequate dose is received.
Nose spray:
Use with caution in pregnancy (B3), breast feeding.
Not for use in children under 12 years.
Use with caution in nose infection.
Use lowest effective dose.
Cream:
Use with caution in pregnancy. May be used in breast feeding and children, but not on breasts.
May aggravate fungal infections of skin.
Use for shortest period of time possible.
Do not use if suffering from any form of skin infection, anal ulcer or broken skin.

SIDE EFFECTS:

Inhaler:
Common: fungal (thrush) infections of mouth, sore throat and mouth, dry mouth.
Unusual: hoarseness, unusual bleeding and bruising, slowed growth.
Severe but rare (stop medication, consult doctor): glaucoma (blurred vision).
Nose spray:
Common: nose irritation.
Uncommon: nose bleeds, taste and smell disturbances, ulceration.
Severe but rare (stop medication, consult doctor): glaucoma (blurred vision).
Cream:
Common: minimal.
Unusual: thinning of skin, itching, burning, stinging, scarring of skin.

INTERACTIONS:

Other drugs:
• ritonavir, ketoconazole.
Herbs:
• liquorice.

PRESCRIPTION:

Yes.

PERMITTED IN SPORT:

Yes.

OVERDOSE:

Unlikely to have any serious effects.
See also Beclomethasone, Budesonide.

Fluvastatin

TRADE NAME:

Lescol.

DRUG CLASS:

Hypolipidaemic.

USES:

Treatment of high blood cholesterol level.

DOSAGE:

 One or two tablets at night.
Maximum 40mg twice daily.

FORMS:

Capsules of 20mg (brown/yellow) and 40mg (brown/orange).

PRECAUTIONS:

Not for use in pregnancy (C) unless medically essential. Use with caution in children.
Use with caution in muscle, liver and kidney disease.
Use with caution in alcoholics.
Regular blood tests to check cholesterol level and liver function necessary.
Do not take if:
 • suffering from liver infection, myopathy (muscle inflammation)
• breast feeding.

SIDE EFFECTS:

Common: nausea, diarrhoea.
Unusual: liver damage, joint and muscle pain, muscle damage.

INTERACTIONS:

Other drugs:
• cimetidine, cyclosporin, erythromycin, gemfibrizol, glibenclamide, nicotinic acid, omeprazole, ranitidine, rifampicin, tolbutamide, warfarin, cholestyramine.
Other substances:
• excess alcohol.
Herbs:
• alfalfa, fenugreek, garlic, ginger.

PRESCRIPTION:

Yes.

PERMITTED IN SPORT:

Yes.

OVERDOSE:

Induce vomiting or administer activated charcoal if taken recently. Seek medical attention.

OTHER INFORMATION:

Introduced in 1996 as an effective means of lowering cholesterol when combined with a low cholesterol diet.
See also Atorvastatin, Cholestyramine, Colestipol, Gemfibrizol, Nicotinic acid, Pravastatin, Simvastatin.

Fluvoxamine

TRADE NAME:

Faverin.

DRUG CLASS:

SSRI antidepressant.

USES:

Depression, obsessive compulsive disorder.

DOSAGE:

Half to three tablets a day. Increase dose very slowly.

FORMS:

Tablets of 50 and 100mg (white).

PRECAUTIONS:

Use with caution in pregnancy (B2), and children.
Use with caution in epilepsy, liver and kidney disease.
Use lower doses in elderly.
Reduce dose slowly before stopping.

Do not take if:

- breast feeding.
- taking MAOI.

SIDE EFFECTS:

Common: generally minimal. Nausea, drowsiness, sweating, tremor, tiredness, dry mouth, sleeplessness, impotence.
Unusual: headache, fever, palpitations, sweating, rash, blurred vision.

INTERACTIONS:

Other drugs:
- MAOI, other SSRI, tryptophan, tricyclic antidepressants, lithium, sumatriptan, anticoagulants (e.g. warfarin), theophylline, clozapine, propranolol, cisapride, benzodiazepines (e.g. diazepam).

Herbs:
- St John's wort, ma huang.

Other substances:
- alcohol.

PRESCRIPTION:

Yes.

PERMITTED IN SPORT:

No.

OVERDOSE:

Symptoms may include nausea, tremor, dilated pupils, dry mouth and irritability.
Death or serious effects unlikely.
Administer activated charcoal or induce vomiting if tablets taken recently. Seek medical attention.

OTHER INFORMATION:

Introduced in 1997 as an effective treatment for depression.

See also Citalopram, Fluoxetine, Paroxetine, Sertraline, Venlafaxine.

Folic acid

TRADE NAMES:

Lexpec.
Ferrograd Folic, Galfer FA, Lexpec with Iron, Pregaday, Slow-Fe Folic (with iron).
Folic acid is also found in numerous other vitamin and mineral preparations.

DRUG CLASS:

Vitamin.

USES:

Some types of anaemia, prevention of anaemia in pregnancy, aids iron absorption.

DOSAGE:

 Tablets and capsules: one or two a day.
Injection: one injection a day.

FORMS:

Capsules, tablets, syrup, injection.

PRECAUTIONS:

Safe to use in pregnancy (A), breast feeding and children.
Use with caution in some types of tumours.

Do not take if:

- suffering from vitamin B12 deficiency.

SIDE EFFECTS:

Common: minimal.
Unusual: nausea, passing excess wind, diarrhoea, irritability, sleep disturbances.

Severe but rare (stop medication, consult doctor): rash, asthma.

INTERACTIONS:

Other drugs:
* anticonvulsants (drugs treating epilepsy), methotrexate, trimethoprim, pyrimethamine, sulfasalazine, gold.
Other substances:
* reacts with alcohol.

PRESCRIPTION:

No.

PERMITTED IN SPORT:

Yes.

OVERDOSE:

No serious effects likely.

OTHER INFORMATION:

Folic acid is essential for the formation of certain proteins in the body that are used in the manufacture of haemoglobin. A lack of folic acid causes anaemia. It is found naturally in liver, dark green leafy vegetables, peanuts, beans, whole grain wheat and yeast. It may be considered to be a vitamin.

See also Iron; VITAMINS.

Folinic acid
See Calcium folinate.

Follicle stimulating hormone
(FSH, Follitropin)

TRADE NAMES:

Gonal-F, Puregon.

DRUG CLASS:

Sex hormone.

USES:

Female and male infertility.

DOSAGE:

 As determined by doctor for each patient.

FORMS:

Injection.

PRECAUTIONS:

Not to be used in pregnancy (B2), breast feeding and children.
Unlikely to be serious effects if used by mistake in pregnancy.

Do not take if:

* suffering from ovarian cysts or enlargement, tumours of the ovaries or other sexual organs, testicular tumours, or undiagnosed vaginal bleeding.
* over 50 years of age.

SIDE EFFECTS:

Common: nausea, diarrhoea, headache.
Unusual: multiple pregnancies, breast tenderness and/or enlargement, acne, weight gain.
Severe but rare: lung and heart effects, vein blood clots.

INTERACTIONS:

Other drugs:
* clomiphene.

PRESCRIPTION:

Yes.

PERMITTED IN SPORT:

Yes.

OTHER INFORMATION:

Widely used and effective medication to assist patients with specific types of infertility.

See also Clomiphene.

Follitropin
See Follicle Stimulating Hormone.

Formaldehyde

TRADE NAME:

Veracur.
Also found in other lotions and gels.

DRUG CLASS:

Keratolytic.

USES:

Plantar warts (veruccae).

DOSAGE:

 Apply twice a day and cover with a dressing.

FORMS:

Gel, lotion.

PRECAUTIONS:

Safe to use on skin in pregnancy, breast feeding and children.
Do not treat warts on face, anus, genitals and other delicate skin.
Try not to apply to normal skin.

SIDE EFFECTS:

Common: skin irritation and redness.

INTERACTIONS:

None significant.

PRESCRIPTION:

No.

PERMITTED IN SPORT:

Yes.

OVERDOSE:

Excessive use may lead to skin damage, burning and pain. Wash off any excess from skin immediately.
Very serious if swallowed. Seek urgent medical attention. Do not cause vomiting, but give milk and antacids.
See also KERATOLYTICS.

Fosinopril

See **ACE INHIBITORS.**

Framycetin

TRADE NAMES:

Soframycin.
Sofradex (with dexamethasone and gramicidin).

DRUG CLASS:

Aminoglycoside antibiotic.

USES:

Ear and eye infections.

DOSAGE:

 Eye drops: insert six times a day.
Ear drops: insert three times a day.
Eye and ear ointment: insert or apply two or three times a day.

FORMS:

Eye drops, eye ointment, ear drops, ear ointment.

PRECAUTIONS:

Must be used with caution in pregnancy (D), but damage to foetus unlikely if used only on body surface. May be used in breast feeding and children.
Do not use ear applications if:
• suffering from perforated ear drum.

SIDE EFFECTS:

Minimal.

INTERACTIONS:

None significant.

PRESCRIPTION:

Yes.

PERMITTED IN SPORT:

Yes.

OTHER INFORMATION:

Very widely used for treatment of swimmer's ear and conjunctivitis.

Frangula

TRADE NAME:

Normacol Plus (with sterculia).
Also found in other fibre supplements.

DRUG CLASS:

Fibre, laxative.

USES:

Constipation.

DOSAGE:

 Take required amount with water two or three times a day.

FORMS:

Granules, powder.

PRECAUTIONS:

Safe in pregnancy.
Not for use in breast feeding and children under 12 years.
Avoid at bedtime.
Not for prolonged use.

Do not take if:

- on a salt, potassium or sugar restricted diet
- suffering from severe constipation with impacted faeces
- suffering from belly pain, nausea or vomiting
- suffering from ulcerative colitis or acute diverticulitis.

SIDE EFFECTS:

Common: minimal.
Unusual: diarrhoea, belly discomfort.

INTERACTIONS:

Other drugs:
- thiazide diuretics, steroids.

Other substances:
- liquorice, high sugar content sweets.

PRESCRIPTION:

No.

PERMITTED IN SPORT:

Yes.

OVERDOSE:

Take additional water. Belly discomfort and passing excess wind only effects.
See also FIBRE.

Frovatriptan

TRADE NAME:

Migard.

DRUG CLASS:

Antimigraine.

USES:

Treatment of migraine.

DOSAGE:

 One tablet at onset of headache, repeat after two hours if necessary. No more than two tablets a day.

FORMS:

Tablets of 2.5mg (white).

PRECAUTIONS:

Should not be used in pregnancy (B3) unless medically essential. Should be used with caution in breast feeding. Not for use in children.
Should be used with caution in liver and kidney disease, and in elderly.
Not to be used for prevention of migraine, only treatment of acute attacks.

Do not take if:

- suffering from angina, poor circulation to heart, recent heart attack, severe high blood pressure, recent stroke, irregular heart beat
- Ergotamine used in previous 24 hours.

SIDE EFFECTS:

Common: chest pain, pain at injection site, tingling sensation, heat, heaviness, flushing, tightness, dizziness, weakness.
Unusual: fatigue, drowsiness, nausea, vomiting.
Severe but rare (stop medication, consult doctor): significant chest pain (angina).

INTERACTIONS:

Other drugs:
• ergotamine, MAOI, fluvoxamine, oral contraceptives.
Other substances:
• does not interact with alcohol.
Other substances:
• St John's wort.

PRESCRIPTION:

Yes.

PERMITTED IN SPORT:

Yes.

OTHER INFORMATION:

Introduced in 2002 as an additional treatment for migraine.

See also Almotriptan, BETA BLOCKERS, Clonidine, Eletriptan, Ergotamine, Methysergide, Naratriptan, NSAIDs, Pizotifen, Rizatripan, Sumatriptan, Zolmitriptan.

Frusemide
(Furosemide)

TRADE NAMES:

Frusol, Lasix.
Lasikal (with potassium).
Fru-Co, Frumil, Lasoride (with amiloride).
Frusene (with triamterene).
Lasilactone (with spironolactone).

DRUG CLASS:

Loop diuretic (increases production of urine).

USES:

Excess fluid in body, high blood pressure, heart failure causing build up of fluid in lungs.

DOSAGE:

 One or more tablets in morning to a maximum of 1500mg Frusemide a day.

FORMS:

Tablets, solution, injection.

PRECAUTIONS:

Should only be used in pregnancy (C) if medically essential. Will reduce production of breast milk and may be used to assist in drying of breast milk in women who have stopped breast feeding.
Safe in children and infants.
Should be used with caution in diabetes, diarrhoea and gout.
Regular blood tests to assess levels of chemicals (electrolytes) in blood are recommended if frusemide used alone.
Use with caution if sensitive to sulpha drugs.

Do not take if:
 • suffering from severe kidney failure, liver failure, jaundice, low blood pressure, difficulty in passing urine, low potassium or salt levels.

SIDE EFFECTS:

Common: passing increased amounts of urine.
Unusual: weakness, dizziness, thirst, muscle cramps, flushing.
Severe but rare (stop medication, consult doctor): dehydration, blood clots, deafness.

INTERACTIONS:

Other drugs:
- digoxin, aspirin, steroids, salicylates, lithium, antibiotics, ethacrynic acid, NSAID, sucralfate.
- medications that lower blood pressure (e.g. ACE inhibitors).

Herbs:
- celery, dandelion, uva ursi.

PRESCRIPTION:

Yes.

PERMITTED IN SPORT:

No.

OVERDOSE:

Severe dehydration may result. Induce vomiting if tablets taken recently. Give extra fluids. Seek medical assistance.

OTHER INFORMATION:

Widely used, safe, and extremely effective medication that has been available since the 1960s. Potassium supplements may be needed.

See also Amiloride, Bumetanide, Spironolactone, THIAZIDE DIURETICS.

FSH

See Follicle stimulating hormone.

Fusafungine

TRADE NAME:

Locabiotal.

DRUG CLASS:

Antibiotic.

USES:

Infections of nose and throat.

DOSAGE:

 One spray every four hours in mouth and both nostrils.

FORMS:

Spray.

PRECAUTIONS:

Safe in pregnancy, breast feeding and children.

SIDE EFFECTS:

Common: nasal irritation.

INTERACTIONS:

None significant.

PRESCRIPTION:

Yes.

PERMITTED IN SPORT:

Yes.

OVERDOSE:

Diarrhoea only likely effect.

OTHER INFORMATION:

Use restricted under the NHS.

Furosemide

See Frusemide.

Fusidic Acid

See Sodium fusidate.

Gabapentin

TRADE NAME:

Neurontin.

DRUG CLASS:

Anticonvulsant.

USES:

Epilepsy, particularly epilepsy that affects only part of the body; nerve pain.

DOSAGE:

 Slowly increasing dosage until desired result obtained. Taken in two or more doses a day. Maximum 2400mg a day.

FORMS:

Capsules of 100mg (white), 300mg (yellow) and 400mg (orange).

PRECAUTIONS:

Use with caution in pregnancy (B1), breast feeding and children under 12 years.
Use with caution in kidney disease, psychiatric disturbances, epilepsy and elderly.
Do not stop suddenly, but reduce dosage slowly.

SIDE EFFECTS:

Common: tiredness, drowsiness, incoordination, nausea, dizziness.
Unusual: vomiting, blurred vision, tremor, weight gain.

INTERACTIONS:

Other drugs:
• antacids, cimetidine.
Herbs:
• evening primrose (linoleic acid), Gingko biloba.
Other substances:
• borage.

PRESCRIPTION:

Yes.

PERMITTED IN SPORT:

Yes.

OVERDOSE:

Unlikely to be lethal. Symptoms may include double vision, slurred speech, drowsiness and diarrhoea.

OTHER INFORMATION:

One of the newer medications for poorly controlled epilepsy that was introduced in the late 1990s. Also very effective in treating intractable nerve pain.

See also Carbamazepine, Clonazepam, Ethosuximide, Lamotrigine, Levetiracetam, Oxcarbazepine, Phenytoin, Primidone, Sodium valproate, Sulthiame, Tiagabine, Topiramate, Vigabatrin.

Galantamine

TRADE NAME:

Reminyl.

USES:

Alzheimer's disease.

DOSAGE:

 4mg to 12mg twice a day. Increase dose slowly.

FORMS:

Tablets of 4mg (off-white), 8mg (pink) and 12mg (orange/brown), solution.

PRECAUTIONS:

Not designed for use in pregnancy (B1), breast feeding and children.
Use with caution with heart rhythm irregularities, peptic ulcer, recent surgery,

epilepsy, severe asthma, emphysema, poor urinary flow and liver disease. Take adequate fluids with medication.

Do not take if:

 • suffering severe liver or kidney disease.

SIDE EFFECTS:

Common: nausea, diarrhoea, weight loss, tiredness, poor appetite.
Unusual: low blood pressure, low blood potassium levels, urinary infection, watery nasal discharge.
Severe but rare (stop medication, consult doctor): irregular heart beat, abnormal bleeding.

INTERACTIONS:

Other drugs:
• anticholinergics, digoxin, beta-blockers, paroxetine, ketoconazole, erythromycin, quinidine, fluoxetine, fluvoxamine.

PRESCRIPTION:

Yes.

PERMITTED IN SPORT:

Yes.

OTHER INFORMATION:

Introduced in 2001. Assists memory and reasoning power in only some patients with Alzheimer's disease. Regular mental tests necessary to assess effectiveness.

See also Donepezil, Rivastigmine.

Gamma Globulin
(Immunoglobulin)

TRADE NAMES:

Flebogamma, Gammabulin, Gammagard, Octagam, Sandoglobulin, Vigam.

DRUG CLASS:

Immunoglobulin.

USES:

Prevention and treatment of hepatitis, polio and measles; adjunctive treatment for bacterial infections; low natural levels of immunoglobulin; some types of leukaemia; Wiskott-Aldrich syndrome; multiple myeloma and congenital AIDS.

DOSAGE:

 For injection as determined by doctor for each patient.

FORMS:

Injection.

PRECAUTIONS:

Safe in pregnancy, breast feeding and children.
Use with caution in idiopathic thrombocytopenia.
Do not use high doses.

Do not take if:

 • suffering from IgA deficiency.

SIDE EFFECTS:

Common: headache, fever, anxiety, flushing, itch.
Unusual: brain irritation, change in blood pressure, chills, muscle aches.
Severe but rare (stop medication, consult doctor): allergy reaction.

INTERACTIONS:

Other drugs:
• live virus vaccines (e.g. Sabin polio).

PRESCRIPTION:

Yes.

PERMITTED IN SPORT:

Yes.

See also IMMUNOGLOBULINS.

Gammalinoleic acid (Evening Primrose oil)

See FATTY ACIDS.

Ganciclovir

TRADE NAMES:

Cymevene, Virgan.

DRUG CLASS:

Antiviral.

USES:

Treatment of cytomegalovirus (CMV) infections of eyes or lungs in patients with AIDS, immunosuppression or transplants; herpes infection of eye.

DOSAGE:

 Four tablets three times a day. One drop of gel five times a day into eye, reducing to three times a day as directed by doctor. By drip into a vein.

FORMS:

Tablets, eye gel, injection.

PRECAUTIONS:

Not to be used in pregnancy (D) or breast feeding.
Not for use in infants. Use with caution in children.
Only use in severe cases of CMV.
Use with caution in poor hydration, kidney disease, and elderly.
Regular blood tests to check blood cell levels essential.

SIDE EFFECTS:

Common: low blood white cell count, low blood platelet count (causes abnormal bleeding), anaemia, nausea, diarrhoea, damage to foetus during pregnancy.
Eye gel: eye stinging.
Unusual: vomiting, reduced fertility long term.

Severe but rare (stop medication, consult doctor): inflamed pancreas (severe belly pain), blood infection.

INTERACTIONS:

Other drugs:
• probenecid, didanosine, zidovudine, cilastin, imipenem.

PRESCRIPTION:

Yes.

PERMITTED IN SPORT:

Yes.

OVERDOSE:

Highly toxic and may cause severe organ damage. Induce vomiting if taken recently. Seek urgent medical attention.

Gemfibrizol

TRADE NAME:

Lopid.

DRUG CLASS:

Hypolipidaemic.

USES:

Reducing excessive blood levels of cholesterol and triglyceride.

DOSAGE:

 One tablet twice daily 30min. before meals.

FORMS:

Tablet of 600mg (white), capsules of 300mg (white/maroon).

PRECAUTIONS:

Use in pregnancy (B3) only if medically essential. Not for use in breast feeding and children.
Patients must remain on a low fat diet.
Use with caution with irregular heart beat, liver disease.
Regular blood tests to check blood fat levels, liver enzymes and blood cells are necessary.

Do not persist for more than three months if ineffective.

Do not take if:

- suffering from severe liver or kidney disease, gall stones.
- trying to get pregnant as drug may reduce fertility.

SIDE EFFECTS:

Common: heartburn, belly pains, diarrhoea, tiredness, nausea, muscle pain.
Unusual: vomiting, eczema, rash, dizziness, constipation, headache.
Severe but rare (stop medication, consult doctor): yellow skin (jaundice), gall stones, disabling muscle pain.

INTERACTIONS:

Other drugs:
- anticoagulants (e.g. warfarin), cerivastatin, colestipol.

Herbs:
- alfalfa, fenugreek, garlic, ginger.

PRESCRIPTION:

Yes.

PERMITTED IN SPORT:

Yes.

OVERDOSE:

No significant problems likely.

OTHER INFORMATION:

Medication introduced in 1995 that is particularly effective and safe in the treatment of excess blood levels of triglycerides and cholesterol.

See also Atorvastatin, Cholestyramine, Colestipol, Fluvastatin, Nicotinic acid, Pravastatin, Probucol, Simvastatin.

Gentamicin

TRADE NAMES:

Cidomycin, Garamycin, Genticin, Minims Gentamicin.
Gentisone HC (with hydrocortisone).

DRUG CLASS:

Aminoglycoside antibiotic.

USES:

Severe infections, particularly bone, lung, soft tissue, eye and belly infections.

DOSAGE:

Injection: every eight hours, or by continuous drip infusion.
Eye drops: two drops every four hours.
Ear drops: two to four drops, three or four times a day.

FORMS:

Injection, eye drops, ear drops.

PRECAUTIONS:

Not to be used in pregnancy (D) unless absolutely essential for mother's well being. Breast feeding must be ceased before use. Use with caution and only when essential in children.
Eye drops and skin preparations may be used with caution in pregnancy and breast feeding.
Use injection with caution in kidney disease.
Blood tests to check that correct dose is being administered are recommended.

SIDE EFFECTS:

Common: eye and ear drops—Minimal. Injection—rash, nausea, headache.
Unusual: ear and kidney damage (dose related), vomiting.
Severe but rare (stop medication, consult doctor): ear noises or deafness, unusual bleeding or bruising.

INTERACTIONS:

Other drugs:
- penicillin, cephalosporins, ethacrynic acid, frusemide, other aminoglycoside antibiotics, vitamin K, narcotics, some general anaesthetics.

PRESCRIPTION:

Yes.

PERMITTED IN SPORT:

Yes.

OVERDOSE:

Ear and kidney damage possible. Give copious fluids to increase excretion through kidneys.

OTHER INFORMATION:

Very useful for the treatment of severe infections. Little risk of serious side effects if dose monitored by blood tests.
See also Amikacin, Gatifloxacin, Neomycin, Tobramycin.

Gestodene

See ORAL CONTRACEPTIVES.

Gestrinone

TRADE NAME:

Dimetriose.

DRUG CLASS:

Sex hormone.

USES:

Endometriosis.

DOSAGE:

 One capsule twice a day for six months.

FORMS:

Capsules (white) of 2.5mg.

PRECAUTIONS:

Must not be used in pregnancy (D), breast feeding or children.
Use with caution in elderly.
Use with caution in diabetes and high blood fat (cholesterol or triglycerides) levels.
Do not take if:

- suffering from significant heart, kidney, liver or metabolic diseases
- suffering from blood vessel disorders
- male.

SIDE EFFECTS:

Common: acne, oily skin, hair growth on face, ankle and foot swelling, excess sweating, low libido, leg cramps, headache, nausea, vomiting, loss of appetite, excess hunger, dizziness, tiredness, rash, hot flushes, reduced breast size.
Unusual: deepening voice, fainting, blurred vision, anxiety, flashing lights in vision, indigestion, diarrhoea, belly pain, weight loss, thirst, muscle cramps, numbness, red face, breast lumps.

INTERACTIONS:

Other drugs:
- epilepsy medications, rifampicin.

PRESCRIPTION:

Yes.

PERMITTED IN SPORT:

No.

OVERDOSE:

Serious exacerbation of side effects likely. Induce vomiting and seek urgent medical attention.

Ginkgo
(Ginkgo biloba)

USES:

Poor circulation, dizziness, ringing in ears (tinnitus), dementia.

DOSAGE:

 40mg to 80mg three times a day.

FORMS:

Capsules, tablets, liquid.

PRECAUTIONS:

Do not use in pregnancy or if trying to become pregnant.
Use with caution in high blood pressure.

SIDE EFFECTS:

Common: nausea, diarrhoea.
Unusual: high blood pressure, vein inflammation (phlebitis).
Severe but rare (stop medication, consult doctor): skin hypersensitivity, abnormal bleeding, infertility, stroke.

INTERACTIONS:

Other drugs:
• anticoagulants (e.g. warfarin), aspirin, NSAIDs.

PRESCRIPTION:

No.

PERMITTED IN SPORT:

Yes.

OVERDOSE:

Muscle spasms and cramps, weakness and incoordination may occur. Seek medical assistance.

OTHER INFORMATION:

Not used in orthodox medicine.

Ginseng

USES:

Fatigue.

DOSAGE:

 1g to 2g of root a day, divided into three or four doses.

FORMS:

Capsules, tablets, liquid, cream.

PRECAUTIONS:

Do not use in pregnancy and breast feeding (masculisation of female foetus and baby possible).
Use with caution in heart disease, diabetes and high blood pressure.

SIDE EFFECTS:

Common: sleeplessness, nose bleeds, headache, nervousness, vomiting.
Unusual: breast tenderness and lumps, vaginal bleeding, high blood pressure.

INTERACTIONS:

Other drugs:
• insulin, hypoglycaemics (for diabetes), warfarin, NSAIDs, aspirin, MAOI, frusemide.
Other substances:
• caffeine.

PRESCRIPTION:

No.

OVERDOSE:

High blood pressure, insomnia, increased muscle tone, fluid retention and tissue swelling occur.

OTHER INFORMATION:

Not used in orthodox medical practice.

GLAUCOMA MEDICATIONS

See Acetazolamide, Apraclonidine, Betaxolol, Bimatoprost, Brimonidine, Brinzolamide, Carbachol, Dipivefrine, Dorzolamide, Latanoprost, Levobunolol, Phenylephrine, Pilocarpine, Timolol, Travoprost.

Glibenclamide

TRADE NAMES:

Daonil, Euglucon, Semi-Daonil.

DRUG CLASS:

Hypoglycaemic.

USES:

Diabetes not requiring insulin injections.

DOSAGE:

 One or two tablets, one to three times a day before meals.
Maximum four tablets a day.

Do not vary from prescribed dose without advice from a doctor.

FORMS:

Tablets of 2.5 and 5mg.

PRECAUTIONS:

Not to be used in pregnancy (C), breast feeding or children.
Use with caution if operating machinery or driving a vehicle.
Use with caution in all forms of kidney disease.
Illness, changes in diet, exercise and stress may change dosage requirements.
Lower doses required in elderly and debilitated patients.
Strict control of carbohydrates and sugars in diet essential.

Do not take if:

- suffering from severe liver or kidney disease.
- insulin dependent diabetic.

SIDE EFFECTS:

Common: minimal.
Unusual: blurred vision, drowsiness, nausea, heartburn, belly discomfort, rash.
Severe but rare (stop medication, consult doctor): low blood sugar (see Overdose below), yellow skin (jaundice), unusual bleeding or bruising.

INTERACTIONS:

Other drugs:
- ACE inhibitors, beta-blockers, other hypoglycaemics, chloramphenicol, clofibrate, clonidine, warfarin, probenecid, MAOI, miconazole, salicylates, tetracycline, sulphonamides, diazoxide, corticosteroids, nicotinic acid, oestrogens, progestogens, phenothiazines, phenytoin, thyroid hormones, laxatives.

Other substances:
- reacts adversely with alcohol.

Herbs:
- alfalfa, celery, eucalyptus, fenugreek, garlic, ginger, ginseng, karela.

PRESCRIPTION:

Yes.

PERMITTED IN SPORT:

Yes.

OVERDOSE:

Serious. Symptoms of low blood sugar (hypoglycaemia) may include tiredness, confusion, chills, palpitations, sweating, vomiting, dizziness, hunger, blurred vision and fainting. Significant overdosage can lead to coma and death. Give sugary drinks or sweets if conscious. Seek emergency medical assistance.

OTHER INFORMATION:

Used mainly in elderly patients who develop maturity onset diabetes that is not severe enough to require insulin injections.

See also Acarbose, Gliclazide, Glimepride, Glipizide, Gliquidone, INSULINS, Metformin, Repaglinide, Rosiglitazone.

Gliclazide

TRADE NAME:

Diamicron.

DRUG CLASS:

Hypoglycaemic.

USES:

Diabetes not requiring insulin injections.

DOSAGE:

 Half to two tablets, one or two times a day before meals. Maximum four tablets a day. Do not vary from prescribed dose without advice from a doctor.

FORMS:

Tablets of 80mg (white).

PRECAUTIONS:

Not to be used in pregnancy (C), breast feeding or children.

Illness, changes in diet, exercise and stress may change dosage requirements. Lower doses required in elderly and debilitated patients.

Strict control of carbohydrates and sugars in diet essential.

Do not take if:

- suffering from severe liver or kidney disease
- an insulin dependent diabetic.

SIDE EFFECTS:

Common: uncommon.

Unusual: blurred vision, drowsiness, nausea, heartburn, belly discomfort, rash.

Severe but rare (stop medication, consult doctor): low blood sugar (see Overdose below), yellow skin (jaundice), unusual bleeding or bruising.

INTERACTIONS:

Other drugs:

- ACE inhibitors, beta-blockers, other hypoglycaemics, chloramphenicol, clofibrate, clonidine, warfarin, probenecid, MAOI, miconazole, salicylates, tetracycline, sulphonamides, diazoxide, corticosteroids, nicotinic acid, oestrogens, progestogens, phenothiazines, phenytoin, thyroid hormones, laxatives.

Other substances:

- reacts adversely with alcohol.

Herbs:

- alfalfa, celery, eucalyptus, fenugreek, garlic, ginger, ginseng, karela.

PRESCRIPTION:

Yes.

PERMITTED IN SPORT:

Yes.

OVERDOSE:

Serious. Symptoms of low blood sugar (hypoglycaemia) may include tiredness, confusion, chills, palpitations, sweating, vomiting, dizziness, hunger, blurred vision and fainting. Significant overdosage can lead to coma and death. Give sugary drinks or sweets if conscious. Seek emergency medical assistance.

OTHER INFORMATION:

Used mainly in elderly patients who develop maturity onset diabetes that is not severe enough to require insulin injections.

See also **Acarbose**, **Glibenclamide**, **Glimepride**, **Glipizide**, **Gliquidone**, **INSULINS**, **Metformin**, **Repaglinide**, **Rosiglitazone**.

Glimepride

TRADE NAME:

Amaryl.

DRUG CLASS:

Hypoglycaemic.

USES:

Diabetes not requiring insulin injections.

DOSAGE:

 Initially 1mg a day at breakfast, increasing very slowly to a maximum of 6mg a day.

FORMS:

Tablets of 1mg (pink), 2mg (green), 3mg (yellow) and 4mg (blue).

PRECAUTIONS:

Not to be used in pregnancy (C), breast feeding and children.

Use with caution with recent surgery, significant infection, poor diet, or other physical stress.

Use with care in elderly.

Regular blood tests of sugar levels and liver function necessary.

Appropriate diet essential.

Do not take if:

- suffering from juvenile (type 1) diabetes, severe kidney or liver disease.

SIDE EFFECTS:

Common: vision disturbances, nausea, diarrhoea.

Unusual: liver damage, blood chemistry

disturbances, low blood sugar.
Severe but rare (stop medication, consult doctor): low blood sugar (see Overdose below), yellow skin (jaundice), unusual bleeding or bruising.

INTERACTIONS:

Other drugs:
• ACE inhibitors, beta-blockers, other hypoglycaemics, chloramphenicol, clofibrate, clonidine, warfarin, probenecid, MAOI, miconazole, salicylates, tetracycline, sulphonamides, diazoxide, corticosteroids, nicotinic acid, oestrogens, progestogen, phenothiazines, phenytoin, thyroid hormones, laxatives.
Other substances:
• reacts adversely with alcohol.
Herbs:
• alfalfa, celery, eucalyptus, fenugreek, garlic, ginger, ginseng, karela.

PRESCRIPTION:

Yes.

PERMITTED IN SPORT:

Yes.

OVERDOSE:

Serious. Symptoms of low blood sugar (hypoglycaemia) may include tiredness, confusion, chills, palpitations, sweating, vomiting, dizziness, hunger, blurred vision and fainting. Significant overdosage can lead to coma and death. Give sugary drinks or sweets if conscious. Seek emergency medical assistance.

See also Acarbose, Glibenclamide, Gliclazide, Glipizide, Gliquidone, INSULINS, Metformin, Repaglinide, Rosiglitazone.

Glipizide

TRADE NAME:

Glibenese, Minodiab.

DRUG CLASS:

Hypoglycaemic.

USES:

Diabetes not requiring insulin injections.

DOSAGE:

 One or two tablets, one to three times a day before meals. Maximum of 20mg a day. Do not vary from prescribed dose without advice from a doctor.

FORMS:

Tablets of 2.5 and 5mg.

PRECAUTIONS:

Not to be used in pregnancy (C), breast feeding or children.
Use with caution in all forms of kidney and liver disease.
Illness, changes in diet, exercise and stress may change dosage requirements. Strict control of carbohydrates and sugars in diet essential.

Do not take if:

 • suffering from severe thyroid, liver or kidney disease.
• uncontrolled infection present.
• an insulin dependent diabetic.
• allergic to sulphas.

SIDE EFFECTS:

Common: nausea, diarrhoea, constipation.
Unusual: blurred vision, drowsiness, dizziness, headache, heartburn, belly discomfort, rash.
Severe but rare (stop medication, consult doctor): low blood sugar (see Overdose below), yellow skin (jaundice), unusual bleeding or bruising.

INTERACTIONS:

Other drugs:
- ACE inhibitors, beta-blockers, other hypoglycaemics, chloramphenicol, clofibrate, clonidine, warfarin, probenecid, MAOI, miconazole, salicylates, tetracycline, sulphonamides, diazoxide, corticosteroids, nicotinic acid, oestrogens, progestogens, phenothiazines, phenytoin, thyroid hormones, laxatives.

Other substances:
- reacts adversely with alcohol.

Herbs:
- alfalfa, celery, eucalyptus, fenugreek, garlic, ginger, ginseng, karela.

PRESCRIPTION:

Yes.

PERMITTED IN SPORT:

Yes.

OVERDOSE:

Serious. Symptoms of low blood sugar (hypoglycaemia) may include tiredness, confusion, chills, palpitations, sweating, vomiting, dizziness, hunger, blurred vision and fainting. Significant overdosage can lead to coma and death. Give sugary drinks or sweets if conscious. Seek emergency medical assistance.

OTHER INFORMATION:

Used mainly in elderly patients who develop maturity onset diabetes that is not severe enough to require insulin injections.

See also Acarbose, Glibenclamide, Gliclazide, Glimepride, Gliquidone, INSULINS, Metformin, Repaglinide, Rosiglitazone.

Gliquidone

TRADE NAME:

Glurenorm.

DRUG CLASS:

Hypoglycaemic.

USES:

Diabetes not requiring insulin injections.

DOSAGE:

 45 to 60mg a day in divided doses before meals. Maximum 180mg a day.

FORMS:

Tablets of 30mg (white).

PRECAUTIONS:

Not to be used in pregnancy (C), breast feeding or children.
Use with caution if operating machinery or driving a vehicle.
Use with caution in all forms of kidney disease.
Illness, changes in diet, exercise and stress may change dosage requirements.
Lower doses required in elderly and debilitated patients.
Strict control of carbohydrates and sugars in diet essential.

Do not take if:

 • suffering from severe liver or kidney disease.

SIDE EFFECTS:

Common: minimal.
Unusual: blurred vision, drowsiness, nausea, heartburn, belly discomfort, rash.
Severe but rare (stop medication, consult doctor): low blood sugar (see Overdose below), yellow skin (jaundice), unusual bleeding or bruising.

INTERACTIONS:

Other drugs:
- ACE inhibitors, beta-blockers, other hypoglycaemics, chloramphenicol, clofibrate, clonidine, warfarin, probenecid, MAOI, miconazole, salicylates, tetracycline, sulphonamides, diazoxide, corticosteroids, nicotinic acid, oestrogens, progestogens, phenothiazines, phenytoin, thyroid hormones, laxatives.

Other substances:
• reacts adversely with alcohol.
Herbs:
• alfalfa, celery, eucalyptus, fenugreek, garlic, ginger, ginseng, karela.

PRESCRIPTION:

Yes.

PERMITTED IN SPORT:

Yes.

OVERDOSE:

Serious. Symptoms of low blood sugar (hypoglycaemia) may include tiredness, confusion, chills, palpitations, sweating, vomiting, dizziness, hunger, blurred vision and fainting. Significant overdosage can lead to coma and death. Give sugary drinks or sweets if conscious. Seek emergency medical assistance.

See also Acarbose, Glibenclamide, Gliclazide, Glimepride, Glipizide, INSULINS, Metformin, Repaglinide, Rosiglitazone.

Glucagon

TRADE NAME:

Glucagen.

USES:

Low blood sugar in diabetics.

DOSAGE:

 Inject contents of ampoule if patient suffers acute low blood sugar not responding to sugar by mouth.

FORMS:

Injection.

PRECAUTIONS:

May be used with caution in pregnancy (B2). Safe to use in breast feeding and children.
Use repeatedly only with caution.
Use with caution in blood clots, heart attack, liver and kidney disease.

Do not take if:

 • suffering from phaeochromocytoma, insulinoma.

SIDE EFFECTS:

Common: nausea, vomiting.

INTERACTIONS:

Other drugs:
• warfarin, beta-blockers (e.g. propranolol).

PRESCRIPTION:

Yes.

PERMITTED IN SPORT:

Yes.

OVERDOSE:

Exacerbation of side effects likely.

OTHER INFORMATION:

May be life saving. Family members and associates should be instructed in use. Diabetics who use too much insulin or eat too little may suffer from sudden low blood sugar that can cause them to rapidly lose consciousness. An injection of Glucagon will revive them rapidly by releasing sugar stored in body.

Glucose

TRADE NAME:

Glucose.
Found in nutritional and electrolyte supplements.
Used as an additive or sweetener in many medications.

DRUG CLASS:

Sugar.

USES:

Correction of severe nutritional loss, correction of insulin overdose, reduction of excessive pressure in brain fluid.

DOSAGE:

 Depends on use. Use as directed by doctor.

FORMS:

Lozenges, injection, solutions.

PRECAUTIONS:

Safe in pregnancy, breast feeding and children.

Do not take if:

• suffering from diabetes, unless suffering insulin overdose.

SIDE EFFECTS:

Minimal.

INTERACTIONS:

None significant.

PRESCRIPTION:

No.

PERMITTED IN SPORT:

Injection: no.
Orally: yes.

OVERDOSE:

No serious consequences. Vomiting likely.

OTHER INFORMATION:

Glucose is a common form of sugar. Works within a couple of minutes after being taken by mouth.

Glutaraldehyde

TRADE NAME:

Glutarol.

DRUG CLASS:

Keratolytic.

USES:

Removal of warts.

DOSAGE:

 Apply twice a day to wart.

FORMS:

Liquid.

PRECAUTIONS:

Safe to use in pregnancy, breast feeding and children.
Avoid warts on face, anus, genitals and other areas of sensitive skin.

SIDE EFFECTS:

Common: skin inflammation and soreness, skin staining.

INTERACTIONS:

None significant.

PRESCRIPTION:

No.

PERMITTED IN SPORT:

Yes.

OVERDOSE:

Serious. Seek urgent medical attention.

See also KERATOLYTICS, PODOPHYLLUMS.

Glycerol

TRADE NAME:

Microlette, Relaxit (with laxatives).
Also used in numerous skin and vaginal preparations.

DRUG CLASS:

Lubricant.

USES:

Constipation, vaginal dryness, skin dryness.

DOSAGE:

 One enema inserted rectally as required.

FORMS:

Enema.

PRECAUTIONS:

Safe in pregnancy, breast feeding, infants and children.
Should not be used repeatedly for prolonged periods.

SIDE EFFECTS:

Minimal.

INTERACTIONS:

None significant.

PRESCRIPTION:

No.

PERMITTED IN SPORT:

Yes.

OVERDOSE:

Causes diarrhoea only.

OTHER INFORMATION:

Very safe ancient remedy.

See also Bisacodyl, Docusate sodium, Fibre, Frangula, Lactulose, Paraffin, Psyllium, Senna, Sodium phosphate, Sodium picosulfate, Sorbitol, Sterculia.

Glyceryl Trinitrate
(GTN, Nitroglycerine)

TRADE NAME:

Coro-Nitro, Deponit, Glytrin, Minitran, Nitro-Dur, Nitrocine, Nitrolingual, Nitromin, Nitronal, Percutol, Suscard Buccal, Sustac, Transiderm Nitro, Trintek.

DRUG CLASS:

Antiangina.

USES:

Relief or prevention of angina.

DOSAGE:

 Tablets: one tablet under tongue every ten minutes as required to a maximum of six a day starting immediately any chest pain experienced. Should not be swallowed.

Spray: one spray under tongue every five minutes as required to a maximum of two sprays per attack starting immediately any chest pain experienced.
Patches: apply to skin of trunk, upper arms or thighs once a day for 16 hours a day.

FORMS:

Tablets, mouth spray, skin patches, injection.
Tablets must not be exposed to light.
Should be stored below 25°C. Discard bottle three months after opening.

PRECAUTIONS:

Should be used with caution in pregnancy (B2) and breast feeding.
Use with caution with strokes, anaemia, severe arteriosclerosis, lung disease, glaucoma, overactive thyroid gland and in the elderly.
Apply patches to different areas with each application.
Tolerance may develop if used constantly.

Do not take if:

 • suffering from head injury, recent stroke, cardiomyopathy.

SIDE EFFECTS:

Common: headache, flushing, rapid heart rate.
Unusual: dizziness, fainting.

INTERACTIONS:

Other drugs:
• sildenafil (Viagra), tadalafil (Cialis): potentially fatal interaction.
Other substances:
• reacts with alcohol. Smoking may exacerbate disease process.

PRESCRIPTION:

Yes.

PERMITTED IN SPORT:

Yes.

OVERDOSE:

Fainting and low blood pressure occur. Red blood cells may be damaged. Administer activated charcoal or induce vomiting if tablets taken recently. Remove patches and ointment. Seek medical assistance.

OTHER INFORMATION:

Tablets under tongue have been used successfully for many decades, but in the last decade better delivery systems in the form of patches and sprays have been developed. Lipstick sized sprays are more convenient, more stable and easier to use than tablets which can deteriorate with time. Nitroglycerine is an incorrect technical name.

See also Isosorbide nitrate, Nicorandil, Perhexiline.

GOLD

See Auranofin, Sodium aurothiomalate.

Gonadotrophin

TRADE NAME:

Choragon, Pregnyl, Profasi.

DRUG CLASS:

Sex hormone.

USES:

Infertility in women, delayed puberty in girls, failure of testicular development, failure of sperm production.

DOSAGE:

 As determined for each patient by doctor.

FORMS:

Injection.

PRECAUTIONS:

Do not use before puberty.
May cause multiple foetus pregnancy.
Use with caution in fluid retention.
Not normally used for more than six months.

Do not take if:

 • suffering from some types of cancer affecting sex organs.

SIDE EFFECTS:

Common: minimal.
Unusual: multiple foetus pregnancy, fluid retention, rash.

INTERACTIONS:

None significant.

PRESCRIPTION:

Yes.

PERMITTED IN SPORT:

No.

OVERDOSE:

Not likely to be serious. Given under strict medical supervision.

Gonadotrophin, menopausal, human

See Menotrophin

Goserelin

TRADE NAME:

Zoladex.

DRUG CLASS:

Cytotoxic.

USES:

Metastatic and severe prostate cancer, advanced breast cancer, fibroids of the uterus, endometriosis.

DOSAGE:

 Implant inserted every one to three months.

FORMS:

Implants of 3.6mg.

PRECAUTIONS:

Not to be used in pregnancy (D), breast feeding or children.
Use with caution in osteoporosis, spinal or ureter disease.

SIDE EFFECTS:

Common: infertility, impotence, decreased libido, hot flushes, headaches, dry vagina, cessation of menstrual periods, changes in blood pressure, breast formation in males, temporary increase in bone pain.
Unusual: breast pain, joint pain, rash, reactions at site of implant or injection, decrease in bone density (osteoporosis).

INTERACTIONS:

Other drugs:
• sex hormones.

PRESCRIPTION:

Yes.

PERMITTED IN SPORT:

Yes.

Gramicidin

TRADE NAME:

Available only in combination with other medications.
Graneodin (with neomycin).
Neosporin (with polymyxin B and neomycin).
Sofradex (with framycetin and dexamethasone).
Soframycin (with framycetin).
Tri-Adcortyl (with triamcinolone, neomycin, nystatin).

DRUG CLASS:

Antibiotic.

USES:

Infections of skin, eyes and ears.

DOSAGE:

 Ear ointment: insert twice a day.
Ear drops: insert two or three times a day (may be used in conjunction with wick in ear).
Cream, ointment: apply three times a day.
Eye drops: insert every three or four hours.
Eye ointment: insert three times a day.

FORMS:

Eye ointment, eye drops (keep cool), ointment, cream, ear drops, ear ointment.

PRECAUTIONS:

Use with caution in pregnancy. May be used in breast feeding and children.

SIDE EFFECTS:

Minimal. Tissue damage possible with prolonged use.

INTERACTIONS:

None significant.

PRESCRIPTION:

Yes.

PERMITTED IN SPORT:

Yes.

OTHER INFORMATION:

Gramicidin is a constituent in some of the most widely used and effective combinations for treating eye, ear and skin infections.
See also Neomycin.

Granisetron

TRADE NAME:

Kytril.

DRUG CLASS:

Antiemetic.

USES:

Nausea and vomiting associated with drugs to treat cancer (cytotoxics).

DOSAGE:

 One or two tablets, once or twice a day.

FORMS:

Tablets of 1 and 2mg (triangular white), liquid, injection, infusion.

PRECAUTIONS:

May be used with caution in pregnancy and children. Not for use in breast feeding.
Use with caution in gut obstruction and liver disease.

SIDE EFFECTS:

Common: headache, constipation.
Unusual: liver damage.

INTERACTIONS:

None significant.

PRESCRIPTION:

Yes.

PERMITTED IN SPORT:

Yes.

OTHER INFORMATION:

Very useful in overcoming the most serious and distressing side-effect of many forms of cancer treatment.

Griseofulvin

TRADE NAME:

Grisovin.

DRUG CLASS:

Antifungal.

USES:

Fungal infection of skin, hair and nails.

DOSAGE:

 One tablet a day after food for several weeks or months.

FORMS:

Tablets of 125 and 500mg (white).

PRECAUTIONS:

Should not be used in pregnancy (B3) unless medically essential. Breast feeding should be ceased before use. May be used in children.
Use with care in liver disease.
Avoid sunlight while using medication.
Use with care if operating machinery or driving a vehicle.
Use with care if allergic to penicillin.
Do not take if:

- suffering from severe liver disease, porphyria, systemic lupus erythematosus (SLE)
- trying to fall pregnant.
- planning to father a child within six months (sperm abnormalities possible).

SIDE EFFECTS:

Common: headache, nausea, sunburn.
Unusual: dizziness, confusion, tiredness, vomiting, sore mouth, furry tongue, rash.

INTERACTIONS:

Other drugs:
- anticoagulants (e.g. warfarin), barbiturates, sedatives, hypnotics, oral contraceptives
- cross reacts with penicillin.
Other substances:
- reacts adversely with alcohol.

PRESCRIPTION:

Yes.

PERMITTED IN SPORT:

Yes.

OVERDOSE:

Unlikely to cause serious effects.

OTHER INFORMATION:

Widely and commonly used for fungal infections, but more effective (and expensive) medications have been recently introduced.

See also Amphotericin, Fluconazole, Itraconazole, Ketoconazole, Terbinafine.

Growth Hormone

See Somatropin.

GTN

See Glyceryl trinitrate.

Guaiphenesin

TRADE NAME:

Ingredient found in numerous non-prescription cough mixtures.

DRUG CLASS:

Expectorant (assists coughing up phlegm).

USES:

Moist chesty cough.

DOSAGE:

 Take every four hours.

FORMS:

Mixture, syrup.

PRECAUTIONS:

Safe to use in pregnancy (A), breast feeding and children.
Use with caution under two years.
Not for long term use.
Does not reduce mucus production.

SIDE EFFECTS:

Common: dizziness, nausea, diarrhoea.
Unusual: drowsiness.

INTERACTIONS:

Other drugs:
• MAOI antidepressants (serious interaction).

PRESCRIPTION:

No.

PERMITTED IN SPORT:

Yes (provided not combined with pseudoephedrine).

OVERDOSE:

Unlikely to have any serious effects.

OTHER INFORMATION:

Old fashioned medication.
See also Camphor, Senega.

Guanethidine

TRADE NAME:

Ismelin.

DRUG CLASS:

Vasodilator.

USES:

Lowering very high blood pressure.

DOSAGE:

 Injection as determined by doctor.

FORMS:

Injection.

PRECAUTIONS:

Safe in pregnancy (A), breast feeding and children.
Use with caution in peptic ulcers, low blood pressure tendency, asthma, kidney disease and diabetes.

Do not take if:

 • suffering from phaeochromocytoma, heart block or abnormal heart rhythm, congestive heart failure.

SIDE EFFECTS:

Common: drowsiness, low blood pressure, faintness, dizziness, slow heart rate.
Unusual: angina, heart failure, nausea, diarrhoea, asthma, impotence, dermatitis, hair loss.
Severe but rare (stop medication, consult doctor): blood cell abnormalities.

INTERACTIONS:

Other drugs:
• MAOI antidepressants (serious interaction), anticoagulants (e.g. warfarin, serious interaction), antiarrhythmics, beta-blockers, digoxin, antihypertensives, sympathomimetics, antipsychotics, tricyclic antidepressants, oral contraceptives, some anaesthetics.
Other substances:
• alcohol.

PRESCRIPTION:

Yes.

PERMITTED IN SPORT:

Yes.

See also Diazoxide, VASODILATORS.

Guarana
(Paullinia cupana)

USES:

Tonic, stimulant.

DOSAGE:

 One gram a day.

FORMS:

Tablets, capsules, liquid.

PRECAUTIONS:

Not for use in pregnancy. Use with caution in breast feeding and children. Use with caution in heart disease, kidney disease, anxiety states, hyperthyroidism (over active thyroid gland), psychoses and muscle spasms (e.g. spasticity).

SIDE EFFECTS:

Common: insomnia (sleeplessness), agitation, increased urine production.
Unusual: low blood potassium levels (hypokalaemia), abnormal bleeding.

INTERACTIONS:

Other drugs:
• digoxin, theophylline.
Other substances:
• caffeine.

PRESCRIPTION:

No.

PERMITTED IN SPORT:

No.

OVERDOSE:

Vomiting, painful and frequent passing of urine, intestinal spasms, irritability and irrational behaviour may occur. Seek medical advice.

OTHER INFORMATION:

Not used in orthodox medicine. Its clinical effects can be explained by the caffeine content of the herb. 250mg of guarana contains about 100mg of caffeine.

H2 RECEPTOR ANTAGONISTS

DISCUSSION:

Peptic ulcers have caused belly pains for millennia and were poorly treated until a significant advance in medication occurred in the late 1970s with the introduction of cimetidine, the first of the H2 receptor antagonists. These drugs are distantly related to antihistamines and act to cure ulcers by reducing the amount of acid secreted into the stomach. This also enables them to control reflux oesophagitis, which may accompany a hiatus hernia. Treatment is usually rapidly effective, but must be continued for weeks or months to prevent relapses.

See Cimetidine, Famotidine, Nizatadine, Ranitidine.

Haemophilus influenzae B vaccine
(HiB vaccine)

TRADE NAMES:

Hiberix, Hibtiter.
ACT-HIB DTP, Infanrix-HIB (with tetanus, whooping cough and diphtheria vaccines).

DRUG CLASS:

Vaccine.

USES:

Prevention of meningitis and epiglottitis (throat infection) caused by Haemophilus influenzae B in children under five years.

DOSAGE:

 Three or four doses, two months apart.

FORMS:

Injection.

PRECAUTIONS:

Not recommended for use in pregnancy (B2) or adults, but unlikely to cause problems if given accidentally during pregnancy or breast feeding. Designed for use in children and infants.
Use with caution in fever, acute infection or immune system problems.
Do not inject into a vein.

SIDE EFFECTS:

Common: redness and soreness at injection site.
Unusual: irritability, tiredness.

INTERACTIONS:

None significant.

PRESCRIPTION:

Yes.

PERMITTED IN SPORT:

Yes.

OTHER INFORMATION:

Introduced in early 1990s to prevent one type of meningitis and a rare but potentially fatal infection that can attack the epiglottis at the back of the throat and block the airway preventing breathing. All children should start a course of this vaccine at two months of age and have follow up injections at four, six and eighteen months. Older children need a shorter course, but greatest risk occurs under twelve months.

HAEMOSTATIC AGENTS

See Phytomenadione.

Halcinonide

TRADE NAME:

Halciderm.

DRUG CLASS:

Corticosteroid.

USES:

Inflammation of skin (eczema, dermatitis, psoriasis etc.).

DOSAGE:

 Apply two or three times a day.

FORMS:

Cream.

PRECAUTIONS:

Should be used with caution in pregnancy, breast feeding and children. Avoid eyes.
Use for shortest period of time possible.
Use with caution on face.

Do not use if:

 • suffering from any form of skin infection or tuberculosis.

SIDE EFFECTS:

Common: minimal.
Unusual: thinning of skin, itching, burning, stinging, scarring of skin.

INTERACTIONS:

None significant.

PRESCRIPTION:

Yes.

PERMITTED IN SPORT:

Yes.

OTHER INFORMATION:

Lowest dose and shortest possible course should be used.

See also Betamethasone, Desoxymethasone, Diflucortolone,

Hydrocortisone, Methylprednisolone, Mometasone, Triamcinolone.

Haloperidol

TRADE NAMES:

Dozic, Haldol, Serenace.

DRUG CLASS:

Antipsychotic.

USES:

Psychotic disorders, acute alcoholism, Tourette's syndrome, severe vomiting, addition to pain killers.

DOSAGE:

 Individualised to patients requirements. Follow doctors instructions carefully.

FORMS:

Tablets, mixture, injection.

PRECAUTIONS:

Should not be used in pregnancy (C) unless medically essential. Breast feeding should be ceased before use. Not for use in children under three years.
Should be used with caution in epilepsy, over active thyroid gland, glaucoma, irregular heart rhythm, liver disease, kidney disease, severe heart disease and hardening of arteries.
Lower doses necessary in elderly.
Use for shortest time possible.

Do not take if:

 • suffering from depression, Parkinson's disease, in a coma
• operating machinery, driving a vehicle or undertaking tasks that require concentration and coordination.

SIDE EFFECTS:

Common: minimal in low doses.
Incoordination, drowsiness, muscle spasms, tremor.

Unusual: depression, anxiety, restlessness, headache, sleeplessness, confusion, dizziness, loss of appetite, rapid heart rate, enlarged breasts (both sexes), increase or decrease in libido. *Severe but rare (stop medication, consult doctor):* repetitive unwanted movements of face, rigid muscles, fever, coma.

INTERACTIONS:

Other drugs:
• narcotics, analgesics, barbiturates, sedatives, anticoagulants (e.g. warfarin), tricyclic antidepressants, quinidine, buspirone, fluoxetine, fluvoxamine, nefazodone, paroxetine, venlafaxine, propranolol, lithium.
Herbs:
• evening primrose (linoleic acid), sparteine (Cytisus scoparius).
Other substances:
• reacts adversely with alcohol and cigarette smoking.

PRESCRIPTION:

Yes.

PERMITTED IN SPORT:

Yes.

OVERDOSE:

May cause sedation, muscle spasms, twitching, convulsions, coma, reduced breathing and death. Administer activated charcoal or induce vomiting if taken recently and patient alert. Seek urgent medical assistance.

See also Amisulpride, Droperidol, Flupenthixol, Lithium Carbonate, Olanzapine, PHENOTHIAZINES, Pimozide, Quetiapine, Risperidone, Thiothixene, Zuclopenthixol.

HCG

See Chorionic gonadotrophin, human.

Heparin

TRADE NAMES:

Canusal, Hepsal, Monoparin, Multipatin.

DRUG CLASS:

Anticoagulant.

USES:

Prevention and treatment of blood clots.

DOSAGE:

 As determined by doctor.

FORMS:

Injection, infusion.

PRECAUTIONS:

Should only be used in pregnancy (C) if medically essential. Breast feeding should be ceased if heparin treatment necessary. May be used in children.
Lower doses required in elderly.
Use with caution in asthma, kidney and liver disease, high blood pressure, eye retina disease.
Regular blood tests to monitor blood clotting time essential.

Do not take if:

 • suffering from bleeding disorders, threatened abortion, heart infection, peptic ulcer, severe high blood pressure, severe liver or kidney disease
• due for surgery.

SIDE EFFECTS:

Common: excessive bleeding, bruising.
Unusual: nose bleeds, vomiting blood, blood in faeces, rash, itch, asthma.

INTERACTIONS:

Other drugs:
• other anticoagulants (e.g. warfarin), aspirin, NSAID, corticosteroids, hydroxychloroquine, ethacrynic acid, sulfinpyrazone, vitamin K,

antihistamines, tetracyclines, digoxin, vitamin C, insulin, nicotine.

Herbs:
• goldenseal.

PRESCRIPTION:

Yes.

PERMITTED IN SPORT:

Yes, but not advised in any active sport.

OVERDOSE:

Extremely serious. Massive bleeding may occur. Antidote available.

OTHER INFORMATION:

Only administered by doctors by injection or infusion (drip) in hospital or strictly controlled outpatient basis. Used for many years to very effectively control life threatening blood clots. Once stabilised, patient is usually switched to an anticoagulant tablet such as warfarin. Available in two forms that vary in their speed and method of action.

See also Calcium Heparin, Dalteparin, Enoxaparin.

Heparinoid

TRADE NAMES:

Hirudoid, Lasonil.
Anacal (with lauromacrogol).

USES:

Blood clots in veins close to skin, inflammation of veins, softening of hard scars, bruises, swelling caused by injury to tissue, sprains, haematomas (blood collections under skin), haemorrhoids.

DOSAGE:

 Apply and massage in once to four times a day.

FORMS:

Cream, gel, ointment.

PRECAUTIONS:

Safe in pregnancy, breast feeding and children.

Do not use on:

 • bleeding areas, infected areas and eye.

SIDE EFFECTS:

Common: skin redness.

INTERACTIONS:

Other drugs:
• heparin, anticoagulants (e.g. warfarin).

PRESCRIPTION:

No.

PERMITTED IN SPORT:

Yes.

OTHER INFORMATION:

Useful and effective medication. Do not use excessive amounts.

See also Benzydamine, Camphor, Capsaicin, Menthol.

Hepatitis A vaccine

TRADE NAMES:

Avaxim, Epaxal, Havrix, VAQTA.
Hepatyrix, Viatim (with typhoid vaccine).
Twinrix (with hepatitis B vaccine).

DRUG CLASS:

Vaccine.

USES:

Prevention of hepatitis A.

DOSAGE:

 Twinrix: three injections at intervals of one month and six to twelve months give at least five years, and possibly far longer protection.
Avaxim, Epaxal, Havrix, Hepatyrix, VAQTA, Viatim: two injections, six to twelve months

apart give at least five years protection.

More frequent revaccination may be necessary for accompanying vaccinations (e.g. typhoid).

FORMS:

Injection.

PRECAUTIONS:

Not designed to be used in pregnancy (B2), but unlikely to cause serious adverse effects if given inadvertently. May be given with caution in breast feeding and children under five years. May be given to children over five years. First injection takes effect after 14 days, and lasts for at least six months. Booster gives long term protection.

Use with caution if exposed to hepatitis A.

Do not take if:

 • suffering from significant fever.

SIDE EFFECTS:

Common: local reaction at injection site.
Unusual: headache, fever, tiredness, nausea, loss of appetite, general unwellness.

INTERACTIONS:

Other drugs:
• immunoglobulin.

PRESCRIPTION:

Yes.

PERMITTED IN SPORT:

Yes.

OVERDOSE:

An inadvertent additional vaccination is unlikely to have any serious effects.

OTHER INFORMATION:

Hepatitis A causes liver damage and is caught from eating contaminated food or poor personal hygiene. Hepatitis A is very common in some developing countries.

See also Salmonella typhi vaccine.

Hepatitis B vaccine

TRADE NAMES:

Engerix B, HBVaxpro.
Twinrix (with hepatitis A vaccine).

DRUG CLASS:

Vaccine.

USES:

Prevention of Hepatitis B.

DOSAGE:

 Three injections at intervals of one month and five months gives at least five years protection.

FORMS:

Injection.

PRECAUTIONS:

Should not be used during pregnancy (B2) unless essential. Accidental vaccination during pregnancy is unlikely to cause any significant problem. Use with caution in breast feeding. May be used in children.

Use with caution if immune system damaged, recently exposed to hepatitis B, or severely ill.

Do not take if:

 • suffering from severe infection or fever.

SIDE EFFECTS:

Common: local soreness, swelling, redness and hardness.
Unusual: headache, dizziness, fever, muscle aches, tiredness, nausea, diarrhoea, joint pain, rash.

INTERACTIONS:

None significant.

PRESCRIPTION:

Yes.

PERMITTED IN SPORT:

Yes.

OVERDOSE:

No adverse effects likely from an inadvertent additional dose.

OTHER INFORMATION:

Hepatitis B is endemic (widely spread) in Aboriginal Australians and South-East Asians. It is spread by sex, blood, sharing needles, blood splashes into eye and possibly by close contact of open wounds.

Heroin

DRUG CLASS:

Narcotic.

USES:

No current recognised medical uses in Britain.
Used in some countries for relief of severe pain.
Used illegally as a psychoactive drug to cause euphoria.

FORMS:

Injection.

PRECAUTIONS:

Should never be used in pregnancy, breast feeding or children.

Do not use if:

- suffering from liver disease, kidney disease, epilepsy, head injury, diabetes, alcoholism, lung disease (e.g. asthma), prostate disease
- driving a car, operating machinery, swimming or undertaking any activity that requires concentration.

SIDE EFFECTS:

Common: constipation, confusion, sweating, contracted pupils, difficulty passing urine, dry mouth, flushing, euphoria (artificial happiness), dizziness, slow heart rate, irregular heart rate, sedation, mood change, rash.
Unusual: itch, blurred vision, low blood pressure, difficulty in breathing, convulsions.

INTERACTIONS:

Other drugs:
- hypnotics, sedatives, marijuana, MAOI, cocaine.
Other substances:
- increases the effect of alcohol.

PRESCRIPTION:

Illegal.

PERMITTED IN SPORT:

No.

OVERDOSE:

Very serious. May cause convulsions, irregular heart beat, difficulty in breathing, coma and death. Seek emergency medical assistance. Antidote available.

OTHER INFORMATION:

Illegal drug of dependence. Highly addictive. Toleration may develop quickly (higher dose required to obtain same effect). Possession may lead to criminal charges. Heroin is closely related to morphine. It may be preferred to morphine in palliative care when available because it is said to produce more calming effects.

See also Alfentanil, Buprenorphine, Codeine, Dextromoramide, Dextropropoxyphene, Fentanyl, Hydromorphone, Methadone, Morphine, Oxycodone, Pentazocine, Pethidine.

Hexachlorophane

TRADE NAME:

Ster-Zac.

DRUG CLASS:

Antiseptic.

USES:

Prevention of bacterial skin infections.

DOSAGE:

 Use once or twice a day.

FORMS:

Cream, powder.

PRECAUTIONS:

Safe to use on skin in pregnancy, breast feeding (not breasts) and children.
Do not use on badly burned or damaged skin.

SIDE EFFECTS:

Common: minimal.
Unusual: light sensitivity, skin irritation.

INTERACTIONS:

None significant.

PRESCRIPTION:

Cream, yes. Powder, no.

PERMITTED IN SPORT:

Yes.

OVERDOSE:

Vomiting and diarrhoea possible if swallowed.

OTHER INFORMATION:

Often used on the cut stump of the umbilical cord of babies after birth.

Hexamine

TRADE NAME:

Hiprex.

DRUG CLASS:

Urinary antiseptic.

USES:

Prevention of recurrent urine infections.

DOSAGE:

 One tablet twice a day.

FORMS:

Tablet (white) of 1g.

PRECAUTIONS:

Safe for use in pregnancy (A), breast feeding and children.
Use with caution in vegetarians.
Do not take if:

 • suffering from severe liver or kidney disease, dehydration, severe kidney infection (without other antibiotic).

SIDE EFFECTS:

Common: nausea, burning urine.
Unusual: vomiting, rash, stomach discomfort.

INTERACTIONS:

Other drugs:
• urinary alkalinisers, sulfonamides.

PRESCRIPTION:

No.

PERMITTED IN SPORT:

Yes.

OVERDOSE:

Exacerbation of side effects likely.

OTHER INFORMATION:

Used mainly in women who have recurrent attacks of cystitis, and in patients with a urinary catheter.
See also URINARY ALKALINISERS.

Hexetedine

TRADE NAME:

Oraldene.

DRUG CLASS:

Antiseptic.

USES:

Mouth infections, thrush and ulcers; bad breath.

DOSAGE:

 Gargle two or three times a day.

FORMS:

Solution.

PRECAUTIONS:

Safe to use in pregnancy, breast feeding and children over six years.

SIDE EFFECTS:

Common: minimal.
Unusual: mouth irritation.

INTERACTIONS:

None significant.

PRESCRIPTION:

No.

PERMITTED IN SPORT:

Yes.

OVERDOSE:

Vomiting and diarrhoea possible if significant amount swallowed.

HiB vaccine

See Haemophilus influenzae B Vaccine.

HORMONE REPLACEMENT THERAPY (HRT)

DISCUSSION:

Concerns about the safety of hormone replacement therapy (HRT) relate to long-term (greater than five years) use of combined (oestrogen and progestogen) HRT. Short term use for up to five years is still apparently safe and is used to control the symptoms of menopause (e.g. hot flushes, dry vagina, aching).

Long term use needs to be weighed for each individual woman according to her risk factors for heart disease, osteoporosis, breast cancer, stroke and blood clot.

Every woman should asses her needs and risks on an individual basis after a discussion with her doctor.
Benefits:
- improved sense of well being
- improved libido and vaginal lubrication
- breast shape retained for longer without drooping
- reduced risk of bowel cancer (risk decreases from 1.6 women in every 1000 developing bowel cancer in any one year to 1.0)
- significantly reduced risk of osteoporosis (risk decreases from 1.5 women in every 1000 having a hip fracture from osteoporosis in any one year to 0.9)
- improved skin quality and tone (fewer wrinkles)
- improves mood and reduces irritability.

Disadvantages:
- increased risk of breast cancer if taken for more than four years (risk rises from 3.1 women in every 1000 developing breast cancer in any one year to 3.9)
- increased risk of heart attacks if taken for more than four years (risk rises from 2.4 women in every 1000 having a heart attack in any one year to 3.1)
- increased risk of blood clots in veins (leg blood clots) (risk rises from 1.1 women in every 1000 developing a blood clot in any one year to 2.9)
- increased risk of stroke (risk rises from 1.9 women in every 1000 developing a stroke in any one year to 2.7)
- breast tenderness and break through bleeding in early stages of use.

Statistics are for postmenopausal women on combined oestrogen and progestogen HRT.

See Oestradiol, Oestriol, Oestrogen, Oestrone, Tibolone.

HORMONES, SEX

See Chorionic gonadotrophin, Cyproterone acetate, Danazol, Dydrogesterone, Ethinyloestradiol, Follicle stimulating

hormone, Gestrinone, **HORMONE REPLACEMENT THERAPY**, Medroxyprogesterone acetate, Mesterolone, Nafarelin, Oestradiol, Oestriol, Oestrogens, Oestrone, **ORAL CONTRACEPTIVES**, Piperazine oestrone sulfate, Testosterone.

HRT

See **HORMONE REPLACEMENT THERAPY**.

Human chorionic gonadotrophin

See Gonadotrophin.

Hyaluronic Acid

TRADE NAME:

Durolane.

USES:

Osteoarthritis of knee.

DOSAGE:

 Injection into knee joint, repeated after six months if necessary.

FORMS:

Injection.

PRECAUTIONS:

Use with caution in pregnancy and breast feeding. Not for use in children.
Excess fluid should be removed from joint before injection.
Use with caution with poor circulation or lymphoedema.
Do not take if:

 • suffering from skin disease or infection at joint site, infection or severe inflammation of knee joint.

SIDE EFFECTS:

Common: knee pain and swelling.
Severe but rare: knee joint infection.

INTERACTIONS:

None significant.

PRESCRIPTION:

Yes.

PERMITTED IN SPORT:

Yes.

OTHER INFORMATION:

Introduced in 2002 as a temporary relief for significant knee arthritis pain.

Hyaluronidase

TRADE NAME:

Hyalase.

USES:

Injection that aids diffusion of fluids through tissue.

DOSAGE:

 As determined by doctor for each patient.

FORMS:

Injection.

PRECAUTIONS:

Safe in pregnancy, breast feeding and children.
Do not use if:

 • suffering from infection or cancer
• not to be injected into a vein.

SIDE EFFECTS:

Minimal.

INTERACTIONS:

None significant.

PRESCRIPTION:

Yes.

PERMITTED IN SPORT:

Yes.

Hydralazine

TRADE NAME:

Apresoline.

DRUG CLASS:

Antihypertensive.

USES:

High blood pressure, often in combination with other medications. Particularly useful in the high blood pressure associated with pre-eclampsia of pregnancy.

DOSAGE:

 One to three tablets four times a day to a maximum of 200mg per day.

FORMS:

Tablets of 25mg (yellow).

PRECAUTIONS:

Should not be used in first seven months of pregnancy (C), and only if medically necessary later in pregnancy. Safe in breast feeding. Should not be used in children.
Take with care if suffering from angina, recent heart attack, other heart diseases, recent stroke, kidney or liver disease. Not for prolonged use.

Do not take if:

 • Suffering from SLE (systemic lupus erythematosus), very rapid pulse, aortic aneurysm, heart failure, cor pulmonale.

SIDE EFFECTS:

Common: slowed reactions, rapid heart rate, palpitations, dizziness, flushing, low blood pressure, angina.

Unusual: headaches, joint pains and swelling, muscle aches, nasal congestion, stomach upsets.
Severe but rare (stop medication, consult doctor): unusual bleeding, irregular heart beat.

INTERACTIONS:

Other drugs:
• vasodilators, calcium channel blockers, ACE inhibitors, diuretics, other medications for high blood pressure, diazoxide, tricyclic antidepressants, tranquillisers, beta-blockers, adrenaline, MAOI (monoamine oxidase inhibitors).
Other substances:
• reacts adversely with alcohol.

PRESCRIPTION:

Yes.

PERMITTED IN SPORT:

Yes.

OVERDOSE:

Results in rapid heart rate, low blood pressure, dizziness, nausea, sweating, irregular heart rate, angina, heart attack and death. If taken recently induce vomiting. Seek urgent medical assistance.

OTHER INFORMATION:

Only used in the most severe and difficult forms of high blood pressure. Interacts with a wide range of other medications.

Hydrochlorothiazide

See THIAZIDE DIURETICS.

Hydrocortisone (Cortisol)

TRADE NAMES:

Colifoam, Corlan, Dioderm, Efcortelan, Efcortesol, Hydrocortistab, Hydrocortone, Mildison Lipocream, Solu-Cortef.
Locoid (Hydrocortisone-17 butyrate).

Actinac (with chloramphenicol, allantoin, sulpha and other ingredients).
Alphaderm (with urea).
Alphosyl HC (with coal tar, allantoin).
Anugesic HC (with pramoxine, zinc oxide, benzyl benzoate and other ingredients).
Anusol HC (with benzyl benzoate, bismuth, zinc oxide and other ingredients).
Calmurid HC (with urea, lactic acid).
Canesten-HC (with clotrimazole).
Daktacort (with miconazole).
Econacort (with econazole).
Eurax-Hydrocortisone (with crotamiton).
Fucidin H (with sodium fusidate).
Gentisone HC (with gentamicin).
Gregoderm (with neomycin, nystatin, polymyxin).
Locoid C (with chlorquinaldol).
Nystaform-HC (with nystatin, chlorhexidine).
Otosporin (with neomycin, polymyxin).
Perinal (with lignocaine).
Proctofoam HC (with pramoxine).
Proctosedyl, Uniroid HC (with cinchocaine).
Terra-Cortril (with oxytetracycline).
Terra-Cortril Nystatin (with oxytetracycline, nystatin).
Timodine (with benzalkonium chloride, dimethicone, nystatin).
Vioform-Hydrocortisone (with clioquinol).
Xyloproct (with lignocaine, zinc oxide, aluminium acetate).

DRUG CLASS:

Corticosteroid.

USES:

Inflammation of skin (eczema, dermatitis, acne etc.), anus (piles), rectum (ulcerative colitis), mouth (mouth ulcers), eyes and other tissues.

DOSAGE:

 Cream and ointment: apply three or four times a day.
Rectal foam: insert twice a day initially, then every two days.
Suppositories: insert up to three times a day initially, then reduce to once a day for up to three weeks.
Eye drops: insert every two to four hours.
Eye ointment: insert two to four times a day.
Tablets: as directed by doctor.
Pellets: one pellet dissolved in mouth four times a day.

FORMS:

Cream, ointment, foam, suppository, eye drops, eye ointment, tablets, pellets, injection, spray.

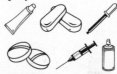

PRECAUTIONS:

Tablets, injections and rectal preparations should be used in pregnancy (C), breast feeding and children only on specific medical advice.
Skin and eye preparations safe in pregnancy, breast feeding and children over three years.
Use tablets, injections and rectal preparations with caution if under stress, and in patients with under active thyroid gland, liver disease, diverticulitis, high blood pressure, myasthenia gravis, or kidney disease.
Avoid eyes with all forms except eye drops and ointment.
Do not use skin preparations for long periods in children.
Medication should not be ceased abruptly, but dosage should be slowly reduced.

Do not take if:

 • suffering from infections, peptic ulcer, osteoporosis
• having a vaccination.

Do not apply to:

 • infected, fungally affected or ulcerated skin or other tissue unless combined with an antibiotic or antifungal.

SIDE EFFECTS:

Most significant side effects occur only with prolonged use of tablets, injections or rectal preparations.

Common: tablets, injections and rectal preparations: bloating, weight gain, rashes and intestinal disturbances. Creams and ointments—rarely cause adverse reactions.

Unusual: tablets, injections and rectal forms: biochemical disturbances of blood, muscle weakness, bone weakness, impaired wound healing, skin thinning, tendon weakness, peptic ulcers, gullet ulcers, bruising, increased sweating, loss of fat under skin, premature ageing, excess facial hair growth in women, pigmentation of skin and nails, acne, convulsions, headaches, dizziness, growth suppression in children, aggravation of diabetes, worsening of infections, cataracts, aggravation of glaucoma, blood clots in veins and sleeplessness.

Severe but rare (stop medication, consult doctor): any significant side effect should be reported to a doctor immediately.

INTERACTIONS:

Other drugs:
- creams do not normally interact with other drugs
- tablets, injections and rectal preparations of hydrocortisone may be affected by oral contraceptives, barbiturates, phenytoin, and rifampicin.

Herbs:
- liquorice.

PRESCRIPTION:

Yes.

PERMITTED IN SPORT:

Creams and ointments: yes.
Other forms: no.

OVERDOSE:

Medical treatment is required. Serious effects and death rare.

OTHER INFORMATION:

Extremely effective and useful medication if used correctly. Safe to use on skin, but other forms must be used with extreme care under strict medical supervision. Lowest dose and shortest possible course should be used. Not addictive.

See also Betamethasone, CORTICOSTEROIDS, Desonide, Methylprednisolone, Mometasone, Prednisolone, Triamcinolone.

Hydroflumethiazide

See THIAZIDE DIURETICS.

Hydrogen peroxide

TRADE NAMES:

Crystacide, Hioxyl.
Hydrogen peroxide 6% mouthwash is prepared under numerous locally made trade names.

DRUG CLASS:

Antiseptic.

USES:

Superficial infections and ulcers of skin and mouth.

DOSAGE:

 Apply or gargle two or three times a day.

FORMS:

Cream, mouthwash.

PRECAUTIONS:

Safe to use in pregnancy, breast feeding and children.
Avoid eyes.
Do not use for more than one month.

SIDE EFFECTS:

Minimal.

INTERACTIONS:

Other drugs:
• iodine, permanganate.

PRESCRIPTION:

No.

PERMITTED IN SPORT:

Yes.

OVERDOSE:

Vomiting and diarrhoea only likely effects if swallowed.

OTHER INFORMATION:

Very old fashioned, but still effective.

Hydromorphone

TRADE NAME:

Palladone.

DRUG CLASS:

Narcotic.

USES:

Relief of severe cancer pain.

DOSAGE:

 One capsule four hourly as required.

FORMS:

Capsules of 1.3mg (orange/clear) and 2.6mg (red/clear).

PRECAUTIONS:

Not for use in pregnancy, breast feeding and children.
Use with caution in underactive thyroid gland, severe lung disease, kidney or adrenal gland disease and enlarged prostate gland.
Reduce dose in elderly.

Do not take if:

 • suffering from poor lung function, in a coma, severe undiagnosed abdominal disease, head injury, convulsions, alcoholism.

SIDE EFFECTS:

Common: constipation, nausea, vomiting, drowsiness.
Unusual: tolerance and dependence.
Severe but rare (stop medication, consult doctor): reduced ability to breathe.

INTERACTIONS:

Other drugs:
• MAOI, sedatives, phenothiazines, some general anaesthetics.
Other substances:
• alcohol.

PRESCRIPTION:

Yes (very restricted).

PERMITTED IN SPORT:

No.

OVERDOSE:

Serious. Sedation, convulsions, coma and death may occur. Administer activated charcoal or induce vomiting if medication taken recently and patient alert. Seek emergency medical assistance. Antidote available.

OTHER INFORMATION:

Highly addictive if used inappropriately. Very effective and unlikely to cause addiction if used appropriately for severe pain. Patients with terminal diseases (e.g. cancer) should use dose adequate to control pain and not be concerned about possibility of addiction. Derived from opium poppy and closely related to heroin.

See also Alfentanil, Buprenorphine, Codeine, Dextromoramide, Dextropropoxyphene, Fentanyl, Heroin, Methadone, Morphine, Oxycodone, Pentazocine, Pethidine.

Hydroxocobalamin
(Vitamin B12)

TRADE NAMES:

Cobalin-H, Neo-Cytamen.
A large number of other preparations
include various forms of vitamin B12
alone or in combination with other
medications.

DRUG CLASS:

Vitamin.

USES:

Pernicious anaemia, pins and needles
sensation of feet, some eye disorders
(optic neuropathy).

DOSAGE:

Injection: once every three
months, or as determined by
doctor.
Recommended daily allowance:
2mcg a day.

FORMS:

Tablets, capsules, mixture, drops,
injection.

PRECAUTIONS:

Safe in pregnancy, breast feeding and
children.
Do not take in high doses or for
prolonged periods of time.
Use with caution in polycythaemia vera.

SIDE EFFECTS:

Common: minimal.
Unusual: low blood potassium, diarrhoea,
itch, swelling sensation.
*Severe but rare (stop medication, consult
doctor):* blood clot in vein.

INTERACTIONS:

Other drugs:
• oral contraceptives, chloramphenicol,
 folic acid.

PRESCRIPTION:

Injection: yes.
Other forms: no.

PERMITTED IN SPORT:

Yes.

OVERDOSE:

Unlikely to cause any serious effects.

OTHER INFORMATION:

Several chemical variations of Vitamin
B12 exist including cyanocobalamin and
hydroxocobalamin. They are identical in
their actions and use. Cyanocobalamin
was the original form of vitamin B12
used medically. Vitamin B12 is a water
soluble vitamin found in animal products.
It is essential for the formation of red
blood cells, normal growth, and normal
fat and sugar metabolism. In pernicious
anaemia, the body loses the ability to
absorb vitamin B12 from the stomach.
Remember, vitamins are merely
chemicals that are essential for the
functioning of the body and if taken to
excess, act as a drug.
See also Cyanocobalamin.

Hydroxyapatite

TRADE NAME:

Ossopan.

DRUG CLASS:

Electrolyte.

USES:

Calcium and phosphorus supplements
may be required in osteoporosis, rickets,
osteomalacia and during breast feeding.

DOSAGE:

Four to eight tablets, or one or
two sachets a day in divided doses.

FORMS:

Tablets, sachets of granules.

PRECAUTIONS:

Safe to use in pregnancy and breast feeding.
Use with caution in children.
Use with caution if a history of kidney stones.

Do not take if:

- suffering from high calcium levels in blood
- immobilised.

SIDE EFFECTS:

Minimal.

INTERACTIONS:

None significant.

PRESCRIPTION:

No.

PERMITTED IN SPORT:

Yes.

OVERDOSE:

Stomach pains, constipation and nausea likely.

Hydroxychloroquine

TRADE NAME:

Plaquenil.

DRUG CLASS:

Antirheumatic, antimalarial.

USES:

Rheumatoid arthritis, systemic lupus erythematosus (SLE), prevention and treatment of malaria.

DOSAGE:

Rheumatoid and SLE: one tablet two or three times a day with meals.
Malaria prevention: two tablets a week.
Malaria treatment: four tablets at once, two tablets eight hours later, then two tablets a day for a further two days.

FORMS:

Tablets (orange) of 200mg.

PRECAUTIONS:

Not to be used in pregnancy (D) as the foetus may be damaged. Use with caution in breast feeding and children.
Use with caution in severe brain disease, severe intestinal disease, porphyria, psoriasis, liver disease and alcoholism.
Exposure to sunlight while taking higher doses may cause excessive sunburn or rash.
Regular eye checks for damage to cornea or retina required if used long term.

Do not take if:

- suffering from macular eye damage.

SIDE EFFECTS:

Common: rash, itching, dry skin, nausea.
Unusual: vomiting, loss of appetite, belly cramps.
Severe but rare (stop medication, consult doctor): blurred vision, unusual bleeding or bruising.

INTERACTIONS:

Other drugs:
- MAOI, digoxin.

PRESCRIPTION:

Yes.

PERMITTED IN SPORT:

Yes.

OVERDOSE:

Very serious. Causes severe liver damage. Symptoms include headache, blurred vision, convulsions, heart failure and death. Administer activated charcoal or induce vomiting if medication taken recently. Seek emergency medical treatment.

OTHER INFORMATION:

Quinine from the bark of the South American chincona tree has been used to treat malaria for centuries.

Hydroxychloroquine is derived from quinine. Found serendipitously to control some rheumatoid conditions and with most forms of malaria now being resistant to Quinine derivatives, it is now used for this purpose far more often than for malaria. Does not cause addiction or dependence.

See also Atovaquone, Artemether and Lumefantrine, Chloroquine, Doxycycline, Mefloquine, Proguanil, Pyrimethamine, Quinine bisulphate.

Hydroxymethylcellulose

See EYE LUBRICANTS.

Hydroxyurea

TRADE NAME:

Hydrea.

USES:

Leukaemia, melanoma, cancer of the ovary.

DOSAGE:

 Must be individualised by doctor for each patient depending on disease, severity and weight of patient.

FORMS:

Capsules (green/pink) of 500mg.

PRECAUTIONS:

Must not be used in pregnancy (D) unless mother's life is at risk as damage to foetus may occur. Breast feeding must be ceased before use. May be used in children if medically essential.

Regular blood and bone marrow tests to check levels of blood and marrow cells and liver function essential.

Adequate contraception must be used by women while Hydroxyurea is being taken.

Use with caution in AIDS, kidney and liver disease.

Do not take if:

 • suffering from anaemia or bone marrow damage.

SIDE EFFECTS:

Common: mouth soreness and ulcers, nausea, loss of appetite, vomiting, diarrhoea, rash.
Unusual: hair loss.
Severe but rare (stop medication, consult doctor): yellow skin (jaundice).

INTERACTIONS:

Other drugs:
• other treatments for cancer, allopurinol.

PRESCRIPTION:

Yes.

PERMITTED IN SPORT:

Yes.

OVERDOSE:

Serious. Induce vomiting if medication taken recently. Seek urgent medical assistance.

See also Methotrexate.

Hydroxyzine

See ANTIHISTAMINES, SEDATING.

Hylan

TRADE NAME:

Synvisc.

USES:

Pain relief in osteoarthritis of the knee.

DOSAGE:

 Weekly injections into knee for three weeks, followed by top up injections every one to six months as necessary.

FORMS:

Injection.

PRECAUTIONS:

Use with caution in pregnancy and children.
To be injected into joint space only.
Use with caution if blood supply to leg poor and severe varicose veins.

Do not take if:

- suffering from poor lymphatic or blood drainage from leg, infected or inflamed joint, large fluid collection in knee joint
- allergic to birds.

SIDE EFFECTS:

Common: temporary pain and swelling of knee joint.
Severe but rare: joint infection.

INTERACTIONS:

None significant.

PRESCRIPTION:

No.

PERMITTED IN SPORT:

Yes.

OTHER INFORMATION:

Expensive artificial joint fluid released onto market in 1999.

Hyoscine

TRADE NAMES:

Buscopan, Scopoderm.
Also found in some locally produced medications for motion sickness and cold remedies.

DRUG CLASS:

Anticholinergic (dries secretions).
Spasmolytic (eases intestinal spasms).
Antiemetic (prevents nausea and vomiting).

USES:

Irritable bowel syndrome, gut spasms and colic, prevents motion sickness, dries excess nasal secretions.

DOSAGE:

 Tablets: 10 to 20mg two to four times a day.
Patch: apply to skin behind ear and leave for up to three days.

FORMS:

Tablets, injection, skin patch.

PRECAUTIONS:

Should be used with caution in pregnancy (B2) and breast feeding.
Use with caution in eye diseases that cause vision problems.

Do not take if:

- suffering from glaucoma, myasthenia gravis, megacolon, enlarged prostate, porphyria, rapid irregular heart rhythm.

SIDE EFFECTS:

Common: drowsiness, dry mouth, reduced sweating.
Unusual: rapid heart rate, difficulty in passing urine, dilated pupil, drowsiness.
Severe but rare (stop medication, consult doctor): hallucinations, confusion, muscle spasm.

INTERACTIONS:

Other drugs:
- dry mouth and drowsiness worsen if used with tricyclic antidepressants, amantadine, quinidine, antihistamines, phenothiazines and monoamine oxidase inhibitors (MAOI)
- rapid heart rate worsens if used with beta-blockers.

Other substances:
- reacts with alcohol to cause excessive drowsiness.

PRESCRIPTION:

Yes.

PERMITTED IN SPORT:

Yes.

OVERDOSE:

No serious effects reported. Induce vomiting. Doctors would use stomach washout and activated charcoal.

See also Atropine, Dicyclomine, Mebeverine.

Hypericum perforatum

See Saint John's Wort.

HYPNOTICS AND SEDATIVES

DISCUSSION:

Medications that sedate, relax and induce sleep.

See BARBITURATES, Chloral hydrate, Chlormethiazole, Flunitrazepam, Midazolam, Nitrazepam, Temazepam, Zaleplon, Zolpidem, Zopiclone.

HYPOGLYCAEMICS

DISCUSSION:

Hypoglycaemics are drugs that lower the level of sugar (glucose) in the bloodstream of diabetics by allowing the sugar to cross the membrane surrounding a cell and to enter the interior of the cell. They are used mainly in the maturity onset (type two) form of diabetes. Alteration to the dosage of all types of hypoglycaemics may be required with changes in exercise, or diet, surgery or the occurrence of other illnesses, particularly if a fever is present. A doctor should be consulted immediately in these situations. As well as treatment with hypoglycaemics, all diabetics must remain on an appropriate diet for the rest of their lives. Regular blood tests and urine tests are essential for the adequate control of all forms of diabetes. Some patients now use small machines the size of a thick credit card, to test their own blood sugar.

Hypoglycaemics fall into two main groups: tablets and injections. Insulins, which is normally produced by the pancreas to transport sugar across the cell membrane, can only be given by injection, and is invariably required in type one diabetes which has its onset in children and young adults. Maturity onset (type two) diabetes has its onset in the middle aged and elderly and is normally treated by hypoglycaemic tablets and diet, but sometimes insulin is also required.

See Acarbose, Glibenclamide, Gliclazide, Glipizide, Gliquidone, INSULINS, Metformin, Nateglinide, Repaglinide, Rosiglitazone.

HYPOLIPIDAEMICS

DISCUSSION:

The term 'hypo' means low (as opposed to 'hyper', meaning high), lipids are fats, and the term 'aemia' refers to the blood (compare 'anaemia', lack of blood), so a hypolipidaemic is a drug that lowers fat in the blood. The fats include both cholesterol and triglycerides. An excess of either, or both, of these in the bloodstream can cause serious diseases such as strokes and heart attacks. A combination of diet and drugs are used to control excess levels of fat in the bloodstream. Diet alone may be sufficient in many patients.

See Acipimox, Atorvastatin, Cerivastatin, Cholestyramine, Ciprofibrate, Colestipol, Fenofibrate, Fluvastatin, Gemfibrizol, Nicotinic acid, Pravastatin, Simvastatin.

Hypromellose

See EYE LUBRICANTS.

I

Ibuprofen

TRADE NAMES:

Brufen, Deep Relief, Fenbid, Fenbid Gel, Ibugel, Ibumousse, Ibuspray, Motrin, Proflex.
Codafen Continus (with codeine).

DRUG CLASS:

NSAID (Nonsteroidal anti-inflammatory drug).

USES:

All forms of arthritis, back pain, period pain, migraine, general pain relief, fevers.

DOSAGE:

 Tablets and capsules: one or two tablets, one to four times a day with food.
Gel and mousse: rub into affected area three or four times a day for up to two weeks.

FORMS:

Tablets, capsules, syrup, gel, mousse.

PRECAUTIONS:

Use with caution in pregnancy (C) and breast feeding.
May be used in children.
Gel and mousse safe in pregnancy.
Use tablets and capsules with caution in asthma, dehydration, high blood pressure, severe infection, heart failure and kidney disease.
Lower doses required in elderly, who may suffer more side effects.

Do not take if:

- suffering from peptic ulcer at present or in recent past
- sensitive to anti-inflammatories or aspirin
- due for surgery (including dental surgery)
- suffering from bleeding disorder or anaemia.

SIDE EFFECTS:

Gel and mousse have much milder side effects.
Common: stomach discomfort, diarrhoea, constipation, heartburn, nausea, headache, dizziness.
Unusual: blurred vision, stomach ulcer, ringing noise in ears, retention of fluid, swelling of tissue, drowsiness, itch, rash, shortness of breath.
Severe but rare (stop medication, consult doctor): vomiting blood, passing blood in faeces, other unusual bleeding, asthma induced by medication.

INTERACTIONS:

Other drugs:
- must never be used with anticoagulants (e.g. warfarin)
- probenecid, diuretics, lithium, methotrexate, beta-blockers, ACE inhibitors
- gel has minimal interactions.

PRESCRIPTION:

Low strength preparations and skin applications: no.
High strength preparations: yes.

PERMITTED IN SPORT:

Yes.

OVERDOSE:

Causes nausea, vomiting, severe headache, dizziness, confusion and convulsions. Administer activated charcoal or induce vomiting if taken recently. Seek medical assistance.

OTHER INFORMATION:

Extensively used to give excellent relief to a wide variety of inflammatory and pain conditions. Significant side effects (particularly on the stomach) in about 5% of patients. Limit their use. Specially coated forms reduce side effects. Minimal side effects with gel, but less effective.

See also Aspirin, Celecoxib, Diclofenac, Diflunisal, Flurbiprofen, Indomethacin, Ketoprofen, Lornoxicam, Mefenamic Acid, Naproxen, NSAID, Piroxicam, Rofecoxib, Salicylic acid, Sulindac, Tenoxicam, Tiaprofenic Acid.

Idarubicin

TRADE NAME:
Zavedos.

DRUG CLASS:
Cytotoxic.

USES:
Leukaemia.

DOSAGE:
 As determined for each patient by doctor.

FORMS:
Capsules of 5mg (orange), 10mg (red/white) and 25mg (orange/white). Injection.

PRECAUTIONS:
Not to be used in pregnancy (D).
Use with caution in breast feeding.
May be used in children.
Use with caution in heart disease and bone marrow suppression.
Use with caution if receiving radiotherapy.
Regular blood tests essential to check liver, kidney and blood cell function.
Use with care if driving or operating machinery.

Do not take if:
 • suffering from severe liver or kidney disease, uncontrolled infection, recent heart attack, or irregular heart rhythm.

SIDE EFFECTS:
Common: nausea, vomiting, mouth inflammation, belly pain, diarrhoea, loss of hair, rash.
Unusual: heart damage, itch, redness of palms and soles, kidney and liver damage, ankle swelling.
Severe but rare (stop medication, consult doctor): abnormal bleeding, abnormal heart rhythm, significant infection.

INTERACTIONS:
Other drugs:
• other medications used to treat leukaemia.

PRESCRIPTION:
Yes.

PERMITTED IN SPORT:
Yes.

OVERDOSE:
Significant heart damage possible, aggravation of side effects likely. Induce vomiting or administer activated charcoal if capsules taken recently. Seek urgent medical attention.

Idoxuridine

TRADE NAME:
Herpid (with dimethyl sulphoxide).

DRUG CLASS:
Antiviral.

USES:
Herpes infections of eyes and skin, cold sores.

DOSAGE:
 Apply four times a day.

FORMS:
Solution.

PRECAUTIONS:

Use with caution in pregnancy (B3), breast feeding and infants. May be used in children.

Continue eye treatment for five days after cure to prevent recurrence.

Do not take internally.

Do not use if:

- suffering from dermographia (skin condition).

SIDE EFFECTS:

Common: minimal.
Unusual: irritation, pain, itch and swelling of eye.

INTERACTIONS:

None significant.

PRESCRIPTION:

Yes.

PERMITTED IN SPORT:

Yes.

OTHER INFORMATION:

Very effective medication, but must be used immediately any sign of infection present (particularly on cold sores).

See also Aciclovir.

Imatinib

TRADE NAME:

Glivec.

DRUG CLASS:

Antineoplastic.

USES:

Chronic myeloid leukaemia.

DOSAGE:

 Complex. Determined by doctor for each patient.

FORMS:

Capsules of 100mg (orange).

PRECAUTIONS:

Not for use in pregnancy (D) or breast feeding. Use with caution in children. Use with caution in liver and kidney disease.

Regular blood tests necessary to check for toxic effects.

SIDE EFFECTS:

Common: nausea, diarrhoea, muscle pains and cramps, bloating.
Unusual: fluid retention, rash, headache, tiredness, joint pains, fever.
Severe but rare (stop medication, consult doctor): gut bleeding, stroke, blood cell damage.

INTERACTIONS:

Other drugs:
- ketoconazole, erythromycin, clarithromycin, itraconazole, antivirals, dexamethasone, phenytoin, carbamazepine, rifampicin, phenobarbitone, warfarin, paracetamol.
Other substances:
- grapefruit juice.

PRESCRIPTION:

Yes.

PERMITTED IN SPORT:

Yes.

OVERDOSE:

Serious, but minimal information available. Induce vomiting or give activated charcoal if taken recently. Seek urgent medical attention.

Imidapril

See ACE INHIBITORS.

IMIDAZOLES

See Clotrimazole, Econazole, Fluconazole, Itraconazole, Ketoconazole, Miconazole, Sulconazole, Tioconazole, Voriconazole.

Imipenem

See Cilastatin and Imipenem.

Imipramine

See TRICYCLIC ANTIDEPRESSANTS.

Imiquimod

TRADE NAME:

Aldara.

DRUG CLASS:

Immunomodifier.

USES:

Treatment of genital and anal warts, and condylomata accuminata.

DOSAGE:

 Apply three times a week at night and leave on for 6 to 10 hours.

FORMS:

Cream.

PRECAUTIONS:

Use with caution in pregnancy (B1), breast feeding and children.
Use with care in vagina and anal canal.
Avoid inflamed skin.
Remove cream before sexual contact.
Uncircumcised men should wash under foreskin daily.
Do not cover treated warts with a bandage.
Use for no more than four months.

Do not take if:

 • suffering from HIV, AIDS or impaired immunity.

SIDE EFFECTS:

Common: skin irritation and redness, swelling of tissue.

Unusual: ulceration and scabbing of skin, burning skin pain, headache.

INTERACTIONS:

Condoms and diaphragms.

PRESCRIPTION:

Yes.

PERMITTED IN SPORT:

Yes.

OTHER INFORMATION:

Released in 1999 as a radical and effective new way to treat a very distressing problem that previously often required minor surgery.

IMMUNOGLOBULINS

TRADE and GENERIC NAMES:

Immunoglobulins against cytomegalovirus (CMV), hepatitis B, rabies, rhesus factor (anti-D), tetanus and zoster (chickenpox) are available as well as pooled normal human immunoglobulin (see gamma globulin).

USES:

Prevention and treatment of specific diseases or as a boost to patients with a deficient immune system.

DOSAGE:

 Depends on disease and individual patient requirements.

FORMS:

Injection.

PRECAUTIONS:

May be used in pregnancy, breast feeding and children.
Should only be used when strictly medically indicated.
Caution must be used with repeat doses.

SIDE EFFECTS:

Common: tenderness at injection site.
Unusual: fever, tiredness, belly

discomfort, flush, headache, rash, itch, shortness of breath, nausea.

INTERACTIONS:

Other drugs:
• vaccines.

PRESCRIPTION:

Yes.

PERMITTED IN SPORT:

Yes.

OVERDOSE:

Inadvertent additional dose may cause allergy reaction (sometimes serious) or exacerbation of side effects.

OTHER INFORMATION:

Purified from blood donations.
See also Gamma Globulin.

IMMUNOMODIFIERS

DISCUSSION:

Immunomodifiers are used to suppress (control or reduce) the immune reaction that occurs after the transplantation of foreign tissue into a body. They may also be used in the treatment of some types of cancer and defects in immunity that allow a few rare diseases to arise within the body. They are the drugs that have made kidney, liver, heart and other transplants possible, as the body normally uses its immune system to reject these donated organs.
See Azathioprine, Cyclosporin, Imiquimod, Interferon, Sirolimus.

IMPOTENCE DRUGS

See Alprostadil, Sildenafil, Tadalafil.

Indapamide

TRADE NAMES:

Natrilix.
Coversyl Plus (with perindopril).

DRUG CLASS:

Diuretic (increases urine production).

USES:

High blood pressure.

DOSAGE:

 One tablet in morning.

FORMS:

Tablet of 1.5 and 2.5mg (white).

PRECAUTIONS:

Should only be used in pregnancy (C) and breast feeding if medically essential. Not for use in children.
Use with caution in systemic lupus erythematosus (SLE), kidney and liver disease.
Regular blood tests necessary to check for irregularities in blood chemistry (electrolytes).

Do not take if:

 • suffering from severe kidney or liver disease.

SIDE EFFECTS:

Common: tiredness, dizziness, headache, muscle cramps, diarrhoea.
Unusual: rash, impotence, sleeplessness, nausea, gout.
Severe but rare (stop medication, consult doctor): fainting.

INTERACTIONS:

Other drugs:
• barbiturates, narcotics, lithium, other diuretics.
Herbs:
• celery, dandelion, uva ursi.
Other substances:
• reacts adversely with alcohol.

PRESCRIPTION:

Yes.

PERMITTED IN SPORT:

No.

OVERDOSE:

No serious effect. Induce vomiting if taken recently.

OTHER INFORMATION:

Often used in combination with other blood pressure medications to increase their effect. Works by increasing output of urine.

Indinavir

TRADE NAME:

Crixivan.

DRUG CLASS:

Antiviral.

USES:

AIDS, HIV infection.

DOSAGE:

 Up to 800mg three times a day. Often combined with other therapy.

FORMS:

Capsules of 100mg, 200mg, 333mg and 400mg (white).

PRECAUTIONS:

Use with considerable caution in pregnancy (B3), breast feeding and children.
Use lower dose in elderly.
Use with caution in liver disease and diabetes.
Ensure adequate fluid intake.

SIDE EFFECTS:

Common: nausea, diarrhoea, headache and others.

Unusual: vomiting, kidney stones, liver damage causing jaundice.
Severe but rare (stop medication, consult doctor): anaemia.

INTERACTIONS:

Other drugs:
• serious interaction with astemizole, alprazolam, cisapride, triazolam, midazolam, pimozide
• calcium channel blockers, didanosine, erythromycin, ketoconazole, itraconazole, efavirenz, sildenafil, rifabutin, rifampicin, SSRI.
Herbs:
• St John's wort.
Other substances:
• grapefruit.

PRESCRIPTION:

Yes.

PERMITTED IN SPORT:

Yes.

See also Abacavir, Amprenavir, Efavirenz, Lamivudine, Nelfinavir, Nevirapine, Ritonavir, Saquinavir, Stavudine, Tenofovir, Zidovudine.

Indomethacin

TRADE NAMES:

Flexin Continus, Indocid, Indomod.

DRUG CLASS:

NSAID (Nonsteroidal anti-inflammatory drug).

USES:

All forms of arthritis, inflammatory disorders, gout, back pain, ankylosing spondylitis, bone pain, period pain, correction of heart defect (patent ductus arteriosus) in premature infants.

DOSAGE:

 50 to 200mg a day in divided doses.

FORMS:

Capsules, suppository, injection.

PRECAUTIONS:

Should not be used in pregnancy (C) unless medically essential. Breast feeding should be ceased if necessary to use NSAID. Not for use in children under two.

Use tablets and capsules with caution in psychiatricaly disturbed patients, epilepsy, severe infection, heart failure and kidney disease.

Lower doses required in elderly, who may suffer more side effects.

Do not take if:

- suffering from peptic ulcer at present or in recent past
- due for surgery (including dental surgery)
- suffering from bleeding disorder or anaemia.

SIDE EFFECTS:

Common: stomach discomfort, diarrhoea, constipation, heartburn, nausea, headache, dizziness.

Unusual: blurred vision, stomach ulcer, ringing noise in ears, retention of fluid, swelling of tissue, drowsiness, itch, rash, shortness of breath.

Severe but rare (stop medication, consult doctor): vomiting blood, passing blood in faeces, other unusual bleeding, asthma induced by medication.

INTERACTIONS:

Other drugs:
- must never be used with anticoagulants (e.g. warfarin)
- probenecid, diuretics, lithium, methotrexate, beta-blockers, ACE inhibitors.

Herbs:
- feverfew.

PRESCRIPTION:

Yes.

PERMITTED IN SPORT:

Yes.

OVERDOSE:

Causes nausea, vomiting, severe headache, dizziness, confusion and convulsions. Administer activated charcoal or induce vomiting if taken recently. Seek medical assistance.

OTHER INFORMATION:

One of the original NSAIDs, and available for nearly 50 years. Extensively used to give excellent relief to a wide variety of inflammatory conditions. Significant side effects (particularly on the stomach) in about 5% of patients. Limit their use.

See also Aspirin, Bufexamac, Celecoxib, Diclofenac, Diflunisal, Flurbiprofen, Ibuprofen, Ketoprofen, Ketorolac trometanol, Mefenamic Acid, Naproxen, NSAID, Piroxicam, Rofecoxib, Salicylic acid, Sulindac, Tenoxicam, Tiaprofenic Acid.

Indoramin

TRADE NAMES:

Baratol, Doralese.

DRUG CLASS:

Alpha blocker.

USES:

Controls high blood pressure, relieves difficulty in passing urine caused by enlarged prostate gland.

DOSAGE:

 Varies from 25mg to 200mg a day in divided doses.

FORMS:

Tablets of 20mg (cream triangular), 25mg (blue) and 50mg (green).

PRECAUTIONS:

May be used with caution in pregnancy, breast feeding and children.

Use with caution in significant heart disease, kidney and liver disease, Parkinson's disease, epilepsy and depression.

Do not take if:

• suffering from heart failure.

SIDE EFFECTS:

Common: drowsiness, dry mouth, stuffy nose.
Unusual: weight gain, difficulty in ejaculation.

INTERACTIONS:

Other drugs:
• MAOI, other medications for high blood pressure.

PRESCRIPTION:

Yes.

PERMITTED IN SPORT:

Yes.

OVERDOSE:

Drowsiness and depressed reflexes most likely effects.

See also Doxazosin, Labetalol, Prazosin, Tamsulosin, Thymoxamine.

Influenza virus vaccine

TRADE NAMES:

Begrivac, Fluarix, Fluvirin, Influvac.

DRUG CLASS:

Vaccine.

USES:

Prevention of influenza.

DOSAGE:

One injection in Autumn every year. Two injections a month apart for first vaccination if under 18 years.

FORMS:

Injection.

PRECAUTIONS:

Not designed to be used in pregnancy (B2), but no adverse effects expected if vaccination given inadvertently. May be used in breast feeding. Use in children only if specifically indicated.

Do not take if:

• suffering from fever
• allergic to eggs, poultry products, neomycin, polymyxin or gentamicin.

SIDE EFFECTS:

Common: local discomfort and redness at injection site.
Unusual: fever, muscle pain.
Severe but rare: vomiting, dizziness, rash, blood vessel inflammation, arthritis.

INTERACTIONS:

Other drugs:
• theophylline, warfarin, phenytoin.

PRESCRIPTION:

Yes.

PERMITTED IN SPORT:

Yes.

OVERDOSE:

An inadvertent additional dose is unlikely to cause any serious effects.

OTHER INFORMATION:

Influenza vaccine gives only limited protection, but this increases with subsequent doses. It should be given to persons over 65 years, persons with debilitating illness, persons with chronic diseases (e.g. of the lung, heart, kidneys etc.), persons undergoing immunotherapy and health and medical personnel. Formulation varies every year to match the strains of flu virus present in the community.

Inositol nicotinate

See Nicotinic Acid.

INSULINS

TRADE and GENERIC NAMES:

ASPART INSULIN: Onset of action, 20–40 minutes; peak action, 4 hours; duration, 6–10 hours.
NovoMix, NovoRapid.
NEUTRAL INSULIN: Onset of action, 30–60 minutes; peak action, 4 hours; duration, 6–10 hours.
Humalog, Human Actrapid, Human Velosulin, Humulin S, Hypurin Bovine Neutral, Hypurine Porcine Neutral, Insuman Rapid, Pork Actrapid.
ISOPHANE INSULIN: Onset of action, 2–4 hours; peak action, 4–12 hours; duration, 24 hours.
Human Insulatard, Humulin I, Hypurin Bovine Isophane, Hypurin Porcine Isophane, Insuman Basal, Pork Insulatard.
PROTAMINE ZINC INSULIN: Onset of action, 4–8 hours; peak action, 16 hours; duration, 36 hours.
Hypurin Bovine PZI.
LENTE INSULIN
(INSULIN ZINC SUSPENSION): Onset of action, 3 hours; peak action, 6–10 hours; duration, 24 hours.
Human Monotard, Humulin Lente, Hypurin Bovine Lente.
ULTRALENTE INSULIN
(CRYSTALLINE INSULIN ZINC-SUSPENSION): Onset of action, 4–6 hours; peak action, 10–30 hours; duration, 24–36 hours.
Human Ultratard, Humulin Zn.
BIPHASIC INSULIN (mixture of Neutral insulin and Isophane insulin): Onset of action, 30–60 minutes; peak action, 4–12 hours; duration, 24 hours.
Humalog Mix25, Human Mixtard, Humulin M, Hypurin Porcine 30/70, Insuman Comb, Pork Mixtard.
INSULIN GLARGINE: Onset of action, 90 minutes; duration 24 hours.
Lantus.

USES:

Diabetes mellitus.

DOSAGE:

As determined by doctor or patient depending on blood sugar levels. Varies from one individual to another, and depends on food intake and exercise.

FORMS:

Injection, injection pens.

PRECAUTIONS:

Safe to use in pregnancy (A), breast feeding and children.
Pregnancy, illness, infections, change in diet, exercise and stress may cause change in insulin requirements.
Regular monitoring of blood sugar levels essential.
Knowledge of dietary requirements by patient essential.
Vary site of insulin injection.
Relatives and close friends should be made aware of symptoms of hypoglycaemia (low blood sugar) and first aid requirements.
Do not inject into vein.

SIDE EFFECTS:

Common: minimal.
Unusual: low blood sugar, loss of fat at site of regular injection.

INTERACTIONS:

Other drugs:
• corticosteroids, thiazides, frusemide, ethacrynic acid, protamine, isoniazid, phenothiazines, salbutamol, phenytoin, anabolic steroids, ACE inhibitors, sulfonamides, oral contraceptives, thyroxine, MAOI, salicylates, beta blockers.
Herbs:
• ginseng, karela.
Other substances:
• alcohol may increase need for insulin.

PRESCRIPTION:

Yes.

PERMITTED IN SPORT:

Yes.

OVERDOSE:

Very serious. Symptoms of low blood sugar (hypoglycaemia) may include tiredness, confusion, palpitations, sweating, vomiting, dizziness, hunger, blurred vision and fainting. Significant overdosage can lead rapidly to coma and death. Give sugary drinks or sweets if conscious. Seek emergency medical assistance.

OTHER INFORMATION:

Insulin is a natural hormone that is essential for the transport of sugar from the blood stream into the cells of the body. It is produced in the pancreas, which lies in the centre of the belly. For the past 70 years, insulin has been derived from the pancreas of cattle or pigs since it was originally identified and isolated by the Canadian doctors, Banting and Best. Because it was derived from animals, there were occasional reactions to the foreign animal protein present in the insulin. In the last few years, genetically engineered human insulin has almost totally replaced the animal insulin. The new form causes virtually no adverse reaction after injection.

See also HYPOGLYCAEMICS.

Interferon

TRADE NAMES:

Intron A, Roferon A, Viraferon (Interferon alpha).
Avonex, Betaferon, Rebif (Interferon beta).
Immukin (Interferon gamma).

DRUG CLASS:

Immunomodifier.

USES:

Some types of leukaemia, genital warts, some skin cancers, multiple myeloma, multiple sclerosis, AIDS, hepatitis B and C and several other rare diseases.

DOSAGE:

 Depends on disease and patient's condition. Must be individualised by doctor.

FORMS:

Injection.

PRECAUTIONS:

Should not be used in pregnancy (C) unless medically essential as risk of miscarriage increased. Breast feeding should be ceased before use. Use with considerable caution in children.
Use with caution in heart disease, psychiatric conditions and psoriasis.
Ensure adequate fluid intake.
Regular medical check ups essential.

Do not take if:

 • suffering from severe liver disease or some autoimmune disease (check with doctor)
 • if a transplanted organ recipient.

SIDE EFFECTS:

Common: fever, fatigue, headache, muscle pain, chills, loss of appetite, nausea, backache, joint pains, rash.
Unusual: dry mouth, altered taste, low blood pressure, vomiting, diarrhoea, dizziness, confusion, sleeplessness, depression, hair loss, sweating.

INTERACTIONS:

Other drugs:
• narcotics, hypnotics, sedatives, theophylline.
Other substances:
• alcohol.

PRESCRIPTION:

Yes.

PERMITTED IN SPORT:

Yes.

OVERDOSE:

Exacerbation of side effects likely.

OTHER INFORMATION:

Wide range of uses from serious exotic diseases to use by general practitioners to treat skin cancers. Once hailed as a miracle cure-all drug when introduced in the early 1980s. Very useful when prescribed appropriately.

INTRA-UTERINE DEVICE

See Levonorgestrel.

Iodine

TRADE NAME:

Betadine (Povidone-iodine).
Other forms of iodine found in numerous non-prescription antiseptics, mineral and vitamin supplements.

DRUG CLASS:

Antiseptic, mineral.

USES:

Prevention and treatment of minor bacterial, viral and fungal infections of skin, mouth and vagina.
Iodine deficiency.

DOSAGE:

 Recommended daily allowance: 120 to 150 mcg a day.
Skin preparations: apply several times a day as needed.
Vaginal pessaries: insert two at night.
Vaginal douche: dilute 1 to 30 with water. Douche each morning for seven to 14 days.

FORMS:

Cream, gargle, lotion, ointment, pads, paint, powder, scrub, spray, swabs, vaginal gel,vaginal douche, vaginal pessary.

PRECAUTIONS:

Safe for use in pregnancy, breast feeding and children.
Vaginal forms should not be used in pregnancy or severe kidney disease.
Not for use on premature infants.
Do not use if:

 • sensitive to Iodine.

SIDE EFFECTS:

None significant.

INTERACTIONS:

Other drugs:
• Vaginal preparations may interact with lithium.

PRESCRIPTION:

No.

PERMITTED IN SPORT:

Yes.

OVERDOSE:

May cause diarrhoea and stomach upsets if significant amount swallowed.

OTHER INFORMATION:

Widely used, safe and effective. Small number of people are excessively sensitive to Iodine.

Iodine, radioactive

See Sodium iodide.

Ipratropium bromide

TRADE NAMES:

Atrovent, Ipratropium Steri-Neb, Respontin, Rinatec.
Combivent (with salbutamol).
Duovent (with fenoterol).

DRUG CLASS:

Bronchodilator.

USES:

Prevention of asthma and hay fever, chronic lung disease.

DOSAGE:

Asthma spray: two inhalations three or four times a day.
Nose spray: two sprays into each nostril two to four times a day.

FORMS:

Inhaler, nebuliser solution, nasal spray.

PRECAUTIONS:

May be used in pregnancy (B1), breast feeding and children.
Use with caution in glaucoma, enlarged prostate gland, difficulty in passing urine, constipation and irregular heart beat.
Avoid contact with eyes.

Do not take if:

• sensitive to soy beans or peanuts.

SIDE EFFECTS:

Common: dry mouth, throat irritation.
Unusual: blurred vision, difficulty in passing urine, cough, headache, nausea.
Severe but rare (stop medication, consult doctor): eye pain or halos seen around objects.

INTERACTIONS:

Other drugs:
• sodium cromoglycate.

PRESCRIPTION:

Yes.

PERMITTED IN SPORT:

Yes.

OVERDOSE:

Exacerbation of side effects only likely consequence.

OTHER INFORMATION:

Commonly used in conjunction with other medication for severe asthma, emphysema and chronic bronchitis. May be used alone in some forms (e.g. exercise induced) of asthma. Very useful and safe medication.
See also Tiotropium.

Irbesartan

See ANGIOTENSIN II RECEPTOR ANTAGONISTS.

IRON

TRADE and GENERIC NAMES:

CosmoFer (Iron-hydroxide dextran).
Ferrograd Folic, Slow-Fe Folic (Ferrous sulphate with folic acid).
Ferrograd, Slow-Fe (Ferrous sulphate).
Fersaday, Fersamal, Galfer (Ferrous fumarate).
Lexpec with Iron (Ferrous ammonium citrate with folic acid).
Niferex (Iron polysaccharide complex).
Plesmet (Ferrous glycine sulphate).
Pregaday (Ferrous fumarate with folic acid).
Sytron (Sodium iron edetate).
Venofer (Iron-hydroxide sucrose).
Numerous other vitamin and mineral supplements also contain various forms of iron (e.g. Ferrous phosphate).
NB: Iron compounds underlined.

DRUG CLASS:

Mineral.

USES:

Iron deficiency, some types of anaemia.

DOSAGE:

One tablet or capsule a day on an empty stomach.
Recommended daily intake: 12 to 16mg a day.

FORMS:

Tablets, capsules, mixture.

PRECAUTIONS:

Safe in pregnancy (A), breast feeding and children.
Cause of any anaemia should be determined before use.
Do not use excessive dose.

Do not take if:

- suffering from haemochromatosis, ulcerative colitis, ileostomy or colostomy, anaemia not due to iron deficiency.

SIDE EFFECTS:

Common: slight stomach upsets, dark coloured faeces.
Unusual: temporary tooth staining.

INTERACTIONS:

Other drugs:
- tetracycline, penicillamine, antacids, calcium, methyldopa, levodopa, chloramphenicol, cimetidine, thyroxine, phenytoin, cholestyramine.

Herbs:
- St John's wort.

PRESCRIPTION:

No.

PERMITTED IN SPORT:

Yes.

OVERDOSE:

Constipation and stomach cramps only likely effects.

OTHER INFORMATION:

Iron is absorbed from the gut at a set rate, and using higher doses is unlikely to have any clinical effect. Iron is found in red meats (particularly liver) and green vegetables. Pregnant women are at risk of iron deficiency because the developing baby needs iron to build muscle and blood cells.

See also Folic acid.

Isometheptene

TRADE NAME:

Midrid (with paracetamol).

DRUG CLASS:

Sympathomimetic.

USES:

Migraine.

DOSAGE:

Two at onset of migraine, then one every hour to a maximum of five in 12 hours.

FORMS:

Capsules (red).

PRECAUTIONS:

Use with caution in pregnancy, breast feeding and children.

Do not take if:

- suffering from kidney, heart and liver disease, stomach irritation, uncontrolled high blood pressure and glaucoma.

SIDE EFFECTS:

Common: minimal.
Unusual: dizziness.

INTERACTIONS:

Other drugs:
- MAOI.

PRESCRIPTION:

Yes.

PERMITTED IN SPORT:

No.

OTHER INFORMATION:

Introduced in 2002.

Isoniazid

TRADE NAMES:

Rifater (with pyrazinamide, rifampicin).
Rifinah, Rimactizid (with rifampicin).

USES:

Tuberculosis (TB).

DOSAGE:

 One tablet, two or three times a day. Dosage adjusted carefully to match weight of patient.

FORMS:

Tablets.

PRECAUTIONS:

May be used safely in pregnancy (A), breast feeding and children.
Use with caution in liver and kidney disease.
Regular checks of eyes recommended.
Regular blood tests to check liver and kidney function recommended.

Do not take if:

 • suffering from severe liver disease.

SIDE EFFECTS:

Common: pins and needles, nausea.
Unusual: vomiting, diarrhoea, belly discomfort, fever, rash.
Severe but rare (stop medication, consult doctor): eye damage, unusual bruising or bleeding, yellow skin (jaundice).

INTERACTIONS:

Other drugs:
• phenytoin, carbamazepine, rifampicin, paracetamol.
Other substances:
• reacts with alcohol
• glucose test strips.

PRESCRIPTION:

Yes.

PERMITTED IN SPORT:

Yes.

OVERDOSE:

Serious. May cause vomiting, dizziness, blurred vision, slurred speech, hallucinations, difficulty in breathing, convulsions and coma. Administer activated charcoal or induce vomiting if medication taken recently. Seek urgent medical assistance.

See also Pyrazinamide, Rifabutin, Rifampicin.

Isophane Insulin

See INSULINS.

Isosorbide

TRADE NAMES:

Cedocard Retard, Isoket (Isosorbide dinitrate).
Elantan, Imdur, Ismo, Isodur XL, Isotard XL, MCR-50, Monit, Monomax (Isosorbide mononitrate).
Imazin XL (Isosorbide mononitrate with aspirin).

DRUG CLASS:

Antiangina.

USES:

Prevention and treatment of angina, some types of heart failure, poor blood supply to heart.

DOSAGE:

 Depends on form.
Long acting tablets: one or two tablets once a day.
Sublingual tablets: one or two tablets under tongue every two or three hours.
Normal tablets: one to three tablets three times a day.
Spray: one or two sprays to the chest once or twice a day.

FORMS:

Tablets, capsules, sublingual (under tongue) tablets, spray.

PRECAUTIONS:

Should be used with caution in pregnancy (B1, B2) and breast feeding. Not for use in children.

Tolerance may develop if used long term. Long acting tablets and capsules not designed for use in acute angina. They should not be ceased suddenly, but withdrawn slowly.
Use with caution in kidney and liver disease, reduced brain blood flow and low blood pressure.

Do not take if:

- suffering from right heart failure, low blood pressure, constrictive pericarditis, severe anaemia, increased brain pressure.

SIDE EFFECTS:

Common: headache, low blood pressure, rapid heart rate, dizziness, poor appetite, nausea, sleep disturbances.
Unusual: flushing, swelling of tissues, rash, vomiting, anaemia.
Severe but rare (stop medication, consult doctor): slow heart rate.

INTERACTIONS:

Other drugs:
- severe interaction with sildenafil, tadalafil
- phenothiazines, tricyclics, anticholinergics, beta-blockers
- drugs that lower blood pressure.

PRESCRIPTION:

Yes.

PERMITTED IN SPORT:

Yes.

OVERDOSE:

Headache, severe low blood pressure, rapid heart rate and collapse may occur. Administer activated charcoal or induce vomiting if tablets taken recently. Seek urgent medical attention.

OTHER INFORMATION:

Used for several decades for treatment and prevention of angina. Slow release long acting forms have far fewer side effects and have dramatically improved the life of patients with angina.

See also Glyceryl trinitrate, Nicorandil.

Isotretinoin

TRADE NAMES:

Isotrex, Roaccutane.
Isotrexin (with erythromycin).

USES:

Severe acne not responding to other medication.

DOSAGE:

Capsules: one or two capsules once or twice a day with food for up to 16 weeks.
Gel: apply sparingly once a day at night.

FORMS:

Capsules of 5mg and 20mg, gel.

PRECAUTIONS:

Absolutely forbidden in pregnancy (X), breast feeding and children under twelve. Must be used with caution in all patients. Adequate contraception essential for all women using Isotretinoin.
Use with caution if cholesterol or triglyceride levels high.
Regular blood tests recommended.
Use with caution in diabetes.
Avoid sun exposure during use.
Never exceed recommended dose or length of course.

Do not take if:

- suffering from liver disease, any form of cancer, high cholesterol or triglycerides, hypervitaminosis A
- taking tetracyclines.

SIDE EFFECTS:

Common: sore mouth and lips, dry eyes, dry mouth, dry skin, nose bleeds, muscle pain, joint pain, joint stiffness, hair thinning, peeling of palms and soles, sun sensitivity.
Unusual: tiredness, headache, depression, gout, diarrhoea, initial worsening of acne, altered blood test results.

Severe but rare (stop medication, consult doctor): severe headache, intractable vomiting, visual disturbances.

INTERACTIONS:

Other drugs:
• tetracycline, minocycline.
Other substances:
• reacts with alcohol
• vitamin A.

PRESCRIPTION:

Yes (capsules restricted to specialist dermatologists and consultant physicians in hospitals only).

PERMITTED IN SPORT:

Yes.

OVERDOSE:

May cause headache, vomiting, flushing, mouth soreness and dryness, abdominal pain and incoordination. Seek medical assistance.

OTHER INFORMATION:

A very potent and potentially dangerous drug, but if used correctly can dramatically and often permanently cure severe chronic acne. Use in pregnancy will always cause severe damage to foetus.
See also Etretinate.

Ispaghula

TRADE NAMES:

Fybogel, Isogel, Ispagel, Regulan.
Fybogel Mebeverine (with mebeverine).
Manevac (with senna).

DRUG CLASS:

Fibre.

USES:

Constipation.

DOSAGE:

 Take required amount with water twice a day.

FORMS:

Granules, powder.

PRECAUTIONS:

Safe in pregnancy and breast feeding.
Do not take if:
 • on a salt restricted diet
• suffering from megacolon or gut obstruction.

SIDE EFFECTS:

Common: minimal.
Unusual: diarrhoea, belly discomfort.

INTERACTIONS:

None significant.

PRESCRIPTION:

No.

PERMITTED IN SPORT:

Yes.

OVERDOSE:

Take additional water. Belly discomfort and passing excess wind only effects.

OTHER INFORMATION:

Widely used, natural fibre supplement.
See also FIBRE, Senna.

Isradipine

TRADE NAMES:

Prescal.

DRUG CLASS:

Calcium channel blocker (calcium antagonist).

USES:

High blood pressure.

DOSAGE:

 One to four tablets, twice a day.

FORMS:

Tablets of 2.5mg (yellow).

PRECAUTIONS:

Should only be used in pregnancy (C) and breast feeding if medically essential. Not designed for use in children.
Use with caution in sick sinus syndrome, poor heart function and diabetes.

Do not take if:

- suffering from severe heart failure, recent heart attack, aortic stenosis, low blood pressure, atrial flutter or fibrillation.

SIDE EFFECTS:

Common: constipation, tiredness, palpitations, headache, dizziness, flushing, indigestion, swelling of feet and ankles.
Unusual: palpitations, slow heart rate, scalp irritation, depression, flushes, nightmares, excess wind, weight gain, rash.
Severe but rare (stop medication, consult doctor): fainting, liver damage.

INTERACTIONS:

Other drugs:
- Beta-blockers (e.g. propranolol), cyclosporin, digoxin, cimetidine, barbiturates, diazepam, amiodarone, quinidine, rifampicin, phenytoin, cisapride, theophylline, terbutaline, salbutamol, diltiazem
- additive effect with other medications for high blood pressure.

Herbs:
- goldenseal, guarana, hawthorn, Korean ginseng, liquorice.

Other substances:
- smoking may aggravate conditions that these medications are treating
- grapefruit juice.

PRESCRIPTION:

Yes.

PERMITTED IN SPORT:

Yes.

OVERDOSE:

May continue to be absorbed for up to 48 hours after overdose. Administer activated charcoal or induce vomiting. Purging should be encouraged to eliminate drug from gut. Overdose may cause low blood pressure, irregular heart rhythm, difficulty in breathing, heart attack and death. Obtain urgent medical attention.

See also Amlodipine, Diltiazem, Felodipine, Lercanidipine, Nifedipine, Nimodipine, Verapamil.

Itraconazole

TRADE NAME:

Sporanox.

DRUG CLASS:

Antifungal.

USES:

Fungal infections of mouth (thrush), skin, vagina and eye.

DOSAGE:

One or two capsules, once or twice a day with food.

FORMS:

Capsules (blue/pink) of 100mg.

PRECAUTIONS:

Not to be used in pregnancy (B3) unless medically essential. Cease breast feeding before use. Use with caution in children. Not to be used long term.
Use with caution in liver disease.

SIDE EFFECTS:

Common: nausea, diarrhoea, headache, dizziness.
Unusual: swelling of tissue, pins and needles sensation.
Severe but rare (stop medication, consult doctor): yellow skin (jaundice), heart failure.

INTERACTIONS:

Other drugs:
- severe interaction with cisapride, astemizole, mizolastine, quinidine, pimozide, simvastatin, midazolam, triazolam
- digoxin, cyclosporin, phenytoin, rifampicin, H2 antagonists, anticoagulants (e.g. warfarin), isoniazid, hypoglycaemics, norethisterone.

Other substances:
- reacts with alcohol.

PRESCRIPTION:

Yes.

PERMITTED IN SPORT:

Yes.

OVERDOSE:

May cause liver damage. Administer activated charcoal or induce vomiting if taken recently. Seek medical assistance.

OTHER INFORMATION:

Introduced 1994. Expensive.

See also Clotrimazole, Econazole, Fluconazole, Griseofulvin, Ketoconazole, Miconazole.

J

No medications have a name starting with the letter J.

K

Kaolin

TRADE NAMES:

Available alone and in combination with other medications in numerous locally produced antidiarrhoeal preparations.

DRUG CLASS:

Antidiarrhoeal.

USES:

Diarrhoea.

DOSAGE:

 30 mLs initially, then 15 to 30 mLs every two to four hours as required for condition.
Take at least an hour away from other medications.

FORMS:

Suspension.

PRECAUTIONS:

Safe in pregnancy, breast feeding and children over three years.

Do not take if:

 • suffering from kidney disease
• for prolonged periods.

SIDE EFFECTS:

Common: minimal.
Unusual: constipation.

INTERACTIONS:

Other drugs:
• kaolin markedly affects the absorption of many other drugs including antibiotics, anticoagulants, H2 antagonists, iron, isoniazid, phenothiazines and aspirin.

PRESCRIPTION:

No.

PERMITTED IN SPORT:

Yes.

OVERDOSE:

Causes constipation, nausea and vomiting.

OTHER INFORMATION:

Kaolin is a form of clay that has been used for thousands of years to treat diarrhoea, but is now considered to be of only slight benefit and has been superseded by more effective medications. Also used in making fine china.

KERATOLYTICS

TRADE and GENERIC NAMES:

Acnecide, Brevoxyl, Panoxyl (Benzoyl peroxide).
Acnisal, Occlusal, Verrugon (Salicylic acid).

Aknemycin Plus (<u>Tretinoin</u> with erythromycin).
Aquasept, Manusept, Ster-Zac Bath (<u>Triclosan</u>).
Aserbine (<u>Benzoic acid</u>, <u>malic acid</u>, <u>salicylic acid</u> and other ingredients).
Avoca (<u>Silver nitrate</u>).
Benzamycin (<u>Benzoyl peroxide</u> with erythromycin).
Brasivol (<u>Aluminium oxide</u>).
Capasal (<u>Salicylic acid</u> with coal tar and oils).
Cocois (<u>Salicylic acid</u> with coal tar, sulphur and oils).
Cuplex (<u>Salicylic acid</u>, <u>lactic acid</u> with copper acetate).
Diprosalic (<u>Salicylic acid</u> with betamethasone).
Duofilm, Salactol, Salatac (<u>Salicylic acid</u>, <u>lactic acid</u>).
Hemocane (<u>Benzoic acid</u> with lignocaine, zinc oxide, bismuth oxide, cinnamic acid).
Meted (<u>Salicylic acid</u> with sulphur).
Monophytol (<u>Salicylic acid</u> with chlorbutol and other ingredients).
Movelat (<u>Salicylic acid</u> with mucopolysaccharide polysulphate).
Oilatum Plus (<u>Triclosan</u> with paraffin, benzalkonium chloride).
Posalfilin (<u>Salicylic acid</u> with podophyllum).
Pragmatar, Sebco (<u>Salicylic acid</u> with coal tar, sulphur).
Psorin (<u>Salicylic acid</u> with coal tar, dithranol).
Pyralvex (<u>Salicylic acid</u> with anthraquinone).
Quinoderm (<u>Benzoyl peroxide</u> with potassium hydroxyquinolone).
Retin-A, Vesanoid (<u>Tretinoin</u>).
Skinoren (<u>Azelaic acid</u>).
Stiedex Lotion (<u>Salicylic acid</u> with desoxymethasone).
NB: keratolytics are underlined.
Formaldehyde, Lactic acid, Isotretinoin and Etretinate (see separate entries) are also Keratolytics.

DRUG CLASS:

Keratolytics remove keratin from skin to thin, dry and soften the skin. Keratin is a protein that creates the horny, hard layers of the skin. Triclosan and azelaic acid also have antiseptic properties.

USES:

Acne, minor skin infections, psoriasis, thickened skin, corns, warts.

DOSAGE:

 Follow directions on packaging, as directions vary with composition, form and strength.

FORMS:

Gel, cream, ointment, liquid, wash, foam, wipes, solution, bar, soap, caustic pencil.

PRECAUTIONS:

Tretinoin should not be used in pregnancy. Other keratolytics may be used in with caution in pregnancy, breast feeding and children. Not designed for use in young children.
Avoid eyes, nostrils, mouth, vagina and anus with all preparations.
Avoid open wound contact.
Avoid sun exposure after use.
Do not exceed recommended dose.

Do not take if:

 • suffering from eczema or sunburn.

SIDE EFFECTS:

Common: stinging, warmth, skin redness.
Unusual: swelling, peeling, sun sensitivity.
Severe but rare (stop medication, consult doctor): skin pain, marked swelling, severe peeling.

INTERACTIONS:

Other drugs:
• other keratolytics, abrasives.
Other substances:
• many cosmetics.

PRESCRIPTION:

Tretinoin: yes.
Others: no.

PERMITTED IN SPORT:

Yes.

OVERDOSE:

Excessive use may lead to skin damage, burning and pain. Wash off any excess from skin immediately.

OTHER INFORMATION:

Keratolytics are skin preparations that are designed to remove the outermost layer of the skin (the keratin layer) and therefore act as the ultimate skin cleanser. They are used to treat diseases such as acne, psoriasis and some forms of dermatitis. Excessive or inappropriate use may cause reddening, burning and discolouration of the skin, particularly on the face. It is wise to make a test application on an area of skin that is not cosmetically important before applying a keratolytic to the face. Tretinoin is a vitamin A derivative. All keratolytics must be used carefully, but if correctly used, may markedly improve acne and other skin diseases.

See also SALICYLATES (Salicylic acid), Acitretin, Formaldehyde, Glutaraldehyde, Isotretinoin, Lactic Acid.

Ketoconazole

TRADE NAME:

Nizoral.

DRUG CLASS:

Antifungal.

USES:

Significant fungal infections of skin and internal organs, severe dandruff, tinea.

DOSAGE:

Tablets: one tablet a day with food.
Cream: apply once or twice a day.
Shampoo: apply to wet scalp for five minutes twice a week for four weeks.

FORMS:

Tablets (white) of 200mg, cream, shampoo.

PRECAUTIONS:

Tablets should not be used in pregnancy (B3) unless medically essential and breast feeding should be ceased before use.
Tablets not to be used in children.
Shampoo and cream may be used in pregnancy, breast feeding and children with caution.
Should not be used long term.
Use with caution in older women.
Use with caution in adrenal disease, if allergic to Penicillin or if Griseofulvin taken recently.
Avoid eye contact with cream and shampoo.

Do not take if:

• suffering from liver disease
• allergic to griseofulvin or penicillin.

SIDE EFFECTS:

Common: tablets—Nausea.
Shampoo and cream—Skin irritation, itch, rash and redness.
Unusual: vomiting, diarrhoea, belly pain, rash, itch, headache, dizziness.
Severe but rare (stop medication, consult doctor): yellow skin (jaundice).

INTERACTIONS:

Other drugs:
• serious interaction with astemizole, mizolastine, cisapride, midazolam, triazolam, pimozide, quinidine, simvastatin.
• tablets—isoniazid, rifampicin, griseofulvin, antacids, ritonavir, warfarin, cyclosporin, sildenafil, digoxin, verapamil, phenytoin.
• shampoo—corticosteroid scalp applications.
Herbs:
• echinacea.

Other substances:
• tablets—alcohol.

PRESCRIPTION:

Yes.

PERMITTED IN SPORT:

Yes.

OVERDOSE:

Induce vomiting if medication taken recently. Seek medical assistance.

OTHER INFORMATION:

Introduced in mid 1980s. Very effective, but may cause liver damage if used inappropriately or for long periods.

See also Clotrimazole, Econazole, Fluconazole, Griseofulvin, Itraconazole, Miconazole.

Ketoprofen

TRADE NAMES:

Ketocid, Orudis, Oruvail, Powergel.

DRUG CLASS:

NSAID (Nonsteroidal anti-inflammatory drug).

USES:

All forms of arthritis, inflammatory disorders, gout, back pain, ankylosing spondylitis, bone pain, pain after surgery, period pain.

DOSAGE:

 100 to 200mg once a day.

FORMS:

Capsules of 50mg, 100mg, 150mg and 200mg, gel, suppositories of 100mg.

PRECAUTIONS:

Should not be used in pregnancy (C) unless medically essential. Breast feeding should be ceased if necessary to use

NSAID. Not for use in children under two. Gel safe in pregnancy.
Use tablets and capsules with caution in psychiatricaly disturbed patients, epilepsy, severe infection, heart failure and kidney disease.
Lower doses required in elderly, who may suffer more side effects.

Do not take if:

 • suffering from peptic ulcer at present or in recent past
• due for surgery (including dental surgery)
• suffering from bleeding disorder or anaemia.

SIDE EFFECTS:

Common: gel—minimal.
Other forms—stomach discomfort, diarrhoea, constipation, heartburn, nausea, headache, dizziness.
Unusual: blurred vision, stomach ulcer, ringing noise in ears, retention of fluid, swelling of tissue, drowsiness, itch, rash, shortness of breath.
Severe but rare (stop medication, consult doctor): vomiting blood, passing blood in faeces, other unusual bleeding, asthma induced by medication.

INTERACTIONS:

Other drugs:
• must never be used with anticoagulants (e.g. warfarin).
• probenecid, diuretics, lithium, methotrexate, beta-blockers, ACE inhibitors, diuretics.
• gel has minimal interactions.

PRESCRIPTION:

Yes.

PERMITTED IN SPORT:

Yes.

OVERDOSE:

Causes nausea, vomiting, severe headache, dizziness, confusion and convulsions. Administer activated charcoal or induce vomiting if taken recently. Seek medical assistance.

OTHER INFORMATION:

Extensively used to give excellent relief to a wide variety of inflammatory conditions. Significant side effects (particularly on the stomach) in about 5% of patients. Limit their use. Specially coated forms reduce side effects. Minimal side effects with gel, but less effective.

See also Aspirin, Celecoxib, Diclofenac, Diflunisal, Flurbiprofen, Ibuprofen, Indomethacin, Ketorolac, Mefenamic Acid, Naproxen, NSAID, Piroxicam, Rofecoxib, Salicylic acid, Sulindac, Tenoxicam, Tiaprofenic Acid.

Ketorolac

TRADE NAMES:

Acular, Toradol.

DRUG CLASS:

NSAID (Nonsteroidal anti-inflammatory drug).

USES:

Post operative pain, allergic conjunctivitis, inflammation during eye surgery.

DOSAGE:

Tablets: one every four to six hours.
Injection: every four to six hours.
Eye drops: one or two drops four times a day.

FORMS:

Tablets of 10mg, injection (Toradol); eye drops (Acular).

PRECAUTIONS:

Should not be used in pregnancy (C) unless medically essential. Breast feeding should be ceased if necessary to use NSAID. Not for use in children under two.
Use tablets and injection with caution in psychiatricaly disturbed patients, epilepsy, severe infection, heart failure and kidney disease.
Lower doses required in elderly, who may suffer more side effects.

Do not take if:

- suffering from peptic ulcer at present or in recent past
- due for surgery (including dental surgery)
- suffering from bleeding disorder or anaemia.

SIDE EFFECTS:

Common: eye drops—stinging, burning, red eye, droopy eyelids, dry eyes. Injection and tablets—stomach discomfort, diarrhoea, constipation, heartburn, nausea, headache, dizziness.
Unusual: blurred vision, stomach ulcer, ringing noise in ears, retention of fluid, swelling of tissue, drowsiness, itch, rash, shortness of breath.
Severe but rare (stop medication, consult doctor): vomiting blood, passing blood in faeces, other unusual bleeding, asthma induced by medication, glaucoma.

INTERACTIONS:

Other drugs:
- must never be used with anticoagulants (e.g. warfarin).
- probenecid, diuretics, lithium, methotrexate, beta-blockers, ACE inhibitors.

PRESCRIPTION:

Yes.

PERMITTED IN SPORT:

Yes.

OVERDOSE:

Causes nausea, vomiting, severe headache, dizziness, confusion and convulsions. Administer activated charcoal or induce vomiting if taken recently. Seek medical assistance.

OTHER INFORMATION:

Used to give excellent relief to a wide variety of inflammatory conditions.

See also Aspirin, Celecoxib, Diclofenac,

Diflunisal, Flurbiprofen, Ibuprofen, Indomethacin, Ketoprofen, Mefenamic Acid, Naproxen, NSAID, Piroxicam, Rofecoxib, Salicylic acid, Sulindac, Tenoxicam, Tiaprofenic Acid.

Ketotifen

TRADE NAME:

Zaditen.

DRUG CLASS:

Antihistamine.

USES:

Allergic conditions, hay fever, allergic conjunctivitis, asthma prevention.

DOSAGE:

 1mg to 2mg twice a day.

FORMS:

Tablets of 1mg (white), capsules of 1mg (white), elixir.

PRECAUTIONS:

Not to be used in pregnancy and breast feeding.
May be used in children over two years of age.
Reduce dose slowly over two or more weeks.

SIDE EFFECTS:

Common: drowsiness, dry mouth, slow reactions.
Unusual: irritability, weight gain, skin reactions, bladder irritation.
Severe but rare (stop medication, consult doctor): convulsions, hepatitis, liver damage.

INTERACTIONS:

Other drugs:
• sedatives, hypoglycaemics (for diabetes), antihistamines.
Other substances:
• alcohol.

PRESCRIPTION:

Yes.

PERMITTED IN SPORT:

Yes.

OVERDOSE:

May result in convulsions, hallucinations, delirium, anxiety, muscle spasms, rapid heart rate, flushing, dry skin, dry mouth and coma. First aid involved inducing vomiting and seeking urgent medical attention.

OTHER INFORMATION:

An unusual antihistamine in that it prevents asthma, as well as the more traditional effects of this class of medication.

See also ANTIHISTAMINES, SEDATING.

Labetalol

TRADE NAME:
Trandate.

DRUG CLASS:
Alpha-Beta-blocker, Antihypertensive.

USES:
High blood pressure.

DOSAGE:
 100mg to 400mg, two to four times a day to a maximum of 2400mg per day.

FORMS:
Tablets (orange) of 50mg, 100mg, 200mg and 400mg.

PRECAUTIONS:
Should not be used in pregnancy (C) unless medically essential. Should be used with caution in breast feeding and elderly. Not recommended in children. Should not be stopped suddenly, but dosage should be slowly reduced over several days.
Use lower doses in elderly.

Do not take if:

• suffering from heart disease, narrowed arteries, Prinzmetal angina, diabetes, overactive thyroid gland, phaeochromocytoma or liver failure.
• having a general anaesthetic. Discuss with doctor.

SIDE EFFECTS:
Common: minimal.
Unusual: slow heart rate, dizziness, headache, tiredness, blurred vision, eye irritation, asthma, rash, difficulty in passing urine.

INTERACTIONS:
Other drugs:
• beta agonists, calcium channel blockers, drugs for treatment of irregular heart beat
• tremor with tricyclic antidepressants
• cimetidine increases blood levels of labetalol
• clonidine, methyldopa, NSAIDs.

PRESCRIPTION:
Yes.

PERMITTED IN SPORT:
No.

OVERDOSE:
Low blood pressure and slow heart rate. Lay patient flat and raise legs. Administer charcoal or induce vomiting if tablets taken recently. Seek medical assistance.

See also Carvedilol, Esmolol, Metoprolol, Oxprenolol, Pindolol, Propranolol, Sotalol.

Lacidipine

TRADE NAME:
Motens.

DRUG CLASS:
Calcium channel blocker (calcium antagonist).

USES:
High blood pressure.

DOSAGE:
 2mg to 6mg once a day.

FORMS:
Tablets of 2mg, and 4mg (white).

PRECAUTIONS:

Should only be used in pregnancy (C) and breast feeding if medically essential. Not designed for use in children.
Use with caution in liver disease.

Do not take if:

- suffering from severe heart failure, low blood pressure, atrial flutter or fibrillation.

SIDE EFFECTS:

Common: flushing, headache, dizziness, indigestion, swelling of feet and ankles.
Unusual: palpitations, slow heart rate, depression, nightmares, excess wind.
Severe but rare (stop medication, consult doctor): fainting, chest pain.

INTERACTIONS:

Other drugs:
- beta-blockers (e.g. propranolol), cyclosporin, digoxin, cimetidine, barbiturates, diazepam, amiodarone, quinidine, rifampicin, phenytoin, cisapride, theophylline, terbutaline, salbutamol, diltiazem
- additive effect with other medications for high blood pressure.

Herbs:
- goldenseal, guarana, hawthorn, Korean ginseng, liquorice.

Other substances:
- smoking may aggravate conditions that these medications are treating
- grapefruit juice.

PRESCRIPTION:

Yes.

PERMITTED IN SPORT:

Yes.

OVERDOSE:

May continue to be absorbed for up to 48 hours after overdose. Administer activated charcoal or induce vomiting. Purging should be encouraged to eliminate drug from gut. Overdose may cause low blood pressure, irregular heart rhythm, difficulty in breathing, heart attack and death.
Obtain urgent medical attention.

See also Amlodipine, Diltiazem, Isradipine, Lercanidipine, Nifedipine, Nimodipine, Verapamil.

Lactic acid

TRADE NAMES:

Available only in combination with other medications.
Calmurid (with urea).
Calmurid HC (with urea, hydrocortisone).
Cuplex (with copper acetate).
Duofilm, Salactol, Salatac (with salicylic acid).
Lacticare (with sodium pyrrolidone carboxylate).
Available in numerous other creams and lotions.

DRUG CLASS:

Acid.

USES:

Thickened skin, warts, corns.

DOSAGE:

 Apply one or two times a day.

FORMS:

Cream, lotion, solution, paint.

PRECAUTIONS:

Safe in pregnancy, breast feeding and children.
Avoid eyes, mouth and nostrils.

SIDE EFFECTS:

Common: stinging.

INTERACTIONS:

None.

PRESCRIPTION:

No.

PERMITTED IN SPORT:

PERMITTED IN SPORT:

Yes.
See also KERATOLYTICS.

Lactulose

TRADE NAMES:

Duphalac, Lactugal.

DRUG CLASS:

Laxative.

USES:

Severe constipation. Also used in rare form of brain inflammation.

DOSAGE:

 30 to 45mLs three or four times a day.

FORMS:

Solution.

PRECAUTIONS:

Safe in pregnancy, breast feeding and children.
Should be used with caution in diabetics.
Should not be used for more than six months without medical check-up.

SIDE EFFECTS:

Common: intestinal cramps, bloating, passing wind.
Unusual: diarrhoea, nausea, loss of appetite, increased thirst.

INTERACTIONS:

Other drugs:
• interacts with neomycin and other antibiotics given by mouth
• antacids.

PRESCRIPTION:

No.

PERMITTED IN SPORT:

Yes.

OVERDOSE:

Diarrhoea and intestinal cramps only problem.

OTHER INFORMATION:

Normally only used for severe constipation when other medications ineffective.
See also Bisacodyl, Docusate sodium, Fibre, Glycerol, Frangula, Paraffin, Psyllium, Senna, Sodium phosphate, Sodium picosulfate, Sorbitol, Sterculia.

Lamivudine

TRADE NAMES:

Epivir, Zeffix.
Combivir (with zidovudine).
Trizivir (with abacavir, zidovudine).

DRUG CLASS:

Antiviral.

USES:

HIV infection, AIDS, chronic hepatitis B.

DOSAGE:

 100 to 150mg, once or twice a day, often in combination with other antivirals.

FORMS:

Tablets, mixture.

PRECAUTIONS:

Use with considerable caution in pregnancy (B3) and children. Use with caution in breast feeding.
Use with caution in kidney and liver disease, diabetes and pancreas disease.
Do not use for HIV/AIDS unless combined with other antivirals.

SIDE EFFECTS:

Common: nausea, headache, tiredness, inability to sleep, rashes.
Unusual: lung and throat infection. Pancreatitis.

INTERACTIONS:

Other drugs:
• trimethoprim, zalcitabine.

PRESCRIPTION:

Yes.

PERMITTED IN SPORT:

Yes.

See also Abacavir, Amprenavir, Efavirenz, Indinavir, Nelfinavir, Nevirapine, Ritonavir, Saquinavir, Stavudine, Tenofovir, Zidovudine.

Lamotrigine

TRADE NAME:

Lamictal.

DRUG CLASS:

Anticonvulsant.

USES:

Epilepsy, particularly seizures that affect only one part of the body and are not controlled by other anticonvulsants.

DOSAGE:

 Gradually increase dose until control obtained, usually between 200mg and 400mg a day taken in two doses. Lower doses used in combination with other anticonvulsants.

FORMS:

Tablets (yellow) of 25mg, 50mg, 100mg and 200mg.

PRECAUTIONS:

Use with great caution in pregnancy (B3), breast feeding and children under 12 years. Use with caution in kidney and liver disease.
Regular blood tests to check liver and kidney function and clotting are necessary.
Do not stop suddenly, but reduce dosage slowly.

SIDE EFFECTS:

Common: rash, dizziness, headache, double vision, incoordination, tiredness, nausea, blurred vision, vomiting.
Uncommon: swelling of tissue, blistering and peeling of skin, blood cell damage.
Severe but rare (stop medication, consult doctor): rash (Stevens-Johnson syndrome or toxic epidermal necrolysis—may be severe and life threatening).

INTERACTIONS:

Other drugs:
• other anticonvulsants, sodium valproate.
Herbs:
• evening primrose (linoleic acid), gingko biloba.
Other substances:
• borage.

PRESCRIPTION:

Yes.

PERMITTED IN SPORT:

Yes.

OVERDOSE:

Sedation, incoordination, double vision and vomiting may occur. Administer charcoal or induce vomiting if taken recently. Seek medical assistance.

OTHER INFORMATION:

Introduced in 1993 to assist the most severe and difficult to control forms of epilepsy. Unfortunately, cost and side effects limit its usefulness.

See also BARBITURATES, BENZODIAZEPINES, Carbamazepine, Clonazepam, Ethosuximide, Gabapentin, Levetiracetam, Oxcarbazepine, Phenytoin, Primidone, Sodium valproate, Sulthiame, Tiagabine, Topiramate, Vigabatrin.

Lansoprazole

See PROTON PUMP INHIBITORS.

Latanoprost

TRADE NAMES:

Xalantan.
Xalacom (with timolol).

USES:

Glaucoma.

DOSAGE:

 One drop in affected eye(s) once a day. Apply pressure to tear duct at inner corner of eye for five minutes after application.

FORMS:

Eye drops.

PRECAUTIONS:

Use with considerable caution in pregnancy (B3). Use with caution in breast feeding and children.
Use with caution in eye inflammation, pigmentary and hereditary glaucoma.

Do not use if:

 • wearing contact lenses.

SIDE EFFECTS:

Common: change in eye colour, irritation of eye surface, redness of eye, blurred vision, eye burning and itching.
Unusual: swelling of eye surface, ulceration of eye surface.

INTERACTIONS:

Other drugs:
• thiomersal drops, acetazolamide.

PRESCRIPTION:

Yes.

PERMITTED IN SPORT:

Yes.

OVERDOSE:

Eye irritation and exacerbation of side effects likely.

OTHER INFORMATION:

Introduced for treatment of glaucoma unresponsive to other medications.
See also Betaxolol, Bimatoprost, Levobunolol, Timolol.

LAXATIVES

DISCUSSION:

When you've just got to go, but you can't go, a laxative may be the answer to a large bowel's prayer. Constipation is a relative matter, as some people consider it normal to pass faeces three times a day, while others consider once a week to be normal. If retained faeces and the attempts to pass them cause pain or discomfort, then constipation needs treatment. Laxatives should be the last resort in the treatment of constipation, after increased fluid intake and alterations to increase the bulk residue of the food in your diet have been tried.

Laxatives vary from simple lubricants, such as paraffin, to bulking agents that contain senna and other fibres, different sugars that draw fluid into the gut (e.g. lactulose) and gut stimulants (e.g. bisacodyl) that actually increase the contractions of the gut. They are available as tablets, mixtures, granules, suppositories and enemas (the last two for anal use). All are available without prescription.

The main complication with laxatives is their overuse. Patients may use laxatives to pass faeces excessively, and become dependent upon them for the natural functioning of the bowel. Patients trying to lose weight by increasing the rate of faeces output may create this type of dependence and it is a practice to be deplored. Laxatives should never be used if there is any suspicion of more sinister disease in the gut. Many patients have treated a pain in the abdomen with laxatives, only to find that they have worsened a case of appendicitis.

Laxatives should be used with great caution in children and during pregnancy. Many other substances, foods and fibres (e.g. senna) are used as laxatives.

See Bisacodyl, Docusate sodium, FIBRE, Lactulose, Macrogol, Paraffin, Poloxamer 188, Senna, Sodium acid phosphate, Sodium phosphate, Sodium picosulfate.

L-Dopa

See **LEVODOPA COMPOUNDS.**

Leflunomide

TRADE NAME:

Arava.

USES:

Treatment of severe rheumatoid arthritis.

DOSAGE:

 100mg a day for three days, then 10mg to 20mg once a day.

FORMS:

Tablets of 10mg (white), 20mg (yellow) and 100mg (white).

PRECAUTIONS:

Never to be used in pregnancy (X) and breast feeding.
May be used with caution in children and the elderly.
Regular blood tests to check liver function and blood cell count necessary.
Use with caution in generalised infection, bone marrow damage, tuberculosis and kidney damage.

Do not take if:

- suffering from immuno-deficiency, low platelet or white cell count, severe infection, Stevens-Johnson syndrome, liver disease or erythema multiforme.
- female partner is pregnant (may be transferred during sex).

SIDE EFFECTS:

Common: skin reactions, nausea, diarrhoea, hair loss.
Unusual: high blood pressure, sore mouth, belly pain, liver and blood cell damage, tendon and muscle pain, headache, dizziness, weight loss, pins and needles sensation, allergy reaction.
Severe but rare (stop medication, consult doctor): severe skin reaction, blistering and loss of skin.

INTERACTIONS:

Other drugs:
- methotrexate, phenytoin, warfarin, tolbutamide, some vaccines, rifampicin, charcoal, cholestyramine, NSAID, celecoxib. rofecoxib, methotrexate.

Other substances:
- alcohol.

PRESCRIPTION:

Yes.

PERMITTED IN SPORT:

Yes (restricted to specialists).

OVERDOSE:

Likely to be serious, but no information available. Seek urgent medical attention.

OTHER INFORMATION:

Introduced in 1999 as a last resort, but effective treatment, for the most severe forms of rheumatoid arthritis.

Lente insulin

See **INSULINS.**

Lercanidipine

TRADE NAME:

Zanidip.

DRUG CLASS:

Antihypertensive, calcium channel blocker.

USES:

Treatment of high blood pressure (hypertension).

DOSAGE:

 One or two tablets once a day.

FORMS:

Tablets of 10mg (yellow).

PRECAUTIONS:

Not to be used in pregnancy (C), breast feeding or children.
Use with caution in the elderly, angina, aortic stenosis, heart failure, recent heart attack, kidney and liver disease.

Do not take if:

 • suffering from severe liver or kidney disease.

SIDE EFFECTS:

Common: constipation, tiredness, headache, dizziness, indigestion, swelling of feet and ankles.
Unusual: flushing, palpitations, slow heart rate, scalp irritation, depression, flushes, nightmares, excess wind.
Severe but rare (stop medication, consult doctor): fainting.

INTERACTIONS:

Other drugs:
• cyclosporin (severe reaction)
• ketoconazole, itraconazole, erythromycin, ritonavir, fluoxetine, phenytoin, carbamazepine, rifampicin, amiodarone, quinidine, metoprolol, propranolol, digoxin, cimetidine, simvastatin.
Other substances:
• alcohol, grapefruit juice.

PRESCRIPTION:

Yes.

PERMITTED IN SPORT:

Yes.

OVERDOSE:

Administer activated charcoal or induce vomiting. Purging should be encouraged to eliminate drug from gut. Overdose may cause low blood pressure, irregular heart rhythm, difficulty in breathing, heart attack and death. Obtain urgent medical attention.

OTHER INFORMATION:

Introduced in 2001 for the management of hypertension.
See also Amlodipine, Diltiazem, Felodipine, Nifedipine, Nimodipine, Verapamil.

Letrozole

TRADE NAME:

Femara.

DRUG CLASS:

Antineoplastic.

USES:

Some types of advanced breast cancer in postmenopausal women.

DOSAGE:

 One tablet a day.

FORMS:

Tablets of 2.5mg (dark yellow).

PRECAUTIONS:

Not to be used in pregnancy (D), breast feeding or children.
Use with caution in kidney and liver disease.

Do not take if:

 • still having menstrual periods.

SIDE EFFECTS:

Common: headache, nausea, diarrhoea, swelling of hands and feet, tiredness, hot flushes, hair thinning, rash, vaginal discharge.

Unusual: weight change, muscle pain, vaginal bleeding, sweating, dizziness, tiredness, increased appetite, joint pain, urgent desire to pass urine, acne, breast enlargement.

Severe but rare (stop medication, consult doctor): blood clot in vein (thrombosis).

INTERACTIONS:

Other drugs:
• tamoxifen.

PRESCRIPTION:

Yes.

PERMITTED IN SPORT:

Restricted for use in sport to women only.

OVERDOSE:

Effect unknown. Induce vomiting or administer activated charcoal if tablets taken recently. Seek medical attention.

OTHER INFORMATION:

Introduced in 1998 for treatment of severe relapses of some types of breast cancer.
See also Tamoxifen, Toremifene.

LEUKOTRENE RECEPTOR ANTAGONISTS

DISCUSSION:

New group of oral medications that prevent and treat asthma.
See Montelukast, Zafirlukast.

Leuprorelin

TRADE NAME:

Prostap.

DRUG CLASS:

Antineoplastic.

USES:

Prostate cancer, endometriosis, fibroids of the uterus prior to surgery.

DOSAGE:

 Monthly or three monthly injection.

FORMS:

Depot injection.

PRECAUTIONS:

Not to be used in pregnancy (D), breast feeding and children.
Use with caution with metastatic cancer involving the spine, urinary tract obstruction.

Do not take if:

 • suffering from osteoporosis, undiagnosed bleeding from the vagina.

SIDE EFFECTS:

Common: hot flushes, sweats, swelling of hands and feet, nausea, diarrhoea.
Unusual: pain at cancer or fibroid sites, shortness of breath, tiredness, headache, emotional instability, palpitations, breast tenderness.
Severe but rare (stop medication, consult doctor): high blood pressure, osteoporosis.

INTERACTIONS:

None significant.

PRESCRIPTION:

Yes.

PERMITTED IN SPORT:

Yes.

Levetiracetam

TRADE NAME:

Keppra.

DRUG CLASS:

Anticonvulsant.

USES:

Partial seizures of epilepsy.

DOSAGE:

 500 to 1500mg twice a day.

FORMS:

Tablets of 250mg (blue), 500mg (yellow) and 1000mg (white).

PRECAUTIONS:

Use with caution in pregnancy (B3) and children under 16 years. Not to be used if breast feeding.
Do not stop tablets suddenly, but reduce dose slowly.
Use with caution with kidney and liver disease.

SIDE EFFECTS:

Common: tiredness, dizziness.
Unusual: aggression, confusion, psychiatric disturbances.

INTERACTIONS:

Other drugs:
• probenecid.

PRESCRIPTION:

Yes.

PERMITTED IN SPORT:

Yes.

OTHER INFORMATION:

Introduced in 2003.

See also BARBITURATES, BENZODIAZEPINES, Carbamazepine, Clonazepam, Ethosuximide, Gabapentin, Lamotrigine, Oxcarbazepine, Phenytoin, Primidone, Sodium valproate, Sulthiame, Tiagabine, Topiramate, Vigabatrin.

Levobunolol

TRADE NAME:

Betagan.

DRUG CLASS:

Beta-blocker.

USES:

Glaucoma.

DOSAGE:

 One drop twice a day.

FORMS:

Eye drops.

PRECAUTIONS:

Should be used with caution in pregnancy (C), but eye drops unlikely to cause problems.
Safe to use in breast feeding.
May be used with caution in children.
Use with care if suffering from alcoholism, liver or kidney failure or about to have surgery.
Use with caution in diabetes, shock, slow heart rate, or enlarged right heart.

Do not take if:

 • suffering from heart failure, asthma, slow heart rate or allergic conditions.

SIDE EFFECTS:

Common: low blood pressure, slow heart rate, burning eyes, stinging, asthma.
Severe but rare (stop medication, consult doctor): severe asthma.

INTERACTIONS:

Other drugs:
• calcium channel blockers, disopyramide, clonidine, adrenaline, other medications for irregular heart beat, lignocaine, ergotamine, indomethacin, chlorpromazine, beta-blocker tablets.

PRESCRIPTION:

Yes.

PERMITTED IN SPORT:

Yes.

OVERDOSE:

Unlikely to be serious effects if eye drops swallowed.

See also Betaxolol, Bimatroprost, Latanoprost, Pilocarpine, Timolol.

Levocabastine

TRADE NAME:

Livostin.

USES:

Allergic conjunctivitis, hay fever.

DOSAGE:

 Eye drops: one drop in eye twice a day.
Nose spray: two sprays in each nostril two to four times a day.

FORMS:

Eye drops, nose spray.

PRECAUTIONS:

Do not use in pregnancy (B3).
Use with caution in breast feeding and kidney disease.
Use with caution if wearing contact lenses.
Do not use continuously for more than eight weeks.

SIDE EFFECTS:

Common: local irritation, headaches.
Unusual: tiredness, nose bleed.

INTERACTIONS:

None significant.

PRESCRIPTION:

Yes.

PERMITTED IN SPORT:

Yes.

OVERDOSE:

Unlikely to be serious.
See also Emedastine.

Levocetirizine

See ANTIHISTAMINES, SEDATING.

LEVODOPA COMPOUNDS (L-dopa)

TRADE and GENERIC NAMES:

Madopar (levodopa and benserazide).
Sinemet (levodopa and carbidopa).

DRUG CLASS:

Antiparkinsonian.

USES:

Parkinson's disease.

DOSAGE:

 Individualised depending on patient's response. Follow doctor's instructions carefully.

FORMS:

Capsules, tablets.

PRECAUTIONS:

Should be used in pregnancy (B3) only if medically essential. Breast feeding should be ceased before use. Not for use in children.
Use with caution in psychiatric conditions, heart disease, peptic ulcers, epilepsy, osteoporosis, glaucoma and osteomalacia.
Do not undertake sudden increases in exercise levels.

Do not take if:

 • suffering from severe heart disease, glandular disease, severe lung disease, liver or kidney disease, psychoses, melanoma, tremor, Huntington's chorea
• under 30 years of age.

SIDE EFFECTS:

Common: nausea, loss of appetite, palpitations, weight gain, constipation, incoordination, twitching, depression, tiredness, hiccups, sleeplessness, muscle cramps, excess excitability, tissue swelling, drowsiness.
Unusual: vomiting, angina, shortness of breath, reduced libido, irregular heart rhythm, diarrhoea, leg pain, fainting,

hallucinations, confusion.
Severe but rare (stop medication, consult doctor): significant psychiatric disturbances.

INTERACTIONS:

Other drugs:
• drugs acting on the heart (e.g. some antihypertensives)
• tricyclic antidepressants, phenothiazines, risperidone, isoniazid, phenytoin, MAOI, selegiline
• drugs used in general anaesthetics.
Herbs:
• kava kava.

PRESCRIPTION:

Yes.

PERMITTED IN SPORT:

Yes.

OVERDOSE:

Symptoms include all side effects above, but exaggerated in severity. Administer activated charcoal or induce vomiting if patient alert and medication taken recently. Seek urgent medical assistance.

OTHER INFORMATION:

Despite their significant side effects, these medications have dramatically improved the quality of life for many patients with Parkinson's disease. Hailed as a miracle cure when introduced in the late 1960s, levodopa is now accepted as just one part of the treatment for this disease. Unfortunately, its effect tends to decrease the longer it is used. An important brain hormone, dopamine is depleted in Parkinson's disease. Providing extra material from which the brain can make dopamine improves the condition for many years.

See also Amantadine, Biperiden, Selegiline.

Levofloxacin

TRADE NAME:

Tavanic.

DRUG CLASS:

Quinolone antibiotic.

USES:

Bacterial infections including sinusitis, acute bronchitis, pneumonia, kidney and bladder infections, skin infections.

DOSAGE:

 250mg to 500mg once or twice a day.

FORMS:

Tablets (off white) of 250 and 500mg.

PRECAUTIONS:

Not to be used in pregnancy and breast feeding. Not recommended in children. Use with caution in porphyria, severe kidney disease and persistent diarrhoea. Avoid strong ultraviolet light.
Do not take if:
 • suffering from epilepsy, drug induced tendon disorders.

SIDE EFFECTS:

Common: nausea, diarrhoea.
Unusual: mild liver damage.
Severe but rare (stop medication, consult doctor): severe liver damage, tendon damage.

INTERACTIONS:

Other drugs:
• iron, antacids, sucralfate, NSAIDs, fenbufen, probenecid, Cimetidine.

PRESCRIPTION:

Yes.

PERMITTED IN SPORT:

Yes.

OVERDOSE:

Exacerbation of side effects most likely result. Induce vomiting if medication taken recently. Maintain adequate fluid intake.

See also Nalidixic acid, Ofloxacin.

Levonorgestrel

TRADE NAME:

Mirena (intra-uterine device, IUD).
Also in numerous oral contraceptives and the 'morning after pill'—see separate entries.

DRUG CLASS:

Sex hormone.

USES:

Contraception.

DOSAGE:

 Intrauterine device replaced every five years.

FORMS:

Intrauterine device.

PRECAUTIONS:

Not for use in pregnancy (D), breast feeding or children.
Not for use in males.
Use IUD with caution in women who have not had children.
Use IUD with care in heart disease, migraine sufferers, liver disease, breast cancer, heart anatomy abnormalities, and with history of sexually transmitted diseases.

Do not use IUD if:

 • suffering from genital or uterine infection, genital cancer, recent abortion, undiagnosed uterine bleeding, abnormal shape of uterus and significant liver disease.

SIDE EFFECTS:

Common: pain low in belly and back, headache, breast tenderness.
Unusual: nausea, acne, abnormal menstrual bleeding, infection of uterus.
Severe but rare (stop medication, consult doctor): perforation of uterus, blood clot (calf pain, short of breath, chest pain).

INTERACTIONS:

Other drugs:
• other sex hormones, primidone, barbiturates, phenytoin, carbamazepine, rifampicin, griseofulvin, phenylbutazone, ritonavir, ampicillin and other antibiotics, hypoglycaemics (used to treat diabetes), insulin.

PRESCRIPTION:

Yes.

PERMITTED IN SPORT:

Yes.

OTHER INFORMATION:

Levonorgestrel IUD introduced in 2001 as a totally new type of contraception.
See also 'MORNING AFTER PILL', ORAL CONTRACEPTIVES.

Licorice

See Liquorice.

Lignocaine

See ANAESTHETICS, LOCAL.

Liniments

DISCUSSION:

Liniments are creams or lotions that are rubbed into the skin to create local warmth and skin redness. There are scores of liniments available from chemists to treat bruises, sprains, fibrositis and arthritic conditions (e.g. camphor, menthol, alcohol, salicylates). They should not be used on the face, near body openings (e.g. anus, vagina), or on grazes or cuts. Many NSAIDs (see separate entry) are also available as creams and gels.

See Benzydamine, Camphor, Capsaicin, Heparinoid, Menthol, SALICYLATES.

Linoleic acid
(Evening primrose oil)

See FATTY ACIDS.

Liothyronine

TRADE NAME:

Tertroxin (T3).

USES:

Severely under active thyroid gland (myxoedema), thyroiditis.

DOSAGE:

 One or two tablets a day on an empty stomach.
Start with low initial dose and slowly increase to a dose determined by doctor after regular blood tests.

FORMS:

Tablets of 20µg (white).

PRECAUTIONS:

Safe to use in pregnancy (A), breast feeding and children.
Use with caution in heart disease and high blood pressure.

Do not take if:

 • suffering from angina, Addison disease.

SIDE EFFECTS:

Only occur with overdosage.

INTERACTIONS:

Other drugs:
• coumarin anticoagulants (e.g. warfarin), barbiturates, narcotics, insulin, catecholamines, tricyclic antidepressants, digoxin, corticosteroids, colestipol, phenytoin, cholestyramine, oral contraceptives.

PRESCRIPTION:

Yes.

PERMITTED IN SPORT:

Yes.

OVERDOSE:

Serious. May cause rapid heart rate, irregular heart beat, angina, restlessness, anxiety, tremor, headache, diarrhoea, vomiting, rapid breathing, fever, heart attack and death. Administer activated charcoal or induce vomiting if medication taken recently. Seek urgent medical assistance.

OTHER INFORMATION:

Widely used to counter the slowly progressive effects of thyroid underactivity, a problem that is common in middle aged women. Does not cause addiction or dependence, but lifelong treatment usually necessary.

See also Thyroxine.

Liquorice
(Glycyrrhizin, Licorice)

USES:

Cough, gastritis (stomach inflammation).

DOSAGE:

 5g to 15g of root a day (200mg to 600mg of glycyrrhizin extract).

FORMS:

Capsules, extract for tea preparation.

PRECAUTIONS:

Do not use in pregnancy and breast feeding.
Do not use long term (over six weeks) as low blood potassium and high blood sodium levels may occur.
Use with caution in fluid retention disorders, high blood pressure and heart disease.

Do not take if:

- suffering from hepatitis, gall bladder disease, cirrhosis, severe kidney disease, diabetes, irregular heart rhythm, untreated high blood pressure, excess muscle tone
- under other circumstances.

SIDE EFFECTS:

Common: retention of fluid, weight gain.
Unusual: high blood pressure.
Severe but rare (stop medication, consult doctor): irregular heart rhythm.

INTERACTIONS:

Other drugs:
- frusemide, thiazide diuretics, digoxin, procainamide, quinidine, steroids.

Other substances:
- smoking tobacco.

PRESCRIPTION:

No.

OVERDOSE:

Blood chemistry disorders may occur, leading to irregular heart rhythm and high blood pressure.

OTHER INFORMATION:

Rarely used in orthodox medical practice.

Lisinopril

See ACE INHIBITORS.

Lithium

TRADE NAMES:

Camcolit, Li-Liquid, Liskonum, Priadel.

DRUG CLASS:

Antipsychotic.

USES:

Manic: depressive psychoses, severe depression, aggressive behaviour, other psychiatric conditions.

DOSAGE:

One or two tablets, two or three times a day.
Sustained release tablets taken once or twice a day.
Dosage must be individualised for each patient.
Follow doctors instructions carefully.

FORMS:

Tablets, liquid.

PRECAUTIONS:

Lithium must not be used in pregnancy (D) except under exceptional circumstances as it may cause malformations of the heart and damage to the thyroid gland of the foetus. Breast feeding must be ceased if Lithium is taken. Not for use in children.
Diet should remain regular during dosage with Lithium as changes in diet and fluid intake can affect blood levels of Lithium.
Regular blood tests to check dosage of Lithium recommended.

Do not take if:

- suffering from significant heart and kidney disease, Addison's disease, underactive thyroid gland.

SIDE EFFECTS:

Common: weight gain, goitre, swelling of tissues (oedema), dermatitis, loss of appetite, nausea, belly discomfort, diarrhoea, tiredness, slurred speech.
Unusual: vomiting, tremor, agitation.

INTERACTIONS:

Other drugs:
- steroids, appetite suppressants, other psychotropic drugs, NSAID, ACE

inhibitors, calcium channel blockers, urea, xanthine, methyldopa, diuretics, antidepressants.

Herbs:
- evening primrose (linoleic acid), psyllium.

PRESCRIPTION:

Yes.

PERMITTED IN SPORT:

Yes.

OVERDOSE:

Extremely serious. Symptoms may include diarrhoea, vomiting, weakness, incoordination, drowsiness, twitching, disorientation, coma and death. Administer activated charcoal or induce vomiting if taken recently and patient alert. Seek emergency medical assistance.

OTHER INFORMATION:

Widely used and effective treatment developed in Australia. Used for some specific types of mental illness. Does not cause addiction or dependence.

See also Amisulpride, Flupenthixol, Haloperidol, Lithium Carbonate, Olanzapine, PHENOTHIAZINES, Pimozide, Quetiapine, Risperidone, Thiothixene, Zuclopenthixol.

LOCAL ANAESTHETICS

See ANAESTHETICS, LOCAL.

Lodoxamide

TRADE NAME:

Alomide.

USES:

Allergic conjunctivitis, keratoconjunctivitis.

DOSAGE:

 One drop in eye four times a day.

FORMS:

Eye drops.

PRECAUTIONS:

May be used with caution in pregnancy (B1), breast feeding and children.
Use with caution if wearing contact lenses.
Do not persist with use if symptoms continue.

SIDE EFFECTS:

Common: eye discomfort, eye itch, blurred vision.
Unusual: crusting of lid margins, dry eye, red eye, excess tears.

INTERACTIONS:

None significant.

PRESCRIPTION:

Yes.

PERMITTED IN SPORT:

Yes.

OVERDOSE:

Unlikely to be serious.

OTHER INFORMATION:

Introduced in 1997 as an effective treatment for allergic reaction in the eye unrelieved by simpler medications.

Lofepramine

See TRICYCLIC ANTIDEPRESSANTS.

Lofexidine

TRADE NAME:

Britlofex.

USES:

Control of withdrawal from narcotics (e.g. heroin, methadone).

DOSAGE:

 Start with one or two tablets a day and slowly increase until symptoms relieved or maximum of 12 tablets a day.

FORMS:

Tablets of 0.2mg (peach).

PRECAUTIONS:

Use with caution in pregnancy, breast feeding and children.
Use with caution in severe heart disease, recent heart attack, slow heart rate, history of depression and chronic kidney disease.

SIDE EFFECTS:

Common: drowsiness, dry mouth and nose.
Unusual: slow heart rate, low blood pressure.

INTERACTIONS:

Other drugs:
• sedatives, tricyclic antidepressants.
Other substances:
• alcohol.

PRESCRIPTION:

Yes.

PERMITTED IN SPORT:

Yes.

OVERDOSE:

Serious. Induce vomiting or administer activated charcoal if swallowed recently. May induce heart attack. Seek urgent medical attention.

LOOP DIURETICS

DISCUSSION:

Subgroup of diuretics that work in a specific way in the kidney (on the loop of Henle apparatus). All diuretics act to increase the production of urine and remove fluid from the body.
See Bumetanide, Frusemide.

Loperamide

TRADE NAMES:

Imodium, Norimode.

DRUG CLASS:

Antidiarrhoeal.

USES:

Diarrhoea.

DOSAGE:

 Two capsules at once, then one capsule after each episode of diarrhoea to a maximum of eight capsules a day.

FORMS:

Capsules, syrup.

PRECAUTIONS:

Should be used in pregnancy (B3) and breast feeding only on medical advice. Not approved for use in children under 12 years.
Do not use for more than 48 hours without medical advice.
Use with caution in ulcerative colitis, Crohn's disease, glaucoma, liver and kidney disease.

Do not take if:

• suffering from cirrhosis of liver or severe kidney disease
• suffering from glaucoma or difficulty in passing urine
• constipated.

SIDE EFFECTS:

Common: excess passage of wind, constipation, nausea, belly pain.
Unusual: giddiness, rash, vomiting, metallic taste, decreased sexual drive, headache, weakness, tiredness, dry mouth, blurred vision.

INTERACTIONS:

Other drugs:
• interacts with tranquillisers in some patients
• may interact with monoamine oxidase inhibitors (MAOI).

Other substances:
• do not take with alcohol.

PRESCRIPTION:

Yes.

PERMITTED IN SPORT:

Yes.

OVERDOSE:

Constipation and vomiting only likely effects.

OTHER INFORMATION:

Widely used and relatively safe medication. Acts to sedate bowel muscles without any effect on the brain.
See also Atropine, Codeine, Diphenoxylate, Kaolin, Pectin.

Lopinavir

See Ritonavir.

Loratadine

See ANTIHISTAMINES, NON-SEDATING.

Lorazepam

TRADE NAME:

Ativan.

DRUG CLASS:

Benzodiazepine (Anxiolytic).

USES:

Relief of anxiety, anxiety associated with depression, preoperative sedation.

DOSAGE:

 One to four tablets a day in one or more doses. Do not exceed dose directed by doctor.

FORMS:

Tablets of 1mg (white) and 2.5mg (yellow).

PRECAUTIONS:

Should be used with caution in pregnancy (C), but not at all if delivery of infant imminent as it may decrease desire to breathe in newborn infant. Should be used with caution in breast feeding. Not for use in children.
Lower dose required in elderly.
Should be used intermittently and not constantly as dependency may develop.
Use with caution in glaucoma, myasthenia gravis, heart disease, kidney or liver disease, psychiatric conditions, schizophrenia, depression and epilepsy.
Do not take if:

 • suffering from severe lung disease, confusion
• tendency to addiction or dependence
• operating machinery, driving a vehicle or undertaking tasks that require concentration and alertness.

SIDE EFFECTS:

Common: reduced alertness, dependence.
Unusual: incoordination, tremor, confusion, increased risk of falls in elderly, rash, low blood pressure, nausea, muscle weakness.
Severe but rare (stop medication, consult doctor): jaundice (yellow skin).

INTERACTIONS:

Other drugs:
• sedatives, other anxiolytics, disulfiram, cimetidine, anticonvulsants, anticholinergics.
Herbs:
• guarana, kava kava, passionflower, St John's wort, valerian.
Other substances:
• reacts with alcohol to cause sedation and confusion.

PRESCRIPTION:

Yes.

PERMITTED IN SPORT:

Yes.

OVERDOSE:

Seldom life threatening. May cause drowsiness, confusion and coma. Induce vomiting if tablets taken recently. Seek medical assistance.

OTHER INFORMATION:

Dependency becoming a significant problem, particularly in elderly, due to overuse.

See also Buspirone, Clobazam, Diazepam, Oxazepam.

Lornoxicam

TRADE NAME:

Xefo.

DRUG CLASS:

NSAID (nonsteroidal anti-inflammatory drug).

USES:

Short term for pain after surgery. Lower back pain, osteoarthritis, rheumatoid arthritis.

DOSAGE:

 4mg to 8mg, once or twice a day immediately after food.

FORMS:

Tablets of 4mg and 8mg (white), injection.

PRECAUTIONS:

Not for use in pregnancy, breast feeding and children.
Use with care in the elderly.
Use with caution if a history of bleeding in the stomach or intestine, high blood pressure, kidney or liver disease, obesity. Blood tests regularly to check liver enzymes and kidney function may be necessary.

Do not take if:

 • suffering from recent peptic (stomach) ulcer, severe kidney disease, bleeding tendencies, severe dehydration or significant heart disease.

SIDE EFFECTS:

Common: nausea, diarrhoea.
Unusual: vomiting, dizziness, headache, tiredness.
Severe but rare (stop medication, consult doctor): vomiting blood, anaemia, black faeces.

INTERACTIONS:

Other drugs:
• anticoagulants (e.g. warfarin, aspirin), sulphonylureas (used for diabetes), other NSAID, diuretics (fluid tablets), cimetidine, methotrexate, digoxin, beta-blockers, ACE inhibitors.

PRESCRIPTION:

Yes.

PERMITTED IN SPORT:

Yes.

OVERDOSE:

Causes nausea, vomiting, severe headache, dizziness, confusion and convulsions. Administer activated charcoal or induce vomiting if taken recently. Seek medical assistance.

OTHER INFORMATION:

Released in 2002 mainly to combat pain of surgery and arthritis.

See also Aspirin, Bufexamac, Celecoxib, Diclofenac, Diflunisal, Flurbiprofen, Ibuprofen, Indomethacin, Ketoprofen, Ketorolac, Mefenamic Acid, Naproxen, Piroxicam, Rofecoxib, SALICYLATES, Sulindac, Tenoxicam, Tiaprofenic Acid.

Losartan

See ANGIOTENSIN II RECEPTOR ANTAGONISTS.

L-Tryptophan

See Tryptophan.

LUBRICANTS, EYE

See EYE LUBRICANTS.

Lumefantrine

See Artemether and Lumefantrine.

Lymecycline

TRADE NAME:

Tetralysal.

DRUG CLASS:

Tetracycline antibiotic.

USES:

Bacterial infections of lungs, ears, skin, sinuses and throat.

DOSAGE:

 One capsule, twice a day.

FORMS:

Capsules (white).

PRECAUTIONS:

Not to be used in pregnancy (D) or children under twelve years as Tetracyclines may cause permanent staining of teeth of foetus or child. Use with caution in breast feeding.
Use with caution in kidney and liver disease.
Never use expired medication as it may become toxic.

Do not take if:

 • suffering from severe kidney disease, systemic lupus erythematosus (SLE), Staphylococcal infection.

SIDE EFFECTS:

Common: loss of appetite, nausea, sore mouth, diarrhoea, difficulty in swallowing, inflamed colon.
Unusual: vomiting, inflamed pancreas, rash, secondary fungal infection (thrush).
Severe but rare (stop medication, consult doctor): severe belly pain, severe diarrhoea, tooth discolouration, significant skin rash.

INTERACTIONS:

Other drugs:
• anticoagulants, penicillin, antacids, iron, oral contraceptives.
Other substances:
• milk may reduce absorption from gut.

PRESCRIPTION:

Yes.

PERMITTED IN SPORT:

Yes.

OVERDOSE:

Exacerbation of side effects only likely effect.

See also Chlortetracycline, Demeclocycline, Doxycycline, Methacycline, Minocycline, Tetracycline.

Lysine aspirin

See Aspirin.

Macrogol

TRADE NAME:

Idrolax.

DRUG CLASS:

Laxative.

USES:

Constipation.

DOSAGE:

 One or two sachets of powder dissolved in water in the morning.

FORMS:

Powder.

PRECAUTIONS:

Safe in pregnancy, breast feeding and children.

Do not take if:

 • suffering from inflammatory bowel disease, painful belly, bowel obstruction, toxic megacolon.

SIDE EFFECTS:

Common: minimal.
Unusual: nausea, bloating.
Severe but rare (stop medication, consult doctor): allergy reaction.

INTERACTIONS:

None significant.

PRESCRIPTION:

No.

PERMITTED IN SPORT:

Yes.

OTHER INFORMATION:

Safe and effective treatment for constipation.

See also LAXATIVES.

MACROLIDES

DISCUSSION:

Macrolides are antibiotics that act against bacteria by interfering with the way their internal chemical reactions occur. They are most commonly used in chest, sinus and ear infections. They can interact with theophylline, which is used by asthmatics and in some cough mixtures. Some people who are allergic to penicillin are also allergic to macrolides.

See Azithromycin, Clarithromycin, Erythromycin, Roxithromycin.

Magnesium

TRADE NAMES:

Magnesium, in various forms, is found in numerous vitamin and mineral supplements.
Magnesium salts are used as antacids (see separate entry).

DRUG CLASS:

Mineral.

USES:

Magnesium deficiency.

DOSAGE:

 Recommended daily intake:
Females: 270mg a day;
Males: 320mg a day.

FORMS:

Tablets, capsules.

PRECAUTIONS:

Safe to use in pregnancy, breast feeding and children.

SIDE EFFECTS:

Minimal.

INTERACTIONS:

None significant.

PRESCRIPTION:

No.

PERMITTED IN SPORT:

Yes.

OVERDOSE:

Stomach and bowel upsets likely.
See also ANTACIDS, ELECTROLYTES.

Magnesium Salts

See ANTACIDS, ELECTROLYTES.

Malathion

TRADE NAMES:

Derbac-M, Prioderm, Suleo-M.

DRUG CLASS:

Insecticide.

USES:

Head and pubic lice, scabies.

DOSAGE:

 Apply to affected area once and leave for 12 hours. Do not use more than once a week for three weeks.

FORMS:

Lotion.

PRECAUTIONS:

Safe to use in pregnancy, breast feeding and children.
Not for use in infants under six months.
Avoid eyes, nose, mouth, anus and vagina.
Use with care in asthma.

SIDE EFFECTS:

Common: minor skin irritation.

INTERACTIONS:

None significant.

PRESCRIPTION:

No.

PERMITTED IN SPORT:

Yes.

OVERDOSE:

Serious effects possible if swallowed.
Seek urgent medical attention.

MAOI
(Monoamine oxidase inhibitors)

TRADE and GENERIC NAMES:

Nardil (Phenelzine).
Parnate (Tranylcypromine).

DRUG CLASS:

Antidepressant.

USES:

Depression, phobias (fears).

DOSAGE:

 One or two tablets, two or three times a day.

FORMS:

Tablets.

PRECAUTIONS:

Should be used in pregnancy only if medically essential. Not for use in breast feeding or children.
Use with caution in kidney disease.
Occasional blood tests to check liver function are recommended.
Regular blood pressure checks to detect low blood pressure are recommended.
Possible serious interactions with food and medication. Read literature supplied by doctor or pharmacist carefully and do not take drug unless you understand instructions completely.

Do not take if:

- suffering from epilepsy, heart disease, stroke, high blood pressure, severe headaches or liver disease
- over 60 years of age.

SIDE EFFECTS:

Common: dizziness, constipation, dry mouth, low blood pressure, drowsiness, weakness, fatigue, swelling of tissues (oedema), nausea.
Unusual: blurred vision, sweating, glaucoma, inability to pass urine.
Severe but rare (stop medication, consult doctor): agitation.

INTERACTIONS:

Other drugs:
- interacts with a very wide range of medications. Do not take ANY medication, including non-prescription and supermarket items, without consulting a doctor.

Other substances:
- reacts adversely with alcohol, particularly wine and beer
- reacts adversely with cheese, broad beans, pickled herrings, yeast extracts (e.g. Marmite) and beef extracts.

Herbs:
- aniseed, capsicum, ginseng, ma huang, parsley.

PRESCRIPTION:

Yes.

PERMITTED IN SPORT:

Yes.

OVERDOSE:

Very serious. Faintness, chest pain, headache, low blood pressure, agitation, clammy skin, fits, coma and death may occur. Administer activated charcoal or induce vomiting if tablets taken recently and patient alert. Seek urgent medical assistance.

OTHER INFORMATION:

A very useful medication in severely depressed patients, but its usefulness is limited by its side effects and severe potential to interact with other drugs and foods. MAOI are potent antidepressants that are only used in severe and chronic cases of depression. They are slow to become effective and their effects may persist for a couple of weeks after they are stopped. Any patient on MAOI should be given by their doctor a list of foods and drugs they must avoid. This list must be observed carefully or serious side effects may occur. If taken correctly, they can dramatically improve a depressed patient's life.
See also ANTIDEPRESSANTS, Selegiline.

Maprotiline

TRADE NAME:

Ludiomil.

DRUG CLASS:

Tetracyclic antidepressant.

USES:

Depression.

DOSAGE:

Usually 25mg to 75mg a day. Maximum 150mg.

FORMS:

Tablets of 10mg (cream), 25m (red), 50mg (orange), 75mg (brown).

PRECAUTIONS:

Use with caution in pregnancy and breast feeding. Not recommended in children. Use with caution in heart disease, low blood pressure, bipolar disorder, over active thyroid gland, schizophrenia, suicidal tendencies and chronic constipation.
Use with care if wearing contact lenses.
Regular blood tests to check liver and kidney function necessary.
Do not stop suddenly, but reduce dose slowly.

Do not take if:

- suffering from mania, severe liver or kidney disease, epilepsy, glaucoma, difficulty in passing urine, recent heart attack, heart electrical problems, alcoholism.

SIDE EFFECTS:

Common: slow reactions.
Unusual: skin rash, dry mouth.
Severe but rare (stop medication, consult doctor): convulsions.

INTERACTIONS:

Other drugs:

- MAOI, other antidepressants, antihypertensives, antipsychotics, anaesthetics, benzodiazepines, cimetidine, warfarin, anticholinergics, quinidine, methylphenidate, diabetic medications.

Other substances:

- alcohol.

PRESCRIPTION:

Yes.

PERMITTED IN SPORT:

Yes.

OVERDOSE:

Serious. Symptoms include drowsiness, high blood pressure, rapid heart rate, coma and death. Administer activated charcoal or induce vomiting if tablets taken recently and patient alert. Seek urgent medical assistance. Patients are often observed in intensive care units.

See also ANTIDEPRESSANTS.

Marijuana

OTHER NAMES:

Pot, cannabis, grass, hash, dope, charas, THC (tetrahydrocannabinol).

DRUG CLASS:

Cannabinoid.

USES:

No recognised medical uses in Britain.

Used experimentally for nausea, vomiting, pain relief, intestinal spasm, sedation, epilepsy, glaucoma, high blood pressure and muscle spasm.
Used illegally as a psychoactive drug to cause euphoria (artificial happiness).

FORMS:

Used experimentally as a tablet or mixture. Used illegally in many forms including smoke and cooked in soup or biscuits.

PRECAUTIONS:

Should never be used in pregnancy, breast feeding or children. Marijuana may damage the foetus.

Do not use if:

- suffering from psychiatric disturbances, asthma, chronic lung disease
- driving a car, operating machinery, swimming or undertaking any activity that requires concentration.

SIDE EFFECTS:

Common: unwanted flash backs, sexual disinhibition, drowsiness, palpitations, rapid pulse, dry mouth, sore and red eyes, dizziness, poor concentration, nausea, poor coordination.
Unusual: hallucinations, vomiting, panic attacks, blackouts, perceptual changes, impotence, infertility.
Long term: increased risk of lung cancer (greater risk than with tobacco smoking) and emphysema. Can bring on certain serious mental illnesses (e.g. schizophrenia).

INTERACTIONS:

Other drugs:

- hypnotics, sedatives, heroin.

Other substances:

- increases the effect of alcohol
- may lead to desire for stronger psychoactive drugs.

PRESCRIPTION:

Illegal.

PERMITTED IN SPORT:

No.

OVERDOSE:

May be serious if swallowed in large quantities. Exacerbation of side effects, convulsions and coma may lead rarely to death. Seek urgent medical attention.

OTHER INFORMATION:

Illegal drug of dependence. Toleration may develop quickly (higher dose required to obtain same effect). Possession may lead to criminal charges. Derived from the Indian Hemp plant. Used at least once by about one third of population. Metabolised slowly by the liver and stored in fat. Complete elimination of a single dose may take up to 6 weeks.

See also Heroin.

Measles vaccine

TRADE NAMES:

MMR II, Priorix (with mumps and rubella vaccines).

DRUG CLASS:

Vaccine.

USES:

Prevention of measles (morbilli).

DOSAGE:

 One injection.

FORMS:

Injection.

PRECAUTIONS:

Should not be used in pregnancy (B2), but unintentional use during pregnancy unlikely to have any serious effect. May be used in breast feeding and children. Use with caution if history of febrile convulsions or head injury.

Do not take if:

- suffering from active infection or tuberculosis
- taking drugs for cancer or leukaemia
- recent blood transfusion or globulin injection
- sensitivity to hen eggs or neomycin.

SIDE EFFECTS:

Common: redness, soreness and lump at injection site; fever.
Unusual: rash.

INTERACTIONS:

Other drugs:
- some other vaccines.

PRESCRIPTION:

Yes.

PERMITTED IN SPORT:

Yes.

OVERDOSE:

An unintentional additional dose is unlikely to have any serious effect.

OTHER INFORMATION:

Measles has been eradicated in most countries by immunisation, but a flare up could still occur if immunisation levels in the community drop. In most cases it is a mild disease, but occasionally it can cause brain damage and death. All children should be vaccinated at one and five years of age. An attenuated live virus vaccine.

See also Mumps vaccine, Rubella vaccine.

Mebendazole

TRADE NAMES:

Pripsen Mebendazole, Vermox.

DRUG CLASS:

Anthelmintic (kills worms).

USES:

Threadworm, roundworm, whipworm and hookworm infestations of the intestine.

DOSAGE:

Threadworm: one tablet as a single dose, repeated in two to four weeks.
Other infestations: one tablet twice a day for three days.

FORMS:

Tablets, suspension.

PRECAUTIONS:

Not for use in pregnancy (B3) unless medically necessary. Breast feeding should be ceased before use. May be used in children over two years.

SIDE EFFECTS:

Common: minimal.
Unusual: diarrhoea, vomiting, belly pains, drowsiness, itch, headache, dizziness.
Severe but rare (stop medication, consult doctor): rash, itch.

INTERACTIONS:

Other drugs:
• cimetidine.

PRESCRIPTION:

Yes.

PERMITTED IN SPORT:

Yes.

OVERDOSE:

Exacerbation of side effects plus possible liver damage. Seek medical attention.

OTHER INFORMATION:

Widely, safely and effectively used.
See also Pyrantel embonate.

Mebeverine

TRADE NAMES:

Colofac.
Fybogel Mebeverine (with ispaghula).

DRUG CLASS:

Antispasmodic.

USES:

Spasms of the intestine. Irritable bowel syndrome.

DOSAGE:

One tablet two or three times a day before food.
One sachet twice a day in water 30 minutes before meals.

FORMS:

Tablets of 200mg and 135mg, liquid, granules.

PRECAUTIONS:

Safe use in pregnancy has not been established. Should be used with caution in breast feeding.
Do not take if:
• suffering from angina, heart disease, severe liver disease, severe kidney disease, lactose intolerance.

SIDE EFFECTS:

Common: minimal
Unusual: indigestion, heartburn, dizziness, sleeplessness, loss of appetite, constipation.

INTERACTIONS:

None significant.

PRESCRIPTION:

Yes.

PERMITTED IN SPORT:

Yes.

OVERDOSE:

No significant problems reported.

OTHER INFORMATION:

Very safe, long established and widely used medication.
See also Alverine citrate, Dicyclomine.

Medroxyprogesterone acetate
(MPA)

TRADE NAMES:

Adgyn Medro, Depo Provera, Fartulal, Provera.
Indivina, Tridestra (with oestradiols).
Premique (with oestrogen).

DRUG CLASS:

Sex hormone.

USES:

Endometriosis, cessation of menstrual periods, abnormal bleeding from uterus, breast cancer, cancer of lining of uterus, some types of kidney cancer.
In combination with oestrogen in the treatment of menopause.
Injection used for contraception.

DOSAGE:

 Tablets: half to three or more tablets a day, depending on diagnosis.
Injection: one injection every three months for contraception.

FORMS:

Tablets, injection.

PRECAUTIONS:

Not to be used in pregnancy (D), breast feeding or children.
Use with caution with a history of blood clots in veins, eye disease, diabetes, depression, high blood pressure, heart failure.

Do not take if:

 • suffering from blood clot, stroke, liver disease, undiagnosed breast disease.
• recent abortion performed.

SIDE EFFECTS:

Common: abnormal vaginal bleeding, headache, reduced fertility.
Unusual: sleeplessness, nervousness, dizziness, tremor, rash, sweating, nausea, breast tenderness, weight gain.
Severe but rare (stop medication, consult doctor): blood clot, calf pain, chest pain, yellow skin (jaundice).

INTERACTIONS:

Other drugs:
• anticoagulants, hypoglycaemics, insulin
• may interfere with laboratory tests.

PRESCRIPTION:

Yes.

PERMITTED IN SPORT:

Yes.

OVERDOSE:

Exacerbation of side effects likely.

OTHER INFORMATION:

Injection used for contraception since late 1960s. Tablets very useful for controlling menstrual period problems and delaying periods that may be due at an awkward time.

See also Cyproterone acetate, Danazol, Dydrogesterone, Ethinyloestradiol, Etonogestrel, HORMONE REPLACEMENT THERAPY, Oestradiol, Oestriol, Oestrogen, ORAL CONTRACEPTIVES, Piperazine.

Mefenamic Acid

TRADE NAME:

Ponstan.

DRUG CLASS:

NSAID (Nonsteroidal anti-inflammatory drug).

USES:

Period pain, migraine, osteoarthritis, general pain relief.

DOSAGE:

 250mg to 500mg three times a day with food.

FORMS:

Capsules of 250mg (white & blue), tablets of 500mg (yellow).

PRECAUTIONS:

Should not be used in pregnancy (C) unless medically essential. Breast feeding should be ceased if necessary to use NSAID. Not for use in children under two.

Use with caution in psychiatricaly disturbed patients, epilepsy, severe infection, heart failure and kidney disease.

Lower doses required in elderly, who may suffer more side effects.

Do not take if:

- suffering from peptic ulcer at present or in recent past
- due for surgery (including dental surgery)
- suffering from bleeding disorder or anaemia.

SIDE EFFECTS:

Common: stomach discomfort, diarrhoea, constipation, heartburn, nausea, headache, dizziness.

Unusual: blurred vision, stomach ulcer, ringing noise in ears, retention of fluid, swelling of tissue, drowsiness, itch, rash, shortness of breath.

Severe but rare (stop medication, consult doctor): vomiting blood, passing blood in faeces, other unusual bleeding, asthma induced by medication.

INTERACTIONS:

Other drugs:

- must never be used with anticoagulants (e.g. warfarin)
- probenecid, diuretics, lithium, methotrexate, beta-blockers, ACE inhibitors.

PRESCRIPTION:

Yes.

PERMITTED IN SPORT:

Yes.

OVERDOSE:

Causes nausea, vomiting, severe headache, dizziness, confusion and convulsions. Administer activated charcoal or induce vomiting if taken recently. Seek medical assistance.

OTHER INFORMATION:

Give excellent relief to many women with period pain. Significant side effects (particularly on the stomach) in about 5% of patients. Limit their use.

See also Aspirin, Celecoxib, Diclofenac, Diflunisal, Flurbiprofen, Ibuprofen, Indomethacin, Ketoprofen, Naproxen, NSAID, Piroxicam, Rofecoxib, Sulindac, Tenoxicam, Tiaprofenic Acid.

Mefloquine

TRADE NAME:

Lariam.

DRUG CLASS:

Antimalarial.

USES:

Prevention and treatment of malaria.

DOSAGE:

 Prevention: one tablet a week for one week before entering, and two weeks after leaving malarious country.

Treatment: three tablets at once, then two tablets six hours later.

FORMS:

Tablets (white) of 250mg.

PRECAUTIONS:

May be used in pregnancy (B3) if medically necessary. Breast feeding should be ceased before use. Not designed for use in children under 14 years.

Use with caution in heart disease and epilepsy.

Do not take if:

- suffering from liver or kidney disease, convulsions, psychiatric disturbances.

SIDE EFFECTS:

Common: dizziness, vomiting.
Unusual: giddiness, faints, pins and needles, muscle pain, fever.
Severe but rare (stop medication, consult doctor): psychiatric disturbances.

INTERACTIONS:

Other drugs:
- quinine, chloroquine, anticonvulsants, beta blockers, beta-blockers (e.g. propranolol, atenolol), calcium channel blockers (e.g. verapamil, nifedipine), antihistamines, tricyclic antidepressants, phenothiazines, typhoid oral vaccine.

PRESCRIPTION:

Yes.

PERMITTED IN SPORT:

Yes.

OVERDOSE:

Exacerbation of side effects likely. Administer activated charcoal or induce vomiting if medication taken recently. Seek medical assistance.

OTHER INFORMATION:

Introduced in the late 1980s to combat the increasing incidence of chloroquine resistant malaria. Effective, easy to use and safe.

See also Atovaquone, Artemether and Lumefantrine, Chloroquine, Doxycycline, Hydroxychloroquine, Primaquine, Proguanil, Pyrimethamine, Quinine bisulphate, Sulfadoxine.

Megestrol

TRADE NAME:

Megace.

USES:

Breast cancer, endometriosis.

DOSAGE:

 One tablet four times a day.

FORMS:

Tablet (white) of 40mg and 160mg.

PRECAUTIONS:

Not to be used in pregnancy (D) unless mother's life at risk as damage to foetus possible. Breast feeding must be ceased before use. Not for use in children. Women must use adequate contraception while taking megestrol.
Regular blood tests to check blood sugar level recommended.
Use with caution in blood clots and diabetes.

SIDE EFFECTS:

Common: nausea, weight gain, fluid retention, abnormal vaginal bleeding.
Unusual: vomiting, tumour pain, bone pain, hot flushes.
Severe but rare (stop medication, consult doctor): blood clot in vein.

INTERACTIONS:

None significant.

PRESCRIPTION:

Yes.

OVERDOSE:

Not likely to be serious. Exacerbation of side effects probable. Seek medical attention.

OTHER INFORMATION:

Used to slow the progress of breast cancer as a last resort after it has spread to other organs.

Meloxicam

TRADE NAME:

Mobic.

DRUG CLASS:

Cox-2 inhibitor.

USES:

Osteoarthritis.

DOSAGE:

 7.5mg to 15mg a day.

FORMS:

Tablets of 7.5mg and 15mg.

PRECAUTIONS:

Use with caution in pregnancy (C) and breast feeding.
Not for use in children.
Use with considerable caution with history of peptic ulcer or stomach bleed.
Use with caution with heart failure, liver disease (e.g. cirrhosis), kidney disease (e.g. nephrotic syndrome), high blood pressure, and the elderly.

Do not take if:

• suffering from asthma, urticaria from aspirin, peptic ulcer disease, severe liver or kidney disease
• under 18 years of age.

SIDE EFFECTS:

Common: nausea.
Unusual: dizziness, headache, mouth ulcers.
Severe but rare (stop medication, consult doctor): stomach pain, ulceration or bleeding.

INTERACTIONS:

Other drugs:
• severe interaction with fluconazole, sulphaphenazone, sulfinpyrazone.
• ketoconazole, itraconazole, erythromycin, astemizole, cyclosporin, amiodarone, quinidine, diuretics, other NSAIDs, anticoagulants (e.g. warfarin), methotrexate, oral contraceptives, hypoglycaemics (used for diabetes), cholestyramine.

PRESCRIPTION:

Yes.

PERMITTED IN SPORT:

Yes.

OVERDOSE:

Exacerbation of side effects likely. Induce vomiting or give activated charcoal if swallowed recently. Seek medical attention.

See also Celecoxib, NSAID, Rofecoxib.

Melphalan

TRADE NAME:

Alkeran.

USES:

Cancer of breast and ovary, sarcoma, melanoma, multiple myeloma, polycythaemia vera.

DOSAGE:

 Must be individualised by doctor for each patient depending on disease, severity, age and weight of patient.

FORMS:

Tablets of 2mg and 5mg (white), injection.

PRECAUTIONS:

Must not be used in pregnancy (D) unless medically essential for the life of the woman. Breast feeding must be ceased before use. Not for use in children unless essential for the life of the child.
Regular blood tests to check blood cells essential.

SIDE EFFECTS:

Common: damage to bone marrow and white blood cells, nausea, vomiting, diarrhoea, sore mouth.
Unusual: hair loss, anaemia, lung damage.

Severe but rare (stop medication, consult doctor): severe abnormal bleeding or bruising.

INTERACTIONS:

Other drugs:
• cyclosporin, nalidixic acid.

PRESCRIPTION:

Yes.

PERMITTED IN SPORT:

Yes.

OVERDOSE:

Very serious. Destruction of bone marrow possible, which may lead to fatal infections. Seek urgent medical attention.

Memantine

TRADE NAME:

Ebixa.

USES:

Moderate to severe Alzheimer's disease.

DOSAGE:

 Start with 5mg a day and slowly increase to 10mg twice a day.

FORMS:

Tablets of 10mg (white), drops.

PRECAUTIONS:

Not to be used in pregnancy, breast feeding and children.
Use with caution in kidney disease, epilepsy, recent heart attack, uncontrolled heart failure and uncontrolled high blood pressure.

Do not take if:

 • suffering from severe kidney disease.

SIDE EFFECTS:

Common: dizziness, headache, tiredness.
Unusual: hallucinations, confusion.

INTERACTIONS:

Other drugs:
• amantadine, ketamine, hydrochlorothiazide, dextromethorphan, levodopa, barbiturates, cimetidine, baclofen, dantrolene, ranitidine, quinidine, procainamide, anticholinergics.
Other substances:
• smoking.

PRESCRIPTION:

Yes.

PERMITTED IN SPORT:

Yes.

OTHER INFORMATION:

Released in 2002 as a novel form of treatment to slow the progression of Alzheimer's disease.

Meningococcal vaccine

TRADE NAMES:

Meningivac A+C, Meningitec, NeisVac-C.

DRUG CLASS:

Vaccine.

USES:

Prevention of meningococcal meningitis caused by Neisseria meningitidis. There are more than a dozen strains of the disease. Mencevax ACWY and Menomune protect against strains A, C, W and Y and are mainly used for short term protection in travellers to poorer countries and during epidemics. Meningitec, Menjugate and NeisVac-C protect only against strain C, which is the strain most likely to cause death, and are used for long term prevention of infection in population based programs.

DOSAGE:

Under one year of age: three
injections a month apart.
Over one year of age: one
injection.

FORMS:

Injection.

PRECAUTIONS:

Not designed to be used in pregnancy
(B2), but inadvertent administration is
unlikely to cause any serious adverse
effect.
Use with caution in malaria, bleeding
disorders or impaired immunity.

Do not take if:

• suffering from significant fever.

SIDE EFFECTS:

Common: injection site pain and redness.
Unusual: headache, rash, muscle pains,
irritability, diarrhoea.

INTERACTIONS:

Other drugs:
• other vaccines (administer in different
limb).

PRESCRIPTION:

Yes.

PERMITTED IN SPORT:

Yes.

OVERDOSE:

An inadvertent additional vaccination is
unlikely to have any serious side effects.

Menopausal gonadotrophin, human

See Menotrophin.

Menotrophin (Menopausal gonadotrophin, human)

TRADE NAMES:

Menogon, Menopur, Merional.

DRUG CLASS:

Hormone.

USES:

Male and female infertility. Stimulates
production of sperm and eggs.

DOSAGE:

As determined by doctor for each
patient.

FORMS:

Injection.

PRECAUTIONS:

Not to be used in pregnancy, breast
feeding and children.
Only for use in specific types of female
infertility caused by failure of egg release
from the ovaries.
Regular blood tests to measure hormone
levels essential.
Regular ultrasound scans to assess size of
ovaries essential.

Do not use if:

• suffering from tumour of ovary,
testes or pituitary gland.

SIDE EFFECTS:

Common: ovarian pain, multiple
pregnancy, injection site pain.

INTERACTIONS:

Other drugs:
• sex hormones.

PRESCRIPTION:

Yes.

PERMITTED IN SPORT:

Yes.

Menthol

TRADE NAMES:

Balmosa (with camphor, methyl salicylate and other ingredients).
Frador (with chlorbutol and other ingredients).
Also found in numerous other lotions, creams, ointments etc.

USES:

Relief of muscular pain, relief of nasal congestion, disguising unwanted aromas.

DOSAGE:

 Varies with form. As directed on packaging.

FORMS:

Gel, cream, ointment, lotion, spray.

PRECAUTIONS:

None.

SIDE EFFECTS:

Minimal.

INTERACTIONS:

None significant.

PRESCRIPTION:

No.

PERMITTED IN SPORT:

Yes.

OVERDOSE:

Not a problem.

OTHER INFORMATION:

Used primarily for its aroma and ability to dissolve other medications. Clinical effects probably minimal.

See also Benzydamine, Camphor, Capsaicin, Heparinoid, LINIMENTS.

Meptazinol

TRADE NAME:

Meptid.

DRUG CLASS:

Analgesic.

USES:

Moderate pain.

DOSAGE:

 One tablet every four hours.

FORMS:

Tablets of 200mg (orange), injection.

PRECAUTIONS:

May be used with caution in pregnancy and breast feeding. Not recommended in children.
Use with caution in liver or kidney disease, severe lung disease.
For short term use only.

SIDE EFFECTS:

Common: dizziness, nausea.

INTERACTIONS:

None significant.

PRESCRIPTION:

Yes.

PERMITTED IN SPORT:

No.

OVERDOSE:

Moderately serious. May cause vomiting, drowsiness, convulsions, reduced breathing, coma and very rarely death. Seek urgent medical attention.

See also ANALGESICS.

Mercaptopurine

TRADE NAME:

Puri-Nethol.

USES:

Leukaemia.

DOSAGE:

 Must be individualised for each patient by doctor depending on response.

FORMS:

Tablets (fawn) of 50mg.

PRECAUTIONS:

Must not be used in pregnancy (D) unless the mother's life is at risk as the foetus may be damaged. Breast feeding must be ceased before use. May be used with caution in children.
Adequate contraception must be used by women taking mercaptopurine.
Regular blood tests to check blood cells and liver function essential.

SIDE EFFECTS:

Common: liver and bone marrow damage.
Unusual: loss of appetite, nausea, vomiting, mouth ulcers.
Severe but rare (stop medication, consult doctor): yellow skin (jaundice), unusual bleeding or bruising.

INTERACTIONS:

Other drugs:
• allopurinol, warfarin, sulfonamides, tranquillisers.

PRESCRIPTION:

Yes.

PERMITTED IN SPORT:

Yes.

OVERDOSE:

May cause fatal damage to liver or bone marrow. Administer activated charcoal or induce vomiting if medication taken recently. Seek urgent medical assistance.

OTHER INFORMATION:

Despite serious side effects, mercaptopurine may save or prolong life in patients with leukaemia.
See also VINCA ALKALOIDS.

Meropenem

TRADE NAME:

Meronem.

DRUG CLASS:

Antibiotic.

USES:

Serious bacterial infections.

DOSAGE:

 500mg to 1000mg by drip into a vein every eight hours.

FORMS:

Injection.

PRECAUTIONS:

Use with caution in pregnancy (B2), breast feeding and infants.
Use with caution in Pseudomonas infections, liver and kidney disease.

SIDE EFFECTS:

Common: injection site redness and pain, diarrhoea.
Unusual: liver damage, large bowel damage, growth of resistant bacteria, damage to white blood cells.
Severe but rare (stop medication, consult doctor): unusual bleeding or bruising.

INTERACTIONS:

Other drugs:
• probenecid, valproic acid.

PRESCRIPTION:

Yes.

PERMITTED IN SPORT:
Yes.

OTHER INFORMATION:
Used only in hospital.

Mesalazine
(Aminosalicylic Acid)

TRADE NAMES:
Asacol, Ipocol, Pentasa, Salofalk.

DRUG CLASS:
Bowel anti-inflammatory.

USES:
Ulcerative colitis, Crohn's disease, other forms of bowel inflammation.

DOSAGE:
 One or two tablets 30 minutes before meals three times a day with plenty of fluid.

FORMS:
Tablet, enema, foam enema, suppositories, granules.

PRECAUTIONS:
Should not be used near the end of pregnancy (C). Should not be used in breast feeding.
Not recommended in children.
Use lower dose in elderly.
Use with caution in patients with liver disease and kidney disease.
Regular blood tests necessary to check for cell damage, liver and kidney function.
Do not take if:
 • allergic to aspirin or salicylates
• suffering from severe kidney or liver disease, peptic ulcer or bleeding disorder.

SIDE EFFECTS:
Common: headache, nausea, rash, belly pains, diarrhoea.

Unusual: kidney damage, pancreas inflammation.
Severe but rare (stop medication, consult doctor): unexplained bleeding or bruising, severe belly pain (pancreatitis).

INTERACTIONS:
Other drugs:
• do not use with lactulose or anticoagulants
• interacts with sulfonylureas, methotrexate, warfarin, frusemide, spironolactone, rifampicin, azathioprine and probenecid.

PRESCRIPTION:
Yes.

PERMITTED IN SPORT:
Yes.

OTHER INFORMATION:
Very effective medication for a number of uncommon diseases.
See also Olsalazine.

Mesna

TRADE NAME:
Uromitexan.

USES:
Prevents damage to lining of urinary tract and kidney that may be caused by powerful anticancer (cytotoxic) drugs.

DOSAGE:
 As determined by doctor individually for each patient.

FORMS:
Injection, tablets (white) of 400 and 600mg.

PRECAUTIONS:
May be used in pregnancy (B1), breast feeding and children.
Use with care in autoimmune diseases.

SIDE EFFECTS:

Common: nausea, diarrhoea.
Unusual: allergy reactions, headache, tiredness.

INTERACTIONS:

Adversely effects laboratory tests on urine.

PRESCRIPTION:

Yes.

PERMITTED IN SPORT:

Yes.

OVERDOSE:

Unlikely to be serious.

Mesterolone

TRADE NAME:

Pro-viron.

DRUG CLASS:

Sex hormone.

USES:

Male infertility, male impotence.

DOSAGE:

 One tablet, one to three times a day.

FORMS:

Tablets of 25mg (white).

PRECAUTIONS:

Not to be used in women or children. Use with caution in prostate disease.

Do not take if:

 • suffering from prostate cancer or liver tumour.

SIDE EFFECTS:

Common: minimal
Unusual: prolonged penile erection.

INTERACTIONS:

None significant.

PRESCRIPTION:

Yes.

PERMITTED IN SPORT:

No.

OVERDOSE:

Painful, damaging, prolonged penile erection possible. Induce vomiting or administer activated charcoal if taken recently. Seek medical attention.

See also Testosterone.

Mestranol

See ORAL CONTRACEPTIVES.

Metformin

TRADE NAME:

Glucophage.

DRUG CLASS:

Hypoglycaemic.

USES:

Diabetes not requiring Insulin injections.

DOSAGE:

 One or two tablets, two or three times a day before meals.
Do not vary from prescribed dose without reference to a doctor.

FORMS:

Tablets of 500mg (white).

PRECAUTIONS:

Not to be used in pregnancy (C), breast feeding or children.
Annual blood tests to check for pernicious anaemia recommended.
Illness, changes in diet, exercise and stress may change dosage requirements.
Lower doses required in elderly and debilitated patients.

Strict control of carbohydrates and sugars in diet essential.

Do not take if:

- suffering from type one diabetes, severe heart disease, blood clot in lungs, pancreatitis, alcoholism, severe liver or kidney disease, recent surgery, severe infection
- using Insulin.

SIDE EFFECTS:

Common: uncommon.
Unusual: nausea, vomiting, belly discomfort, weakness.
Severe but rare (stop medication, consult doctor): low blood sugar (see Overdose below), yellow skin (jaundice), unusual bleeding or bruising, rash.

INTERACTIONS:

Other drugs:
- cimetidine, other hypoglycaemics, beta-blockers, diclofenac, ACE inhibitors, corticosteroids, anticoagulants (e.g. warfarin), thiazide diuretics, thyroxine.
Other substances:
- reacts adversely with alcohol.
Herbs:
- alfalfa, celery, eucalyptus, fenugreek, garlic, ginger, ginseng, karela.

PRESCRIPTION:

Yes.

PERMITTED IN SPORT:

Yes.

OVERDOSE:

Serious. Symptoms of low blood sugar (hypoglycaemia) may include tiredness, confusion, chills, palpitations, sweating, vomiting, dizziness, hunger, blurred vision and fainting. Significant overdosage can lead to coma and death. Give sugary drinks or sweets if conscious. Seek emergency medical assistance.

OTHER INFORMATION:

Used mainly in elderly patients who develop maturity onset diabetes that is not severe enough to require insulin injections.

See also Acarbose, Glibenclamide, Gliclazide, Glipizide, Gliquidone, INSULINS, Repaglinide, Rosiglitazone.

Methadone

TRADE NAME:

Physeptone.

DRUG CLASS:

Narcotic, Analgesic.

USES:

Severe pain, narcotic addiction.

DOSAGE:

One or two tablets every six to eight hours. 2mLs to 10mLs of syrup a day.

FORMS:

Tablets (white) of 5mg, injection.

PRECAUTIONS:

Not to be used in the last stages of pregnancy (C) as methadone may cause the newborn infant to have difficulty in breathing. Use with caution in breast feeding and children.
Not designed for prolonged use.

Do not take if:

- suffering from severe lung disease
- operating machinery or driving a vehicle.

SIDE EFFECTS:

Common: dizziness, drowsiness, vomiting, mood changes.
Unusual: difficulty in breathing.

INTERACTIONS:

Other drugs:
- MAOI, rifampicin, phenytoin, carbamazepine, propranolol.
Other substances:
- alcohol should not be used with

methadone.

PRESCRIPTION:

Yes (very restricted).

PERMITTED IN SPORT:

No.

OVERDOSE:

Serious. Symptoms may not appear for some hours after medication taken and may include drowsiness, difficulty in breathing and coma. Administer activated charcoal or induce vomiting if medication taken recently and patient alert. Seek urgent medical attention. Antidote available.

OTHER INFORMATION:

Used in a slowly reducing dose to ease heroin addicts off their addiction. May itself be addictive if used inappropriately.

See also Alfentanil, Buprenorphine, Codeine, Dextromoramide, Dextropropoxyphene, Fentanyl, Heroin, Hydromorphone, Morphine, Oxycodone, Pentazocine, Pethidine.

Methionine

TRADE NAMES:

Methionine.
Paradote (with paracetamol).

DRUG CLASS:

Antidote.

USES:

Counteracts overdosage with Paracetamol, liver damage.
Paradote combines paracetamol and methionine to prevent liver damage in case of overdose.

DOSAGE:

 Paracetamol overdose: five tablets at once, repeated at four hour intervals for a total of four doses. Paradote: two every four hours to a maximum of eight a day.

FORMS:

Tablets.

PRECAUTIONS:

May be used in pregnancy, breast feeding and children.
Administer activated charcoal or induce vomiting if medication or poison taken recently.
Treatment must be undertaken immediately after vomiting has been successfully induced, before any signs of poisoning are evident.
Medication does not replace hospital care and other treatments.
Hospitals usually measure levels of paracetamol before starting specific treatment.

SIDE EFFECTS:

Minimal.

INTERACTIONS:

None significant.

PRESCRIPTION:

No.

PERMITTED IN SPORT:

Yes.

OTHER INFORMATION:

Overdosage with paracetamol may cause fatal liver damage. Methionine may prevent this damage if given within ten hours of the overdose being taken.

Methocarbamol

TRADE NAME:

Robaxin.

USES:

Muscle spasms.

DOSAGE:

 Two tablets, four times a day.

FORMS:

Tablets (white) of 750mg.

PRECAUTIONS:

Use with caution in pregnancy and breast feeding. Not recommended in children.
Use with caution in kidney and liver disease.

Do not take if:

 • suffering from brain damage, epilepsy, myasthenia gravis or in a coma.

SIDE EFFECTS:

Common: drowsiness.
Unusual: allergic reaction.

INTERACTIONS:

Other drugs:
• sedatives, stimulants, anticholinergics.
Other substances:
• alcohol.

PRESCRIPTION:

Yes.

PERMITTED IN SPORT:

Yes.

Methotrexate

TRADE NAME:

Maxtrex.

USES:

Numerous types of cancer including cancer of breast and uterus, leukaemia, severe psoriasis, severe rheumatoid arthritis.

DOSAGE:

Must be individualised for each patient by doctor depending on disease, severity and weight of patient. Often given once a week.

FORMS:

Tablets of 2.5 and 10mg (yellow), injection.

PRECAUTIONS:

Must not be used in pregnancy (D) unless mother's life is at risk, as the foetus may be damaged. Breast feeding must be ceased before use. May be used in children if medically essential.
Regular blood tests to check blood cells and liver function are essential.
Adequate contraception must be used by women while Methotrexate is being taken.
Use with caution in infection, peptic ulcer and ulcerative colitis.

Do not take if:

• suffering from severe liver or kidney disease, significant infection, bone marrow disease, low level of white blood cells, low level of blood platelets, significant anaemia, immune deficiency (e.g. AIDS), alcoholism.

SIDE EFFECTS:

Common: mouth ulcers, nausea, belly pains, diarrhoea.
Unusual: tiredness, chills, dizziness, reduced resistance to infection, rash, infertility.
Severe but rare (stop medication, consult doctor): yellow skin (jaundice), unusual bleeding or bruising, bone marrow damage, vision changes.

INTERACTIONS:

Other drugs:
• NSAID, aspirin, sulfonamides, phenytoin, tetracyclines, chloramphenicol, folic acid, probenecid, co-trimoxazole, NSAIDs, drugs used to lower cholesterol levels, other cytotoxics.
Herbs:
• echinacea, willow bark.

PRESCRIPTION:

Yes.

PERMITTED IN SPORT:

Yes.

OVERDOSE:

Serious. Administer activated charcoal or induce vomiting if medication taken recently. Seek urgent medical assistance. Antidote available (calcium folinate).

OTHER INFORMATION:

Despite risk of significant side effects, methotrexate may save the life, or improve the quality of life, of many patients.

See also Hydroxyurea, Thioguanine.

Methotrimeprazine

See PHENOTHIAZINES.

Methyl aminolaevulinate

TRADE NAME:

Metvix.

USES:

Keratoses of skin, some forms of basal cell carcinoma (BCC).

DOSAGE:

 Apply thin layer to spot and 5mm around with spatula (flat stick). Cover with dressing for three hours. Remove dressing, clean skin with saline, then expose to special frequency red light.

FORMS:

Cream.

PRECAUTIONS:

Not for use in pregnancy, breast feeding and children.
Must only be used under specialist doctor supervision.
Avoid ultraviolet light.

Do not take if:

 • suffering from porphyria, some forms of BCC.

SIDE EFFECTS:

Common: local skin burning and irritation.

INTERACTIONS:

None significant.

PRESCRIPTION:

Yes.

PERMITTED IN SPORT:

Yes.

OTHER INFORMATION:

Introduced in 2002 for treatment of keratoses and BCC when other treatments inappropriate.

Methylcellulose

TRADE NAME:

Celevac.

DRUG CLASS:

Fibre.

USES:

Constipation, fibre supplementation, appetite suppression, diverticulitis.

DOSAGE:

 Two to five tablets three times a day with water before meals.

FORMS:

Tablets (pink).

PRECAUTIONS:

Safe in pregnancy and breast feeding.
Ensure adequate fluid intake.
Not recommended for children.

Do not take if:

 • suffering from bowel blockage.

SIDE EFFECTS:

Common: loose bulky motions.

INTERACTIONS:

Other drugs:
• may affect the absorption of a wide range of medications.

PRESCRIPTION:

No.

PERMITTED IN SPORT:

Yes.

OVERDOSE:

No adverse effects likely.

OTHER INFORMATION:

Totally inactive in body and merely acts to add bulk to faeces.

See also See Frangula, Ispaghula, Pectin, Psyllium, Sterculia.

Methyldopa

TRADE NAME:

Aldomet.

DRUG CLASS:

Antihypertensive.

USES:

High blood pressure.

DOSAGE:

 One or two tablets two or three times a day to a maximum of 3000mg a day.

FORMS:

Tablets of 125mg, 250mg and 500mg (yellow).

PRECAUTIONS:

Safe in pregnancy (A), breast feeding and children.
Should be used with caution in patients with a history of depression.

Do not take if:

 • suffering from liver disease.

SIDE EFFECTS:

Common: fever, sedation, headache.
Unusual: aggravation of angina, swelling of tissues.
Severe but rare (stop medication, consult doctor): unusual bleeding, severe tiredness.

INTERACTIONS:

Other drugs:
• significant interaction with MAOI
• interacts with some anaesthetics, lithium and other medications that lower blood pressure.
Other substances:
• smoking aggravates high blood pressure.

PRESCRIPTION:

Yes.

PERMITTED IN SPORT:

Yes.

OVERDOSE:

Causes low blood pressure, sedation, weakness, dizziness, slow heart rate, diarrhoea, nausea and vomiting. Rarely fatal. If taken recently, administer activated charcoal or induce vomiting. If taken more than two hours earlier, give patient additional fluids. Seek medical assistance.

OTHER INFORMATION:

An oldie but a goodie. One of the first effective treatments for high blood pressure.

See also ANTIHYPERTENSIVES.

Methylphenidate

TRADE NAMES:

Concerta XL, Equasym, Ritalin, Tranquilyn.

DRUG CLASS:

Stimulant.

USES:

Attention deficit hyperactivity disorder, narcolepsy.

DOSAGE:

 Individualised. Start with low dose and gradually increase as determined by doctor until adequate response obtained.

FORMS:

Tablets of 5, 10 and 20mg.

PRECAUTIONS:

Not for use in pregnancy unless medically essential. Not for use in breast feeding. Not for use in children under six years. Use with caution in high blood pressure and epilepsy.
If possible, should not be used for prolonged periods of time.

Do not take if:

 • suffering from depression, psychoses, anxiety, agitation, twitches, Tourette syndrome, glaucoma, overactive thyroid gland, irregular heart beat or angina.

SIDE EFFECTS:

Common: sleeplessness, irritability, drowsiness, loss of appetite, belly pains, nausea, tolerance and dependency.
Unusual: vomiting, irregular heart beat, rash, growth retardation, blurred vision, psychiatric disturbances, angina, fever, hair loss, liver damage.

INTERACTIONS:

Other drugs:
• tricyclic antidepressants, MAOI, anticoagulants (e.g. warfarin), anticonvulsants, phenylbutazone, guanethidine, medications for treatment of high blood pressure.
Other substances:
• alcohol.

PRESCRIPTION:

Yes (restricted).

PERMITTED IN SPORT:

No.

OVERDOSE:

Very serious. May cause vomiting, agitation, tremors, twitching, confusion, hallucinations, convulsions, coma and death. Administer activated charcoal or induce vomiting if tablets taken recently. Seek urgent medical attention.

OTHER INFORMATION:

May cause dependence and addiction if used inappropriately. May make a dramatic improvement in the quality of life for some hyperactive children and their parents, but use is still controversial as correct diagnosis of ADHD is difficult to determine.

Methylprednisolone

TRADE NAMES:

Depo-Medrone, Medrone, Solu-Medrone.
Depo-Medrone with Lidocaine (with lidocaine).

DRUG CLASS:

Corticosteroid.

USES:

Severe asthma, rheumatoid and other forms of severe arthritis, autoimmune diseases (e.g. Sjögren Syndrome), severe allergy reactions and other severe and chronic inflammatory diseases.

DOSAGE:

 Tablets: strictly as directed by doctor.

FORMS:

Tablets, injection.

PRECAUTIONS:

Should be used in pregnancy (C), breast feeding and children only on specific medical advice.

Use with caution if under stress and in patients with under active thyroid gland, liver disease, diverticulitis, high blood pressure, myasthenia gravis or kidney disease.

Use for shortest period of time possible. Medication should not be ceased abruptly, but dosage should be slowly reduced.

Do not use if:

- suffering from any form of infection, peptic ulcer or osteoporosis.
- having a vaccination

SIDE EFFECTS:

Most significant side effects occur only with prolonged use.

Common: bloating, weight gain, rashes and intestinal disturbances.

Unusual: biochemical disturbances of blood, muscle weakness, bone weakness, impaired wound healing, skin thinning, tendon weakness, peptic ulcers, gullet ulcers, bruising, increased sweating, loss of fat under skin, premature ageing, excess facial hair growth in women, pigmentation of skin and nails, acne, convulsions, headaches, dizziness, growth suppression in children, aggravation of diabetes, worsening of infections, cataracts, aggravation of glaucoma, blood clots in veins and sleeplessness.

Severe but rare (stop medication, consult doctor): any significant side effect should be reported to a doctor immediately.

INTERACTIONS:

Other drugs:
- tablets: oral contraceptives, barbiturates, phenytoin, rifampicin.

PRESCRIPTION:

Yes.

PERMITTED IN SPORT:

No.

OVERDOSE:

Medical treatment is required. Serious effects and death rare.

OTHER INFORMATION:

Extremely effective and useful medication if used correctly. Tablets must be used with extreme care under strict medical supervision. Lowest dose and shortest possible course should be used. Not addictive.

Methyl salicylate

TRADE NAMES:

Balmosa (with menthol, camphor and other ingredients).
Monophytol (with propyl salicylate, salicylic acid, chlorbutol, methyl undecenoate and other ingredients).
Radian B (with menthol, camphor, aspirin).

DRUG CLASS:

Rubefacient.

USES:

Temporary relief of pain (e.g. muscular, arthritic, gums).
Monophytol is used for skin fungal infections.

DOSAGE:

 Massage into clean dry skin two or three times a day.

FORMS:

Cream, paint, lotion.

PRECAUTIONS:

Safe in pregnancy and breast feeding. Use with caution in children under five years.
Avoid contact with eyes, mouth, nose, anus and vagina.

Use sparingly on face, skin folds and thin skin.

May stain clothing.

Do not use if:

- suffering from broken or infected skin.

SIDE EFFECTS:

Minimal.

INTERACTIONS:

None significant.

PRESCRIPTION:

No.

PERMITTED IN SPORT:

Yes.

OVERDOSE:

May have serious effects in the unlikely event of the liniment being swallowed.

See also Aspirin (Acetylsalicylic acid), Balsalazide, KERATOLYTICS, Salicylates.

Methyl undecenoate

TRADE NAME:

Monophytol (with chlorbutol, salicylic acid and other ingredients).

DRUG CLASS:

Antifungal.

USES:

Fungal infections of feet (athlete's foot).

DOSAGE:

 Apply twice daily until two weeks after condition has settled, then once a week.

FORMS:

Paint.

PRECAUTIONS:

Not for use in pregnancy, breast feeding and children.

SIDE EFFECTS:

Common: minimal.
Unusual: skin irritation.

INTERACTIONS:

None significant.

PRESCRIPTION:

No.

PERMITTED IN SPORT:

Yes.

See also ANTIFUNGALS.

Methysergide

TRADE NAME:

Deseril.

DRUG CLASS:

Antimigraine.

USES:

Prevention of migraine and cluster headaches.

DOSAGE:

 One to four tablets, two or three times a day with food.

FORMS:

Tablets of 1mg (white).

PRECAUTIONS:

Should not be used in pregnancy (C), breast feeding or children.

Sudden cessation may cause rebound migraine, reduce dosage slowly when ceasing.

Do not take if:

- suffering from poor circulation to arms and legs, poor circulation to heart, hardening of arteries, vein inflammation, severe infections, high blood pressure, collagen diseases, severe kidney or liver disease, urinary tract disease
- do not take constantly for more than six months.

SIDE EFFECTS:

Common: nausea, vomiting.
Unusual: sleeplessness, dizziness, rash, tissue swelling, chest pain, belly pain, pins and needles sensation.
Severe but rare (stop medication, consult doctor): difficulty in producing urine, backache, pain on passing urine, poor blood supply to legs.

INTERACTIONS:

None significant.

PRESCRIPTION:

Yes.

PERMITTED IN SPORT:

Yes.

OVERDOSE:

Administer activated charcoal or induce vomiting if tablets taken recently. Symptoms include vomiting, diarrhoea, thirst, cold skin, itch, rapid weak pulse, tingling, confusion. Seek medical assistance.

OTHER INFORMATION:

One of several medications that may be used to prevent migraines. Trial and error between these medications if often necessary to find the best one. Because of very rare but serious complications with long term use (retroperitoneal fibrosis, scar tissue forming at back of belly around kidneys), methysergide is often towards the bottom of the list of medications considered.
See also Pizotifen.

Metipranolol

TRADE NAME:

Minims Metipranolol.

DRUG CLASS:

Beta-blocker.

USES:

Glaucoma, increased pressure in eye.

DOSAGE:

 One drop in eye twice a day.

FORMS:

Eye drop in single dose package.

PRECAUTIONS:

May be used with caution in pregnancy, breast feeding and children.
Use with caution with heart diseases.
Do not take if:
 • suffering from asthma, heart failure, slow heart rate.

SIDE EFFECTS:

Common: stinging in eye.
Unusual: headache.
Severe but rare (stop medication, consult doctor): slow heart rate, asthma.

INTERACTIONS:

Other drugs:
• other beta-blockers, verapamil.

PRESCRIPTION:

Yes.

PERMITTED IN SPORT:

No.
See also BETA-BLOCKERS, Timolol.

Metoclopramide

TRADE NAMES:

Gastrobid Continus, Maxolon.
Migramax (with aspirin).
Paramax (with paracetamol).

DRUG CLASS:

Antiemetic.

USES:

Nausea, vomiting, during investigative procedures.

DOSAGE:

 One tablet three times a day.

FORMS:

Tablets, syrup, injection.

PRECAUTIONS:

Safe in pregnancy (A), breast feeding and children.
Use with caution in epilepsy, liver and kidney disease.
Lower doses required in elderly.
Do not persist with medication if vomiting continues, but seek further medical assessment.

Do not take if:

 • suffering from phaeochromocytoma.

SIDE EFFECTS:

Common: drowsiness, restlessness, tiredness.
Unusual: sleeplessness, headache, dizziness, diarrhoea.
Severe but rare (stop medication, consult doctor): incoordination, twitching, muscle spasms.

INTERACTIONS:

Other drugs:
• narcotics, sedatives, anticholinergics, tetracycline, L-dopa, digoxin.
Other substances:
• reacts adversely with alcohol.

PRESCRIPTION:

Yes.

PERMITTED IN SPORT:

Yes.

OVERDOSE:

Abnormal muscle twitching, muscle spasms and incoordination may occur.
Seek medical advice.

OTHER INFORMATION:

Very widely used, safe and effective medication. Does not cause addiction or dependence.

See also Domperidone, Prochlorperazine, Promethazine.

Metolazone

See THIAZIDE DIURETICS.

Metoprolol

TRADE NAMES:

Betaloc, Lopresor.
Co-Betaloc (with hydrochlorothiazide).

DRUG CLASS:

Beta-blocker.

USES:

High blood pressure, angina, rapid heart rate, irregular heart beat, paroxysmal atrial tachycardia, heart attack, overactive thyroid gland.

DOSAGE:

 50 to 400mg a day in divided doses.

FORMS:

Tablets.

PRECAUTIONS:

Should be used in pregnancy (C) only if medically essential.
Safe to use in breast feeding.
May be used with caution in children.
Use with care if suffering from alcoholism, diabetes, prinzmetal angina, over active thyroid gland, liver or kidney failure or about to have surgery.

Do not take if:

 • suffering from asthma or allergic conditions
• suffering from heart failure,

shock, slow heart rate, enlarged right side of heart or phaeochromocytoma
• if undertaking prolonged fast.

SIDE EFFECTS:

Common: low blood pressure, slow heart rate, cold hands and feet, asthma.
Unusual: loss of appetite, nausea, diarrhoea, impotence, tiredness, sleeplessness, nightmares, rash, loss of libido, hair loss, noises in ears.
Severe but rare (stop medication, consult doctor): severe asthma.

INTERACTIONS:

Other drugs:
• calcium channel blockers, prazosin, MAOI, disopyramide, clonidine, adrenaline, other medications for irregular heart beat, lignocaine, ergotamine, indomethacin, chlorpromazine.

PRESCRIPTION:

Yes.

PERMITTED IN SPORT:

No.

OVERDOSE:

Slow heart rate, low blood pressure, asthma and heart failure may result. Administer activated charcoal or induce vomiting if tablets taken recently. Use salbutamol or other asthma sprays for difficulty in breathing. Seek medical assistance.

OTHER INFORMATION:

Except for asthmatics, very safe and effective. First released in 1970s.

See also Atenolol, BETA-BLOCKERS, Carvedilol, Esmolol, Labetalol, Oxprenolol, Pindolol, Propranolol, Sotalol.

Metronidazole

TRADE NAMES:

Acea, Anabact, Flagyl, Metrogel, Metrosa, Metrotop, Rozex, Zidoval, Zyomet.
Flagyl Compak (with nystatin).
Helimet (with lansoprazole and clarithromycin).

DRUG CLASS:

Antibiotic.

USES:

Bacterial infections of gut and vagina, particularly Giardiasis of gut and Trichomonal infections of vagina.
Acne rosacea.

DOSAGE:

Tablets: one or two tablets three times a day.
Gel and ointment: apply thinly twice daily after washing.

FORMS:

Tablets, suppository, ointment, gel, suspension, infusion.

PRECAUTIONS:

Use with caution in pregnancy (B2) and breast feeding. Safe to use in children.
Avoid eyes, nostrils, mouth, vagina and anus with skin preparations.
Not designed for long term use.
Use with caution in kidney and liver disease.

Do not take if:

• suffering from brain disease, blood cell abnormalities.

SIDE EFFECTS:

Common: tablets—bad taste, nausea, diarrhoea, headache.
Skin preparations—redness, dryness, burning, irritation.
Unusual: vomiting, loss of appetite, belly discomfort.

INTERACTIONS:

Other drugs:
- skin preparations have minimal interactions
- warfarin, cyclophosphamide, phenytoin, phenobarbitone, cimetidine, lithium, cyclosporin, 5-fluorouracil.

Other substances:
- reacts adversely with alcohol
- may affect some laboratory blood test results.

PRESCRIPTION:

Yes.

PERMITTED IN SPORT:

Yes.

OVERDOSE:

With tablet overdosage disorientation and vomiting only likely effects.

OTHER INFORMATION:

Widely used. Very safe and effective. Often used in combination with other antibiotics for infections of female pelvic organs. Most effective treatment for the unusual skin condition of acne rosacea. Bad taste with tablets occurs in virtually every patient, as drug comes to taste buds on tongue through blood stream and not from mouth, and so cannot usually be removed by sucking pleasantly flavoured sweets.

See also Tinidazole.

Metyrapone

TRADE NAME:

Metopirone.

USES:

Diagnosis of adrenal gland dysfunction, hyperaldosteronism, Cushing syndrome.

DOSAGE:

 Strictly as directed and determined by doctor.

FORMS:

Capsules (cream) of 250mg.

PRECAUTIONS:

Use with care (B2) in pregnancy, breast feeding and children.
Use with care in liver, pituitary gland and thyroid disease.

Do not take if:

 • suffering from adrenocortical insufficiency.

SIDE EFFECTS:

Common: nausea, diarrhoea, dizziness, sedation, headache.
Unusual: low blood pressure, belly pain, excess hair growth.

INTERACTIONS:

Other drugs:
- may interact with numerous medications.

PRESCRIPTION:

Yes.

PERMITTED IN SPORT:

Yes.

OVERDOSE:

Very serious damage to numerous glands may occur.

OTHER INFORMATION:

Normally only used in hospitals as a diagnostic tool.

Mexiletine

TRADE NAME:

Mexitil.

DRUG CLASS:

Antiarrhythmic.

USES:

Serious heart beat irregularities in the heart ventricles.

DOSAGE:

 Variable from one patient to another. Usually about 200mg three times a day. Follow doctors instructions carefully.

FORMS:

Capsules of 50mg (red/purple), 200mg (red) and 360mg (red/turquoise), injection.

PRECAUTIONS:

Should be used with caution in pregnancy (B1) and breast feeding. Not designed for use in children.
Use with caution with low blood pressure, slow heart rate, liver or kidney failure.
Should not be stopped suddenly, but dose should be slowly decreased over several days.

Do not take if:

- suffering from recent heart attack
- you are hypersensitive to local anaesthetics.

SIDE EFFECTS:

Common: usually only on commencement of medication due to blood concentrations being too high. Minimal on long term use.
Unusual: nausea, vomiting, hiccups, bad tastes, drowsiness, confusion, dizziness, double vision, tremor, blurred vision, palpitations.

INTERACTIONS:

Other drugs:
- other medications that treat heart rhythm irregularities
- theophylline, warfarin, narcotics.
Other substances:
- reacts with alcohol and caffeine.

PRESCRIPTION:

Yes.

PERMITTED IN SPORT:

Yes.

OVERDOSE:

Very serious. Administer activated charcoal or induce vomiting if tablets taken recently. Seek urgent medical assistance. Symptoms may include vomiting, drowsiness, confusion, slow heart rate, heart attack and death.
See also Amiodarone, Disopyramide, Flecainide, Procainamide, Quinidine, Sotalol, Verapamil.

Miconazole

TRADE NAMES:

Daktarin, Gyno-Daktarin.
Daktacort (with hydrocortisone).

DRUG CLASS:

Imidazole antifungal.

USES:

Treatment of fungal infections of skin (tinea, athlete's foot, pityriasis versicolor), vagina (thrush) and mouth (oral thrush).

DOSAGE:

 Skin and mouth: apply two or three times a day.
Vagina: insert pessary or cream once a day at night.

FORMS:

Cream, mouth gel, vaginal pessaries and cream.

PRECAUTIONS:

Safe to use in pregnancy (A), breast feeding and children.
Should not be used in eyes.
Use with care on open wounds.

SIDE EFFECTS:

Common: none.
Unusual: skin irritation, rash.

INTERACTIONS:

None significant.

PRESCRIPTION:

No.

PERMITTED IN SPORT:

Yes.

OTHER INFORMATION:

This class of medication dramatically improved the treatment of fungal infections when introduced in the early 1970s. Very safe and effective.

See Clotrimazole, Econazole, Fluconazole, Itraconazole, Ketoconazole, Sulconazole.

Midazolam

TRADE NAME:

Hypnovel.

DRUG CLASS:

Sedative/Hypnotic, Benzodiazepine.

USES:

Short acting sedation for procedures (e.g. Gastroscopy), continuous sedation of acutely ill patients, sedation prior to anaesthesia.

DOSAGE:

 As given by doctor.

FORMS:

Injection.

PRECAUTIONS:

Should be used with caution in pregnancy (C), but not at all if delivery of infant imminent as it may decrease desire to breathe in newborn infant. Should be used with caution in breast feeding and children.

Do not take if:

 • suffering from myasthenia gravis, shock, alcoholism or glaucoma.

SIDE EFFECTS:

Common: reduces lung and heart activity.
Rare: hiccups, nausea, vomiting, memory loss of events immediately before and after injection.

INTERACTIONS:

Other drugs:
• cimetidine, erythromycin, other sedatives, sodium valproate.
Herbs:
• guarana, kava kava, passionflower, St John's wort, valerian, celery, camomile, goldenseal.
Other substances:
• reacts adversely with alcohol.

PRESCRIPTION:

Yes.

OTHER INFORMATION:

Excellent medication to allow many non-painful but uncomfortable and frightening procedures to be performed with minimal risk.

See also BARBITURATES, Flunitrazepam, Nitrazepam, Temazepam.

Mifepristone
(RU486)

TRADE NAME:

Mifegyne.

USES:

Termination of pregnancy up to 49 days after last menstrual period.

DOSAGE:

 Three tablets taken once. Often followed two days later by a prostaglandin.

FORMS:

Tablets of 200mg (yellow).

PRECAUTIONS:

Not to be used in pregnancy (X) unless termination of pregnancy desired.
Not to be used in breast feeding and children.
Follow up visit at 12 to 14 days after taking drug essential to confirm complete abortion.

Do not take if:

- suffering from bleeding disorders.

SIDE EFFECTS:

Common: nausea, vomiting, diarrhoea, chills, fever. Abdominal pain, cramping and vaginal bleeding, from the abortion process.
Unusual: excessive vaginal bleeding, incomplete abortion,ongoing pregnancy which requires an abortion.
Severe but rare (stop medication, consult doctor): torrential vaginal bleeding.

INTERACTIONS:

None significant.

PRESCRIPTION:

Yes.

PERMITTED IN SPORT:

Yes.

OTHER INFORMATION:

Introduced in France in 1988, this medication has been surrounded by controversy because of its action, but despite this, it is a safe and effective way of terminating a pregnancy. Usually used in conjunction with misoprostol, which causes contraction of the uterus.

See also Amiodarone, Disopyramide, Mexiletine, Quinidine, Sotalol, Verapamil.

MINERALS

DISCUSSION:

Minerals are inorganic substances (i.e. not vegetable or animal in origin) that are necessary for the normal functioning of the body.

See Calcium, Copper, Fluoride, Iodine, Iron, Magnesium, Phosphorus, Potassium, Selenomethionine (Selenium), Zinc.

MINI-PILL

See Norethisterone.

Minocycline

TRADE NAMES:

Aknemin, Minocin.

DRUG CLASS:

Tetracycline antibiotic.

USES:

Infections caused by susceptible bacteria, prevention and treatment of acne.

DOSAGE:

Treatment: 100mg a day.
Prevention: 50mg a day.

FORMS:

Capsules of 50mg and 100mg, tablets of 50mg, injection.

PRECAUTIONS:

Not to be used in pregnancy (D) or children under twelve as Minocycline may cause permanent staining of teeth of foetus or child. Use with caution in breast feeding.
Use with caution in kidney disease.

Do not take if:

- suffering from severe kidney disease, systemic lupus erythematosus (SLE), Staphylococcal infection.

SIDE EFFECTS:

Common: loss of appetite, nausea, sore mouth, diarrhoea, difficulty in swallowing, inflamed colon.
Unusual: vomiting, inflamed pancreas, rash, secondary fungal infection (thrush).
Severe but rare (stop medication, consult doctor): severe belly pain, severe diarrhoea, tooth discolouration.

INTERACTIONS:

Other drugs:
- anticoagulants (e.g. warfarin), penicillin, antacids, iron, oral contraceptives, diuretics (fluid tablets).
Other substances:
- milk may reduce absorption from gut.

PRESCRIPTION:

Yes.

PERMITTED IN SPORT:

Yes.

OVERDOSE:

Exacerbation of side effects only likely effect.

OTHER INFORMATION:

Used for a wide range of infections in general practice, including prevention of acne. Does not cause dependence or addiction.
See also Demeclocycline, Doxycycline, Methacycline, Tetracycline.

Minoxidil

TRADE NAMES:

Loniten.

DRUG CLASS:

Antihypertensive.

USES:

Severe high blood pressure.

DOSAGE:

5mg to 50mg a day, usually as a single dose.

FORMS:

Tablets of 2.5mg, 5mg and 10mg.

PRECAUTIONS:

Use in pregnancy (C) and breast feeding only if medically necessary.
Should not be used for mild high blood pressure.
Fluid intake must be controlled carefully.
May be necessary to check heart with regular cardiographs (ECG).

Do not take if:

- suffering from recent heart attack.

SIDE EFFECTS:

Common: excess hair growth on face and scalp, darkening and thickening of fine body hair, weight gain, fluid retention, increased heart rate.
Unusual: low blood pressure, breast tenderness, rash, nausea, diarrhoea.

INTERACTIONS:

None significant.

PRESCRIPTION:

Yes.

PERMITTED IN SPORT:

Yes.

OVERDOSE:

Low blood pressure only likely effect.

OTHER INFORMATION:

Ability to reverse male baldness found by accident in patients taking drug for blood pressure. Success in baldness varies greatly between patients and long term use is required. Used for only most severe forms of high blood pressure.

MIOTICS

DISCUSSION:

Medications that are used to contract the pupil in the eye, usually for the treatment of glaucoma.

See Acetylcholine chloride, Carbachol.

Mirtazapine

TRADE NAME:

Zispin.

DRUG CLASS:

Antidepressant.

USES:

Depression.

DOSAGE:

 Half to two tablets at night.

FORMS:

Tablets of 30mg (reddish brown).

PRECAUTIONS:

Not to be used in pregnancy, breast feeding and children.
Do not stop suddenly, but reduce dose slowly.
Use with caution in kidney and liver disease, epilepsy, low blood pressure, glaucoma, diabetes, prostate gland enlargement, angina and other heart conditions.

SIDE EFFECTS:

Common: increased appetite and subsequent weight gain, swelling, dizziness.
Unusual: headache, drowsiness (eases with time), nausea, joint and muscle pain.
Severe but rare (stop medication, consult doctor): rash, bone marrow damage, jaundice (yellow skin).

INTERACTIONS:

Other drugs:
• severe interaction with MAOI
• benzodiazepines (e.g. diazepam), erythromycin, clotrimazole, econazole, fluconazole, itraconazole, ketoconazole, miconazole, erythromycin, nefazodone, carbamazepine, rifampicin, phenytoin, cimetidine.
Herbs:
• ma huang.
Other substances:
• reacts with alcohol.

PRESCRIPTION:

Yes.

PERMITTED IN SPORT:

Yes.

OVERDOSE:

Induce vomiting or administer activated charcoal if tablets taken recently. Seek medical attention.

OTHER INFORMATION:

Introduced in 2002 as an additional effective treatment for most types of depression.

See also ANTIDEPRESSANTS, TRICYCLIC ANTIDEPRESSANTS.

Misoprostol

TRADE NAMES:

Cytotec.
Arthrotec (with diclofenac).
Napratec (with naproxen).

DRUG CLASS:

Antiulcerant, Prostaglandin analogue.

USES:

Treatment of ulcers of the stomach and duodenum (upper small intestine).
Prevention of ulcers in patients who are likely to develop them.

DOSAGE:

 Up to 800ug a day divided into two to four doses.

FORMS:

Tablets.

PRECAUTIONS:

Extremely dangerous in pregnancy (X). Pregnancy must be prevented in any woman using this medication by adequate contraception. May cause miscarriage and serious damage to the foetus. Not recommended in children and breast feeding.

Do not take if:

- Epileptic, likely to suffer from low blood pressure or asthma.

SIDE EFFECTS:

Common: diarrhoea, belly pains.
Unusual: belly cramps, menstrual disorders, nausea, headache, passing wind, constipation.

INTERACTIONS:

None significant.

PRESCRIPTION:

Yes.

PERMITTED IN SPORT:

Yes.

OVERDOSE:

The effects of an overdose are unknown.

OTHER INFORMATION:

A very potent and effective form of treatment for ulcers that have failed to heal by other methods. Widely used in severely injured or ill patients to prevent stomach ulcers. Must never be used in pregnancy as it causes contraction of the uterus.

See also PROTON PUMP INHIBITORS.

Mizolastine

See ANTIHISTAMINES, SEDATING.

Moclobemide

TRADE NAME:

Manerix.

DRUG CLASS:

Antidepressant, RIMA (reversible inhibitor of monoamine oxidase type A).

USES:

Depression.

DOSAGE:

 150 to 600mg, once or twice a day after a meal.

FORMS:

Tablets of 150mg (yellow) and 300mg (white).

PRECAUTIONS:

Should be used in pregnancy (B3) and breast feeding only with great caution. Not for use in children.
Use with caution in excited and agitated patients, schizophrenia, high blood pressure, thyroid disease, liver and kidney disease.
Lower doses should be used in elderly.

Do not take if:

- suffering from schizophrenia and similar psychiatric conditions.

SIDE EFFECTS:

Common: usually minimal. Dizziness, nausea, sleeplessness, headache.
Unusual: dry mouth, constipation, diarrhoea, anxiety, restlessness.

INTERACTIONS:

Other drugs:
- metoprolol, cimetidine, pethidine, selegiline, clomipramine, SSRI antidepressants (citalopram, fluoxetine, fluvoxamine, paroxetine, sertraline, venlafaxine), dextromethorphan.
Herbs:
- ma huang, sparteine (Cytisus scoparius).

PRESCRIPTION:

Yes.

PERMITTED IN SPORT:

Yes.

OVERDOSE:

Drowsiness, low blood pressure and rapid heart rate may occur. Not serious. Seek medical advice.

OTHER INFORMATION:

Released in the early 1990s it has improved the treatment of depression because of its safety and lack of side effects. May take up to two weeks for patient to notice any improvement in depression.

See also ANTIDEPRESSANTS.

Modafinil

TRADE NAME:

Provigil.

USES:

Narcolepsy. Promotes awakening.

DOSAGE:

 Two to four tablets, in morning and again at noon if necessary.

FORMS:

Tablets of 100mg (white).

PRECAUTIONS:

Not to be used in pregnancy, breast feeding and children.
Ensure adequate contraception used in women.
Use with caution in liver or kidney disease and anxiety disorders.
Blood pressure must be checked regularly.

Do not take if:

 • suffering from high blood pressure, irregular heart beat or other heart disease.

SIDE EFFECTS:

Common: excitement, nervousness, aggression, inability to sleep.
Unusual: personality disorders, loss of appetite, headache, excessive happiness, belly pains, dry mouth, palpitations, high blood pressure, rapid heart rate, tremor, itchy skin.
Severe but rare (stop medication, consult doctor): facial muscle spasms.

INTERACTIONS:

Other drugs:
• oral contraceptives, methylphenidate, triazolam, MAOI, diazepam, phenytoin, propranolol, tricyclic antidepressants, cyclosporin, rifampicin, ketoconazole, itraconazole, warfarin.
Herbs:
• ma huang.

PRESCRIPTION:

Yes.

PERMITTED IN SPORT:

No.

OVERDOSE:

Serious. Seek urgent medical attention. Heart damage likely.

OTHER INFORMATION:

Use must be carefully monitored. Addictive.

See also Methylphenidate.

Moexipril

See ACE INHIBITORS.

Mometasone

TRADE NAMES:

Asmanex, Elocon, Nasonex.

DRUG CLASS:

Corticosteroid.

USES:

Severe inflammation of skin (eczema, dermatitis etc.).
Hay fever, allergic rhinitis.
Prevention of asthma.

DOSAGE:

 Skin: apply once a day.
Nose: two sprays in each nostril once a day.
Inhaler: one inhalation, once or twice a day.

FORMS:

Cream, ointment, nose spray, inhaler.

PRECAUTIONS:

Should be used with caution in pregnancy (B3), breast feeding and children.
Avoid eyes.
Use skin preparations for shortest period of time possible.
Rinse mouth with water after using inhaler.

Do not use cream if:

 • suffering from any form of skin infection.

Do not use nose spray if:

• suffering from fungal nose infection.

Do not use inhaler if:

• suffering from untreated lung infection.

SIDE EFFECTS:

Common: skin—minimal.
Nose spray—headache, nose bleed, nose irritation.
Inhaler—thrush in mouth, hoarseness.
Unusual: skin—thinning of skin, itching, burning, stinging, scarring of skin.
Nose—nasal ulcers.
Inhaler—sore throat, headache.

INTERACTIONS:

Inhaler interacts with ketoconazole.

PRESCRIPTION:

Yes.

PERMITTED IN SPORT:

Yes.

OTHER INFORMATION:

Extremely effective and useful skin medication, that is just as effective as other steroid creams that are used two or three times a day.

See also Betamethasone, Budesonide, Desonide, Fluticasone, Hydrocortisone, Methylprednisolone, Triamcinolone.

Montelukast

TRADE NAME:

Singulair.

USES:

Prevention and treatment of chronic asthma.

DOSAGE:

 10mg at bedtime.

FORMS:

Tablets of 4mg (pink), 5mg (pink) and 10mg (beige).

PRECAUTIONS:

May be used with care in pregnancy (B1), breast feeding and children.
Not for treatment of acute asthma.
Two 5mg tablets are NOT equivalent to one 10mg tablet.

SIDE EFFECTS:

Common: belly pain, headache.
Unusual: nausea, diarrhoea, rash, insomnia, dizziness, joint and muscle pains, tiredness.

INTERACTIONS:

Other drugs:
• aspirin, NSAID, phenobarbitone, phenytoin, rifampicin.

PRESCRIPTION:

Yes.

PERMITTED IN SPORT:

Yes.

OVERDOSE:

Exacerbation of side effects likely.

OTHER INFORMATION:

Released 1999 for the management of more difficult cases of persistent asthma. A remarkably effective an easy to use form of asthma prevention with virtually no side effects. May also be used (without approval) for hay fever and other allergy conditions.

See Zafirlukast.

'MORNING AFTER PILL'

TRADE NAME:

Levonelle-2 (Levonorgestrel).

DRUG CLASS:

Sex hormone.

USES:

Contraception after, but within 72 hours of, unprotected sexual intercourse.

DOSAGE:

 One tablet immediately, and a second tablet twelve hours later. Often combined with medication to reduce risk of vomiting.

FORMS:

Tablets.

PRECAUTIONS:

Not for use more than 72 hours after sexual intercourse. Should be kept out of reach of children and are obviously not for use in children, although accidental usage by children is unlikely to be serious.

Use with caution in heart disease, history of blood clots, epilepsy, migraine, diabetes, severe depression and sickle cell anaemia.

Diarrhoea, vomiting or use of antibiotics may affect action.

Do not take if:

 • suffering from high blood pressure, blood clots, stroke, very high cholesterol blood levels, severe liver disease, Dubin-Johnson syndrome, liver tumour, systemic lupus erythematosus, sex organ or breast cancer, jaundice, otosclerosis or severe skin irritation
• male.

SIDE EFFECTS:

Common: nausea, vomiting, headache, breast tenderness.
Unusual: break through bleeding.
Severe but rare (stop medication, consult doctor): severe headache, blood clot, calf or chest pain, severe shortness of breath.

INTERACTIONS:

Other drugs:
• antibiotics, phenytoin, primidone, barbiturates, rifampicin, anticoagulants, medications that treat diabetes, imipramine.
Other substances:
• smoking increases risk of serious side effects.

PRESCRIPTION:

Yes.

PERMITTED IN SPORT:

Yes.

OVERDOSE:

Vomiting and abnormal vaginal bleeding only likely effects.

OTHER INFORMATION:

Not designed to replace pregnancy prevention by oral contraceptives or other methods. Should not be used repeatedly.

See also ORAL CONTRACEPTIVES.

Morphine

TRADE NAMES:

Morcap SR, MST Continus, MXL, Oramorph, Sevredol, Zomorph. Cyclimorph (with cyclizine).

DRUG CLASS:

Narcotic.

USES:

Severe pain.

DOSAGE:

 Depends on form and level of pain. Follow doctors directions strictly.

FORMS:

Tablets, slow release capsules and tablets, mixture, injection.

PRECAUTIONS:

Should only be used during pregnancy (C) if medically essential. Use with caution in breast feeding. May be used in children.

Use with caution in colic caused by gall stones, pancreatitis, ulcerative colitis, underactive thyroid gland, enlarged prostate gland, head injury and shock.

Do not take if:

- suffering from heart failure, severe head injury, acute diabetes, severe liver disease, severe alcoholism, poor lung function or convulsions
- do not operate machinery, drive a vehicle or undertake tasks requiring concentration after use of morphine.

SIDE EFFECTS:

Common: sedation, constipation, confusion, sweating, nausea, loss of appetite.
Unusual: vomiting, difficulty passing urine, flushing, dizziness, slow heart rate, irregular heart rate, fainting, mood changes.

Severe but rare (stop medication, consult doctor): difficulty in breathing, convulsions.

INTERACTIONS:

Other drugs:
- MAOI, sedatives, cimetidine, warfarin, zidovudine, pentazocine, thiopentone, diazepam, barbiturates, phenothiazines, amphetamines, chlorpromazine, beta-blockers (e.g. propranolol).

Other substances:
- should not be used with alcohol.

PRESCRIPTION:

Yes (very restricted).

PERMITTED IN SPORT:

No.

OVERDOSE:

Serious. Sedation, convulsions, coma and death may occur. Administer activated charcoal or induce vomiting if medication taken recently and patient alert. Seek emergency medical assistance. Antidote available.

OTHER INFORMATION:

Highly addictive if used inappropriately. Very effective and unlikely to cause addiction if used appropriately for severe pain. Patients with terminal diseases (e.g. cancer) should use dose adequate to control pain, and not be concerned about possibility of addiction. Derived from opium poppy and closely related to heroin, but not as addictive.

See also Alfentanil, Buprenorphine, Codeine phosphate, Dextromoramide, Dextropropoxyphene, Fentanyl, Heroin, Hydromorphone, Methadone, NARCOTICS, Oxycodone, Pentazocine, Pethidine.

Moxifloxacin

TRADE NAME:

Avelox.

DRUG CLASS:

Quinolone antibiotic.

USES:

Acute exacerbations of chronic bronchitis, pneumonia, sinusitis.

DOSAGE:

 One tablet a day.

FORMS:

Tablets of 400mg.

PRECAUTIONS:

Not for use in pregnancy, breast feeding and children.
Use with caution in epilepsy, recent heart attack, cystic fibrosis and kidney disease.
Designed for short term use.
Avoid excess sunlight exposure.

Do not take if:

 • suffering from heart electrical conduction problems, tendon problems related to quinolones, very slow heart rate, irregular heart rhythm, severe liver or kidney disease.

SIDE EFFECTS:

Common: belly pain, headache, dizziness, nausea.
Unusual: diarrhoea, vomiting, abnormal taste.
Severe but rare (stop medication, consult doctor): muscle or limb pain, irregular heart rate, significant diarrhoea.

INTERACTIONS:

Other drugs:
• drugs used to treat irregular heart rhythm, antidepressants, muscle relaxants, antihistamines, cisapride, antacids, sucralfate, iron, zinc, anticoagulants (e.g. warfarin), steroids.

PRESCRIPTION:

Yes.

PERMITTED IN SPORT:

The medication can be taken legally while competing in high standards of sport.

OTHER INFORMATION:

Released in 2002 to treat more difficult respiratory infections.

See also See Cinoxacin, Ciprofloxacin, Levofloxacin, Norfloxacin, Ofloxacin.

Moxonidine

TRADE NAME:

Physiotens.

DRUG CLASS:

Antihypertensive.

USES:

High blood pressure (hypertension).

DOSAGE:

 200 to 600ug a day.

FORMS:

Tablets of 200ug (pink) and 400ug (red).

PRECAUTIONS:

Use with caution in pregnancy and breast feeding. Not recommended in children.
Use with caution in kidney and liver disease, Raynaud's disease, epilepsy, Parkinson's disease, glaucoma and depression.
Do not stop suddenly, but reduce dose gradually.

Do not take if:

 • suffering from angioneurotic oedema, some types of irregular heart beat, unstable angina, slow heart beat, heart failure, narrowed coronary (heart) arteries, severe liver or kidney disease.

SIDE EFFECTS:

Common: dry mouth, headaches, tiredness.
Unusual: dizziness, nausea, insomnia, dilation of blood vessels.

INTERACTIONS:

Other drugs:
• sedatives.
Other substances:
• alcohol.

PRESCRIPTION:

Yes.

PERMITTED IN SPORT:

Yes.

OVERDOSE:

Serious heart effects possible. Seek urgent medical attention.

See also ANTIHYPERTENSIVES.

MPA

See Medroxyprogesterone acetate.

MUCOLYTICS

DISCUSSION:

Mucolytics liquefy and break down thick mucus. Mucus produced during colds, flu, bronchitis and other infections of the airways, is often sticky and tenacious. Mucolytics make this phlegm watery and runny, so that coughing and sneezing can more easily clear it from the body. They are available as tablets and mixtures.

See Carbocisteine.

Mumps vaccine

TRADE NAMES:

MMR II, Priorix (with measles and rubella vaccines).

DRUG CLASS:

Vaccine.

USES:

Prevention of mumps.

DOSAGE:

 One injection at twelve months and a second one at four or five years of age.

FORMS:

Injection.

PRECAUTIONS:

Not designed for use in pregnancy (B2), but unlikely to cause adverse effects if given inadvertently. May be used in children and breast feeding.
Use with caution in history of febrile convulsions or brain injury.

Do not take if:

• suffering from allergy to eggs, poultry or neomycin
• significant fever, immune system disease (e.g. AIDS)
• blood transfusion within three months
• suffering from TB, bone marrow disease, or leukaemia.

SIDE EFFECTS:

Common: burning at site of injection.
Unusual: fever, enlarged glands, itch, rash.
Severe but rare: brain inflammation.

INTERACTIONS:

None significant.

PRESCRIPTION:

Yes.

PERMITTED IN SPORT:

Yes.

OVERDOSE:

An additional inadvertent dose is unlikely to have any serious side effects.

OTHER INFORMATION:

Mumps is usually a mild disease, but may rarely cause infertility, brain damage and death. Vaccination with rubella, measles and mumps routine in childhood.

Mupirocin

TRADE NAME:

Bactroban.

DRUG CLASS:

Antibiotic.

USES:

Bacterial skin and nasal infections, school sores (impetigo).

DOSAGE:

 Apply three times a day.

FORMS:

Ointment, nasal ointment.

PRECAUTIONS:

Use with caution in pregnancy and breast feeding. May be used in children.
Not for use in eyes or mouth.

SIDE EFFECTS:

Common: minimal.
Unusual: skin irritation.

INTERACTIONS:

None significant.

PRESCRIPTION:

Yes.

PERMITTED IN SPORT:

Yes.

OTHER INFORMATION:

Excellent and safe medication for treating minor skin infections. Introduced in late 1980s.

See also Chlorhexidine, Neomycin, Sodium fusidate.

MUSCLE RELAXANTS

DISCUSSION:

Muscle relaxants are used to relieve muscle cramps and the spasms associated with spasticity (cerebral palsy), paralysis (paraplegia and quadriplegia), multiple sclerosis and some rare brain diseases.

See Baclofen, Botulinum toxin, Carisoprodol, Dantrolene sodium, Orphenadrine, Tizanidine.

Mycophenolate

TRADE NAME:

Celicept.

DRUG CLASS:

Immune system modifier.

USES:

Prevention of rejection of kidney or heart transplant.

DOSAGE:

 1000mg twice a day.

FORMS:

Capsules of 250mg (blue/brown), tablet of 500mg (lavender), infusion.

PRECAUTIONS:

Must not be used in pregnancy (D). May be used with caution in children and breast feeding.
Regular blood tests to monitor blood cell function essential.
Use with caution in stomach, intestine and severe kidney disease.

SIDE EFFECTS:

Common: skin cancer incidence increased, infection, low white blood cell count, diarrhoea, bleeding from intestine.
Unusual: severe abdominal pain.

Severe but rare (stop medication, consult doctor): cancer of lymph nodes, perforation of intestine.

INTERACTIONS:

Other drugs:
- aciclovir, ganciclovir, iron, magnesium salts and aluminium salts (e.g. in antacids), oral contraceptives, probenecid, drugs secreted in kidney, cholestyramine. Check with doctor before using any other medication
- live vaccines (e.g. polio).

Other substances:
- alcohol.

PRESCRIPTION:

Yes.

PERMITTED IN SPORT:

Yes.

OVERDOSE:

Extremely serious organ damage may occur. Induce vomiting or administer activated charcoal if taken recently. Seek emergency medical attention.

OTHER INFORMATION:

Introduced in 1997.

MYDRIATICS

TRADE and GENERIC NAMES:

Mydrilate (Cyclopentolate).
Minims Mydriatics (Atropine, cyclopentolate, phenylephrine, tropicamide).
Mydriacyl (Tropicamide).

DRUG CLASS:

Anticholinergic.

USES:

Dilates pupil for examination and surgery.

DOSAGE:

 Use drops as directed by doctor. Often used by doctors in their surgery or operating theatre.

FORMS:

Eye drops.

PRECAUTIONS:

May be used in pregnancy and breast feeding. Use with caution in children. Not designed for prolonged use.

Do not take if:

 • suffering from glaucoma.

SIDE EFFECTS:

Common: irritation of eye with prolonged use, sensitivity to bright light.
Unusual: disorientation, blurred vision, dry mouth, incoordination, rapid heart rate.

INTERACTIONS:

None significant.

PRESCRIPTION:

Yes.

PERMITTED IN SPORT:

Yes.

OTHER INFORMATION:

Mainly used before eye examinations, and before and during eye surgery.

See also Atropine.

Nabumetone

TRADE NAME:

Relifex.

DRUG CLASS:

Nonsteroidal anti-inflammatory drug
(NSAID).

USES:

Osteoarthritis and rheumatoid arthritis.

DOSAGE:

 Two tablets at night or twice a day.

FORMS:

Tablet of 500mg (red), dispersible tablet
of 500mg (white), suspension.

PRECAUTIONS:

Not for use in pregnancy or breast
feeding. Use with care in children.
Use with caution in kidney disease,
history of peptic ulcer, liver disease and
the elderly (lower dose necessary).

Do not take if:

 • suffering from active peptic
ulcer, aspirin allergy, severe liver
disease (e.g. cirrhosis).

SIDE EFFECTS:

Common: nausea, heartburn, diarrhoea,
headache.
Unusual: dizziness, rash, sedation.
*Severe but rare (stop medication, consult
doctor):* vomiting blood, passing black
faeces.

INTERACTIONS:

Other drugs:
• warfarin and other anticoagulants, some
anticonvulsants (for epilepsy), some
hypoglycaemics (for diabetes).

PRESCRIPTION:

Yes.

PERMITTED IN SPORT:

Yes.

OVERDOSE:

Causes nausea, vomiting, severe
headache, dizziness, confusion and
convulsions. Administer activated
charcoal or induce vomiting if taken
recently. Seek medical assistance.

**See also See Aceclofenac, Acemetacin,
Diclofenac, Diflunisal, Etodolac, Felbinac,
Fenbufen, Fenoprofen, Flurbiprofen,
Ibuprofen, Indomethacin, Ketoprofen,
Lornoxicam, Meloxicam, Naproxen,
NSAID, Piroxicam, Sulindac, Tenoxicam.**

Nadolol

TRADE NAMES:

Corgard.
Corgaretic (with bendrofluazide).

DRUG CLASS:

Beta-blocker.

USES:

High blood pressure, overactive thyroid
gland (thyrotoxicosis).

DOSAGE:

 80mg to 240mg a day.

FORMS:

Tablets.

PRECAUTIONS:

Should be used in pregnancy (C) only if
medically essential. Safe to use in breast
feeding. May be used with caution in
children.

Use with care if suffering from alcoholism, diabetes, prinzmetal angina, over active thyroid gland, liver or kidney failure or about to have surgery.

Do not take if:

- suffering from chronic bronchitis, asthma, emphysema, some forms of heart rhythm abnormalities, very slow heart rate, poor circulation, heart failure, low blood pressure, very enlarged heart, phaeochromocytoma (rare adrenal tumour).

SIDE EFFECTS:

Common: low blood pressure, slow heart rate, cold hands and feet, asthma.
Unusual: loss of appetite, nausea, diarrhoea, impotence, tiredness, sleeplessness, nightmares, rash, loss of libido, hair loss, noises in ears.
Severe but rare (stop medication, consult doctor): severe asthma.

INTERACTIONS:

Other drugs:

- calcium channel blockers, prazosin, MAOI, disopyramide, clonidine, adrenaline, other medications for irregular heart beat, lignocaine, ergotamine, indomethacin, chlorpromazine.

PRESCRIPTION:

Yes.

PERMITTED IN SPORT:

No.

OVERDOSE:

Slow heart rate, low blood pressure, asthma and heart failure may result. Administer activated charcoal or induce vomiting if tablets taken recently. Use Salbutamol or other asthma sprays for difficulty in breathing. Seek medical assistance.

See also Atenolol, BETA-BLOCKERS, Carvedilol, Esmolol, Labetalol, Metoprolol, Nebivolol, Oxprenolol, Pindolol, Propranolol, Sotalol.

Naferelin

TRADE NAME:

Synarel.

DRUG CLASS:

Sex hormone.

USES:

Treatment of endometriosis. Preliminary treatment to stimulate ovary before in vitro fertilisation (IVF).

DOSAGE:

One or two sprays into different nostrils, twice a day commencing two to four days after menstrual period starts.

FORMS:

Nasal spray.

PRECAUTIONS:

Must never be used in pregnancy (D), breast feeding or children.
Use with caution in osteoporosis, polycystic ovaries and hay fever.
Use with caution under 18 years.

Do not use if:

- suffering from unusual vaginal bleeding.
- male.

SIDE EFFECTS:

Common: ovarian pain, ovarian cysts, belly pain, dry vagina, breast shrinkage, hot flushes, poor libido, headaches, acne.
Unusual: emotional changes, muscle pains, nasal irritation.

INTERACTIONS:

Other drugs:
- other sex hormones.

PRESCRIPTION:

Yes.

PERMITTED IN SPORT:

No.

OVERDOSE:

Unlikely to be serious.

OTHER INFORMATION:

Introduced in the mid 1990s as a radically new and effective treatment for endometriosis via a novel route which overcomes the necessity for injections, and side effects caused by swallowing tablets.

Naftidrofuryl

TRADE NAME:

Praxilene.

DRUG CLASS:

Vasodilator.

USES:

Poor circulation of blood to brain and other tissues.

DOSAGE:

 One or two capsules three times a day.

FORMS:

Capsules of 100mg (pink).

PRECAUTIONS:

Use with caution in pregnancy and breast feeding. Not recommended in children.

Do not use if:

 • suffering from calcium balance problems in the body or kidney stones containing calcium.

SIDE EFFECTS:

Common: nausea.
Unusual: belly pain, rash.
Severe but rare (stop medication, consult doctor): jaundice (yellow skin) from liver damage, kidney stones.

INTERACTIONS:

None significant.

PRESCRIPTION:

Yes.

PERMITTED IN SPORT:

No.

Nalbuphine

TRADE NAME:

Nubain.

DRUG CLASS:

Narcotic.

USES:

Moderate to severe pain (e.g. heart attack), after surgery.

DOSAGE:

 One or two ampoules in injection as determined by doctor.

FORMS:

Injection.

PRECAUTIONS:

Use with caution in pregnancy, breast feeding and children.
Use with caution if lung function reduced (e.g. emphysema, asthma), head injury, kidney and liver disease.
Beware of use in patients with a history of narcotic abuse.

SIDE EFFECTS:

Common: sedation, sweating, dry mouth.
Unusual: dizziness, fainting.

INTERACTIONS:

Other drugs:
• sedatives, other narcotics.

PRESCRIPTION:

Yes.

PERMITTED IN SPORT:

No.

OVERDOSE:

May be serious. Symptoms may not appear for some hours after injection given and may include drowsiness, difficulty in breathing and coma. Seek urgent medical attention. Antidote available.

OTHER INFORMATION:

May be addictive if used inappropriately.

Nalidixic acid

TRADE NAMES:

Negram, Uriben.

DRUG CLASS:

Antibiotic.

USES:

Bacterial infections of urine.

DOSAGE:

 One or two tablets four times a day.

FORMS:

Tablets (beige) of 500mg, granules, suspension.

PRECAUTIONS:

Safe to use in pregnancy (A) and breast feeding. Use with caution in children. Use with caution in epilepsy, hardening of arteries, liver and kidney disease.

Do not take if:

 • suffering from convulsions.

SIDE EFFECTS:

Common: drowsiness, headache, dizziness, sensitivity to bright light, nausea, belly discomfort, rash.
Unusual: vomiting, diarrhoea, itch, sun sensitive skin.
Severe but rare (stop medication, consult doctor): yellow skin (jaundice).

INTERACTIONS:

Other drugs:
• nitrofurantoin, anticoagulants, antacids, cyclosporin.

Other substances:
• reacts with caffeine.

PRESCRIPTION:

Yes.

PERMITTED IN SPORT:

Yes.

OVERDOSE:

Exacerbation of side effects likely.

OTHER INFORMATION:

Often used long term to prevent infections of urine (e.g. cystitis). Does not cause dependence or addiction.

Naloxone

TRADE NAME:

Narcan.

DRUG CLASS:

Antidote.

USES:

Reversal of effects of overdosage with narcotics (e.g. morphine, heroin).

DOSAGE:

 Repeated injections at intervals of two or three minutes until desired effect achieved.

FORMS:

Injection.

PRECAUTIONS:

May be used in pregnancy (B1), breast feeding and children of all ages.
Use with caution in narcotic addicts, heart disease.
Exclude other poisons that may be responsible for symptoms.
Patient must be monitored closely by doctors.

SIDE EFFECTS:

Common: high blood pressure, irregular heart beat, shortness of breath, convulsions.
Unusual: heart attack.

INTERACTIONS:

None significant.

PRESCRIPTION:

Yes.

PERMITTED IN SPORT:

Yes.

OTHER INFORMATION:

Often life saving in addicts who take a heroin overdose, or in newborn infants of mothers who are heroin addicts. May precipitate withdrawal in narcotic addicts.

Naltrexone

TRADE NAME:

Nalorex.

USES:

Narcotic drug and alcohol dependence.

DOSAGE:

 50mg once or twice a day for three to 12 months. Half dose given initially in narcotic drug addiction.

FORMS:

Tablet of 50mg (yellow).

PRECAUTIONS:

Use with caution in pregnancy (B3) and breast feeding.
Use with caution in children.
Use with caution in liver and kidney disease.
Patients must have a negative urine test for narcotics before first dose given, and must never use narcotics.

Do not take if:

 • taking any narcotic or opiate medications (e.g. codeine, morphine) or illegal drugs (e.g. heroin). May result in fatal reaction.
• suffering from acute hepatitis or liver failure.

SIDE EFFECTS:

Common: severe withdrawal effects if not previously completely withdrawn from alcohol or narcotics, diarrhoea, nausea, dizziness, tiredness.
Unusual: liver damage, nervousness, fatigue, anxiety, joint and muscle pains.

INTERACTIONS:

Other drugs:
• all narcotic drugs (e.g. codeine, pethidine, morphine, heroin, opium—may result in death).
• thioridazine.
Other substances:
• alcohol.

PRESCRIPTION:

Yes.

PERMITTED IN SPORT:

Yes.

OVERDOSE:

Exacerbation of side effects likely. Seek medical attention.

OTHER INFORMATION:

Should be combined with a drug or alcohol withdrawal program.

See also Acamprosate.

Nandrolone decanoate

TRADE NAME:

Deca Durabolin.

DRUG CLASS:

Anabolic steroid.

USES:

Kidney failure, inoperable breast cancer, severe osteoporosis, aplastic anaemia, suppression of white cells, in addition to corticosteroids used long term.
Used dangerously and in an unapproved manner by body builders and athletes.

DOSAGE:

 As directed and determined by doctor. Usually one injection a week.

FORMS:

Injection.

PRECAUTIONS:

Must not be used in pregnancy (D) or breast feeding. Use with caution in children as growth suppression may occur.

Use with caution in heart disease, enlarged prostate gland, diabetes.

Do not take if:

 • suffering from prostate and testicular cancer, heart failure, breast cancer, liver and kidney disease.

SIDE EFFECTS:

Common: increased hairiness and decreased breast size in women, voice deepening in women, acne, frequent unwanted erections, infertility.
Unusual: anaemia, enlargement of clitoris in women, cessation of menstrual periods, decrease in testicular size, impotence, breast enlargement in males, baldness in females, reduced libido.
Severe but rare (stop medication, consult doctor): unusual bruising or bleeding, calcium deposits (lumps) in tissue, jaundice (yellow skin).

INTERACTIONS:

Other drugs:
• insulin, warfarin, hypoglycaemics (used for diabetes).
Herbs:
• echinacea.

PRESCRIPTION:

Yes.

PERMITTED IN SPORT:

No. Although increasing muscle bulk, there is no evidence that this medication enhances athletic ability. Long term inappropriate use may cause permanent damage to the body.

OVERDOSE:

Exacerbation of side effects likely.

OTHER INFORMATION:

Does not cause dependence or addiction. Short term gains in muscle bulk when used inappropriately by body builders, may result in long term permanent body damage that may lead to early heart attacks, infertility, bone weakness, liver disease and premature death. The bottom line is, don't use it except under strict medical supervision when indicated for specific diseases.

Naproxen

TRADE NAMES:

Naprosyn, Nycopren, Synflex. Napratec (with misoprostol).

DRUG CLASS:

NSAID (Nonsteroidal anti-inflammatory drug).

USES:

All forms of arthritis, inflammatory disorders, gout, back pain, ankylosing spondylitis, bone pain, period pain, migraine, general pain relief.

DOSAGE:

 250 to 1000mg a day with food. May be given in one or more doses.

FORMS:

Tablets, capsules.

PRECAUTIONS:

Should not be used in pregnancy (C) unless medically essential. Napratec must never be used in pregnancy. Breast feeding should be ceased if necessary to use NSAID. Not for use in children under two.

Use with caution in psychiatricaly disturbed patients, epilepsy, severe infection, heart failure and kidney disease.

Lower doses required in elderly, who may suffer more side effects.

Do not take if:

- suffering from peptic ulcer at present or in recent past
- due for surgery (including dental surgery)
- suffering from bleeding disorder or anaemia.

SIDE EFFECTS:

Common: stomach discomfort, diarrhoea, constipation, heartburn, nausea, headache, dizziness.

Unusual: blurred vision, stomach ulcer, ringing noise in ears, retention of fluid, swelling of tissue, drowsiness, itch, rash, shortness of breath.

Severe but rare (stop medication, consult doctor): vomiting blood, passing blood in faeces, other unusual bleeding, asthma induced by medication.

INTERACTIONS:

Other drugs:

- must never be used with anticoagulants (e.g. warfarin).
- probenecid, diuretics, lithium, methotrexate, beta-blockers, ACE inhibitors.

Herbs:

- feverfew.

PRESCRIPTION:

Yes.

PERMITTED IN SPORT:

Yes.

OVERDOSE:

Causes nausea, vomiting, severe headache, dizziness, confusion and convulsions. Administer activated charcoal or induce vomiting if taken recently. Seek medical assistance.

OTHER INFORMATION:

Extensively used to give excellent relief to a wide variety of inflammatory conditions. Significant side effects (particularly on the stomach) in about 5% of patients. Limit their use. Specially coated forms reduce side effects.

See also See Aceclofenac, Acemetacin, Diclofenac, Diflunisal, Etodolac, Felbinac, Fenbufen, Fenoprofen, Flurbiprofen, Ibuprofen, Indomethacin, Ketoprofen, Lornoxicam, Meloxicam, Nabumetone, NSAID, Piroxicam, Sulindac, Tenoxicam.

Naratriptan

TRADE NAME:

Naramig.

DRUG CLASS:

Antimigraine.

USES:

Treatment of acute migraine.

DOSAGE:

Take one tablet at onset of migraine. Repeat after four hours if necessary.

FORMS:

Tablets of 2.5mg (green).

PRECAUTIONS:

May be used with caution in pregnancy (B3), breast feeding, the elderly and children.

Use with caution in paralysis and visual disturbances due to migraine (exclude other serious causes).

Use with caution in heart disease, kidney and liver disease.

May cross react in patients with a sulphur allergy.

Do not take if:

- suffering from angina, heart attack, stroke, TIAs (transient ischaemic attacks), poor circulation, uncontrolled high blood pressure, severe liver or kidney disease.

SIDE EFFECTS:

Common: tiredness, fatigue, dizziness,tingling, heat sensation.
Unusual: chest heaviness, pressure, tightness, slow or rapid heart rate, disturbed vision.

INTERACTIONS:

Other drugs:
• other migraine treatments, ergotamine, methysergide.
Herbs:
• St John's wort.

PRESCRIPTION:

Yes.

PERMITTED IN SPORT:

Yes.

OVERDOSE:

Causes high blood pressure and may affect heart. Recovery within eight hours usual unless heart damaged. Seek medical attention.

OTHER INFORMATION:

Introduced in 1998. Not addictive.
See also Ergotamine, Sumatriptan, Zolmitriptan.

NARCOTICS

DISCUSSION:

Narcotics are strong, addictive and effective painkillers derived from opium. They are highly restricted in their use, and must be kept in safes by chemists and doctors. If they are used appropriately, they give relief from severe pain to patients with acute injuries, and pain from diseases such as cancer and kidney stones. They are often used before, during and after operations to ease the pain of the procedure. If used in this way, it is unlikely that addiction will occur.
If narcotics are used excessively, a psychological and physical addiction can

rapidly develop. Heroin is an infamous illegal narcotic which is broken down to morphine in the body. Narcotics not only relieve severe pain, they also reduce anxiety, stop coughs, sedate and cause euphoria (artificial happiness). They should be used with caution in asthma and other lung diseases, liver disease and after head injuries.

See Alfentanil, Buprenorphine, Codeine, Dextromoramide, Dextropropoxyphene, Ethoheptazine, Fentanyl, Heroin, Hydromorphone, Methadone, Morphine, Nalbuphine, Oxycodone, Pentazocine, Pethidine, Phenazocine.

Nateglinide

TRADE NAME:

Starlix.

DRUG CLASS:

Hypoglycaemic.

USES:

Type two diabetes in combination with metformin.

DOSAGE:

 60mg to 180mg before meals three times a day.

FORMS:

Tablets of 60mg (pink), 120mg (yellow) and 180mg (red).

PRECAUTIONS:

Not for use in pregnancy, breast feeding and children.
Use with caution in liver disease, adrenal or pituitary gland disease, poor nutrition and episodes of low blood sugar (hypo-glycaemia) on other diabetes medication.

Do not take if:
• suffering from type one diabetes or complicated diabetes type two
• suffering from severe liver disease.

SIDE EFFECTS:

Common: low blood sugar.
Unusual: allergy reaction.
Severe but rare (stop medication, consult doctor): liver damage (jaundice).

INTERACTIONS:

Other drugs:
• ACE inhibitors (for blood pressure and heart failure), steroids, salbutamol, terbutaline.
Other substances:
• alcohol.

PRESCRIPTION:

Yes.

PERMITTED IN SPORT:

Yes.

OTHER INFORMATION:

Introduced in 2002 for difficult to control diabetes type two.

See also Acarbose, Glibenclamide, Gliclazide, Glipizide, Gliquidone, HYPOGLYCAEMICS, INSULINS, Metformin, Repaglinide, Rosiglitazone.

Nebivolol

TRADE NAME:

Nebilet.

DRUG CLASS:

Beta-blocker.

USES:

High blood pressure.

DOSAGE:

 Half to one tablet a day.

FORMS:

Tablets of 5mg (white).

PRECAUTIONS:

Should be used in pregnancy (C) only if medically essential. Safe to use in breast feeding. May be used with caution in children.

Use with care if suffering from alcoholism, diabetes, prinzmetal angina, over active thyroid gland, liver or kidney failure or about to have surgery.

Do not take if:

 • suffering from chronic bronchitis, asthma, emphysema, some forms of heart rhythm abnormalities, very slow heart rate, poor circulation, heart failure, low blood pressure, very enlarged heart, phaeochromo-cytoma (rare adrenal tumour).

SIDE EFFECTS:

Common: low blood pressure, slow heart rate, cold hands and feet, asthma.
Unusual: loss of appetite, nausea, diarrhoea, impotence, tiredness, sleeplessness, nightmares, rash, loss of libido, hair loss, noises in ears.
Severe but rare (stop medication, consult doctor): severe asthma.

INTERACTIONS:

Other drugs:
• calcium channel blockers, prazosin, MAOI, disopyramide, clonidine, adrena-line, other medications for irregular heart beat, lignocaine, ergotamine, indomethacin, chlorpromazine.

PRESCRIPTION:

Yes.

PERMITTED IN SPORT:

No.

OVERDOSE:

Slow heart rate, low blood pressure, asthma and heart failure may result. Administer activated charcoal or induce vomiting if tablets taken recently. Use Salbutamol or other asthma sprays for difficulty in breathing. Seek medical assistance.

See also Atenolol, BETA-BLOCKERS, Carvedilol, Esmolol, Labetalol, Metoprolol, Nadolol, Oxprenolol, Pindolol, Propranolol, Sotalol.

Nedocromil

TRADE NAMES:

Rapitil, Tilade.

USES:

Prevention of asthma, allergic conjunctivitis.

DOSAGE:

 Inhaler: two puffs, two to four times a day.
Drops: one drop in each eye, two to four times a day.

FORMS:

Inhaler, eye drops.

PRECAUTIONS:

Safe to use with caution in pregnancy (B1), breast feeding and children over 12 years.
Not to be used for the relief of acute asthma attacks.

Do not take if:

 • sensitive to aerosol propellants. Do not use eye drops
• if wearing contact lenses.

SIDE EFFECTS:

Common: inhaler—unpleasant taste.
Eye drops—temporary irritation.
Unusual: headache, nausea, cough.

INTERACTIONS:

None significant.

PRESCRIPTION:

Yes.

PERMITTED IN SPORT:

Yes.

OVERDOSE:

Unlikely to cause any serious problems.

OTHER INFORMATION:

A very effective preventer of inflammation in the lungs.
See also Sodium cromoglycate.

Nefopam

TRADE NAME:

Acupan.

DRUG CLASS:

Analgesic.

USES:

Pain, particularly after surgery.

DOSAGE:

 One tablet up to three times a day.

FORMS:

Tablets of 30mg (white).

PRECAUTIONS:

Use with caution in pregnancy. May be used in breast feeding. Not recommended in children.
Use with caution in liver and kidney disease, and difficulty in passing urine.

Do not take if:

 • suffering from epilepsy or recent heart attack.

SIDE EFFECTS:

Common: nausea, nervousness, dry mouth, dizziness.

INTERACTIONS:

Other drugs:
• MAOI, anticholinergics, sympathomimetics, tricyclic antidepressants.
Other substances:
• alcohol.

PRESCRIPTION:

Yes.

PERMITTED IN SPORT:

No.
See also ANALGESICS.

Neisseria meningitidis vaccine

See Meningococcal Vaccine.

Nelfinavir

TRADE NAME:

Viracept.

DRUG CLASS:

Antiviral.

USES:

HIV (AIDS) infection.

DOSAGE:

 Three tablets, three times a day.

FORMS:

Tablets of 250mg (light blue).

PRECAUTIONS:

May be used with care in pregnancy (B2), breast feeding and children.
Use with caution in diabetes, kidney disease, liver disease and haemophilia.
Must be used in combination with other antivirals.

SIDE EFFECTS:

Common: diarrhoea.
Unusual: diabetes develops.

INTERACTIONS:

Other drugs:
• serious interaction with astemizole, cisapride, midazolam, triazolam, ergotamine, amiodarone, quinidine
• rifampicin, rifabutin, simvastatin, atorvastatin, oral contraceptives and anticonvulsants
Other substances:
• St John's wort.

PRESCRIPTION:

Yes.

PERMITTED IN SPORT:

Yes.

OTHER INFORMATION:

Always used in combination with other antivirals. Introduced in 2000.
See also Abacavir, Efavirenz, Indinavir, Lamivudine, Nevirapine, Ritonavir, Saquinavir, Stavudine, Tenofovir, Zalcitabine, Zidovudine.

Neomycin

TRADE NAMES:

Nivermycin.
Audicort (with triamcinolone).
Betnesol-N (with betamethasone).
Cicatrin (with bacitracin).
Dermovate NN (with nystatin, clobetasol).
Graneodin (with gramicidin).
Gregoderm, Otosporin (with polymyxin B, hydrocortisone).
Maxitrol (with dexamethasone, polymyxin B).
Naseptin (with chlorhexidine).
Neosporin (with polymyxin B, gramicidin).
Otomize (with dexamethasone, acetic acid).
Predsol-N (with prednisolone).
Synalar-N (with fluocinolone).
Tri-Adcortyl (with triamcinolone, gramicidin, nystatin).
Tri-Adcortyl Otic (with triamcinolone, gramicidin).

DRUG CLASS:

Aminoglycoside antibiotic.

USES:

Infections of eye, ear, skin and bowel.

DOSAGE:

 Tablets: two tablets every four hours.
Skin: apply two or three times a day.

Eye drops: two drops four times
a day.
Eye and ear ointment: apply twice
a day.

FORMS:

Tablets, irrigation solution, ear drops, ear
ointment, eye drops, eye ointment, cream,
lotion, powder.

PRECAUTIONS:

Skin, eye and ear preparations may be
used with caution in pregnancy, breast
feeding and children.
Tablets must not be used in pregnancy
(D) or breast feeding.
Use tablets with caution in kidney disease
and hearing damage.
Tablets are designed for very short term
use.
Avoid eye contact with forms not
designed for use in eye.
Skin preparations should not be used on
viral infections.

Do not take tablets if:

• suffering from ulcerative colitis
or bowel obstruction.

SIDE EFFECTS:

Common: tablets—diarrhoea.
Other forms—minimal.
Unusual: tablets—ear and kidney
damage.

INTERACTIONS:

Other drugs:
• tablets—penicillin, cephalosporins,
frusemide, warfarin, methotrexate,
vitamin B12, digoxin.

PRESCRIPTION:

Yes.

PERMITTED IN SPORT:

Yes.

OVERDOSE:

Tablets may cause severe diarrhoea, ear
and kidney damage.

OTHER INFORMATION:

Widely used for superficial mild
infections. Available for over forty years.
**See Amikacin, Gatifloxacin, Gentamicin,
Tobramycin.**

Neostigmine

TRADE NAME:

Robinul Neostigmine (with
glycopyrronium bromide).

DRUG CLASS:

Anticholinesterase.

USES:

Before anaesthetic to dry secretions,
myasthenia gravis, inability to pass urine.

DOSAGE:

 As determined by doctor.

FORMS:

Injection.

PRECAUTIONS:

May be used in pregnancy (B2) with
caution. Safe for use in breast feeding.
Use with caution in children.
Dosage must be carefully monitored by
doctor.
Use with caution in epilepsy, slow heart
rate, asthma, recent heart attack, irregular
heart beat, overactive thyroid gland, and
peptic ulcer.

Do not take if:

 • suffering from gut obstruction or
peritonitis.

SIDE EFFECTS:

Common: slow heart rate, headache,
nausea, diarrhoea, excess salivation,
cough, wheeze, bowel noises.
Unusual: confusion, slurred speech,
vomiting, belly cramps, desire to pass

urine, muscle cramps, contracted pupils. *Severe but rare (stop medication, consult doctor):* difficulty breathing, chest pain.

INTERACTIONS:

Other drugs:

• muscle relaxants, atropine, aminoglycosides, drugs used to treat irregular heart beat, some anaesthetics.

PRESCRIPTION:

Yes.

PERMITTED IN SPORT:

Yes.

See also Donepezil, Pyridostigmine.

Netilmicin

TRADE NAME:

Netilin.

DRUG CLASS:

Antibiotic.

USES:

Severe bacterial infections.

DOSAGE:

 By injection into a muscle, or slow infusion by a drip into a vein, dosage as determined by doctor for each patient.

FORMS:

Injection.

PRECAUTIONS:

Must not be used in pregnancy (D). Use with caution breast feeding and children. Use with caution in kidney disease, myasthenia gravis and low blood calcium levels.
Beware of dehydration.
Reduce dose in elderly.
Not for prolonged use.

SIDE EFFECTS:

Common: adverse effects on ear, nerve and kidney function.
Unusual: resistant infection.

INTERACTIONS:

Other drugs:

• frusemide, other diuretics, anaesthetics, cephalosporins, numerous other medications.

Other substances:

• some forms of blood transfusion.

PRESCRIPTION:

Yes.

PERMITTED IN SPORT:

Yes.

OTHER INFORMATION:

Introduced in 1996 for the treatment of more difficult and severe infections.

Neutral insulin

See INSULINS.

Nevirapine

TRADE NAME:

Viramune.

DRUG CLASS:

Antiviral.

USES:

AIDS, HIV infection.

DOSAGE:

 One or two tablets a day in combination with other antiviral treatment.

FORMS:

Tablets of 200mg (white), suspension.

PRECAUTIONS:

Use with caution in pregnancy (B3), breast feeding and children.
Use with caution in kidney and liver disease.

SIDE EFFECTS:

Common: rash, itch, fever, nausea, headache.
Unusual: severe skin reactions, vomiting, liver damage.
Severe but rare (stop medication, consult doctor): jaundice (yellow skin).

INTERACTIONS:

Other drugs:
• rifampicin, rifabutin, sex hormones, oral contraceptives, methadone, prednisolone, saquinavir, ketoconazole.
Herbs:
• St John's wort.

PRESCRIPTION:

Yes.

PERMITTED IN SPORT:

Yes.

OVERDOSE:

May cause serious organ damage. Induce vomiting or give activated charcoal if taken recently. Seek urgent medical attention.

OTHER INFORMATION:

Introduced in 1997 as an additive medication for the management of HIV (Human Immunodeficiency Virus) infection.
See also Abacavir, Efavirenz, Indinavir, Lamivudine, Nelfinavir, Ritonavir, Saquinavir, Stavudine, Tenofovir, Zalcitabine, Zidovudine.

Niacin

See Nicotinic acid.

Nicardipine

TRADE NAMES:

Cardene.

DRUG CLASS:

Calcium channel blocker (calcium antagonist).

USES:

High blood pressure.

DOSAGE:

 20mg to 60mg two or three times a day. Maximum 120mg a day.

FORMS:

Capsules of 20mg, 30mg and 45mg in standard or sustained release (SR) forms.

PRECAUTIONS:

Should only be used in pregnancy (C) and breast feeding if medically essential. Not designed for use in children.
Use with caution in heart failure, after a stroke, liver or kidney disease.
Do not take if:

 • suffering from severe heart failure, low blood pressure, atrial flutter or fibrillation, aortic stenosis, recent heart attack.

SIDE EFFECTS:

Common: constipation, tiredness, headache, dizziness, indigestion, swelling of feet and ankles.
Unusual: flushing, palpitations, slow heart rate, scalp irritation, depression, flushes, nightmares, excess wind.
Severe but rare (stop medication, consult doctor): fainting, angina (chest pain).

INTERACTIONS:

Other drugs:
• beta-blockers (e.g. propranolol), cyclosporin, digoxin, cimetidine, barbiturates, diazepam, amiodarone, quinidine, rifampicin, phenytoin, cisapride, theophylline, terbutaline, salbutamol, diltiazem
• additive effect with other medications for high blood pressure.

Herbs:
- goldenseal, guarana, hawthorn, Korean ginseng, liquorice.

Other substances:
- smoking may aggravate conditions that these medications are treating
- grapefruit juice.

PRESCRIPTION:
Yes.

PERMITTED IN SPORT:
Yes.

OVERDOSE:
May continue to be absorbed for up to 48 hours after overdose. Administer activated charcoal or induce vomiting. Purging should be encouraged to eliminate drug from gut. Overdose may cause low blood pressure, irregular heart rhythm, difficulty in breathing, heart attack and death. Obtain urgent medical attention.

See also Amlodipine, CALCIUM CHANNEL BLOCKERS, Diltiazem, Isradipine, Lacidipine, Lercanidipine, Nifedipine, Nimodipine, Verapamil.

Nicorandil

TRADE NAME:
Ikorel.

DRUG CLASS:
Antiangina, vasodilator.

USES:
Angina (heart pain).

DOSAGE:
 5mg to 20mg twice a day. Use minimum effective dose.

FORMS:
Tablets of 10mg and 20mg (white).

PRECAUTIONS:
Use with caution in pregnancy (B3), breast feeding and children.

Do not take if:

- suffering from low blood pressure or heart failure
- sensitive to nicotinic acid.

SIDE EFFECTS:
Common: headache, muscle pain, tiredness, palpitations, dizziness, nausea.
Unusual: high blood pressure, diarrhoea, shortness of breath.
Severe but rare (stop medication, consult doctor): low blood pressure.

INTERACTIONS:
Other drugs:
- other vasodilators, tricyclic antidepressants, sildenafil (Viagra), other medications that aid penile erection, medications that lower blood pressure.

Other substances:
- alcohol.

PRESCRIPTION:
Yes.

PERMITTED IN SPORT:
Yes.

OVERDOSE:
Low blood pressure, rapid heart rate and collapse may occur. Induce vomiting or administer activated charcoal if tablets taken recently. Seek medical assistance.

OTHER INFORMATION:
Introduced in 1998. Does not cause addiction or dependence.

See also Glyceryl trinitrate, Isosorbide nitrate, Perhexiline.

Nicotinamide
See Nicotinic acid.

Nicotine

TRADE NAMES:

Nicorette, Nicotinell, Niquitin CQ.
Nicotine is also one of the active chemicals in tobacco.

DRUG CLASS:

Stimulant.

USES:

Assists in stopping smoking.

DOSAGE:

 Chewable gum: chew one or two at a time when urge to smoke is felt. Maximum 60mg a day. Reduce frequency of use over time. Skin patches: apply to different place on non-hairy skin of trunk or upper arm once a day in morning. Instructions vary with brands. Follow doctors directions. Progressively reduce strength of patch over ten to twelve weeks. Under tongue dissolvable tablets: one or two tablets placed under tongue every hour. Inhaler: six to twelve cartridges inhaled a day. Nasal spray: one spray into each nostril every 30 minutes as required. Slowly reduce dose of all forms over several months.

FORMS:

Chewable gum, skin patches, under tongue dissolvable tablets, inhaler, nasal spray.

PRECAUTIONS:

Not to be used in pregnancy (D) (NB: smoking is also harmful to the foetus in pregnancy). Breast feeding should be ceased before use. Not designed for use in children under 14 years.
Not designed for long term use.

Use chewable gum with caution if:
• wearing dentures or having dental work
• suffering from mouth ulcers or inflammation
• suffering from peptic ulcer or inflamed stomach.
Use all forms in caution with heart disease.
Use patches with caution in dermatitis and eczema.

Do not take if:

 • suffering from recent heart attack, angina, irregular heart rate or recent stroke
• continuing to smoke.

SIDE EFFECTS:

Common: patches—rash at application site.
Inhaler—cough, headache, nausea.
Unusual: dizziness, nausea, diarrhoea, sore mouth or throat (with gum and inhaler).

INTERACTIONS:

Other drugs:
• cessation of smoking may result in altered availability of many medications and may require alteration in their doses
• phenacetin, theophylline, imipramine, oxazepam, paracetamol, pentazocine, propranolol, frusemide, insulin.
Other substances:
• continued smoking while using nicotine may cause significant serious adverse effects
• caffeine.

PRESCRIPTION:

No.

PERMITTED IN SPORT:

Yes.

OVERDOSE:

Nausea and vomiting only likely effects.

OTHER INFORMATION:

Nicotine medications work best if used with an appropriate smoking cessation program. Will only work if the patient wants to stop smoking and is prepared to use nicotine as assistance to his or her own determination. Nicotine by itself will not stop someone from smoking. Nicotine medications may cause dependence. Nicotine is highly addictive.

See also Bupropion.

Nicotinic Acid
(Niacin, Nicotinyl and Nicotinamide)
(Vitamin B3)

TRADE NAMES:

Nicotinic Acid.
Hexopal (Inositol nicotinate).
Nicam (Nicotinamide).
Also found in numerous vitamin and mineral supplements.

DRUG CLASS:

Vitamin, Hypolipidaemic, Vasodilator.

USES:

High levels of blood cholesterol and triglycerides, pellagra, poor circulation, acne.

DOSAGE:

 Pellagra: 500mg a day.
High cholesterol/triglyceride: 250mg to 1500mg three times a day after meals.
Poor circulation: one or two tablets, three or four times a day.
Acne: apply sparingly twice a day.

FORMS:

Tablets, capsules, gel.

PRECAUTIONS:

Use with caution in pregnancy (B2) and breast feeding.
Blood tests to check liver function, uric acid levels and blood fat levels recommended.
Use with caution with low blood pressure and poor liver function.

Do not take if:

 • suffering from peptic ulcer, stomach upsets, recent heart attack, severe liver disease, diabetes, gout, heart disease, gall bladder disease, glaucoma, tendency to bleed easily.

SIDE EFFECTS:

Common: rashes, itchy skin, changes in heart function, stomach upsets, nervousness.
Unusual: dry skin, skin pigmentation.
Severe but rare (stop medication, consult doctor): yellow skin.

INTERACTIONS:

Other drugs:
• drugs used to treat high blood pressure
• steroids, hallucinogens, reserpine, chlordiazepoxide.
Herbs:
• alfalfa, fenugreek, garlic, ginger.
Other substances:
• other vitamins may affect nicotinic acid absorption.

PRESCRIPTION:

No.

PERMITTED IN SPORT:

Yes.

OVERDOSE:

Causes flushing, itch, vomiting, diarrhoea, heartburn, belly cramps, fainting. Induce vomiting if tablets taken recently. Seek medical assistance.

OTHER INFORMATION:

Used as a starting point in the treatment of high cholesterol blood levels and poor circulation. Remember, vitamins are merely chemicals that are essential for the functioning of the body and if taken to excess, act as a drug.

See also Acipimox, VASODILATORS.

Nicoumalone

TRADE NAME:
Sinthrome.

DRUG CLASS:
Anticoagulant.

USES:
Prevention and treatment of blood clots in arteries and veins.

DOSAGE:
 Dosage carefully adjusted by doctor on a regular basis depending on blood test results.

FORMS:
Tablets of 1mg (white).

PRECAUTIONS:
Must not be used in pregnancy (D) as it may cause foetal damage and death. Breast feeding should be ceased if use is medically necessary. Not recommended in children.
Regular blood tests to check blood clotting time essential.
Other illnesses (e.g. infection) may require an adjustment of dosage.
Read literature accompanying medication very carefully. Ask questions of doctor about anything you do not understand.
Use with caution in high blood pressure and heart failure.
Do not undertake any activity that may result in falls, bruising or extreme exertion.

Do not take if:

- suffering from bleeding tendency, peptic ulcer, dementia, mental diseases, severe high blood pressure, significant liver or kidney disease, endocarditis, abnormal blood cells
- due to have essential surgery, including dental surgery
- unable to cooperate with doctor and instructions.

SIDE EFFECTS:
Common: abnormal bleeding and bruising.
Severe but rare (stop medication, consult doctor): allergy reactions, hair loss, liver damage (jaundice—yellow skin), skin damage.

INTERACTIONS:
Other drugs:
- NSAID, aspirin, hypoglycaemics, sulphonamides, quinidine, antibiotics, phenformin, cimetidine, corticosteroids
- many other drugs may affect dosage levels.

PRESCRIPTION:
Yes.

PERMITTED IN SPORT:
Yes.

OVERDOSE:
Extremely serious. Administer activated charcoal or induce vomiting only if tablets taken very recently. Seek emergency medical assistance. Massive internal bleeding may cause sudden death. Antidote (Vitamin K) available. Blood transfusion may be necessary.
See also Warfarin.

Nifedipine

TRADE NAMES:
Adalat, Adipine MR, Cardilate MR, Coracten, Fortipine LA, Tensipine MR. Beta-Adalat, Tenif (with atenolol).

DRUG CLASS:
Calcium channel blocker (calcium antagonist).

USES:
High blood pressure, angina.

DOSAGE:
 10 to 40mg a day.
Do not vary dosage without medical advice.

FORMS:

Tablets, capsules, slow release tablets.

PRECAUTIONS:

Should only be used in pregnancy (C) and breast feeding if medically essential. Not designed for use in children.
Use with caution in heart failure, diabetes and dialysis patients.

Do not take if:

 • suffering from severe heart failure, low blood pressure, atrial flutter or fibrillation, unstable angina, aortic stenosis, recent heart attack.

SIDE EFFECTS:

Common: constipation, tiredness, headache, dizziness, indigestion, swelling of feet and ankles.
Unusual: flushing, palpitations, slow heart rate, scalp irritation, depression, flushes, nightmares, excess wind.
Severe but rare (stop medication, consult doctor): fainting.

INTERACTIONS:

Other drugs:
• beta-blockers (e.g. propranolol), cyclosporin, digoxin, cimetidine, diazepam, amiodarone, quinidine, rifampicin, phenytoin, cisapride, theophylline, terbutaline, salbutamol, diltiazem
• additive effect with other medications for high blood pressure.
Herbs:
• goldenseal, guarana, hawthorn, Korean ginseng, liquorice.
Other substances:
• smoking may aggravate conditions that these medications are treating
• grapefruit juice.

PRESCRIPTION:

Yes.

PERMITTED IN SPORT:

Yes.

OVERDOSE:

May continue to be absorbed for up to 48 hours after overdose. Administer activated charcoal or induce vomiting. Purging should be encouraged to eliminate drug from gut. Overdose may cause low blood pressure, irregular heart rhythm, difficulty in breathing, heart attack and death. Obtain urgent medical attention.

OTHER INFORMATION:

Commonly used as a first line medication in high blood pressure and to prevent angina.

See also Amlodipine, CALCIUM CHANNEL BLOCKERS, Diltiazem, Felodipine, Nicardipine, Nimodipine, Verapamil.

Nimodipine

TRADE NAME:

Nimotop.

DRUG CLASS:

Calcium channel blocker (calcium antagonist).

USES:

Poor blood supply to brain after haemorrhage into brain (stroke).

DOSAGE:

 As determined by doctor. Start within four days of stroke.

FORMS:

Tablets of 30mg (yellow), injection.

PRECAUTIONS:

Should only be used in pregnancy (C) and breast feeding if medically essential. Not designed for use in children.
Use with caution in swelling of brain, kidney disease, cirrhosis.

Do not take if:

- suffering from severe heart failure, low blood pressure, atrial flutter or fibrillation, recent heart attack.

SIDE EFFECTS:

Common: constipation, tiredness, headache, dizziness, indigestion, swelling of feet and ankles, low blood pressure.
Unusual: flushing, palpitations, slow heart rate, scalp irritation, depression, flushes, nightmares, excess wind.
Severe but rare (stop medication, consult doctor): fainting.

INTERACTIONS:

Other drugs:
- beta-blockers (e.g. propranolol), cyclosporin, digoxin, cimetidine, diazepam, amiodarone, quinidine, rifampicin, phenytoin, cisapride, theophylline, terbutaline, salbutamol, diltiazem
- additive effect with other medications for high blood pressure.
Herbs:
- goldenseal, guarana, hawthorn, Korean ginseng, liquorice.
Other substances:
- smoking may aggravate conditions that these medications are treating
- grapefruit juice.

PRESCRIPTION:

Yes.

PERMITTED IN SPORT:

Yes.

OVERDOSE:

May continue to be absorbed for up to 48 hours after overdose. Administer activated charcoal or induce vomiting. Purging should be encouraged to eliminate drug from gut. Overdose may cause low blood pressure, irregular heart rhythm, difficulty in breathing, heart attack and death. Obtain urgent medical attention.

See also Amlodipine, CALCIUM CHANNEL BLOCKERS, Diltiazem, Felodipine, Nifedipine, Verapamil.

Nisoldipine

TRADE NAME:

Syscor MR.

DRUG CLASS:

Calcium channel blocker (calcium antagonist).

USES:

High blood pressure.

DOSAGE:

 10 to 40mg once a day.

FORMS:

Slow release tablets of 10mg, 20mg and 30mg.

PRECAUTIONS:

Should only be used in pregnancy (C) and breast feeding if medically essential. Not designed for use in children.
Use with caution in heart failure, diabetes and dialysis patients.

Do not take if:

- suffering from severe heart failure, low blood pressure, atrial flutter or fibrillation, unstable angina, aortic stenosis, recent heart attack.

SIDE EFFECTS:

Common: constipation, tiredness, headache, dizziness, indigestion, swelling of feet and ankles.
Unusual: flushing, palpitations, slow heart rate, scalp irritation, depression, flushes, nightmares, excess wind.
Severe but rare (stop medication, consult doctor): fainting.

INTERACTIONS:

Other drugs:
- beta-blockers (e.g. propranolol), cyclosporin, digoxin, cimetidine, diazepam, amiodarone, quinidine, rifampicin, phenytoin, cisapride, theophylline, terbutaline, salbutamol, diltiazem

- additive effect with other medications for high blood pressure.

Herbs:
- goldenseal, guarana, hawthorn, Korean ginseng, liquorice.

Other substances:
- smoking may aggravate conditions that these medications are treating
- grapefruit juice.

PRESCRIPTION:
Yes.

PERMITTED IN SPORT:
Yes.

OVERDOSE:
May continue to be absorbed for up to 48 hours after overdose. Administer activated charcoal or induce vomiting. Purging should be encouraged to eliminate drug from gut. Overdose may cause low blood pressure, irregular heart rhythm, difficulty in breathing, heart attack and death. Obtain urgent medical attention.

See also Amlodipine, CALCIUM CHANNEL BLOCKERS, Diltiazem, Felodipine, Nicardipine, Nimodipine, Verapamil.

Nitrazepam

TRADE NAME:
Mogadon.

DRUG CLASS:
Sedative/hypnotic, Benzodiazepine.

USES:
Relieves insomnia (sleeplessness).

DOSAGE:
 One or two at bedtime.

FORMS:
Tablet of 5mg (white).

PRECAUTIONS:
Should be used with caution in pregnancy (C), but not at all if delivery of infant imminent as it may decrease desire to breathe in newborn infant. Should be used with caution in breast feeding. Not for use in children.

Lower dose required in elderly.

Should be used intermittently and not constantly as dependency may develop. Stopping suddenly after prolonged constant use may cause withdrawal symptoms.

Use with caution in glaucoma, myasthenia gravis, heart disease, kidney or liver disease, psychiatric conditions, depression and epilepsy.

Do not take if:

- suffering from severe lung disease, confusion.
- tendency to addiction or dependence.

SIDE EFFECTS:
Common: confusion and falls in elderly, impaired alertness.

Unusual: dizziness, incoordination, poor memory, headache, hangover in morning, slurred speech, nightmares.

INTERACTIONS:
Other drugs:
- other medications that reduce alertness (e.g. barbiturates, antihistamines, antianxiety drugs)
- disulfiram, cimetidine, anticonvulsants, anticholinergics, antihistamines.

Herbs:
- guarana, kava kava, passionflower, St John's wort, valerian, celery, camomile, goldenseal.

Other substances:
- reacts with alcohol to cause excessive drowsiness.

PRESCRIPTION:
Yes.

PERMITTED IN SPORT:
Yes.

OVERDOSE:
Seldom life threatening. May cause drowsiness, confusion and coma.

Administer activated charcoal or induce vomiting if tablets taken recently. Seek medical assistance.

OTHER INFORMATION:

In use for almost thirty years. Very safe and effective, but dependence (inability to sleep or function without medication) a problem if used regularly.
See also Zolpidem, Zopiclone.

Nitrofurantoin

TRADE NAMES:

Furadantin, Macrobid, Macrodantin.

DRUG CLASS:

Antibiotic.

USES:

Bacterial infections of urine.

DOSAGE:

 One or two capsules four times a day with food.

FORMS:

Capsules and tablets of 50 and 100mg.

PRECAUTIONS:

Safe to use in pregnancy (A), breast feeding and children. Not for use during labour of pregnancy or if labour imminent. Not for use under one month of age.
Not designed for long term use.
Use with caution in kidney function disorders, diabetes, blood chemistry (electrolyte) disorders.
Do not take if:

 • suffering from severe kidney failure.

SIDE EFFECTS:

Common: nausea, vomiting.
Unusual: brown urine.

Severe but rare (stop medication, consult doctor): numbness or tingling, yellow skin (jaundice).

INTERACTIONS:

Other drugs:
• barbiturates, antacids, urinary acidifiers and alkalinisers.

PRESCRIPTION:

Yes.

PERMITTED IN SPORT:

Yes.

OVERDOSE:

Exacerbation of side effects likely. Give additional fluids by mouth to increase rate of excretion.

OTHER INFORMATION:

Useful and effective medication.
See also Hexamine hippurate.

Nitroglycerine

See Glyceryl Trinitrate.

Nizatadine

TRADE NAME:

Axid.

DRUG CLASS:

Antiulcerant, H2 receptor antagonist.

USES:

Prevention and treatment of ulcers of the stomach, oesophagus (gullet) and duodenum (upper small intestine). Prevention of acid reflux into the oesophagus (heartburn).

DOSAGE:

 300mg a day in one or two doses.

FORMS:

Capsules of 150 (cream/yellow) and 300mg (yellow/brown).

PRECAUTIONS:

Care should be taken with use in pregnancy (B3) and breast feeding. Safety in children not established.

Do not take if:

- suffering from severe kidney disease or phenylketonuria
- suffering from stomach cancer.

SIDE EFFECTS:

Common: anaemia, tiredness, drowsiness, rash.
Unusual: constipation, breast enlargement and tenderness (both sexes).
Severe but rare (stop medication, consult doctor): hepatitis (jaundice), rapid or irregular heart beat.

INTERACTIONS:

Other drugs:
- aspirin.
Herbs:
- alfalfa, capsicum, eucalyptus, senega.

PRESCRIPTION:

Yes.

PERMITTED IN SPORT:

Yes.

OVERDOSE:

No serious effects reported.

OTHER INFORMATION:

Very safe and effective H2 receptor antagonist that may be more effective in reflux oesophagitis than others in this class. Introduced in 1992.
See also Cimetidine, Famotidine, Ranitidine.

Nonoxynol 9

TRADE NAMES:

Delfen, Durex Duragel, Gynol II, Ortho-Creme, Ortho-Forms.

DRUG CLASS:

Contraceptive, Spermicide.

USES:

For use in combination with a diaphragm or condom to prevent pregnancy, kills sperm.

DOSAGE:

 Varies with form and product. Use strictly in accordance with directions on packaging.

FORMS:

Cream, foam, gel.

PRECAUTIONS:

Safe if used accidentally in pregnancy (A). Safe in breast feeding. Not designed for use in children.
Wait six to eight hours after sex before removing diaphragm or using douche. Do not retain diaphragm for more than 24 hours.
Ensure hands and diaphragm are completely clean before insertion.

SIDE EFFECTS:

Common: minimal.
Unusual: irritation of vagina or penis.

INTERACTIONS:

None.

PRESCRIPTION:

No.

PERMITTED IN SPORT:

Yes.

OTHER INFORMATION:

Not a reliable form of contraception if used alone. Even in combination with a diaphragm or condom, spermicides have a failure rate of about 5% (i.e. five out of 100 women using this method of

contraception for a year will fall pregnant). Does not protect against venereal disease.
See also ORAL CONTRACEPTIVES.

Norelgestren

TRADE NAME:
Evra (with ethinyloestradiol).

DRUG CLASS:
Sex hormone.

USES:
Contraception.

DOSAGE:
 Apply first patch on first day of menstrual period to intact, non-hairy, smooth, soft area of skin (e.g. lower abdomen, buttocks). Change patch once a week on same day of week, and apply at different site. After using three patches, cease for one week then start cycle again.

FORMS:
Skin patch.

PRECAUTIONS:
Not for use in pregnancy (D), breast feeding or children.
Take other precautions against pregnancy if patch falls off, or is left on for more than a week.
Do not use if:
 • suffering from severe liver disease, jaundice or blood clots
• male.

SIDE EFFECTS:
Common: breast tenderness, rash under patch.
Unusual: headache, abnormal vaginal bleeding.

INTERACTIONS:
Other drugs:
• other sex hormones.

Other substances:
• smoking increases risk of serious side effects.

PRESCRIPTION:
Yes.

PERMITTED IN SPORT:
Yes.

OTHER INFORMATION:
Introduced in 2002 as a new method of contraception.
See also ORAL CONTRACEPTIVES.

Norethisterone

TRADE NAMES:
Micronor, Noriday, Noristerat, Primolut-N, Utovlan.
Adgyn Combi, Climagest, Climesse, Elleste Duet, Estracombi, Evorel, FemTab Continuous, Kliofem, Kliovance, Novofem, Nuvelle Continuous, Trisequens (with oestradiol).
Used in numerous oral contraceptives (e.g. **BiNovum, Brevinor, Loestrin, Norimin, Norinyl-1, Ovysmen, Synphase, TriNovum**), see separate entry.

DRUG CLASS:
Sex hormone.

USES:
Abnormal bleeding from uterus, failure of menstrual period, premenstrual tension, breast tenderness, endometriosis, as an addition to oestrogen in menopausal hormone replacement therapy (HRT). Contraception (as contraceptive mini-pill in Micronor, Noriday, Noristerat, Utovlan).

DOSAGE:
 Tablets: one or two tablets, one to three times a day with fluid.
Patches: apply once or twice a week.

FORMS:
Tablets, patches.

PRECAUTIONS:

Not for use in pregnancy (D), breast feeding or children.
Use with caution in diabetes.

Do not take if:

- suffering from severe liver disease, jaundice or blood clots
- male.

SIDE EFFECTS:

Common: abnormal vaginal bleeding, headache.
Unusual: sleeplessness, nervousness, dizziness, tremor, rash, sweating, nausea, breast tenderness, weight gain.
Severe but rare (stop medication, consult doctor): blood clot, calf pain, chest pain, yellow skin (jaundice).

INTERACTIONS:

Other drugs:
- other sex hormones.

Other substances:
- smoking increases risk of serious side effects.

PRESCRIPTION:

Yes.

PERMITTED IN SPORT:

Yes.

OVERDOSE:

Unlikely to be serious. Vomiting and abnormal vaginal bleeding likely.

OTHER INFORMATION:

Widely used and safe medication. Useful for delaying menstrual period that may be due at an awkward time, or as an additive to menopausal treatments to prevent over stimulation of the uterine lining. Does not cause addiction or dependence. Mini-pill often used as a contraceptive in women who are breast feeding, although they must be taken at the same time each day to be reliable.

See also HORMONE REPLACEMENT THERAPY, ORAL CONTRACEPTIVES.

Norfloxacin

TRADE NAME:

Utinor.

DRUG CLASS:

Quinolone antibiotic.

USES:

Urinary infections.

DOSAGE:

 One tablet twice a day.

FORMS:

Tablet (white) of 400mg.

PRECAUTIONS:

Not to be used in pregnancy (B3) and breast feeding unless medically essential.
Not for use in children.
Ensure adequate fluid intake.
Use with caution in epilepsy and kidney disease.
Avoid excessive sun exposure while taking medication.

SIDE EFFECTS:

Common: nausea, headache, dizziness.
Unusual: tiredness, rash, belly pain, depression, sleeplessness, constipation, excess wind, constipation.
Severe but rare (stop medication, consult doctor): bloody diarrhoea, unusual bruising or bleeding, tender tendons.

INTERACTIONS:

Other drugs:
- antacids, nitrofurantoin, theophylline, cyclosporin, probenecid, anticoagulants.

Other substances:
- reacts with caffeine.

PRESCRIPTION:

Yes.

PERMITTED IN SPORT:

Yes.

OVERDOSE:

Exacerbation of side effects most likely result. Induce vomiting if medication taken recently. Maintain adequate fluid intake.

OTHER INFORMATION:

Introduced in late 1980s. Very effective in treating the more difficult infections of the bladder and kidneys.

See also Ciprofloxacin.

Norgestimate

See ORAL CONTRACEPTIVES.

Norgestrel

See ORAL CONTRACEPTIVES.

Normal Immunoglobulin

See Gamma globulin.

Nortriptyline

See TRICYCLICS.

NSAIDs
(NONSTEROIDAL ANTI-INFLAMMATORY DRUGS)

DISCUSSION:

Despite their long name and unpronounceable acronym, the NSAIDs are some of the most widely used drugs in modern medicine. They are drugs that reduce inflammation in tissue, without being steroids (see separate entry), which are the most potent anti-inflammatory drugs available.

Inflammation is the redness, swelling, pain and heat that occurs in tissue that is subjected to some form of irritation or injury. NSAIDs not only reduce inflammation but also ease pain and lower fevers. Their main uses are in the treatment of rheumatoid and osteoarthritis, sporting injuries to joints, muscles and tendons, and to reduce the inflammation in the pelvis associated with menstrual period pain. They are all available as tablets or capsules, but some are also available as injections, and even as creams, gels and a rub-on lotion.

A subgroup of the NSAIDs are the salicylates, which are all derived from salicylic acid. The most commonly known member of this subgroup is aspirin which acts as a painkiller (analgesic), fever-reducing agent (antipyretic) and anti-inflammatory medication. It has the same side effects as the other NSAIDs.

The greatest problem with the use of NSAIDs is the possibility of causing peptic ulcers in the stomach or small intestine. Unfortunately, a significant proportion of the patients using these medications will develop some intestinal problem. This can be prevented to some extent by always taking the drugs after food, or in conjunction with an antacid or other ulcer-preventing medication. Any patient who develops stomach pains, vomits blood or passes black stools while on NSAIDs must cease them and see a doctor immediately.

Despite the problems associated with the use of NSAIDs, many patients with arthritis find that these drugs have improved their lives dramatically by controlling their previously painful and swollen joints. They can also enable sportsmen and women to overcome painful sprains and strains to enable them to return to competition as quickly as possible.

See Aceclofenac, Acemetacin, Aspirin, Azapropazone, Dexketoprofen, Diclofenac, Diflunisal, Etodolac, Felbinac, Fenbufen, Fenoprofen, Flurbiprofen, Ibuprofen, Indomethacin, Ketoprofen, Ketorolac, Lornoxicam, Mefenamic acid, Meloxicam,

Nabumetone, Naproxen, Piroxicam,
Salicylic acid, Sulindac, Tenoxicam,
Tiaprofenic Acid, Tolfenamic acid.

Nystatin

TRADE NAMES:

Nystan.
Dermovate-NN (with clobetasol,
neomycin).
Flagyl Compak (with metronidazole).
Gregoderm (with neomycin, polymyxin
B, hydrocortisone).
Nystaform (with chlorhexidine).
Nystaform-HC (with chlorhexidine,
hydrocortisone).
Terra-Cortril Nystatin (with
oxytetracycline, hydrocortisone).
Timodine (with hydrocortisone,
benzalkonium chloride, dimethicone).
Tinaderm-M (with tolnaftate).
Tri-Adcortyl (with triamcinolone,
neomycin and gramicidin).
Trimovate (with clobetasone,
oxytetracycline).

DRUG CLASS:

Antifungal.

USES:

Treatment and prevention of fungal
infections of skin (tinea), mouth, vagina
(thrush) and intestine (candidiasis).

DOSAGE:

Tablets: one or two, three times
a day.
Skin preparations: apply three
times a day.
Vaginal preparations: one pessary
or applicator of cream at night for
14 days.

FORMS:

Tablets, cream, ointment, suspension,
lozenges, vaginal cream, vaginal pessary.

PRECAUTIONS:

Safe to use in pregnancy, breast feeding
and children.
Applicator of vaginal preparations must
be used with care in pregnancy.

SIDE EFFECTS:

Minimal.

INTERACTIONS:

None significant.

PRESCRIPTION:

Yes.

PERMITTED IN SPORT:

Yes.

OVERDOSE:

Diarrhoea, nausea and vomiting only
likely effects.

OTHER INFORMATION:

Does not cause dependence or addiction.
Available for over thirty years. Very safe.
Use decreasing in recent years with
introduction of more potent antifungals
(e.g. Imidazoles). Often combined with
other medications (particularly steroids)
in skin preparations.

See also ANTIFUNGALS, Clotrimazole,
Econazole, Fluconazole, Itraconazole,
Ketoconazole, Miconazole.

OBESITY DRUGS

See Methylcellulose, Orlistat, Silbutramine.

Octreotide

TRADE NAME:

Sandostatin.

USES:

Acromegaly (bone overgrowth caused by tumour of pituitary gland), relief of carcinoid tumour symptoms.

DOSAGE:

 One or more injections a day as determined by doctor.

FORMS:

Injection.

PRECAUTIONS:

Must not be used in pregnancy (C) or breast feeding. Use in children only when medically essential.
Use with caution in diabetes.
Regular checks on gall bladder and pituitary gland necessary.
Designed for short term or intermittent use.

SIDE EFFECTS:

Common: pain at injection site, nausea, vomiting, loss of appetite, bloating, excess wind, diarrhoea.
Unusual: headache, dizziness, fatigue, flushing.

INTERACTIONS:

Other drugs:
• cyclosporin, cimetidine, bromocriptine.

PRESCRIPTION:

Yes.

PERMITTED IN SPORT:

Yes.

Oestradiol
(Estradiol)

TRADE NAMES:

Adgyn Estro, Aerodiol, Climaval, Dermestril, Elleste Solo, Estraderm, Estrapak, Estring, Evorel, Fematrix, Femseven, FemTab, Menorest, Menoring, Oestrogel, Progynova, Sandrena, Vagifem, Zumenon.
Adgyn Combi, Climagest, Climesse, Elleste Duet, Estracombi, Evorel Conti, Evorel Sequi, Evorel-Pak, FemTab Continuous, FemTab Sequi, Kliofem, Kliovance, Novofem, Nuvelle Continuous, Oestradiol, Trisequens (with norethisterone).
Cyclo-Progynova, Femseven Conti, Femseven Sequi, Nuvelle, Nuvelle TS (with levonorgestrel).
Femapak, Femoston (with dydrogesterone).
Hormonin (with oestrone, oestriol).
Indivina, Tridestra (with medroxyprogesterone acetate).

DRUG CLASS:

Sex hormone.

USES:

Oestrogen (female hormone) replacement in menopause.

DOSAGE:

 Tablets: dosage individualised by doctor. Usually one tablet once a day.
Patch: apply once or twice a week.
Nasal spray: one or two sprays in each nostril once a day. Do not inhale during spray, or blow nose for five minutes afterwards.

Pessary: one pessary in vagina every night initially, reducing to twice a week. Vaginal ring: one inserted into vagina and replaced every three months.

FORMS:

Tablets, patches, nasal spray, vaginal pessary, vaginal cream, vaginal ring, injection, implant.

PRECAUTIONS:

Not to be used in pregnancy (B1), breast feeding or children. Accidental usage in these situations unlikely to be harmful. Not to be used by males.
Use with caution in epilepsy, migraine, heart failure, high blood pressure, kidney disease, diabetes, porphyria or uterine disease.

Do not take if:

 • suffering from liver disease, breast or genital cancer, blood clots, sickle cell anaemia, undiagnosed bleeding from vagina, severe high blood pressure, or endometriosis.

SIDE EFFECTS:

Common: abnormal uterine bleeding, vaginal thrush, nausea, fluid retention, weight gain, breast tenderness.
Unusual: rash at site of patch application, blurred vision, vomiting, bloating, intestinal cramps, pigmentation of skin on face, nose bleeds with nasal spray use.
Severe but rare (stop medication, consult doctor): blood clots, calf or chest pain, yellow skin (jaundice).

INTERACTIONS:

Other drugs:
• other sex hormones, antibiotics, diabetes medications (hypoglycaemics), warfarin, epilepsy medications (anticonvulsants), imipramine, corticosteroids, thyroxine
• do not use oestradiol nose spray at same time as other nose sprays.

Herbs:
• saw palmetto, alfalfa, dong quai, ginseng, liquorice, red clover.
Other substances:
• smoking increases risk of serious side effects.

PRESCRIPTION:

Yes.

PERMITTED IN SPORT:

Yes.

OVERDOSE:

Vomiting and abnormal vaginal bleeding only likely effects.

OTHER INFORMATION:

Does not cause addiction or dependence. Very useful in managing the effects of menopause, and reduces the risk of osteoporosis and heart disease after the menopause.

See also Cyproterone acetate, Danazol, Dydrogesterone, Estropipate, Ethinyloestradiol, Etonogestrel, HORMONE REPLACEMENT THERAPY, Medroxyprogesterone acetate, Oestriol, Oestrogen, Oestrone, ORAL CONTRACEPTIVES, Piperazine, Testosterone, Tibolone.

Oestriol

TRADE NAMES:

Ortho-Gynest, Ovestin.
Hormonin (with oestradiol, oestrone).
Trisequens (with oestradiol, norethisterone).

DRUG CLASS:

Sex Hormone.

USES:

Oestrogen (female hormone) replacement in menopause.

DOSAGE:

 Tablets: dosage individualised by doctor. Usually one tablet once a day.

Vaginal cream and pessaries: use daily at bed time initially, reduce to once or twice a week long term.

FORMS:

Tablets (white) of 1mg, vaginal cream, vaginal pessaries.

PRECAUTIONS:

Not to be used in pregnancy (B1), breast feeding or children. Accidental usage in these situations unlikely to be harmful. Use with caution in epilepsy, migraine, heart failure, high blood pressure, kidney disease, diabetes, porphyria or uterine disease.

Do not take if:

- suffering from liver disease, breast or genital cancer, blood clots, undiagnosed vaginal bleeding, endometriosis, porphyria or otosclerosis.

SIDE EFFECTS:

Common: abnormal uterine bleeding, vaginal thrush, nausea, fluid retention, weight gain, breast tenderness.
Unusual: rash, blurred vision, vomiting, bloating, intestinal cramps, pigmentation of skin on face.
Severe but rare (stop medication, consult doctor): blood clots, calf or chest pain, yellow skin (jaundice).

INTERACTIONS:

Other drugs:
- other sex hormones.
Other substances:
- smoking increases risk of serious side effects.

PRESCRIPTION:

Yes.

PERMITTED IN SPORT:

Yes.

OVERDOSE:

Vomiting and abnormal vaginal bleeding only likely effects.

OTHER INFORMATION:

Does not cause addiction or dependence. Very useful in managing the effects of menopause and reduces the risk of osteoporosis and heart disease after the menopause.

See also Ethinyloestradiol, Estropipate, Etonogestrel, HORMONE REPLACEMENT THERAPY, Oestradiol, Oestrogen, Oestrone, Oxandrolone, Piperazine.

Oestrogen

TRADE NAMES:

Premarin, Prempak-C.
Premique (with medroxyprogesterone).

DRUG CLASS:

Sex hormone.

USES:

Female hormone replacement in menopause.

DOSAGE:

 Tablets: dosage individualised by doctor. usually one tablet once a day.
Vaginal cream: insert daily, three weeks per month.

FORMS:

Tablets, vaginal cream, injection.

PRECAUTIONS:

Not to be used in pregnancy (B1), breast feeding or children. Accidental usage in these situations unlikely to be harmful. Use with caution in epilepsy, migraine, heart failure, high blood pressure, kidney disease, diabetes, porphyria or uterine disease.

Do not take if:

- suffering from liver disease, breast or genital cancer, blood clots, undiagnosed vaginal bleeding.

SIDE EFFECTS:

Common: abnormal uterine bleeding, vaginal thrush, nausea, fluid retention, weight gain, breast tenderness.
Unusual: rash, blurred vision, vomiting, bloating, intestinal cramps, pigmentation of skin on face.
Severe but rare (stop medication, consult doctor): blood clots, calf or chest pain, yellow skin (jaundice).

INTERACTIONS:

Other drugs:
• other sex hormones, rifampicin.
Herbs:
• saw palmetto, alfalfa, dong quai, ginseng, liquorice, red clover.
Other substances:
• smoking increases risk of serious side effects.

PRESCRIPTION:

Yes.

PERMITTED IN SPORT:

Yes.

OVERDOSE:

Vomiting and abnormal vaginal bleeding only likely effects.

OTHER INFORMATION:

Does not cause addiction or dependence. Very useful in managing the effects of menopause and reduces the risk of osteoporosis and heart disease after the menopause.

See also Cyproterone acetate, Danazol, Dydrogesterone, Estropipate, Ethinyloestradiol, Etonogestrel, HORMONE REPLACEMENT THERAPY, Medroxyprogesterone acetate, Oestradiol, Oestriol, Oestrone, ORAL CONTRACEPTIVES, Oxandrolone, Piperazine oestrone sulfate.

Oestrone

TRADE NAME:

Only used in combination with other forms of oestrogen.
Hormonin (with oestradiol, oestriol).

DRUG CLASS:

Sex Hormone.

USES:

Oestrogen (female hormone) replacement in menopause.

DOSAGE:

 One or two tablets a day, continuously or cyclically.

FORMS:

Tablets (pink).

PRECAUTIONS:

Not to be used in pregnancy (B1), breast feeding or children. Accidental usage in these situations unlikely to be harmful. Use with caution in epilepsy, migraine, heart failure, high blood pressure, kidney disease, diabetes, porphyria or uterine disease.

Do not take if:

 • suffering from liver disease, breast or genital cancer, blood clots.

SIDE EFFECTS:

Common: abnormal uterine bleeding, vaginal thrush, nausea, fluid retention, weight gain, breast tenderness.
Unusual: rash, blurred vision, vomiting, bloating, intestinal cramps, pigmentation of skin on face.
Severe but rare (stop medication, consult doctor): blood clots, calf or chest pain, yellow skin (jaundice).

INTERACTIONS:

Other drugs:
• other sex hormones, rifampicin.

Herbs:
- saw palmetto, alfalfa, dong quai, ginseng, liquorice, red clover.

Other substances:
- smoking increases risk of serious side effects.

PRESCRIPTION:
Yes.

PERMITTED IN SPORT:
Yes.

OVERDOSE:
Vomiting and abnormal vaginal bleeding only likely effects.

See also HORMONE REPLACEMENT THERAPY, Oestradiol, Oestriol, Oestrogen.

Ofloxacin

TRADE NAMES:
Exocin, Tarivid.

DRUG CLASS:
Quinolone antibiotic.

USES:
Severe bacterial infections.

DOSAGE:

Tablets: one tablet three times a day.
Eye drops: one drop in affected eye(s) every four to six hours for maximum of ten days.

FORMS:
Tablets of 200mg (off white), 400mg (yellow), eye drops.

PRECAUTIONS:
Use with caution in pregnancy (B3), breast feeding and children.
Use with caution in diabetes, syphilis, tuberculosis, epilepsy, brain disorders, liver and kidney disease.
Ensure adequate hydration.
Not for prolonged use.

SIDE EFFECTS:
Common: fever, rash, inflammation of veins, inflammation of lungs, liver and kidney stress, dizziness, drowsiness,
Unusual: psychosis, brain pressure and stimulation, persistent diarrhoea, sensitivity to light, weakening of tendons, vomiting.
Severe but rare (stop medication, consult doctor): seizures, jaundice.

INTERACTIONS:
Other drugs:
- antacids, zinc, cyclosporin, cimetidine, NSAIDs, probenecid, warfarin, theophylline, other antibiotics.

PRESCRIPTION:
Yes.

PERMITTED IN SPORT:
Yes.

OVERDOSE:
Serious exacerbation of side effects likely. Administer activated charcoal or induce vomiting if tablets taken recently. Seek urgent medical attention.

OTHER INFORMATION:
Introduced in 1997 for the treatment of serious infections unresponsive to other antibiotics.

See also Ciprofloxacin.

Olanzapine

TRADE NAME:
Zyprexa.

DRUG CLASS:
Antipsychotic.

USES:
Schizophrenia, psychoses, dementia, other psychiatric conditions.

DOSAGE:

2.5 to 20mg once a day. Increase dose slowly.

FORMS:

Tablets of 2.5mg, 5mg, 7.5mg, 10mg and 15mg.
Dispersible wafers of 5mg, 10mg and 15mg.

PRECAUTIONS:

Use with caution in pregnancy (B3), breast feeding and children.
Use with caution in enlarged prostate gland, glaucoma, diabetes, poor small bowel function, epilepsy, kidney and liver disease.
Use low doses in elderly.
Regular blood tests to check function of blood cells and bone marrow necessary.

Do not take if:

 • suffering from leukaemia, bone marrow disease.

SIDE EFFECTS:

Common: sleepiness, tiredness, weight gain, dizziness, low blood pressure, swelling of feet and hands, dry mouth.
Unusual: liver damage, poor coordination, breast milk production.
Severe but rare (stop medication, consult doctor): severe infection, jaundice (yellow skin).

INTERACTIONS:

Other drugs:
• drugs affecting heart function, drugs acting on the brain, carbamazepine, fluoxetine, fluvoxamine.
Herbs:
• evening primrose (linoleic acid).
Other substances:
• alcohol, smoking.

PRESCRIPTION:

Yes.

PERMITTED IN SPORT:

Yes.

OVERDOSE:

Serious exacerbation of side effects likely. Induce vomiting or administer activated charcoal if taken recently. Seek urgent medical attention.

OTHER INFORMATION:

Extraordinarily effective drug introduced in 1997 for the treatment of the more difficult forms of schizophrenia and behaviour problems associated with dementia.

See also Amisulpride, Flupenthixol, Haloperidol, Lithium Carbonate, PHENOTHIAZINES, Pimozide, Quetiapine, Risperidone, Thiothixene, Zuclopenthixol.

Olopatadine

TRADE NAME:

Opatanol.

USES:

Allergic conjunctivitis.

DOSAGE:

 One or two drops into affected eye, once or twice a day.

FORMS:

Eye drops.

PRECAUTIONS:

Use with caution in pregnancy (B1).
Not for use in breast feeding.
Not for long term use over 14 weeks.
Use with caution if wearing soft contact lenses.
Do not use other eye medication within ten minutes.

SIDE EFFECTS:

Common: temporary blurred vision.
Unusual: headaches, tiredness, eye burning and stinging, dry eye, irritated eye, red eye, swollen eyelid, abnormal taste.

INTERACTIONS:

None significant.

PRESCRIPTION:

Yes.

PERMITTED IN SPORT:

Yes.

See also Levocabastine.

Olsalazine

TRADE NAME:

Dipentum.

USES:

Treatment of complicated cases of ulcerative colitis.

DOSAGE:

 250 to 1000mg three times a day after meals.

FORMS:

Capsule of 250mg (light brown), tablets of 500mg (yellow).

PRECAUTIONS:

Should be used with caution in pregnancy (B2) and breast feeding.
Should be used with caution in severe kidney disease.

Do not take if:

- sensitive to salicylates
- suffering from a bleeding disorder or peptic ulcer.

SIDE EFFECTS:

Common: diarrhoea (very common), nausea, belly pains.
Unusual: rash, headache, joint pains.
Severe but rare (stop medication, consult doctor): many rare and serious effects reported including blood cell abnormalities and liver damage.

INTERACTIONS:

Other drugs:
- serious interaction with anticoagulants (e.g. warfarin).

PRESCRIPTION:

Yes.

PERMITTED IN SPORT:

Yes.

OTHER INFORMATION:

Used in only very special circumstances in the uncommon condition of ulcerative colitis.

See also Mesalazine.

Omeprazole

See PROTON PUMP INHIBITORS.

Ondansetron

TRADE NAME:

Zofran.

USES:

Stops nausea and vomiting caused by cancer treating drugs, radiotherapy or surgery.

DOSAGE:

One to four tablets twice a day.

FORMS:

Tablets (yellow) of 4mg, syrup, soluble tablet of 4mg, suppositories, injection.

PRECAUTIONS:

May be used with caution in pregnancy (B1), breast feeding and children over four years.
Use with caution in liver disease.

SIDE EFFECTS:

Common: hot flush, headache, upper belly discomfort.
Unusual: dry mouth, constipation, hiccups.

INTERACTIONS:

Other drugs:
• phenytoin, carbamazepine.

PRESCRIPTION:

Yes.

PERMITTED IN SPORT:

Yes.

OVERDOSE:

Exacerbation of side effects likely.

OTHER INFORMATION:

Introduced in 1993 to relieve the severe vomiting that may be caused by some anticancer drugs. More effective if given by injection.

See also Chlorpromazine, Metoclopramide, Prochlorperazine.

OPIATES

DISCUSSION:

Opiates (also known as narcotics) are strong, addictive and effective painkillers derived from the opium poppy. They are highly restricted in their use and must be kept in safes by chemists and doctors. If they are used appropriately, they give relief from severe pain to patients with acute injuries, and pain from diseases such as cancer and kidney stones. They are often used before, during and after operations to ease the pain of the procedure. If used in this way, it is unlikely that addiction will occur. If used excessively, a psychological and physical addiction can rapidly develop. Heroin is an infamous illegal opiate which is broken down to morphine in the body. Opiates not only relieve severe pain, they also reduce anxiety, stop coughs, sedate and cause euphoria (artificial happiness). They should be used with caution in asthma and other lung diseases, liver disease and after head injuries.

See Alfentanil, Buprenorphine, Codeine, Dextromoramide, Dextropropoxyphene, Ethoheptazine, Fentanyl, Heroin, Hydromorphone, Methadone, Morphine, Nalbuphine, Oxycodone, Pentazocine, Pethidine, Phenazocine.

ORAL CONTRACEPTIVES (CONTRACEPTIVE PILLS)

TRADE and GENERIC NAMES:

In this section, the various oral contraceptive pills are divided into groups, depending on:
Whether they contain:
  • two hormones (combined Oestrogen and Progestogen).
  • one hormone (Progestogen only mini pill)
Whether the dosage:
  • does not vary (monophasic) during the month
  • varies twice (biphasic) during the month
  • varies three times (triphasic) during the month.

MONOPHASIC COMBINED OESTROGEN AND PROGESTOGEN PILLS:
Brevinor, Loestrin, Norimin, Ovysmen (ethinyloestradiol, norethisterone).
Cilest (ethinyloestradiol, norgestimate).
Femodene, Femodette, Minulet (ethinyloestradiol, gestodene).
Dianette (cyproterone acetate, ethinyloestradiol).
Eugynon 30, Microgynon 30, Ovranette (ethinyloestradiol, levonorgestrel).
Evra Patch (ethinyloestradiol, norelgestromin).
Marvelon, Mercilon (desogestrel, ethinyloestradiol).
Norinyl-1 (mestranol, norethisterone).
Yasmin (ethinyloestradiol, drospirenone).
BIPHASIC COMBINED OESTROGEN AND PROGESTOGEN PILLS:
Binovum (ethinyloestradiol, norethisterone).

TRIPHASIC COMBINED OESTROGEN
AND PROGESTOGEN PILLS:
Synphase, Trinovum (ethinyloestradiol,
norethisterone).
Logynon, Trinordiol (ethinyloestradiol,
levonorgestrel).
Triminulet, Triadene (gestodene,
ethinyloestradiol).
PROGESTOGEN ONLY (MINI) PILLS:
Cerazetta (desogestrel).
Femulen (etynodiol diacetate).
Microval, Norgeston (levonorgestrel).
Micronor, Noriday (norethisterone).
Neogest (norgestrel).

DRUG CLASS:

Sex hormones.

USES:

Prevention of pregnancy, control of
irregular or painful menstrual cycle
(combined forms only), control of acne in
women (Dianette particularly).

DOSAGE:

One tablet a day on the day
indicated on the pack for 21 or
28 days a month.
Evra patch—one patch weekly for
three weeks, then use no patch for
a week.
May fail as a contraceptive if
progestogen only pill missed by
more than four hours of normal
time of taking, or if low dose
combined pill missed by more than
eight hours of normal time.
If a contraceptive pill is missed,
take the missed pill with the next
remembered pill, continue taking
the pill, but use other forms of
contraception (e.g. condoms) for the
next seven days, but if this seven
day period extends into the inactive
(sugar) pill section of the pack or
into the pill free days of a 21 day
pack, do not take the inactive pills
or have a break, but continue with
the next active pill in a new pack.

FORMS:

Tablets, patch (Evra).

PRECAUTIONS:

Not for use in pregnancy (B3), but serious
effects from taking oral contraceptive
accidentally during pregnancy are
unlikely. Progestogen only pills are
recommended during breast feeding, but
low dose combined pills may be used if
necessary. Should be kept out of reach of
children and are obviously not for use in
children, although accidental usage by
children is unlikely to be serious.
Use with caution in heart disease, history
of blood clots, epilepsy, migraine,
diabetes, severe depression and sickle cell
anaemia.
Not to be used in pubertal girls until
menstruation well established.
Before prescribing, a thorough history
and physical check should be performed
by a doctor.
Annual checks of blood pressure and
breasts necessary.
Two yearly Pap smears and urine
screening tests advisable.
Diarrhoea, vomiting or use of antibiotics
may affect contraceptive action.
Do not take if:
 • suffering from high blood
pressure, blood clots, stroke, very
high cholesterol blood levels,
severe liver disease, Dubin-
Johnson syndrome, liver tumour,
systemic lupus erythematosus,
sex organ or breast cancer,
jaundice, otosclerosis or severe
skin irritation.
• male.

SIDE EFFECTS:

Common: nausea, pigmentation of facial
skin and nipples, headache, breast
tenderness, weight change (up or down).
Unusual: depression, increased sex drive,
break through bleeding.
*Severe but rare (stop medication, consult
doctor):* severe headache, blood clot, calf
or chest pain, severe shortness of breath,
yellow skin (jaundice).

INTERACTIONS:

Other drugs:
• antibiotics, phenytoin, primidone, barbiturates, rifampicin, anticoagulants (e.g. warfarin), hypoglycaemics (medications that treat diabetes), imipramine.

Herbs:
• St John's wort, liquorice.

Other substances:
• smoking increases risk of serious side effects.
• vitamin C (ascorbic acid).

PRESCRIPTION:

Yes.

PERMITTED IN SPORT:

Yes.

OVERDOSE:

Vomiting and abnormal vaginal bleeding only likely effects.

OTHER INFORMATION:

Sex hormones used as a contraceptive pill come in several different forms, but are mainly divided into the combined pill which contains both an oestrogen and progestogen and the mini-pill which has only progestogen. Some of the combined pills have a two or three phase variation in their dosage during the month.

In 1961, a woman taking the first form of the oral contraceptive pill was taking more than 32 times the amount of hormone every month than the modern woman on the latest three-phase type of pill. Over the past few decades, the pill has been subjected to more clinical trials and more intensive investigation than any other medication used by womankind. There is no doubt that it is now much safer to take the contraceptive pill for many years than it is to have one pregnancy and that is the realistic basis on which to judge the safety of any contraceptive.

Two different hormones (oestrogen and progestogen) control the menstrual cycle.

At the time of ovulation, the levels of oestrogen drops and progestogen rises, triggering the egg's release from the ovary. When the hormones revert to their previous level two weeks later, the lining of the womb is no longer able to survive and breaks away, giving the woman a period. The contraceptive pill maintains a more constant hormone level and thus prevents the release of the egg. With the triphasic pills, the level of both hormones rises at the normal time of ovulation and then drops slightly thereafter to give a more natural hormonal cycle to the woman, while still preventing the release of an egg. When the pill is stopped (or the sugar pills started) at the end of the month, the sudden drop in hormone levels cause a menstrual period to start.

The so-called mini-pill contains only one hormone (a progestogen) which is taken constantly without any sugar pills or break at the end of each month. This type of pill must be taken very carefully, as even missing it by four hours one day may drop the hormone levels sufficiently to allow ovulation and pregnancy. The failure rate of the mini-pill is significantly higher than that of the combined pill.

The pill has several positive benefits besides almost perfect prevention of pregnancy. It regulates irregular periods, reduces menstrual pain and premenstrual tension, may increase the size of the breasts, reduces the severity of acne in some women, and libido (the desire for sex) is often increased. It even reduces the incidence of some types of gynaecological cancer. Women who have unwanted side effects from the pill can be assessed by a doctor and a pill containing a different balance of hormones can be prescribed.

If taken correctly, the pill is very effective as a contraceptive, but missing a pill, or suffering from diarrhoea or vomiting can have a very pregnant result. Some antibiotics can also interfere with the pill, as can vitamin C. There is no need these days to take a break from the pill every year or so, as may have been the case in earlier years. On the other hand, many women find they can successfully skip a period by continuing to take the active pills of a monophasic combined contraceptive pill (does not work with biphasic, triphasic or progestogen only pills).

The effects of the pill are readily reversible. If a woman decides to become pregnant, she can find herself in that state in as little as two weeks after ceasing it, with no adverse effects on the mother or child.

Diane and Marvelon were introduced in 1994. Diane is particularly useful in women with acne.

Femoden, Minulet, Tri-Minulet and Trioden introduced in 1995 and are particularly useful in controlling heavy and irregular periods.

Yasmin was introduced in 2001 as a new combination of hormones that suits some women better than those used traditionally.

The 'morning after' pill is described under its active ingredient: levonorgestrel.

The contraceptive implant is described under etonogestrel.

The contraceptive injection is described under medroxyprogesterone acetate.

See also Cyproterone acetate, Etonogestrel, HORMONE REPLACEMENT THERAPY, Levonorgestrel, Medroxyprogesterone acetate, SPERMICIDES.

Orciprenaline

TRADE NAME:

Alupent.

DRUG CLASS:

Bronchodilator.

USES:

Asthma, bronchitis.

DOSAGE:

 Inhaler: one or two inhalations three or four times a day.
Tablets: one four times a day.

FORMS:

Inhaler, tablet of 20mg (off white), syrup.

PRECAUTIONS:

Safe to use in pregnancy (A), breast feeding and older children.
Use with caution in high blood pressure, heart disease, diabetes and labour of pregnancy.
Tolerance may develop with overuse.

Do not take if:

 • suffering from irregular or rapid heart beat, aortic disease or overactive thyroid gland.

SIDE EFFECTS:

Common: palpitations, tremor, restlessness, flush, headache.
Unusual: nausea, giddiness, sleeplessness.
Severe but rare (stop medication, consult doctor): chest pain (angina).

INTERACTIONS:

Other drugs:
• sympathomimetics, beta-blockers, MAOI, diuretics.
Other substances:
• caffeine and alcohol.

PRESCRIPTION:

Yes.

PERMITTED IN SPORT:

No.

OVERDOSE:

Exacerbation of side effects likely. These may become distressing and may be serious in patients with heart disease or high blood pressure.

OTHER INFORMATION:

One of the early treatments for asthma that is no longer widely used.
See also Salbutamol.

Orlistat

TRADE NAME:

Xenical.

USES:

Treatment of obesity.

DOSAGE:

 One tablet three times a day with meals.

FORMS:

Capsules (turquoise) of 120mg.

PRECAUTIONS:

Use with caution in pregnancy (B1) and children.
Use with caution with peptic ulcers, psychiatric disturbances, adhesions in belly, kidney stones, serious heart, liver and kidney disease.

Do not take if:

- breast feeding
- suffering from pancreatitis, malabsorption, recent major surgery or some types of gall bladder disease
- normal or under weight.

SIDE EFFECTS:

Common: diarrhoea (worse if fat eaten), flatulence, liquid faeces, headache.
Unusual: incontinence of faeces, nausea, indigestion, bowel noises, anal irritation, dizziness, muscle pains.
Severe but rare (stop medication, consult doctor): liver damage.

INTERACTIONS:

Other drugs:
- cyclosporin, pravastatin, other drugs for obesity.

Other substances:
- vitamins within two hours.

PRESCRIPTION:

Yes.

PERMITTED IN SPORT:

Yes.

OVERDOSE:

Unlikely to be serious.

OTHER INFORMATION:

Introduced 2000 as a totally new type of anti-obesity drug that acts by preventing the absorption of fat from the intestine.
See also Methylcellulose, Silbutramine.

Orphenadrine

TRADE NAMES:

Biorphen, Disipal.

DRUG CLASS:

Antiparkinsonian, muscle relaxant.

USES:

Parkinsonism, severe dizziness, other movement disorders, muscle spasm.

DOSAGE:

 One to three tablets, three times a day with food.

FORMS:

Tablets, solution.

PRECAUTIONS:

Should be used with caution in pregnancy (B2) and breast feeding. Not for use in children.
Use with caution with rapid heart rate and heart disease.
Use short term if possible.

Do not take if:

- suffering from glaucoma, myasthenia gravis, enlarged prostate gland.

SIDE EFFECTS:

Common: minimal. Dry mouth, blurred vision, light headedness.
Unusual: excitation.

INTERACTIONS:

None significant.

PRESCRIPTION:

Yes.

PERMITTED IN SPORT:

Yes.

OVERDOSE:

May cause excitement, confusion, convulsions, rapid heart rate, inability to pass urine and coma. Administer activated charcoal or induce vomiting if medication taken recently. Seek medical assistance.

OTHER INFORMATION:

Does not cause addiction or dependence.
See also Baclofen, LEVODOPA.

Use with care with significant kidney disease.
Course not to be repeated immediately.

SIDE EFFECTS:

Common: nausea, vomiting.
Unusual: sleeplessness, diarrhoea, dizziness.

INTERACTIONS:

None significant.

PRESCRIPTION:

Yes.

PERMITTED IN SPORT:

Yes.

OVERDOSE:

Nausea and vomiting only likely effects.

OTHER INFORMATION:

Released in 2001 as a new way of combating influenza, but only if taken as soon as possible after symptoms first appear.
See also Zanamivir.

Oseltamivir

TRADE NAME:

Tamiflu.

DRUG CLASS:

Antiviral.

USES:

Treatment of influenza.

DOSAGE:

 One capsule twice a day for five days, starting within 48 hours of onset of symptoms.

FORMS:

Capsules of 75mg (cream/grey), suspension.

PRECAUTIONS:

Use with caution in pregnancy (B1) and breast feeding.
Not for use in children under 12 years.

Oxcarbazepine

TRADE NAME:

Trileptal.

DRUG CLASS:

Antiepileptic.

USES:

Partial epileptic seizures.

DOSAGE:

300 to 1200mg twice a day.

FORMS:

Tablets of 150, 300 and 600mg.

PRECAUTIONS:

Not to be used in pregnancy or breast feeding.
May be used in children over six years of age.

Use with caution in kidney and heart disease.
Use lower doses in elderly.
Regular blood tests to measure sodium levels necessary.
Reduce dosage slowly, do not stop suddenly.

SIDE EFFECTS:

Common: biochemical abnormalities (low blood sodium levels), liver damage, tiredness, dizziness, headache.
Unusual: acne, alopecia (hair loss), rash, nausea, diarrhoea.
Severe but rare (stop medication, consult doctor): double vision, liver damage (jaundice), altered blood sodium levels.

INTERACTIONS:

Other drugs:
• NSAID (arthritis medication), oral contraceptives, phenobarbitone, phenytoin, citalopram, diazepam, imipramine, omeprazole, propranolol, clomipramine, amitriptyline, pantoprazole, lansoprazole, progesterone, cyclophosphamide.
Other substances:
• alcohol, borage.
Herbs:
• St John's wort, evening primrose (linoleic acid), Gingko biloba.

PRESCRIPTION:

Yes.

PERMITTED IN SPORT:

Yes.

OTHER INFORMATION:

Introduced in 1999 to treat more difficult cases of epilepsy.
See also BARBITURATES, BENZODIAZEPINES, Carbamazepine, Clonazepam, Ethosuximide, Gabapentin, Lamotrigine, Levetiracetam, Phenytoin, Primidone, Sodium valproate, Sulthiame, Tiagabine, Topiramate, Vigabatrin.

Oxerutin

TRADE NAME:

Paroven.

USES:

Poor arterial and venous circulation, swelling of ankles and other tissue, varicose veins, piles, night cramps.

DOSAGE:

 Two capsules twice a day.

FORMS:

Capsules of 250mg (yellow).

PRECAUTIONS:

Safe in all but first three months of pregnancy. Safe in breast feeding. Not recommended in children.
Eat diet high in fibre and protein.

SIDE EFFECTS:

Common: minimal.
Unusual: nausea, indigestion, constipation, diarrhoea, flushes, headache.

INTERACTIONS:

None significant.

PRESCRIPTION:

No.

PERMITTED IN SPORT:

Yes.

OVERDOSE:

Constipation only likely effect.

OTHER INFORMATION:

Successfully used for for many years to prevent tired aching legs, particularly in women who must stand for a long period of time in their work. Very safe. Does not cause dependence.

Oxethazine

See ANTACIDS.

Oxitropium

TRADE NAME:

Oxivent.

DRUG CLASS:

Anticholinergic.

USES:

Asthma, emphysema, chronic obstructive airways disease.

DOSAGE:

 Two inhalations, two or three times a day.

FORMS:

Inhaler, autohaler.

PRECAUTIONS:

Not for use in pregnancy, breast feeding and children.
Use with caution in glaucoma, prostate enlargement.
Avoid eyes.
Cease if wheeze or cough worsens.

SIDE EFFECTS:

Common: local mouth irritation.
Unusual: nausea, dry mouth.

INTERACTIONS:

None significant.

PRESCRIPTION:

Yes.

PERMITTED IN SPORT:

Yes.

OVERDOSE:

Exacerbation of side effects only likely consequence.

OTHER INFORMATION:

Not addictive.
See also Ipratropium.

Oxpentifylline

TRADE NAME:

Trental.

USES:

Poor arterial circulation to legs and arms.

DOSAGE:

 One tablet three times a day with meals and liquid.

FORMS:

Tablet of 400mg (pink).

PRECAUTIONS:

Should be used with caution in pregnancy, breast feeding and in children.
Should be used with caution in low blood pressure, kidney and liver disease.
Lower dose may be required in elderly.
Do not take if:

 • suffering from heart attack, peptic ulcer or excessive bleeding.

SIDE EFFECTS:

Common: nausea, heartburn, burping, dizziness, headache, flushing, palpitations.
Unusual: vomiting, tremor, shortness of breath, loss of appetite, anxiety, nose bleed, brittle finger nails, blurred vision, bad taste.
Severe but rare (stop medication, consult doctor): unusual bleeding.

INTERACTIONS:

Other drugs:
• warfarin, antihypertensives (treat high blood pressure), beta-blockers, diuretics (fluid tablets), theophylline, hypoglycaemics (treat diabetes).

PRESCRIPTION:

Yes.

PERMITTED IN SPORT:

Yes.

OVERDOSE:

Flushing, low blood pressure, convulsions, fever and coma may occur. No deaths reported. Seek medical assistance.

OTHER INFORMATION:

Unique drug that works by making cells slip more easily through the smallest capillaries. Introduced in the 1980s, it has had only limited use because of its cost, despite excellent clinical results.

Oxprenolol

TRADE NAMES:

Slow-Trasicor, Trasicor.
Trasidrex (with cyclopenthiazide).

DRUG CLASS:

Beta-blocker.

USES:

High blood pressure, angina, rapid heart rate, irregular heart beat, paroxysmal atrial tachycardia.

DOSAGE:

 20 to 160mg a day in divided doses.

FORMS:

Tablets.

PRECAUTIONS:

Should be used in pregnancy (C) only if medically essential.
Safe to use in breast feeding.
May be used with caution in children.
Use with care if suffering from alcoholism, poor circulation to limbs, angina, over active thyroid gland

(hyperthyroidism), liver or kidney failure or about to have surgery.
Do not stop suddenly, but reduce dose slowly.

Do not take if:

- suffering from diabetes, asthma, or allergic conditions
- suffering from heart failure, shock, slow heart rate, or enlarged right heart
- if undertaking prolonged fast.

SIDE EFFECTS:

Common: low blood pressure, slow heart rate, cold hands and feet, asthma.
Unusual: loss of appetite, nausea, diarrhoea, impotence, tiredness, sleeplessness, nightmares, rash, loss of libido, hair loss, noises in ears, depression.
Severe but rare (stop medication, consult doctor): severe asthma.

INTERACTIONS:

Other drugs:
- calcium channel blockers, disopyramide, clonidine, adrenaline, other medications for irregular heart beat, lignocaine, ergotamine, indomethacin, chlorpromazine.

PRESCRIPTION:

Yes.

PERMITTED IN SPORT:

Yes.

OVERDOSE:

Slow heart rate, low blood pressure, asthma and heart failure may result. Administer activated charcoal or induce vomiting if tablets taken recently. Use Salbutamol or other asthma sprays for difficulty in breathing. Seek medical assistance.

See also Atenolol, Carvedilol, Esmolol, Labetalol, Metoprolol, Pindolol, Propranolol, Sotalol.

Oxybuprocaine

See **ANAESTHETICS, LOCAL.**

Oxybutynin

TRADE NAMES:

Cystrin, Ditropan, Lyrinel XL.

DRUG CLASS:

Anticholinergic.

USES:

Relieves some forms of difficulty in passing urine caused by muscle spasm, unstable bladder function.

DOSAGE:

 One tablet two or three times a day.

FORMS:

Tablet of 2.5mg, 3mg, 5mg and 10mg, elixir.

PRECAUTIONS:

Use with caution in pregnancy (B1), and children under five years. Not to be used in breast feeding, as breast milk production may be reduced.
Use with caution in hot climates.
Avoid vigourous exercise while using Oxybutinin.
Use with caution in ulcerative colitis, reflux oesophagitis, over active thyroid gland, heart disease, high blood pressure, enlarged prostate gland, liver and kidney disease.
Regular consultations with doctor necessary to monitor bladder function.

Do not take if:

- suffering from glaucoma, gut obstruction, megacolon, severe ulcerative colitis, myasthenia gravis, acute bleeding.

SIDE EFFECTS:

Common: palpitations, rapid heart rate, decreased sweating, constipation, dry mouth, nausea, dizziness.
Unusual: impotence, rash, drowsiness, hallucinations, dry eyes.

INTERACTIONS:

Other drugs:
- sedatives, other anticholinergics.
Other substances:
- reacts adversely with alcohol.

PRESCRIPTION:

Yes.

PERMITTED IN SPORT:

Yes.

OVERDOSE:

Serious. Symptoms may include restlessness, irrational behaviour, flushing, low blood pressure, difficulty in breathing, paralysis, coma and death. Administer activated charcoal or induce vomiting if medication taken recently and patient alert. Seek urgent medical assistance.

OTHER INFORMATION:

Does not cause addiction or dependence. Released in 1994.

Oxycodone

TRADE NAMES:

OxyContin, OxyNorm.

DRUG CLASS:

Narcotic, Analgesic.

USES:

Moderate to severe pain.

DOSAGE:

 One tablet every six to twelve hours with food.

FORMS:

Tablets, solution.

PRECAUTIONS:

Should be used in pregnancy (C) only if medically essential as use of oxycodone immediately before birth may cause difficulty in breathing for the infant. Use with caution in breast feeding. Not for use in children.

Not designed for prolonged use except in patients with terminal disease.

Do not stop suddenly, but reduce dosage slowly.

Use with caution in severe lung disease, myasthenia gravis, underactive thyroid gland, liver and kidney disease, enlarged prostate gland, shock or bowel obstruction.

Lower doses necessary in elderly and debilitated patients.

Do not take if:

- suffering from severe asthma, severe lung disease, irregular heart beat, brain tumour, alcoholism, head injury, convulsions, gut obstruction
- operating machinery or driving a vehicle.

SIDE EFFECTS:

Common: nausea, constipation, drowsiness, confusion.

Unusual: vomiting, difficulty in passing urine, dry mouth, sweating, flushing, faintness, loss of appetite, dizziness, slow heart rate, mood changes.

Severe but rare (stop medication, consult doctor): severe headache, convulsions, difficulty in breathing.

INTERACTIONS:

Other drugs:
- MAOI, amphetamines, chlorpromazine, sedatives, antihistamines,beta-blockers, anticoagulants (e.g. warfarin), anticholinergics, metoclopramide.

Other substances:
- do not use alcohol with oxycodone.

PRESCRIPTION:

Yes (restricted).

PERMITTED IN SPORT:

No.

OVERDOSE:

Very serious. Symptoms may include drowsiness, difficulty in breathing, muscle weakness, coma, heart failure and death. Administer activated charcoal or induce vomiting if medication taken recently and patient alert. Seek urgent medical attention. Antidote available.

OTHER INFORMATION:

May cause addiction if taken inappropriately for long periods of time.

See also Alfentanil, Buprenorphine, Codeine, Dextromoramide, Dextropropoxyphene, Fentanyl, Heroin, Hydromorphone, Methadone, Morphine, Pentazocine, Pethidine.

Oxymetholone

DRUG CLASS:

Anabolic steroid.

USES:

Used dangerously and in an unapproved manner by body builders and athletes.

PRECAUTIONS:

Must not be used in pregnancy (D) or breast feeding.

Use with caution in heart disease, enlarged prostate gland, diabetes.

Do not take if:

- suffering from prostate and testicular cancer, breast cancer, liver and kidney disease.

SIDE EFFECTS:

Common: increased hairiness and decreased breast size in women, voice deepening in women, acne, frequent unwanted erections, infertility.

Unusual: anaemia, enlargement of clitoris in women, cessation of menstrual periods, decrease in testicular size, impotence, breast enlargement in males, baldness in females, reduced libido.

Severe but rare (stop medication, consult doctor): unusual bruising or bleeding, calcium deposits (lumps) in tissue, jaundice (yellow skin).

INTERACTIONS:

Other drugs:
• anticoagulants.

PRESCRIPTION:

Not legally available.

PERMITTED IN SPORT:

No. Although increasing muscle bulk, there is no evidence that this medication enhances athletic ability. Long term inappropriate use may cause permanent damage to the body.

OVERDOSE:

Exacerbation of side effects likely.

OTHER INFORMATION:

Illegal drug, but imported and used by some body builders and sportsmen. Does not cause dependence or addiction. Short term gains in muscle bulk when used inappropriately may result in long term permanent body damage that may lead to early heart attacks, infertility, bone weakness, liver disease and premature death. Bottom line is, don't use it.

Oxytetracycline

TRADE NAMES:

Terra-Cortril (with hydrocortisone).
Terra-Cortril Nystatin (with hydrocortisone, nystatin).
Trimovate (with clobetasone, nystatin).

DRUG CLASS:

Antibiotic.

USES:

Bacterial infections of the skin.

DOSAGE:

 Apply two to four times a day for up to one week.

FORMS:

Cream, ointment.

PRECAUTIONS:

Cream and ointment safe to use in pregnancy, breast feeding and children.

SIDE EFFECTS:

Common: minimal.
Unusual: skin irritation.
Severe but rare (stop medication, consult doctor): skin damage with prolonged use.

INTERACTIONS:

Minimal as ointment and cream.

PRESCRIPTION:

Yes.

PERMITTED IN SPORT:

Yes.

See also Tetracycline.

Oxytocin

TRADE NAMES:

Syntocinon.
Syntometrine (with ergometrine).

USES:

Starting labour in pregnancy, stopping abnormal bleeding after delivery.

DOSAGE:

 As determined by doctor. May be given by drip infusion.

FORMS:

Injection.

PRECAUTIONS:

Safe to use for induction of labour in pregnancy (A), but should not otherwise be used in pregnancy. Safe for use in breast feeding. Not for use in children. Use with caution in heart disease.

Do not take injection if:

• previous Caesarean section.

SIDE EFFECTS:

Common: rapid heart rate, retention of fluid.
Unusual: low blood pressure.

PRESCRIPTION:

Yes.

PERMITTED IN SPORT:

Yes.

OVERDOSE:

Unlikely to have serious effects.

OTHER INFORMATION:

Injection commonly used to increase intensity of labour and immediately after delivery to reduce bleeding.

See also Ergometrine.

Paclitaxel

TRADE NAME:

Taxol.

DRUG CLASS:

Antimetabolite.

USES:

Cancer of the breast and ovaries.

DOSAGE:

 As determined by doctor for each patient.

FORMS:

Injection.

PRECAUTIONS:

Must not be used in pregnancy (D) or children. Use with caution in breast feeding.
Regular blood tests to check function of blood cells essential.
Use with caution in neuropathy (nerve disease).

SIDE EFFECTS:

Common: flushes, rash, shortness of breath, chest pain, fainting, joint and muscle pain.
Unusual: low blood pressure, slow heart rate, damage to nerves (pins and needles sensation, numbness), damage to liver.
Severe but rare (stop medication, consult doctor): jaundice (yellow skin).

INTERACTIONS:

Other drugs:
• sex hormones.

PRESCRIPTION:

Yes.

PERMITTED IN SPORT:

Yes.

OVERDOSE:

Serious damage to bone marrow and nerves likely.

Pamidronate
(Disodium pamidronate)

TRADE NAME:

Aredia.

DRUG CLASS:

Bisphosphonate.

USES:

High blood calcium levels, Paget's disease, bone secondary cancer, multiple myeloma.

DOSAGE:

 As determined by doctor.

FORMS:

Intravenous infusion.

PRECAUTIONS:

Use with caution in pregnancy (B3) and breast feeding. Not for use in children.
Not to be injected into muscle or quickly into vein.
Use with caution in hyperparathyroidism, kidney and heart disease.
Regular blood tests to check calcium and phosphate levels and kidney function, necessary.

SIDE EFFECTS:

Common: low blood calcium, fever, other biochemical abnormalities, muscle pain, nausea, diarrhoea.

Unusual: vomiting, headache, drowsiness.
Severe but rare (stop medication, consult doctor): seizures, damaged blood cells, fluid in lungs, high or low blood pressure, heart failure, kidney failure.

INTERACTIONS:

Other drugs:
• other bisphosphonates, calcium.

PRESCRIPTION:

Yes.

PERMITTED IN SPORT:

Yes.

Pancreatin

TRADE NAMES:

Creon, Nutizym GR, Pancrease, Pancrex V.

USES:

Deficiency of pancreatic enzymes due to disease (e.g. cystic fibrosis, chronic pancreatitis) or surgery.

DOSAGE:

 Taken with each meal in sufficient quantity to adequately digest food.
Dosage varies for each person.

FORMS:

Capsules, tablets, pellets.

PRECAUTIONS:

Safe in pregnancy, breast feeding and children.
Ensure adequate fluid intake.
Do not take if:

 • suffering from acute pancreatitis.
• allergic to pork.

SIDE EFFECTS:

Common: minimal. Usually dose related.
Unusual: nausea, diarrhoea, passing excess wind, mouth soreness.
Severe but rare (stop medication, consult doctor): gout.

INTERACTIONS:

Other drugs:
• antacids.

PRESCRIPTION:

No.

PERMITTED IN SPORT:

Yes.

OVERDOSE:

Diarrhoea only likely effect.

OTHER INFORMATION:

Totally natural products used to replace a missing digestive enzyme.
See also Tilactase.

Panthenol
See Pantothenic Acid.

Pantoprazole
See PROTON PUMP INHIBITORS.

Pantothenic acid
(Panthenol, Vitamin B5)

TRADE NAMES:

A large number of preparations include pantothenic acid (vitamin B5) or its derivative panthenol, alone or in combination with other vitamins and minerals.

DRUG CLASS:

Vitamin.

USES:

Vitamin B deficiency.
Cream used for mild burns, nappy rash and sore nipples.

DOSAGE:

Recommended daily allowance:
4 to 7mg a day.
Apply creams several times a day as required.

FORMS:

Tablets, capsules, mixtures, drops, creams.

PRECAUTIONS:

Safe in pregnancy, breast feeding and children.
Do not take in high doses or for prolonged periods of time.

SIDE EFFECTS:

Minimal.

INTERACTIONS:

None significant.

PRESCRIPTION:

No.

PERMITTED IN SPORT:

Yes.

OVERDOSE:

Unlikely to have serious adverse effects.

OTHER INFORMATION:

Pantothenic acid is a water soluble vitamin. Remember, vitamins are merely chemicals that are essential for the functioning of the body and if taken to excess, act as a drug.

Paracetamol
(Acetaminophen)

TRADE NAMES:

Alvedon, Calpol, Infadrops, Medinol.
Distalgesic (with dextropropoxyphene).
Domperamol (with domperidone).
Fortagesic (with pentazocine).
Kapake, Solpadol, Tylex, Zapain (with codeine).
Midrid (with isometheptene).
Migraleve (with buclizine, codeine).
Paradote (with methionine).
Paramax (with metoclopramide).
Remedeine (with dihydrocodeine).

DRUG CLASS:

Analgesic.

USES:

Mild to moderate pain relief, fever.

DOSAGE:

One or two tablets every three or four hours.
Other forms as directed by directions on packaging, doctor or pharmacist.

FORMS:

Tablets, capsules, soluble tablets, chewable tablets, mixture, drops, suppository, powder.

PRECAUTIONS:

Safe in pregnancy (A), breast feeding, children and infants over one month of age.
Use with caution in severe liver and kidney disease.
Never exceed recommended dose.

SIDE EFFECTS:

Common: minimal.
Unusual: nausea, irritability, insomnia, rash, inability to pass urine.

INTERACTIONS:

Other drugs:
• anticoagulants (e.g. warfarin), metoclopramide, propantheline, chloramphenicol, antidepressants, narcotics, anticonvulsants (treat epilepsy).

PRESCRIPTION:

No.
Prescription required in some forms combined with narcotics.

PERMITTED IN SPORT:

Yes.

OVERDOSE:

Very serious, particularly in children. Symptoms may include vomiting, belly pain and sweating. Delayed effect can be serious liver damage that may cause liver failure, jaundice and death. Administer activated charcoal or induce vomiting if medication taken recently. Seek urgent medical attention. Antidote is methionine.

OTHER INFORMATION:

The most widely used pain killer in the world. Very effective, and often underrated in its effectiveness. Extremely safe if taken according to directions. Up to eight tablets a day can be taken for years on end. Found in a wide variety of cold and flu preparations. Paracetamol is given the generic name Acetaminophen in the United States.
See also Aspirin, Ibuprofen.

Paraffin

TRADE NAMES:

Alcoderm, Cetraben, E45 Wash, Keri, Oilatum Crean, Oilatum Emollient, Oilatum Gel.
Diprobath, Epaderm, Hydromol, Ultrabase, Unguentum M (with other ingredients).
E45 Bath Oil (with dimethicone).
Alpha Keri, E45 Cream, E45 Lotion (with lanolin).

Polytar (with tar, arachis oil and other ingredients).
Dermalo (with wool alcohol).
Dermol (with chlorhexidine, benzalkonium chloride and other ingredients).
Diprobase (with cetomacrogol and other ingredients).
Doublebase (with isopropyl myristate).
Emulsiderm (with benzalkonium chloride and other ingredients).
Imuderm, Infaderm (with almond oil).
Lacri-Lube, Lubri-Tears (with wool fat).
Lipobase (with cetomacrogol).
Oilatum Plus (with triclosan, benzalkonium chloride).
Also used as a lubricant in many other skin and eye preparations.

DRUG CLASS:

Lubricant, moisturiser, laxative.

USES:

Skin dryness, skin itch, eye dryness, vaginal dryness, constipation.

DOSAGE:

 Use externally as often as necessary.

FORMS:

Cream, oil, lotion, wash, liquid.

PRECAUTIONS:

May be used in pregnancy (B2), breast feeding and children.
Should be used long term as a laxative only under medical advice.

SIDE EFFECTS:

Minimal.

INTERACTIONS:

None significant.

PRESCRIPTION:

No.

PERMITTED IN SPORT:

Yes.

OVERDOSE:

Diarrhoea only effect if swallowed.

OTHER INFORMATION:

Safe and widely used laxative that has been available for thousands of years. White soft paraffin and liquid paraffin are used in many creams as a vehicle for other medications.

See also EYE LUBRICANTS.

Parecoxib

TRADE NAME:

Dynastat.

DRUG CLASS:

COX-2 Inhibitor.

USES:

Short-term use for pain after surgery.

DOSAGE:

 20mg to 40mg, two to four times a day.

FORMS:

Injection.

PRECAUTIONS:

Use with considerable caution in pregnancy (B3) and breast feeding.
Not for use in children.
Use with caution with previous peptic ulcer, high blood pressure, fluid retention, heart failure, asthma, dehydration, liver or kidney disease, sulpha allergy.
Lower doses may be necessary in the elderly and with long term use.

Do not take if:

 • asthma occurs with NSAID medications or aspirin, severe liver disease, peptic ulcer, severe heart failure.

SIDE EFFECTS:

Common: fluid retention (swollen feet).
Unusual: gut irritation, indigestion, altered blood pressure, back pain.
Severe but rare (stop medication, consult doctor): liver and kidney damage.

INTERACTIONS:

Other drugs:
• Nonsteroidal anti-inflammatory drugs (NSAID), steroids, anticoagulants (e.g. warfarin), diuretics, ACE inhibitors, lithium, antacids, fluconazole.

PRESCRIPTION:

Yes.

PERMITTED IN SPORT:

Yes.

OVERDOSE:

Lethargy, drowsiness, nausea, vomiting and indigestion may occur. Give activated charcoal. Seek medical attention.

OTHER INFORMATION:

Revolutionary new class of medications first released in 1999 to treat all forms of arthritis and inflammation with reduced side effects.

See also Celecoxib, Meloxicam, NSAID, Rofecoxib.

Paroxetine

TRADE NAME:

Seroxat.

DRUG CLASS:

SSRI antidepressant.

USES:

Depression.

DOSAGE:

 One or two tablets a day in morning with food.

FORMS:

Tablet of 20mg (white) and 30mg (blue), liquid.

PRECAUTIONS:

Should be used in pregnancy (B3) with considerable caution. Breast feeding should be ceased if Paroxetine prescribed. Not for use in children.
Should be used with caution in mania, epilepsy and heart disease.
Should not be stopped suddenly, but dose should be slowly reduced over several days.

Do not take if:

• taking MAOI antidepressants.

SIDE EFFECTS:

Common: generally minimal and ease with continued use. Nausea, drowsiness, sweating, tremor, tiredness, dry mouth, sleeplessness, impotence.
Unusual: headache, fever, poor libido, palpitations, sweating, rash, blurred vision, decreased appetite.
Severe but rare (stop medication, consult doctor): seizures (fits).

INTERACTIONS:

Other drugs:
• serious interaction with MAOI
• anticoagulants (e.g. warfarin), thioridazine, phenytoin, tryptophan.
Herbs:
• St John's wort, ma huang.
Other substances:
• use of alcohol with paroxetine is not advised.

PRESCRIPTION:

Yes.

PERMITTED IN SPORT:

Yes.

OVERDOSE:

Symptoms may include nausea, tremor, dilated pupils, dry mouth and irritability.

Death or serious effects have not occurred. Seek medical attention.

OTHER INFORMATION:

One of the newer antidepressants released in the 1990s that has dramatically improved the treatment of depression because of its safety and lack of side effects. May take up to two weeks for patient to notice any improvement in depression.

See also Citalopram, Fluoxetine, Fluvoxamine, Sertraline, Venlafaxine.

Pectin

TRADE NAMES:

Orabase (with carmellose and other ingredients).
Also found in some locally produced antidiarrhoeal medications.

DRUG CLASS:

Fibre.

USES:

Mouth and other ulcers.
Mild diarrhoea.

DOSAGE:

 Apply to ulcer as required.
Take as required to control diarrhoea.

FORMS:

Powder, ointment, liquid.

PRECAUTIONS:

Safe in pregnancy, breast feeding and children.
Use with caution in reduced intestinal absorption.

SIDE EFFECTS:

Minimal.

INTERACTIONS:

Other drugs:
• may affect absorption of some drugs (e.g. digoxin) if swallowed.

PRESCRIPTION:

No.

PERMITTED IN SPORT:

Yes.

OVERDOSE:

Not likely to be harmful if excess swallowed.

OTHER INFORMATION:

Derived from apple fibre.

Penciclovir

TRADE NAME:

Vectavir.

DRUG CLASS:

Antiviral.

USES:

Cold sores, Herpes simplex infections.

DOSAGE:

 Apply every two hours from first sign of infection.

FORMS:

Cream.

PRECAUTIONS:

May be used in pregnancy (B1), breast feeding and children over 12 years.
Use with caution in infants.
Avoid contact with eyes, inside of mouth, nostrils and other moist membranes.

Do not take if:

 • suffering from immune deficiency.

SIDE EFFECTS:

Minimal.

INTERACTIONS:

None significant.

PRESCRIPTION:

Yes.

PERMITTED IN SPORT:

Yes.

See also Aciclovir.

Penicillamine

TRADE NAME:

Distamine.

USES:

Severe rheumatoid arthritis, Wilson's disease, cystinuria, heavy metal poisoning (e.g. lead).

DOSAGE:

 Rheumatoid disease: one or two tablets, one to three times a day. Other conditions: up to 2000mg a day depending upon severity and response.

FORMS:

Tablets (white) of 125mg and 250mg.

PRECAUTIONS:

Must not be used in pregnancy (D) unless essential for the life of the mother. Breast feeding should be ceased before use. May be used in children when medically indicated.
Use with caution in liver and kidney disease, brain disorders or feverish.
Avoid surgery if possible.
Regular blood tests essential.
Regular checks of skin, eyes and temperature necessary.
Ensure adequate vitamin B intake.
Patient must be made aware of the adverse effects of this medication before use.

Do not take if:

• using gold or chloroquine.

SIDE EFFECTS:

Common: rash, fever, joint pains, enlarged glands, itch.
Unusual: hair loss, ringing noise in ears, abnormal blood tests, nausea, loss of appetite, vomiting, diarrhoea, blood clots, taste changes.
Severe but rare (stop medication, consult doctor): significant rash, severe belly pain, yellow skin (jaundice), vision disturbances, unusual bleeding or bruising.

INTERACTIONS:

Other drugs:
• gold, antimalarial drugs
  (e.g. chloroquine), isoniazid.

PRESCRIPTION:

Yes.

PERMITTED IN SPORT:

Yes.

OVERDOSE:

May cause permanent organ damage. Administer activated charcoal or induce vomiting if medication taken recently. Seek medical attention.

OTHER INFORMATION:

Although it has serious side effects, Penicillamine may give great relief to sufferers of severe rheumatoid arthritis, and may be life saving in heavy metal poisoning. Risks minimal if taken under close supervision of a competent physician.
See also GOLD.

PENICILLINS

DISCUSSION:

Penicillins are the most widely used antibiotics in the world. There are many different types of penicillin now available. They are broad-spectrum antibiotics that kill a wide range of bacteria, and have been used for almost every conceivable type of infection at some time. Unfortunately many bacteria are now becoming resistant to penicillins. Allergies to penicillin are not more common than to other drugs, but appear to be so because it is so widely used. Patients who know they have a penicillin allergy should tell their doctors and wear a warning pendant or bracelet. Penicillins may cause a skin rash if given to a patient with glandular fever, and may start a vaginal thrush infection in some women.
See Amoxycillin, Ampicillin, Cloxacillin, Flucloxacillin, Penicillin G, Piperacillin, Pivmecillinam, Ticarcillin.

Penicillin G
(Benzyl Penicillin)

TRADE NAME:

Crystapen.

DRUG CLASS:

Penicillin antibiotic.

USES:

Treatment of infections caused by susceptible bacteria.

DOSAGE:

Two to four injections a day, or by drip into a vein.

FORMS:

Injection.

PRECAUTIONS:

Safe in pregnancy (A), children and breast feeding.
Use with caution in kidney failure and leukaemia.
Do not take if:

• allergic to Penicillin.
• suffering from glandular fever.

SIDE EFFECTS:

Common: mild diarrhoea, nausea, vomiting.
Unusual: fever, headache, dizziness, hot flushes, tiredness, black tongue.
Severe but rare (stop medication, consult doctor): itchy rash, hives, severe diarrhoea, yellow skin (jaundice), muscle pains, throat tightness.

INTERACTIONS:

None significant.

PRESCRIPTION:

Yes.

PERMITTED IN SPORT:

Yes.

OVERDOSE:

Not life threatening unless allergic to Penicillin. Vomiting and diarrhoea only likely effects.

OTHER INFORMATION:

One of the older types of Penicillin. Does not cause dependence or addiction.

See also Amoxycillin, Ampicillin, Cloxacillin, Flucloxacillin, Piperacillin, Pivmecillinam, Ticarcillin.

Pentazocine
(Pentazocine hydrochloride and Pentazocine lactate)

TRADE NAMES:

Fortral.

DRUG CLASS:

Narcotic analgesic.

USES:

Moderate to severe pain.

DOSAGE:

 25 to 100mg every three or four hours after food.

FORMS:

Fortral: tablets of 25mg (white), capsules of 50mg (yellow/grey), injection.

PRECAUTIONS:

Not for use in pregnancy (C) unless medically necessary. May cause difficulty in breathing for the newborn if given in the few hours before birth. Use with caution in breast feeding. May be used in children over one year.
Use with caution in severe kidney disease, severe lung disease, severe liver disease, asthma, thyroid disease, pituitary disease, epilepsy, heart attack or head injury.

Do not take if:

 • Using machinery or driving a vehicle.

SIDE EFFECTS:

Common: nausea, dizziness, sedation, mood changes, headache, sweating.
Unusual: vomiting, contracted pupils, hallucinations, rapid heart rate.
Severe but rare (stop medication, consult doctor): difficulty in breathing.

INTERACTIONS:

Other drugs:
• MAOI, sedatives, tetracycline, phenytoin.
Other substances:
• do not use alcohol while taking pentazocine.

PRESCRIPTION:

Yes (restricted).

PERMITTED IN SPORT:

No.

OVERDOSE:

Serious. May cause convulsions, sedation, coma, difficulty in breathing and rarely death. Administer activated charcoal or induce vomiting if medication taken recently and patient alert. Seek urgent medical attention. Antidote available.

OTHER INFORMATION:

May cause dependence or addiction if used inappropriately. Available since the late 1960s.

See also Codeine, Dextropropoxyphene, Hydromorphone, Methadone, Morphine, Oxycodone, Pethidine.

Peppermint oil

TRADE NAMES:

Colpermin, Mintec.
Also found in numerous liniments, soothing creams and other medications for indigestion.

DRUG CLASS:

Antispasmodic.

USES:

Irritable bowel, excess bowel gas, passing excess wind.

DOSAGE:

 Take three or four times a day 30 minutes before food as needed.

FORMS:

Capsules, tablets.

PRECAUTIONS:

Safe to use in pregnancy, breast feeding and children over six years.
Use with caution in heartburn.

SIDE EFFECTS:

Common: minimal.
Unusual: heartburn, anal irritation, rash.

INTERACTIONS:

None significant.

PRESCRIPTION:

No.

PERMITTED IN SPORT:

Yes.

OVERDOSE:

Exacerbation of side effects likely.

OTHER INFORMATION:

Very safe and effective ancient remedy.

Pergolide

TRADE NAME:

Celance.

DRUG CLASS:

Antiparkinsonian.

USES:

Parkinson's disease.

DOSAGE:

 Gradually increasing dose taken three times a day until dose adequate to control condition.

FORMS:

Tablets of 0.05mg (white), 0.25mg (green) and 1mg (pink).

PRECAUTIONS:

Not to be used in pregnancy (C), breast feeding or children.
Use with care in irregular heart beat, liver and kidney disease.
Should not be stopped suddenly, but dosage should be reduced slowly over some weeks.
Designed to be used only in combination with levodopa.

Do not take if:

• sensitive to ergot.

SIDE EFFECTS:

Common: generalised pain, nausea, incoordination, runny nose, double vision, fainting.
Unusual: belly pain, hallucinations, tiredness, sleeplessness, shortness of breath.

Severe but rare (stop medication, consult doctor): irregular heart rhythm.

INTERACTIONS:

Other drugs:
• phenothiazines, metoclopramide, medications to lower blood pressure.

PRESCRIPTION:

Yes.

PERMITTED IN SPORT:

Yes.

OVERDOSE:

May cause vomiting, convulsions, fainting, agitation, hallucinations and twitching. Induce vomiting if medication taken recently. Seek medical assistance.

OTHER INFORMATION:

Used only in combination with Levodopa compounds. Not addictive. Released in 1993.
See also LEVODOPA COMPOUNDS.

Pericyazine

See PHENOTHIAZINES.

Perindopril

See ACE INHIBITORS.

Permethrin

TRADE NAME:

Lyclear.

DRUG CLASS:

Antiparasitic.

USES:

Head lice, scabies.

DOSAGE:

 Lotion: apply to just washed hair. Leave for ten minutes then rinse out.

Cream: apply to whole body except head and face. Wash off eight to 12 hours later. Reapply after one week.

FORMS:

Cream, lotion.

PRECAUTIONS:

Use with caution in pregnancy (B2), breast feeding and children. Not for use under six months of age.
Avoid contact with eyes, nostrils, mouth, anus and vagina.
Use with caution in elderly.

SIDE EFFECTS:

Common: skin stinging and burning, itch.

INTERACTIONS:

None significant.

PRESCRIPTION:

No.

PERMITTED IN SPORT:

Yes.

OVERDOSE:

If swallowed may cause alcohol intoxication, belly pain, nausea and vomiting. Seek medical attention.

OTHER INFORMATION:

Treat all members of family and other close contacts at same time. Use fine comb repeatedly on hair to remove egg cases. Repeat treatment in one week if necessary.

Perphenazine

See PHENOTHIAZINES.

Pertussis Vaccine

See Whooping Cough Vaccine.

Pethidine

TRADE NAMES:

Pethidine.
Pamergan (with promethazine).

DRUG CLASS:

Narcotic analgesic.

USES:

Severe pain.

DOSAGE:

 As directed by doctor. Usually four hourly.

FORMS:

Injection.

PRECAUTIONS:

Should only be used during the later stages of pregnancy (C) if medically essential as it may reduce the desire to breathe in newborn infants. Use with caution in breast feeding. May be used in children.

Use with caution in colic caused by gall stones, glaucoma, diabetes, pancreatitis, kidney and liver disease, heart disease, ulcerative colitis, underactive thyroid gland, enlarged prostate gland, head injury and shock.

Not designed for long term use. Use lowest dose possible for the shortest time possible.

Do not stop medication suddenly, but reduce dosage slowly.

Lower doses necessary in elderly.

Do not take if:

- suffering from heart failure, irregular heart rhythm, severe head injury, brain tumour, acute diabetes, severe liver disease, severe alcoholism, eclampsia of pregnancy, poor lung function or convulsions
- operating machinery, driving a vehicle or undertaking tasks requiring concentration.

SIDE EFFECTS:

Common: sedation, constipation, confusion, sweating, nausea, vomiting, loss of appetite.
Unusual: difficulty passing urine, flushing, dizziness, slow heart rate, irregular heart rate, fainting, mood changes.
Severe but rare (stop medication, consult doctor): difficulty in breathing, convulsions.

INTERACTIONS:

Other drugs:
- severe interaction with MAOI
- sedatives, pentazocine, phenytoin, paracetamol, barbiturates, phenothiazines, amphetamines, other narcotics.

Other substances:
- should not be used with alcohol.

PRESCRIPTION:

Yes (restricted).

PERMITTED IN SPORT:

No.

OVERDOSE:

Serious. Sedation, convulsions, coma and death may occur. Administer activated charcoal or induce vomiting if medication taken recently and patient alert. Seek emergency medical assistance. Antidote available.

OTHER INFORMATION:

Highly addictive if used inappropriately. Very effective and unlikely to cause addiction if used appropriately for severe pain. Patients with terminal diseases (e.g. cancer) should use dose adequate to control pain and not be concerned about possibility of addiction. Derived from opium poppy and closely related to morphine and heroin, but not as addictive.

See Alfentanil, Buprenorphine, Codeine, Dextromoramide, Dextropropoxyphene, Ethoheptazine, Fentanyl, Heroin, Hydromorphone, Methadone, Morphine, Nalbuphine, Oxycodone, Pentazocine, Phenazocine.

Phenelzine

See MAOI.

Phenobarbitone

See BARBITURATES.

PHENOTHIAZINES

TRADE and GENERIC NAMES:

Clozaril (Clozapine).
Fentazine (Perphenazine).
Largactil (Chlorpromazine).
Melleril (Thioridazine).
Modecate, Moditen (Fluphenazine).
Motival (Fluphenazine with nortriptyline).
Neulactil (Pericyazine).
Nozinan (Methotrimeprazine).
Piportil Depot (Pipothiazine).
Stelazine (Trifluoperazine).
Triptafen (Perphenazine with amitriptyline).
NB: phenothiazines are underlined.

DRUG CLASS:

Antipsychotics, Antiemetics (chlorpromazine and perphenazine).

USES:

Schizophrenia, mania, psychoses, senile agitation, severe agitation in children, intractable vomiting, intractable hiccups, severe anxiety, other psychiatric conditions, increasing the effect of pain killers.

DOSAGE:

 One to three tablets or capsules, two or three times a day. Dosage varies widely from one form to another depending on length of action and potency. Follow doctors instructions carefully.

FORMS:

Tablets, capsules, mixture, suppository, injection.

PRECAUTIONS:

Should only be used in pregnancy (C) if medically necessary. High doses should be avoided late in pregnancy. Should be used with caution in breast feeding. Most forms may be used in children.
Should be used with caution in epilepsy, under active thyroid gland (hypothyroidism), enlarged prostate gland, glaucoma, Parkinsonism, hypoparathyroidism, myasthenia gravis, low blood pressure, liver and kidney diseases.
Use with caution if operating machinery or driving a vehicle.

Do not take if:

 • suffering from depression, very poor circulation, uncontrolled epilepsy, phaeochromocytoma, liver disease or bone marrow disease
• having a spinal anaesthetic
• intoxicated with alcohol or marijuana.

SIDE EFFECTS:

Common: drowsiness, reduced alertness, abnormal body temperature, low blood pressure, dermatitis, dry mouth, constipation, weight gain, blurred vision, stuffy nose.
Unusual: itch, difficulty passing urine, confusion, dizziness, incoordination, tremor, slow breathing, irregular heart beat, skin pigmentation.
Severe but rare (stop medication, consult doctor): yellow skin (jaundice), convulsions, repetitive unwanted movements, muscle rigidity, fever, coma.

INTERACTIONS:

Other drugs:
• adrenaline, tricyclic antidepressants, guanethidine, antacids, sedatives,

barbiturates, phenytoin, lithium, levodopa, sedatives, amphetamines, beta-blockers, hypoglycaemics (treat diabetes), MAOI, quinidine, suxamethonium.

Herbs:
• evening primrose (linoleic acid), ginseng.

Other substances:
• reacts adversely with alcohol and some foods.
• marijuana.

PRESCRIPTION:
Yes.

PERMITTED IN SPORT:
Yes.

OVERDOSE:
Very serious. Symptoms include drowsiness, confusion, restlessness, rapid heart rate, tremor, convulsions, difficulty in breathing and swallowing, coma and death. Administer activated charcoal or induce vomiting if taken recently and patient alert. Seek urgent medical attention.

OTHER INFORMATION:
These drugs have revolutionised the lives of many psychiatric patients to the point where they can lead completely normal lives. First introduced in 1960s. Do not cause addiction or dependence.

See also Amisulpride, Benperidol, Droperidol, Flupenthixol, Haloperidol, Lithium Carbonate, Olanzapine, Pimozide, Prochlorperazine, Quetiapine, Risperidone, Thiothixene, Zotepine, Zuclopenthixol.

Phenylephrine

TRADE NAMES:
Minims Phenylephrine.
Isopto Frin (with hypromellose).
Also found in numerous cold and flu preparations.

DRUG CLASS:
Sympathomimetic (constricts blood vessels), decongestant.

USES:
Minor eye irritations, nasal congestion.

DOSAGE:
 Eye drops: one or two drops every three or four hours.

FORMS:
Eye drops, nose sprays.

PRECAUTIONS:
Safe to use in pregnancy (B2), breast feeding and children.
Use with caution in high blood pressure. Do not use nasal sprays long term.

Do not use eye drops if:
 • suffering from glaucoma.

SIDE EFFECTS:
Minimal.

INTERACTIONS:
Other drugs:
• antidepressants, sedatives.
Other substances:
• reacts with alcohol if taken by mouth.

PRESCRIPTION:
No.

PERMITTED IN SPORT:
If taken by mouth: no.
Other preparations: yes.

OVERDOSE:
If taken by mouth may cause irritability, convulsions, palpitations, high blood pressure, angina and difficulty in passing urine. Administer activated charcoal or induce vomiting if medication taken recently. Seek urgent medical assistance. Nasal preparations if used excessively may cause rebound nasal stuffiness and congestion.

OTHER INFORMATION:

Used widely in cold mixtures, eye drops and nasal sprays to ease irritation and congestion. Safe and effective if taken as directed, but do not take more than recommended dose or over use nose drops and sprays.

See also GLAUCOMA MEDICATIONS, MYDRIATICS, Oxymetazoline, Pseudoephedrine, Tramazoline, VASOCONSTRICTORS.

Phenytoin

TRADE NAME:

Epanutin.

DRUG CLASS:

Anticonvulsant.

USES:

Epilepsy, some forms of irregular heart beat.

DOSAGE:

 One or two tablets, two or three times a day with water and food.

FORMS:

Capsules, tablets, mixture, injection.

PRECAUTIONS:

Not for use in pregnancy (D) unless absolutely essential, as the risk of foetal deformity is increased.
Use with caution in breast feeding. May be used in children.
Lower doses required in elderly.
Use with caution in liver disease, heart disease, low blood pressure, porphyria.
Do not stop suddenly, but reduce dosage slowly over several weeks.

Do not take if:

 • suffering from some forms of heart disease.

SIDE EFFECTS:

Common: most side effects eased by slight reduction in dose. Slurred speech, incoordination, jerky eye movements, confusion.
Unusual: dizziness, sleeplessness, nervous twitching, headache.
Severe but rare (stop medication, consult doctor): enlarged glands in neck, groin or armpits.

INTERACTIONS:

Other drugs:
• wide range of medications can affect the blood levels of phenytoin. Do not take any prescription medication without checking possible interactions with a doctor or pharmacist
• non-prescription medications that interact with phenytoin include aspirin, antacids, calcium, vitamin D and folic acid
• oral contraceptive pill.
Herbs:
• St John's wort, evening primrose (linoleic acid), gingko biloba, piperine (Ayurvedic Piper nigrum), shankhapushpl.
Other substances:
• reacts adversely with alcohol.
• borage.

PRESCRIPTION:

Yes.

PERMITTED IN SPORT:

Yes.

OVERDOSE:

Doses of over 2000mg to 5000mg (depending on size, sex etc.) may be fatal. Symptoms include incoordination, incoherent speech, tremor, tiredness, vomiting, slow heart rate, coma, dilated pupils and death. Administer activated charcoal or induce vomiting if tablets taken recently and patient alert. Seek urgent medical assistance.

OTHER INFORMATION:

For decades, phenytoin has been the mainstay of epilepsy treatment world wide. Does not cause addiction or dependence.

See also **BARBITURATES, BENZODIAZEPINES, Carbamazepine, Clonazepam, Ethosuximide, Gabapentin, Lamotrigine, Levetiracetam, Oxcarbazepine, Primidone, Sodium valproate, Sulthiame, Tiagabine, Topiramate, Vigabatrin.**

Pholcodine

TRADE NAMES:
Galenphol, Pavacol-D.

DRUG CLASS:
Cough suppressant.

USES:
Control of dry cough.

DOSAGE:
 Take 5 to 15mLs four times a day.

FORMS:
Mixture.

PRECAUTIONS:
Safe to use in pregnancy (A), breast feeding and children.
Not for long term use.

SIDE EFFECTS:
Common: minimal.
Unusual: nausea, drowsiness.

INTERACTIONS:
Other substances:
• alcohol.

PRESCRIPTION:
No.

PERMITTED IN SPORT:
Yes.

OVERDOSE:
Serious adverse effects unlikely.

OTHER INFORMATION:
Very old medication. Widely used and very safe.

See also **COUGH SUPPRESSANTS, EXPECTORANTS.**

Phosphorus

TRADE NAMES:
Added to numerous non-prescription vitamin and mineral supplements.

DRUG CLASS:
Mineral.

USES:
Nutritional deficiency, hyperparathyroidism, multiple myeloma, some form of rickets, bone cancer.

DOSAGE:
 Recommended daily dose 1000mg. Higher doses used in treating diseases listed above.

FORMS:
Tablets, mixture.

PRECAUTIONS:
Safe to use in pregnancy, breast feeding and children.
Use with caution in kidney disease.
If high doses used, regular blood tests to check balance of all minerals in blood necessary.

SIDE EFFECTS:
Common: diarrhoea.
Unusual: tissue calcium deposits, kidney stones.

INTERACTIONS:
None significant.

PRESCRIPTION:
No.

PERMITTED IN SPORT:
Yes.

OVERDOSE:

Unlikely to be serious.

OTHER INFORMATION:

Phosphorus is a mineral found naturally in many foods including dairy foods, meat, fish, nuts, eggs and cereals. A natural deficiency is very unusual.

See also MINERALS.

Phytomenadione
(Vitamin K)

TRADE NAME:

Konakion.

DRUG CLASS:

Haemostatic.

USES:

Treatment and prevention of excessive bleeding (particularly in newborn infants), overdose of anticoagulants.

DOSAGE:

 Depends on severity of bleeding.

FORMS:

Tablets, injection.

PRECAUTIONS:

Should be used with caution in pregnancy, breast feeding and children.

Do not take if:

 • suffering from severe allergy tendency.

SIDE EFFECTS:

Common: minimal.
Severe but rare (stop medication, consult doctor): yellow skin (jaundice), allergy reaction.

INTERACTIONS:

None significant.

PRESCRIPTION:

No.

PERMITTED IN SPORT:

Yes.

OVERDOSE:

No serious effects, except in infants where anaemia may occur.

OTHER INFORMATION:

Vitamin K is a fat soluble group of compounds essential for the formation of the factors that clot blood. It is found in most foods (particularly green leafy vegetables) and is also made by bacteria that live in the gut. The adequate daily allowance is 1mg A lack of vitamin K is rare, but may occur if fat absorption from the gut is abnormal. Newborn infants can be low on vitamin K and are often given vitamin K at birth to prevent excessive bleeding.

See also Aminocaproic Acid, Tranexamic acid.

PILL, CONTRACEPTIVE

See ORAL CONTRACEPTIVES.

Pilocarpine

TRADE NAMES:

Minims Pilocarpine, Pilogel, Salagen.

USES:

Glaucoma, dry mouth, Sjögren syndrome.

DOSAGE:

 Eye drops: two drops three or four times a day.
Tablets: one or two three times a day after meals.

FORMS:

Eye drops, eye gel, tablets.

PRECAUTIONS:

Safe to use in pregnancy, breast feeding and children.
Do not exceed prescribed dose.

Do not take if:

 • suffering from acute iritis.

SIDE EFFECTS:

Common: blurred vision.
Unusual: red eye.

INTERACTIONS:

None significant.

PRESCRIPTION:

Yes.

PERMITTED IN SPORT:

Yes.

OVERDOSE:

Seek medical advice. Unlikely to be serious.

OTHER INFORMATION:

Commonly used medication for the treatment of glaucoma.
See also Betaxolol, Bimatoprost, Latanoprost, Levobunolol, Timolol.

Pimozide

TRADE NAME:

Orap.

DRUG CLASS:

Antipsychotic.

USES:

Chronic psychotic disorders (e.g. schizophrenia).

DOSAGE:

 One or more tablets once a day to a maximum of 20mg a day.

FORMS:

Tablet of 2mg (white), 4mg (green) and 10mg (white).

PRECAUTIONS:

Use with caution in pregnancy (B1), breast feeding and children.
Use with caution in heart disease, severe anxiety, aggressive behaviour, liver and kidney disease.

Do not take if:

• suffering from active drug or alcohol abuse, depression, irregular heart beat, Parkinson's disease.

SIDE EFFECTS:

Common: tremor, excess salivation, muscle stiffness, dizziness.
Unusual: difficulty in swallowing, disorientation, sleeplessness, rapid heart rate, restlessness, constipation, loss of appetite, menstrual irregularities.
Severe but rare (stop medication, consult doctor): unwanted and uncontrolled muscle movements particularly of face, rigid muscles, fever.

INTERACTIONS:

Other drugs:
• severe interaction with ketoconazole, erythromycin, nefazodone, quinidine
• anticonvulsants, sedatives, stimulants, atropine, antihypertensives, antiarrhythmics, levodopa, phenothiazines, tricyclic antidepressants.
Herbs:
• evening primrose (linoleic acid).
Other substances:
• reacts adversely with alcohol.

PRESCRIPTION:

Yes.

PERMITTED IN SPORT:

Yes.

OVERDOSE:

Relatively safe. Confusion and drowsiness most likely symptoms.

Administer activated charcoal or induce vomiting if taken recently. Seek medical assistance.

See also Amisulpride, Flupenthixol, Haloperidol, Lithium Carbonate, Olanzapine, PHENOTHIAZINES, Quetiapine, Risperidone, Thiothixene, Zuclopenthixol.

Pindolol

TRADE NAMES:

Visken.
Viskaldix (with clopamide).

DRUG CLASS:

Beta-blocker.

USES:

High blood pressure, angina, rapid heart rate, irregular heart beat, paroxysmal atrial tachycardia, heart attack.

DOSAGE:

 10 to 30mg a day.

FORMS:

Tablets.

PRECAUTIONS:

Should be used in pregnancy (C) only if medically essential.
Safe to use in breast feeding.
May be used with caution in children.
Use with care if suffering from alcoholism, poor circulation, diabetes, hyperthyroidism (over active thyroid gland), liver or kidney failure or about to have surgery.

Do not take if:

- suffering from asthma or allergic conditions
- suffering from heart failure, shock, slow heart rate, or enlarged right heart
- if undertaking prolonged fast.

SIDE EFFECTS:

Common: low blood pressure, slow heart rate, dizziness, headache, cold hands and feet, asthma.
Unusual: loss of appetite, nausea, diarrhoea, impotence, tiredness, sleeplessness, nightmares, rash, loss of libido, hair loss, noises in ears.
Severe but rare (stop medication, consult doctor): severe asthma.

INTERACTIONS:

Other drugs:
- calcium channel blockers, disopyramide, clonidine, adrenaline, other medications for irregular heart beat, lignocaine, ergotamine, indomethacin, chlorpromazine.

PRESCRIPTION:

Yes.

PERMITTED IN SPORT:

No.

OVERDOSE:

Slow heart rate, low blood pressure, asthma and heart failure may result. Administer activated charcoal or induce vomiting if tablets taken recently. Use Salbutamol or other asthma sprays for difficulty in breathing. Seek medical assistance.

OTHER INFORMATION:

Except for asthmatics, very safe and effective.

See also Atenolol, Carvedilol, Esmolol, Labetalol, Metoprolol, Oxprenolol, Propranolol, Sotalol.

Pine tar

See Tar.

Pioglitazone

TRADE NAME:

Actos.

DRUG CLASS:

Hypoglycaemic.

USES:

Type two (non-insulin dependent) diabetes.

DOSAGE:

 15mg to 45mg once a day. Low dose initially, then slowly increased.

FORMS:

Tablets of 15mg and 30mg.

PRECAUTIONS:

Use with caution in pregnancy (B3), breast feeding and children.
Use with care in heart failure, liver and kidney disease.
Normally used in combination with other diabetes medications.

SIDE EFFECTS:

Common: oedema (swelling of tissue).
Unusual: anaemia, liver damage, weight gain.

INTERACTIONS:

Other drugs:
• oral contraceptives, insulin, NSAID (used for arthritis).

PRESCRIPTION:

Yes.

PERMITTED IN SPORT:

Yes.

OVERDOSE:

May be serious. Seek urgent medical attention.

OTHER INFORMATION:

Released in 2002 to treat more difficult cases of type two diabetes.

See also Acarbose, Glibenclamide, Gliclazide, Glimepride, Glipizide, Gliquidone, INSULINS, Metformin, Repaglinide, Rosiglitazone.

Piperacillin

TRADE NAMES:

Tazocin (with tazobactam).

DRUG CLASS:

Penicillin antibiotic.

USES:

Treatment of infections caused by susceptible bacteria.

DOSAGE:

 One injection every three to six hours or by continuous drip infusion.

FORMS:

Injection.

PRECAUTIONS:

May be used in pregnancy (B1), children and breast feeding when medically appropriate.
Use with caution in kidney failure, liver disease, meningitis, and venereal disease.
Not for prolonged use over three weeks.

Do not take if:

 • allergic to penicillin
• suffering from glandular fever.

SIDE EFFECTS:

Common: pain at injection site, diarrhoea.
Unusual: itch or rash, headache, nausea, dizziness, hot flushes, tiredness.
Severe but rare (stop medication, consult doctor): itchy rash, hives, severe diarrhoea, yellow skin (jaundice), unusual bleeding or bruising.

INTERACTIONS:

Other drugs:
• vercuronium, heparin, warfarin, methotrexate.

PRESCRIPTION:

Yes.

PERMITTED IN SPORT:

Yes.

OVERDOSE:

Vomiting and diarrhoea likely.

OTHER INFORMATION:

Used for more severe and unusual infections.

See Amoxycillin, Ampicillin, Cloxacillin, Flucloxacillin, Penicillin G, Pivmecillinam, Ticarcillin.

Piperazine

TRADE NAME:

Pripsen (with senna).

DRUG CLASS:

Anthelmintic.

USES:

Threadworm and roundworm infestations of the gut.

DOSAGE:

 One sachet, repeated after two weeks.

FORMS:

Sachet of powder.

PRECAUTIONS:

May be used in pregnancy and children over three months of age.
Use with caution in breast feeding.
Use with caution in brain disturbances.

Do not take if:

 • suffering from epilepsy, kidney and liver disease.

SIDE EFFECTS:

Common: minimal.
Unusual: dizziness.
Severe but rare (stop medication, consult doctor): visual disturbances.

INTERACTIONS:

None significant.

PRESCRIPTION:

No.

PERMITTED IN SPORT:

Yes.

OVERDOSE:

Unlikely to be serious.
See also Mebendazole.

Pipothiazine

See PHENOTHIAZINES.

Piracetam

TRADE NAME:

Nootropil.

DRUG CLASS:

Anticonvulsant.

USES:

Muscle spasms associated with seizures.

DOSAGE:

 Slowly increase dosage as directed by doctor. Maximum 20g a day.

FORMS:

Tablets of 800 and 1200mg (white), solution.

PRECAUTIONS:

Not to be used in pregnancy, breast feeding and children.
Use with caution in all kidney disease.
Reduce dose in elderly.
Do not stop suddenly, but reduce dose slowly.

Do not take if:

• suffering from severe kidney and liver disease.

SIDE EFFECTS:

Common: restlessness, sleeplessness, weight gain.
Unusual: tiredness, nervousness, depression, diarrhoea, rash.

INTERACTIONS:

Other drugs:
• thyroid hormones.
Other substances:
• alcohol.

PRESCRIPTION:

Yes.

PERMITTED IN SPORT:

Yes.

OTHER INFORMATION:

Medication introduced in 2000 that is almost invariably combined with other medications to control epilepsy.

Piroxicam

TRADE NAMES:

Feldene, GenRx Piroxicam, Mobilis, Pirohexal, Rosig.

DRUG CLASS:

NSAID (Nonsteroidal anti-inflammatory drug).

USES:

All forms of arthritis, inflammatory disorders, gout, back pain, ankylosing spondylitis.

DOSAGE:

 Tablets and capsules: 10 to 20mg once a day with food.
Gel: rub into affected area three or four times a day for up to two weeks.

FORMS:

Capsules, tablets, gel.

PRECAUTIONS:

Should not be used in pregnancy (C) unless medically essential. Breast feeding should be ceased if necessary to use NSAID. Not for use in children under two. Gel safe in pregnancy.
Use tablets and capsules with caution in psychiatricaly disturbed patients, epilepsy, severe infection, heart failure and kidney disease.
Lower doses required in elderly, who may suffer more side effects.

Do not take if:

 • suffering from peptic ulcer at present or in recent past
• due for surgery (including dental surgery)
• suffering from bleeding disorder or anaemia.

SIDE EFFECTS:

Common: gel—minimal.
Other forms—stomach discomfort, diarrhoea, constipation, heartburn, nausea, headache, dizziness.
Unusual: blurred vision, stomach ulcer, ringing noise in ears, retention of fluid, swelling of tissue, drowsiness, itch, rash, shortness of breath.
Severe but rare (stop medication, consult doctor): vomiting blood, passing blood in faeces, other unusual bleeding, asthma induced by medication.

INTERACTIONS:

Other drugs:
• must never be used with anticoagulants (e.g. warfarin)
• probenecid, diuretics, lithium, methotrexate, beta-blockers, ACE inhibitors.
• gel has minimal interactions.
Herbs:
• St John's wort.

PRESCRIPTION:

Gel: no.
Capsules and tablets: yes.

PERMITTED IN SPORT:

Yes.

OVERDOSE:

Causes nausea, vomiting, severe headache, dizziness, confusion and convulsions. Administer activated charcoal or induce vomiting if taken recently. Seek medical assistance.

OTHER INFORMATION:

Used to give excellent relief to a wide variety of inflammatory conditions. Significant side effects (particularly on the stomach) in about 5% of patients. Limit their use. Specially coated forms reduce side effects. Minimal side effects with gels, but less effective.

See also Dexketoprofen, Diclofenac, Diflunisal, Felbinac, Fenbufen, Fenoprofen, Flurbiprofen, Ibuprofen, Indomethacin, Ketoprofen, Ketorolac, Mefenamic acid, Meloxicam, Naproxen, NSAID, Piroxicam, Sulindac, Tenoxicam.

Pivmecillinam

TRADE NAME:

Selexid.

DRUG CLASS:

Penicillin antibiotic.

USES:

Prevention or treatment of urinary infections.

DOSAGE:

 Prevention: two tablets, three or four times a day.
Treatment: two tablets at once, then one tablet three times a day for three days.

FORMS:

Tablets of 200mg (white).

PRECAUTIONS:

Use with caution in pregnancy.
May be used in breast feeding and children.
Use with caution in kidney disease.

Do not take if:

 • suffering from oesophageal strictures, intestinal obstruction
• allergic to penicillin.

SIDE EFFECTS:

Common: nausea, diarrhoea.
Unusual: rash.

INTERACTIONS:

Other drugs:
• methotrexate, valproate.

PRESCRIPTION:

Yes.

PERMITTED IN SPORT:

Yes.

OVERDOSE:

Exacerbation of side effects likely.
See also PENICILLINS.

Pizotifen

TRADE NAME:

Sanomigran.

DRUG CLASS:

Antimigraine.

USES:

Prevention of migraine.

DOSAGE:

 0.5 to 3mg a day as a single dose. Maximum 6mg a day.

FORMS:

Tablet of 0.5 and 1.5mg (white).

PRECAUTIONS:

Should be used with caution in pregnancy (B1), breast feeding and children.
Pizotifen has no effect on acute migraine attacks.

Do not take if:

 • suffering from glaucoma, difficulty in passing urine.

SIDE EFFECTS:

Common: sedation, increased appetite
Unusual: dizziness, dry mouth, constipation, nervousness in children, swelling of tissues, headache, rash, muscle aches, tingling sensation, impotence.

INTERACTIONS:

Other drugs:
• increased sedation with sedatives, hypnotics and antihistamines.
Other substances:
• reacts with alcohol to cause drowsiness.

PRESCRIPTION:

Yes.

PERMITTED IN SPORT:

Yes.

OVERDOSE:

Serious. Administer activated charcoal or induce vomiting if taken recently. Symptoms include drowsiness, nausea, dizziness, reduced breathing, convulsions, coma. Seek urgent medical assistance.

OTHER INFORMATION:

Older, widely used medication. Large doses often necessary. Increase dosage slowly.
See also Clonidine, Methysergide, Propranolol.

Plague vaccine

See Yersinia pestis vaccine.

Pneumococcal vaccine

TRADE NAMES:

Pneumovax II, Pnu-Imune, Prevenar.

DRUG CLASS:

Vaccine.

USES:

Prevention of infections caused by Pneumococcal bacteria (usually a type of pneumonia).
Recommended for most people over 65 years, those who have had a splenectomy (spleen removal) and anyone with poor immunity.

DOSAGE:

 Single injection.

FORMS:

Injection.

PRECAUTIONS:

Not designed for use in pregnancy. May be used in breast feeding and children over two years.
Use with caution in heart and lung disease, reduced immunity, fever, current antibiotic treatment.
Do not take if:
 • receiving chemotherapy for Hodgkin's disease
• previously vaccinated with this vaccine.

SIDE EFFECTS:

Common: local soreness and redness at site of injection.
Unusual: rash, joint pain, fever, joint pains, headache, tiredness, enlarged lymph nodes.

INTERACTIONS:

Other drugs:
• immunosuppressives (used in cancer treatment).

PRESCRIPTION:

Yes.

PERMITTED IN SPORT:

Yes.

OVERDOSE:

Significant adverse reactions and allergy reactions may occur if a second vaccination is given to an adult. Children may require a second vaccination.

OTHER INFORMATION:

Not used routinely but restricted to patients who are elderly, have lung diseases, have (or are about to have) their spleen removed, who are chronically ill, or who are in an institution where the disease has occurred.

PODOPHYLLUMS

TRADE and GENERIC NAMES:

Condyline, Warticon (podophyllotoxin). **Posalfilin** (podophyllum resin with salicylic acid).

USES:

Warts.

DOSAGE:

 Cream and ointment: apply two or three times a week.
Paint: apply once or twice a day.

FORMS:

Cream, ointment, paint.

PRECAUTIONS:

Not to be used in pregnancy or breast feeding. Not for use in infants. Use with caution in children.
Use with caution in diabetes and poor circulation.
Do not use on moles, birthmarks or unusual warts, but seek medical advice.
Use on only a limited number of warts at one time.
Avoid use on normal and broken skin.
Be careful to avoid eyes, nose, vagina.

SIDE EFFECTS:

Common: burning, redness of skin.
Unusual: skin pain.

INTERACTIONS:

None significant.

PRESCRIPTION:

Yes.

PERMITTED IN SPORT:

Yes.

OTHER INFORMATION:

Ancient and commonly used remedy for warts that is usually effective.
See also Glutaraldehyde, KERATOLYTICS, SALICYLATES.

Podophyllotoxin

See PODOPHYLLUMS.

Poliomyelitis vaccine

TRADE NAME:

Polio Sabin.

DRUG CLASS:

Vaccine.

USES:

Prevention of poliomyelitis.

DOSAGE:

 Three drops on a spoon or lump of sugar given three times at two monthly intervals. Booster dose at five years.

FORMS:

Drops (must be carefully stored at 4°C).

PRECAUTIONS:

Not designed to be used during pregnancy (B2), but inadvertent use unlikely to cause any serious effect. May be used during breast feeding, in children and infants.
Use with caution in diarrhoea, vomiting or infection.

Do not take if:

- suffering from fever or reduced immunity.

SIDE EFFECTS:

Common: minimal.
Unusual: headache, vomiting, diarrhoea.

INTERACTIONS:

Other drugs:
- other live vaccines.

PRESCRIPTION:

Yes.

PERMITTED IN SPORT:

Yes.

OVERDOSE:

Unintentional additional dose is unlikely to have any serious effect.

OTHER INFORMATION:

Poliomyelitis is a viral infection that causes muscle paralysis and sometimes death. It has been eradicated from Britain, Europe and all developed countries by vaccination, but is still widespread in many poorer countries.

Poloxamer 188

TRADE NAME:

Codalax (with danthron).

DRUG CLASS:

Laxative.

USES:

Constipation, particularly if caused by use of powerful pain killers.

DOSAGE:

 5 to 10mLs at night.

FORMS:

Liquid.

PRECAUTIONS:

Safe in pregnancy (A), breast feeding and children over three months.
Not for long term use. May cause intestinal dependence.

Do not take if:

- suffering from suspected appendicitis, bleeding from anus, belly pain, obstructed gut.

SIDE EFFECTS:

Common: minimal.
Unusual: colic, belly pain, diarrhoea.

INTERACTIONS:

Other drugs:
- other laxatives.

PRESCRIPTION:

No.

PERMITTED IN SPORT:

Yes.

OVERDOSE:

Diarrhoea and belly cramps only likely effects.
See also LAXATIVES.

Polymyxin B

TRADE NAMES:

Only available in combination with other medications.
Gregoderm (with nystatin, hydrocortisone).
Maxitrol (with dexamethasone, neomycin, hypromellose).
Neosporin (with neomycin, gramicidin).
Otosporin (with neomycin, hydrocortisone).
Polyfax (with bacitracin).
Polytrim (with trimethoprim).

DRUG CLASS:

Antibiotic.

USES:

Bacterial infections of skin and eyes.

DOSAGE:

Eye drops and ointment: insert every three to six hours.
Ear drops: two drops, three times a day.
Skin ointment: apply two or three times a day.

FORMS:

Eye drops, eye ointment, ear drops, ointment.

PRECAUTIONS:

Safe to use in pregnancy, breast feeding and children.
Not designed for long term regular use.
Do not use on large areas of skin or in ear with perforated ear drum.

SIDE EFFECTS:

Common: minimal.
Severe but rare (stop medication, consult doctor): skin or eye irritation.

INTERACTIONS:

None significant.

PRESCRIPTION:

Yes.

PERMITTED IN SPORT:

Yes.
See also Neomycin.

Polystyrene sulfonate
(Sodium polystyrene sulfonate)

TRADE NAME:

Calcium Resonium, Resonium A.

DRUG CLASS:

Detoxifying agent.

USES:

Reducing very high blood potassium levels.

DOSAGE:

15g by mouth one to four times a day. May also be used rectally in double dose.

FORMS:

Powder.

PRECAUTIONS:

May be used in pregnancy, breast feeding and children.
Use with caution in heart disease, high blood pressure and tissue swelling.
Regular blood tests to monitor effect on blood chemistry essential.

SIDE EFFECTS:

Common: loss of appetite, bowel discomfort, constipation, nausea, vomiting.
Unusual: impaction of faeces.

INTERACTIONS:

Other drugs:
• digoxin, antacids, laxatives.
Other substances:
• reacts with fruit juices.

PRESCRIPTION:

Yes.

PERMITTED IN SPORT:

Yes.

OVERDOSE:

Severe constipation possible.

OTHER INFORMATION:

Resonium A is not absorbed from the gut, but draws Potassium out of the body to pass out in the faeces.

Polyvinyl alcohol
See EYE LUBRICANTS.

Potassium bicarbonate
See ELECTROLYTES.

Potassium chloride

See ELECTROLYTES.

Potassium clavulanate

See Clavulanic acid.

Potassium hydroxyquinoline

TRADE NAMES:

Quinoderm (with benzoyl peroxide).

DRUG CLASS:

Antifungal, antibiotic.

USES:

Gel: acne.
Cream: mild fungal and bacterial skin infections combined with dermatitis.

DOSAGE:

 Gel: massage into affected skin one to three times a day.
Cream: apply two or three times a day.

FORMS:

Cream, gel.

PRECAUTIONS:

Safe to use in pregnancy, breast feeding and children.
Avoid eyes, mouth and nostrils.

SIDE EFFECTS:

Common: minimal.
Unusual: skin irritation.

INTERACTIONS:

None significant.

PRESCRIPTION:

No.

PERMITTED IN SPORT:

Yes.

Potassium p-Aminobenzoate

See Aminobenzoic Acid.

Povidone

See EYE LUBRICANTS.

Povidone-Iodine

See Iodine.

Pramipexole

TRADE NAME:

Mirapexin.

DRUG CLASS:

Antiparkinsonian.

USES:

Parkinson's disease.

DOSAGE:

 Initially 125mg three times a day. Dose slowly increased as directed by doctor. Maximum 4.5mg a day.

FORMS:

Tablets (white) of 0.125, 0.25 and 1mg.

PRECAUTIONS:

Not to be used in breast feeding and children.
Use with considerable caution in pregnancy.
Use with caution in kidney disease, psychoses, schizophrenia and severe heart disease.
Blood pressure must be checked regularly.
Eye checks must be performed regularly.

SIDE EFFECTS:

Common: nausea, constipation, sudden and unpredictable onset of sleep.
Unusual: tiredness, incoordination, hallucinations.
Severe but rare (stop medication, consult doctor): high blood pressure, eye damage.

INTERACTIONS:

Other drugs:
• cimetidine, diltiazem, quinidine, quinine, ranitidine, procainamide, digoxin, triamterene, amantadine, verapamil, trimethoprim, sedatives.
Other substances:
• alcohol.

PRESCRIPTION:

Yes.

PERMITTED IN SPORT:

Yes.

OVERDOSE:

May be serious. Seek urgent medical attention. Induce vomiting or give activated charcoal if taken recently.

OTHER INFORMATION:

Almost invariably used in combination with Levodopa. Introduced 1999 for the management of more severe forms of Parkinson's disease.

See Amantadine, Apomorphine, Benzhexol, Benztropine, Biperiden, Bromocriptine, Entacapone, LEVODOPA COMPOUNDS, Orphenadrine, Pergolide, Procyclidine, Ropinirole, Selegiline.

Pravastatin

TRADE NAME:

Lipostat.

DRUG CLASS:

Hypolipidaemic.

USES:

High blood levels of cholesterol.

DOSAGE:

 10mg to 40mg taken at bedtime on an empty stomach.

FORMS:

Tablets (yellow) of 10mg, 20mg and 40mg.

PRECAUTIONS:

Must not be taken in pregnancy (C) as Pravastatin may cause miscarriage or foetal abnormalities. Adequate contraception must be used by all women of child bearing potential who are taking this medication. Not to be used in breast feeding or children.
Must be used with caution in elderly, with kidney and liver disease, and alcoholism. Regular blood tests to check cholesterol level and liver function necessary.

Do not take if:
• suffering from liver or kidney disease, alcoholism.

SIDE EFFECTS:

Common: muscle pains, rash, headache, nausea, diarrhoea, constipation, excess wind.
Unusual: chest pain, vomiting, belly pains, heartburn, fatigue, joint pain, muscle weakness.
Severe but rare (stop medication, consult doctor): liver damage (yellow skin), severe muscle pain and weakness.

INTERACTIONS:

Other drugs:
• gemfibrizol, nicotinic acid, cyclosporin, erythromycin, cimetidine, cholestyramine, colestipol.
Other substances:
• reacts with alcohol.
Herbs:
• alfalfa, fenugreek, garlic, ginger.

PRESCRIPTION:

Yes.

PERMITTED IN SPORT:

Yes.

OVERDOSE:

No information available.

OTHER INFORMATION:

Introduced in the early 1990s. Dangerous in pregnancy.

See also Atorvastatin, Cholestyramine, Colestipol, Fluvastatin, Gemfibrizol, Nicotinic acid, Simvastatin.

Prazosin

TRADE NAME:

Hypovase.

DRUG CLASS:

Antihypertensive, Alpha blocker.

USES:

High blood pressure, severe heart failure, Raynaud's phenomenon, enlargement of prostate gland.

DOSAGE:

 Taken two or three times a day to a maximum of 20mg per day.

FORMS:

Tablets of 0.5mg (white),1mg (orange), and 2mg (white).

PRECAUTIONS:

Should be used with caution in pregnancy (B2) and breast feeding. Not designed to be used in children.
Always start at a very low dose and increase slowly.
Use with caution in angina, heart valve narrowing causing heart failure, liver and kidney disease.

Do not take if:

 • suffering from phaeochromocytoma, low blood pressure on standing or poor liver function.

SIDE EFFECTS:

Common: headache, drowsiness, palpitations, swelling of tissue, nausea, nasal congestion, blurred vision, low blood pressure on standing.
Unusual: vomiting, itchy skin.
Severe but rare (stop medication, consult doctor): fainting.

INTERACTIONS:

Other drugs:
• additive effect from diuretics
• other antihypertensives.

PRESCRIPTION:

Yes.

PERMITTED IN SPORT:

Yes.

OVERDOSE:

Drowsiness and depressed reflexes only effects.

OTHER INFORMATION:

Very effective in high blood pressure. Found to temporarily reduce the size of the prostate gland and make it easier to pass urine. Delays prostate surgery, but does not remove long term necessity for surgery.

See also ANTIHYPERTENSIVES.

Prednisolone

TRADE NAMES:

Deltacortril, Deltastab, Minims Prednisolone, Pred Forte, Predenema, Predfoam, Predsol.
Predsol-N (with neomycin).
Scheriproct (with cinchocaine).

DRUG CLASS:

Corticosteroid.

USES:

Severe inflammation of skin (eczema, dermatitis etc.), anus (piles), rectum (ulcerative colitis), eyes and other tissues. Severe asthma, rheumatoid and other forms of severe arthritis, autoimmune diseases (e.g. Sjögren syndrome), severe allergy reactions and other severe and chronic inflammatory diseases.

DOSAGE:

Enema: insert once a day for up to four weeks.
Suppositories: insert twice a day for up to three weeks.
Eye and ear drops: insert every two to four hours.
Tablets and mixture: as directed by doctor.

FORMS:

Ear drops, enema, eye drops, mixture, suppository, tablets, foam.

PRECAUTIONS:

Should be used in pregnancy (C), breast feeding and children only on specific medical advice.
Eye preparations safe in pregnancy, breast feeding and children over three years.
Use with caution if under stress and in patients with under active thyroid gland, liver disease, diverticulitis, high blood pressure, myasthenia gravis or kidney disease.
Avoid eyes with all forms except eye drops.
Use for shortest period of time possible. Medication should not be ceased abruptly, but dosage should be slowly reduced.

Do not use if:

- suffering from any form of infection, peptic ulcer or osteoporosis
- having a vaccination.

SIDE EFFECTS:

Most significant side effects occur only with prolonged use of tablets or rectal preparations.

Common: may cause bloating, weight gain, rashes and intestinal disturbances. Eye and ear drops rarely cause adverse reactions away from eyes and ears.
Unusual: biochemical disturbances of blood, muscle weakness, bone weakness, impaired wound healing, skin thinning, tendon weakness, peptic ulcers, gullet ulcers, bruising, increased sweating, loss of fat under skin, premature ageing, excess facial hair growth in women, pigmentation of skin and nails, acne, convulsions, headaches, dizziness, growth suppression in children, aggravation of diabetes, worsening of infections, cataracts, aggravation of glaucoma, blood clots in veins and sleeplessness.
Severe but rare (stop medication, consult doctor): any significant side effect should be reported to a doctor immediately.

INTERACTIONS:

Other drugs:
- tablets and rectal preparations may be affected by oral contraceptives, barbiturates, phenytoin and rifampicin.
Herbs:
- liquorice, echinacea, ginseng, salboku-to, magnolia, poria cocos.
Other substances:
- zinc.

PRESCRIPTION:

Yes.

PERMITTED IN SPORT:

Most forms: no.
Eye drops: yes.

OVERDOSE:

Medical treatment is required. Serious effects and death rare.

OTHER INFORMATION:

Extremely effective and useful medication if used correctly. Must be used with extreme care under strict medical supervision. Lowest dose and shortest possible course should be used. Not addictive.

See also CORTICOSTEROIDS, Cortisone acetate, Dexamethasone, Fludrocortisone, Flumethasone, Fluorometholone,

Fluticasone, Hydrocortisone, Methylprednisolone.

Prilocaine

See ANAESTHETICS, LOCAL.

Primidone

TRADE NAME:

Mysoline.

DRUG CLASS:

Anticonvulsant.

USES:

Epilepsy.

DOSAGE:

 Requires individual planning by a doctor, depending on nature and timing of convulsions.

FORMS:

Tablets of 250mg (white).

PRECAUTIONS:

Not to be used in pregnancy (D) unless absolutely necessary as it may cause bleeding problems in the newborn infant. Use with caution in breast feeding. May be used in children.
Use with caution in kidney, liver and lung disease.
Lower doses necessary in elderly.
Do not stop suddenly, but reduce dosage slowly.
Use with caution if operating machinery, driving a vehicle or undertaking tasks that require coordination and alertness.

Do not take if:

 • suffering from porphyria.

SIDE EFFECTS:

Common: usually minimal and dose related. Drowsiness, vision disturbances.
Unusual: nausea, headache, dizziness, vomiting, rash, poor coordination, personality changes, joint pains
Severe but rare (stop medication, consult doctor): blood cell abnormalities, anaemia, liver damage (jaundice).

INTERACTIONS:

Other drugs:
• anticonvulsants, anticoagulants (e.g. warfarin), oral contraceptive pill, sedatives.
Herbs:
• gingko biloba.
Other substances:
• reacts adversely with alcohol
• borage.

PRESCRIPTION:

Yes.

PERMITTED IN SPORT:

Yes.

OVERDOSE:

Serious. Symptoms may include incoordination, reduced breathing and coma. Administer activated charcoal or induce vomiting if medication taken recently and patient alert. Seek urgent medical assistance.

See also BARBITURATES, BENZODIAZEPINES, Carbamazepine, Clonazepam, Ethosuximide, Gabapentin, Lamotrigine, Levetiracetam, Oxcarbazepine, Phenytoin, Sodium valproate, Sulthiame, Tiagabine, Topiramate, Vigabatrin.

Procainamide

TRADE NAME:

Pronestyl.

DRUG CLASS:

Antiarrhythmic.

USES:

Control and prevention of some types of heart beat irregularities.

DOSAGE:

 One or two tablets, four to six times a day.

FORMS:

Tablets of 250mg (white), injection.

PRECAUTIONS:

Should be used with caution in pregnancy (B2). Should not be used in breast feeding. Should be used only if medically essential in children.
Should be used with caution in kidney and liver disease.
Routine blood tests may be required with long term treatment to check on cell types and numbers.

Do not take if:

 • suffering from myasthenia gravis, SLE or atrio-ventricular heart conduction block.

SIDE EFFECTS:

Common: generally well tolerated. Low blood pressure, stomach upsets.
Unusual: depression, dizziness, hallucinations, fever, rash, flush, shivering, itchy skin, mild arthritis, bad taste.
Severe but rare (stop medication, consult doctor): blood cell abnormalities.

INTERACTIONS:

Other drugs:
• amiodarone, propranolol, other antiarrhythmics, cimetidine, anticholinergics, antihypertensives, captopril, sulphonamides, trimethoprim.
Other substances:
• alcohol.

PRESCRIPTION:

Yes.

PERMITTED IN SPORT:

Yes.

OVERDOSE:

Rapid heart rate, vomiting and low blood pressure may occur. Administer activated charcoal or induce vomiting if tablets taken recently. Seek medical assistance.
See also Amiodarone, Disopyramide, Flecainide, Mexiletine, Quinidine, Sotalol, Verapamil.

Prochlorperazine

TRADE NAMES:

Buccastem, Stemetil.

DRUG CLASS:

Antiemetic, Antihistamine.

USES:

Nausea, vomiting, dizziness, Ménière's disease.

DOSAGE:

 Tablets: one tablet two to four times a day.
Buccal tablets: dissolve between upper lip and gum once or twice a day.
Suppository: one every six to eight hours as needed.

FORMS:

Tablets (cream) of 5mg, buccal tablets (yellow), suppositories, granules in sachet, syrup, injection.

PRECAUTIONS:

Should be used in pregnancy (C) only if medically essential. Use with caution in breast feeding. Not for use in children under two years or less than 10kg.
Use with caution in epilepsy, Parkinson's disease, underactive thyroid gland, myasthenia gravis, Reye's syndrome, phaeochromocytoma, enlarged prostate gland, low calcium states, kidney or liver disease.
Lower doses necessary in elderly.

Do not take if:

 • suffering from shock, brain diseases, bone marrow disease.

SIDE EFFECTS:

Common: constipation, dry mouth, drowsiness, tremor, blurred vision.
Unusual: swelling of tissues (oedema), low blood pressure, irregular heart beat, rash, difficulty in passing urine, headache, sleeplessness.
Severe but rare (stop medication, consult doctor): yellow skin (jaundice), difficulty in breathing, convulsion.

INTERACTIONS:

Other drugs:
• sedatives, desferrioxamine, anticholinergics, procarbazine, L-Dopa, anticoagulants, thiazides, propranolol, guanethidine, phenytoin, warfarin, tricyclic antidepressants.
Other substances:
• reacts adversely with alcohol.

PRESCRIPTION:

Yes.

PERMITTED IN SPORT:

Yes.

OVERDOSE:

Serious, particularly in children. Symptoms include confusion, restlessness, rapid heart rate, tremor, twitching, convulsions, difficulty breathing, coma and rarely death. Administer activated charcoal or induce vomiting if medication taken recently and patient alert. Seek urgent medical assistance.

OTHER INFORMATION:

Widely used and effective. Available for over 30 years. Does not cause addiction or dependence. Related to the Phenothiazines.
See also Domperidone, Metoclopramide, Promethazine.

Procyclidine

TRADE NAMES:

Arpicolin, Kemadrin.

DRUG CLASS:

Antiparkinsonian.

USES:

Parkinson's disease, other muscle movement disorders.

DOSAGE:

 Half to two tablets three times a day.

FORMS:

Tablet of 5mg (white), syrup.

PRECAUTIONS:

Safe for use in pregnancy (A). Use with caution in breast feeding and children. Use with caution in glaucoma, intestinal obstruction, enlarged prostate gland and psychiatric conditions.
Use with caution in elderly.

SIDE EFFECTS:

Common: dry mouth, blurred vision, nausea.
Unusual: vomiting, rash, dizziness, hallucinations.

PRESCRIPTION:

Yes.

PERMITTED IN SPORT:

Yes.

OVERDOSE:

Unlikely to be serious. Seek medical advice.

OTHER INFORMATION:

Does not cause addiction or dependence.
See also ANTIPARKINSONIANS.

Progesterone

TRADE NAMES:
Crinone, Cyclogest, Gestone.

DRUG CLASS:
Sex hormone.

USES:
Premenstrual tension (PMT), abnormal vaginal bleeding, adjunct to oestrogen in hormone replacement therapy, endometriosis, maintenance of early pregnancy, aid to infertility, postnatal depression.

DOSAGE:

Vaginal gel: second daily for last two weeks of menstrual cycle for PMT.
Suppository: insert rectally or vaginally once or twice a day for last two weeks of menstrual cycle for PMT.

FORMS:
Vaginal gel, suppository, injection.

PRECAUTIONS:
May be used with care in pregnancy and breast feeding.
Not for use in children.
Use with caution in diabetes, migraine, epilepsy, liver disease.
Do not take if:

- suffering from breast cancer, liver disease, undiagnosed abnormal vaginal bleeding
- history of blood clots.

SIDE EFFECTS:
Common: abnormal vaginal bleeding, headache.

INTERACTIONS:
Other drugs:
- anticoagulants, hypoglycaemics, insulin.

PRESCRIPTION:
Yes.

PERMITTED IN SPORT:
Yes.
See also Norethisterone.

Proguanil

TRADE NAMES:
Paludrine.
Malarone (with atovaquone).

DRUG CLASS:
Antimalarial.

USES:
Prevention (Paludrine) and treatment (Malarone) of malaria.

DOSAGE:

Prevention: two tablets a day.
Treatment: four tablets a day with food for three days.

FORMS:
Paludrine: tablets of 100mg (white).
Malarone: tablets (pink).

PRECAUTIONS:
Use with caution in pregnancy (B2) and breast feeding.
Use with caution in kidney disease.

SIDE EFFECTS:
Common: loss of appetite, nausea, diarrhoea, headache.
Unusual: vomiting, rash, dizziness, hair loss.

INTERACTIONS:
Other drugs:
- magnesium salts (antacids).

PRESCRIPTION:
Yes.

PERMITTED IN SPORT:
Yes.

OVERDOSE:
Very serious. May be fatal. Administer activated charcoal or induce vomiting if

taken recently. Seek urgent medical attention.

OTHER INFORMATION:

Not addictive or dependence forming.

See also ANTIMALARIALS.

Promethazine

See ANTIHISTAMINES, SEDATING.

Propafenone

TRADE NAME:

Arythmol.

DRUG CLASS:

Antiarrhythmic.

USES:

Prevention and treatment of some forms of abnormal heart rhythm.

DOSAGE:

 150 to 300mg, two or three times a day.

FORMS:

Tablets (white) of 150 and 300mg.

PRECAUTIONS:

Not to be used in pregnancy, breast feeding and children.
Use with caution in asthma, liver and kidney disease, heart structure abnormalities, and any type of heart failure.
Treatment should be started in hospital.
Use lower doses in elderly.
Use care if pacemaker present.

Do not take if:

 • suffering from uncontrolled congestive cardiac failure, shock, very slow heart rate, blood electrolyte disturbances, severe lung diseases, very low blood pressure, myasthenia gravis,

some types of irregular heart rhythm.

SIDE EFFECTS:

Common: dizziness, nausea, bitter taste, irregular bowel habits, headache.
Unusual: fatigue, vomiting, skin rashes, slow heart rate.
Severe but rare (stop medication, consult doctor): worsening heart beat irregularities.

INTERACTIONS:

Other drugs:
• other antiarrhythmics, digoxin, cimetidine, warfarin, propranolol, metoprolol, rifampicin, tricyclic antidepressants, cyclosporin,theophylline.
Other substances:
• alcohol.

PRESCRIPTION:

Yes.

PERMITTED IN SPORT:

Yes.

OVERDOSE:

Very serious. Seek urgent medical attention. Induce vomiting or give activated charcoal if swallowed recently.

OTHER INFORMATION:

Used only for serious, difficult to control, heart beat rhythm abnormalities.

See also Amiodarone, Disopyramide, Flecainide, Mexiletine, Procainamide, Quinidine, Sotalol, Verapamil.

Propamidine isethionate
(Dibromopropamide isethionate)

TRADE NAME:

Golden Eye Ointment.

DRUG CLASS:

Antiseptic.

USES:

Mild eye infections.

DOSAGE:

 Apply two or three times a day.

FORMS:

Eye drops, eye ointment.

PRECAUTIONS:

Safe to use in pregnancy, breast feeding and children.
Not to be used regularly for longer than one week.

SIDE EFFECTS:

Minimal.

INTERACTIONS:

None significant.

PRESCRIPTION:

No.

PERMITTED IN SPORT:

Yes.

OTHER INFORMATION:

Commonly used as first line treatment for conjunctivitis.
See also Chloramphenicol, Neomycin, Sulfacetamide.

Propionic Acid
(Sub-class of nonsteroidal anti-inflammatory drugs: NSAID)

See Fenbufen, Flurbiprofen, Ibuprofen, Ketoprofen, Naproxen.

Propiverine

TRADE NAME:

Detrunorm.

DRUG CLASS:

Anticholinergic.

USES:

Unstable bladder control, urinary incontinence, urinary urgency.

DOSAGE:

 One tablet, two to four times a day.

FORMS:

Tablets of 15mg (pink).

PRECAUTIONS:

Not to be used in pregnancy, breast feeding and children.
Use with caution in overactive thyroid gland, angina, coronary artery disease, heart failure, irregular heart beat rhythm, rapid heart rate, enlarged prostate, heartburn and hiatus hernia.

Do not take if:

 • suffering from bladder outflow obstruction, myasthenia gravis, bowel obstruction, severe ulcerative colitis, megacolon, glaucoma, severe liver or kidney disease.

SIDE EFFECTS:

Common: dry mouth, blurred vision, drowsiness.
Unusual: nausea, diarrhoea, difficulty passing urine, tiredness.
Severe but rare (stop medication, consult doctor): unable to pass urine.

INTERACTIONS:

Other drugs:
• tricyclic antidepressants, tranquillisers, anticholinergics, amantadine, salbutamol, isoniazid, sedatives.

PRESCRIPTION:

Yes.

PERMITTED IN SPORT:

Yes.

OVERDOSE:

Exacerbation of side effects only likely effects.

Propranolol

TRADE NAMES:

**Beta-Progane, Inderal, Syprol.
Inderetic, Inderex** (with bendrofluazide).

DRUG CLASS:

Beta-blocker.

USES:

High blood pressure, angina, over active thyroid gland, rapid heart rate, irregular heart beat, paroxysmal atrial tachycardia, heart attack, prevention of migraine, tremors, phaeochromocytoma, prevention of anxiety related symptoms (e.g. stage fright, exam nerves)

DOSAGE:

 10 to 320mg a day.

FORMS:

Tablets, long acting tablets.

PRECAUTIONS:

Should be used in pregnancy (C) only if medically essential.
Safe to use in breast feeding.
May be used with caution in children.
Use with care if suffering from alcoholism, liver or kidney failure, heart failure, diabetes or about to have surgery.

Do not take if:

- suffering from asthma or related allergic conditions
- suffering from uncontrolled heart failure, shock, low blood pressure, slow heart rate, or enlarged right heart
- if undertaking prolonged fast.

SIDE EFFECTS:

Common: low blood pressure, slow heart rate, cold hands and feet, asthma.
Unusual: loss of appetite, nausea, diarrhoea, impotence, tiredness, sleeplessness, nightmares, rash, loss of libido, hair loss, noises in ears.

Severe but rare (stop medication, consult doctor): severe asthma.

INTERACTIONS:

Other drugs:
- calcium channel blockers, disopyramide, clonidine, adrenaline, other medications for irregular heart beat, lignocaine, ergotamine, indomethacin, chlorpromazine.

PRESCRIPTION:

Yes.

PERMITTED IN SPORT:

No.

OVERDOSE:

Slow heart rate, low blood pressure, asthma and heart failure may result. Administer activated charcoal or induce vomiting if tablets taken recently. Use Salbutamol or other asthma sprays for difficulty in breathing. Seek medical assistance.

OTHER INFORMATION:

An amazing drug that can help an extraordinarily wide range of problems. Except for asthmatics, very safe and effective. First developed in 1960s.

See also Atenolol, BETA-BLOCKERS, Carvedilol, Esmolol, Labetalol, Metoprolol, Oxprenolol, Pindolol, Sotalol.

Propyl salicylate

See SALICYLATES.

Prostaglandin E1

See Alprostadil.

Protamine zinc insulin

See INSULINS.

PROTON PUMP INHIBITORS

TRADE and GENERIC NAMES:

Zoton (Lansoprazole).
Heliclear (<u>Lansoprazole</u> with clarithromycin, amoxycillin).
Helimet (<u>Lansoprazole</u> with clarithromycin, metronidazole).
Losec (Omeprazole).
Nexium (Esomoprazole).
Pariet (Rabeprazole).
Protiun (Pantoprazole).

DRUG CLASS:

Anti-ulcer.

USES:

Peptic ulcers of the stomach and duodenum, ulcers of the oesophagus, over production of acid in stomach (e.g. Zollinger Ellison syndrome).

DOSAGE:

 One or two capsules once a day. Swallow capsule whole.

FORMS:

Capsules, tablets.

PRECAUTIONS:

Safe use in pregnancy (B3) and while breast feeding not proven, but may be used if essential.

SIDE EFFECTS:

Common: minimal.
Unusual: nausea, vomiting, diarrhoea, constipation, belly pains, passing wind, headache, dry mouth and throat, tiredness, joint pains.
Severe but rare (stop medication, consult doctor): skin rash, breast enlargement in both sexes.

INTERACTIONS:

Other drugs:
• diazepam (sedation), phenytoin (increases effect of phenytoin), warfarin (dosage of warfarin may need to be decreased), ketoconazole, theophylline, carbamazepine, low dose oral contraceptives, sucralfate, iron.
Herbs:
• cranberry juice.

PRESCRIPTION:

Yes.

PERMITTED IN SPORT:

Yes.

OVERDOSE:

Unlikely to be serious.

OTHER INFORMATION:

This very effective class of medications was first introduced in 1991 and has revolutionised the treatment of more resistant peptic ulcers and persistent reflux oesophagitis. They act by inhibiting the activity of the enzyme in the stomach lining that is responsible for acid production.

See also ANTACIDS, Cimetidine, Famotidine, Nizatadine, Ranitidine.

Proxymetacaine

See ANAESTHETICS, LOCAL.

Pseudoephedrine

TRADE NAMES:

Galpseud, Sudafed.
Dimotane Plus (with brompheniramine).
Galpseud Plus (with chlorpheniramine).
Sudafed Plus (with triprolidine).
Also found in numerous other non-prescription cold and flu remedies.

DRUG CLASS:

Decongestant.

USES:

Congestion of nose and sinuses.

DOSAGE:

 One tablet or capsule two to four times a day.

FORMS:

Tablets, capsules, mixture, syrup.

PRECAUTIONS:

Use with caution in pregnancy (B2) and breast feeding. May be used in children. Use with caution in treated high blood pressure, enlarged prostate gland and bladder problems.

Do not take if:

- suffering from uncontrolled blood pressure or angina.

SIDE EFFECTS:

Common: sleeplessness, rapid heart rate.
Unusual: hallucinations, sweating, flushing, difficulty in passing urine.
Severe but rare (stop medication, consult doctor): chest pain.

INTERACTIONS:

Other drugs:
- other decongestants, MAOI, furazolidone, medications used to treat high blood pressure.

PRESCRIPTION:

No.

PERMITTED IN SPORT:

No.

OVERDOSE:

Serious. May cause irritability, convulsions, palpitations, high blood pressure, angina and difficulty in passing urine. Administer activated charcoal or induce vomiting if medication taken recently. Seek urgent medical assistance.

OTHER INFORMATION:

Very widely used medication for colds and flu. Safe and effective if taken in recommended dose. Should not be used to combat drowsiness.

See also Phenylephrine.

PSYCHOTROPICS

DISCUSSION:

Medications that alter the functioning of the brain and can ease problems as widespread as depression and anxiety, but also include some illegally used drugs.

See ANTIDEPRESSANTS, ANTIPSYCHOTICS, ANXIOLYTICS, Marijuana.

Psyllium

TRADE NAMES:

Used in some bulking agents and fibre supplements.

DRUG CLASS:

Fibre.

USES:

Constipation.

DOSAGE:

 Take required amount with water two or three times a day.

FORMS:

Granules, powder.

PRECAUTIONS:

Safe in pregnancy and breast feeding.

Do not take if:

- on a salt, potassium or sugar restricted diet
- suffering from severe constipation with impacted faeces
- suffering from belly pain, nausea or vomiting.

SIDE EFFECTS:

Common: minimal.
Unusual: diarrhoea, belly discomfort.

INTERACTIONS:

Other drugs:
- can affect the absorption of other drugs for up to two hours after use.

PRESCRIPTION:

No.

PERMITTED IN SPORT:

Yes.

OVERDOSE:

Take additional water. Belly discomfort and passing excess wind only effects.

OTHER INFORMATION:

Widely used, natural fibre supplement.
See also FIBRE.

Pyrazinamide

TRADE NAMES:

Rifater (with isoniazid, rifampicin).

USES:

Tuberculosis.

DOSAGE:

 One tablet three or four times a day in combination with other medication for the treatment of tuberculosis.

FORMS:

Zinamide: Tablets (white) of 500mg.

PRECAUTIONS:

Should be used in pregnancy only if medically essential. Breast feeding should be ceased before use. Use with caution in children.
Use with caution in gout, diabetes and kidney disease.
Regular blood tests to check liver function and blood count necessary.
Do not take if:

 • suffering from liver disease, acute gout.

SIDE EFFECTS:

Common: fever, loss of appetite.
Unusual: liver tenderness and enlargement, gout, nausea, vomiting.

Severe but rare (stop medication, consult doctor): yellow skin (jaundice), severe joint pain.

INTERACTIONS:

None significant.

PRESCRIPTION:

Yes.

PERMITTED IN SPORT:

Yes.

OVERDOSE:

Attacks the brain to cause convulsions and coma. Administer activated charcoal or induce vomiting if medication taken recently. Seek urgent medical attention.
See also Isoniazid, Rifampicin.

Pyridostigmine

TRADE NAME:

Mestinon.

DRUG CLASS:

Anticholinesterase.

USES:

Myasthenia gravis, inability to pass urine, paralysis of small intestine.

DOSAGE:

 One to three tablets once or twice a day.

FORMS:

Tablets of 60mg (white).

PRECAUTIONS:

Should be used in pregnancy (C) only when medically essential. Safe for use in breast feeding. Use with caution in children.
Dosage must be carefully monitored by doctor.
Use with caution in epilepsy, slow heart rate, asthma, recent heart attack, irregular heart beat, overactive thyroid gland, and peptic ulcer.

Do not take if:

- suffering from gut obstruction.

SIDE EFFECTS:

Common: slow heart rate, headache, nausea, diarrhoea, excess salivation, cough, wheeze, bowel noises.
Unusual: confusion, slurred speech, vomiting, belly cramps, desire to pass urine, muscle cramps, contracted pupils.
Severe but rare (stop medication, consult doctor): difficulty breathing, chest pain.

INTERACTIONS:

Other drugs:
- muscle relaxants, atropine, aminoglycosides, drugs used to treat irregular heart beat, some anaesthetics.

PRESCRIPTION:

Yes.

PERMITTED IN SPORT:

Yes.

OVERDOSE:

Serious. May cause diarrhoea, vomiting, difficulty in breathing, weakness, low blood pressure, slow heart rate and heart attack. Seek urgent medical attention.

OTHER INFORMATION:

Useful for the few patients with the distressing muscle disease of myasthenia gravis.
See also Donepezil, Neostigmine.

Pyridoxine
(Vitamin B6)

TRADE NAMES:

A large number of non-prescription preparations include pyridoxine (vitamin B6) alone or in combination with other vitamins and minerals.

DRUG CLASS:

Vitamin.

USES:

Vitamin B deficiency, nervous tension, mouth ulcers, premenstrual tension, hardening of arteries.

DOSAGE:

Recommended daily allowance:
Females: 0.9 to 1.4mg a day.
Males: 1.3 to 1.9mg a day.

FORMS:

Tablets, capsules, mixture, drops, injection.

PRECAUTIONS:

Safe in pregnancy, breast feeding and children.
Do not take in high doses or for prolonged periods of time.
Ensure adequate protein intake in diet.

SIDE EFFECTS:

Common: minimal.
Unusual: sensory nerve damage.

INTERACTIONS:

Other drugs:
- oral contraceptives, L-dopa.

PRESCRIPTION:

No.

PERMITTED IN SPORT:

Yes.

OVERDOSE:

May cause sensory nerve damage.

OTHER INFORMATION:

Pyridoxine is a water soluble vitamin. It is essential for the metabolism of protein. Remember, vitamins are merely chemicals that are essential for the functioning of the body and if taken to excess, act as a drug.
See also VITAMINS.

Pyrimethamine

TRADE NAMES:

Daraprim.
Fansidar (with sulfadoxine).

DRUG CLASS:

Antimalarial.

USES:

Prevention and treatment of malaria, toxoplasmosis.

DOSAGE:

 Prevention: one tablet a week.
Treatment: two tablets at once, then one tablet a day.

FORMS:

Tablets, injection.

PRECAUTIONS:

Should not be used in pregnancy (B3) unless medically essential. May be used in breast feeding and children.
Use with caution in liver and kidney disease.
Ensure adequate fluid intake.
Do not take if:

 • suffering from folate deficiency.

SIDE EFFECTS:

Common: minimal.
Unusual: rash, nausea, colic, vomiting, diarrhoea.
Severe but rare (stop medication, consult doctor): blood cell abnormalities.

INTERACTIONS:

Other drugs:
• co-trimoxazole, lorazepam, cytotoxics.

PRESCRIPTION:

Yes.

PERMITTED IN SPORT:

Yes.

OVERDOSE:

Serious. Induce vomiting if taken recently. Give additional fluids. Seek urgent medical assistance.

OTHER INFORMATION:

Used in areas where chloroquine resistant malaria occurs (e.g. New Guinea, Solomon Islands, southeast Asia).
See also ANTIMALARIALS.

Pyrithione zinc

TRADE NAMES:

Polytar AF (with tar and arachis oil).
Numerous other over the counter antiseptic and antidandruff shampoos contain pyrithione zinc, usually combined with other ingredients.

DRUG CLASS:

Antiseptic, antifungal.

USES:

Dandruff.

DOSAGE:

 Apply once every day or two.

FORMS:

Shampoo, cream.

PRECAUTIONS:

Safe to use in pregnancy, breast feeding and children.
Avoid eye contact.

SIDE EFFECTS:

Minimal.

INTERACTIONS:

None.

PRESCRIPTION:

No.

PERMITTED IN SPORT:

Yes.

Quetiapine

TRADE NAME:

Seroquel.

DRUG CLASS:

Antipsychotic.

USES:

Treatment of schizophrenia.

DOSAGE:

 Gradually increased from 25mg twice a day to maximum dose of 350mg twice a day.

FORMS:

Tablets of 25mg (peach), 100mg (yellow), 150mg (cream) and 200mg (white).

PRECAUTIONS:

Use with caution in pregnancy (B3), breast feeding and children.
Use with caution in heart and liver disease, poor brain circulation, recent strokes, low blood pressure and epilepsy. Lower doses necessary in elderly.

SIDE EFFECTS:

Common: dizziness and light headedness from low blood pressure, tiredness, dry mouth, runny nose, indigestion and constipation. Side effects often settle after two weeks.
Unusual: rapid heart rate, fainting.
Severe but rare (stop medication, consult doctor): seizures.

INTERACTIONS:

Other drugs:
• sedatives, sleeping medication (benzodiazepines), thioridazine, phenytoin, barbiturates, rifampicin, carbamazepine, erythromycin, ketoconazole.

Herbs:
• evening primrose (linoleic acid).
Other substances:
• alcohol.

PRESCRIPTION:

Yes.

PERMITTED IN SPORT:

Yes.

OVERDOSE:

Unlikely to have serious consequences other than worsening of side effects. Seek medical attention.

OTHER INFORMATION:

Introduced in 2000 to treat previously uncontrolled patients with schizophrenia.
See also Amisulpride, Flupenthixol, Haloperidol, Lithium Carbonate, Olanzapine, PHENOTHIAZINES, Pimozide, Risperidone, Thiothixene, Zuclopenthixol.

Quinagolide

TRADE NAME:

Norprolac.

USES:

Hyperprolactinaemia (overactive pituitary gland producing excess breast milk).

DOSAGE:

 Start with 25ug at night, increasing slowly to a maximum of 150ug at night.

FORMS:

Tablets of 25ug (pink), 50ug (blue), 75ug (white) and 150ug (white).

PRECAUTIONS:

Not to be used in pregnancy, breast feeding and children.

Non-hormonal contraception must be used.

Use with caution if history of psychotic disorders.

Check blood pressure regularly.

Do not take if:

- suffering from kidney or liver disease.

SIDE EFFECTS:

Common: nausea, diarrhoea, headache, dizziness.
Unusual: tiredness, loss of appetite, sleeplessness, swelling of tissue, nasal congestion.
Severe but rare (stop medication, consult doctor): low blood pressure, psychotic reactions.

INTERACTIONS:

Other drugs:
- none significant.
Other substances:
- alcohol.

PRESCRIPTION:

Yes.

PERMITTED IN SPORT:

Yes.

OVERDOSE:

May be serious. Seek urgent medical attention. Induce vomiting or give activated charcoal if swallowed recently.

Quinalbarbitone

See BARBITURATES.

Quinapril

See ACE INHIBITORS.

Quinidine bisulphate

TRADE NAME:

Kinidin Durules.

DRUG CLASS:

Antiarrhythmic.

USES:

Prevents some types of irregular heart beats.

DOSAGE:

 Two to five tablets twice a day.

FORMS:

Tablets of 250mg (white).

PRECAUTIONS:

Should only be used in pregnancy (C) if medically essential. Should not be used in breast feeding or children.

Do not take if:

- suffering from thrombocytopenia, low blood pressure, bowel obstruction or kidney failure.

SIDE EFFECTS:

Common: nausea, vomiting, loss of appetite, diarrhoea, dizziness, noises in ears, blurred vision, headache.
Unusual: psychiatric disturbances, fever, rash, worsening of asthma, anaemia.
Severe but rare (stop medication, consult doctor): unusual bleeding, yellow skin, asthma.

INTERACTIONS:

Other drugs:
- digoxin (severe reaction), anticoagulants (e.g. warfarin), cimetidine, phenytoin, barbiturates, rifampicin, procainamide, propranolol, verapamil, amiodarone, nifedipine
- absorption of quinidine slowed by antacids.

Herbs:
• sparteine (Cytisus scoparius).

PRESCRIPTION:

Yes.

PERMITTED IN SPORT:

Yes.

OVERDOSE:

Very serious. Administer activated charcoal or induce vomiting if tablets taken recently. Seek urgent medical assistance. Symptoms include blurred vision, deafness, weakness, dizziness, headache, nausea, vomiting, low blood pressure, diarrhoea, irregular heart rate and death.

OTHER INFORMATION:

Old fashioned but useful drug for specific types of heart beat irregularities.

See also Amiodarone, Disopyramide, Flecainide, Mexiletine, Procainamide, Sotalol, Verapamil.

QUINOLONES

DISCUSSION:

A group of widely used and very effective antibiotics.

See Cinoxacin, Ciprofloxacin, Levofloxacin, Moxifloxacin, Norfloxacin, Ofloxacin.

R

Rabeprazole

See PROTON PUMP INHIBITORS.

Rabies vaccine

TRADE NAME:

Rabipur.

DRUG CLASS:

Vaccine.

USES:

Prevention of rabies.

DOSAGE:

 Prevention: Four injections one week apart, repeat every two to five years.
After suspect animal bite: series of frequent injections as determined by doctor.

FORMS:

Injection.

PRECAUTIONS:

Not designed for use in pregnancy, but must be used if mother exposed to bite from rabid animal. May be used in breast feeding and children.
Use with caution in immune deficiency and history of allergy.

SIDE EFFECTS:

Common: local redness, soreness and hardness at injection site.
Unusual: fever, muscle pains, nausea, diarrhoea.

INTERACTIONS:

Other drugs:
• corticosteroids, immunosupressants.

PRESCRIPTION:

Yes.

PERMITTED IN SPORT:

Yes.

OVERDOSE:

An inadvertent additional injection is unlikely to have any serious adverse effects.

OTHER INFORMATION:

Routinely given only to veterinarians and others working with animals in areas affected by rabies. Given after any bite by an animal in an area affected by rabies. Once symptoms of rabies occur, it is inevitably fatal. Rabies does not occur in Britain, but is widespread in Europe.

Raloxifene

TRADE NAME:

Evista.

USES:

Prevention and treatment of osteoporosis after the menopause.

DOSAGE:

 One tablet a day.

FORMS:

Tablet (white) of 60mg.

PRECAUTIONS:

Must never be used in pregnancy (X)(causes deformities of foetus), breast feeding or children.
Use with caution in liver disease.
Abnormal uterine bleeding must be diagnosed before use.

Do not take if:

 • still menstruating. For use in postmenopausal women only
• medical history of blood clots
• male.

SIDE EFFECTS:

Common: hot flushes, leg cramps, sinus congestion.
Severe but rare (stop medication, consult doctor): blood clots.

INTERACTIONS:

Other drugs:
• oestrogen supplements, cholestyramine, ampicillin, warfarin.

PRESCRIPTION:

Yes.

PERMITTED IN SPORT:

Yes.

OVERDOSE:

Unlikely to result in serious consequences. Exacerbation of side effects likely. Seek medical assistance.

OTHER INFORMATION:

Released in 1999 to assist women who are unable to tolerate normal postmenopausal hormone replacement therapy.
See also Alendronate sodium, Disodium etidronate, Salcatonin.

Ramipril
See ACE INHIBITORS.

Ranitidine

TRADE NAMES:

Zantac.
Pylorid (with bismuth citrate).

DRUG CLASS:

Antiulcerant, H2 receptor antagonist.

USES:

Prevention and treatment of ulcers of the stomach, oesophagus (gullet) and duodenum (upper small intestine). Prevention of acid reflux into the oesophagus (heartburn).

DOSAGE:

 Up to 600mg a day in one or two doses.

FORMS:

Tablets, effervescent tablets, syrup, injection.

PRECAUTIONS:

Care should be taken with use in pregnancy (B1) and breast feeding. Children under twelve may be treated at the discretion of the doctor.
Cause of ulceration or pain must be determined (e.g. by gastroscopy) if symptoms persist on treatment.
Use with caution in porphyria or on low salt diet.
Do not take if:
• suffering from severe kidney disease or phenylketonuria.

SIDE EFFECTS:

Common: headache, diarrhoea, rash.
Unusual: tiredness, dizziness, sleeplessness, speeding or slowing of heart rate, constipation, joint pains, breast tenderness (both sexes).
Severe but rare (stop medication, consult doctor): hepatitis (jaundice), pancreatitis (severe stomach pain).

INTERACTIONS:

Other drugs:
• sucralfate.
Herbs:
• alfalfa, capsicum, eucalyptus, senega.

PRESCRIPTION:

Yes.

PERMITTED IN SPORT:

Yes.

OVERDOSE:

No serious effects reported.

OTHER INFORMATION:

Most widely used medication for the treatment of peptic ulcers. Very safe and effective.

See also Cimetidine, Famotidine, Nizatadine.

Reboxetine

TRADE NAME:

Edronax.

DRUG CLASS:

SSRI antidepressant.

USES:

Depression.

DOSAGE:

 One or two tablets twice a day.

FORMS:

Tablet (white) of 4mg.

PRECAUTIONS:

May be used with care in pregnancy (B1), breast feeding and children.
Use with caution in epilepsy, bipolar disorders, heart disease, stroke, high blood pressure, dehydration, hyperthyroidism (over active thyroid gland), liver and kidney disease, urine retention and enlarged prostate gland.

Do not take if:

 • suffering from glaucoma.

SIDE EFFECTS:

Common: headache, rapid heart rate, nausea, sleeplessness.
Unusual: low blood pressure, sweating, dizziness, constipation, dry mouth.
Severe but rare (stop medication, consult doctor): retention of urine.

INTERACTIONS:

Other drugs:
• severe interaction with MAOI
• antihypertensives (lower blood pressure), ketoconazole, erythromycin, fluvoxamine, carbamazepine, lithium, thiazide diuretics (fluid tablets).
Other substances:
• ergot.

PRESCRIPTION:

Yes.

PERMITTED IN SPORT:

Yes.

OVERDOSE:

Symptoms may include nausea, tremor, dilated pupils, dry mouth and irritability. Death or serious effects have not occurred. Seek medical attention.

OTHER INFORMATION:

One of the newer antidepressants released in the late 1990s. May take up to two weeks for patient to notice any improvement in depression.

See also Citalopram, Fluoxetine, Fluvoxamine, Paroxetine, Sertraline, Venlafaxine.

Repaglinide

TRADE NAME:

Novonorm.

DRUG CLASS:

Hypoglycaemic.

USES:

Complicated type two (maturity onset, non-insulin dependent) diabetes.

DOSAGE:

 0.5 to 4mg before meals three times a day.

FORMS:

Tablets of 0.5mg (white), 1mg (yellow) and 2mg (red).

PRECAUTIONS:

Not to be used in pregnancy (C), breast feeding or children.

Only to be used when other treatments for type two diabetes are not controlling disease.

Use with caution in kidney and liver disease.

Do not take if:

 • suffering from type one (juvenile, insulin dependent) diabetes, severe liver disease or ketoacidosis.

SIDE EFFECTS:

Common: nausea, dyspepsia, headache.
Unusual: vomiting, pins and needles sensation, chest pain.
Severe but rare (stop medication, consult doctor): jaundice (yellow skin from liver damage), low blood sugar (hypoglycaemia).

INTERACTIONS:

Other drugs:
• oral contraceptives, metformin, insulin, thiazides, corticosteroids, danazol, thyroid hormones, MAOI, beta-blockers, ACE inhibitors, salicylates, NSAID, octreotide, anabolic steroids.
Other substances:
• alcohol.
Herbs:
• alfalfa, celery, eucalyptus, fenugreek, garlic, ginger.

PRESCRIPTION:

Yes.

PERMITTED IN SPORT:

Yes.

OVERDOSE:

Low blood sugar with dizziness, headache, tremor, sweating and convulsions may occur. Give sweet drinks or injections of sugar. Seek medical assistance.

OTHER INFORMATION:

Introduced in 2000 as an additional treatment for severe forms of type two diabetes. Normally used in combination with metformin. Tolerance may gradually develop necessitating an increase in dosage.
See also HYPOGLYCAEMICS.

Resorcinol

TRADE NAMES:

Found in some locally produced acne and psoriasis preparations.

USES:

Skin peeling agent, acne, psoriasis.

DOSAGE:

 Varies between preparations. Follow directions on packaging.

FORMS:

Gel, cream, solution, ointment.

PRECAUTIONS:

Safe in pregnancy and breast feeding.
Not for use in infants.
Use with caution in children.
Avoid contact with eyes, mouth, nose, anus and vagina.

Do not use on:

• inflamed or broken skin (cuts, grazes, burns etc.).

SIDE EFFECTS:

Common: skin inflammation.

INTERACTIONS:

Other drugs:
• other skin acne and psoriasis preparations.

PRESCRIPTION:

No.

PERMITTED IN SPORT:

Yes.

Retinol
(Vitamin A)

TRADE NAMES:

Found in numerous vitamin and mineral preparations, as well as soothing and healing creams and lotions.

DRUG CLASS:

Vitamin.

USES:

Vitamin A deficiency, malnutrition, poor diet, soothing agent in creams for minor burns.

DOSAGE:

 Recommended daily allowance: 2500 International Units a day.

FORMS:

Capsules, tablets, mixture, lotion, cream.

PRECAUTIONS:

Must not be used in pregnancy (D) as high doses may cause birth defects. May be used in breast feeding and with caution in children. Skin preparations safe in pregnancy.
Do not exceed recommended dose.
Use with caution in Vitamin K deficiency.

SIDE EFFECTS:

Common: minimal.
Severe but rare (stop medication, consult doctor): yellow skin, particularly of palms and soles.

INTERACTIONS:

None significant.

PRESCRIPTION:

No.

PERMITTED IN SPORT:

Yes.

OVERDOSE:

Chronic overdosage will lead to carotenaemia in which excess Retinol is deposited in skin (causes it to turn yellow) and may cause damage to organs.

OTHER INFORMATION:

Fat soluble vitamin. Dangerous in pregnancy and overdose. Remember, vitamins are merely chemicals that are essential for the functioning of the body, and if taken to excess, act as a drug.
See also Betacarotene, Cod liver oil, VITAMINS.

REVERSIBLE INHIBITORS OF MONOAMINE OXIDASE
(RIMA)

See Moclobemide.

Riboflavine
(Vitamin B2)

TRADE NAMES:

A large number of preparations include riboflavine (vitamin B2) alone or in combination with other vitamins and minerals.

DRUG CLASS:

Vitamin.

USES:

Vitamin B deficiency, arabinoflavinosis.

DOSAGE:

 Recommended daily allowance: 1.0 to 1.7mg a day

FORMS:

Tablets, capsules, mixture, drops.

PRECAUTIONS:

Safe in pregnancy, breast feeding and children.

SIDE EFFECTS:

Minimal.

INTERACTIONS:

None significant.

PRESCRIPTION:

No.

PERMITTED IN SPORT:

Yes.

OVERDOSE:

Not harmful.

OTHER INFORMATION:

Riboflavine is a water soluble vitamin found in dairy products, offal and green leafy vegetables. It is essential for the effective working of the lungs. Remember, vitamins are merely chemicals that are essential for the functioning of the body and if taken to excess, act as a drug.

See also VITAMINS.

Rifabutin

TRADE NAME:

Mycobutin.

USES:

Tuberculosis (TB).

DOSAGE:

 One or two capsules once a day.

FORMS:

Capsule (red/brown) of 150mg.

PRECAUTIONS:

Not to be used in pregnancy (C) unless medically essential. Breast feeding should be ceased before use. Not to be used in children.

Use with caution in liver and kidney disease and eye inflammation.
Regular blood tests to check white cells, platelets and liver function essential.
Soft contact lenses may be stained.
Check eyes regularly for inflammation.

SIDE EFFECTS:

Common: nausea, vomiting, yellow skin (jaundice), unusual bruising, anaemia, arthritis, muscle pains, orange urine, fever, rash.
Unusual: eye inflammation, asthma.

INTERACTIONS:

Other drugs:
• severe interaction with ritonavir and delavirdine
• dapsone, narcotics, anticoagulants (e.g. warfarin), corticosteroids, quinidine, hypoglycaemics, clarithromycin, oral contraceptives.

PRESCRIPTION:

Yes.

PERMITTED IN SPORT:

Yes.

OVERDOSE:

May be serious. Seek medical assistance.

OTHER INFORMATION:

Introduced in 1994 to treat resistant forms of tuberculosis.

See also Isoniazid, Pyrazinamide, Rifampicin.

Rifampicin

TRADE NAMES:

Rifadin, Rimactane.
Rifater (with isoniazid, pyrazinamide).
Rifinah, Rimactazid (with isoniazid).

USES:

Treatment of tuberculosis and leprosy, prevention of Meningococcal and Haemophilus bacterial infections.

DOSAGE:

 450mg to 600mg a day as a single daily dose in combination with other treatments on a regular basis for at least six months.

FORMS:

Capsules, tablets, syrup, infusion.

PRECAUTIONS:

Should not be used in pregnancy (C) unless medically essential. Not to be used in breast feeding or infants. May be used with caution in children.
Use with caution in liver disease.
Designed to be used continuously long term.

Do not take if:

- suffering from jaundice (yellow skin).

SIDE EFFECTS:

Common: heartburn, nausea, loss of appetite, intestinal cramps.
Unusual: vomiting, headache, diarrhoea, drowsiness, fatigue, dizziness.
Severe but rare (stop medication, consult doctor): yellow skin (jaundice).

INTERACTIONS:

Other drugs:
- anticoagulants (e.g. warfarin), corticosteroids, cyclosporin, digoxin, quinidine, hypoglycaemics (used to treat diabetes), dapsone, narcotics, oral contraceptives.

PRESCRIPTION:

Yes.

PERMITTED IN SPORT:

Yes.

OVERDOSE:

Serious. Nausea, vomiting, drowsiness, brown stain to body fluids, convulsions, coma, jaundice and liver failure may occur. Administer activated charcoal or induce vomiting if medication taken recently. Seek urgent medical assistance.
See also Isoniazid, Pyrazinamide, Rifabutin.

Riluzole

TRADE NAME:

Rilutek.

USES:

Amyotrophic lateral sclerosis (Lou Gehrig disease), motor neurone disease.

DOSAGE:

 One tablet twice a day.

FORMS:

Tablets of 50mg (white).

PRECAUTIONS:

Not to be used in pregnancy, breast feeding or children.
Use with caution in liver and kidney disease.
Commence under specialist supervision.
Regular blood tests to check liver function and white blood cells necessary.

Do not take if:

- suffering from severe liver disease.

SIDE EFFECTS:

Common: tiredness, nausea, vomiting, headache, belly pains, dizziness.
Unusual: rapid heart rate, sleepiness, pins and needles around mouth.
Severe but rare (stop medication, consult doctor): fever, low white cell count.

INTERACTIONS:

Other drugs:
- not known.

PRESCRIPTION:

Yes.

PERMITTED IN SPORT:

Yes.

OVERDOSE:

Seek urgent medical attention. Induce vomiting or administer activated charcoal if swallowed recently.

RIMA
(Reversible Inhibitor of Monoamine Oxidase Type A)

See Moclobemide.

Rimexolone

TRADE NAME:

Vexol.

DRUG CLASS:

Corticosteroid.

USES:

Eye inflammation after surgery, uveitis, inflamed conjunctiva.

DOSAGE:

 One drop into eye four to twelve times a day.

FORMS:

Eye drops.

PRECAUTIONS:

May be used with caution in pregnancy and breast feeding. Not recommended in children.
Not for prolonged use.
Monitor eye pressure regularly.

Do not take if:

 • suffering from any form of eye infection.

SIDE EFFECTS:

Common: intermittent blurred vision.

Unusual: eye discharge, eye discomfort or temporary pain, foreign body sensation.
Severe but rare (stop medication, consult doctor): raised pressure in eye (haloes around objects, constantly blurred vision).

INTERACTIONS:

Other drugs:
• other eye preparations.

PRESCRIPTION:

Yes.

PERMITTED IN SPORT:

Yes.

OVERDOSE:

Unlikely to be serious if swallowed.

Risedronate

TRADE NAME:

Actonel.

DRUG CLASS:

Bisphosphonate.

USES:

Osteoporosis, lose off calcium from bone, Paget's disease of bone.

DOSAGE:

 One 5mg tablet a day or one 35mg tablet a week. Swallow tablet whole in an upright position with water, at least half an hour before first food or drink of day, or at least two hours after eating. Do not lie down for 30 minutes. Tablet must not be chewed, sucked or broken.

FORMS:

Tablets of 5mg (yellow) and 35mg (orange).

PRECAUTIONS:

Not to be used in pregnancy, breast feeding or children.
Use with caution in kidney disease,

oesophageal disease, mineral metabolism disorders.

Ensure adequate dietary calcium and vitamin D intake.

Do not take if:

- suffering from severe kidney disease, low blood calcium levels
- unable to sit upright or stand for 30 minutes after taking tablet.

SIDE EFFECTS:

Common: nausea, diarrhoea, flu symptoms, chest pain, dizziness.
Unusual: muscle pain, headache, rash, swelling of tissues, weight loss, shortness of breath, sinus congestion, eye irritation, dry eye, blurred vision, ringing in ears, passing urine at night.
Severe but rare (stop medication, consult doctor): liver damage.

INTERACTIONS:

Other drugs:
- antacids, calcium supplements, aspirin, NSAIDs, other drugs used to treat osteoporosis.

Other substances:
- minerals (e.g. iron, magnesium).

PRESCRIPTION:

Yes.

PERMITTED IN SPORT:

Yes.

OVERDOSE:

Serious. Symptoms include loss of appetite, tiredness, vomiting, diarrhoea, sweating, excess urine production, extreme thirst and headache. This may progress to high blood pressure and kidney failure. Administer activated charcoal or induce vomiting if taken recently. Seek medical assistance.

OTHER INFORMATION:

Introduced in 2000 as a new way of preventing vertebral fractures and subsequent curvature of the spine in older women.

See also Alendronate.

Risperidone

TRADE NAME:

Risperdal.

DRUG CLASS:

Antipsychotic.

USES:

Schizophrenia.

DOSAGE:

 Start with low dose and gradually increase at direction of doctor. Maximum 8mg twice a day.

FORMS:

Tablets of 0.5mg (red), 1mg (white), 2mg (orange), 3mg (yellow), 4mg (green) and 6mg (yellow), liquid, injection.

PRECAUTIONS:

Use with caution and only when necessary in pregnancy (B3) and breast feeding. Not for use in children under 15. Use with caution in heart disease, low blood pressure, epilepsy or seizures, Parkinson's disease, liver or kidney disease.
Lower doses necessary in elderly.

SIDE EFFECTS:

Common: low blood pressure, sleeplessness, agitation, anxiety, headache.
Unusual: tiredness, dizziness, constipation, nausea, poor concentration, weight gain, blurred vision, belly pain, impotence.

INTERACTIONS:

Other drugs:
- levodopa, antihypertensives (treat high blood pressure), carbamazepine, tricyclic antidepressants, quinidine, phenothiazines, beta-blockers.

Herbs:
- evening primrose (linoleic acid).

PRESCRIPTION:

Yes.

PERMITTED IN SPORT:

Yes.

OVERDOSE:

Drowsiness, sedation, rapid heart rate and low blood pressure may occur.
Administer activated charcoal or induce vomiting if taken recently. Seek medical attention.

OTHER INFORMATION:

Often very effective, but very expensive.

See also Amisulpride, Flupenthixol, Haloperidol, Lithium Carbonate, Olanzapine, PHENOTHIAZINES, Pimozide, Quetiapine, Thiothixene, Zuclopenthixol.

Ritodrine hydrochloride

TRADE NAME:

Yutopar.

USES:

Stops labour of pregnancy, reduces intensity of uterine contractions during labour.

DOSAGE:

 Normally given by intravenous injection or infusion initially, then tablets are taken to continue effect.

FORMS:

Injection, tablets (pale yellow) of 10mg.

PRECAUTIONS:

Not to be used in any situation other than during premature or excessively severe labour of pregnancy.
Not to be used in pregnancy before 24 weeks.
Use with caution in heart disease, high blood pressure, diabetes, liver and kidney disease.
Close monitoring of mother and foetus essential.

Do not take if:

 • suffering from overactive thyroid gland, pre-eclampsia.

SIDE EFFECTS:

Common: rapid heart rate, lung congestion, palpitations, nausea, vomiting.

INTERACTIONS:

Other drugs:
• corticosteroids, sympathomimetics, beta-blockers, digoxin, MAOI, tricyclic antidepressants.

PRESCRIPTION:

Yes.

OVERDOSE:

Exacerbation of side effects likely.

OTHER INFORMATION:

Introduced in early 1980s, and has proved very useful in preventing premature births in some situations.

Ritonavir

TRADE NAMES:

Norvir.
Kaletra (with lopinavir).

DRUG CLASS:

Antiviral.

USES:

HIV infection, AIDS.

DOSAGE:

 Twice a day with food.

FORMS:

Capsules, solution.

PRECAUTIONS:

Use with considerable caution in pregnancy (B3), breast feeding and children.
Use with caution in liver disease.

SIDE EFFECTS:

Common: tiredness, raised triglyceride (fat) levels in blood, nausea, diarrhoea, abnormal pain, pins and needles sensation.
Unusual: vomiting, dizziness, abnormal taste.

INTERACTIONS:

Other drugs:
• do NOT use with amiodarone, benzodiazepines, cisapride, clonazepam, dextropropoxyphene, flecainide, quinidine, pethidine, piroxicam, rifabutin
• hypnotics, sedatives, oral contraceptives, other antivirals.
Herbs:
• St John's wort.

PRESCRIPTION:

Yes.

PERMITTED IN SPORT:

Yes.

OVERDOSE:

May be serious. Induce vomiting or administer activated charcoal if medication taken recently. Seek immediate medical attention.

OTHER INFORMATION:

Introduced in 1997. Treatment usually started only in hospital.
See Abacavir, Efavirenz, Indinavir, Lamivudine, Nelfinavir, Nevirapine, Saquinavir, Stavudine, Tenofovir, Zalcitabine, Zidovudine.

Rivastigmine

TRADE NAME:

Exelon.

DRUG CLASS:

Anticholinesterase.

USES:

Dementia of Alzheimer's disease.

DOSAGE:

 Initially 1.5mg twice a day, slowly increasing to a maximum of 6mg twice a day.

FORMS:

Capsules of 1.5mg (yellow), 3mg (orange), 4.5mg (red) and 6mg (orange/red).

PRECAUTIONS:

Not to be used in pregnancy, breast feeding or children.
Treatment should be initiated by specialist.
Use with caution in heart disease, peptic ulcer history, asthma, emphysema, chronic bronchitis, enlarged prostate gland, and liver disease.
Monitor weight loss carefully.
Do not take if:
• suffering from severe liver disease.

SIDE EFFECTS:

Common: tiredness, loss of appetite, dizziness, belly pains.
Unusual: agitation, confusion, depression, diarrhoea, sweating, weight loss, tremor, headache, sleeplessness, respiratory and urinary infections.
Severe but rare (stop medication, consult doctor): angina, bleeding from gut, fainting.

INTERACTIONS:

Other drugs:
• other anticholinergics.
Other substances:
• smoking.

PRESCRIPTION:

Yes.

PERMITTED IN SPORT:

Yes.

OVERDOSE:

Serious. May cause diarrhoea, vomiting, difficulty in breathing, weakness, low blood pressure, slow heart rate and heart attack. Seek urgent medical attention.

OTHER INFORMATION:

Introduced in 1999 as a totally new treatment to slow the progress of Alzheimer's disease. Success rate relatively low and effectiveness should be proved by serial tests on mental function. **See also Donepezil, Galantamine.**

Rizatripan

TRADE NAME:

Maxalt.

DRUG CLASS:

Antimigraine.

USES:

Treatment of some types of migraine.

DOSAGE:

 10mg swallowed or dissolved on tongue. Repeat after two hours if necessary.

FORMS:

Tablets (pink) of 5mg, soluble wafers of 10mg.

PRECAUTIONS:

Use with caution in pregnancy and breast feeding. Not recommended in children. Patient must be carefully evaluated to exclude poor circulation to heart, brain and other organs before starting treatment.
Use with caution in kidney and liver disease, and phenylketonuria.
Do not take if:

 • suffering from severe kidney or liver disease, history of strokes or poor blood supply to brain, angina, significant heart disease, poor circulation, high blood pressure, paralysing migraine or other types of headache.

SIDE EFFECTS:

Common: dizziness, tiredness, muscle pains, chest and belly pains, palpitations.
Unusual: rapid heart rate, nausea, diarrhoea, throat discomfort, shortness of breath, skin rash, blurred vision, hot flushes.
Severe but rare (stop medication, consult doctor): angina, stroke, heart attack.

INTERACTIONS:

Other drugs:
• MAOI, ergotamine, propranolol.

PRESCRIPTION:

Yes.

PERMITTED IN SPORT:

Yes.

OVERDOSE:

Serious. Seek urgent medical attention.

OTHER INFORMATION:

Introduced in 1999 to help patients with more serious and intractable cases of migraine.
See also Almotriptan, BETA BLOCKERS, Clonidine, Eletriptan, Ergotamine, Frovatriptan, Methysergide, Naratriptan, Pizotifen, Sumatriptan, Zolmitriptan.

Rofecoxib

TRADE NAME:

Vioxx.

DRUG CLASS:

COX-2 inhibitor.

USES:

Osteoarthritis.

DOSAGE:

 12.5 to 50mg once a day.

FORMS:

Tablets of 12.5mg (white), 25mg (yellow) and 50mg (orange), suspension.

PRECAUTIONS:

Not for use in pregnancy (C). Use with caution in breast feeding and children.
Use with caution if history of peptic ulcer or intestinal bleeding.
Use with caution in smokers, alcoholics, dehydration, asthma, high blood pressure, heart failure, infection, liver or kidney disease.
Use with care in elderly.

Do not take if:

 • suffering from active peptic ulcer, intestinal bleeding, active asthma, urticaria (hives).

SIDE EFFECTS:

Common: minimal.
Unusual: intestinal upsets, allergy, anaemia, fluid retention.
Severe but rare (stop medication, consult doctor): peptic ulcer.

INTERACTIONS:

Other drugs:
• NSAID, aspirin, steroids, anticoagulants (e.g. warfarin), rifampicin, methotrexate, ACE Inhibitors (treat high blood pressure and heart disorders), lithium, diuretics (fluid tablets), theophylline, amitriptyline, tacrine.
Other substances:
• smoking increases risk of stomach ulcer.

PRESCRIPTION:

Yes.

PERMITTED IN SPORT:

Yes.

OVERDOSE:

Exacerbation of side effects likely. Induce vomiting or give activated charcoal if swallowed recently. Seek medical attention.

OTHER INFORMATION:

Introduced 2000. Far less likely than other treatments for arthritis (e.g. NSAIDs) to cause intestinal bleeding.
See also Celecoxib, Meloxicam, Valdecoxib.

Ropinirole

TRADE NAME:

Requip.

DRUG CLASS:

Antiparkinsonian.

USES:

Parkinson's disease.

DOSAGE:

 Start with 0.25mg three times a day. Increase each dose by 0.25mg weekly as necessary, up to 3mg three times a day. Maximum dose 24mg a day.

FORMS:

Tablets of 0.25mg (white), 1mg (green), 2mg (pink) and 5mg (blue).

PRECAUTIONS:

Not to be used in pregnancy, breast feeding and children.
Use with caution in significant heart disease and psychoses.
Do not stop suddenly but withdraw slowly.

Do not take if:

• suffering from severe liver or kidney disease.

SIDE EFFECTS:

Common: nausea, tiredness, leg swelling.
Unusual: belly pain, fainting, vomiting, low blood pressure, slow heart rate.

INTERACTIONS:

Other drugs:
• blood pressure lowering medications, medications to control irregular heart beat, oestrogens.
Other substances:
• alcohol.

PRESCRIPTION:

Yes.

PERMITTED IN SPORT:

Yes.

OVERDOSE:

Serious. Seek urgent medical attention. Induce vomiting or give activated charcoal if swallowed recently.

OTHER INFORMATION:

Does not cause addiction or dependence.

See also Amantadine, Apomorphine, Benzhexol, Benztropine, Biperiden, Bromocriptine, Entacapone, LEVODOPA COMPOUNDS, Orphenadrine, Pergolide, Pramipexole, Procyclidine, Selegiline.

Ropivacaine

See ANAESTHETICS, LOCAL.

Rosiglitazone

TRADE NAME:

Avandia.

DRUG CLASS:

Hypoglycaemic.

USES:

Maturity onset (type 2) diabetes.

DOSAGE:

 4 to 8mg a day.

FORMS:

Tablets of 4mg (orange) and 8mg (red/brown).

PRECAUTIONS:

Use with considerable caution in pregnancy (B3), breast feeding or children.
Use with caution in polycystic ovary disease, heart failure and severe liver disease.
Regular blood tests to check sugar levels and liver function necessary.

SIDE EFFECTS:

Common: swelling of tissue.
Unusual: liver damage, high cholesterol, weight gain, anaemia.

INTERACTIONS:

Other drugs:
• troglitazone.
Herbs:
• alfalfa, celery, eucalyptus, fenugreek, garlic, ginger.

PRESCRIPTION:

Yes.

PERMITTED IN SPORT:

Yes.

OVERDOSE:

Not likely to be very serious. Give glucose drinks and seek medical attention.

OTHER INFORMATION:

Introduced in 2000.

See also Acarbose, Glibenclamide, Gliclazide, Glimepride, Glipizide, Gliquidone, INSULINS, Metformin, Repaglinide.

RU486

See Mifepristone.

RUBEFACIENTS

DISCUSSION:

Rubefacients are a type on liniment that causes redness of the skin.

See Capsaicin, Diethylamine salicylate, Menthol, Salicylic acid.

Rubella vaccine

TRADE NAMES:

Erevax.
MMR II, Priorix (with measles and mumps vaccines).

DRUG CLASS:

Vaccine.

USES:

Prevention of rubella (German measles).

DOSAGE:

 Single injection. Repeat in early teen years if first dose given under five years of age.
Lifelong protection usual.

FORMS:

Injection.

PRECAUTIONS:

Not to be used in pregnancy (B2), but inadvertent use unlikely to have serious effects. May be used in breast feeding and children.
Use with caution if history of convulsions.

Do not take if:

• suffering from fever, immune system deficiency
• blood transfusion within three months
• allergic to neomycin.

SIDE EFFECTS:

Common: pain, soreness, redness, firmness at site of injection.
Unusual: fever, rash, headache, joint pains, sore throat, tender glands.

INTERACTIONS:

Other drugs:
• immunoglobulin, other live vaccines at same site.
Other substances:
• blood transfusion.

PRESCRIPTION:

Yes.

PERMITTED IN SPORT:

Yes.

OVERDOSE:

No adverse effects likely from an inadvertent additional dose.

OTHER INFORMATION:

Rubella (German measles) is usually a minor disease, although it may cause significant arthritis, headache and fever, but if caught by the mother during the first three months of pregnancy it may cause serious damage to the foetus.

RUTOSIDES

See Oxerutin.

Sabin vaccine

See Poliomyelitis vaccine.

Saint John's Wort
(Hypericum perforatum)

USES:

Mild depression and anxiety, skin inflammation, bruises and burns.

DOSAGE:

 Varies with form of preparation. Generally 300mg of standardised extract three times a day.
Apply topically three times a day.

FORMS:

Capsules, tablets, oils, creams, dried herb (for tea making).

PRECAUTIONS:

None significant.

SIDE EFFECTS:

Common: constipation, dry mouth, bloating, restlessness, tiredness.
Unusual: diarrhoea, loss of appetite, nausea, belly pain, red skin, itchy skin, skin becomes sun sensitive (sunburn).
Severe but rare (stop medication, consult doctor): sperm damage and infertility, nerve damage.

INTERACTIONS:

Other drugs:
• severe interaction with MAOI
• SSRI antidepressants, iron, oral contraceptive pill, theophylline, digoxin, sertraline, nefazadine, tetracyclines, sulfa antibiotics, quinolone antibiotics, thiazide diuretics, piroxicam, narcotics, barbiturates, cyclosporin, indinavir.

PRESCRIPTION:

No.

PERMITTED IN SPORT:

Yes.

OVERDOSE:

Exacerbation of side effects likely.

OTHER INFORMATION:

Not used in orthodox medical practice.

Salbutamol

TRADE NAMES:

Airolin, Airomir, Asmasal, Pulvinal Salbutamol, Salamol, Salbulin, Ventmax SR, Ventodisks, Ventolin, Volmax.
Aerocrom (with sodium cromoglycate).
Combivent (with ipratropium bromide).

DRUG CLASS:

Bronchodilators (Beta-2 agonist).

USES:

Asthma, bronchitis, emphysema, spasm of airways in lung, prevention of labour in childbirth.

DOSAGE:

 Inhalers and sprays: one or two inhalations every four hours.
Tablets: one three times a day.
Elixir: 5mLs to 10mLs three or four times a day.

FORMS:

Injection, spray, inhaler, nebuliser solution, dischaler, rotacaps, syrup.

PRECAUTIONS:

Safe to use in pregnancy (A), breast feeding and children.

Not designed for long term constant use. Use with care in high blood pressure, heart disease, overactive thyroid gland, diabetes, liver and kidney disease. Lower doses necessary in elderly. Seek urgent medical assistance if no response to medication.

SIDE EFFECTS:

Common: tremor, rapid heart rate, palpitations, headache.
Unusual: nausea, flush, mouth irritation.

INTERACTIONS:

Other drugs:
• sympathomimetics, beta-blockers, theophyllines, steroids, diuretics, digoxin, imipramine, chlordiazepoxide.
Other substances:
• tablets and capsules may react with alcohol and caffeine.

PRESCRIPTION:

Yes.

PERMITTED IN SPORT:

Yes, but only under specific conditions set out by each sport. Must be declared by athlete to sport administrators.

OVERDOSE:

Exacerbation of side effects likely. May be dangerous in patients with heart disease or high blood pressure.

OTHER INFORMATION:

Designed for intermittent occasional use, and not to be taken regularly. Other medication should be used to prevent asthma if repeated doses of this medication are needed. Does not cause dependence or addiction. First introduced in the 1960s, beta-agonists have revolutionised life for asthmatics.
See also Fenoterol, Salmeterol, Terbutaline.

Salcatonin
(Calcitonin)

TRADE NAMES:

Calsynar, Miacalcic.

USES:

Paget's disease of bone, excess blood calcium levels (hypercalcaemia).

DOSAGE:

 By injection in a dose determined by doctor for each patient.

FORMS:

Injection.

PRECAUTIONS:

Not to be used in pregnancy, or breast feeding.
Use with great caution in children.
Not for long term use.

SIDE EFFECTS:

Common: nausea, vomiting, injection site inflammation.
Unusual: dizziness, pain.

INTERACTIONS:

Other drugs:
• digoxin.

PRESCRIPTION:

Yes.

PERMITTED IN SPORT:

Yes.

OTHER INFORMATION:

Derived from a natural hormone found in salmon.

SALICYLATES

See Aspirin, Choline salicylate, Diethylamine salicylate, Methyl salicylate, Salicylic acid.

Salicylic acid

TRADE NAMES:

Acnisal, Occlusal, Verrugon.
Aserbine (with malic acid, benzoic acid and other ingredients).
Capasal (with coal tar and other ingredients).
Cocois (with coal tar, coconut oil and sulphur).
Cuplex (with lactic acid and copper).
Diprosalic (with betamethasone).
Duofilm (with lactic acid).
Meted (with sulphur).
Monophytol (with methyl salicylate, propyl salicylate, chlorbutol, methyl undecenoate and other ingredients).
Movelat, Pyralvex (with other ingredients).
Posalfilin (with podophyllum).
Pragmatar, Sebco (with coal tar and sulphur).
Psorin (with coal tar and dithranol).
Salactol, Salatac (with lactic acid).
Stiedex lotion (with desoxymethasone).

DRUG CLASS:

Rubefacient, Acid.

USES:

Temporary relief of pain (e.g. muscular, arthritic, gums).
Psoriasis, acne.

DOSAGE:

 Muscle and joint pain: massage liniments into clean dry skin two or three times a day.
Mouth ulcers: apply every three hours.
Psoriasis and acne: apply to affected skin, leave for ten minutes, then wash off.

FORMS:

Lotion, gel, cream, ointment, paint, shampoo, soap, spray.

PRECAUTIONS:

Safe in pregnancy and breast feeding.
Use with caution in children under five years.
Avoid contact with eyes, mouth, nose, anus and vagina.
Use sparingly on face, skin folds and thin skin.
May stain clothing.
Do not use if:
 • suffering from broken or infected skin.

SIDE EFFECTS:

Minimal.

INTERACTIONS:

Other drugs:
• aspirin interacts with mouth gels.

PRESCRIPTION:

No.
If combined with steroids: Yes.

PERMITTED IN SPORT:

Yes.

OVERDOSE:

May have serious effects in the unlikely event of the liniment being swallowed.

OTHER INFORMATION:

Widely used and very safe.
See also Aspirin (Acetylsalicylic acid), Balsalazide, KERATOLYTICS, Methyl salicylate.

Salmeterol

TRADE NAMES:

Serevent.
Seretide (with fluticasone).

DRUG CLASS:

Bronchodilator.

USES:

Long term control of asthma.

DOSAGE:

 Two inhalations twice a day.

FORMS:

Inhaler, accuhaler, diskhaler.

PRECAUTIONS:

Use with caution in pregnancy (B3), breast feeding and children.
Do not exceed recommended dosage.
Use with caution in thyroid disease.
Not for treatment of acute asthma.
Regular checks of lung function advisable.

Do not use if:

 • under four years.

SIDE EFFECTS:

Common: tremor, rapid pulse, palpitations, headache.
Unusual: temporary worsening of wheeze immediately after use.

INTERACTIONS:

None significant.

PRESCRIPTION:

Yes.

PERMITTED IN SPORT:

No.

OVERDOSE:

Dramatic worsening of side effects may occur. Seek medical assistance.

OTHER INFORMATION:

Introduced in 1993 to assist in the control of severe chronic asthma. Does not cause addiction or dependence, but must be used under medical supervision.

See also Eformoterol.

Salmonella typhi (Typhoid) vaccine

TRADE NAMES:

Typherix, Typhim Vi.

DRUG CLASS:

Vaccine.

USES:

Prevention of typhoid.

DOSAGE:

 Single injection gives three years protection.

FORMS:

Injection.

PRECAUTIONS:

Not designed for use in pregnancy (B2), but unintentional use in pregnancy is unlikely to have any serious effects. Use with caution in breast feeding. Not for use in children under six years.
Use with caution in immune diseases.

Do not take if:

 • suffering from significant infection.

SIDE EFFECTS:

Common: local pain, redness and swelling at injection site.
Unusual: fever, nausea, diarrhoea, headache, tiredness.

INTERACTIONS:

Other drugs: administer other injected vaccines at different site.

PRESCRIPTION:

Yes.

PERMITTED IN SPORT:

Yes.

OVERDOSE:

Inadvertent additional vaccination unlikely to cause any serious adverse effects.

OTHER INFORMATION:

Not used routinely. Only given to persons travelling to or living in poorer countries where typhoid is widespread. Typhoid causes severe diarrhoea and vomiting and is caught from contaminated food or poor personal hygiene.

Salt (Sodium chloride)

See ELECTROLYTES.

Saquinavir

TRADE NAMES:

Fortovase, Invirase.

DRUG CLASS:

Antiviral.

USES:

AIDS, HIV infection.

DOSAGE:

 600 to 1200mg three times a day after a large meal and usually in combination with other antiviral agents.

FORMS:

Capsules of 200mg (light brown/green), gelcaps of 200mg (beige).

PRECAUTIONS:

Use with caution in pregnancy (B1), breast feeding and children.
Use with caution in diarrhoea, liver and kidney disease.
Use lower doses in elderly.
Should be used in combination with other medications for HIV infection.

SIDE EFFECTS:

Common: tiredness, nausea, diarrhoea, abnormal pain, abnormal sensation.
Unusual: vomiting, dizziness.

INTERACTIONS:

Other drugs:
• severe interaction with astemizole, cisapride, pimozide, triazolam, midazolam, rifampicin, rifabutin, pentamidine

• nifedipine, clindamycin, nevirapine, efavirenz, indinavir, clarithromycin, ketoconazole, delavirdine, sildenafil, other drugs affecting liver function.
Other substances:
• grapefruit juice
Herbs:
• St John's wort.

PRESCRIPTION:

Yes.

PERMITTED IN SPORT:

Yes.

OVERDOSE:

No information available. Induce vomiting or administer activated charcoal if taken recently. Seek urgent medical attention.

See also Abacavir, Efavirenz, Indinavir, Lamivudine, Nelfinavir, Nevirapine, Ritonavir, Stavudine, Tenofovir, Zidovudine.

SEDATIVES AND HYPNOTICS

DISCUSSION:

Medications that sedate, relax and induce sleep.

See BARBITURATES, Chlormethiazole, Flunitrazepam, Midazolam, Nitrazepam, Zolpidem, Zopiclone.

SELECTIVE SEROTONIN REUPTAKE INHIBITORS (SSRI)

DISCUSSION:

Class of medication widely used for depression and excessive anxiety.

See Citalopram, Fluoxetine, Fluvoxamine, Paroxetine, Reboxetine, Sertraline, Venlafaxine.

Selegiline

TRADE NAMES:

Eldepryl, Zelapar.

DRUG CLASS:

Antiparkinsonian. MAOI.

USES:

Advanced forms of Parkinson's disease.

DOSAGE:

 One or two tablets once or twice a day.

FORMS:

Tablets of 1.25, 5 and 10mg, syrup.

PRECAUTIONS:

Use with caution in pregnancy (B2), breast feeding and children.
Use with caution in heart disease, peptic ulcer, high blood pressure, angina and psychiatric conditions.

Do not take if:

 • Other MAOI, pethidine or fluoxetine taken recently.

SIDE EFFECTS:

Common: tremor, dry mouth, nausea, slow urination, sweating.
Unusual: restlessness, hallucinations, headache, irregular heart beat, vomiting, constipation, facial hair growth.

INTERACTIONS:

Other drugs:
• MAOI, pethidine, fluoxetine, moclobemide, SSRI, tricyclic antidepressants, tetracyclic antidepressants, clozapine, oral contraceptives, dopamine, tramadol, sympathomimetics.
Other substances:
• ecstasy.

PRESCRIPTION:

Yes.

PERMITTED IN SPORT:

Yes.

OVERDOSE:

Very serious. Up to a 12 hour delay between taking overdose and onset of symptoms. May cause drowsiness, dizziness, headache, hallucinations, convulsions, coma, irregular heart beat and death. Administer activated charcoal or induce vomiting if medication taken recently. Seek urgent medical attention.

OTHER INFORMATION:

Does not cause addiction or dependence. Often used in conjunction with levodopa.
See also LEVODOPA COMPOUNDS; MAOI.

Selenium sulfide

TRADE NAME:

Selsun.

DRUG CLASS:

Antifungal.

USES:

Dandruff, mild fungal infections of skin and scalp.

DOSAGE:

 Apply to scalp for five minutes two or three times a week.

FORMS:

Lotion.

PRECAUTIONS:

Safe to use in pregnancy, breast feeding and children.
Avoid eyes.

Do not use if:

 • suffering from inflamed skin
• permanent wave, tinting or bleaching of hair within two days.

SIDE EFFECTS:

Common: minimal.
Severe but rare (stop medication, consult doctor): skin irritation.

INTERACTIONS:

None significant.

PRESCRIPTION:

No.

PERMITTED IN SPORT:

Yes.

OVERDOSE:

Diarrhoea, nausea and vomiting may occur if swallowed.

OTHER INFORMATION:

Simple and effective treatment for dandruff and pityriasis versicolor (a common fungal skin condition that shows on skin as white or pink patches).

Senna

TRADE NAMES:

Senokot.
Manevac (with ispaghula).
Pripsen (with piperazine).

DRUG CLASS:

Laxative.

USES:

Constipation.

DOSAGE:

 Tablets: two to four tablets once (before going to bed) or twice a day.
Granules: one or two teaspoonfuls a day.

FORMS:

Tablets, granules, syrup.

PRECAUTIONS:

Safe in pregnancy (A) and breast feeding. May be used in children over six years. Do not use long term without medical advice.

Do not take if:

 • suffering from stomach pain or gut obstruction, nausea, vomiting or diarrhoea.

SIDE EFFECTS:

Common: minimal.
Unusual: belly discomfort.
Severe but rare (stop medication, consult doctor): severe belly pain.

INTERACTIONS:

None significant.

PRESCRIPTION:

No.

PERMITTED IN SPORT:

Yes.

OVERDOSE:

Diarrhoea and belly cramps only effects.

OTHER INFORMATION:

Safe and widely used.
See also Ispaghula.

Sertraline

TRADE NAME:

Lustral.

DRUG CLASS:

SSRI antidepressant.

USES:

Depression.

DOSAGE:

 One to four tablets a day in morning with or without food.

FORMS:

Tablet (white) of 50mg and 100mg.

PRECAUTIONS:

Should be used in pregnancy (B3) with considerable caution. Breast feeding should be ceased if Paroxetine prescribed. Not for use in children.
Should be used with caution in mania, epilepsy, liver and kidney disease.

Do not take if:

 • taking MAOI antidepressants.

SIDE EFFECTS:

Common: generally minimal. Nausea, drowsiness, sweating, tremor, tiredness, dry mouth, sleeplessness, impotence.
Unusual: headache, fever, palpitations, sweating, rash, blurred vision.

INTERACTIONS:

Other drugs:
• severe interaction with MAOI
• anticoagulants (e.g. warfarin), phenytoin, tryptophan, lithium, tolbutamide, sumatriptan, fenfluramine.
Herbs:
• St John's wort, ma huang.
Other substances:
• use of alcohol is not advised.

PRESCRIPTION:

Yes.

PERMITTED IN SPORT:

Yes.

OVERDOSE:

Symptoms may include nausea, tremor, dilated pupils, dry mouth and irritability. Death or serious effects unlikely. Seek medical attention.

OTHER INFORMATION:

One of the newer antidepressants released in the 1990s that has dramatically improved the treatment of depression because of its safety and lack of side effects. May take up to two weeks for patient to notice any improvement in depression.
See also Citalopram, Fluoxetine, Fluvoxamine, Paroxetine, Venlafaxine.

Sevelamer

TRADE NAME:

Renagel.

USES:

Excess levels of phosphate in blood, usually caused by haemodialysis.

DOSAGE:

 As determined by doctor after consulting blood test results.

FORMS:

Capsules of 403mg (white).

PRECAUTIONS:

Use with caution in pregnancy, breast feeding and children.
Use with caution if swallowing is difficult, stomach retains food or history of major bowel surgery.
Use with caution in inflammatory bowel disease.
Regular blood tests necessary to monitor electrolytes.
Vitamin supplements may be necessary.

Do not take if:

 • suffering from bowel obstruction.

SIDE EFFECTS:

Unknown.

INTERACTIONS:

Unknown.

PRESCRIPTION:

Yes.

PERMITTED IN SPORT:

Yes.

OVERDOSE:

Unknown. Seek urgent medical attention.

OTHER INFORMATION:

Only released in 1999 and used by very few patients.

SEX HORMONES

DISCUSSION:

Sex hormones are produced by the ovaries in the woman and the testes in the man to give each sex its characteristic appearance. In men, they are responsible for the enlargement of the penis and scrotum at puberty, the development of facial hair and the ability to produce sperm and ejaculate. In women, the sex hormones that are produced for the first time at puberty cause breast enlargement, hair growth in the armpit and groin, ovulation, the start of menstrual periods, and later act to maintain a pregnancy.

If the sex hormones are reduced or lacking, these characteristics disappear. This happens naturally during the female menopause. During the transition from normal sex hormone production to no production in the menopause, there may be some irregular or inappropriate release of these hormones, causing the symptoms commonly associated with menopause such as irregular periods, irritability and hot flushes. After the menopause, the breasts sag, pubic and armpit hair becomes scanty and the periods cease due to this lack of sex hormones. Men also go through a form of menopause, but more gradually, so the effects are far less obvious than in the female.

Sex hormones and many synthesised drugs that act artificially as sex hormones, are used in medicine in two main areas— to correct natural deficiencies in sex hormone production and to alter the balance between the two female hormones (oestrogen and progestogen) that cause ovulation, to prevent ovulation and therefore act as a contraceptive.

It is now well recognised that hormone replacement therapy (HRT) in middle-aged women who have entered the menopause significantly improves their quality of life by not only controlling the symptoms of the menopause itself, but by preventing osteoporosis (bone weakening), reducing the apparent rate of ageing, reducing the risk of dementia, and reducing the risk of bowel cancer after the menopause. Women who have both their ovaries removed surgically at a time before their natural menopause, will also require sex hormones to be given regularly by mouth, patch or injection.

Female sex hormones can also be used to control some forms of recurrent miscarriage and prolong a pregnancy until a baby is mature enough to deliver, to control a disease called endometriosis, and to treat certain types of cancer.

See Cyproterone acetate, Danazol, Dydrogesterone, Ethinyloestradiol, Etonogestrel, HORMONE REPLACEMENT THERAPY, Medroxyprogesterone acetate, MORNING AFTER PILL, Oestradiol, Oestriol, Oestrogen, ORAL CONTRACEPTIVES, Oxandrolone, Piperazine oestrone sulfate, Stilboestrol, Testosterone.

Sibutramine

TRADE NAME:

Reductil.

DRUG CLASS:

Anorectic.

USES:

Obesity in conjunction with diet and exercise program.

DOSAGE:

 One capsule a day.

FORMS:

Capsules of 10mg (blue/yellow) and 15mg (blue/white).

PRECAUTIONS:

Not for use in pregnancy (C), breast feeding and children.
Use with caution in liver and kidney disease, gallstones and epilepsy.

Regular checks of blood pressure and pulse necessary.
Not for long term use.

Do not take if:

- suffering from mental illness leading to excessive eating, Tourette syndrome, heart disease, recent stroke, uncontrolled high blood pressure, over active thyroid gland (hyperthyroidism), enlarged prostate gland, glaucoma, history of drug abuse, severe liver or kidney disease
- elderly.

SIDE EFFECTS:

Common: rapid heart rate, dry mouth, sleeplessness.
Unusual: high blood pressure, nausea, diarrhoea.
Severe but rare (stop medication, consult doctor): seizure.

INTERACTIONS:

Other drugs:
- serious interactions with diethylpropion hydrochloride, orlistat, phentermine, MAOI
- sumatriptan, lithium, ketoconazole, macrolide antibiotics (e.g. erythromycin), phenytoin, dexamethasone.

Other substances:
- tryptophan.
- excess alcohol.

PRESCRIPTION:

Yes.

PERMITTED IN SPORT:

No.

OVERDOSE:

Serious. May cause restlessness, tremor, rapid breathing, irregular heart beat, high blood pressure, confusion, hallucinations, violence, panic state, vomiting, diarrhoea, coma, convulsions and death. Administer activated charcoal or induce vomiting if medication taken recently. Seek urgent medical attention.

OTHER INFORMATION:

Introduced in 2001. Must always be used in conjunction with an appropriate diet and exercise program. May be addictive.
See also Orlistat.

Sildenafil

TRADE NAME:

Viagra.

USES:

Impotence, inability to obtain erection of the penis with appropriate stimulation.

DOSAGE:

25 to 100mg one to four hours before erection desired.

FORMS:

Tablets (blue) of 25, 50 and 100mg.

PRECAUTIONS:

No for use in pregnancy (B1), breast feeding or by children.
Not recommended for use by women.
Use with caution in all heart diseases, abnormal anatomy of the penis (e.g. Peyronie's disease), bleeding disorders, peptic ulcer disease, untreated diabetes and all diseases of the retina in the eye.

Do not take if:

- taking medications containing nitrates (e.g. antiangina medication such as glyceryl trinitrate)
- suffering from angina, untreated high blood pressure or recent stroke
- inherited disorders of the retina
- suffering from significant liver disease.

SIDE EFFECTS:

Common: headache, flush, indigestion.
Unusual: blue halos in vision, blurred vision.

Severe but rare (stop medication, consult doctor): serious adverse effects on the heart and circulation of blood.

INTERACTIONS:

Other drugs:
• nitrate containing angina medications, other drugs for impotence, cimetidine, rifampicin, erythromycin, ketoconazole, saquinavir, ritonavir.
Herbs:
• korean ginseng.
Other substances:
• alcohol.

PRESCRIPTION:

Yes (restricted on the NHS to men who have impotence due to prostate cancer, spinal injury, diabetes mellitus, kidney failure, multiple sclerosis, prostate surgery and a number of other specific conditions).

PERMITTED IN SPORT:

Yes.

OVERDOSE:

May have adverse effects on the heart and circulation. Seek medical attention.

OTHER INFORMATION:

Introduced in 1998. Very effective, and generally very safe if precautions followed.
See also Alprostadil, Tadalafil, Vardenafil.

Silver nitrate
See KERATOLYTICS.

Silver sulfadiazine
(SSD)

TRADE NAME:
Flamazine.

DRUG CLASS:
Sulphonamide antibiotic.

USES:
Burns, skin ulcers, sores, grazes.

DOSAGE:
 Apply very thickly once every day or two.

FORMS:
Cream.

PRECAUTIONS:
Not to be used in pregnancy (C) or newborn infants. May be used in breast feeding (but not on breast) and older children.
Use with caution in liver and kidney disease.
Do not use if:
 • suffering from sulphur drug allergy.

SIDE EFFECTS:
Common: minimal.
Unusual: diarrhoea.
Severe but rare (stop medication, consult doctor): damage to blood cells.

INTERACTIONS:
Other drugs:
• oral hypoglycaemics (treat type 2 diabetes), phenytoin, cimetidine.

PRESCRIPTION:
Yes.

PERMITTED IN SPORT:
Yes.

OTHER INFORMATION:
Excellent cream for soothing serious burns and preventing or treating infection in burns and skin ulcers. Usually covered by a non-adhesive dressing over a thick (3 to 5mm) layer of cream.

Simethicone
See Dimethicone.

Simvastatin

TRADE NAME:

Zocor.

DRUG CLASS:

Hypolipidaemic.

USES:

Excess blood levels of cholesterol and triglycerides (fats).

DOSAGE:

 10 to 80mg a day at night.

FORMS:

Tablets of 10mg (peach), 20mg (tan), 40mg (red) and 80mg (red).

PRECAUTIONS:

Should not be used in pregnancy (C) unless no alternative available. Not for use in breast feeding or children. Regular blood tests to check blood fats and liver enzymes are necessary. Use with caution in liver and kidney disease.

Do not take if:

• suffering from severe liver disease, myopathy.

SIDE EFFECTS:

Common: constipation, diarrhoea, excess wind, nausea, headache.
Unusual: vomiting, heartburn, back pain, muscle pain, dizziness, sleeplessness, cough, bronchitis, pins and needles sensation, rash, sinusitis, blurred vision, depression.
Severe but rare (stop medication, consult doctor): yellow skin (jaundice), severe muscle pain and weakness.

INTERACTIONS:

Other drugs:
• anticoagulants (e.g. warfarin), niacin, nicotinic acid, digoxin, verapamil, gemfibrizol, cyclosporin, nefazodone, ketoconazole, itraconazole, macrolide antibiotics (e.g. erythromycin, clarithromycin).
Other treatments:
• immunosuppressive treatment.
Herbs:
• alfalfa, fenugreek, garlic, ginger.
Other substances:
• grapefruit juice.

PRESCRIPTION:

Yes (restricted to high blood cholesterol levels not controlled by diet).

PERMITTED IN SPORT:

Yes.

OVERDOSE:

Liver stress only likely effect.

OTHER INFORMATION:

Drug released in the late 1980s that has improved the treatment of excess cholesterol. Very safe and generally well tolerated.

See also Atorvastatin, Cholestyramine, Colestipol, Fluvastatin, Gemfibrizol, Nicotinic acid, Pravastatin.

Sirolimus

TRADE NAME:

Rapamune.

DRUG CLASS:

Immunomodifier.

USES:

Prevents rejection of kidney transplants.

DOSAGE:

 2mg once a day initially, then adjust depending on results of blood tests. Take solution with orange juice.

FORMS:

Triangular tablets of 1mg (white) and 2mg (beige), solution.

PRECAUTIONS:

Use with significant caution in pregnancy (C), breast feeding and children under 13 years.
Use with caution in liver disease.
Avoid excess sunlight and UV rays.
Increased risk of cancers and infections.
Regular blood tests essential to monitor kidney function.

SIDE EFFECTS:

Common: fever, tissue swelling, poor healing, belly pain, diarrhoea.
Unusual: high cholesterol levels, anaemia, abnormal blood chemistry, joint pains, acne.
Severe but rare (stop medication, consult doctor): blood clots (thrombosis), lung damage, liver damage.

INTERACTIONS:

Other drugs:
• cyclosporin, drugs that lower cholesterol, rifampicin, ketoconazole, diltiazem.
• live vaccines (e.g. polio).
Other substances:
• grapefruit juice.

PRESCRIPTION:

Yes.

PERMITTED IN SPORT:

Yes.

OTHER INFORMATION:

Introduced in 2002. Must be taken regularly and consistently to be effective.

Sodium acid phosphate

TRADE NAMES:

Carbalax (with sodium bicarbonate).
Fleet, Fleet Phospho-Soda, Fletcher's Phosphate (with sodium phosphate).

DRUG CLASS:

Laxative.

USES:

To clean bowel prior to surgery or colonoscopy, severe constipation.

DOSAGE:

 Suppositories: one or two a day.
Solution: 45mLs with water twice a day.

FORMS:

Enema, solution, suppository.

PRECAUTIONS:

Use with care in pregnancy, breast feeding and children.
Use with caution in colostomy, poor kidney function and any heart disease.
Do not take if:
 • suffering from heart failure, intestinal obstruction, megacolon, kidney failure, ulcerative colitis, diverticulitis, undiagnosed abdominal pain, vomiting.
• under 12 years of age.

SIDE EFFECTS:

Common: diarrhoea, nausea.

INTERACTIONS:

Other drugs:
• diuretics, lithium
• will affect absorption of all swallowed medications, including oral contraceptive pill.

PRESCRIPTION:

No.

PERMITTED IN SPORT:

Yes.

OVERDOSE:

Severe diarrhoea and electrolyte deficiencies likely.

OTHER INFORMATION:

Usually used when other laxatives have failed.
See also Sodium Phosphate.

Sodium alginate

See ANTACIDS.

Sodium aurothiomalate
(Gold)

TRADE NAME:

Myocrisin.

DRUG CLASS:

Antirheumatic.

USES:

Rheumatoid arthritis.

DOSAGE:

 Weekly injections until condition controlled, then reduce frequency slowly.

FORMS:

Injection.

PRECAUTIONS:

Should be used with caution in pregnancy (B2), breast feeding and children.
Use with caution in liver and kidney disease.
Regular blood and urine tests required to assess kidney and liver function, blood cells and effectiveness of treatment.
Do not take if:

 • suffering from severe liver or kidney disease, diabetes, severe eczema, some blood diseases.

SIDE EFFECTS:

Common: dermatitis, itch, mouth ulcers, flushing, fainting.
Unusual: sweating, dizziness, weakness, feeling unwell, eye damage, kidney damage.
Severe but rare (stop medication, consult doctor): severe rash, unusual bleeding or bruising.

INTERACTIONS:

Other drugs:
• phenylbutazone, penicillamine, ACE inhibitors.

PRESCRIPTION:

Yes.

PERMITTED IN SPORT:

Yes.

OTHER INFORMATION:

An unusual but remarkably effective treatment that has been used for over thirty years. Careful monitoring of blood tests and skin reactions essential. Gold is not addictive when swallowed or injected, only when collected!
See also Auranofin.

Sodium bicarbonate

See ANTACIDS, ELECTROLYTES.

Sodium chloride
(Common Salt)

See ELECTROLYTES.

Sodium citrate

See ELECTROLYTES.

Sodium clodronate

TRADE NAME:

Bonefos.

USES:

High levels of calcium in blood and bone pain due to bone tumours.

DOSAGE:

 2400 to 3200mg once a day initially, reducing to 1600mg once a day. Do not take within two hours of food.

FORMS:

Capsules of 400mg (yellow), tablets of 400mg (white), infusion.

PRECAUTIONS:

Use with considerable caution in pregnancy (B3), breast feeding and children.
Use with caution in dehydration and kidney disease.
Regular blood tests to check calcium levels necessary.
Maintain adequate fluid intake.
Do not take if:

- suffering from severe intestinal inflammation.

SIDE EFFECTS:

Common: low blood calcium, stomach upsets.
Severe but rare (stop medication, consult doctor): blood chemistry disorders, kidney failure.

INTERACTIONS:

Other drugs:
- other medications affecting phosphorus or calcium levels
- estamustine, NSAIDs, antacids.

PRESCRIPTION:

Yes.

PERMITTED IN SPORT:

Yes.

OVERDOSE:

Serious blood chemistry disorders possible that may lead to major organ failure. Seek urgent medical attention. Induce vomiting or give activated charcoal if swallowed recently.

Sodium cromoglycate
(Cromolyn sodium, Disodium cromoglycate)

TRADE NAMES:

Hay-Crom, Opticrom for use in eye.
Cromogen, Intal for use in lungs.
Aerocrom (with salbutamol) for use in lungs.
Rynacrom for use in nose.
Nalcrom for use in gut.

USES:

Prevention (but not treatment) of asthma.
Prevention (but not treatment) of hay fever.
Prevention (but not treatment) of allergic reactions in the eye.
Prevention (but not treatment) of food allergies.

DOSAGE:

Inhaler: two inhalations up to four times a day.
Nasal spray: one spray to each nostril, two to four times a day.
Eye drops: one or two drops into eye, four to six times a day.
Capsules: two capsules, four times a day before food.

FORMS:

For use in eye: drops (keep in door of refrigerator).
For use in lungs: capsules for spinhaler (keep cool), metered aerosol, inhaler.
For use in nose: nasal spray.
For use in gut: capsules of 100mg (clear).

PRECAUTIONS:

Safe in pregnancy (A), children and breast feeding.
Do not stop suddenly from full dose, as recurrence of asthma or allergic condition may occur.

SIDE EFFECTS:

Common: hoarse voice and bad taste with inhaled forms.

Unusual: headache, stuffy nose, nosebleed, throat irritation.
Severe but rare (stop medication, consult doctor): rash, hives, increased wheezing, joint pain, muscle pain, palpitations.

INTERACTIONS:

None significant.

PRESCRIPTION:

Yes.

PERMITTED IN SPORT:

Yes.

OVERDOSE:

No problems encountered other than increased likelihood of side effects.

OTHER INFORMATION:

Excellent cheap and effective medication for prevention of many allergies and asthma. Minimal side effects. Very safe. In use for 25 years and actions well understood. Newer presentation in pressurised inhaler and higher doses has increased use in recent years. Does not cause dependence or addiction. Cromoglycate is a preventative medication and cannot be used to treat asthma, hay fever or allergy reactions in the eye.

See also Beclomethasone, Budesonide, Fluticasone, Montelukast.

Sodium fluoride

See Fluoride.

Sodium fusidate and Fusidic acid

TRADE NAMES:

Fucidin, Fucithalmic.
Fucibet (with betamethasone).
Fucidin H (with hydrocortisone).

DRUG CLASS:

Antibiotic.

USES:

Infections caused by susceptible bacteria, particularly lung, heart, eye and skin infections.

DOSAGE:

 Tablets: two tablets three times a day with meals.
Ointment: apply two or three times a day for seven days.
Eye drops: one drop twice a day.

FORMS:

Gel, cream, tablets, suspension, infusion, eye drops.

PRECAUTIONS:

Should not be used in pregnancy (C) unless medically essential. Should be used with caution in breast feeding and infants. Safe for use in children.
Not designed for long term use.
Use with caution in liver disease.

SIDE EFFECTS:

Common: ointment—skin irritation, skin pain.
Swallowed forms—nausea, loss of appetite, diarrhoea.
Eye drops—temporary irritation.
Unusual: belly discomfort, vomiting, dizziness.
Severe but rare (stop medication, consult doctor): yellow skin (jaundice).

INTERACTIONS:

Other drugs:
• lincomycin, rifampicin.

PRESCRIPTION:

Yes.

PERMITTED IN SPORT:

Yes.

OVERDOSE:

Belly pain and diarrhoea likely. Long term overdosage may cause liver damage.

OTHER INFORMATION:

Used only for more severe and complex infections, particularly in cystic fibrosis.

Sodium hyaluronate

TRADE NAMES:

Cystistat, Fermathron, Hyalgan, Ostenil, Supartz, Suplasyn.
Solaraze (with diclofenac).

USES:

Osteoarthritic pain in the knee, protection of cornea during eye operations, actinic keratoses, interstitial cystitis (bladder inflammation).

DOSAGE:

 Eye drops: one or two drops in eye as often as needed.
Injection: one injection into knee every week for five weeks gives up to six months relief of arthritis pain.

FORMS:

Injection, solution, eye drops, gel.

PRECAUTIONS:

Eye drops may be used safely in pregnancy and breast feeding.
Do not use other eye drops within five minutes.

Do not have injection if:

 • suffering from skin disease or infection near knee
• under 16 years.

SIDE EFFECTS:

Common: eye drops—short term blurred vision after use.
Injection—temporary pain, swelling and inflammation of knee.
Severe but rare (stop medication, consult doctor): injection—infection of knee joint.

INTERACTIONS:

None significant.

PRESCRIPTION:

Yes.

PERMITTED IN SPORT:

Yes.

OTHER INFORMATION:

Injection introduced in 2000 as a radical new form of treatment for otherwise intractable arthritis. Used in eyes for many years.

Sodium iodide
(Radioactive iodine, I^{131})

TRADE NAME:

Sodium iodide.

USES:

Overactive thyroid gland (hyperthyroidism), thyroid cancer.

DOSAGE:

 Very strictly as directed by doctor.

FORMS:

Capsules (yellow), injection.

PRECAUTIONS:

Absolutely forbidden in pregnancy (X), breast feeding and children.
Ensure adequate contraception for at least two months before and after dosage.
Patient should avoid close contact with children for ten days after dosage.
Ensure high fluid intake for ten days after dosage.

Do not take if:

 • suffering from kidney disease, vomiting or diarrhoea.

SIDE EFFECTS:

Common: nausea, diarrhoea, itch, rapid heart rate.
Unusual: vomiting, inflamed salivary glands, radiation sickness, lung damage, anaemia, bone marrow damage.
Severe but rare: critical thyroid reaction, death.

INTERACTIONS:

Other drugs:
• antithyroid drugs (e.g. propylthiouracil), thyroxine, x-ray contract dye.

Other substances:
• seafood, iodine containing foods.

PRESCRIPTION:

No.

OVERDOSE:

Significant overdose likely to be fatal.

OTHER INFORMATION:

Radioactive iodine is taken up specifically by the thyroid gland and selectively destroys the most active cells in that gland. Very effective and commonly used treatment for both thyroid cancer and hyperthyroidism.

Sodium iron edetate

See Iron.

Sodium lauryl sulfoacetate

TRADE NAME:

Relaxit (with sodium citrate, sorbic acid, glycerol and sorbitol).

USES:

Constipation.

DOSAGE:

 One tube rectally at night.

FORMS:

Rectal enema.

PRECAUTIONS:

Safe in pregnancy, breast feeding and children.
Insert only half nozzle length in children under three years.

SIDE EFFECTS:

Minimal.

INTERACTIONS:

None significant.

PRESCRIPTION:

No.

PERMITTED IN SPORT:

Yes.

OVERDOSE:

Diarrhoea only effect.

OTHER INFORMATION:

Commonly used in elderly. Very safe and effective.

See also Bisacodyl, Docusate sodium, Fibre, Glycerol, Frangula, Lactulose, Paraffin, Psyllium, Senna, Sodium phosphate, Sodium picosulfate, Sorbitol, Sterculia.

Sodium perborate

TRADE NAME:

Bocasan.

DRUG CLASS:

Antiseptic.

USES:

Mouth and gum inflammation and soreness.

DOSAGE:

 One sachet dissolved in water and used as mouthwash four times a day after meals.

FORMS:

Powder.

PRECAUTIONS:

Safe to use in pregnancy, breast feeding and children.
Do not swallow.

SIDE EFFECTS:
Minimal.

INTERACTIONS:
None significant.

PRESCRIPTION:
No.

PERMITTED IN SPORT:
Yes.

OVERDOSE:
Diarrhoea and nausea only likely effects if swallowed in large quantities.

Sodium phosphate

TRADE NAMES:
Fleet Enema, Fleet Phospho-Soda, Fletchers Phosphate (with sodium acid phosphate).

DRUG CLASS:
Laxative.

USES:
To clean bowel prior to surgery or colonoscopy, constipation.

DOSAGE:

Use enema once a day.
45mLs solution with water twice a day.

FORMS:
Solution, enema.

PRECAUTIONS:
Use with caution in pregnancy and breast feeding.
Use with caution in diabetes, kidney disease, electrolyte disturbances, colostomy, belly pain, vomiting, people prone to dehydration.
Reduce dose in elderly.
Not for repeated use.

Do not take if:

• suffering from bowel obstruction, bowel paralysis, impacted faeces, megacolon, ascites, poor kidney function, congestive heart failure, dehydration, ileostomy
• under 12 years of age.

SIDE EFFECTS:
Common: dehydration, nausea, electrolyte imbalances.
Unusual: vomiting, allergic reactions.

INTERACTIONS:
Other drugs:
• diuretics, lithium.
• will affect absorption of all swallowed medications, including contraceptive pill.

PRESCRIPTION:
No.

PERMITTED IN SPORT:
Yes (guaranteed to cause failure in almost any sport!).

OVERDOSE:
Severe diarrhoea and dehydration with significant electrolyte disturbances that may lead to organ damage and heart attack. Vomiting likely after overdose as side effect of medication.

OTHER INFORMATION:
Normally only used as a preparation for a medical procedure on the large bowel in association with a strict diet.

See also Bisacodyl, Docusate sodium, Fibre, Glycerol, Frangula, Lactulose, Paraffin, Psyllium, Senna, Sodium lauryl sulfoacetate, Sodium picosulfate, Sorbitol, Sterculia.

Sodium picosulfate

TRADE NAMES:

Laxoberal.
Picolax (with magnesium citrate).

DRUG CLASS:

Laxative.

USES:

Preparation of bowel for surgery or colonoscopy, constipation.

DOSAGE:

 5 to 15mLs of solution once a day at night.
Powder in sachet dissolved in water once or twice a day.

FORMS:

Powder for solution, liquid.

PRECAUTIONS:

Not to be used in pregnancy (C) or children under 20kg.
Use with caution in breast feeding and children.
Use with caution in heart disease, phenylketonuria, dehydration, electrolyte disturbances, if prone to aspiration.
Reduce dose in elderly.

Do not take if:

 • suffering from bowel obstruction, bowel paralysis, belly pain, colitis, bowel inflammation.

SIDE EFFECTS:

Common: nausea, bloating, anal irritation, belly discomfort.
Unusual: vomiting, recurrence of constipation.

INTERACTIONS:

Other drugs:
• affects absorption of all swallowed medications, including contraceptive pill.

PRESCRIPTION:

No.

PERMITTED IN SPORT:

Yes.

OVERDOSE:

Severe diarrhoea and dehydration with significant electrolyte disturbances that may lead to organ damage and heart attack. Vomiting likely after overdose as side effect of medication.

See also Bisacodyl, Docusate sodium, Fibre, Glycerol, Frangula, Lactulose, Paraffin, Psyllium, Senna, Sodium lauryl sulfoacetate, Sodium phosphate, Sorbitol, Sterculia.

Sodium polystyrene sulfonate

See Polystyrene sulfonate.

Sodium valproate

TRADE NAME:

Epilim.

DRUG CLASS:

Anticonvulsant.

USES:

Epilepsy.

DOSAGE:

 Dosage increased slowly until desired control achieved, usually between 1000mg and 2000mg a day taken in one or more doses with or after food.

FORMS:

Tablets, coated tablets, syrup, injection.

PRECAUTIONS:

Not to be taken in pregnancy (D) unless medically essential as the risk of foetal abnormality is significantly increased.

Use with caution in breast feeding. May be used in children.

Use with caution in in kidney disease and during surgery (may increase bleeding). Do not stop medication suddenly, but reduce dosage slowly.

Do not take if:

- suffering from liver disease
- family history of severe liver disease.

SIDE EFFECTS:

Common: usually reduced by using slow release form or reducing dosage. Nausea, belly cramps, loss of appetite, diarrhoea.
Unusual: drowsiness, hair loss, rash, irregular menstrual periods, swelling of tissues.
Severe but rare (stop medication, consult doctor): unusual bleeding or bruising, yellow skin (jaundice), severe belly pain.

INTERACTIONS:

Other drugs:
- other anticonvulsants (e.g. ethosuximide), sedatives, lorazepam, midazolam, clozapine, diazepam, clonazepam, aspirin, anticoagulants (e.g. warfarin), psychotropics (e.g. chlorpromazine), fluoxetine, MAOI.
Herbs:
- evening primrose (linoleic acid), Gingko biloba.
Other substances:
- reacts adversely with alcohol
- borage.

PRESCRIPTION:

Yes.

PERMITTED IN SPORT:

Yes.

OVERDOSE:

Death possible but rare. Symptoms include drowsiness, slow breathing, incoordination, confusion and coma. Administer activated charcoal or induce vomiting if taken recently and patient alert. Seek urgent medical attention.

OTHER INFORMATION:

Very effective and relatively safe medication that has improved the life of many epileptics. Not addictive or dependence forming.

See also Carbamazepine, Clonazepam, Ethosuximide, Gabapentin, Lamotrigine, Levetiracetam, Oxcarbazepine, Phenytoin, Primidone, Sulthiame, Tiagabine, Topiramate, Vigabatrin.

Somatropin
(Growth hormone)

TRADE NAMES:

Genotropin, Humatrope, Norditropin, Saizen, Zomacton.

DRUG CLASS:

Hormone.

USES:

Short stature due to growth hormone deficiency in children.

DOSAGE:

 Administered weekly by injection.

FORMS:

Injection, injector pen.

PRECAUTIONS:

Not for use in pregnancy or breast feeding.
Use with caution in diabetes, ACTH deficiency, underactive thyroid gland, slipped epiphysis, increased pressure within brain.
Do not exceed recommended dose.

Do not take if:

- suffering from active tumour, cancer, brain growths
- adult.

SIDE EFFECTS:

Common: irritation at injection site, allergy reaction, fluid retention, fat loss.
Unusual: underactive thyroid gland, diabetes, slipped bony epiphysis.
Severe but rare (stop medication, consult doctor): increased pressure of fluid within brain.

INTERACTIONS:

Other drugs:
• steroids, sex hormones, cyclosporin.

PRESCRIPTION:

Yes.

PERMITTED IN SPORT:

No.

OVERDOSE:

Overgrowth of bones leading to pressure on nerves and brain (acromegaly), and imbalance in body's ability to deal with glucose.

OTHER INFORMATION:

Used illegally by some sportsmen to aid body building.

Sorbide Nitrate

See Isosorbide.

Sorbitol

TRADE NAMES:

Glandosane (with carboxymethylcellulose sodium).
Relaxit (with glycerol, sodium citrate and sodium lauryl sulfoacetate).

DRUG CLASS:

Laxative, Softening agent.

USES:

Softening faeces in constipation, lubricant.

DOSAGE:

 Enema: once a day into rectum.
Mouth spray: spray as often as required for dry mouth.

FORMS:

Mouth spray, suspension, enema, liquid.

PRECAUTIONS:

Usually safe to use in pregnancy, breast feeding and children.
Not for prolonged use.
Use with caution in diabetes.
Do not take if:
 • suffering from appendicitis, undiagnosed abdominal pain
• intolerant to fructose.

SIDE EFFECTS:

Common: passing excess wind, diarrhoea.
Severe but rare (stop medication, consult doctor): disturbances to blood chemistry (electrolytes).

INTERACTIONS:

Other drugs:
• other laxatives, may interfere with absorption of any medication taken by mouth, including oral contraceptives.
Other substances:
• fructose containing foods.

PRESCRIPTION:

No.

PERMITTED IN SPORT:

Yes.

OVERDOSE:

Exacerbation of side effects likely. May cause serious blood chemistry disorders.

OTHER INFORMATION:

Widely used and safe in correct dosage.
See Bisacodyl, Docusate sodium, Fibre, Frangula, Glycerol, Lactulose, Paraffin, Poloxamer, Psyllium, Sennosides, Sodium phosphate, Sodium picosulfate, Sterculia.

Sotalol

TRADE NAMES:

Beta-Cardone, Sotacor.

DRUG CLASS:

Beta-blocker.

USES:

Irregular heart beat, paroxysmal atrial tachycardia.

DOSAGE:

 80 to 400mg a day in divided doses.

FORMS:

Tablets of 40mg, 80mg, 160mg and 200mg; injection.

PRECAUTIONS:

Should be used in pregnancy (C) only if medically essential.
Safe to use in breast feeding.
May be used with caution in children.
Use with care if suffering from alcoholism, diabetes, psoriasis, hyperthyroidism (overactive thyroid gland), liver or kidney failure, or about to have surgery.
Regular checks on heart rhythm essential.
Do not stop suddenly, but reduce dose gradually.

Do not take if:

- suffering from diabetes, asthma, or allergic conditions
- suffering from heart failure, shock, slow heart rate, or enlarged right heart
- if undertaking prolonged fast.

SIDE EFFECTS:

Common: low blood pressure, slow heart rate, cold hands and feet, asthma.
Unusual: loss of appetite, nausea, diarrhoea, impotence, tiredness, sleeplessness, nightmares, rash, loss of libido, hair loss, noises in ears, dizziness.
Severe but rare (stop medication, consult doctor): severe asthma.

INTERACTIONS:

Other drugs:
- calcium channel blockers, disopyramide, clonidine, adrenaline, other medications for irregular heart beat, lignocaine, ergotamine, indomethacin, chlorpromazine.

PRESCRIPTION:

Yes.

PERMITTED IN SPORT:

Restricted in some sports (e.g. shooting, archery). Check with sport's governing body.

OVERDOSE:

Slow heart rate, low blood pressure, asthma and heart failure may result. Administer activated charcoal or induce vomiting if tablets taken recently. Use Salbutamol or other asthma sprays for difficulty in breathing. Seek medical assistance.

See also Atenolol, Carvedilol, Esmolol, Labetalol, Metoprolol, Oxprenolol, Pindolol, Propranolol.

SPASMOLYTICS

DISCUSSION:

Medications that ease spasms of the intestine to prevent colic.

See Alverine citrate, Dicyclomine, Hyoscine, Mebeverine.

SPERMICIDES

See Nonoxynol-9.

Spironolactone

TRADE NAMES:

Aldactone.
Aldactide (with hydroflumethiazide).
Lasilactone (with frusemide).

DRUG CLASS:

Diuretic (aldosterone antagonist).

USES:

High blood pressure, congestive cardiac failure, excess fluid retention, cirrhosis of liver, low blood potassium levels, excessive body and face hair in women, primary hyperaldosteronism.

DOSAGE:

 Varies depending on usage from 25mg to 400mg a day in one or several doses.

FORMS:

Tablets.

PRECAUTIONS:

Should not be used in pregnancy (B3) unless medically essential. Should not be used in breast feeding or children. Regular blood tests for level of blood chemicals (electrolytes) may be necessary.

Do not take if:

 • suffering from kidney failure, excess potassium in blood.

SIDE EFFECTS:

Common: breast enlargement (both sexes), diarrhoea, gut cramps.
Unusual: tiredness, headache, confusion, rash, fever, incoordination, impotence, irregular menstruation.
Severe but rare (stop medication, consult doctor): unusual bleeding.

INTERACTIONS:

Other drugs:
• do not take with potassium supplements, amiloride or triamterene
• reacts with carbenoxolone, digoxin
• ACE inhibitors, NSAIDs.
Herbs:
• celery, dandelion, liquorice, uva ursi.

PRESCRIPTION:

Yes.

PERMITTED IN SPORT:

No.

OVERDOSE:

Large doses required for adverse effects. Pins and needles sensation, weakness, muscle spasms and paralysis are possible symptoms. Induce vomiting if tablets taken recently. Give extra fluids. Seek medical assistance.

OTHER INFORMATION:

An old fashioned medication for removal of excess fluid from the body that has recently been given a new life because of its ability to reduce excess facial hair (hirsutism) in women. Must be taken for many months for this purpose.

See also Amiloride, Bumetanide, Frusemide, THIAZIDE DIURETICS.

SSD

See Silver sulfadiazine.

SSRI
(SELECTIVE SEROTONIN REUPTAKE INHIBITORS)
(Treat depression and abnormal anxiety)

See Citalopram, Fluoxetine, Fluvoxamine, Paroxetine, Reboxetine, Sertraline, Venlafaxine.

Stavudine

TRADE NAME:

Zerit.

DRUG CLASS:

Antiviral.

USES:

HIV infection, AIDS.

DOSAGE:

 Dosage as determined by doctor taken twice a day one hour before meals.

FORMS:

Capsules of 15mg (yellow/red), 20mg (brown), 30mg (light orange/dark orange), 40mg (dark orange), solution.

PRECAUTIONS:

Use with caution in pregnancy (B3), breast feeding and children under 12 years.
Use with caution in peripheral neuropathy (nerve inflammation), pancreatitis, liver disease.

SIDE EFFECTS:

Common: nerve pain and inflammation, inflammation of pancreas.
Unusual: liver damage.

INTERACTIONS:

Other drugs:
• zidovudine, didanosine, hydroxyurea, trimethoprim.

PRESCRIPTION:

Yes.

PERMITTED IN SPORT:

Yes.

OVERDOSE:

No information available. Seek urgent medical attention. Induce vomiting or administer activated charcoal if taken recently.

OTHER INFORMATION:

Introduced in 1997.
See Abacavir, Efavirenz, Indinavir, Lamivudine, Nelfinavir, Nevirapine, Ritonavir, Saquinavir, Tenofovir, Zidovudine.

Sterculia

TRADE NAMES:

Normacol.
Normacol Plus (with frangula).
Spasmonal Fibre (with alverine citrate).

DRUG CLASS:

Fibre.

USES:

Constipation, irritable bowel syndrome.

DOSAGE:

 Take one or two heaped teaspoons with water twice a day at least two hours before bed time.

FORMS:

Granules.

PRECAUTIONS:

Safe in pregnancy and breast feeding.
Safe in children over six years.
Do not take if:
 • about to go to bed.
• suffering from ulcerative colitis.

SIDE EFFECTS:

Common: minimal.
Unusual: diarrhoea, belly discomfort.

INTERACTIONS:

None significant.

PRESCRIPTION:

No.

PERMITTED IN SPORT:

Yes.

OVERDOSE:

Take additional water. Belly discomfort and passing excess wind only effects.

OTHER INFORMATION:

Widely used, natural fibre supplement.
See also FIBRE.

STEROIDS (CORTICOSTEROIDS)

DISCUSSION:

Cholesterol is the base substance from which the body produces natural steroids. There are many different types of steroids, including sex hormones, anabolic steroids (that are often abused by athletes) and trophic hormones (see separate entries). The type being described here are more correctly called corticosteroid hormones. They act as powerful reducers of inflammation in damaged tissue. Artificial steroids have been synthesised to control a wide range of diseases, including asthma, arthritis, dermatitis, eczema and severe allergy reactions.

Steroids are available as tablets, mixtures, injections, creams, nasal sprays, inhaled sprays, eye drops, ear drops and suppositories. They are therefore an extremely useful group of drugs in a wide variety of conditions.

The actions of steroids include shrinking down inflamed tissue (e.g. in allergies, injuries, piles) to normal, reducing itching (e.g. in eczema and bites) and opening up airways by reducing mucus secretion and shrinking swollen tissue (e.g. hay fever, asthma).

When used on the skin or on the surface of the airways (lungs, nose), side effects are uncommon. Overuse of sprays used for asthma is quite safe, but overuse in the nose can cause tissue damage. Creams and ointments that contain strong steroids should not be overused, particularly in children and on the face, as they can cause skin thinning and damage. Taken as injection into joints, steroids are very successful at controlling arthritis, but again, overuse may cause weakness and damage to the joint tissue instead of controlling the disease.

The greatest dangers occur when steroids are taken as tablets. Short courses, in which a high dose is given at the start and then reduced rapidly to zero over a couple of weeks, are quite safe. Low doses given for quite long periods of time are also relatively safe, but when high doses are given for months on end, damage can occur in the body.

Side effects of prolonged steroid tablet use include tissue swelling, an imbalance in blood chemicals, high blood pressure, weight gain, peptic ulcers, brittle bones (fracturing easily), heart failure, muscle weakness, delayed wound healing, headache, abnormal menstrual periods, fatty deposits under the skin, blood clots, cataracts, glaucoma and a host of rarer conditions. It is therefore obvious why doctors use these remarkably effective drugs with great caution. In some situations, the seriousness of the disease warrants taking the risk of using steroids to give a patient relief, or even saving a life.

If used judiciously, steroids can dramatically improve a patient's quality of life, but doctors must always be aware of the pros and cons of their use in every individual.

See Beclomethasone, Betamethasone, Budesonide, Clobetasol, Clobetasone, Cortisone, Deflazacort, Desoxymethasone, Dexamethasone, Diflucortolone, Fludrocortisone, Flucinolone, Fluocinonide, Fluocortolone, Fluorometholone, Flurandrelone, Fluticasone, Halcinonide, Hydrocortisone, Mometasone, Prednisolone, Rimexolone, Triamcinolone.

Stilboestrol

TRADE NAME:

Tampovagan.

DRUG CLASS:

Sex hormone.

USES:

Female hormone replacement in menopause, vaginal dryness after menopause.

DOSAGE:

 Insert one or two high into vagina at night.

FORMS:

Vaginal pessary.

PRECAUTIONS:

Not to be used in pregnancy (B1), breast feeding or children. Accidental usage in these situations unlikely to be harmful. Use with caution in epilepsy, migraine, heart failure, high blood pressure, kidney disease, diabetes, porphyria or uterine disease.

Do not take if:

 • suffering from liver disease, breast or genital cancer, blood clots.

SIDE EFFECTS:

Common: abnormal uterine bleeding, vaginal thrush, fluid retention, weight gain, breast tenderness.
Unusual: rash, bloating, intestinal cramps.
Severe but rare (stop medication, consult doctor): blood clots, calf or chest pain, yellow skin (jaundice).

INTERACTIONS:

Other drugs:
• other sex hormones.
Other substances:
• smoking increases risk of serious side effects.

PRESCRIPTION:

Yes.

PERMITTED IN SPORT:

Yes.

OVERDOSE:

Vomiting and abnormal vaginal bleeding only likely effects if swallowed.

STIMULANTS

DISCUSSION:

Stimulants are used in medicine to treat disorders of excessive sleep, some types of senility and (rather strangely) overactivity in children. They have been known to be abused by long-distance truck drivers and others who wish to stay awake for long periods of time. Dependence upon these drugs can develop rapidly.

See Caffeine, Cocaine, Dexamphetamine, Methylphenidate, Nicotine.

St John's Wort

See Saint John's Wort.

Streptodornase

See FIBRINOLYTICS.

Streptokinase

See FIBRINOLYTICS.

Sucralfate

TRADE NAME:

Antepsin.

DRUG CLASS:

Antiulcerant.

USES:

Protects the lining of the stomach. Treats and prevents ulcers of the stomach and duodenum (upper small intestine).

DOSAGE:

 One tablet three times a day one hour before meals, and a fourth tablet last thing at night before bed. Course usually limited to eight weeks.

FORMS:

Tablets of 1g (white), suspension.

PRECAUTIONS:

Use with caution in pregnancy (B1). Not recommended for use in children.
Cause of symptoms must be determined (e.g. by gastroscopy) if symptoms persist or return after use.
Use with caution if swallowing difficult.

Do not take if:

• suffering from stomach cancer, bleeding ulcer or significant kidney disease.

SIDE EFFECTS:

Common: constipation, headache, itchy rash, nausea.
Unusual: indigestion, dry mouth, diarrhoea, back pain, sleepiness, dizziness.

INTERACTIONS:

Other drugs:

• antacids should not be taken within half an hour
• tetracycline, phenytoin, digoxin, norfloxacin, ciprofloxacin, warfarin and cimetidine may have their effectiveness reduced while taking sucralfate.

PRESCRIPTION:

Yes.

PERMITTED IN SPORT:

Yes.

OVERDOSE:

Constipation and nausea only effects.

See also ANTACIDS, Cimetidine, Misoprostol, Nizatadine, PROTON PUMP INHIBITORS, Ranitidine.

SUGAR

See Glucose.

Sulconazole

TRADE NAMES:

Exelderm.

DRUG CLASS:

Imidazole antifungal.

USES:

Treatment of fungal infections of skin (e.g. tinea, athlete's foot).

DOSAGE:

 Apply twice a day.

FORMS:

Cream.

PRECAUTIONS:

Safe to use in pregnancy (A), breast feeding and children.
Should not be used in eyes.
Use with care on open wounds.

SIDE EFFECTS:

Common: none.
Unusual: skin irritation, rash.

INTERACTIONS:

None significant.

PRESCRIPTION:

No.

PERMITTED IN SPORT:

Yes.

OTHER INFORMATION:

This class of medication dramatically improved the treatment of fungal infections when introduced in the early 1970s. Very safe and effective.

See Clotrimazole, Econazole, Fluconazole, Itraconazole, Ketoconazole, Miconazole.

Sulfadoxine

TRADE NAME:

Fansidar (with pyrimethamine).

DRUG CLASS:

Antimalarial.

USES:

Prevention and treatment of malaria.

OTHER INFORMATION:

Only available in combination with pyrimethamine. See pyrimethamine entry for further information.

Sulfonamides

See Sulphonamides.

Sulindac

TRADE NAMES:

Clinoril.

DRUG CLASS:

NSAID (Nonsteroidal anti-inflammatory drug).

USES:

All forms of arthritis, inflammatory disorders, gout, back pain, ankylosing spondylitis, rheumatoid arthritis.

DOSAGE:

 One or two tablets, twice a day with food.

FORMS:

Tablets of 100mg and 200mg.

PRECAUTIONS:

Should not be used in pregnancy (C) unless medically essential. Breast feeding should be ceased if necessary to use NSAID. Not for use in children under two.

Use with caution in psychiatricaly disturbed patients, epilepsy, severe infection, heart failure and kidney disease.
Lower doses required in elderly, who may suffer more side effects.

Do not take if:

- suffering from peptic ulcer at present or in recent past
- due for surgery (including dental surgery)
- suffering from bleeding disorder or anaemia.

SIDE EFFECTS:

Common: stomach discomfort, diarrhoea, constipation, heartburn, nausea, headache, dizziness.
Unusual: blurred vision, stomach ulcer, ringing noise in ears, retention of fluid, swelling of tissue, drowsiness, itch, rash, shortness of breath.
Severe but rare (stop medication, consult doctor): vomiting blood, passing blood in faeces, other unusual bleeding, asthma induced by medication.

INTERACTIONS:

Other drugs:
- must never be used with anticoagulants (e.g. warfarin).
- probenecid, diuretics, lithium, methotrexate, beta-blockers, ACE inhibitors.

PRESCRIPTION:

Yes.

PERMITTED IN SPORT:

Yes.

OVERDOSE:

Causes nausea, vomiting, severe headache, dizziness, confusion and convulsions. Administer activated charcoal or induce vomiting if taken recently. Seek medical assistance.

OTHER INFORMATION:

Significant side effects (particularly on the stomach) in about 5% of patients. Limit their use.

See also Aspirin, Bufexamac, Celecoxib, Diclofenac, Diflunisal, Flurbiprofen, Ibuprofen, Indomethacin, Ketoprofen, Ketorolac trometanol, Mefenamic Acid, Naproxen, Piroxicam, Rofecoxib, Tenoxicam, Tiaprofenic Acid.

Sulphabenzamide, Sulphacetamide, Sulphathiazole

TRADE and GENERIC NAMES:

Sultrin (combination of sulphathiazole, sulphacetamide and sulphabenzamide).

DRUG CLASS:

Antibiotic.

USES:

Treat bacterial vaginal infections.

DOSAGE:

 One application once or twice a day into vagina.

FORMS:

Vaginal cream.

PRECAUTIONS:

Not to be used in pregnancy (C), breast feeding or infants. Safe for use in children.
Use with caution in liver or kidney disease.

SIDE EFFECTS:

Common: itch, redness, swelling.
Severe but rare (stop medication, consult doctor): rash, severe belly pain, kidney damage.

INTERACTIONS:

Other substances:
• latex condoms and diaphragms.

PRESCRIPTION:

Yes.

PERMITTED IN SPORT:

Yes.

OTHER INFORMATION:

Sulfonamides were the first antibiotics in the 1930s. Used less frequently now due to resistant forms of bacteria developing. Allergy to Sulfonamides a problem in some patients.

Sulphamethoxazole

TRADE NAME:

Only available in combination with trimethoprim—this combination is known as co-trimoxazole.
Septrin (with trimethoprim).

DRUG CLASS:

Sulphonamide antibiotic.

USES:

Infections caused by susceptible bacteria, particularly infections of sinuses, lungs, urine and skin.

DOSAGE:

 One or two tablets twice a day.

FORMS:

Tablets, suspension, injection.

PRECAUTIONS:

Should not be used in pregnancy (C). Use with caution in breast feeding. May be used in children over two years.
Use with caution in AIDS, blood disorders, asthma, allergic conditions, kidney and liver disease.
Not designed for long term use.
Lower doses and caution necessary in elderly.
Give additional fluids to dilute.

Do not take if:

- suffering from severe liver disease, abnormal blood cells, bone marrow damage, severe kidney disease
- under three months of age.

SIDE EFFECTS:

Common: nausea, loss of appetite, rash.
Unusual: vomiting, diarrhoea.
Severe but rare (stop medication, consult doctor): unusual bleeding or bruising, yellow skin (jaundice).

INTERACTIONS:

Other drugs:

- hypoglycaemics, methotrexate, urinary acidifiers, anticoagulants (e.g. warfarin), NSAID, salicylates, sulfinpyrazone, phenytoin, rifampicin, cyclosporin, thiazide diuretics, pyrimethamine, acetazolamide.

PRESCRIPTION:

Yes.

PERMITTED IN SPORT:

Yes.

OVERDOSE:

Exacerbation of side effects likely. Administer activated charcoal or induce vomiting if tablets taken recently. Take as much fluid as possible. Kidney damage possible. Seek medical assistance.

OTHER INFORMATION:

Widely used for two decades after its introduction in the mid 1960s, but now more effective antibiotics tend to be used where possible.

See also Sulphonamides.

Sulphasalazine

TRADE NAME:

Salazopyrin.

DRUG CLASS:

Sulphonamide antibiotic.

USES:

Ulcerative colitis, Crohn's disease, rheumatoid arthritis.

DOSAGE:

Tablets: 250mg to 2000mg up to four times a day with plenty of fluids.
Suppository: 500mg to 1000mg once or twice a day.

FORMS:

Tablets of 500mg (yellow), enteric coated tablets of 500mg (yellow), suppositories of 500mg, enema, suspension.

PRECAUTIONS:

Safe in pregnancy (A). Use with caution in breast feeding.
Blood and urine tests must be taken regularly during treatment to detect any adverse effects.
Use with caution if suffering from a G6PD deficiency.
Ensure adequate fluids are drunk.

Do not take if:

- suffering from allergy conditions, porphyria, blood cell disorders, gut or urinary obstruction, significant liver or kidney disease, sensitivity to aspirin or sulfonamides.

SIDE EFFECTS:

Common: nausea, vomiting, loss of appetite, fever, red skin, itchy skin, headache.
Unusual: reversible infertility, belly pain, diarrhoea, pins and needles sensation, depression, dizziness, sleeplessness, cough.
Severe but rare (stop medication, consult doctor): fever, bleeding, bruising, jaundice, sore throat. These symptoms may be signs of a severe blood disorder that may rarely occur with sulphasalazine.

INTERACTIONS:

Other drugs:
- interacts with anticoagulants (e.g. warfarin), methotrexate, sulfonylureas (used in diabetes), sulfonamides, penicillin, digoxin
- increased effect of sulfasalazine occurs if taken with indomethacin, phenylbutazone, urinary acidifiers or salicylates.

Other substances:
- iron.

PRESCRIPTION:

Yes.

PERMITTED IN SPORT:

Yes.

OVERDOSE:

Diarrhoea, bloody urine and kidney damage may occur. Seek urgent medical attention.

OTHER INFORMATION:

Used for many years to successfully control intestinal inflammation. Found serendipitously to also control some forms of rheumatoid arthritis.

See also SULPHONAMIDES.

Sulphathiazole

See Sulphabenzamide, Sulphacetamide, Sulphathiazole.

Sulphinpyrazone

TRADE NAME:

Anturan.

DRUG CLASS:

Uricosuric.

USES:

Prevention of gout.

DOSAGE:

 One or two tablets two to four times a day with food or milk.

FORMS:

Tablet (yellow) of 100 and 200mg.

PRECAUTIONS:

Use with caution in pregnancy (B2) and breast feeding. Not for use in children. Use with caution in kidney stones, porphyria, kidney disease, heart failure, asthma.
Regular blood tests to check blood cells recommended.
Ensure adequate fluids are swallowed.

Do not take if:

 • suffering from acute gout, peptic ulcer, severe liver or kidney disease, hay fever, skin allergies.

SIDE EFFECTS:

Common: nausea, diarrhoea.
Unusual: vomiting, stomach ulcer, rash.
Severe but rare (stop medication, consult doctor): yellow skin (jaundice).

INTERACTIONS:

Other drugs:
- diuretics, urinary alkalinisers, anticoagulants, aspirin, penicillins, sulphonamides, sulphonylureas, theophylline, phenytoin.

Other substances:
- alcohol may aggravate gout.

PRESCRIPTION:

Yes.

PERMITTED IN SPORT:

Yes.

OVERDOSE:

Serious. May cause vomiting, diarrhoea, belly pains, irregular heart beat, low blood pressure, difficulty in breathing, convulsions, coma, liver and kidney failure and death. Administer activated charcoal or induce vomiting if medication taken recently and patient alert. Seek urgent medical attention.

OTHER INFORMATION:

Does not cause addiction or dependence. **See also Allopurinol.**

SULPHONAMIDES

DISCUSSION:

Sulphur (sulfur—the American spelling is becoming more widespread in pharmacology) containing antibiotics were the very first antibiotics developed, but the ones available in the late 1930s had severe side effects and were not very effective. Sulphonamides today are not as widely used as other antibiotics but still play a part in the treatment of some types of infections. The most commonly prescribed sulpha preparation is co-trimoxazole, which has a sulpha antibiotic (sulphasalazine) combined with a second type of antibiotic. They should be avoided in patients with liver disease and used with caution in the elderly.

See Silver sulfadiazine, Sulfadoxine, Sulphabenzamide, Sulphacetamide, Sulphamethoxazole, Sulphasalazine, Sulphathiazole.

Sulphur

TRADE NAMES:

Actinac (with chloramphenicol, hydrocortisone, allantoin and other ingredients).
Cocois (with coal tar, salicylic acid, coconut oil).
Meted (with salicylic acid).
Pragmatar, Sebco (with coal tar, salicylic acid).
Also found in many other skin preparations.

USES:

Acne, psoriasis.

DOSAGE:

 Varies. Apply medication as directed on label.

FORMS:

Cream, gel, lotion, ointment, shampoo.

PRECAUTIONS:

Most forms safe in pregnancy and breast feeding.
Use with caution in children.
For external use only, do not swallow.
Avoid eyes, nostrils, mouth, ears, anus, vagina.

Do not use if:

- skin broken, burnt or grazed
- suffering from infected pustular acne or psoriasis.

SIDE EFFECTS:

Common: skin inflammation.

INTERACTIONS:

None.

PRESCRIPTION:

Most forms: no.
Actinac: yes.

PERMITTED IN SPORT:

Yes.

OTHER INFORMATION:

Normally only available in combination with other medications.

Sulpride

TRADE NAMES:

Dolmatil, Sulpitil, Sulpor.

DRUG CLASS:

Antipsychotic.

USES:

Schizophrenia.

DOSAGE:

 Start with 200 to 400mg twice a day, increasing slowly to a maximum of 1200mg twice a day.

FORMS:

Tablets of 200 and 400mg.

PRECAUTIONS:

Use with caution in pregnancy and breast feeding.
Not for use in children under 14 years. Use with caution in epilepsy, kidney disease and hypomania.

Do not take if:

 • suffering from phaeochromocytoma, severe liver or kidney disease, blood cell disorders.

SIDE EFFECTS:

Common: drowsiness, reduced alertness, abnormal body temperature, low blood pressure, dermatitis, dry mouth, constipation, weight gain, blurred vision, stuffy nose.
Unusual: itch, difficulty passing urine, confusion, dizziness, incoordination, tremor, slow breathing, irregular heart beat, skin pigmentation.
Severe but rare (stop medication, consult doctor): yellow skin (jaundice), convulsions, repetitive unwanted movements, muscle rigidity, fever, coma.

INTERACTIONS:

Other drugs:
• adrenaline, tricyclic antidepressants, guanethidine, antacids, barbiturates, phenytoin, lithium, levodopa, sedatives, amphetamines, beta-blockers, hypoglycaemics, MAOI, quinidine, suxamethonium.
Other substances:
• reacts adversely with alcohol and some foods.

PRESCRIPTION:

Yes.

PERMITTED IN SPORT:

Yes.

OVERDOSE:

Very serious. Symptoms include drowsiness, confusion, restlessness, rapid heart rate, tremor, convulsions, difficulty in breathing and swallowing, coma and death. Administer activated charcoal or induce vomiting if taken recently and patient alert. Seek urgent medical attention.

See also ANTIPSYCHOTICS.

Sumatriptan

TRADE NAME:

Imigran.

DRUG CLASS:

Antimigraine.

USES:

Treatment of acute migraine and cluster headache.

DOSAGE:

 Tablets: one tablet immediately symptoms of migraine appear. Repeat if necessary. Maximum of three tablets a day.
Nasal spray: one spray into one nostril at onset of migraine. Repeat after two hours if necessary.
Injection: self inject immediately symptoms of migraine appear. Repeat once in no less than one hour if necessary.

FORMS:

Tablets of 50mg (pink) and 100mg (white), nasal spray, injection (auto-injector kit available).

PRECAUTIONS:

Should not be used in pregnancy (B3) unless medically essential. Should be used with caution in breast feeding. Not for use in children.

Should be used with caution in liver and kidney disease, and in elderly.

Not to be used for prevention of migraine, only treatment of acute attacks.

Must not be injected into a vein.

Do not take if:

- suffering from angina, poor circulation to heart or limbs, recent heart attack, severe high blood pressure, recent stroke, irregular heart beat, significant liver disease
- Ergotamine used in previous 24 hours.

SIDE EFFECTS:

Common: chest pain, pain at injection site, tingling sensation, heat, heaviness, flushing, tightness, dizziness, weakness. Bitter taste with nasal spray.

Unusual: fatigue, drowsiness, nausea, vomiting.

Severe but rare (stop medication, consult doctor): significant chest pain (angina).

INTERACTIONS:

Other drugs:
- ergotamine, MAOI.

Herbs:
- St John's wort.

Other substances:
- does NOT interact with alcohol.

PRESCRIPTION:

Yes.

PERMITTED IN SPORT:

Yes.

OVERDOSE:

Exacerbation of side effects only.

OTHER INFORMATION:

Considered a wonder drug when introduced in the early 1990s, Sumatriptan has given instant relief with minimal side effects to millions of migraine sufferers. Works far more effectively as an injection or nasal spray than if taken as tablets. Patients should use medication to prevent migraines in preference to treating migraines regularly.

See also Ergotamine, Naratriptan, Zolmitriptan.

SYMPATHOMIMETICS (DECONGESTANTS)

DISCUSSION:

Medications that clear blocked nose and sinuses in patients with a cold, flu or hay fever.

See Ephedrine, Isometheptene, Phenylephrine, Pseudoephedrine.

T3, T4

See THYROID HORMONES.

Tacalcitol

TRADE NAME:

Curatoderm.

USES:

Psoriasis plaques.

DOSAGE:

 Apply sparingly to plaques once a day at bedtime.

FORMS:

Ointment.

PRECAUTIONS:

Use with care in pregnancy and breast feeding.
Not for use in children.
Use with caution in kidney disease, pustular and flaking psoriasis.
Do not use for more than 12 months.

Do not take if:

 • suffering from high blood calcium levels.

SIDE EFFECTS:

Common: local skin redness.

INTERACTIONS:

None significant.

PRESCRIPTION:

Yes.

PERMITTED IN SPORT:

Yes.

See also Dithranol, Tar.

Tacrolimus

TRADE NAME:

Prograf, Protopic.

DRUG CLASS:

Immunosupressant.

USES:

Prevention of rejection of kidney and liver transplants.
Resistant forms of atopic dermatitis.

DOSAGE:

 Capsules complex: must be determined individually for each patient by doctor.
Ointment: apply twice daily, reducing strength of ointment after three weeks.

FORMS:

Capsules of 0.5mg (yellow), 1mg (white) and 5mg (grey/red), injection, ointment.

PRECAUTIONS:

Not to be used in pregnancy (C) except under exceptional circumstances. Use with caution in breast feeding and children.
Use with caution with liver diseases and erythroderma.
Avoid bright sunlight while using ointment.
Do not use ointment on infected skin, or near eyes, nose or lips.
Careful monitoring of dosage and blood cells and body chemistry essential.

Do not take if:

• suffering from sensitivity to macrolide antibiotics.

SIDE EFFECTS:

Common: capsules—tremor, headache, pins and needles sensation, nausea, diarrhoea.

Ointment—burning, itching, redness.
Unusual: capsules—high blood pressure, excess sugar in blood, excess calcium in blood, skin rashes, wheeze.
Ointment—skin infections, acne.
Severe but rare (stop medication, consult doctor): heart damage, diabetes, kidney and liver damage.

INTERACTIONS:

Other drugs:
• cyclosporin (serious interaction), aminoglycosides, NSAIDs, vancomycin, amphotericin B, co-trimoxazole, aciclovir, ganciclovir, potassium supplements, amiloride, some vaccines, oral contraceptives.
Other substances:
• grapefruit juice, alcohol.

PRESCRIPTION:

Yes.

PERMITTED IN SPORT:

Yes.

OVERDOSE:

Likely to be very serious. Induce vomiting or give activated charcoal if swallowed recently. Seek urgent medical attention.

Tadalafil

TRADE NAME:

Cialis

USES:

Impotence and erectile dysfunction in men.

DOSAGE:

 10mg or 20mg once a day. The lower dose is usually reserved for the elderly and those with and those with kidney disease.

FORMS:

Tablets of 10mg and 20mg (yellow).

PRECAUTIONS:

Not for use in women or children.
Use with caution in liver and kidney disease, and low blood pressure.

Do not take if:

 • suffering from severe heart disease (e.g. unstable angina, congestive heart failure)
• using nitrate medications (e.g. glyceryl trinitrate for angina)

SIDE EFFECTS:

Common: headache, indigestion.
Unusual: muscle aches, flushing.
Severe but rare (stop medication, consult doctor): chest pain.

INTERACTIONS:

Other drugs:
• never use with glyceryl nitrate or other nitrate medications
• erythromycin, ritonavir, saquinavir, clarithromycin, itraconazole, rifampicin, phenobarb, phenytoin, angiotensin II receptor blockers (used for high blood pressure), warfarin.

PRESCRIPTION:

Yes (very restricted access on NHS).

PERMITTED IN SPORT:

Yes.

OVERDOSE:

Exacerbation of side effects likely.

OTHER INFORMATION:

Released in 2003 as a competitor to sildenafil (Viagra). Initial information indicates that it works faster, lasts longer, and has fewer side effects than its famous competitor.
See also Alprostadil, Sildenafil, Vardenafil.

Tamoxifen

TRADE NAMES:

Nolvadex, Soltamox.

USES:

Breast cancer, infertility.

DOSAGE:

 10 to 20mg once a day.

FORMS:

Tablets.

PRECAUTIONS:

Must not be used in pregnancy (D) unless mother's life is at risk as damage to foetus probable. Breast feeding must be ceased before use. Not for use in children. Adequate contraception must be used by all fertile women during use of tamoxifen. Use with caution in bleeding disorders and blood cell abnormalities.
Regular gynaecological checks essential.

SIDE EFFECTS:

Common: hot flushes, abnormal vaginal bleeding, itchy vulva, fluid retention, light headedness, nausea, vomiting, diarrhoea.
Unusual: vaginal discharge, headache, blood clots (thrombosis), bone pain, vision changes.
Severe but rare (stop medication, consult doctor): damage to uterus and ovary, blood cell changes.

INTERACTIONS:

Other drugs:
• Anticoagulants (e.g. warfarin).
Herbs:
• dong quai.

PRESCRIPTION:

Yes.

PERMITTED IN SPORT:

Yes.

OVERDOSE:

Exacerbation of side effects likely.

OTHER INFORMATION:

This medication has saved the lives of thousands of women with breast cancer and has prevented recurrences in thousands more. Very useful and effective. Introduced in late 1980s.
See also Letrozole, Toremifene.

Tamsulosin

TRADE NAME:

Flomax.

DRUG CLASS:

Alpha one adrenergic blocker (alpha blocker).

USES:

Reduces size of enlarged prostate gland.

DOSAGE:

 One capsule a day, half hour before breakfast.

FORMS:

Capsule of 400µg (orange/brown).

PRECAUTIONS:

To be used only in males. If unintentionally taken during pregnancy (B2) or breast feeding, unlikely to be harmful.
Not for use in children.
Prostate cancer must be excluded before use.
Use with caution if heart attack within six previous months.
Do not take if:
 • suffering from low blood pressure, severe liver or kidney disease.

SIDE EFFECTS:

Common: palpitations, dizziness, low blood pressure, inability to ejaculate during sexual intercourse.
Unusual: itch, urinary tract infection, sleeplessness, diarrhoea.

Severe but rare (stop medication, consult doctor): sudden drop in blood pressure with changes in position resulting in falls.

INTERACTIONS:

Other drugs:
• other alpha blockers, cimetidine, diclofenac, warfarin, frusemide.

PRESCRIPTION:

Yes.

PERMITTED IN SPORT:

Yes.

OVERDOSE:

Severe low blood pressure may occur. Give activated charcoal and seek medical attention.

OTHER INFORMATION:

Introduced in 2000 as a more specifically targeted drug against the prostate gland. Other alpha blockers lower blood pressure as well as shrinking the prostate.

See also **ALPHA BLOCKERS.**

Tar
(Coal Tar)

TRADE NAMES:

Alphosyl (Coal tar with allantoin).
Alphosyl HC (Coal tar with hydrocortisone).
Capasal (Coal tar with salicylic acid and other ingredients).
Carbo-Dome, Clinitar, Exorex, Pentrax, Psoriderm, T Gel (Coal tar).
Cocois, Pragmatar, Sebco (Coal tar with sulphur, salicylic acid and other ingredients).
Polytar (Tar with other ingredients).
Psorin (Coal tar with dithranol, salicylic acid).
Also found in numerous other skin preparations and soaps.

USES:

Itchy skin, itchy anus, prickly heat, mild dermatitis, psoriasis, dandruff, skin ulcers.

DOSAGE:

 Apply several times a day, or add to bath water.

FORMS:

Lotion, cream, ointment, solution, bar, shampoo, bandage.

PRECAUTIONS:

Safe to use in pregnancy, breast feeding and children.

SIDE EFFECTS:

Common: minimal.
Unusual: skin irritation.

INTERACTIONS:

None significant.

PRESCRIPTION:

No, unless combined with a medication requiring a prescription (e.g. hydrocortisone).

PERMITTED IN SPORT:

Yes.

OTHER INFORMATION:

The original dermatitis treatment, in use for thousands of years.

Tazarotene

TRADE NAME:

Zorac.

DRUG CLASS:

Retinoid.

USES:

Psoriasis with plaques.

DOSAGE:

 Apply sparingly to plaques once a day in evening.

FORMS:

Gel.

PRECAUTIONS:

Never to be used in pregnancy (X), breast feeding and children.
Ensure adequate contraception during use.
Do not use for more than three months.
Avoid skin folds, face, scalp, eyes, genitals and inflamed skin.
Do not apply to normal skin.
Avoid excess exposure to sunlight of treated areas.

SIDE EFFECTS:

Common: skin itching, redness, burning and irritation.
Unusual: skin pealing, rash, skin pain.
Severe but rare (stop medication, consult doctor): blistering of skin.

INTERACTIONS:

Other substances:
• moisturisers, cosmetics.

PRESCRIPTION:

Yes.

PERMITTED IN SPORT:

Yes.
See also Calcipotriol, Dithranol.

Tazobactam

TRADE NAME:

Tazocin (with piperacillin).

DRUG CLASS:

Antibiotic.

USES:

Severe bacterial infections in hospital.

DOSAGE:

 4.5 grams every eight hours by injection into muscle or slow infusion by a drip into a vein.

FORMS:

Injection.

PRECAUTIONS:

May be used with care in pregnancy (B1), breast feeding and children.
Use with caution in syphilis, kidney and liver disease.
Not for prolonged use.
Blood tests to check electrolyte balance, blood cells, kidney and liver function necessary.

SIDE EFFECTS:

Common: nausea, diarrhoea, rash, vein inflammation.
Unusual: vomiting, blood clots.
Severe but rare (stop medication, consult doctor): bloody diarrhoea, other abnormal bleeding.

INTERACTIONS:

Other drugs:
• heparin, anticoagulants (e.g. warfarin), aminoglycoside antibiotics, methotrexate.

PRESCRIPTION:

Yes.

PERMITTED IN SPORT:

Yes.
See also Piperacillin.

TB vaccine

See BCG Vaccine.

Tegafur and Uracil

TRADE NAME:

Uftoral (only available as combination of the two medications).

DRUG CLASS:

Antineoplastic.

USES:

Metastatic colon cancer.

DOSAGE:

 Complex cycles of treatment. Follow doctors instructions carefully. Normally used in combination with other antineoplastics (e.g. calcium folinate).

FORMS:

Capsule (white).

PRECAUTIONS:

Not to be used in pregnancy, breast feeding and children.
Contraception essential for three months after treatment course completed.
Use with care in elderly, kidney disease, bowel obstruction and heart disease.
Regular blood tests to monitor liver function necessary.

Do not take if:

 • suffering from severe liver disease, bone marrow disease.

SIDE EFFECTS:

Common: nausea, diarrhoea, belly pain, anaemia, low white cell count, bleeding disorders, sore mouth, tiredness.
Unusual: fever, headache, dehydration, muscle pains, fungal infections, weight loss, dry mouth, loss of taste, watery eyes, red eyes, swelling of hands and feet, shortness of breath, hair loss, cough, sore throat, rashes, sweating, nail damage, back pain, joint pain.
Severe but rare (stop medication, consult doctor): blood clot in veins, jaundice (yellow skin from liver damage).

INTERACTIONS:

Other drugs:
• anticoagulants (e.g. warfarin), other antineoplastics, other drugs that affect liver function.

PRESCRIPTION:

Yes.

PERMITTED IN SPORT:

Yes.

OVERDOSE:

Very serious. Seek urgent medical attention.

OTHER INFORMATION:

Introduced in 2001 as a first line treatment for metastatic large bowel cancer.

See also ANTINEOPLASTICS.

Teicoplanin

TRADE NAME:

Targocid.

DRUG CLASS:

Antibiotic.

USES:

Osteomyelitis (bone infection), septic arthritis (joint infection), septicaemia (blood infection).

DOSAGE:

 Intravenous infusion as determined by doctor.

FORMS:

Injection.

PRECAUTIONS:

May be used with caution in pregnancy (B3), breast feeding and children.
Use with caution in kidney disease and elderly.
Blood tests to check liver, kidney and blood cell function necessary.
Not for prolonged use.

SIDE EFFECTS:

Common: nausea, diarrhoea.
Unusual: vomiting.
Severe but rare (stop medication, consult doctor): liver and kidney damage, hearing or balance changes.

INTERACTIONS:

Other drugs:
- aminoglycosides, amphotericin, cyclosporin, frusemide.

PRESCRIPTION:

Yes.

PERMITTED IN SPORT:

Yes.

Telithromycin

TRADE NAME:

Ketek.

DRUG CLASS:

Antibiotic.

USES:

Treatment of bacterial bronchitis, pneumonia, sinusitis, tonsillitis, throat infections and other infections caused by the bacteria *Streptococcus*.

DOSAGE:

 800mg once a day.

FORMS:

Tablets (orange) of 400mg.

PRECAUTIONS:

May be used with caution in pregnancy. Not for use in breast feeding or children. Use with caution in liver and kidney disease, heart disease, slow heart rate and low potassium levels in blood.

Do not take if:

 • suffering from pseudomembranous colitis, heart electrical conductivity problems.

SIDE EFFECTS:

Common: nausea, diarrhoea.
Unusual: liver stress, headache, dizziness, taste disturbances.

Severe but rare (stop medication, consult doctor): jaundice (yellow skin from liver damage).

INTERACTIONS:

Other drugs:
- terfenadine, cisapride, pimozide, astemizole, simvastatin, atorvastatin, lovastatin, digoxin, warfarin, theophylline.

Herbs:
- ergot.

PRESCRIPTION:

Yes.

PERMITTED IN SPORT:

Yes.

OTHER INFORMATION:

Introduced in 2002 as a second line antibiotic for use when other antibiotics inappropriate or ineffective.

Telmisartan

See ANGIOTENSIN II RECEPTOR ANTAGONISTS.

Temozolomide

TRADE NAME:

Temodal.

DRUG CLASS:

Cytotoxic.

USES:

Brain cancers (glioma, astrocytoma).

DOSAGE:

 Complex. As determined for each patient by doctor.

FORMS:

Capsules (white) of 5, 20, 100 and 250mg.

PRECAUTIONS:

Not to be used in pregnancy (D) and breast feeding.
Use with caution in children.
Partners of males using medication must not fall pregnant.
Use with caution in liver and kidney disease.
Regular blood tests essential.
Use lower dose in elderly.

Do not take if:

 • suffering from immunosuppression (e.g. AIDS).

SIDE EFFECTS:

Common: nausea, diarrhoea, headache, tiredness.
Unusual: vomiting, infertility.

INTERACTIONS:

Other drugs:
• other cancer treating drugs.
Other substances:
• alcohol.

PRESCRIPTION:

Yes.

PERMITTED IN SPORT:

Yes.

OVERDOSE:

Likely to cause serious organ damage. Seek urgent medical attention. Induce vomiting or give activated charcoal if swallowed recently.

OTHER INFORMATION:

Introduced in 1998 for treatment of more resistant forms of brain cancer.

Tenofovir

TRADE NAME:

Viread.

DRUG CLASS:

Antiviral.

USES:

HIV (AIDS).

DOSAGE:

 One tablet a day with food.

FORMS:

Tablets of 245mg (light blue).

PRECAUTIONS:

Use with caution in pregnancy (B3). Not for use in breast feeding and children under 18 years.
Use with caution in kidney disease and if used long term.
Always used in combination with other medications to treat HIV.
Regular blood tests recommended to assess kidney, liver and blood cell function.

Do not take if:

 • suffering from kidney failure.

SIDE EFFECTS:

Common: nausea, diarrhoea, tiredness.
Unusual: vomiting, dizziness, shortness of breath, rash.
Severe but rare (stop medication, consult doctor): kidney damage, bone damage, pancreatitis (severe belly pain).

INTERACTIONS:

Other drugs:
• didanosine.

PRESCRIPTION:

Yes.

PERMITTED IN SPORT:

Yes.

See also Nelfinavir, Nevirapine, Stavudine.

Tenoxicam

TRADE NAME:

Mobiflex.

DRUG CLASS:

NSAID (Nonsteroidal anti-inflammatory drug).

USES:

All forms of arthritis, inflammatory disorders, gout, back pain.

DOSAGE:

 One tablet a day with food.

FORMS:

Tablets (brown) of 20mg.

PRECAUTIONS:

Should not be used in pregnancy (C) unless medically essential. Breast feeding should be ceased if necessary to use NSAID. Not for use in children under two.

Use tablets and capsules with caution in psychiatricaly disturbed patients, epilepsy, severe infection, heart failure and kidney disease.

Lower doses required in elderly, who may suffer more side effects.

Do not take if:

* suffering from peptic ulcer at present or in recent past
* due for surgery (including dental surgery)
* suffering from bleeding disorder or anaemia.

SIDE EFFECTS:

Common: stomach discomfort, diarrhoea, constipation, heartburn, nausea, headache, dizziness.

Unusual: blurred vision, stomach ulcer, ringing noise in ears, retention of fluid, swelling of tissue, drowsiness, itch, rash, shortness of breath.

Severe but rare (stop medication, consult doctor): vomiting blood, passing blood in faeces, other unusual bleeding, asthma induced by medication.

INTERACTIONS:

Other drugs:
* must never be used with anticoagulants (e.g. warfarin)
* Probenecid, diuretics, lithium, methotrexate, beta-blockers, ACE inhibitors.

PRESCRIPTION:

Yes.

PERMITTED IN SPORT:

Yes.

OVERDOSE:

Causes nausea, vomiting, severe headache, dizziness, confusion and convulsions. Administer activated charcoal or induce vomiting if taken recently. Seek medical assistance.

OTHER INFORMATION:

Significant side effects (particularly on the stomach) in about 5% of patients. Limit their use.

See also Celecoxib, Diclofenac, Ibuprofen, Indomethacin, Ketoprofen, Naproxen, NSAID, Piroxicam, Rofecoxib, Sulindac.

Terazosin

TRADE NAME:

Hytrin.

USES:

Benign enlargement of prostate gland, high blood pressure.

DOSAGE:

 Slowly increasing dosage for three weeks to a maintenance level of 5mg to 10mg once a day in the morning.

FORMS:

Tablets of 1mg (white), 2mg (yellow), 5mg (brown), and 10mg (blue).

PRECAUTIONS:

Should be used with caution in pregnancy (B2), breast feeding.
Not recommended for children.
Use with caution if history of fainting.
Beware of sudden drop in blood pressure with first dose.

SIDE EFFECTS:

Common: dizziness, light headedness, palpitations, blurred vision, tiredness.
Unusual: low blood pressure, nasal congestion, faint, swelling of ankles, feet and hands.

INTERACTIONS:

Other drugs:
• other antihypertensives, diuretics, beta-blockers, NSAIDs.

PRESCRIPTION:

Yes.

PERMITTED IN SPORT:

Yes.

OVERDOSE:

Severe low blood pressure could result.

OTHER INFORMATION:

Does not cause addiction or dependence.
Introduced in 1994.
See also Finasteride, Tamsulosin.

Terbinafine

TRADE NAME:

Lamisil.

DRUG CLASS:

Antifungal.

USES:

Fungal infections of skin (ringworm) and nails.

DOSAGE:

 Tablets: one tablet a day for several weeks.
Cream: apply once or twice a day to dry skin.

FORMS:

Tablet (white) of 250mg, cream.

PRECAUTIONS:

Use with caution in pregnancy (B1), breast feeding and children.
Use with caution in liver and kidney disease.
Avoid eye contact with cream.
Do not take if:
• suffering from severe liver disease.

SIDE EFFECTS:

Common: cream—redness, itching, stinging.
Tablets—nausea, diarrhoea, rash, itch, headache, dizziness.
Unusual: vomiting, red skin, tiredness, chest pain, light headedness.

INTERACTIONS:

Other drugs:
• tablets—oral contraceptives, cimetidine, rifampicin, tricyclic antidepressants, beta-blockers, SSRI antidepressants, MAOI.
Other substances:
• tablets react with alcohol.

PRESCRIPTION:

Yes.

PERMITTED IN SPORT:

Yes.

OVERDOSE:

Unlikely to have serious effects. Seek medical advice.

OTHER INFORMATION:

Introduced in 1993. Very effective and safe, but quite expensive.
See also Amphotericin, Fluconazole, Griseofulvin, Itraconazole, Ketoconazole.

Terbutaline

TRADE NAME:

Bricanyl.

DRUG CLASS:

Bronchodilators (Beta-2 agonist).

USES:

Asthma, bronchitis, spasm of airways in lung.

DOSAGE:

 Inhalers and sprays: one or two inhalations every four to six hours. Tablets: half to one tablet three times a day.
Sustained action tablets (SA): one tablet twice a day.
Mixture: 10 to 15mLs three times a day.

FORMS:

Spray, inhaler, nebuliser solution, tablets, sustained action tablets (SA), mixture, injection.

PRECAUTIONS:

Safe to use in pregnancy (A), breast feeding and children.
Not designed for long term constant use.
Use with care in high blood pressure, heart disease, overactive thyroid gland, diabetes, liver and kidney disease.
Lower doses necessary in elderly and children.
Seek urgent medical assistance if no response to medication.

SIDE EFFECTS:

Common: tremor, rapid heart rate, palpitations, headache.
Unusual: nausea, diarrhoea, flush, mouth irritation.
Severe but rare (stop medication, consult doctor): irregular heart rhythm. low blood pressure.

INTERACTIONS:

Other drugs:
• sympathomimetics, beta-blockers, theophyllines, steroids, diuretics, digoxin.
Other substances:
• mixture may react with alcohol and caffeine.

PRESCRIPTION:

Yes.

PERMITTED IN SPORT:

Yes.

OVERDOSE:

Exacerbation of side effects likely. May be dangerous in patients with heart disease or high blood pressure.

OTHER INFORMATION:

Designed for intermittent occasional use, and not to be taken regularly. Other medication should be used to prevent asthma if repeated doses of this medication are needed. Does not cause dependence or addiction. First introduced in the 1960s, beta-agonists have revolutionised life for asthmatics.

See also Fenoterol, Salbutamol, Salmeterol.

Testosterone

TRADE NAMES:

Andropatch, Restandol, Sustanon, Testogel, Viromone.

DRUG CLASS:

Sex hormone.

USES:

Testosterone deficiency in males, male infertility, male osteoporosis, Klinefelter's syndrome.
In combination with oestrogen used for menopause and after removal of ovaries in women.
Breast cancer in women.
Low libido in women (experimental).

DOSAGE:

 Capsules: one to three capsules a day after food.
Patch: apply one at night. Replace every 24 hours.
Gel: apply one or two sachets of gel as thin layer without rubbing once a day to clean soft skin on abdomen.

FORMS:

Patches of 2.5, 5 and 6mg, capsules of 40mg (brown), gel in sachet, injection.

PRECAUTIONS:

Not to be used in pregnancy (D), breast feeding or children.
Not to be used in women except in combination with Oestrogen.
Use with caution in heart disease, kidney disease, high blood pressure.

Do not take if:

 • suffering from prostate cancer, breast cancer
• before puberty.

SIDE EFFECTS:

Common: unwanted penile erections, retention of fluid, nausea, oily faeces.

INTERACTIONS:

Other drugs:
• cyclosporin, hypoglycaemics (treat diabetes).

PRESCRIPTION:

Yes.

PERMITTED IN SPORT:

No.

OVERDOSE:

No specific problems short term. Long term inappropriate use may cause infertility, shrinking of testes, increased muscle bulk, high blood pressure, heart failure and increased risk of heart attack.

OTHER INFORMATION:

Does not cause addiction or dependence. Sometimes used illegally and inappropriately by athletes and body builders with potentially serious consequences.
See also SEX HORMONES.

Tetanus vaccine

TRADE NAMES:

Clostet.
Tetabulin (Tetanus antitoxin).
ACT-HIB DTP, Infanrix-HIB (with Haemophilus influenzae B, diphtheria and whooping cough vaccines).
Diftavax (with diphtheria vaccine).
Infanrix (with diphtheria and whooping cough vaccines).

DRUG CLASS:

Vaccine.

USES:

Prevention of tetanus.

DOSAGE:

 Injections at two, four and six months, four years and then every ten years throughout life.

FORMS:

Injection.

PRECAUTIONS:

Safe for use in pregnancy (A), breast feeding, children and infants.

Do not take if:

 • suffering from significant chest, throat, ear, nose or sinus infection
• having treatment for some types of cancer and leukaemia.

SIDE EFFECTS:

Common: redness, swelling, soreness and lump at injection site.
Unusual: fever, tiredness, allergic reaction.

INTERACTIONS:

Other drugs:
• chloramphenicol.

PRESCRIPTION:

Yes.

PERMITTED IN SPORT:

Yes.

OVERDOSE:

An unintentional additional vaccination is unlikely to have any significant adverse effect.

OTHER INFORMATION:

Tetanus is a world wide disease that is caught from spores in the soil entering a wound. This disease kills about half its victims, but it can be completely prevented by vaccination.

See also Diphtheria vaccine, Whooping cough vaccine.

Tetrabenazine

TRADE NAME:

Xenazine.

USES:

Chorea, muscle movement disorders.

DOSAGE:

 One to four tablets twice a day.

FORMS:

Tablets of 25mg (yellow).

PRECAUTIONS:

Should be used with considerable caution in pregnancy (B2). Breast feeding should be ceased if prescribed.

Do not take if:

 • suffering from Parkinsonism, depression.

SIDE EFFECTS:

Common: drowsiness, muscle stiffness, tremor, depression, difficulty swallowing.
Unusual: agitation, sleeplessness, confusion, fainting, tiredness.

INTERACTIONS:

Other drugs:
• severe interaction with levodopa, reserpine and MAOI
• blood pressure medication, stimulants, tricyclic antidepressants.
Other substances:
• reacts very adversely with alcohol.

PRESCRIPTION:

Yes.

PERMITTED IN SPORT:

Yes.

OVERDOSE:

May cause drowsiness, sweating and semi-comatose state. Administer activated charcoal or induce vomiting if medication taken recently and patient alert. Seek medical assistance.

OTHER INFORMATION:

Not addictive or dependence forming. Useful in a number of rare diseases affecting muscle action.

Tetrocosactrin

TRADE NAME:

Synacthen depot.

DRUG CLASS:

Trophic hormone.

USES:

Multiple sclerosis, some rare movement disorders.

DOSAGE:

 Initially injection twice a day, reducing to once or twice a week.

FORMS:

Injection.

PRECAUTIONS:

Not for use in pregnancy (D) and children under one year.

Use with caution in breast feeding, ulcerative colitis, diverticulitis, kidney disease, blood clots, osteoporosis, myasthenia gravis, underactive thyroid gland, liver disease (e.g. cirrhosis), recent surgery, and unstable mental state.
Do not stop suddenly but reduce dose slowly.

Do not take if:

- suffering from significant viral or bacterial infection, asthma, serious allergy, diabetes, untreated high blood pressure, severe psychiatric disturbance, peptic ulcer, Cushing syndrome, uncontrolled heart failure, or adrenogenital syndrome
- after recent live vaccination (e.g. polio).

SIDE EFFECTS:

Common: fluid retention, muscle pains, joint pains, nausea, rash.
Unusual: allergy reaction, vomiting, diarrhoea.
Severe but rare (stop medication, consult doctor): psychological or mental disturbance, severe allergy, vision changes.

INTERACTIONS:

Other drugs:
- hypoglycaemics (treat diabetes), antihypertensives (treat high blood pressure).

PRESCRIPTION:

Yes.

PERMITTED IN SPORT:

No.

TETRACYCLIC ANTIDEPRESSANT

See Maprotiline.

Tetracycline

TRADE NAMES:

Deteclo (tetracycline hydrochloride, chlortetracycline and demeclocycline).
Topicycline (tetracycline hydrochloride).

DRUG CLASS:

Antibiotic.

USES:

Ear, nose, throat, eye, lung, urinary, gut and skin (e.g. acne) infections.

DOSAGE:

Tablets: one every 12 hours, two hours after meals.
Solution: apply twice a day.

FORMS:

Tablets, solution.

PRECAUTIONS:

Not to be used in pregnancy (D) or children under eight years as tetracyclines may cause permanent staining of teeth of foetus or child. Use with caution in breast feeding. Eye ointment safe to use in pregnancy, breast feeding and children. Use capsules with caution in kidney disease. Never use expired medication as it may become toxic.

Do not take capsules if:

- suffering from severe kidney disease, systemic lupus erythematosus (SLE), Staphylococcal infection.

SIDE EFFECTS:

Common: capsules—loss of appetite, nausea, sore mouth, diarrhoea, difficulty in swallowing, inflamed colon.
Solution—stinging, burning sensation, sun sensitivity.
Unusual: capsules—vomiting, inflamed pancreas, rash, secondary fungal infection (thrush), sun sensitivity.
Severe but rare (stop medication, consult doctor): severe belly pain, severe diarrhoea, tooth discolouration, significant skin rash.

INTERACTIONS:

Other drugs:
• anticoagulants (e.g. warfarin), penicillin, antacids, iron, oral contraceptives.
Herbs:
• dong quai, St John's wort.
Other substances:
• milk may reduce absorption from gut.

PRESCRIPTION:

Yes.

PERMITTED IN SPORT:

Yes.

OVERDOSE:

Exacerbation of side effects only likely effect.

OTHER INFORMATION:

Used for a wide range of infections. Tetracycline has been superseded by more sophisticated antibiotics in the same group (e.g. doxycycline, minocycline) in the last decade.

See also Chlortetracycline, Demeclocycline, Doxycycline, Methacycline, Minocycline, Oxytetracycline.

Theophylline

TRADE NAMES:

**Nuelin, Slo-Phyllin, Uniphyllin.
Franol** (with ephedrine).

DRUG CLASS:

Bronchodilator.

USES:

Asthma, emphysema, chronic bronchitis.

DOSAGE:

Liquid: 10mLs to 20mLs four times a day.
Tablets: one every six hours.
Sustained release capsules: one twice a day.

FORMS:

Tablets, sustained release tablets, capsules, liquid.

PRECAUTIONS:

Safe to use in pregnancy (A), breast feeding and children. Use with caution in infants.
Use with caution in acute asthma.
Use with caution in heart disease, stomach ulcers, heartburn, kidney disease and liver disease.
Lower doses necessary in elderly and lighter patients.
Higher doses may be necessary in smokers.
Blood tests to monitor blood level of theophylline may be necessary.

SIDE EFFECTS:

Common: nausea, vomiting, belly discomfort, rapid heart rate, tremor, palpitations.
Unusual: irregular heart rate, convulsions, angina.

INTERACTIONS:

Other drugs:
• cimetidine, allopurinol, propranolol, quinolone antibiotics, oral contraceptives, erythromycin, phenobarbitone, phenytoin, carbamazepine, rifampicin.
Herbs:
• St John's wort, piperine (Ayurvedic piper nigrum).
Other substances:
• reacts with alcohol, caffeine and nicotine
• marijuana.

PRESCRIPTION:

No.

PERMITTED IN SPORT:

Yes.

OVERDOSE:

Serious. May cause vomiting, headache, irritability, rapid heart rate, confusion, fever, delirium and convulsions. Seek urgent medical assistance.

OTHER INFORMATION:

An old fashioned treatment for asthma that is still very useful. Dose must be finely adjusted to give adequate clinical response while avoiding side effects.
See also Terbutaline.

Thiamine
(Vitamin B1)

TRADE NAME:

Benerva.
A large number of other preparations include thiamine (Vitamin B1) alone or in combination with other vitamins and minerals.

DRUG CLASS:

Vitamin.

USES:

Vitamin B deficiency from fad diets, starvation and over cooked foods.
Beriberi.

DOSAGE:

One tablet a day.
Recommended daily allowance:
Females: 0.8mg; Males: 1.1mg.

FORMS:

Tablets of 50mg.

PRECAUTIONS:

Safe in pregnancy, breast feeding and children.

SIDE EFFECTS:

Minimal.

INTERACTIONS:

Other drugs:
• diuretics, some laxatives.

PRESCRIPTION:

No.

PERMITTED IN SPORT:

Yes.

OVERDOSE:

No serious effects.

OTHER INFORMATION:

Thiamine is a water soluble vitamin found in liver, kidney, pork and whole grain. It is essential for the normal metabolism of carbohydrate foods. The symptoms of vitamin B deficiency include loss of appetite, muscle cramps, pins and needles sensation and ankle swelling. Remember, vitamins are merely chemicals that are essential for the functioning of the body and if taken to excess, act as a drug.
See also VITAMINS.

THIAZIDE DIURETICS

TRADE and GENERIC NAMES:

Accuretic (Hydrochlorothiazide with quinapril).
Acezide, Capozide (Hydrochlorothiazide with captopril).
Aldactide (Hydroflumethiazide with spironolactone).
Amil-Co, Moducren, Moduret, Moduretic (Hydrochlorothiazide with amiloride).
Aprinox, Neo-Naclex (Bendrofluazide).
Carace Plus, Zestoretic (Hydrochlorothiazide with lisinopril).
Centyl K, Neo-Naclex K (Bendrofluazide with potassium chloride).
CoApprovel (Hydrochlorothiazide with irbesartan).
Co-Betaloc (Hydrochlorothiazide with metoprolol).
Corgaretic (Bendrofluazide, nadolol).
Cozaar-Comp (Hydrochlorothiazide with losartan).
Diurexan (Xipamide: thiazide analogue diuretic).
Dyazide, Triam-Co (Hydrochlorothiazide with triamterene).
Dytide (Benzthiazide, triamterene).
Hygroton (Chlorthalidone: thiazide analogue diuretic).

Inderetic, Inderex (<u>Bendrofluazide</u> with propranolol).
Innozide (<u>Hydrochlorothiazide</u> with enalapril).
Kalspare (<u>Chlorthalidone</u> with triamterene).
Kalten (<u>Hydrochlorothiazide</u> with atenolol).
Metenix (Metolazone: thiazide analogue diuretic)
Micardis Plus (<u>Hydrochlorothiazide</u> with telmisartan).
Navidrex (<u>Cyclopenthiazide</u>).
Navispare (<u>Cyclopenthiazide</u> with amiloride).
Prestim, Tenben (<u>Bendrofluazide</u> with timolol).
Secadrex (<u>Hydrochlorothiazide</u> with acebutolol).
Tenoret, Tenoretic (<u>Chlorthalidone</u> with atenolol).
Trasidrex (<u>Cyclopenthiazide</u> with oxprenolol).
Viskaldix (<u>Clopamide</u> with pindolol).
NB: thiazides are underlined. Analogues are drugs that act like another drug.

DRUG CLASS:

Diuretic (increases urine production).

USES:

High blood pressure, tissue swelling, excess fluid states, heart failure.

DOSAGE:

 One or two tablets in morning.

FORMS:

Tablets.

PRECAUTIONS:

Should not be used in pregnancy (C) unless medically essential. May reduce volume of milk in breast feeding and are sometimes used for this purpose in women who wish to stop breast feeding. Use with caution in children.
Use with caution in kidney disease, liver disease, diabetes, SLE and asthma.

Do not take if:

 • suffering from complete kidney failure, gout.

SIDE EFFECTS:

Common: increased urinary frequency.
Unusual: nausea, vomiting, gut cramps, diarrhoea, dizziness, headache, rash.
Severe but rare (stop medication, consult doctor): unusual bleeding, fainting.

INTERACTIONS:

Other drugs:
• lithium, barbiturates, digoxin, insulin, steroids, NSAIDs
• tablets for controlling maturity onset diabetes
• beneficial interaction with most medications that lower blood pressure.
Herbs:
• guarana, liquorice, celery, dandelion, uva ursi.
Other substances:
• reacts with alcohol.

PRESCRIPTION:

Yes.

PERMITTED IN SPORT:

No.

OVERDOSE:

Confusion, dizziness and gut spasms due to chemical (electrolyte) imbalances occur. Administer activated charcoal or induce vomiting if tablets taken recently. Give extra fluids. Seek medical assistance.

OTHER INFORMATION:

Widely used for fluid problems for over forty years. Combined in low doses with many blood pressure medications to improve their effect.

See also Amiloride, Bumetanide, Diazoxide, Frusemide, Spironolactone, Triamterene.

Thioguanine

TRADE NAME:

Lanvis.

USES:

Leukaemia.

DOSAGE:

 Must be individually determined by doctor for each patient depending on severity of disease, age and weight of patient.

FORMS:

Tablets (yellow) of 40mg.

PRECAUTIONS:

Must not be used in pregnancy (D) unless mother's life is at risk as damage to foetus may occur. Breast feeding must be ceased before use. May be used in children if medically essential.
Use with caution if infection present.
Regular blood tests to check blood cells and liver function essential.

Do not take if:

 • suffering from severe liver or kidney disease, significant viral infection, blood cell damage.

SIDE EFFECTS:

Common: nausea, vomiting, diarrhoea, mouth soreness.
Severe but rare (stop medication, consult doctor): yellow skin (jaundice), unusual bleeding or bruising.

INTERACTIONS:

Other drugs:
• busulfan.

PRESCRIPTION:

Yes.

PERMITTED IN SPORT:

Yes.

OVERDOSE:

Serious. Induce vomiting if medication taken recently. Seek urgent medical assistance.

OTHER INFORMATION:

One of the original medications used to treat leukaemia, but still useful today.
See also VINCA ALKALOIDS.

Thioridazine

See PHENOTHIAZINES.

Thymoxamine

TRADE NAME:

Opilon.

DRUG CLASS:

Alpha blocker.

USES:

Raynaud's phenomenon (spasm of arteries causing poor circulation to fingers and toes).

DOSAGE:

 One or two tablets, four times a day.

FORMS:

Tablets of 40mg (cream).

PRECAUTIONS:

Not for use in pregnancy, breast feeding and children.
Use with caution in diabetes.
Not for long term use.

Do not take if:

 • suffering from active liver disease.

SIDE EFFECTS:

Common: nausea, diarrhoea, dizziness, headache.
Unusual: facial flushing, rash.
Severe but rare (stop medication, consult doctor): liver damage (jaundice, yellow skin).

INTERACTIONS:

Other drugs:
• tricyclic antidepressants, blood pressure medications.

PRESCRIPTION:

Yes.

PERMITTED IN SPORT:

Yes.

OVERDOSE:

Low blood pressure, drowsiness and depressed reflexes only effects.

Thyroxine

TRADE NAMES:

Eltroxin.

USES:

Under active thyroid gland, thyroiditis.

DOSAGE:

 25µg to 200µg a day on an empty stomach.
Start with low initial dose and slowly increase to a dose determined by doctor after regular blood tests.

FORMS:

Tablets (white) of 25µg, 50µg and 100µg.

PRECAUTIONS:

Safe to use in pregnancy (A), breast feeding and children.
Use with caution in heart disease, diabetes insipidus and high blood pressure.
Lower doses necessary in elderly.

Do not take if:

• suffering from angina, over active thyroid gland (hyperthyroidism), recent heart attack.

SIDE EFFECTS:

Only occur with overdosage.

INTERACTIONS:

Other drugs:
• coumarin anticoagulants (e.g. warfarin), barbiturates, narcotics, catecholamines, insulin, tricyclic antidepressants, digoxin, corticosteroids, colestipol, phenytoin.
Herbs:
• horseradish, kelp, myrrh.

PRESCRIPTION:

Yes.

PERMITTED IN SPORT:

Yes.

OVERDOSE:

Serious. May cause rapid heart rate, irregular heart beat, angina, restlessness, anxiety, tremor, headache, diarrhoea, vomiting, rapid breathing, fever, heart attack and death. Administer activated charcoal or induce vomiting if medication taken recently. Seek urgent medical assistance.

OTHER INFORMATION:

Widely used to counter the slowly progressive effects of thyroid underactivity, a problem that is common in middle aged women. Does not cause addiction or dependence, but lifelong treatment usually necessary.
See also Liothyronine.

Tiagabine

TRADE NAME:

Gabitril.

DRUG CLASS:

Anticonvulsant.

USES:

Some types of epilepsy causing partial seizures.

DOSAGE:

 7.5mg to 70mg a day in three divided doses with meals, usually in combination with other anticonvulsants.

FORMS:

Tablets of 5mg, 10mg and 15mg (white).

PRECAUTIONS:

Use with caution in pregnancy (B3) and breast feeding. May be used in children. Start with a very low dose and increase slowly.
Use with caution in elderly.
Do not stop suddenly, but reduce dose slowly.

Do not take if:

 • suffering from severe liver disease.

SIDE EFFECTS:

Common: dizziness, tiredness, nervousness, tremor, diarrhoea.
Unusual: depression, temperamental.
Severe but rare (stop medication, consult doctor): aggravation of epilepsy.

INTERACTIONS:

Other drugs:
• phenytoin, carbamazepine, primidone, phenobarbitone.
Herbs:
• evening primrose (linoleic acid), gingko biloba.
Other substances:
• alcohol, borage.

PRESCRIPTION:

Yes.

PERMITTED IN SPORT:

Yes.

OVERDOSE:

Tiredness, dizziness, incoordination, dazed appearance and coma may occur. Induce vomiting or give activated charcoal if tablets taken recently. Seek medical assistance.

OTHER INFORMATION:

Introduced in 1998 for the management of more difficult and resistant cases of partial epilepsy.

See also Carbamazepine, Clonazepam, Ethosuximide, Gabapentin, Lamotrigine, Levetiracetam, Oxcarbazepine, Phenytoin, Primidone, Sodium valproate, Sulthiame, Topiramate, Vigabatrin.

Tiaprofenic acid

TRADE NAME:

Surgam.

DRUG CLASS:

NSAID (Nonsteroidal anti-inflammatory drug).

USES:

All forms of arthritis, inflammatory disorders, gout, ankylosing spondylitis, muscle inflammation and pain.

DOSAGE:

 Tablets: one tablet twice a day with food.
Capsules: two capsules, once a day with food.

FORMS:

Tablets (white) of 200 and 300mg, slow release capsule of 300mg (maroon/pink).

PRECAUTIONS:

Should not be used in pregnancy (C) unless medically essential. Breast feeding should be ceased if necessary to use NSAID. Not for use in children under three.
Use with caution in psychiatricaly disturbed patients, epilepsy, severe infection, heart failure and kidney disease.
Lower doses required in elderly, who may suffer more side effects.

Do not take if:

 • suffering from peptic ulcer at present or in recent past
• due for surgery (including dental surgery)
• suffering from bleeding disorder or anaemia.

SIDE EFFECTS:

Common: stomach discomfort, diarrhoea, constipation, heartburn, nausea, headache, dizziness.

Unusual: bladder irritation and inflammation, blurred vision, stomach ulcer, ringing noise in ears, retention of fluid, swelling of tissue, drowsiness, itch, rash, shortness of breath.

Severe but rare (stop medication, consult doctor): vomiting blood, passing blood in faeces, other unusual bleeding, asthma induced by medication.

INTERACTIONS:

Other drugs:
• must never be used with anticoagulants (e.g. warfarin)
• probenecid, diuretics, lithium, methotrexate, beta-blockers, ACE inhibitors.

PRESCRIPTION:

Yes.

PERMITTED IN SPORT:

Yes.

OVERDOSE:

Causes nausea, vomiting, severe headache, dizziness, confusion and convulsions. Administer activated charcoal or induce vomiting if taken recently. Seek medical assistance.

OTHER INFORMATION:

Used to give excellent relief to a wide variety of inflammatory conditions. Significant side effects (particularly on the stomach) in about 5% of patients. Limit their use.

See also Celecoxib, Diclofenac, Diflunisal, Flurbiprofen, Ibuprofen, Indomethacin, Ketoprofen, Mefenamic Acid, Naproxen, NSAID, Piroxicam, Rofecoxib, Sulindac.

Tibolone

TRADE NAME:

Livial.

USES:

Symptoms of menopause, prevention of osteoporosis after menopause.

DOSAGE:

 One tablet a day.

FORMS:

Tablets of 2.5mg (white).

PRECAUTIONS:

Not to be used in pregnancy (D), breast feeding and children.

Use with caution in high cholesterol or triglycerides, liver disease or risk of blood clots (thromboses).

Do not commence in menopause until a year after last menstrual bleed.

Do not take if:

 • suffering from undiagnosed vaginal bleeding, hormone dependent tumours (e.g. breast cancer), significant heart disease, recent stroke, blood clots or severe liver disorders
• male.

SIDE EFFECTS:

Common: weight gain, dizziness, headache, belly pain.

Unusual: migraine, dermatitis, disturbed vision, skin irritation, nausea, constipation, breast pain, vaginal irritation.

Severe but rare (stop medication, consult doctor): blood clots, liver damage, abnormal vaginal bleeding.

INTERACTIONS:

Other drugs:
• hormone replacement therapies used in menopause, anticoagulants (e.g. warfarin), barbiturates, carbamazepine, rifampicin.

PRESCRIPTION:

Yes.

PERMITTED IN SPORT:

Yes.

OVERDOSE:

Nausea and abnormal vaginal bleeding only likely effects.

OTHER INFORMATION:

Released in 2000 as a completely new method of managing bone density loss after the menopause. Tibolone has none of the risks of conventional hormone replacement therapy. Seems to suit many women very well, while others cannot tolerate it.

See also Norethisterone, Oestradiol, Oestriol.

Ticarcillin

TRADE NAME:

Timentin (with clavulanic acid).

DRUG CLASS:

Penicillin antibiotic.

USES:

Treatment of infections caused by susceptible bacteria (e.g. septicaemia, pneumonia, bronchitis, osteomyelitis, septic arthritis, urinary infections, gynaecological infections and serious skin infections).

DOSAGE:

 Usually given by continuous drip infusion.

FORMS:

Injection.

PRECAUTIONS:

May be used in pregnancy (B1), children and breast feeding if clinically indicated. Use with caution in kidney failure and heart disease.

Do not take if:

 • allergic to penicillin
• suffering from glandular fever.

SIDE EFFECTS:

Common: mild diarrhoea, nausea, vomiting.
Unusual: itch, rash, headache, dizziness, hot flushes, tiredness.
Severe but rare (stop medication, consult doctor): severe itchy rash, hives, severe diarrhoea, yellow skin (jaundice), unusual bruising or bleeding.

INTERACTIONS:

Other drugs:
• probenecid, aminoglycoside antibiotics.

PRESCRIPTION:

Yes.

PERMITTED IN SPORT:

Yes.

OVERDOSE:

Vomiting and diarrhoea likely.

OTHER INFORMATION:

Used in more severe infections.

See also Amoxycillin, Ampicillin, Clavulanic acid, Dicloxacillin, Flucloxacillin, Phenoxymethyl penicillin, Piperacillin, Procaine penicillin.

Tiludronic acid
(Tiludronate disodium)

TRADE NAME:

Skelid.

DRUG CLASS:

Bisphosphonate.

USES:

Paget's disease of bone.

DOSAGE:

 Two tablets once a day two hours before or after food, with water, for three months. Do not reuse for six months.

FORMS:

Tablets of 200mg (white).

PRECAUTIONS:

Use with caution in pregnancy (B2), breast feeding and children.
Ensure adequate calcium and vitamin D intake.
Use with caution in kidney disease.

Do not take if:

 • suffering from severe kidney disease.

SIDE EFFECTS:

Common: nausea, diarrhoea.
Unusual: dizziness, giddiness, headache, tiredness, skin reaction.

INTERACTIONS:

Other drugs:
• indomethacin, antacids, mineral supplements.
Other substances:
• food containing calcium.

PRESCRIPTION:

Yes.

PERMITTED IN SPORT:

Yes.

OVERDOSE:

Serious. Symptoms include loss of appetite, tiredness, vomiting, diarrhoea, sweating, excess urine production, extreme thirst and headache. This may progress to high blood pressure and kidney failure. Administer activated charcoal or induce vomiting if taken recently. Seek medical assistance.

Timolol

TRADE NAMES:

Betim, Nyogel, Timoptol.
Cosopt (with dorzolamide).
Prestim (with bendrofluazide).
Xalacom (with latanoprost).

DRUG CLASS:

Beta-blocker.

USES:

Glaucoma.
High blood pressure (hypertension).

DOSAGE:

 Drops: one drop, once or twice a day.
Tablets (Prestim): one to four tablets a day.

FORMS:

Eye drops (for glaucoma), tablet (for hypertension).

PRECAUTIONS:

Should be used with caution in pregnancy (C), but eye drops unlikely to cause problems.
Safe to use in breast feeding.
May be used with caution in children.
Use with care if suffering from alcoholism, liver or kidney failure or about to have surgery.
Use with caution in heart disease, shock or enlarged right heart.

Do not take if:

• suffering from diabetes, asthma, heart block, heart failure, slow heart rate, or allergic conditions.

SIDE EFFECTS:

Common: low blood pressure, slow heart rate, burning eyes, stinging, asthma.
Severe but rare (stop medication, consult doctor): severe asthma.

INTERACTIONS:

Other drugs:
• calcium channel blockers, disopyramide, clonidine, adrenaline, other medications for irregular heart beat, lignocaine, ergotamine, indomethacin, chlorpromazine, beta-blocker tablets.

PRESCRIPTION:

Yes.

PERMITTED IN SPORT:

Yes.

OVERDOSE:

Unlikely to be serious effects if eye drops swallowed other than exacerbation of side effects.

See also BETA BLOCKERS, Betaxolol, Bimatoprost, Brimonidine, Brinzolamide, Levobunolol, Metipranolol, Pilocarpine, Travoprost.

Tinidazole

TRADE NAMES:

Fasigyn.

DRUG CLASS:

Antibiotic.

USES:

Infections caused by susceptible bacteria (particularly infections of gut and vagina), giardiasis, amoebic dysentery.

DOSAGE:

 Four tablets as a single dose.

FORMS:

Tablets of 500mg (white).

PRECAUTIONS:

Should not be used in pregnancy (B3) or breast feeding. Use with caution in children.
Use with caution in kidney disease.
Do not take if:

 • suffering from brain disease, blood cell abnormalities.

SIDE EFFECTS:

Common: bad taste, nausea, loss of appetite, diarrhoea.
Unusual: vomiting, headache, constipation, dizziness, rash.

INTERACTIONS:

Other drugs:
• anticoagulants (e.g. warfarin).
Other substances:
• reacts with alcohol.

PRESCRIPTION:

Yes.

PERMITTED IN SPORT:

Yes.

OVERDOSE:

Exacerbation of side effects only likely effect.

OTHER INFORMATION:

Introduced in the early 1980s as a rapid and effective form of treatment for Giardia of gut and Trichomonal infections of vagina.

See also Metronidazole.

Tioconazole

TRADE NAME:

Trosyl.

DRUG CLASS:

Imidazole antifungal.

USES:

Fungal nail infections.

DOSAGE:

 Apply to nail and surrounding skin twice a day for six to twelve months.

FORMS:

Solution.

PRECAUTIONS:

Not for use in pregnancy and children.

SIDE EFFECTS:

Common: skin irritation.

INTERACTIONS:

None significant.

PRESCRIPTION:

Yes.

PERMITTED IN SPORT:

Yes.

OVERDOSE:

Seek medical advice if swallowed.
Unlikely to have serious consequences.
Hallucinations and mental disturbance
may occur.

See also ANTIFUNGALS; IMIDAZOLES.

Tiotropium

TRADE NAME:

Spiriva.

DRUG CLASS:

Anticholinergic.

USES:

Chronic obstructive airways disease,
emphysema, chronic bronchitis.

DOSAGE:

 One capsule inhaled once a day.

FORMS:

Capsule (light green) of powder for
inhalation through specific inhaler
(Handihaler).

PRECAUTIONS:

Not designed for use in pregnancy (B1),
breast feeding and children.
Not for acute treatment of wheeze or
breathlessness.
Use with caution in severe kidney
disease, glaucoma, or enlarged prostate.

Do not take if:

 • adverse reaction to atropine.

SIDE EFFECTS:

Common: dry mouth.

Unusual: constipation, throat irritation,
rapid heart rate.
*Severe but rare (stop medication, consult
doctor):* inability to pass urine, irregular
heart rate.

INTERACTIONS:

Other drugs:

• atropine, dicyclomine, homatropine
methylbromide, hyoscine, ipratropium,
oxitropium, oxybutynin, propiverine,
tiotropium, tolterodine.

PRESCRIPTION:

Yes.

PERMITTED IN SPORT:

Yes.

OVERDOSE:

Excessive inhalation causes worsening of
side effects. Swallowing capsules is
harmless.

OTHER INFORMATION:

Introduced in 2003 as a new method of
treating the very difficult to manage
symptoms of lung damage caused by
recurrent lung infections, smoking and
other inhaled irritants.

See also Ipratropium.

Tizanidine

TRADE NAME:

Zanaflex.

DRUG CLASS:

Muscle relaxant.

USES:

Muscle spasm caused by multiple
sclerosis or spinal cord injury.

DOSAGE:

Increase dose very slowly to a
maximum of 36mg a day given in
three or four doses.

FORMS:

Tablets of 2 and 4mg (white).

PRECAUTIONS:

Use with caution in pregnancy, breast feeding and children.
Use with caution in kidney disease.
Regular blood tests to check liver function necessary.

Do not take if:

 • suffering from liver disease.

SIDE EFFECTS:

Common: drowsiness, tiredness, dizziness, dry mouth.
Unusual: nausea, diarrhoea, low blood pressure, sleeplessness, slow heart rate.
Severe but rare (stop medication, consult doctor): hallucinations, liver damage (jaundice, yellow skin).

INTERACTIONS:

Other drugs:
• diuretics, beta-blockers, blood pressure medications, digoxin, oral contraceptives, sedatives.
Other substances:
• alcohol.

PRESCRIPTION:

Yes.

PERMITTED IN SPORT:

Yes.

OVERDOSE:

Seek medical attention. Liver damage likely. Give activated charcoal or induce vomiting if swallowed recently.

Tobramycin

TRADE NAMES:

Nebcin, TOBI.
Tobradex (with dexamethasone).

DRUG CLASS:

Aminoglycoside antibiotic.

USES:

Severe infections, particularly meningitis, blood, eye and belly infections.
Prevention and control of chronic lung infections.
Prevention of eye infections.

DOSAGE:

 Injection: every eight hours, or by continuous drip infusion.
Nebuliser: use twice a day for a month, then stop for a month before restarting cycle.
Eye drops: one drop every four to six hours.

FORMS:

Injection, nebuliser solution, eye drops.

PRECAUTIONS:

Not to be used in pregnancy (D) unless absolutely essential for mother's well being. Breast feeding must be ceased before use. Use with caution and only when essential in children.
Use with caution in kidney disease and muscle disorders.
Blood tests to check that correct dose is being administered are recommended.
Ensure adequate fluid intake during administration of medication.

SIDE EFFECTS:

Common: rash, nausea, headache.
Unusual: ear and kidney damage (dose related), vomiting, delayed wound healing (eye).
Severe but rare (stop medication, consult doctor): ear noises or deafness, unusual bleeding or bruising.

INTERACTIONS:

Other drugs:
• penicillin, cephalosporins, ethacrynic acid, frusemide, vitamin K.

PRESCRIPTION:

Yes.

PERMITTED IN SPORT:

Yes.

OVERDOSE:

Ear and kidney damage possible. Give copious fluids to increase excretion through kidneys.

OTHER INFORMATION:

Very useful for the treatment of severe infections. Introduced in early 1980s.

See Amikacin, Gatifloxacin, Gentamicin, Neomycin.

Tocopherols
(Vitamin E)

TRADE NAMES:

A large number of preparations include Tocopherols (Vitamin E) alone or in combination with other medications.

DRUG CLASS:

Vitamin.

USES:

Used in many soothing and healing creams, red blood cell disorders, fat absorption disorders.

DOSAGE:

 Recommended daily allowance: 8 to 10mg a day.

FORMS:

Tablets, capsules, mixture, cream.

PRECAUTIONS:

Use with caution in pregnancy, breast feeding and children.
Do not take in high doses or for prolonged periods of time.

SIDE EFFECTS:

Minimal.

INTERACTIONS:

None significant.

PRESCRIPTION:

No.

PERMITTED IN SPORT:

Yes.

OVERDOSE:

Dangerous. May cause blood clots, high blood pressure, breast lumps, headaches, vaginal bleeding, vision disturbances, muscle weakness and bowel disturbances if taken in high doses for a prolonged period of time.

OTHER INFORMATION:

Tocopherol is a fat soluble vitamin found in polyunsaturated fatty acids in a wide variety of foods. Remember, vitamins are merely chemicals that are essential for the functioning of the body and if taken to excess, act as a drug.

See also VITAMINS.

Tolfenamic acid

TRADE NAME:

Clotam.

DRUG CLASS:

NSAID.

USES:

Migraine.

DOSAGE:

 One tablet at start of migraine. Repeat once after one or two hours if necessary.

FORMS:

Tablet of 200mg (white).

PRECAUTIONS:

Not for use in last three months of pregnancy or in children. May be used with breast feeding.
Use with caution with past history of peptic ulcer.

Do not take if:

- suffering from peptic ulcer, allergic to aspirin, or significant liver or kidney disease.

SIDE EFFECTS:

Common: diarrhoea, nausea, heartburn, rash.

Unusual: pain passing urine, inflamed stomach, headache, tremor.

Severe but rare (stop medication, consult doctor): peptic ulcer, asthma, blood cell damage, liver damage (jaundice).

INTERACTIONS:

Other drugs:

- must never be used with anticoagulants (e.g. warfarin)
- frusemide, lithium.

Herbs:

- feverfew.

PRESCRIPTION:

Yes.

PERMITTED IN SPORT:

Yes.

OVERDOSE:

Causes nausea, vomiting, severe headache, dizziness, confusion and convulsions. Administer activated charcoal or induce vomiting if taken recently. Seek medical assistance.

OTHER INFORMATION:

Introduced in 2002 specifically for the treatment of migraine. Most NSAIDs are used for arthritic and muscular pain.

See also Diclofenac, Diflunisal, Felbinac, Fenbufen, Fenoprofen, Flurbiprofen, Ibuprofen, Indomethacin, Ketoprofen, NSAID, Piroxicam, Sulindac, Tenoxicam.

Tolnaftate

TRADE NAME:

Tinaderm-M (with nystatin).

DRUG CLASS:

Antifungal.

USES:

Fungal infections (tinea) of skin.

DOSAGE:

 Apply two or three times a day.

FORMS:

Cream.

PRECAUTIONS:

Safe to use in pregnancy, breast feeding and children.

Avoid eyes, nostrils, mouth, vagina and anus.

Seek medical advice if no improvement in ten days.

SIDE EFFECTS:

Common: skin irritation.

INTERACTIONS:

None significant.

PRESCRIPTION:

Yes.

PERMITTED IN SPORT:

Yes.

OTHER INFORMATION:

Old fashioned, but very widely used, safe and generally effective.

See also IMIDAZOLES, Ketoconazole, Nystatin.

Tolterodine

TRADE NAME:

Detrusitol.

DRUG CLASS:

Anticholinergic.

USES:

Urgency and frequency of urination, urinary incontinence.

DOSAGE:

 2mg twice a day.

FORMS:

Tablets (white) of 1 and 2mg.

PRECAUTIONS:

Not for use in pregnancy, breast feeding and children.
Use with caution in enlarged prostate, constipation, kidney and liver disease, hiatus hernia and some forms of neuropathy (nerve disease).

Do not take if:

 • suffering from urinary retention, uncontrolled glaucoma, myasthenia gravis, ulcerative colitis or megacolon.

SIDE EFFECTS:

Common: dry mouth, nausea, constipation.
Unusual: dry eyes, dry skin, tiredness, nervousness, pins and needles sensation.

INTERACTIONS:

Other drugs:
• some antifungals, macrolide antibiotics, other anticholinergics, cisapride, metoclopramide.

PRESCRIPTION:

Yes.

PERMITTED IN SPORT:

Yes.

OVERDOSE:

May be very serious, depending upon dose. Seek urgent medical advice.

See also ANTICHOLINERGICS.

Topiramate

TRADE NAME:

Topamax.

DRUG CLASS:

Anticonvulsant.

USES:

Additional treatment for some forms of partial epilepsy.

DOSAGE:

 25mg to 200mg twice a day. Increase dosage slowly.

FORMS:

Tablets of 25mg (white), 50mg (cream), 100mg (yellow), and 200mg (pink), sprinkle.

PRECAUTIONS:

Use with considerable caution in pregnancy (B3), breast feeding and children.
Use with caution in liver and kidney disease, psychiatric disorders.
Do not stop medication suddenly. Must be gradually withdrawn.

Do not take if:

• suffering from kidney stones.

SIDE EFFECTS:

Common: drowsiness, dizziness, poor coordination, nausea, diarrhoea.
Unusual: psychiatric disturbances, vomiting, low white blood cell count.
Severe but rare (stop medication, consult doctor): kidney stones.

INTERACTIONS:

Other drugs:
• phenytoin, carbamazepine, digoxin, sedatives, hypnotics, low dose oral contraceptives, phenobarbitone.
Herbs:
• evening primrose (linoleic acid), Gingko biloba.

Other substances:
• alcohol, borage.

PRESCRIPTION:

Yes.

PERMITTED IN SPORT:

Yes.

OVERDOSE:

No information available. Induce vomiting or administer activated charcoal if taken recently. Seek urgent medical attention.

OTHER INFORMATION:

Introduced in 1997 to assist patient with poorly controlled epilepsy despite maximum use of existing medications. Not addictive.

See also Carbamazepine, Clonazepam, Ethosuximide, Gabapentin, Lamotrigine, Levetiracetam, Oxcarbazepine, Phenytoin, Primidone, Sodium valproate, Sulthiame, Tiagabine, Vigabatrin.

Torasemide

TRADE NAME:

Torem.

DRUG CLASS:

Diuretic.

USES:

Removing excess fluid from body in heart failure, kidney disease, lung disease and high blood pressure.

DOSAGE:

 5 to 40mg a day in morning.

FORMS:

Tablets (white) of 2.5mg, 5mg and 10mg.

PRECAUTIONS:

Not to be used in pregnancy, breast feeding and children.
Regular blood tests to check electrolyte levels and blood cells necessary.
Use with caution in gout and diabetes.

Do not take if:

 • suffering from severe kidney failure, severe liver disease, low blood pressure
• sensitive to sulphas.

SIDE EFFECTS:

Common: dry mouth, headache, dizziness.
Unusual: muscle cramps, blood chemistry (electrolyte) disorders, nausea, diarrhoea, pins and needles sensation.
Severe but rare (stop medication, consult doctor): blood cell damage.

INTERACTIONS:

Other drugs:
• digoxin, corticosteroids, other blood pressure medications, aminoglycoside antibiotics, cephalosporin antibiotics, lithium, ACE inhibitors, diabetes medications, probenecid, NSAIDs, cholestyramine, theophylline and cisplatin.

Other substances:
• alcohol.

PRESCRIPTION:

Yes.

PERMITTED IN SPORT:

No.

OVERDOSE:

Severe dehydration may result. Induce vomiting if tablets taken recently. Give extra fluids. Seek medical assistance.

See also Frusemide.

Toremifene

TRADE NAME:

Fareston.

DRUG CLASS:

Antineoplastic.

USES:
Some types of breast cancer in postmenopausal women.

DOSAGE:
 One tablet a day.

FORMS:
Tablets of 60mg (white).

PRECAUTIONS:
Not to be used in pregnancy (B3) unless essential for the health of the mother. Not for use in breast feeding or children. Use with caution in angina, heart disease, diabetes or history of recent blood clots. Not for prolonged use.

Do not take if:

- suffering severe liver disease or some conditions affecting the lining of the uterus
- cancer of breast is oestrogen receptor negative.

SIDE EFFECTS:
Common: excess calcium in blood, hot flushes, sweating, dizziness, diarrhoea, nausea, vaginal discharge.
Unusual: vomiting, unusual bleeding from vagina, swelling of tissue, muscle pain.
Severe but rare (stop medication, consult doctor): blood clots.

INTERACTIONS:
Other drugs:
- phenytoin, carbamazepine, phenobarbitone, thiazide diuretics, warfarin, ketoconazole, macrolide antibiotics.

PRESCRIPTION:
Yes.

PERMITTED IN SPORT:
Yes.

OVERDOSE:
Exacerbation of side effects likely. Induce vomiting or administer activated charcoal if tablets taken recently. Seek medical assistance.

OTHER INFORMATION:
Released in 1998 as a new initial treatment for some types of breast cancer.
See also Letrozole, Tamoxifen.

Tramadol

TRADE NAMES:
Dromadol, Tramake, Zamadol, Zydol.

DRUG CLASS:
Narcotic.

USES:
Moderate to severe pain.

DOSAGE:
 50 to 100mg every six to twelve hours as needed. Maximum 600mg a day.

FORMS:
Capsules, tablets, powder in sachets, injection.

PRECAUTIONS:
Use with considerable caution in pregnancy, breast feeding and children. For short term use only.
Use with caution in undiagnosed abdominal pain, poor lung function, head injury, kidney and liver disease, and epilepsy.

Do not take if:
- suffering from alcoholism.
- addicted to narcotics (e.g. heroin).

SIDE EFFECTS:
Common: nausea, dizziness, constipation, sedation, sweating.
Unusual: vomiting, convulsions, allergy reactions.

INTERACTIONS:

Other drugs:
- hypnotics, other analgesics and narcotics, psychotropics, sedatives, general anaesthetics, buprenorphine, pentazocine, drugs used for depression (e.g. SSRI, tricyclic antidepressants), antipsychotics, MAOI, carbamazepine, quinidine, ketoconazole, erythromycin.

Other substances:
- alcohol.

PRESCRIPTION:

Yes.

PERMITTED IN SPORT:

Yes.

OVERDOSE:

Symptoms may include drowsiness, confusion, difficulty in breathing and coma. Induce vomiting if medication taken recently and patient alert. Seek urgent medical attention.

OTHER INFORMATION:

May cause dependence and addiction. Introduced in 1999 for the short term control of severe pain.

See also Buprenorphine, Codeine, Dextropropoxyphene, Methadone, Oxycodone.

Tramazoline

TRADE NAME:

Dexa-Rhinaspray Duo (with dexamethasone).

DRUG CLASS:

Vasoconstrictor.

USES:

Congestion of nose, hay fever.

DOSAGE:

 One spray to each nostril three to six times a day.

FORMS:

Nasal spray.

PRECAUTIONS:

Use in pregnancy only if medically essential. Use with caution in breast feeding and children. Not for use in children under six years.
Use with caution in high blood pressure, glaucoma and thyroid disease.
Avoid eye contact.
Not to be used regularly long term.

Do not take if:

 • suffering from glaucoma.

SIDE EFFECTS:

Common: tingling and burning of nose.
Unusual: worsening of congestion in nose if used long term.

INTERACTIONS:

Other drugs:
- MAOI, tricyclic antidepressants.
Other substances:
- reacts with alcohol.

PRESCRIPTION:

Yes.

PERMITTED IN SPORT:

Yes.

OVERDOSE:

Nasal congestion worsens if over used.

OTHER INFORMATION:

Very effective medication in stuffy noses from any cause.

See also VASOCONSTRICTORS, Xylometazoline.

Trandolapril

See ACE INHIBITORS.

Tranexamic acid

TRADE NAME:

Cyklokapron.

DRUG CLASS:

Haemostatic.

USES:

Hereditary angioedema, severe heavy periods (menorrhagia), hyphaemia, control of bleeding during surgery.

DOSAGE:

 As determined by doctor for each patient depending upon use.

FORMS:

Tablets of 500mg (white), injection.

PRECAUTIONS:

May be used with caution in pregnancy (B1), breast feeding and children.
Use with caution in kidney disease, blood in urine due to kidney disease, bleeding into body cavities.

Do not take if:

 • suffering from blood clots, recent history of blood clots, colour vision disturbances, bleeding around brain.

SIDE EFFECTS:

Common: nausea, diarrhoea.
Unusual: impaired colour vision, rash.

INTERACTIONS:

None significant.

PRESCRIPTION:

Yes.

PERMITTED IN SPORT:

Yes.

OVERDOSE:

Nausea and vomiting likely.
See also HAEMOSTATIC AGENTS.

Tranylcypromine

See MAOI.

Travoprost

TRADE NAME:

Travatan.

USES:

Glaucoma.

DOSAGE:

 One drop in eye in evening. Use at least five minutes away from other eye drops. Remove contact lenses before use, and do not replace for 15 minutes. Apply pressure to tear duct at inner corner of eye for two minutes after using drop. may be used in conjunction with timolol drops.

FORMS:

Eye drops.

PRECAUTIONS:

Not for use in pregnancy (B3), breast feeding and children.
Use with caution in dry eyes and inflammatory eye conditions.

SIDE EFFECTS:

Common: red and itchy eye, eye discomfort.
Unusual: changes in eyelash colour, dry eye.

INTERACTIONS:

None significant.

PRESCRIPTION:

Yes.

PERMITTED IN SPORT:

Yes.

OVERDOSE:

May have serious effects if eye drops swallowed. Seek urgent medical advice.

OTHER INFORMATION:

Introduced in 2002.

See also Betaxolol, Bimatoprost, Lantaprost, Levobunolol, Timolol.

Trazodone

TRADE NAME:

Molipaxin.

DRUG CLASS:

Antidepressant.

USES:

Depression, abnormal anxiety.

DOSAGE:

 50mg to 300mg once or twice a day. Most commonly 150mg once a day.

FORMS:

Tablets of 150mg (pink), capsules of 50mg (violet/green) and 100mg (violet/fawn), slow release tablets of 150mg (blue octagonal).

PRECAUTIONS:

May be used with caution in pregnancy, breast feeding and children.
Use with caution in epilepsy, heart disease, liver and kidney disease.

SIDE EFFECTS:

Common: drowsiness, dizziness, headache.
Unusual: nausea, light headedness, fainting.
Severe but rare (stop medication, consult doctor): prolonged erection of penis, liver damage, blood cell damage.

INTERACTIONS:

Other drugs:
• muscle relaxants, MAOI, Phenytoin, Clonidine, Digoxin, Sedatives.
Other substances:
• alcohol.

PRESCRIPTION:

Yes.

PERMITTED IN SPORT:

Yes.

OVERDOSE:

Seek medical attention. Give activated charcoal or induce vomiting if swallowed recently.

See also Citalopram, Fluoxetine, Fluvoxamine, Maprotiline, Mirtazapine, Moclobemide, Nefazodone, Paroxetine, Reboxetine, Sertraline, Venlafaxine.

Tretinoin

See KERATOLYTICS.

Triamcinolone

TRADE NAMES:

Adcortyl, Adcortyl in Orabase, Kenalog, Nasacort.
Audicort (with neomycin).
Aureocort (with chlortetracycline).
Tri-Adcortyl (with neomycin, gramicidin, nystatin).

DRUG CLASS:

Corticosteroid.

USES:

Severe inflammation of skin (eczema, dermatitis etc.), mouth and other tissues.
Severe rheumatoid and other forms of severe arthritis, autoimmune diseases, and other severe and chronic inflammatory diseases.

DOSAGE:

 Skin preparations: apply two or three times a day.
Ear drops: insert two drops twice a day.
Injection: limited number of injections to affected site or joint once or twice a week.

FORMS:

Cream, ointment, paste, ear drops, injection.

PRECAUTIONS:

Should be used in pregnancy (C), breast feeding and children only on specific medical advice.

Skin and ear preparations safe in pregnancy, breast feeding and children. Use injection with caution if under stress, and in patients with under active thyroid gland, liver disease, diverticulitis, high blood pressure, myasthenia gravis or kidney disease.

Avoid eyes with all forms.

Use for shortest period of time possible.

Do not use injection if:

- suffering from any form of infection, peptic ulcer, or osteoporosis
- having a vaccination.

Do not use cream if:

- suffering any form of fungal, viral or bacterial skin infection.

SIDE EFFECTS:

Most significant side effects occur only with prolonged use.

Common: injection—may cause bloating, weight gain, rashes and intestinal disturbances.

Ear drops and skin preparations—rarely cause adverse reactions.

Unusual: injection—dose related effects. Biochemical disturbances of blood, muscle weakness, bone weakness, impaired wound healing, skin thinning, tendon weakness, peptic ulcers, gullet ulcers, bruising, increased sweating, loss of fat under skin, premature ageing, excess facial hair growth in women, pigmentation of skin and nails, acne, convulsions, headaches, dizziness, growth suppression in children, aggravation of diabetes, worsening of infections, cataracts, aggravation of glaucoma, blood clots in veins and sleeplessness.

Skin preparations—thinning of skin, scarring of skin, premature ageing of skin. *Severe but rare (stop medication, consult doctor):* any significant side effect should be reported to a doctor immediately.

INTERACTIONS:

None significant.

PRESCRIPTION:

Yes.

PERMITTED IN SPORT:

Yes.

OVERDOSE:

Exacerbation of side effects likely.

OTHER INFORMATION:

Extremely effective and useful medication if used correctly. Lowest dose and shortest possible course should be used. Not addictive.

See also Betamethasone, Desonide, Hydrocortisone, Methylprednisolone, Mometasone.

Triamterene

TRADE NAMES:

Only available in combination with other medications.
Dyazide, Triam-Co (with hydrochlorothiazide).
Dytide (with benzthiazide).
Frusene (with frusemide).
Kalspare (with chlorthalidone).

DRUG CLASS:

Potassium sparing diuretic.

USES:

Excess fluid in body, conserving potassium stores in body.

DOSAGE:

 One tablet, one to three times a day after meals.

FORMS:

Tablets, capsules.

PRECAUTIONS:

Should only be used in pregnancy if medically indicated. Not for use in breast feeding or children.

Do not take if:

 • suffering from liver or severe kidney disease.

SIDE EFFECTS:

Common: minimal.
Unusual: nausea, vomiting, diarrhoea, weakness.

INTERACTIONS:

Other drugs:
• ACE inhibitors, lithium, indomethacin
• medications used to treat high blood pressure
• should not be taken with potassium supplements.

PRESCRIPTION:

Yes.

PERMITTED IN SPORT:

No.

OVERDOSE:

No serious effects. If tablets taken recently induce vomiting. Seek medical assistance.

OTHER INFORMATION:

Normally used in combination with a diuretic to prevent potassium being washed out of the body.

Tribavirin

TRADE NAMES:

Copegus, Rebetol, Virazole.

DRUG CLASS:

Antiviral.

USES:

Hepatitis C, severe bronchiolitis caused by the respiratory syncitial virus.

DOSAGE:

 Complex. Individualised for each patient by doctor.

FORMS:

Capsules of 200mg, nebuliser powder.

PRECAUTIONS:

Absolutely forbidden in pregnancy (X) and breast feeding. Severe damage to foetus likely if taken during pregnancy. Adequate contraception must be used for at least seven months after use of tribavirin.
Female sexual partners of patients using tribavirin must use adequate contraception as drug may pass to woman in semen.
Capsules not recommended in children.
Nebuliser powder may be used in children.
Regular blood tests necessary to check blood cells, kidney and liver function when taking capsules.
An ECG to check heart function should be taken before and during treatment with capsules.
Use capsules with caution in heart failure, recent heart attack, liver disease, irregular heart beat, gout, mood disorders and thyroid disorders.
Nebuliser equipment must be monitored carefully to check for precipitation of powder in tubing.

Do not take if:

 • suffering from severe heart disease, thalassaemia, sickle cell anaemia, chronic kidney failure, history of significant psychiatric disturbances, severe liver disease (e.g. cirrhosis), uncontrolled thyroid disease, and autoimmune disorders.

SIDE EFFECTS:

Capsules:
Damage to red blood cells, psychiatric disturbances, thyroid gland disorders, suicide, excess uric acid in blood, gout.
Nebuliser powder:
Secondary bacterial infection, pneumonia, pneumothorax.

INTERACTIONS:

Other drugs:
• other antivirals.

PRESCRIPTION:

Yes.

PERMITTED IN SPORT:

Yes.

OVERDOSE:

Very serious. Likely to cause severe organ damage. No further information available.

OTHER INFORMATION:

Introduced 1999 to treat very specific severe and life threatening viral infections.

Triclosan

TRADE NAMES:

Aquasept, Manusept, Ster-Zac Bath Concentrate.
Oilatum Plus (with paraffin and benzalkonium chloride).

DRUG CLASS:

Antiseptic.

USES:

Minor skin infections.

DOSAGE:

 Depends on form. Usually once or twice a day, or as hand wash as required.

FORMS:

Liquid.

PRECAUTIONS:

Safe to use in pregnancy, breast feeding and children.
Avoid eyes.
Not for long term use.

SIDE EFFECTS:

Minimal.

INTERACTIONS:

None significant.

PRESCRIPTION:

No.

PERMITTED IN SPORT:

Yes.

OVERDOSE:

Diarrhoea and vomiting only likely effects if swallowed.

OTHER INFORMATION:

Very widely used and safe.
See also ANTISEPTICS.

TRICYCLIC ANTIDEPRESSANTS

TRADE and GENERIC NAMES:

Allegron (<u>Nortriptyline</u>).
Anafranil (<u>Clomipramine</u>).
Asendis (<u>Amoxapine</u>).
Gamanil, Lomont (<u>Lofepramine</u>).
Motival (<u>Nortriptyline</u> with fluphenazine).
Prothiaden (<u>Dothiepin</u>).
Sinequan (<u>Doxepin</u>).
Surmontil (<u>Trimipramine</u>).
Tofranil (<u>Imipramine</u>).
Triptafen (<u>Amitriptyline</u> with perphenazine).
NB: tricyclics are underlined.

DRUG CLASS:

Antidepressants.

USES:

Depression, sleeplessness (insomnia), bed wetting (amitriptyline and imipramine only).

DOSAGE:

 One to four or more tablets or capsules usually taken in evening, but may be divided in equal or unequal doses through day when larger amount of medication taken.

FORMS:

Tablets, capsules, mixture.

PRECAUTIONS:

Should not be used in pregnancy (C) or breast feeding unless medically essential. May be used with caution in children. Potentially suicidal patients should be watched carefully.

Use with caution in heart disease, kidney and liver disease.

Lower doses required in elderly.

Do not stop medication suddenly, but gradually reduce dosage over some days or weeks.

Do not take if:

 • suffering from glaucoma or difficulty in passing urine.

SIDE EFFECTS:

Common: drowsiness, dry mouth, dizziness, tremor, nausea, constipation, rapid heart rate.

Unusual: confusion, difficulty in passing urine, decreased libido, vomiting, blurred vision, poor concentration, hallucinations, breast enlargement, intestinal cramps, rash.

Severe but rare (stop medication, consult doctor): yellow skin (jaundice).

INTERACTIONS:

Other drugs:
• severe interaction with MAOI
• sedatives, anxiolytics, cimetidine, quinidine, barbiturates, guanethidine, antihistamines, phenytoin, carbamazepine, sympathomimetics, other antidepressants.

Herbs:
• ma huang, yohimbine.

Other substances:
• reacts with alcohol to cause drowsiness.

PRESCRIPTION:

Yes.

PERMITTED IN SPORT:

Yes.

OVERDOSE:

May be very serious. Symptoms include blurred vision, inability to pass urine, delirium, agitation, incoordination, convulsions, reduced breathing, coma and death. Administer activated charcoal or induce vomiting if taken recently and patient alert. Seek urgent medical assistance. Patients with tricyclic overdose are often observed in intensive care.

OTHER INFORMATION:

Tricyclics are widely used and are the main medication for control of depression. Slow acting and may take two or more weeks for any positive effect to occur. In use for over 40 years.

See also ANTIDEPRESSANTS, Citalopram, Fluoxetine, Fluvoxamine, MAOI, Mianserin, Mirtazapine, Moclobemide, Nefazodone, Paroxetine, Reboxetine, Sertraline, Venlafaxine.

Trifluoperazine

See PHENOTHIAZINES.

Triglycerides

See Fatty acids.

Trigonella

See Fenugreek.

Trilostane

TRADE NAME:

Modrenal.

USES:

Breast cancer, hyperaldosteronism, excess activity of adrenal gland.

DOSAGE:

 60 to 240mg four times a day.

FORMS:

Capsules of 60mg (pink/black) and 120mg (pink/yellow).

PRECAUTIONS:

Must not to be used in pregnancy, breast feeding and children.
Non-hormonal contraception must be used by women.
Use with caution with physical stress, or any kidney or liver disease.

Do not take if:

 • suffering from severe kidney or liver disease.

SIDE EFFECTS:

Common: flushing, nausea, runny nose, diarrhoea.
Unusual: vomiting.

INTERACTIONS:

Other drugs:
• potassium, amiloride, triamterene.
Other substances:
• high potassium foods (e.g. bananas, apricots).

PRESCRIPTION:

Yes.

PERMITTED IN SPORT:

Yes.

Trimeprazine

See ANTIHISTAMINES, SEDATING.

Trimethoprim

TRADE NAMES:

Monotrim, Trimopan.
Septrin (with sulphamethoxazole—this combination is known as co-trimoxazole).
Polytrim (with polymyxin B).

DRUG CLASS:

Antibiotic.

USES:

Urinary tract (bladder and kidney) infections.
Co-trimoxazole used for a wide variety of infections.

DOSAGE:

 One tablet a day at night with food.
Co-trimoxazole: one tablet twice a day.

FORMS:

Tablets, suspension, drops, ointment.

PRECAUTIONS:

Use in pregnancy (B3) only if medically essential. Not to be used in breast feeding, or in children under six years.
Use with caution in folate deficiency, liver and kidney disease.
Lower doses may be necessary in elderly.
Normally not for constant long term use.

Do not take if:

 • suffering from blood disorders, pernicious anaemia, severe liver and kidney disease.

SIDE EFFECTS:

Common: itch, rash.
Unusual: nausea, vomiting, fever.
Severe but rare (stop medication, consult doctor): unusual bleeding or bruising.

INTERACTIONS:

Other drugs:
• anticoagulants (e.g. warfarin), methotrexate, pyrimethamine.

PRESCRIPTION:

Yes.

PERMITTED IN SPORT:

Yes.

OVERDOSE:

Nausea, vomiting, dizziness, headache, depression, confusion and damage to bone marrow may occur. Administer activated charcoal or induce vomiting if medication taken recently. Seek medical assistance.

OTHER INFORMATION:

Widely used for minor to moderate urinary infections. Synthetic antibiotic. Does not cause dependence or addiction. **See also ANTIBIOTICS.**

Trimipramine

See TRICYCLIC ANTIDEPRESSANTS.

Tripotassium dicitratobismuthate

TRADE NAMES:

DeNoltab.

DRUG CLASS:

Antiulcerant.

USES:

Treatment of stomach and duodenal (upper small intestine) ulcers.

DOSAGE:

 Up to four tablets a day, in two to four doses, half hour before meals and last thing at night.

FORMS:

Tablets of 120mg (white).

PRECAUTIONS:

Safety in pregnancy and breast feeding not established.

Do not take if:

 • suffering from kidney failure.

SIDE EFFECTS:

Common: Black faeces, coated tongue and teeth, nausea, vomiting.

INTERACTIONS:

Other drugs:
• do not take Antacids within one hour of bismuth subcitrate
• tetracycline efficacy may be reduced

• efficacy of cimetidine, ranitidine, nizatadine and other antiulcerants may be reduced.
Other substances:
• reacts with food and milk to reduce drugs efficiency
• avoid carbonated drinks (e.g. beer).

PRESCRIPTION:

No.

PERMITTED IN SPORT:

Yes.

OVERDOSE:

Giving activated charcoal, or induction of vomiting and stomach washout recommended. No reported serious effects.

See also Nizatadine, PROTON PUMP INHIBITORS, Ranitidine.

Triprolidine

See ANTIHISTAMINES, SEDATING.

TROPHIC HORMONES

DISCUSSION:

Trophic hormones are given as injections to aid infertility, prevent miscarriages, stimulate sperm production in men, control breast pain due to hormone imbalances, to start puberty in cases where it has been delayed and to control some patients with asthma and arthritis. There are a number of rarer diseases in which they are also useful. Commonly used trophic hormones include menopausal gonadotrophin, chorionic gonadotrophin, and tetrocosactrin. Adverse reactions are uncommon but severe when they do occur. They include nausea, headaches, peptic ulcers, fluid retention, high blood pressure, inappropriate sexual development and skin markings.

See Gonadotrophin, Menotrophin, Tetrocosactrin.

Tropicamide

See MYDRIATICS.

Tropisetron

TRADE NAME:

Navoban.

USES:

Prevention of nausea and vomiting caused by cancer treatments and surgery.

DOSAGE:

 One capsule in morning immediately on waking, one hour before food.

FORMS:

Capsule (yellow/white) of 5mg, injection.

PRECAUTIONS:

Should not be used in pregnancy (B3) or children unless medically essential. Breast feeding should be ceased before use.
Use caution if operating machinery or driving a vehicle.
Use with caution in high blood pressure, irregular heart rhythm, kidney and liver disease.

SIDE EFFECTS:

Common: tiredness, headache, dizziness, constipation.
Unusual: diarrhoea, loss of appetite.

INTERACTIONS:

Other drugs:
• rifampicin, barbiturates.
Other substances:
• avoid food for one hour after taking capsule.

PRESCRIPTION:

Yes.

PERMITTED IN SPORT:

Yes.

OVERDOSE:

Hallucinations and high blood pressure may occur. Seek medical assistance.

OTHER INFORMATION:

Introduced in 1995.
See also Metoclopramide.

Trospium

TRADE NAME:

Regurin.

DRUG CLASS:

Anticholinergic.

USES:

Passing urine frequently or urgently, incontinence of urine.

DOSAGE:

 One tablet twice a day before meals.

FORMS:

Tablets of 20mg (yellow).

PRECAUTIONS:

Use with caution in pregnancy and breast feeding. Not for use in children.
Use with caution in kidney disease, bowel obstruction, hiatus hernia, overactive thyroid gland (hyperthyroidism), angina or heart failure.

Do not take if:

 • suffering from retention of urine, glaucoma, myasthenia gravis, rapid irregular heart beat, ulcerative colitis, liver disease or kidney failure.

SIDE EFFECTS:

Common: dry mouth, constipation.

INTERACTIONS:

Other drugs:
• amantadine, tricyclic antidepressants, quinidine, antihistamines, disopyramide,

metoclopramide, cisapride, colestipol, cholestyramine and salbutamol.

PRESCRIPTION:

Yes.

PERMITTED IN SPORT:

Yes.

OVERDOSE:

May be very serious, depending upon dose. Seek urgent medical advice.

OTHER INFORMATION:

Introduced in 2002 specifically to aid bladder control.

See also ANTICHOLINERGICS.

Tryptophan
(L-Tryptophan)

TRADE NAME:

Optimax.

DRUG CLASS:

Antidepressant.

USES:

Severe, prolonged, intractable depression.

DOSAGE:

 Two to four tablets, three times a day.

FORMS:

Tablets (white) of 500mg.

PRECAUTIONS:

Use with caution in pregnancy, breast feeding and children.

Use with caution in kidney and liver disease.
Use lower doses in elderly.

Do not take if:

• suffering from eosinophilia myalgia syndrome.

SIDE EFFECTS:

Common: drowsiness, nausea, headache.
Severe but rare (stop medication, consult doctor): eosinophilia myalgia syndrome.

INTERACTIONS:

Other drugs:
• MAOI, phenothiazines, diazepam and other benzodiazepines.

PRESCRIPTION:

Yes (restricted to specific doctors in some hospitals only).

PERMITTED IN SPORT:

Yes.

OVERDOSE:

No specific information. Seek urgent medical attention.

See also ANTIDEPRESSANTS.

Tuberculosis vaccine

See BCG vaccine.

Typhoid vaccine

See Salmonella typhi vaccine.

Ultralente insulin

See INSULINS.

Undecenoic acid

TRADE NAMES:

Ceanel (with cetrimide and other ingredients).
Monophytol (with salicylates and other ingredients).

DRUG CLASS:

Antifungal.

USES:

Psoriasis and dermatitis of scalp, tinea pedis (athlete's foot).

DOSAGE:

 Use as shampoo two or three times a week.
Paint feet twice daily until two weeks after apparent cure.

FORMS:

Liquid, paint.

PRECAUTIONS:

Safe to use in pregnancy, breast feeding and children.
Monophytol not to be used in pregnancy due to other ingredients.
Avoid eyes, nose and mouth.
Use with caution on broken skin.

SIDE EFFECTS:

Minimal.

INTERACTIONS:

None significant.

PRESCRIPTION:

No.

PERMITTED IN SPORT:

Yes.

OVERDOSE:

Unlikely to have serious effects if swallowed.

Uracil

See Tegafur and Uracil.

Urea

TRADE NAMES:

Aquadrate, Eucerin, Nutraplus.
Alphaderm (with hydrocortisone).
Balneum Plus (with lauromacrogols).
Calmurid (with lactic acid).
Calmurid HC (with lactic acid and hydrocortisone).
Found in numerous other creams in combination with other medications.

USES:

Skin moisturiser for dry skin, eczema, irritated skin.

DOSAGE:

 Apply as required. Use Hydrocortisone combinations twice a day.

FORMS:

Cream.

PRECAUTIONS:

Safe to use in pregnancy, breast feeding and children.

SIDE EFFECTS:

None.

INTERACTIONS:

None.

PRESCRIPTION:

No.
Yes if combined with Hydrocortisone.

PERMITTED IN SPORT:

Yes.

OTHER INFORMATION:

Safe, simple, cheap and effective. In use for hundreds of years as a moisturiser.
See also TAR, Zinc oxide.

Urea hydrogen peroxide

TRADE NAME:

Exterol (with glycerine).

USES:

Softening hard ear wax.

DOSAGE:

Five drops twice a day for three to four days. Retain in ear.

FORMS:

Ear drops.

PRECAUTIONS:

Safe to use in pregnancy), breast feeding and children.

Do not take if:

• suffering from perforated ear drum.

SIDE EFFECTS:

Common: effervescent sensation, discomfort.

INTERACTIONS:

None in ear.

PRESCRIPTION:

No.

PERMITTED IN SPORT:

Yes.

OVERDOSE:

Unlikely to have serious effects if swallowed.

URICOSURICS

DESCRIPTION:

Medications that reduce levels of uric acid in blood by increasing its loss in urine to prevent gout.
See Allopurinol, Probenecid, Sulphinpyrazone.

URINARY ACIDIFIERS

DISCUSSION:

Medications that make urine more acid.
See Ammonium chloride.

URINARY ALKALINISERS

TRADE and GENERIC NAMES:

Effercitrate, (Citric acid and potassium citrate).
Mictral (<u>Citric acid</u>, <u>sodium bicarbonate</u> and <u>sodium citrate</u> with nalidixic acid).
Optiflo G, Uriflex G, Uro-Tainer G (Citric acid, sodium bicarbonate, disodium edetate and other ingredients).
Optiflo R, Uriflex R, Uro-Tainer R (Citric acid, gluconolactone, disodium edetate and other ingredients).
Uro-Tainer Suby G (Sodium bicarbonate with other ingredients).

USES:

Bladder and kidney infection, excess stomach acid.

DOSAGE:

One or two sachets dissolved in water, three or four times a day.

FORMS:

Powder in sachet, granules in sachet, capsules, effervescent tablet, liquid.

PRECAUTIONS:

Safe to use in pregnancy, breast feeding and children.
Use with caution in heart disease.

Do not take if:

- suffering from kidney failure.

SIDE EFFECTS:

Common: minimal.
Unusual: diarrhoea.

INTERACTIONS:

Other drugs:
- hexamine, quinolone antibiotics, antacids, laxatives, lithium.

PRESCRIPTION:

No.

PERMITTED IN SPORT:

Yes.

OVERDOSE:

Severe diarrhoea likely.

OTHER INFORMATION:

Widely used to ease the symptoms of urinary infections and prevent recurrences. Does not cause addiction or dependence.
See also Hexamine hippurate.

URINARY ANTISEPTICS

DISCUSSION:

Medications used to prevent urinary infections.
See Hexamine hippurate, URINARY ALKALINISERS.

Ursodeoxycholic acid

TRADE NAMES:

Destolit, Urdox, Ursofalk.

USES:

Cirrhosis of liver, dissolving some types of gall stones.

DOSAGE:

Complex. Must be determined individually for each patient by doctor.

FORMS:

Capsules of 150mg, 250mg and 300mg.

PRECAUTIONS:

Not for use in pregnancy and breast feeding.
Use with caution in children.
Regular blood tests to check liver function necessary.

Do not take if:

- suffering from cholecystitis, bile duct inflammation, bile duct obstruction, inflamed bowel or peptic ulcer.

SIDE EFFECTS:

Common: minimal.
Unusual: diarrhoea, itchy skin, nausea, vomiting, sleep disturbances.
Severe but rare (stop medication, consult doctor): worsening liver disease.

INTERACTIONS:

Other drugs:
- ciprofloxacin, cyclosporin, cholestyramine, charcoal, colestipol, antacids, oral contraceptives, oestrogen.

PRESCRIPTION:

Yes.

PERMITTED IN SPORT:

Yes.

OVERDOSE:

No information available. Seek medical attention.

VACCINES

DISCUSSION:

Vaccines prevent diseases caused by viruses and bacteria by specifically stimulating the immune system to produce antibodies against the infecting agent.

See BCG (TB) vaccine, Chickenpox vaccine, Diphtheria vaccine, Haemophilus influenzae B (HiB) vaccine, Hepatitis A vaccine, Hepatitis B vaccine, Influenza vaccine, Measles vaccine, Meningococcal Vaccine, Mumps vaccine, Poliomyelitis (Sabin) vaccine, Pneumococcal vaccine, Rabies vaccine, Rubella (German measles) vaccine, Salmonelli typhi (typhoid) vaccine, Tetanus vaccine, Whooping cough vaccine, Yellow fever vaccine, Yersinia (plague) vaccine.

Valaciclovir

TRADE NAME:

Valtrex.

DRUG CLASS:

Antiviral.

USES:

Shingles, genital herpes, herpes infection of eye.

DOSAGE:

 Shingles: two tablets three times a day for a week. Must be started within 72 hours of first sign of rash. Herpes: one tablet twice a day.

FORMS:

Tablets of 500mg (white).

PRECAUTIONS:

Use with considerable caution in pregnancy (B3). Use with caution in breast feeding. Safe in children. Use with caution in dehydration, kidney disease and immunosuppression.

SIDE EFFECTS:

Common: headache, nausea.

INTERACTIONS:

Other drugs:
• diuretics, probenecid, cimetidine, cyclosporin.

PRESCRIPTION:

Yes.

PERMITTED IN SPORT:

Yes.

OVERDOSE:

Exacerbation of side effects only likely problem.

OTHER INFORMATION:

Introduced in 1997 as a very effective antiviral.
See also Aciclovir, Famciclovir.

Valdecoxib

TRADE NAME:

Bextra.

DRUG CLASS:

COX-2 inhibitor.

USES:

Osteoarthritis, rheumatoid arthritis, painful periods.

DOSAGE:

 10mg to 40mg once a day.

FORMS:

Tablets of 10mg (white), 20mg (white) and 40mg (yellow).

PRECAUTIONS:

Not for use in pregnancy (C) or if trying to fall pregnant. Use with caution in breast feeding and children.
Use with caution if history of peptic ulcer or intestinal bleeding.
Use with caution in smokers, alcoholics, dehydration, asthma, high blood pressure, heart failure, infection, liver or kidney disease.
Use with care in elderly.

Do not take if:

- suffering from active peptic ulcer, intestinal bleeding, active asthma, urticaria (hives), severe heart failure.

SIDE EFFECTS:

Common: dry mouth.
Unusual: intestinal upsets, allergy, anaemia, fluid retention, high blood pressure.
Severe but rare (stop medication, consult doctor): peptic ulcer.

INTERACTIONS:

Other drugs:
- NSAID, aspirin, cyclosporin, steroids, anticoagulants (e.g. warfarin), rifampicin, methotrexate, ACE Inhibitors (treat high blood pressure and heart disorders), lithium, diuretics (fluid tablets), theophylline, amitriptyline, tacrolimus, oral contraceptives.

Other substances:
- smoking increases risk of stomach ulcer.

PRESCRIPTION:

Yes.

PERMITTED IN SPORT:

Yes.

OVERDOSE:

Exacerbation of side effects likely. Induce vomiting or give activated charcoal if swallowed recently. Seek medical attention.

OTHER INFORMATION:

Introduced 2002. Far less likely than other treatments for arthritis (e.g. NSAIDs) to cause intestinal bleeding.
See also Celecoxib, Meloxicam, Parecoxib, Rofecoxib.

Valerian

USES:

Insomnia, anxiety.

DOSAGE:

 100mg to 1800mg a day divided into several doses.

FORMS:

Capsules, liquid, tablets, tea bags.

PRECAUTIONS:

Do not use in pregnancy or breast feeding.
Use care with driving or operating machinery after use.

SIDE EFFECTS:

Common: nausea, diarrhoea.
Unusual: headache, restlessness, insomnia, irregular heart rhythm.

INTERACTIONS:

Other drugs:
- sedatives, barbiturates, benzodiazepines (e.g. diazepam).

Other substances:
- alcohol.

PRESCRIPTION:

No.

PERMITTED IN SPORT:

Yes.

OVERDOSE:

Exacerbation of side effects likely.

OTHER INFORMATION:

Not used in orthodox medical practice.

Valganciclovir

TRADE NAME:

Valcyte.

DRUG CLASS:

Antiviral.

USES:

Cytomegalovirus (CMV) infections of the eye in patients with AIDS.

DOSAGE:

 Initially, two tablets twice a day with food. After three weeks, reduce to one tablet twice a day.

FORMS:

Tablets of 450mg (pink).

PRECAUTIONS:

Not for use in pregnancy, breast feeding and children.
Use with care in kidney and liver disease, blood cell damage, and radiotherapy.
Men must use barrier contraception during use and for 90 days afterwards.
Regular blood tests to check blood cells necessary.

Do not take if:

- having haemodialysis
- suffering from low haemoglobin, white cell or platelet count.

SIDE EFFECTS:

Common: thrush in mouth, poor appetite, weight loss, depression, anxiety.
Unusual: blood cell damage, headache, taste disturbances, altered sensations, eye damage, cough, nausea, diarrhoea, sweating, itch, fever, back pain, dizziness.
Severe but rare (stop medication, consult doctor): liver damage (jaundice), blindness (retinal haemorrhage).

INTERACTIONS:

Other drugs:
- severe interaction with ganciclovir, aciclovir, valaciclovir
- imipenem, cilastin, didanosine, cancer treating drugs (cytotoxics), probenecid.

PRESCRIPTION:

Yes.

PERMITTED IN SPORT:

Yes.

OVERDOSE:

Very serious. Seek urgent medical assistance.

OTHER INFORMATION:

Introduced in 2002 to treat a specific uncommon eye complication of AIDS.

See also Abacavir, Delavirdine, Didanosine, Efavirenz, Indinavir, Lamivudine, Nelfinavir, Nevirapine, Ritonavir, Saquinavir, Stavudine, Tenofovir, Zidovudine.

Valproate

See Sodium valproate, Valproic acid.

Valproic acid

TRADE NAME:

Convulex, Depakote.

DRUG CLASS:

Anticonvulsant.

USES:

Epilepsy, manic episodes of bipolar disorder (manic-depressive psychosis).

DOSAGE:

 300 to 1000mg twice a day.

FORMS:

Capsules of 150mg, 250mg, 300mg and 500mg.

PRECAUTIONS:

Use with caution in pregnancy, breast feeding and children.
Use with caution in elderly.
Regular blood tests to check liver function necessary.

Do not take if:

- suffering from liver disease, porphyria, pancreatitis.

SIDE EFFECTS:

Common: standard urine tests show false positive for ketones (not a serious effect), nausea, diarrhoea.
Unusual: liver damage, abnormal bleeding, dizziness, weight gain, hair loss, tremor, drowsiness, cessation of menstrual periods, rash.
Severe but rare (stop medication, consult doctor): jaundice (yellow skin), blistering rash.

INTERACTIONS:

Other drugs:
- barbiturates, antidepressants, muscle relaxants, salicylates, MAOI, antipsychotics, benzodiazepines, carbamazepine, lamotrigine, primidone, phenytoin, zidovudine, cimetidine, mefloquine, warfarin, erythromycin, cholestyramine.

Other substances:
- Alcohol.

PRESCRIPTION:

Yes.

PERMITTED IN SPORT:

Yes.

OVERDOSE:

Severe liver damage may occur. Induce vomiting or give activated charcoal if swallowed recently. Seek urgent medical attention.

See also Sodium valproate.

Valsartan

See ANGIOTENSIN II RECEPTOR ANTAGONISTS.

Vancomycin

TRADE NAME:

Vancocin.

DRUG CLASS:

Antibiotic.

USES:

Capsules: severe intestinal infections.
Injection, infusion: very severe infections of heart, bone, lungs, blood and soft tissue.

DOSAGE:

 One capsule every six hours.

FORMS:

Capsules of 125mg (peach/blue) and 250mg (grey/blue), injection, infusion.

PRECAUTIONS:

Use with caution in pregnancy (B2) and breast feeding. May be used when appropriate in children.
Use with caution in kidney disease, bowel inflammation and hearing loss.
Lower doses necessary in elderly.
Not designed for long term use.

SIDE EFFECTS:

Common: indigestion, nausea, chills, diarrhoea.
Unusual: vomiting, hearing loss, rash, muscle pain.
Severe but rare (stop medication, consult doctor): noises in ears or reduced hearing.

INTERACTIONS:

Other drugs:
- aspirin, some other antibiotics.

PRESCRIPTION:

Yes.

PERMITTED IN SPORT:

Yes.

OVERDOSE:

May cause kidney damage. Seek medical assistance.

OTHER INFORMATION:

Very potent and effective antibiotic when used appropriately.

Vardenafil

TRADE NAME:

Levitra.

USES:

Impotence and erectile failure in men.

DOSAGE:

 10mg to 20mg taken 30 to 60 minutes before sex.

FORMS:

Tablets of 5mg, 10mg and 20mg (orange).

PRECAUTIONS:

Not to be used by women or children. Use with caution in liver and kidney disease, deformed penis, sickle cell anaemia, history of priapism (prolonged erections of penis), multiple myeloma, leukaemia, bleeding disorders and active peptic ulcer.
Use lower doses in elderly.

Do not take if:

 • suffering from significant heart disease, angina, severe kidney or liver disease, low blood pressure, recent stroke or heart attack, inherited retinal diseases of the eye.

SIDE EFFECTS:

Common: nausea, heartburn, dizziness.
Unusual: flushing, watery nose, headache, light sensitive eyes, blurred vision.
Severe but rare (stop medication, consult doctor): muscle spasms, fainting, low blood pressure.

INTERACTIONS:

Other drugs:
• severe interaction with nitrates used for angina
• erythromycin, amyl nitrate, ritonavir, ketoconazole, indinavir, itraconazole, alpha-blockers.
Herbs:
• grapefruit juice.

PRESCRIPTION:

Yes (very limited availability on the NHS).

PERMITTED IN SPORT:

Yes.

OTHER INFORMATION:

Introduced in 2003 as an additional form of treatment for erectile impotence.
See also Alprostadil, Sildenafil, Tadalafil.

Varicella Zoster Vaccine

See Chickenpox Vaccine.

VASOCONSTRICTORS

DISCUSSION:

Vasoconstrictors are drugs that constrict (reduce in size) blood vessels (arteries in particular) and raise blood pressure. When a patient collapses with a heart attack, severe allergy or shock, it is often due to the sudden overdilation of all the arteries in the body, which causes a very low blood pressure. This can be corrected by a doctor giving an injection of a vasoconstrictor such as adrenaline. Otherwise, vasoconstrictors are used mainly as drops in the eye and nose, and as additives (e.g. pseudoephedrine) to some cold and hay fever remedies. Vasoconstrictor eye drops constrict any dilated arteries criss-crossing the white of the eye to leave it looking and feeling much better. Nose drops and sprays containing phenylephrine shrink down the dilated arteries in the nose that develop with hay fever. They can therefore ease the congestion and stuffiness in the nose and allow victims to breathe more easily. Overuse can cause a rebound effect and the nose becomes inflamed because the drops cause it to swell again. All swallowed or injected vasoconstrictors should be used with caution in patients with high blood pressure, diabetes, thyroid disease or heart disease.

See Adrenaline, Antazoline, Phenylephrine, Pseudoephedrine, Tramazoline, Xylometazoline.

VASODILATORS

DISCUSSION:

Arteries and to a lesser extent veins, are surrounded by tiny muscles that control the diameter of the blood vessel tube by contracting and relaxing it. If arteries in the arms and legs are excessively contracted or blocked by plaques of cholesterol (atherosclerosis), the amount of blood reaching the distant parts of the body may be insufficient for them to work properly. The earliest sign of a poor blood supply is pallor of the skin. This is followed by muscle weakness and pain. Vasodilators will relax the tiny muscles around the artery, enabling it to dilate to its maximum extent and allowing the greatest possible amount of blood to reach the affected areas. Vasodilators can also be used in the emergency treatment of very high blood pressure.

See Betahistine, Diazoxide, Guanethidine, Naftidrofuryl, Nicorandil, Nicotinic Acid.

Vasopressin
(Antidiuretic hormone)

TRADE NAME:

Pitressin.

DRUG CLASS:

Antidiuretic.

USES:

Diabetes insipidus, some investigations.

DOSAGE:

 May be given by injection, or soaked onto cotton buds which are inserted into nose.

FORMS:

Injection.

PRECAUTIONS:

Use with caution in pregnancy (B2), breast feeding and children.
Must not be given by intravenous injection.
Use with caution in artery disease, heart disease, angina, kidney disease, epilepsy, migraine, asthma, goitre, heart attack, blood clots, hardening of arteries.

SIDE EFFECTS:

Common: minimal.
Unusual: sweating, tremor, dizziness, fainting, headache, nausea, gut cramps.

INTERACTIONS:

None significant.

PRESCRIPTION:

Yes.

PERMITTED IN SPORT:

Yes.

OVERDOSE:

Unlikely to cause serious effects.

OTHER INFORMATION:

One of the few effective treatments for the rare disease diabetes insipidus, which is completely unrelated to sugar diabetes (diabetes mellitus).

See also Desmopressin acetate.

Venlafaxine

TRADE NAME:

Efexor.

DRUG CLASS:

Antidepressant.

USES:

Depression.

DOSAGE:

 Tablets: 37.5mg to 75mg twice a day. Increase dose slowly. Capsules: one a day with food.

FORMS:

Tablets (peach) of 37.5mg, 50mg and 75mg, sustained release capsules (peach) of 75mg and 150mg.

PRECAUTIONS:

Use with caution in pregnancy (B2), breast feeding and children.
Use with caution in higher doses.
Check blood pressure regularly.
Use with caution in epilepsy, other psychiatric conditions, liver and kidney diseases.
Watch patient carefully if suicidal.
Do not stop suddenly, but reduce dose slowly.

Do not take if:

• taking MAOI.

SIDE EFFECTS:

Common: dizziness, sleeplessness, nervousness, nausea, diarrhoea, dry mouth.
Unusual: tiredness, vomiting, excess sweating, impotence, general tiredness.
Severe but rare (stop medication, consult doctor): high blood pressure.

INTERACTIONS:

Other drugs:
• MAOI may cause very serious effects
• other antidepressants
• haloperidol, clozapine, imipramine, desipramine, warfarin, amiodarone, erythromycin, fluconazole, quinidine.
Herbs:
• St John's wort, ma huang.
Other substances:
• grapefruit.

PRESCRIPTION:

Yes.

PERMITTED IN SPORT:

Yes.

OVERDOSE:

May be serious. Induce vomiting or give activated charcoal if taken recently. Seek urgent medical attention.

OTHER INFORMATION:

Introduced in 1997 for the effective management of depression.
See also Citalopram, Fluoxetine, Fluvoxamine, Paroxetine, Reboxetine, Sertraline.

Verapamil

TRADE NAMES:

Cordilox, Securon, Univer, Vertab SR, Zolvera.
Tarka (with trandolapril).

DRUG CLASS:

Calcium channel blocker (calcium antagonist).

USES:

High blood pressure, angina, rapid heart rate.

DOSAGE:

 40mg to 120mg two or three times a day, or 180mg to 240mg. once a day. Maximum dose 480mg a day.

FORMS:

Tablets of 40mg, 80mg, 120mg, 180 and 240mg, solution, injection.

PRECAUTIONS:

Should only be used in pregnancy (C) and breast feeding if medically essential. Not designed for use in children.

Do not take if:

- suffering from severe heart failure, low blood pressure, atrial flutter or fibrillation.

SIDE EFFECTS:

Common: constipation, tiredness, headache, dizziness, indigestion, swelling of feet and ankles.
Unusual: flushing, palpitations, slow heart rate, scalp irritation, depression, flushes, nightmares, excess wind.
Severe but rare (stop medication, consult doctor): fainting.

INTERACTIONS:

Other drugs:
- Beta-blockers (e.g. propranolol), cyclosporin, digoxin, cimetidine, diazepam, amiodarone, quinidine, rifampicin, phenytoin, cisapride, theophylline, terbutaline, salbutamol, diltiazem
- additive effect with other medications for high blood pressure.

Herbs:
- goldenseal, guarana, hawthorn, Korean ginseng, liquorice.

Other substances:
- smoking may aggravate conditions that these medications are treating
- grapefruit juice.

PRESCRIPTION:

Yes.

PERMITTED IN SPORT:

Yes.

OVERDOSE:

May continue to be absorbed for up to 48 hours after overdose. Administer activated charcoal or induce vomiting. Purging should be encouraged to eliminate drug from gut. Overdose may cause low blood pressure, irregular heart rhythm, difficulty in breathing, heart attack and death. Obtain urgent medical attention.

OTHER INFORMATION:

Commonly used as a first line medication in high blood pressure and to prevent angina.

See also Amlodipine, Diltiazem, Felodipine, Nifedipine, Nimodipine.

Vigabatrin

TRADE NAME:

Sabril.

DRUG CLASS:

Anticonvulsant.

USES:

Epilepsy, particularly difficult to control epilepsy.

DOSAGE:

 One or two tablets twice a day.

FORMS:

Tablets (white) of 500mg, powder in sachet.

PRECAUTIONS:

Not to be used in pregnancy (D) or breast feeding.
Use with care in psychiatric conditions and kidney disease.
Response to medication must be checked regularly by a doctor.
Use with caution in elderly.
Medication should not be stopped suddenly.
Interferes with some laboratory blood tests.

SIDE EFFECTS:

Common: drowsiness, weight gain, nausea, diarrhoea.
Unusual: disturbed brain function, disturbed bowel function, vomiting, reduced alertness.

INTERACTIONS:

Other drugs:
• phenytoin.
Herbs:
• evening primrose (linoleic acid), gingko biloba.
Other substances:
• borage.

PRESCRIPTION:

Yes.

PERMITTED IN SPORT:

Yes.

OTHER INFORMATION:

Released in 1994. Not addictive or dependence forming.

See also Carbamazepine, Clonazepam, Ethosuximide, Gabapentin, Lamotrigine, Levetiracetam, Phenytoin, Primidone, Sodium valproate, Sulthiame, Tiagabine, Topiramate.

Vinblastine

See **VINCA ALKALOIDS**.

VINCA ALKALOIDS

TRADE and GENERIC NAMES:

Eldisine (Vindesine sulfate).
Navelbine (Vinorelbine).
Oncovin (Vincristine sulfate).
Velbe (Vinblastine sulfate).

USES:

Leukaemia, some lung cancers, blood disorders, Hodgkin's disease, advanced breast cancer, some other forms of cancer.

DOSAGE:

 Must be individualised for each patient by doctor depending on disease, severity, response and weight of patient.

FORMS:

Injection, infusion.

PRECAUTIONS:

Must not be used in pregnancy (D) unless mother's life is at risk as foetus may be damaged. Breast feeding must be ceased before use. May be used with caution in children.
Adequate contraception must be used by all women during treatment.
Regular blood and marrow tests to check blood and marrow cells and liver function essential.
Use with caution in nerve, muscle and lung disease.

Do not take if:

 • suffering from serious infection, nerve damage, thrombocytopenia (bleeding disorder due to low blood platelet count).

SIDE EFFECTS:

Common: loss of all body hair, pins and needles, nerve pain, muscle weakness, nausea, vomiting.
Unusual: paralysis of some muscles, convulsions, constipation or diarrhoea, depression, headache, rash, fever, anaemia, jaw pain.
Severe but rare (stop medication, consult doctor): unusual bleeding or bruising, yellow skin (jaundice).

INTERACTIONS:

Other drugs:
• phenytoin, mitomycin, cisplatin
• live virus vaccines (e.g. Sabin polio).
Other substances:
• alcohol should be avoided during treatment.

PRESCRIPTION:

Yes.

OVERDOSE:

Frequently fatal.

OTHER INFORMATION:

Despite significant side effects, these drugs may save the life of patients with leukaemia and other cancers.

See also Amascrine, Busulphan, Chlorambucil, Cyclophosphamide, Cytarabine, Daunorubicin, Mercaptopurine, Thioguanine.

Vincristine

See VINCA ALKALOIDS.

Vindesine

See VINCA ALKALOIDS.

Vinorelbine

See VINCA ALKALOIDS.

VITAMINS

DISCUSSION:

Vitamins are a group of totally unrelated chemicals that have only one thing in common: they are essential (usually in tiny amounts) for the normal functioning of the body. All vitamins have been given letter codes, sometimes with an additional number to differentiate vitamins within a group. The missing letters and numbers in the series are due to substances initially having been identified as vitamins but later being found to lack the essentials for the classification.

See Ascorbic acid (Vitamin C); Biotin (Vitamin H); Calcitriol, Cholecalciferol, Ergocalciferol (Vitamin D); Cyanocobalamin(Vitamin B12); Folic acid; Hydroxocobalamin (Vitamin B12); Nicotinic Acid (Vitamin B3); Pantothenic acid (Vitamin B5); Phytomenadione (Vitamin K); Pyridoxine (Vitamin B6); Retinol (Vitamin A); Riboflavine (Vitamin B2); Thiamine (Vitamin B1); Tocopherols (Vitamin E).

Vitamin A

See Retinol.

Vitamin B1

See Thiamine.

Vitamin B2

See Riboflavine.

Vitamin B3

See Nicotinic acid.

Vitamin B5

See Panthenol (Pantothenic acid).

Vitamin B6

See Pyridoxine.

Vitamin B12

See Cyanocobalamin; Hydroxocobalamin.

Vitamin C

See Ascorbic acid.

Vitamin D

See Cholecalciferol, Calcitriol and Ergocalciferol.

Vitamin E

See Tocopherols.

Vitamin H

See Biotin.

Vitamin K

See Phytomenadione.

Voriconazole

TRADE NAME:

Vfend.

DRUG CLASS:

Imidazole antifungal.

USES:

Severe invading fungal infections such as aspergillosis and systemic candidiasis. Severe fungal infections in immune suppressed patients (e.g. AIDS).

DOSAGE:

 Varies depending on body weight. Initial loading dose necessary. Take twice a day one hour away from food.

FORMS:

Tablets of 50mg and 200mg (white).

PRECAUTIONS:

Not for use in pregnancy and breast feeding. may be used with caution in children.

Women should ensure adequate contraception used.
Use with caution in kidney disease, liver disease (e.g. cirrhosis).
Avoid sun exposure.
Regular blood tests to monitor blood chemistry advisable.

SIDE EFFECTS:

Common: rash, red skin, muscle pains, swelling of feet, hands and feet.
Unusual: palpitations, nausea, diarrhoea.
Severe but rare (stop medication, consult doctor): blood chemistry disturbances, shortness of breath, disturbed vision, kidney failure.

INTERACTIONS:

Other drugs:
• phenytoin, rifabutin, rifampicin, carbamazepine, barbiturates, terfenadine, cisapride, pimozide, quinidine, astemizole, sirolimus, ergots, and other imidazole antifungals.
Herbs:
• echinacea.

PRESCRIPTION:

Yes.

PERMITTED IN SPORT:

Yes.

OTHER INFORMATION:

Introduced in 2003 to treat serious complicated fungal infections.

See also Clotrimazole, Econazole, Fluconazole, Itraconazole, Ketoconazole, Miconazole, Sulconazole, Tioconazole.

Warfarin

TRADE NAME:

Marevan.

DRUG CLASS:

Anticoagulant.

USES:

Prevention and treatment of blood clots (e.g. lung clots, heart clots).

DOSAGE:

 Precise dose as directed by doctor once a day at the same time.

FORMS:

Tablets of 0.5mg (white), 1mg (brown), 3mg (blue) and 5mg (pink).

PRECAUTIONS:

Must not be used in pregnancy (D) as it may cause foetal damage and death. Breast feeding should be ceased if use is medically necessary. May be used with caution in children.
Regular blood tests to check blood clotting time essential.
Other illnesses (e.g. infection) may require an adjustment of warfarin dosage. Read literature accompanying medication very carefully. Ask questions of doctor about anything you do not understand. Do not undertake any activity that may result in falls, bruising or extreme exertion.

Do not take if:

- suffering from bleeding tendency, peptic ulcer, dementia, mental diseases, severe high blood pressure, blood cell abnormalities, alcoholism
- due to have essential surgery, including dental surgery.

SIDE EFFECTS:

Common: bruising, nose bleeds.
Unusual: hair loss, itch, rash, fever, nausea, diarrhoea, belly pains.
Severe but rare (stop medication, consult doctor): significant bleeding, blood in urine, blood in faeces, vomiting blood, black patch of skin.

INTERACTIONS:

Other drugs:
- interacts with a very wide range of medications. Do not take any medication (including cold mixtures, vitamins, and other chemist and supermarket lines) without checking with a doctor
- never take aspirin or arthritis (NSAID) drugs with warfarin.

Herbs:
- alfalfa, bilberry, celery, camomile, clove, devil's claw, dong quai, fenugreek, feverfew, garlic, ginger, ginkgo biloba, ginseng, guarana, Korean ginseng, liquorice, papaya, pau d'arco, red clover, slippery elm bark, St John's wort, tumeric, willow bark.

Other substances:
- reacts with alcohol and caffeine
- reacts with many foods. Do not alter diet without discussing with a doctor.
- eat a constant amount of green leafy vegetables, meat and dairy products as a variation may affect the effect of warfarin
- do not diet or binge eat without discussing with a doctor.

PRESCRIPTION:

Yes.

PERMITTED IN SPORT:

Yes, but not recommended in active sport. Body contact sport forbidden.

OVERDOSE:

Extremely serious. Administer activated charcoal or induce vomiting only if tablets taken very recently. Seek emergency medical assistance. Massive internal bleeding may cause sudden death. Antidote (Vitamin K) available. Blood transfusion may be necessary.

OTHER INFORMATION:

Warfarin is the active ingredient of many rat poisons. If used correctly and carefully, warfarin can save and prolong life with minimal or no side effects. Slightest variation of dose may cause adverse effects. Wearing a bracelet or charm with information about the medication is advised for anyone using warfarin long term.

See also Heparin.

WEIGHT LOSS DRUGS

See ANORECTICS, Methylcellulose, Orlistat, Silbutramine.

Whooping cough vaccine (Pertussis vaccine)

TRADE NAMES:

Only available in combination with other vaccines.
Infanrix (with tetanus and diphtheria vaccines).
Act-Hib DTP, Infanrix-HiB (with HiB, diphtheria and tetanus vaccines).

DRUG CLASS:

Vaccine.

USES:

Prevention of whooping cough.

DOSAGE:

 Three injections at monthly intervals starting at two months of age.

FORMS:

Injection.

PRECAUTIONS:

Not designed for use over two years of age.
Use with caution if history of brain disease or convulsions.

Do not take if:

 • suffering from acute illness, significant fever or epilepsy
• previously infected with whooping cough.

SIDE EFFECTS:

Common: local redness and tenderness at injection site, persistent lump, fever.
Unusual: tiredness, irritability, faint.
Severe but rare: convulsion, brain inflammation.

INTERACTIONS:

Vaccines other than poliomyelitis (Sabin) vaccine.

PRESCRIPTION:

Yes.

PERMITTED IN SPORT:

Yes.

OVERDOSE:

An unintentional additional dose is unlikely to have any serious effect.

OTHER INFORMATION:

Vaccination that should be given to all infants. Whooping cough infections still occur in Britain and may cause brain damage and death.

See also Diphtheria vaccine, Hepatitis B vaccine, Tetanus vaccine.

Xipamide

See THIAZIDE DIURETICS.

Xylitol

TRADE NAMES:

Oralbalance.
AS Saliva Orthana (with mucin).

USES:

Artificial saliva for use in conditions causing a dry mouth.

DOSAGE:

 Use freely as required.

FORMS:

Spray, gel.

PRECAUTIONS:

Safe in pregnancy, breast feeding and children.
No precautions necessary.

SIDE EFFECTS:

None significant.

INTERACTIONS:

None significant.

PRESCRIPTION:

No.

PERMITTED IN SPORT:

Yes.

OVERDOSE:

Safe.

Xylometazoline

TRADE NAMES:

Otrivin.
Otrivin-Anthistin (with antazoline).
Rynacrom Co (with sodium cromoglycate).

DRUG CLASS:

Vasoconstrictor.

USES:

Nasal congestion, hay fever, eye inflammation, eye allergy.

DOSAGE:

 Nose: use in each nostril one to four times a day.
Eye: one or two drops two or three times a day.

FORMS:

Nose drops and spray, eye drops.

PRECAUTIONS:

Safe to use in pregnancy, breast feeding and children.
Ensure children strength and not adult strength nose preparations used in children.
Use eye drops with caution in children.
Not to be used in nose long term.

Do not take any form if:

 • suffering from glaucoma or serious eye disease.

Do not use eye drops if:

 • using contact lenses.

Do not use nose drops if:

 • recent brain surgery performed through nose.

SIDE EFFECTS:

Common: eye drops—temporary blurred vision, stinging.
Nose drops—burning, stinging, sneezing, dry nose.
Unusual: nose drops—worsening nasal congestion if over used, sleeplessness, light headedness, palpitations, headache.

INTERACTIONS:

Other drugs:
• MAOI
Other substances:
• reacts with alcohol.

PRESCRIPTION:

No.

PERMITTED IN SPORT:

Yes.

OVERDOSE:

If used excessively, nasal congestion rather than relief may occur.
If swallowed, sedation, high blood pressure, rapid irregular heart rate and coma may occur. Seek medical assistance.

OTHER INFORMATION:

Ensure instructions are followed and medication is not over used.

See also Tramazoline, VASOCONSTRICTORS.

Yellow fever vaccine

TRADE NAME:

Arilvax, Stamaril.

DRUG CLASS:

Vaccine.

USES:

Prevention of yellow fever.

DOSAGE:

 Single injection gives ten years protection.

FORMS:

Injection.

PRECAUTIONS:

Not to be used in pregnancy. May be used with caution in breast feeding and children over one year.

Do not take if:

 • suffering from significant illness, cancer or immune disease
• allergic to poultry or eggs.

SIDE EFFECTS:

Common: fever, tiredness, joint pains.

INTERACTIONS:

None significant.

PRESCRIPTION:

Yes (only available from specifically registered centres).

PERMITTED IN SPORT:

Yes.

OVERDOSE:

An inadvertent additional vaccination is unlikely to have any serious consequences.

OTHER INFORMATION:

Not routinely used. Only given to persons travelling to or resident in, countries of tropical Africa and South America where yellow fever occurs. The disease is spread by mosquitoes.

Yersinia pestis vaccine (Plague vaccine)

TRADE NAME:

Plague Vaccine.

DRUG CLASS:

Vaccine.

USES:

Prevention of plague (black death).

DOSAGE:

 Two injections at an interval of one to four weeks. Third injection necessary for children under twelve. Additional booster doses required every six months.

FORMS:

Injection.

PRECAUTIONS:

Use with caution in pregnancy. May be used in breast feeding and children. Use with caution in fever from infection.

SIDE EFFECTS:

Common: minimal.
Unusual: fever, muscle spasms, loss of appetite.
Severe but rare: brain inflammation, speech disorders, muscle wasting.

INTERACTIONS:

Other drugs:
• other vaccines.

PRESCRIPTION:

Yes.

PERMITTED IN SPORT:

Yes.

OVERDOSE:

Additional inadvertent vaccination
unlikely to have any serious
consequences.

OTHER INFORMATION:

Not a routine travel vaccination. Only
given to residents and visitors to an area
where plague occurs.

Z

Zafirlukast

TRADE NAME:

Accolate.

DRUG CLASS:

Leukotrene receptor antagonist.

USES:

Prevention and treatment of asthma.

DOSAGE:

 One or two tablets twice a day.

FORMS:

Tablets (white) of 20mg.

PRECAUTIONS:

May be used with caution in pregnancy (B1) and breast feeding. Use with caution in children.
Use with caution in unstable and sudden onset asthma.
Do not stop medication suddenly.
Use with caution if withdrawing from steroids.
Use with caution in liver disease.

SIDE EFFECTS:

Common: chest infection.
Unusual: abnormal bleeding.
Severe but rare (stop medication, consult doctor): liver and white blood cell damage.

INTERACTIONS:

Other drugs:
• warfarin, theophylline, erythromycin, terfenadine, aspirin.

PRESCRIPTION:

Yes.

PERMITTED IN SPORT:

Yes.

OVERDOSE:

May cause damage to liver and blood cells. Induce vomiting or give activated charcoal if taken recently. Seek urgent medical attention.

OTHER INFORMATION:

Expensive medication introduced in 1999 to assist asthmatics who are not adequately controlled by other medications.
See Montelukast.

Zalcitabine

TRADE NAME:

Hivid.

DRUG CLASS:

Antiviral.

USES:

AIDS, HIV infection.

DOSAGE:

 One or two tablets three times a day. Often used in combination with zidovudine.

FORMS:

Tablets of 0.375mg (beige) and 0.75mg (grey).

PRECAUTIONS:

Must not be used in pregnancy (D). Use with caution in breast feeding and children.
Use with caution in peripheral neuropathy, pancreatitis, kidney and liver disease.
Regular blood tests to check liver and kidney function, and blood cells, are necessary.

SIDE EFFECTS:

Common: mouth ulcers, nausea, rash, itch, headache, muscle pain, tiredness.
Unusual: pain on swallowing, loss of appetite, vomiting, dizziness, throat inflammation.
Severe but rare (stop medication, consult doctor): belly pain (pancreatitis), numbness and burning in hands and feet (neuropathy).

INTERACTIONS:

Other drugs:
• aminoglycosides, amphotericin, foscarnet, chloramphenicol, cisplatin, dapsone, didanosine, disulfiram, glutethamide, hydralazine, iodoquinol, isoniazid, nitrofurantoin, phenytoin, ribavirin, vincristine.

PRESCRIPTION:

Yes.

PERMITTED IN SPORT:

Yes.

OVERDOSE:

No information available. Induce vomiting or administer activated charcoal if taken recently. Seek urgent medical attention.

OTHER INFORMATION:

Usually combined with other medications used to treat HIV infections.

See Abacavir, Efavirenz, Indinavir, Lamivudine, Nelfinavir, Nevirapine, Ritonavir, Saquinavir, Stavudine, Tenofovir, Zidovudine.

Zaleplon

TRADE NAME:

Sonata.

DRUG CLASS:

Hypnotic.

USES:

Severe insomnia resistant to other forms of treatment.

DOSAGE:

 5 to 10mg at bedtime.

FORMS:

Capsules of 5mg (white/light brown with gold band) and 10mg (white with pink band).

PRECAUTIONS:

Not to be used in pregnancy, breast feeding and children.
Not to be used for more than two weeks.
Use with caution in liver disease, depression and poor lung function.
Use with caution if history of alcohol or drug abuse.

Do not take if:
• suffering from severe liver disease, sleep apnoea, myasthenia gravis, severe lung disease, psychiatric disturbances
• history or suspicion of suicide.

SIDE EFFECTS:

Common: rebound anxiety and insomnia when medication finished, dependence upon drug, loss of memory, headache, tiredness, drowsiness.
Unusual: dizziness, poor reactions.
Severe but rare (stop medication, consult doctor): psychiatric disturbances, liver damage.

INTERACTIONS:

Other drugs:
• antipsychotics, hypnotics, sedatives, narcotics, antidepressants, antihistamines, anticonvulsants, ketoconazole, cimetidine, erythromycin, barbiturates, rifampicin and carbamazepine.
Other substances:
• alcohol, marijuana, heroin.

PRESCRIPTION:

Yes.

PERMITTED IN SPORT:

Yes.

OVERDOSE:

May be very serious. Induce vomiting or give activated charcoal if swallowed recently. Seek urgent medical attention.

OTHER INFORMATION:

May be addictive if used for more than a couple of weeks.

Zanamivir

TRADE NAME:

Relenza.

DRUG CLASS:

Antiviral.

USES:

Treatment of influenza. Must be started within 48 hours of first symptoms of influenza appearing.

DOSAGE:

 Two inhalations twice daily for five days.

FORMS:

Disc inhaler.

PRECAUTIONS:

Use with caution in pregnancy (B1) and breast feeding.
Use with caution in severe asthma.
Not for prevention of influenza.

SIDE EFFECTS:

Common: minimal.
Unusual: dizziness, diarrhoea.
Severe but rare (stop medication, consult doctor): asthma.

INTERACTIONS:

None significant.

PRESCRIPTION:

Yes.

PERMITTED IN SPORT:

Yes.

OVERDOSE:

Additional inhalations unlikely to have any serious effects.

OTHER INFORMATION:

Released in 1999 as the first medication for the treatment of influenza. Developed in Australia.
See also Oseltamivir.

Zidovudine
(Azidothymidine, AZT)

TRADE NAMES:

Retrovir.
Combivir (with lamivudine).
Trivizir (with abacavir, lamivudine).

DRUG CLASS:

Antiviral.

USES:

AIDS (acquired immune deficiency syndrome), HIV (human immunodeficiency virus) positive patients.

DOSAGE:

 As determined by doctor, depending on medication combinations and severity of disease.

FORMS:

Capsules, syrup.

PRECAUTIONS:

Not to be used in pregnancy (B3) unless medically essential. Breast feeding should be ceased before use. Not to be used in children unless medically essential. Regular blood tests to check for organ and blood cell damage essential.

Patients must be fully informed of risks associated with this treatment by their doctor.

Do not take if:

- not suffering from HIV/AIDS
- planning to father children
- low red or white blood cell count present.

SIDE EFFECTS:

Many side effects of zidovudine may be caused by the disease (AIDS) it is treating.

Common: tiredness, fever, headache, loss of appetite, nausea, vomiting, muscle aches, sleeplessness, rash, blood cell damage.

Unusual: belly discomfort, dizziness, pins and needles, shortness of breath.

Severe but rare: impairs fertility, may cause cancer.

INTERACTIONS:

Other drugs:

- codeine, methadone, morphine, paracetamol, NSAIDs, oxazepam, lorazepam, cimetidine, probenecid, phenytoin, ribavirin, clofibrate, dapsone, stavudine.

PRESCRIPTION:

Yes.

PERMITTED IN SPORT:

Yes.

OVERDOSE:

Causes vomiting. Uneventful recovery likely.

OTHER INFORMATION:

Introduced in early 1990s in an attempt to slow the progress of HIV/AIDS, but does not cure the disease. Normally used in combination with other antivirals.

See Abacavir, Efavirenz, Indinavir, Lamivudine, Nelfinavir, Nevirapine, Ritonavir, Saquinavir, Stavudine, Tenofovir, Zalcitabine.

Zinc oxide

TRADE NAMES:

Anugesic-HC (with hydrocortisone, pramoxine, benzyl benzoate and other ingredients).
Anusol (with benzyl benzoate, bismuth and other ingredients).
Anusol HC (with hydrocortisone, benzyl benzoate, bismuth and other ingredients).
E45 Sun Block (with titanium oxide).
Hemocane (with lignocaine, bismuth oxide, benzoic acid and other ingredients).
Hewletts Cream (with lanolin).
Morhulin (with cod liver oil).
Sprilon (with dimethicone).
Sudocrem (with wool fat, benzyl benzoate and other ingredients).
Vasogen (with dimethicone and calamine).
Xyloproct (with hydrocortisone, aluminium acetate, lignocaine).
Also found in numerous other locally produced barrier creams.

DRUG CLASS:

Mineral.

USES:

Skin protection, skin inflammation, mild fungal infections of skin, piles, skin ulcers, aid to healing.

DOSAGE:

 Applied to affected area as needed.

FORMS:

Cream, ointment, lotion, suppository, impregnated bandage.

PRECAUTIONS:

Safe in pregnancy, breast feeding and children of all ages.

SIDE EFFECTS:

Common: minimal.
Unusual: sensitivity reactions.

INTERACTIONS:

Other drugs:

• may prevent other creams from reaching skin and acting on skin if zinc oxide is applied first.

PRESCRIPTION:

Most forms: no.
Combined with hydrocortisone: yes.

PERMITTED IN SPORT:

Yes.

OTHER INFORMATION:

Zinc oxide has been used for centuries to protect skin from injury, and to soothe irritation.

See also Urea.

Zinc pyrithione

See Pyrithione zinc.

Zinc sulphate

TRADE NAMES:

Solvazinc.
Zinc sulphate is also found in numerous other locally produced mineral and vitamin supplements.

DRUG CLASS:

Mineral.

USES:

Mineral supplement, dermatitis, acne.

DOSAGE:

 One tablet, one to three times a day.

FORMS:

Tablets of 125mg.

PRECAUTIONS:

Use tablets with caution in pregnancy and children. May be used in breast feeding. Do not exceed recommended dose.

Do not take tablets constantly, but suspend medication intermittently. Ensure adequate intake of fibre while taking tablets.

SIDE EFFECTS:

Minimal.

INTERACTIONS:

None significant.

PRESCRIPTION:

No.

PERMITTED IN SPORT:

Yes.

OVERDOSE:

Constipation only likely serious effect.

OTHER INFORMATION:

Low levels of zinc in the blood may reduce the body's ability to repair damage. May improve acne healing. Recommended daily intake 12mg per day.

Zolmitriptan

TRADE NAME:

Zomig.

DRUG CLASS:

Antimigraine.

USES:

Treatment of acute migraine.

DOSAGE:

 One tablet at onset of migraine. Repeat after two hours if necessary.

FORMS:

Tablets of 2.5mg (yellow).

PRECAUTIONS:

Use with considerable caution in pregnancy (B3), breast feeding and children.
Use with caution in irregular heart rhythm and liver disease.

Do not take if:

- suffering from angina, serious heart disease, poor circulation, significant high blood pressure, poor kidney function
- history of recent heart attack, stroke or transient ischaemic attack.

SIDE EFFECTS:

Common: tiredness, nausea, dizziness, warm sensation, pins and needles sensation.
Unusual: dry mouth, throat pressure, muscle aches.
Severe but rare (stop medication, consult doctor): chest pain.

INTERACTIONS:

Other drugs:
- ergotamine, MAOI, cimetidine, fluvoxamine, quinolone antibiotics.
Herbs:
- St John's wort.

PRESCRIPTION:

Yes.

PERMITTED IN SPORT:

Yes.

OVERDOSE:

Sedation only likely effect.

OTHER INFORMATION:

Very effective medication, particularly if taken immediately migraine starts.
See Almotriptan, Clonidine, Eletriptan, Ergotamine, Frovatriptan, Naratriptan, Rizatripan, Sumatriptan.

Zolpidem

TRADE NAME:

Stilnoct.

DRUG CLASS:

Hypnotic.

USES:

Insomnia.

DOSAGE:

 5 or 10mg at bedtime.

FORMS:

Tablets (white) of 5mg and 10mg.

PRECAUTIONS:

Use with caution in pregnancy and breast feeding.
Not recommended in children.
Not to be used long term.
Use with caution in lung and liver diseases, depression.

Do not take if:

- suffering from sleep apnoea, myasthenia gravis, severe lung or liver disease, psychiatric disturbances
- history of drug abuse.

SIDE EFFECTS:

Common: rebound inability to sleep when medication ceased, nausea, diarrhoea, dizziness, tiredness.
Unusual: headache.
Severe but rare (stop medication, consult doctor): memory loss, confusion, depression, tremor, hallucinations.

INTERACTIONS:

Other drugs:
- other sedatives, rifampicin, ketoconazole.
Herbs:
- celery, camomile.
Other substances:
- alcohol, heroin, marijuana.

PRESCRIPTION:

Yes.

PERMITTED IN SPORT:

Yes.

OVERDOSE:

May be serious, but rarely life threatening. Induce vomiting or give activated charcoal if swallowed recently. Seek urgent medical attention.

OTHER INFORMATION:

May cause dependence and addiction if used excessively.

See also Nitrazepam, Zaleplon.

Zopiclone

TRADE NAME:

Zimovane.

DRUG CLASS:

Sedative/Hypnotic.

USES:

Insomnia (sleeplessness).

DOSAGE:

 One tablet 30 minutes before bedtime.

FORMS:

Tablet of 3.75mg (blue) and 7.5mg (white).

PRECAUTIONS:

Should not be used in pregnancy (C), breast feeding or children.
Designed for short term use only.
Use with caution in severe kidney and liver disease, poor thyroid function, depression and epilepsy.
Lower doses needed in elderly.
Dependence possible.

Do not take if:

• suffering from myasthenia gravis, severe lung disease, sleep apnoea, recent stroke
• operating machinery, driving a vehicle or undertaking tasks that require concentration and alertness.

SIDE EFFECTS:

Common: drowsiness, headache, fatigue, taste disturbances, dry mouth.
Unusual: dependency on medication.

INTERACTIONS:

Other drugs:
• other sedatives.
Other substances:
• reacts with alcohol to increase sedation.

PRESCRIPTION:

Yes.

PERMITTED IN SPORT:

Yes.

OVERDOSE:

Seldom life threatening. May cause drowsiness, confusion and coma. Induce vomiting if tablets taken recently. Seek medical assistance.

OTHER INFORMATION:

Introduced in 1993. Very safe and effective. May cause dependence.

See also Nitrazepam, Zolpidem.

Zotepine

TRADE NAME:

Zoleptil.

DRUG CLASS:

Antipsychotic.

USES:

Schizophrenia.

DOSAGE:

 25 to 100mg three times a day. Increase dosage slowly.

FORMS:

Tablets of 25mg (white), 50mg (yellow) and 100mg (pink).

PRECAUTIONS:

May be used with considerable caution in pregnancy. Not to be used in breast feeding or children.
Use with caution in epilepsy, heart disease, low blood pressure, kidney and liver disease, prostate gland enlargement,

difficulty in passing urine, glaucoma, Parkinson's disease and adrenal tumours. Check blood pressure and blood chemistry regularly.

Do not take if:

- suffering from acute gout, alcoholism
- intoxicated.

SIDE EFFECTS:

Common: tiredness, fever, headache.
Unusual: infections, unusual pains, low blood pressure, fainting, altered appetite, tissue swelling, excess thirst, blurred vision, conjunctivitis, impotence, urinary incontinence.
Severe but rare (stop medication, consult doctor): liver damage (jaundice—yellow skin).

INTERACTIONS:

Other drugs:
- sedatives, other antipsychotics, fluoxetine, diazepam, anaesthetics.
Other substances:
- alcohol.

PRESCRIPTION:

Yes.

PERMITTED IN SPORT:

Yes.

OVERDOSE:

Very serious. Symptoms include drowsiness, confusion, restlessness, rapid heart rate, tremor, convulsions, difficulty in breathing and swallowing, coma and death. Administer activated charcoal or induce vomiting if taken recently and patient alert. Seek urgent medical attention.

OTHER INFORMATION:

Introduced in 1999 to help more serious cases of schizophrenia.
See also PHENOTHIAZINES.

Zuclopenthixol

TRADE NAME:

Clopixol.

DRUG CLASS:

Antipsychotic.

USES:

Schizophrenia, severe psychoses, mania.

DOSAGE:

 Capsules: 10mg to 50mg a day in divided doses.
Depot injection: one injection every two to four weeks.
Injection: one injection every two to four days.

FORMS:

Tablets of 2mg (pink), 10mg (light brown), 25mg (brown).
Injection, depot injection.

PRECAUTIONS:

Use only as a last resort in pregnancy (C). Use with caution in breast feeding and children.
Use with caution in Parkinsonism, epilepsy, glaucoma, poor blood supply to brain, severe hardening of arteries and heart disease, kidney and liver disease.
Use with caution in climates with high temperatures.
Regular blood tests to check liver and blood cell function recommended.
Consider options carefully before using for prolonged period.
Avoid contact with organophosphate insecticides.

Do not take if:

- suffering from coma, brain injury, abnormal blood cells in past or present, phaeochromocytoma
- alcohol, narcotics or barbiturates recently consumed.

SIDE EFFECTS:

Common: drowsiness, twitching, dry mouth, constipation.
Unusual: uncontrolled movements, liver damage, blood cell damage, inability to vomit.
Severe but rare (stop medication, consult doctor): high fever, jaundice (yellow skin).

INTERACTIONS:

Other drugs:
• anticholinergics, sedatives, hypnotics, tricyclic antidepressants, metoclopramide, piperazine.
Herbs:
• celery, camomile, evening primrose (linoleic acid).
Other substances:
• alcohol
• organophosphate insecticides.

PRESCRIPTION:

Yes.

PERMITTED IN SPORT:

Yes.

OVERDOSE:

Tiredness, convulsions, coma, low blood pressure and altered temperature may occur. Induce vomiting or give activated charcoal if capsules taken recently. Seek urgent medical attention.

OTHER INFORMATION:

Introduced in 1996 to control more difficult cases of schizophrenia and other psychiatric conditions. Does not cause addiction or dependence.

See also Amisulpride, Flupenthixol, Haloperidol, Lithium, Olanzapine, PHENOTHIAZINES, Pimozide, Quetiapine, Risperidone, Thiothixene.